GUINNESS WORLD RECORDS DAY
CERTIFICATE
世界記録に挑戦中
Salina
5500
Größtes Trachtenkleid („Dirndl") der Welt

LARGEST OBJECT LIFTED BY HELIUM BALLOONS

Inspired by the animated movie *Up* (USA, 2009), the National Geographic Channel (USA) floated a house weighing 4,335 lb (1,966 kg) – including the frame, ballast, rigging, and pilot – to a height of 10,000 ft (3,050 m) over Los Angeles, USA, using a cluster of 300 helium-filled balloons 10 stories tall. The project, which took two weeks to realize in February and March 2011, was filmed for the TV series *How Hard Can it Be?*

AIR

GREATEST DISTANCE FLOWN IN A WING SUIT

Shinichi Ito (Japan) flew a horizontal, straight-line distance of 10.19 miles (16.4 km) after jumping from an airplane 33,430 ft (10,550 m) above Yolo County, California, USA. He flew for 4 min 57 sec on September 24, 2010, reaching a maximum speed of 178.3 mi/h (287 km/h) and deploying his parachute at an altitude of 3,050 ft (929.6 m). During his record attempt, he wore a "Blade II" wing suit, manufactured by Birdman, Inc. (Finland).

FARTHEST FLIGHT BY A PAPER AIRCRAFT

Stephen Krieger (USA) flew a paper aircraft 207 ft 4 in (63.19 m) in a hangar near Moses Lake, Washington, USA, on September 6, 2003.

MOST AIRCRAFT FLOWN IN BY ONE PASSENGER

Edwin A Shackleton (UK) had flown in a total of 841 different types of aircraft by January 2007.

LARGEST WHOOPEE CUSHION

Measuring 10 ft (3.05 m) in diameter, the largest whoopee cushion ever was made by Steve Mesure (UK) on behalf of the Street Vibe music project for an event at The Scoop in London, UK, on June 14, 2008. Volunteers were encouraged to sit on the cushion to demonstrate how wind instruments work.

FARTHEST DISTANCE TRAVELED BY A HUMAN VOICE

The normal intelligible outdoor range of the male human voice in still air is 590 ft (180 m). *Silbo Gomero*, the whistled language of the Spanish-speaking inhabitants of the Canary Island of La Gomera, is intelligible under ideal conditions at 5 miles (8 km).

Largest bubblegum bubble blown
20 in (50.8 cm), by Chad Fell (USA), Winston County, Alabama, USA, April 24, 2004.

Largest free-floating soap bubble
483 ft^3 (13.67 m^3), by Jarom Watts (USA), Spokane, Washington, USA, February 21, 2009.

Largest frozen soap bubble
0.15 ft^3 (4,315.7 cm^3) by Sam "Samsam Bubbleman" Heath (UK), London, UK, June 28, 2010.

Most people inside a soap bubble
94, by Hammou Bensalah (Algeria), Soltau, Germany, September 24, 2009.

LONGEST-DURATION MALTESER BLOWING

Dermot Whelan (Ireland) kept a Malteser suspended in the air for 3.18 seconds by blowing, in Dublin, Ireland, on September 16, 2008.

MOST KITES FLOWN SIMULTANEOUSLY BY ONE PERSON

In Weifang City, China, 43 kites were flown at the same time by Ma Qinghua (China) on November 7, 2006.

10.19-MILE FLIGHT

UPDATED RECORD
NEW RECORD

THE LIGHT STUFF
The **least dense solid** is an aerogel made by Lawrence Livermore National Laboratory (USA). With a density of just 0.25 grains/in^3 (1 mg/cm^3), it is lighter than air.

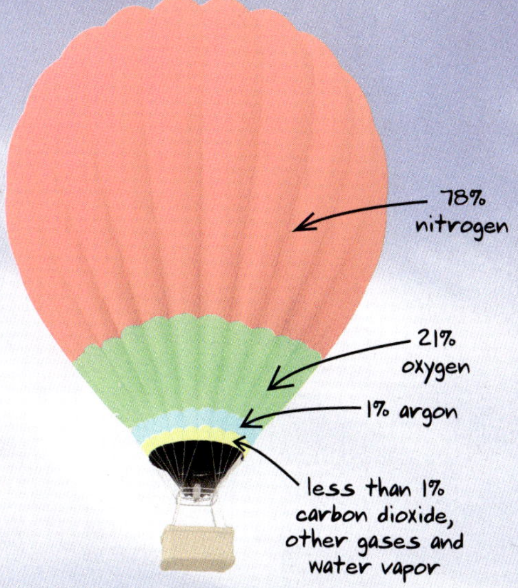

What is air?
Air is, in fact, a mixture of gases. The air pressing down on us – the atmosphere – is about 74 miles (120 km) thick and weighs 2,204.62 lb (1 metric ton). We can't feel its weight because the air pressure inside our bodies is the same as that outside them. If it wasn't, we'd be crushed. The higher you go, the less air there is pressing down on you. If you climbed Mount Everest you would have gone through 70% of the atmosphere, so the weight pressing down on you would be less. The atmosphere thins further still until you reach outer space.

LONGEST-DURATION FLIGHT BY HELIUM BALLOONS

Piloted by Jonathan Trappe (USA), the *Spirit Cluster* (made up of 57 balloons) flew for 13 hr 36 min 57 sec across North Carolina, USA, from April 10 to 11, 2010. In total, Jonathan covered 109 miles (175 km) during his flight and reached a peak altitude of 7,474 ft (2,278 m).

MOST AIR GUITAR WORLD CHAMPIONSHIP WINS

The Oulu Music Video Festival's Air Guitar World Championships, held in Oulu, Finland, have been won by Zac "The Magnet" Monro (UK, below) in 2001 and 2002, and by Ochi "Dainoji" Yosuke (Japan) in 2006 and 2007.

AIR GUITAR CONTESTS USE A 6.0 SCALE FOR SCORING – LIKE FIGURE SKATING

MOST MODELING BALLOON SCULPTURES MADE IN ONE MINUTE

John Cassidy (USA) made 13 balloon sculptures in one minute in New York City, USA, on November 21, 2005. John sculpted a bone, bracelet, crocodile, dagger, dachshund, dog (no breed), dragonfly, elephant, fish, hat, honeybee, Indian headdress, and sword.

British Library Cataloging-in-Publication Data:
A catalog record for this book is available from the British Library

ISBN: 978-1-897553-11-4

Special thanks: Matthew White. For a complete list of credits and acknowledgments, turn to p.284.

If you wish to make a record claim, find out how on p.14. Always contact us before making a record attempt.

Check the official website **www.guinnessworldrecords.com** regularly for record-breaking news, plus video footage of record attempts. You can also join and interact with the GWR online community.

Sustainability
The trees that are harvested to print *Guinness World Records* are carefully selected from managed forests to avoid the devastation of the landscape.

The paper contained within this edition is manufactured by Stora Enso Veitsiluoto, Finland. The production site is Chain-of-Custody certified, and operates within environmental systems certificated to ISO 14001 to ensure sustainable production.

Typefaces
This edition of *Guinness World Records* is set in Myriad Pro, a beautifully proportioned and highly readable *sans serif* typeface designed in the early 1990s by Robert Slimbach and Carol Twombly (both USA).
The display typeface is **Digital Sans EF**, designed by Veronika Elsner and Günther Flake (both Germany) in 1974. Clean and crisp with a futuristic flavor, it combines with Myriad Pro to help set the fresh, understated tone of this year's design.

Pictured on the opposite page is Chanel Tapper (USA), who has the longest tongue of any woman on the planet – find out just how long it is on p.82.

OFFICIALLY AMAZING

THE JIM PATTISON GROUP

EDITOR-IN-CHIEF
Craig Glenday

SENIOR MANAGING EDITOR
Stephen Fall

LAYOUT EDITORS
Rob Dimery, Alex Meloy

EDITORIAL TEAM
Chris Bernstein (index), Rob Cave ("Global Connections"), Tadg Farrington ("Average Life"), Carla Masson (sports reference), Matthew White (proofreading)

DESIGN
Nigel Wright and Janice Browne at XAB Design Ltd, London, UK

VP PUBLISHING
Frank Chambers

DIRECTOR OF PROCUREMENT
Patricia Magill

PUBLISHING MANAGER
Jane Boatfield

PUBLISHING ASSISTANT
Charlie Peacock

PRODUCTION CONSULTANTS
Esteve Font Canadell, Roger Hawkins, Julian Townsend

PRINTING & BINDING
Rotocayfo S.L., Barcelona, Spain

COVER PRODUCTION
Spectratek Technologies, Inc.

PICTURE EDITOR
Michael Whitty

DEPUTY PICTURE EDITOR
Laura Nieberg

PICTURE RESEARCHER
Fran Morales

ORIGINAL PHOTOGRAPHY
Richard Bradbury, Chris Granger, Stuart Hendry, Paul Michael Hughes, Shinsuke Kamioka, Ranald Mackechnie, Ryan Schude, David Torrence, Jay Williams, John Wright

COLOR ORIGINATION
Resmiye Kahraman at FMG, London, UK

EDITORIAL CONSULTANTS
Dr Mark Aston
Dr Eleanor Clarke
Joshua Dowling
Dick Fiddy
David Fischer
Mike Flynn
Ben Hagger
David Hawksett
Alan Howard
Dave McAleer
Christian Marais
Ocean Rowing Society
Stephen Wrigley
Eric Sakowski
Dr Karl Shuker
Dr Glenn Speer
Stewart Wolpin
World Speed Sailing Records Council
Robert Young

RECORDS MANAGEMENT
VP Records: Marco Frigatti (Italy)
Head of Records Management (UK): Andrea Bánfi (Hungary)
Head of Records Management (US): Carlos Martínez (Spain)
Records Management & Adjudications: Jack Brockbank (UK), Dong Cheng (China), Gareth Deaves (UK), Danny Girton Jr. (USA), Ralph Hannah (UK/Paraguay), Johanna Hessling (USA), Freddie Hoff (Denmark), Louise Ireland (UK), Kaoru Ishikawa (Japan), Mike Janela (USA), Olaf Kuchenbecker (Germany), Annabel Lawday (UK), Dougal McLachlan (NZ), Amanda Mochan (USA), Erika Ogawa (Japan), Anna Orford (France), Kimberly Partrick (USA), Talal Omar (Yemen), Vin Sharma (UK), Chris Sheedy (Australia), Lucia Sinigagliesi (Italy), Elizabeth Smith (UK), Şeyda Subaşi-Gemici (Turkey), Kristian Teufel (Germany), Louise Toms (UK), Carim Valerio (Italy), Tarika Vara (UK), Lorenzo Veltri (Italy), Aleksandr Vypirailenko (Lithuania), Xiaohong Wu (China)

COMMUNICATIONS
SVP USA & Global Marketing: Samantha Fay
Marketing Manager (US): Stuart E F Claxton
Senior PR Executive (US): Jamie Panas
Publishing, Sales & Product Manager (US): Jennifer Gilmour
Licensing, Promotions & Events (US): David Cohen
PR & Marketing Assistant (US): Sara Wilcox

Senior Marketing Manager: Nicola Eyre
Marketing Manager: Justine Bourdariat

Senior PR Manager: Amarilis Whitty
PR Manager: Claire Burgess
PR Executive: Damian Field

Director of Digital Media: Katie Forde
Video Content Manager: Adam Moore
Community Manager: Dan Barrett

GUINNESS WORLD RECORDS
Managing Director: Alistair Richards
SVP Finance: Alison Ozanne
Finance Manager (UK): Neelish Dawett
Finance Manager (USA & Japan): Jason Curran
Accounts Payable Manager: Kimberley Dennis
Accounts Receivable Manager & Contracts Administrator: Lisa Gibbs
Head of Legal & Business Affairs: Raymond Marshall
IT Manager: Graham Pullman
Web Applications Developer: Imran Javed

TELEVISION
SVP Programming & TV Sales: Christopher Skala
Director of Television: Rob Molloy
TV Distribution Manager: Denise Carter Steel
Television Assistant: Jonny Sanders

COMMERCIAL
VP Commercial: Paul O'Neill
Creative Director: Adam Wide
Licensing Manager: Chris Taday
Live Event Manager: Fern Holland

PUBLISHING SALES
Global Sales Director – Publishing: Nadine Causey
Senior National Accounts Manager: John Pilley
Sales & Distribution Executive: Richard Stenning

SVP Japan: Frank Foley
Business Development Manager (Japan): Erika Ogawa
Sales & Marketing Executives (Japan): Momoko Cunneen, Shaun Cunneen

HR: Kelly Garrett, Clare McEvoy
UK Office Manager: Jennifer Robson
US Administrator: Morgan Wilber

ACCREDITATION
Guinness World Records Limited has a very thorough accreditation system for records verification. However, while every effort is made to ensure accuracy, Guinness World Records Limited cannot be held responsible for any errors contained in this work. Feedback from our readers on any point of accuracy is always welcomed.

ABBREVIATIONS & MEASUREMENTS
Guinness World Records Limited uses both metric and imperial measurements. The sole exceptions are for some scientific data where metric measurements only are universally accepted, and for some sports data. Where a specific date is given, the exchange rate is calculated according to the currency values that were in operation at the time. Where only a year date is given, the exchange rate is calculated from December of that year. "One billion" is taken to mean one thousand million. "GDR" (the German Democratic Republic) refers to the East German state, which was unified with West Germany in 1990. The abbreviation is used for sports records broken before 1990. The USSR (Union of Soviet Socialist Republics) split into a number of parts in 1991, the largest of these being Russia. The CIS (Commonwealth of Independent States) replaced it and the abbreviation is used mainly for sporting records broken at the 1992 Olympic Games. Guinness World Records Limited does not claim to own any right, title or interest in the trademarks of others reproduced in this book.

GENERAL WARNING
Attempting to break records or set new records can be dangerous. Appropriate advice should be taken first and all record attempts are undertaken at the participant's risk. In no circumstances will Guinness World Records Limited have any liability for death or injury suffered in any record attempt. Guinness World Records Limited has complete discretion over whether or not to include any particular records in the book. Being a Guinness World Records record holder does not guarantee you a place in the book.

GUINNESS
WORLD
RECORDS
2012
GUINNESS WORLD RECORDS

Introduction

CONTENTS

Look out for these "fact snakes": bite-sized stats about record holders

Timelines place records in historical context

Q. What are these colored boxes for?

A. They're full of surprising, record-related teasers that will challenge what you think you know – rather like our "Mythconceptions" feature (see pp.16–17).

Our photographers have traveled the globe to bring you the most exciting and dynamic images

Every colored circle provides extra background info or additional records

RECORD BUBBLES
Popping up across the book you'll find these bubbles, each featuring another Guinness World Records feat. **Brand new records** get a ●. Those that are **updates of existing records** get a ●.

Color-coded sections

Guinness World Records takes you on a global tour of record-breaking with these bottom-of-the-page entries. Records on the left-hand page will be from a particular country, and will have a particular theme…

122 Number of facts about your life listed in this book! At the top of most spreads you'll find this fact box, written by Tadg Farrington, author of *The Average Life of the Average Person*, based on the typical reader of Guinness World Records.

THIS IS YOUR LIFE

On average, how many times will you sneeze during your life? And how much will you sweat? Uncover a wealth of fun facts about yourself, courtesy of writer and researcher Tadg Farrington.

Lists and tables pack the pages with even more world-beating records

Notes and annotations add a new dimension to the photos and help you find out even more about the record holders

Fact Files – Each chapter opens with a special feature exploring one particular aspect of record-breaking

THESE BOXES GIVE A CROSS-REFERENCE TO A RELATED FEATURE ON ANOTHER PAGE.

...the theme is then picked up in a record listed here, at the bottom of the right-hand page. This record will be from a different country. On the following page you'll find another record from the same country. And so on, around the world!

EDITOR'S LETTER

OFFICIALLY AMAZING!

No two words better sum up Guinness World Records than "Officially Amazing". As the global authority on superlative achievements, we process thousands of record applications from around the world each year, applying our expertise and experience to fully investigate each claim. And the result? An annual book bringing you the very best, most awe-inspiring, and entertaining accomplishments…

LONGEST JOURNEY BY MOTORCYCLE IN ONE COUNTRY

It was a pleasure and honor to meet Canadian brothers Ryan and Colin Pyle following their epic tour of China – a 10,091-mile (16,240-km) ride starting and finishing in Shanghai. Find out more about their epic trip on p.121.

FASTEST MARATHON BY A MASCOT

Dressed as "Jefferson", the canine mascot of MyNextRace.com, Peter Donato (Canada) ran the ScotiaBank Toronto Waterfront Marathon in Toronto, Canada, in 4 hr 16 min 43 sec on September 26, 2010. Turn to pp.252–53 to see where Peter's time would have placed him among his fellow fancy dressers in the 2011 London Marathon...

Welcome to the new, fully updated edition of the world's **best-selling copyright book**. We've spent the last 12 months processing more claims than ever before, and the result is an unrivaled compendium of superlatives that will blow your mind. This year's book is full to bursting with the most thrilling, awesome, inspiring adventures from the world of record-breaking – illustrated with some of the world's most amazing photos.

With the London Olympics on the horizon – and, if certain astrologers are correct, the end of the world – then 2012 is going to be an explosive year! To mark London's third time as the host of the Olympiad, we've compiled an extended Olympics feature (pp.230–37). Sports fans will see that we've also completely restructured the Sports section (pp.228–77) – you'll find all your favorite subjects as usual, but this year ordered by theme.

If you're intrigued by the idea that the world's going to

MAKE A CONNECTION

At the foot of every page this year, you'll find a flag icon and a record relating to that flag's country. At the foot of the opposite page, you'll find a related record from another country. This country is featured again on the following page, and so the pattern continues, making record-breaking connections around the world, from country to country. We start our journey here, with a record from China, followed opposite by a related fact from Austria. Let's see how connected we all are…

China is the country with the **highest consumption of cigarettes**. A breathtaking 1.69 trillion cigarettes are smoked in China each year, and one out of every three cigarettes smoked in the world is smoked there.

HEAVIEST HOUSE PULLED
First he pulled a 126,200-lb (57,243-kg) fire truck, then a 416,299-lb (188.83-tonne) airplane… now, the ripped Reverend Kevin Fast has outdone himself by hauling a house! Find out how heavy it was on p.104.

end, as predicted by the Maya (see p.66), then our pages on asteroids (p.26) and killer climates (p.44) might make you panic!

For those of you who think (probably rightly!) that the world *won't* end in 2012, there's always Alan Turing Year to look forward to. Turing was a major pioneer in the history of computing and code-breaking, and we celebrate the life of this Great British scientist with an exciting new spread on Codes & Cryptography (p.158) and a Computing Fact File (p.162) that explores the history of computer technology.

Indeed, history plays a big part in this year's book – we've dedicated an entire chapter to bringing you a superlative (if brief) history of the world (Time Tales, pp.66–77).

Talking of which, history was being made just as we went to press, with Prince William marrying Catherine Middleton, watched by a record online audience – YouTube's Royal Channel hosted 72 million streams during the nuptials, which is the **most live streams for a single event**. And with the fast-approaching diamond jubilee of Queen Elizabeth II (**longest reigning queen – living**), it seemed a good time to explore some more superlative sovereigns in our Royalty & Monarchies spread (p.156).

Another feature of this year's book is a unique series of photographs documenting some of the best of the recent adventuring world records. The brainchild of GWR's Picture Editor, Michael Whitty, Spirit of Adventure (pp.116–31) is a visual celebration of young pioneers and proof – were it needed – that our planet continues to be a thrilling, challenging, and dangerous place to explore… and that you're never too young to achieve greatness!

MOST PINCH-HIT HOME RUNS IN AN MLB CAREER
Canada's Matt Stairs racked up an historic 23rd pinch-hit home run on September 14, 2010 – the most ever scored by a Major League Baseball player. And if *you're* feeling sporty, we've got it covered – flick straight to our bumper Sports section (pp.228–77) for more sporting achievements.

LARGEST GLOWSTICK DESIGN

The Département de Chimie of Université Laval in Quebec City, Quebec, was literally glowing with pride on March 25, 2011 when their efforts – and those of 308 volunteers – were rewarded with an official GWR certificate for their giant glowstick design.

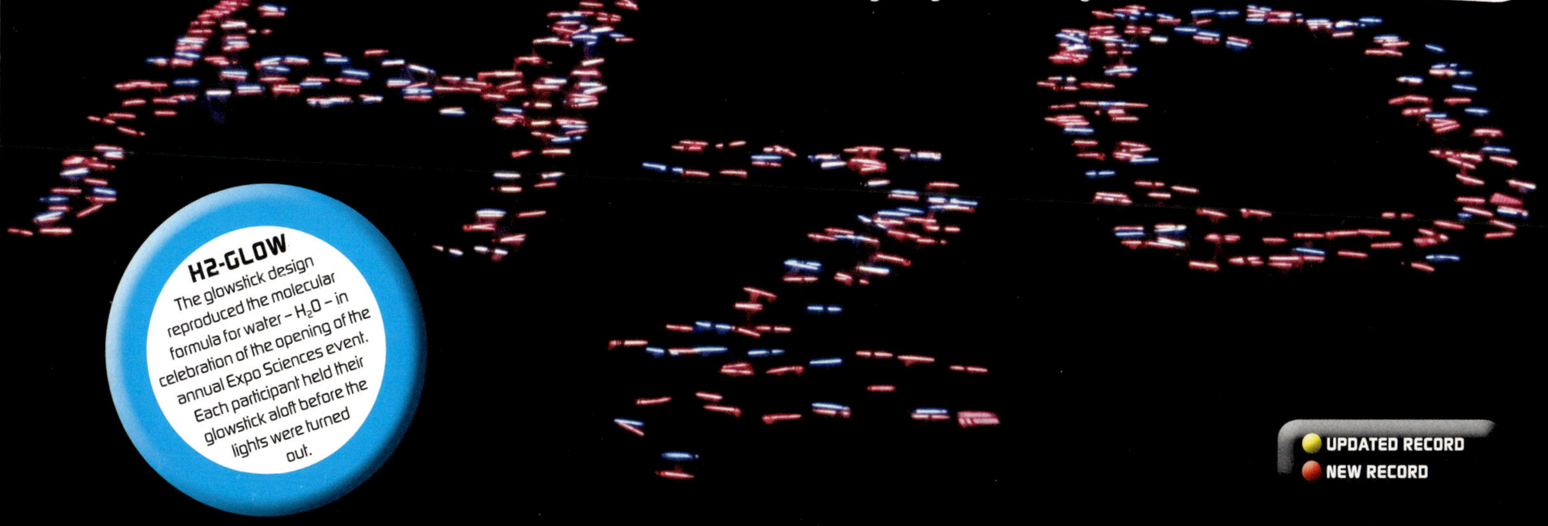

H2-GLOW
The glowstick design reproduced the molecular formula for water – H_2O – in celebration of the opening of the annual Expo Sciences event. Each participant held their glowstick aloft before the lights were turned out.

UPDATED RECORD
NEW RECORD

Measured per capita, the world's **heaviest smokers** are the Austrians – 36.3% of the population indulge in this habit regularly.

EDITOR'S LETTER

● LARGEST BLEEP TEST: An incredible 324 out of 443 people made it to fitness level 5 in the world's largest bleep test, held at Lower Canada College in Montreal, on October 27, 2010.

● LARGEST KILT RACE: On June 26, 2010, a record 1,089 runners donned the tartan and hit the road for the Perth Kilt Run in Perth, Ontario.

LONGEST JOURNEY BY POWERED PARAGLIDER

When Canada's Benjamin Jordan crossed from Tofino in British Columbia to Bay St Lawrence in Nova Scotia, he decided to take the scenic route in his powered paraglider. Meet him and discover more about his epic journey in our Big Air feature on p.262.

FLIGHTS OF FANCY

Benjamin's trans-Canadian trip is just one of many aerial escapades featured in this year's book – you'll find more Flights of Fancy and breathtaking round-the-world adventures on pp.128–131...

● MOST PEOPLE IN A NURSERY RHYME RELAY

To gain first-hand experience of record-breaking, and to understand the effort required, 154 delegates from the Jim Pattison Group (Canada) – the company that owns Guinness World Records – took it in turns to recite the lines of various nursery rhymes in San Antonio, Texas, on March 12, 2011.

WANT MORE DARE-DEVILRY? TURN TO P.92!

Austria has the world's **highest proportion of organic farming**, with an amazing 10% of its entire land area dedicated to organic production.

2 Minutes per day that the average person spends reading reference books, compared with seven minutes of reading online. Hopefully this edition will inspire you to read for a bit longer each day – otherwise, you'll only spend four years of your life learning from books.

LARGEST GATHERING OF PEOPLE DRESSED AS GNOMES

To mark Family Day in Canada on February 21, 2011, a record 266 people got dressed up as garden gnomes for a special screening of the film *Gnomeo & Juliet* (UK, 2011) in Toronto, Ontario, organized by eOne Films Canada. In fact, 2011 was a great year for fancy dress gatherings all over the world – discover more on p.102.

We could be here all day listing the new features, so why not just jump right in now and see what you find? And remember – if you come across something you think you can do better, then let us know about it. You'll find out How to be a Record-Breaker on p.14. Who knows – perhaps this time next year, you'll find your name listed alongside the new Olympic greats, the latest Oscar winners, and the rest of 2012's record-breaking community. Of course, that's assuming the world doesn't come to an end in December! Good luck!

Craig Glenday
Editor-in-Chief
twitter.com/craigglenday

LARGEST STREET HOCKEY TOURNAMENT

From June 4–6, 2010, a record 2,096 players in 205 teams took part in the fourth annual Walter Gretzky Street Hockey Tournament in Brantford, Ontario. The tournament is named after the father of Wayne Gretzky, Canada's greatest ice hockey player, who makes his own appearance in this year's book on p.240.

If you can't explore the world, then discovering *Guinness World Records 2012* is the next best thing. Visit the spectacular UNESCO World Heritage sites in World of Wonders (p.40) and Water World (p.42) without leaving the comfort of your own armchair; find out how to climb Mount Everest (p.118), the **highest peak** on Earth; and if the world is not enough, you can explore our fully updated features on the *International Space Station* (p.28) and Space Disasters (p.30). Or perhaps you'd prefer to wile away the time with some record recreations such as Juggling (p.112) or even Collectible Card Gaming (p.206).

FASTEST TIME TO PEEL 50 LB OF ONIONS

Proving you can become a record-breaker without setting foot outside your own front door, multiple record holder Bob Blumer (Canada) demonstrates his latest kitchen-based skills – at the expense of 31 onions – on p.106.

TESSA AND SCOTT ARE THE WORLD AND OLYMPIC CHAMPIONS

HIGHEST SCORE IN FIGURE SKATING – ICE DANCE, SHORT DANCE

On February 17, 2011, Canadian pair Tessa Virtue and Scott Moir pleased both the crowd and the judges at the ISU Four Continents Championships in Taipei, Taiwan, notching up a record score of 69.40 in the short dance event. And if dancing is your thing, then waltz your way over to our special Planet Dance feature on p.98.

UPDATED RECORD
NEW RECORD

The **largest consumers of organic food** are the Danish, who spend $350 million on organic produce every year – equivalent to $65.88 per person.

GWR DAY

NOVEMBER 17

... is the date for Guinness World Records Day 2011. Each year, people worldwide try to set or break a Guinness World Record on this special day – as these photos from GWR Day 2010 show. Want to break a record of your own? Find out how at www.guinnessworldrecords.com!

LARGEST SCREW ARTWORK: Saimir Strati (Albania) used 235,500 metal screws in an artwork depicting the poet Homer in Tirana, Albania, unveiled specially on GWR Day.

MOST HEADSPINS IN ONE MINUTE: Aichi Ono (Japan) performed a dizzying 135 headspins on the set of Mino Monta no Asazuba (TBS) for GWR Day 2010.

MOST FLAMES BLOWN IN ONE MINUTE: Hot, hot, hot! Fire-breather Preacher Muad'dib (Ireland) managed to blast out 69 fire torches in 60 seconds by London's iconic Tower Bridge.

LARGEST MELODICA ENSEMBLE: A group of 158 children from the Jyosei Elementary School in Hikone, Japan, played "Twinkle Twinkle Little Star."

MOST SIMULTANEOUS HIGH KICKS IN 30 SECONDS BY A CHORUS LINE: Moulin Rouge cancan dancers performed 720 high kicks at the Moulin Rouge theater, Paris.

MOST ARROWS CAUGHT IN TWO MINUTES: Joe Alexander (Germany) caught 43 arrows by hand, from 26 ft 3 in (8 m) away, in Hamburg, Germany.

MOST DOGS IN FANCY DRESS: The Suncoast Animal League (USA) assembled 426 dressed-up dogs during their annual Dogtoberfest in Dunedin, Florida, USA.

LARGEST TUG OF WAR TOURNAMENT: A total of 1,290 students from Het Nieuwe Lyceum and De Werkplaats (both Netherlands) took the strain for GWR Day.

LARGEST PAINTING BY NUMBERS: The Ecole de Dessin in Lagos State, Nigeria, unveiled a 208-ft 4-in (63.5-m) x 161-ft 9-in (49.3-m) painting by numbers.

UPDATED RECORD
NEW RECORD

The Danes can boast the world's **oldest movie theater still in operation**. Denmark's Korsør Biograf Teater opened on August 7, 1908.

ALL THIS HAPPENED IN JUST ONE DAY.
FOR RECORDS THAT WERE ACHIEVED IN JUST ONE HOUR, TURN TO P.96.

MOST BASKETBALL SLAM DUNKS WITH A TRAMPOLINE IN ONE MINUTE: Norway's Team Kangaroos sank 28 trampoline-powered slam dunks in Marienlysthallen, Norway.

LONGEST MARATHON SLICING MEAT: Francisco Alonso (Spain) spent 24 hr 54 min 6 sec cutting ham in Tenerife, Spain, piling up 166 lb 12 oz (75.641 kg) of meat in total!

LARGEST GATHERING OF WIZARD OF OZ CHARACTERS: Mile Oak Primary School, Brighton, UK, assembled 446 people dressed up as Oz folk.

FARTHEST DISTANCE TO RIDE A WATER SLIDE IN FOUR HOURS: A mixed German team covered 199.27 miles (320.68 km) on a water slide in just four hours.

OLDEST WING WALKER: Veteran wing walker Thomas Lackey (UK, b. May 22, 1920) took to the skies over Cirencester, Gloucestershire, UK, at the age of 90.

LARGEST MAPLE LEAF: In October 2010, Joseph Donato (Canada) discovered a maple leaf – Canada's national symbol – 13.6 in (34.61 cm) wide and 11.5 in (29.21 cm) long.

GWR DAY

Guinness World Records Day 2010 was actively celebrated by over 250,000 people, in over 15 countries, breaking 56 records. We'd like to thank everyone who took part – you made it the best GWR Day yet!

ON THE SAME DAY

- Farthest distance static cycling in three minutes: 3.6 miles (5.8 km), by Miguel Angel Castro (Spain).
- Most jokes told in one minute: 17, shared by Ted Robbins, BBC Lancashire, and Ben Day, Touch FM (both UK).
- Tightrope walking – greatest distance in 24 hours: 9.74 miles (5.68 km), by Joey Kelly (Germany).
- Most rotations while juggling in one minute (five clubs): 735, by Mario Berousek (Czech Republic) at the Moulin Rouge in Paris, France.
- Heaviest shoes walked in: 323 lb (146.5 kg), by Ashrita Furman (USA).
- Largest rice ball mosaic: 566.5 ft^2 (52.63 m^2), by 500 participants at the Gohanshoku Network Conference (Japan).
- Longest line of bunting: 8,982 ft (2,737.72 m), by Malbank Secondary School and Sixth Form College (UK).
- Most capital cities named in a minute: 33, by James Way (UK).
- Most concrete blocks broken while holding a raw egg: 24, by Joe Alexander (Germany).
- Most consecutive Double Dutch-style skips (team): 371, by Summerwind Skippers (USA).
- Most spinning splits in 30 seconds: 34, by Adonis Kosmadakis (Greece) and Nicolas Pihiliangegedera (France). Shared record.
- Largest game of leapfrog: 1,348 students and visitors to the Canterbury Agricultural & Pastoral (A&P) Show in Christchurch, New Zealand.
- Most words spelled backward in a minute: 14, by Emma Britton (UK).
- Tallest tower of paper cups built in 30 seconds: 10.63 in (27 cm), by Masato Kajiwara (Japan).

The **first operating movie theater** was the Cinématographe Lumière at the Salon Indien, 14 Boulevard de Capucines, Paris, France, which opened on December 28, 1895.

HOW TO BE A RECORD-BREAKER

ARE YOU **OFFICIALLY** AMAZING?

There are now more ways than ever to earn yourself a much-coveted Guinness World Records certificate. Record-breaking is free and open to everyone, so if you've got a special skill or a talented pet, tell us about it now! You can attempt a record at one of our live events, or make a star appearance on a global TV show… you might even get your name listed in the world's **best-selling copyright book**!

STEP 1 – APPLY ONLINE
Your first step on the path to glory begins at the GWR website: **www.guinnessworldrecords.com**. Choose the "Break a Record" option and tell us as much as you can about the record you want to set or break. We want the Who, What, Where, When, and Why to help us decide if it really is worthy of the name Guinness World Records! Aim to do this about three weeks before your attempt.

STEP 2 – GET THE GUIDELINES
If we like your idea – or if you want to try to break an existing record – we'll send you the official rules that you must follow when attempting the record. (If we reject your proposal, we'll tell you why.) Everyone MUST follow the same guidelines so that each attempt can be fairly judged.

STEP 3 – ATTEMPT YOUR RECORD
Now it's time to plan and practice, practice, practice! Be sure to video your efforts, and get lots of witnesses and at least two independent eyewitness statements. Don't worry about taking notes now – full instructions are in the guidelines.

STEP 4 – SEND YOUR EVIDENCE
Collate all your evidence as per the guidelines and post it to GWR HQ. There, our Records Management Team will sift through your clips, photos, witness statements, logbooks, and so on, and make a decision. If you're successful then you'll know about it when your official GWR certificate arrives in the post. This is the confirmation that you are OFFICIALLY AMAZING!

TELEVISION

RECORDS

RECORDS MANAGEMENT
Our team of multilingual Records Managers travels the world to adjudicate records. This team also writes the rules for record attempts and processes around 1,000 claims a week. You'll get to meet a member of this talented team if you apply for an onsite adjudicator.

MARCO PRONTO!
Here's the Head of Records, Marco Frigatti, presenting a GWR certificate to Khagendra Thapa Magar, the world's **shortest man**. "It's only a world record when we say so," says Marco!

Lucien Laurent's goal for France against Mexico on July 13, at the 1930 World Cup in Uruguay, was the **first FIFA World Cup goal**.

TV STATS

GWR TV shows have been seen by a quarter of a billion people in over 90 countries. Will you be TV's next record-breaking star? If your talents are particularly exciting and dramatic, you could find yourself on the box!

TV

Only the most visually spectacular record attempts get picked for our TV shows. GWR TV is filmed and shown all around the world, and if you're lucky enough to be shortlisted, you could find yourself in China, India, Australia, Italy... just some of the locations in which we've filmed over the past 12 months!

DIGITAL

Whether it's online, or via ebooks or iPad apps, GWR Digital provides the 24/7 face of record-breaking. Check out the site, **guinnessworldrecords.com**, for record-breaking news, and search for some of your all-time favorite record holders. It's also your chance to make a claim or mail your attempt directly to our video channel. When you're there, sign up to our Facebook and Twitter feeds and meet the Challengers team, who'll help you realize your record-breaking dreams!

EXPERTS

Pictured here are just a few of the dozens of consultants who advise us in every field of knowledge – from astronomy to zoology. They're always on the lookout for new world records, and, if we've got a query, these are the mavens we turn to.

LIVE!

Experience the heart-in-your-mouth thrill and excitement of attempting a Guinness World Records challenge LIVE and in front of a crowd of onlookers at one of the GWR LIVE! roadshow events. One minute you're an idle bystander and the next you're a record holder! It's so immediate, you won't know what's hit you! Our LIVE! helpers are there to make sure you get the most fun out of your experience, so visit guinnessworld records.com/live to find a LIVE! event near you...

LIVE! ACTION

These roadshow visitors became instant record-breakers when they built the **tallest coffee cup tower in three minutes**, measuring 6 ft 10 in (2.08 m), at the GWR LIVE! event in Barcelona, Spain, on May 14, 2010.

José Batista's (Uruguay) first-minute sending-off for fouling Scotland's Gordon Strachan at Mexico '86 was the **fastest red card in a World Cup finals match**. The game was played at the Estadio Neza '86, Nezahualcoyotl, Mexico, on June 13, 1986.

MYTHCONCEPTIONS

PUT YOUR RECORD-BREAKING KNOWLEDGE TO THE TEST...

So, Everest is the tallest mountain, is it? And you can see the Great Wall of China from the Moon? And we all know that the Sahara is the largest desert, right? Wrong, wrong, and wrong again. Forget what you think you know and take our quirky quiz of common myths and misconceptions...

CAN YOU NAME THE WORLD'S TALLEST MOUNTAIN?

No, not Mount Everest! At 29,029 ft (8,848 m), Everest is the ***highest* mountain** on Earth – in that it reaches the highest altitude – but the ***tallest*** is actually Mauna Kea in Hawaii, USA. You can only see 13,796 ft (4,205 m) of it (the rest is underwater), but from its submarine base in the Hawaiian Trough, it reaches up for a total of 33,480 ft (10,205 m).

WHAT IS THE MOST DANGEROUS ANIMAL?

The great white shark? The poison-dart frog? What about the huntsman spider? Yes, these creatures are extremely dangerous, but would you be surprised to hear that the answer is the mosquito? It may be just 0.12 in (3 mm) long but mosquitoes of the genus *Anopheles* – and specifically its malarial parasites of the genus *Plasmodium* – have been responsible for approximately 50% of all human deaths since the Stone Age (excluding wars and accidents).

AND WHAT'S THE LONGEST ANIMAL?

Surprisingly, it's not the 90-ft-long (27-m) blue whale or even the lengthy *praya dubia* – the jellyfish-like siphonophore that can reach 160 ft (50 m) long. The **longest creature** is the bootlace worm (*Lineus longissimus*), a species of nemertean or ribbon worm inhabiting shallow waters of the North Sea. The longest known specimen, washed ashore in Fife, UK, in 1864, measured more than 180 ft (55 m) long.

HOW DO BATS SEE?

With their eyes, of course! Bats have the **most acute hearing of any non-aquatic animal** – some can hear frequencies as high as 250 kHz (compared with just 20 kHz for a human) – and they do use echolocation to find prey and communicate, but they're not blind. To be fair, many bat species have under-developed eyesight but not one of them is blind. Indeed, Old World fruit bats have relatively large eyes with decent light-gathering capacity. Bats are mostly active at night to avoid competition from other animals, so they need all the sensory input they can get.

WHO IS THE MOST PROLIFIC AUTHOR OF JAMES BOND NOVELS?

Perhaps surprisingly, James Bond creator Ian Fleming was *not* the most prolific writer of Bond novels – between 1981 and 1996, John Gardner (UK) wrote 14 Bond novels and two screenplay adaptations, surpassing Fleming's output of 12 novels and two short-story collections.

LONGEST PREGNANCY? Not the elephant (22 months) or the blue whale (11.5 months) but the common frilled shark (*Chlamydoselachus anguineus*), whose young gestate for 42 months!

WHERE IS THE LARGEST POPULATION OF WILD CAMELS?

There are up to one million wild camels living in – no, not Mongolia or Arabia – Australia! Imported there in the 19th century as a form of desert transportation, the camels escaped into the wild, where they now thrive.

UPDATED RECORD
NEW RECORD

The **largest revolving restaurant** is Bellini, located on the 45th floor of Mexico City's World Trade Center in Mexico. The restaurant has an area of 11,244.58 ft^2 (1,044.66 m^2).

MOST TORNADO-HIT COUNTRY? By area, the Netherlands has more twisters than any country, with one for every 769 miles² (1,991 km²) of land! The USA has one per 3,161 miles² (8,187 km²).

TALLEST KNOWN MOUNTAIN? If you said Everest, then you'd be wrong by a factor of three – the tallest mountain known to man is Olympus Mons on the planet Mars at a whopping 15 miles (25 km)!

With a total length of at least 2,150 miles (3,460 km), the Great Wall of China is the "longest wall in the world." But – contrary to popular belief – it is not visible from the surface of the Moon. This was confirmed by the Apollo astronauts who actually visited the Moon.

China's first taikonaut (or "yǔhángyuán"), Yang Liwei, admitted that he never saw the Great Wall during his maiden space flight in October 2003.

Things you *can* see from space – especially in low orbit – include cities, airports, major highway systems, bridges, and reservoirs.

WHO WERE THE FIRST PASSENGERS IN A HOT-AIR BALLOON?

The Montgolfier brothers? Good answer, but no. Joseph-Michel and Jacques-Etienne Montgolfier (France) did invent and build a hot-air balloon for a test in front of French royals Louis XVI and Marie Antoinette in 1783, but the effects of flight on a human were unknown, and it was decided to test the venture with a sheep (named Montauciel, or "Reach the Sky"), a duck, and a rooster – the **first living creatures to take flight in a man-made craft**.

WHO WAS FIRST TO SAIL AROUND THE WORLD?

Ferdinand Magellan, you say? The man who gave his name to the Straits of Magellan, the Magellanic penguin, and the Magellanic cloud? Erm, no. The Portuguese explorer may have set off on the **first circumnavigation of the world** in 1519 but he never completed the journey. Instead, he was hacked to death in the Philippines in March 1521, leaving the Spanish navigator Juan Sebastian de Elcano to complete the trip. Theories abound of earlier circumnavigations by others, but these are impossible to date and verify accurately.

WHEN A TOURIST IN LONDON BOUGHT WHAT HE *THOUGHT* WAS TOWER BRIDGE, WHAT DID HE END UP BUYING INSTEAD?

This story involves the record for the **farthest distance to move a bridge** – but it's not the apocryphal tale of the tourist who bought the *wrong* bridge. The story goes that a US tourist in London bought what he thought was Tower Bridge and had it shipped back home – only to discover he'd bought the less iconic London Bridge. Only part of this tale is true. The American was Robert McCulloch, and in 1962 he *did* buy London Bridge – but he did so willingly, and had it rebuilt 5,300 miles (8,530 km) away at Lake Havasu City in Arizona, USA, as a tourist attraction.

IN ANTARCTICA – THE LARGEST ARID EXPANSE ON EARTH – THE AVERAGE TEMPERATURE IS –4°F

WHERE IS THE LARGEST DESERT?

The Sahara in north Africa covers 3.5 million miles² (9.1 million km²) and is the largest *hot* desert. But a "desert" is simply an area that has no or very little rainfall, so by this definition the largest must be Antarctica (5.4 million miles²; 14 million km²), with about 2 in (50 mm) of precipitation per year.

To find the restaurant with the **largest menu** you will have to visit Hungary. The menu at the restaurant Mofarguru in the capital city, Budapest, features a whopping 1,810 different items.

LARGEST LOCAL GALAXY

Andromeda is the largest galaxy in the "Local Group," the cluster that includes Earth's own galaxy, the Milky Way. This composite image shows Andromeda's dust lanes in infrared (orange) and its X-ray binary star systems (blue), which probably contain black holes or neutron stars. Containing about a trillion stars, and at a distance of around 2.5 million light years, the Andromeda galaxy is the farthest object visible to the naked eye.

The ● **largest serving of pastries** took place in Hungary on May 23, 2009 during the Életfa-Hosök tornája, when 10,000 were dished out at the Puskas Stadium in Budapest.

If big baking is your thing, head for Portugal. The **longest loaf of bread** measured 3,975 ft (1,211.6 m) and was achieved at the Bread and Bakers' Party held in Vagos on July 10, 2005.

STAR LIVES

LIFE CYCLE OF A STAR

Stars are born, have a lifespan, then die, and the stars we can see in the night sky are all at various different stages of this life cycle. Our star – the Sun – was born about 4.57 billion years ago, and is expected to reach the ripe old age of 14 billion years. The life story of a star is shaped by its mass – smaller stars go down one avenue of evolution, and larger stars down another…

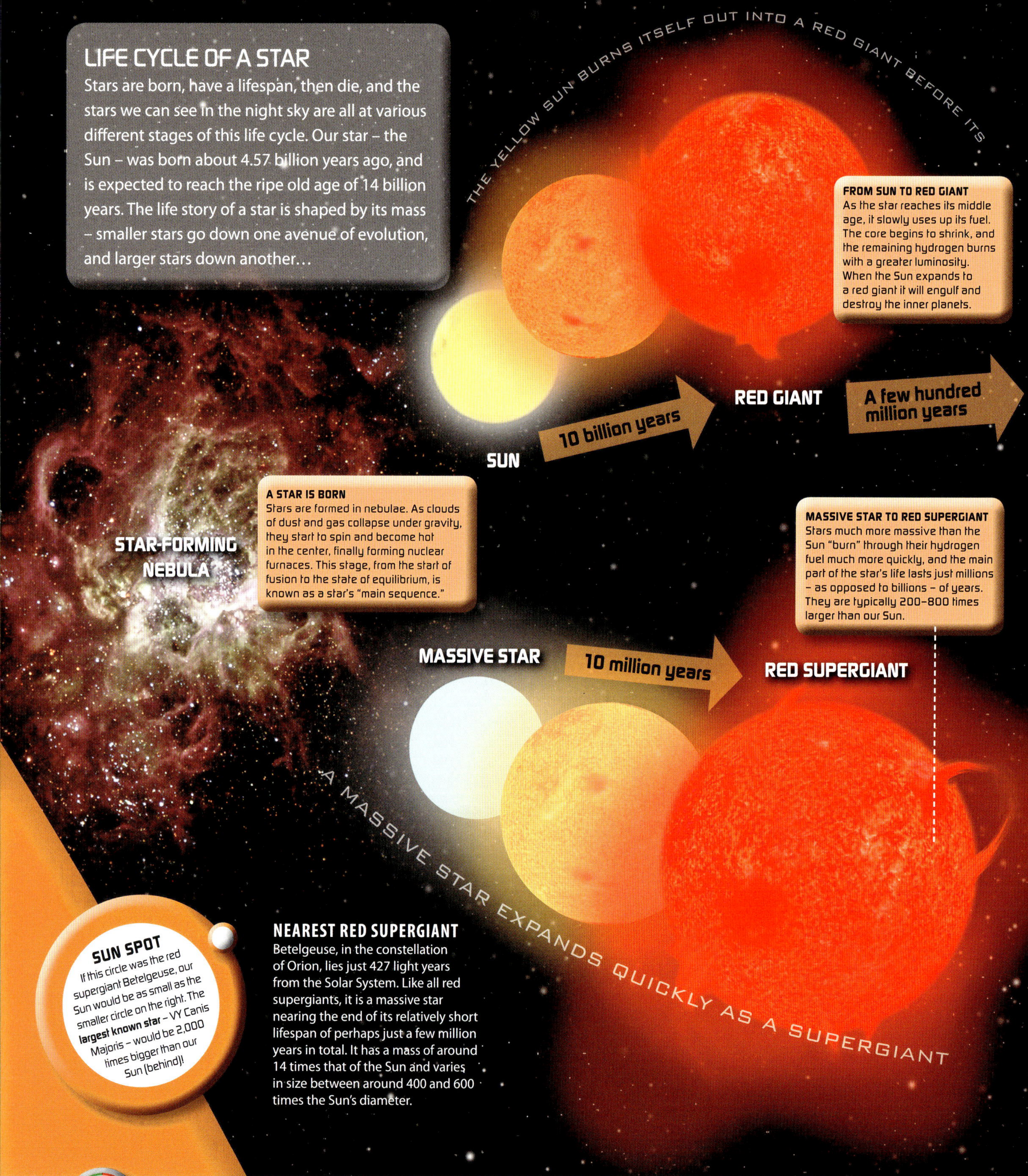

FROM SUN TO RED GIANT
As the star reaches its middle age, it slowly uses up its fuel. The core begins to shrink, and the remaining hydrogen burns with a greater luminosity. When the Sun expands to a red giant it will engulf and destroy the inner planets.

A STAR IS BORN
Stars are formed in nebulae. As clouds of dust and gas collapse under gravity, they start to spin and become hot in the center, finally forming nuclear furnaces. This stage, from the start of fusion to the state of equilibrium, is known as a star's "main sequence."

MASSIVE STAR TO RED SUPERGIANT
Stars much more massive than the Sun "burn" through their hydrogen fuel much more quickly, and the main part of the star's life lasts just millions – as opposed to billions – of years. They are typically 200–800 times larger than our Sun.

SUN SPOT
If this circle was the red supergiant Betelgeuse, our Sun would be as small as the smaller circle on the right. The **largest known star** – VY Canis Majoris – would be 2,000 times bigger than our Sun (behind)!

NEAREST RED SUPERGIANT

Betelgeuse, in the constellation of Orion, lies just 427 light years from the Solar System. Like all red supergiants, it is a massive star nearing the end of its relatively short lifespan of perhaps just a few million years in total. It has a mass of around 14 times that of the Sun and varies in size between around 400 and 600 times the Sun's diameter.

The **largest firework display** consisted of 66,326 fireworks and was achieved by Macedo's Pirotecnia Lda. in Funchal, Madeira, Portugal, on December 31, 2006.

7,350 Apples you will eat in a lifetime. Just 6,000 of the 3 septillion stars in the universe can be seen by the naked eye, so you'll eat more apples than there are visible stars in the sky.

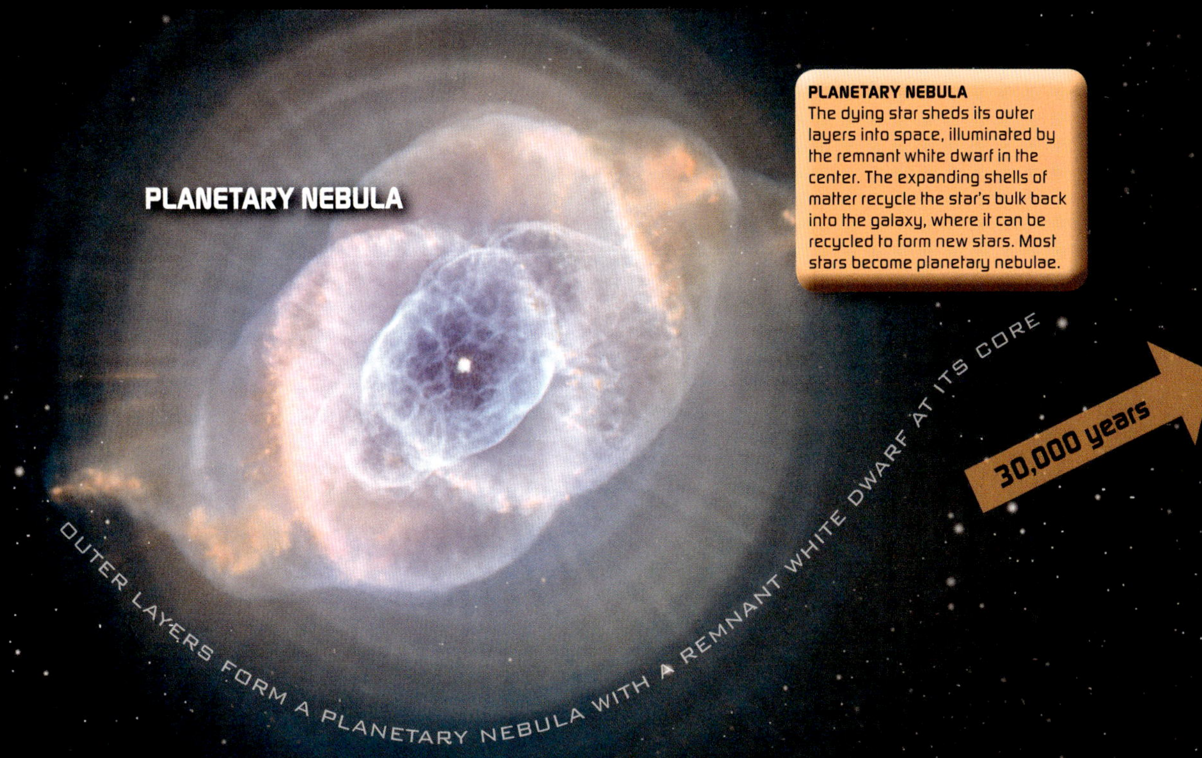

PLANETARY NEBULA
The dying star sheds its outer layers into space, illuminated by the remnant white dwarf in the center. The expanding shells of matter recycle the star's bulk back into the galaxy, where it can be recycled to form new stars. Most stars become planetary nebulae.

WHITE DWARF
The star ends its life as an incredibly dense mass of carbon and oxygen at a fraction of its original size (scientists predict that our Sun will end up as small as Earth). Now out of fuel, this "white dwarf" will continue to cool. As it solidifies into pure carbon, white dwarfs crystallize into the **largest diamonds in the universe**.

NEAREST PLANETARY NEBULA

The Helix Nebula (also known as NGC 7293), at a distance of around 400 light years, is the closest planetary nebula to the Earth. It formed when a dying star threw off its outer layers, which are gradually expanding into space. They are called planetary nebulae because astronomers originally believed they were new planets, owing to their often spherical shapes.

The **youngest planetary nebula** is the Stingray Nebula in the southern constellation of Ara. It was observed as a star in the 1970s, but in the last 30 years its central star had heated up enough to make its surrounding ejected gas shells glow as a planetary nebula.

SUPERNOVA
When a massive star exhausts its hydrogen, it then fuses its helium into heavier elements. When this process reaches the element iron, fusion can no longer occur and the star's core collapses catastrophically, resulting in a titanic supernova explosion that can outshine an entire galaxy.

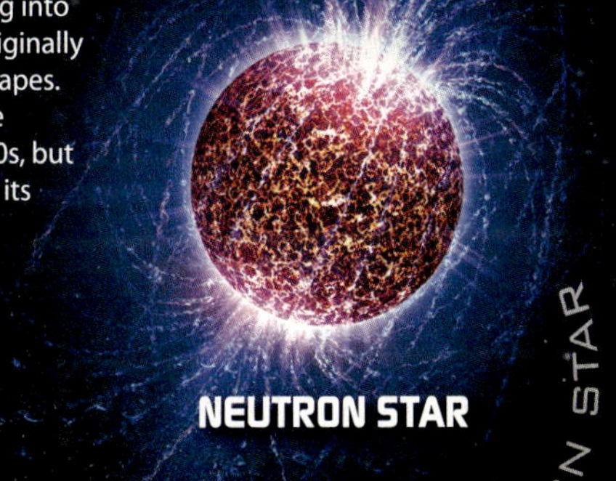

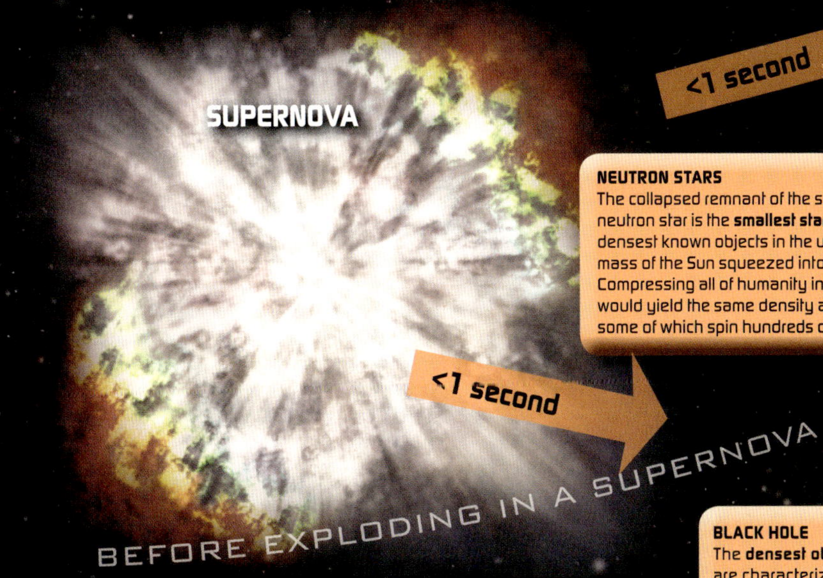

NEUTRON STARS
The collapsed remnant of the star's core, a neutron star is the **smallest star** and one of the densest known objects in the universe, with the mass of the Sun squeezed into the size of a city. Compressing all of humanity into a sugar cube would yield the same density as a neutron star, some of which spin hundreds of times per second.

BLACK HOLE
The **densest objects in the universe**, black holes are characterized by a region of space in which gravity is so strong that not even light can escape. At the center is the "singularity," where the mass of the dead star is compressed to a single point of zero size and infinite density.

The **largest chocolate firework** measured 9.8 ft (3 m) in height and contained 132 lb (60 kg) of Swiss Cailler chocolates. It was released at the Hechtplatz, Zürich, Switzerland, on December 31, 2002.

DEPTHS OF SPACE

UPDATED RECORD
NEW RECORD

FARTHEST OBJECT IN THE UNIVERSE

In January 2011, NASA scientists announced that the Hubble Space Telescope had photographed a galaxy so old that its light has taken 13.2 billion years to reach us. The galaxy as we see it today was formed less than 480 million years after the Big Bang, and is the earliest known object to have formed in the universe.

MOST DISTANT BLACK HOLE

In June 2007, astronomers announced that results from the Canada-France-Hawaii Telescope (CFHT) and the Gemini South 8m-class telescope had revealed a quasar containing a supermassive black hole with a redshift of 6.43. (A quasar is a very distant, old, and bright celestial object emitting high levels of electromagnetic radiation.) Named CFHQS J2329-0301, the quasar is in the constellation of Pisces and is estimated to be 2 million light-years farther away from Earth than the previous record holder. At just under 13 billion light-years' distance, it is only 0.7 billion years younger than the estimated age of the universe from the moment of the Big Bang.

MOST DISTANT OBSERVED SUPERNOVA

Astronomers led by Jeff Cooke (USA) have found what is thought to be a Type IIn supernova – a massive exploding star – in a distant galaxy some 11 billion light-years from Earth. Using data from the CFHT, the astronomers noticed a galaxy that brightened momentarily, with a spectrum that is characterized by a very narrow color band of light emitted from burning hydrogen.

Study of this type of supernova could help scientists to discover more about the true size – and origins – of the universe. The results from the analysis of the data were announced in July 2009.

MOST DISTANT EXTRASOLAR PLANET

OGLE-2005-BLG-390Lb is 21,500 ± 3,300 light-years away from Earth, near the center of the Milky Way. It orbits a star located in the constellation of Scorpius (see artist's impression, right) at a distance that would put it somewhere in the region between Mars and Jupiter in our own solar system. It may be the most distant Earth-like planet yet found – that is, a planet with a rocky core and a shell atmosphere.

MOST DISTANT OBJECT IN THE SOLAR SYSTEM

The dwarf planet Sedna has a highly elliptical orbit taking it 84 billion miles (130 billion km) from the Sun, which it takes around 10,500 years to orbit. Scientists at Mount Palomar Observatory, California, USA, discovered it on November 14, 2003. The picture above shows an artist's impression of a view of the Sun from the surface of Sedna.

IN THE TIME IT TAKES YOU TO READ THIS SENTENCE, VOYAGER 1 HAS TRAVELED 31 MILES (51 KM)

MOST REMOTE MAN-MADE OBJECT

NASA's *Voyager 1*, launched on September 5, 1977, encountered Jupiter in March 1979, and then Saturn in November 1980. The flybys produced slingshot effects whereby *Voyager 1* was flung upward out of the plane of the Solar System. As of February 4, 2011, it was 14,135,000,000 miles (17,367,000,000 km) from the Sun.

FOR RECORD-BREAKING AVIATION, TAKE OFF FOR P.130.

The **largest ski lesson** was attended by 594 skiers who were instructed by Hansjürg Gredig (Switzerland) of the Swiss-Snowsport School at Sarn-Heinzenberg (Graubünden), Switzerland, on February 23, 2008.

518 Weight in pounds of salt you will eat during your lifetime. If each individual grain weighs 2.06352677 × 10^{-6} ounces, your 518 lb contains 4,017,094,017 grains of salt. That's four grains for every star in the Milky Way.

FASTEST MATTER

The fastest objects observed in the universe are blobs of superheated plasma, ejected from black holes in the cores of extremely active galaxies known as blazars. These blobs, with as much mass as the planet Jupiter, have been observed moving at 99.99% of the speed of light.

The **fastest speed possible in the universe** is the speed of light, achieved only by light and other forms of electromagnetic radiation, such as radio waves, X-rays, or infrared radiation. The speed of light varies depending on what it passes through. It is fastest traveling in a vacuum, when its velocity is 983,571,056 ft/s (299,792,458 m/s). This means that when you look at the Moon, you are actually seeing it as it was about 1.3 seconds ago, while you see the Sun as it was around 8.3 minutes in the past.

FASTEST STAR IN THE GALAXY

On February 8, 2005, a team of astronomers from the Harvard-Smithsonian Center for Astrophysics in Cambridge, Massachusetts, USA, announced their discovery of a star traveling at a speed of over 1.5 million mi/h (2.4 million km/h). The star, named SDSS J090745.0+24507, had probably been accelerated by an encounter with the supermassive black hole at the center of our Milky Way galaxy slightly less than 80 million years ago.

ALTHOUGH FIRST SEEN IN 1846, NEPTUNE'S EXISTENCE HAD BEEN MATHEMATICALLY PREDICTED BEFOREHAND

FASTEST APPROACHING GALAXY

Despite the overall expansion of the universe, a few galaxies are approaching our own. M86, a lenticular galaxy around 52 million light-years away in the Virgo Cluster, is moving toward our Milky Way at 260 mi/s (419 km/s).

LARGEST STRUCTURE IN THE UNIVERSE

In October 2003, a team of astronomers led by Richard Gott III and Mario Juric (both USA) of Princeton University, New Jersey, USA, announced the discovery of a huge wall of galaxies some 1.37 billion light-years long. They used data from the Sloan Digital Sky Survey, which is mapping 1 million galaxies in the universe.

GREATEST EXPLOSION

Most astronomers now believe that the universe began about 13.7 billion years ago in a cataclysmic explosion we call the Big Bang. All of the matter and energy in the universe had its origins in this event, as did time itself.

At the very instant of the Big Bang, the universe is thought to have had infinite temperature (the **highest temperature ever**), as it existed as a single, infinitely small and infinitely dense point. Just 10^{-43} seconds later, the universe had expanded to a size of around 10^{-33}cm across and cooled to roughly 10^{32} kelvin (0°C = 273.15 kelvin).

COLDEST PLACE IN THE MILKY WAY

The Boomerang Nebula is a cloud of dust and gases 5,000 light-years from Earth. It has a temperature of -457.6°F (-272°C) and is formed by the rapid expansion of gas and dust flowing away from its central, ageing star.

CLOSEST PLANETARY BINARY SYSTEM TO EARTH

The term "binary system" refers to two objects in space that are close enough for their respective gravities to influence each other, causing the objects to orbit around a common point. The minor planet Pluto (716.44 miles, or 1,153 km, in diameter) and its moon Charon (375 miles, or 603.5 km, in diameter) form the only true planetary binary system in the Solar System. Charon is so large in relation to Pluto that they orbit a common point in space above the surface of Pluto. For a normal moon orbiting a planet, the point in space about which they both orbit is near the center of the planet involved, and so produces only a small wobble in the planet's orbit. True binary systems orbit a point in space outside either body.

BRIGHTEST RADIO SOURCE IN THE NIGHT SKY

Lying in the Cassiopeia constellation, the supernova remnant Cassiopeia A is the brightest radio source seen from Earth. It is the result of a supernova explosion some 11,000 years ago. Light from the explosion (and the radio waves we see today) was thought to have reached Earth about 300 years ago, but interstellar dust may have made this hard to see at the time.

I WANDER... Ancient astronomers saw that while some heavenly bodies moved together in a fixed pattern, others seemed to travel along their own paths. The ancient Greeks called these "planetes," meaning "wanderers."

FARTHEST PLANET IN THE SOLAR SYSTEM

Since the International Astronomical Union (IAU) demoted Pluto in 2006, Neptune is regarded as the farthest major planet from the Sun. It is 2.8 billion miles (4.5 billion km) from the Sun, which it orbits at 3.38 mi/s (5.45 km/s), taking 164.79 years to make one orbit. Neptune is also home to the **fastest winds in the Solar System**, measured at around 1,500 mi/h (2,400 km/h).

Q. Why is Pluto now a "minor" planet?

A. New criteria from the IAU stated that a planet must have gravity strong enough to stop other celestial objects floating around it ("clear its neighborhood," as the IAU puts it). Pluto doesn't.

The **largest indoor ski resort** is Ski Dubai in the United Arab Emirates. With a total area of 242,187 ft^2 (22,500 m^2) covered with 13 million lb (6,000 metric tons) of real snow all year around, it has room for 1,500 visitors.

JUPITER

PLANET WITH THE SHORTEST DAY

Jupiter has the shortest day of all eight major planets in the Solar System, performing a full rotation on its axis once every 9 hr 55 min 29.69 sec.

LARGEST METALLIC HYDROGEN OCEAN

Inside Jupiter is an ocean of metallic hydrogen up to 34,175 miles (55,000 km) deep. Metallic hydrogen forms when liquid hydrogen is subjected to enormous pressures and becomes ionized. This gives the hydrogen metallic properties, thus turning it into an electrical conductor and creating the **strongest magnetic field in the Solar System** – around 19,000 times stronger than Earth's.

FIRST JUPITER FLYBY

Launched in 1972, the unmanned NASA spacecraft *Pioneer 10* reached Jupiter on December 3, 1973. After becoming the first spacecraft to travel through the asteroid belt, it passed by the planet at a distance of 80,778 miles (130,000 km). The encounter yielded not only the first close-up images of the planet but also data on its magnetic field, and proved Jupiter to be a mostly liquid planet.

MOST SPACECRAFT TO VISIT AN OUTER PLANET

Jupiter has been visited by eight spacecraft. After *Pioneer 10*'s visit in 1973, *Pioneer 11* performed a flyby in 1974, with *Voyagers 1* and *2* following in 1979. *Ulysses* made two long-distance flybys in 1992 and 2004, while *Galileo* orbited Jupiter between 1995 and 2003. *Cassini-Huygens* and *New Horizons* both used Jupiter as a slingshot on their journeys to Saturn in 2000 and Pluto in 2007, respectively.

LONGEST ORBITAL SURVEY OF AN OUTER PLANET

NASA's *Galileo* spacecraft was launched on October 18, 1989 and reached Jupiter on December 7, 1995, where it slowed to enter the planet's orbit and became the first probe to orbit a world in the outer Solar System. It lasted nearly eight years, ending on September 21, 2003 when *Galileo*'s power began to fail and the craft burned up in the atmosphere.

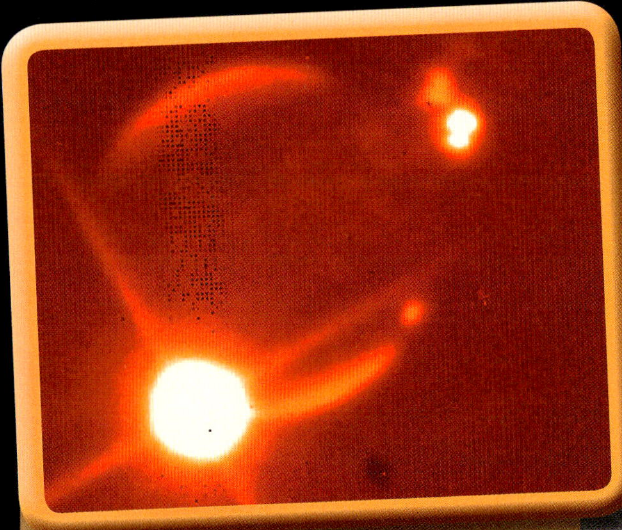

LARGEST RECORDED IMPACT IN THE SOLAR SYSTEM

On July 16–22, 1994, fragments of comet Shoemaker-Levy 9 collided with Jupiter. The greatest impact was of the "G" fragment (pictured), which exploded with the energy of roughly 6 million megatons of TNT (600 times the nuclear arsenal of the world). Jupiter has also taken the brunt of the **largest asteroid impact in the Solar System**. On June 3, 2010, amateur astronomer Anthony Wesley (Australia) observed an asteroid of around 26–43 ft (8–13 m) across crashing into the planet.

JUPITER AT A GLANCE

Namesake: King of the Roman gods

Adjective: Jovian

Date of discovery: Unknown

Mean distance from Sun: 484,632,000 miles (778,330,000 km)

Diameter: 89,405 miles (143,884 km)

Mass: 318 Earths; 1,898,130,000,000,000, 000,000,000,000 kg

Orbital period: 11.86 years

Rotation period: 9 hr 55 min 29.69 sec

Designation: Outer planet; Gas giant

Satellites: 63, four of which are significant bodies in the Solar System (see right); also has a thin, wispy system of dust rings discovered in 1979

INSIDE THE GAS GIANT

Jupiter has a mass 318 times greater than Earth – indeed, it has nearly three times the mass of all the other Solar System planets added together. Despite this, it's composed mostly of gases and liquids around a relatively small, solid core.

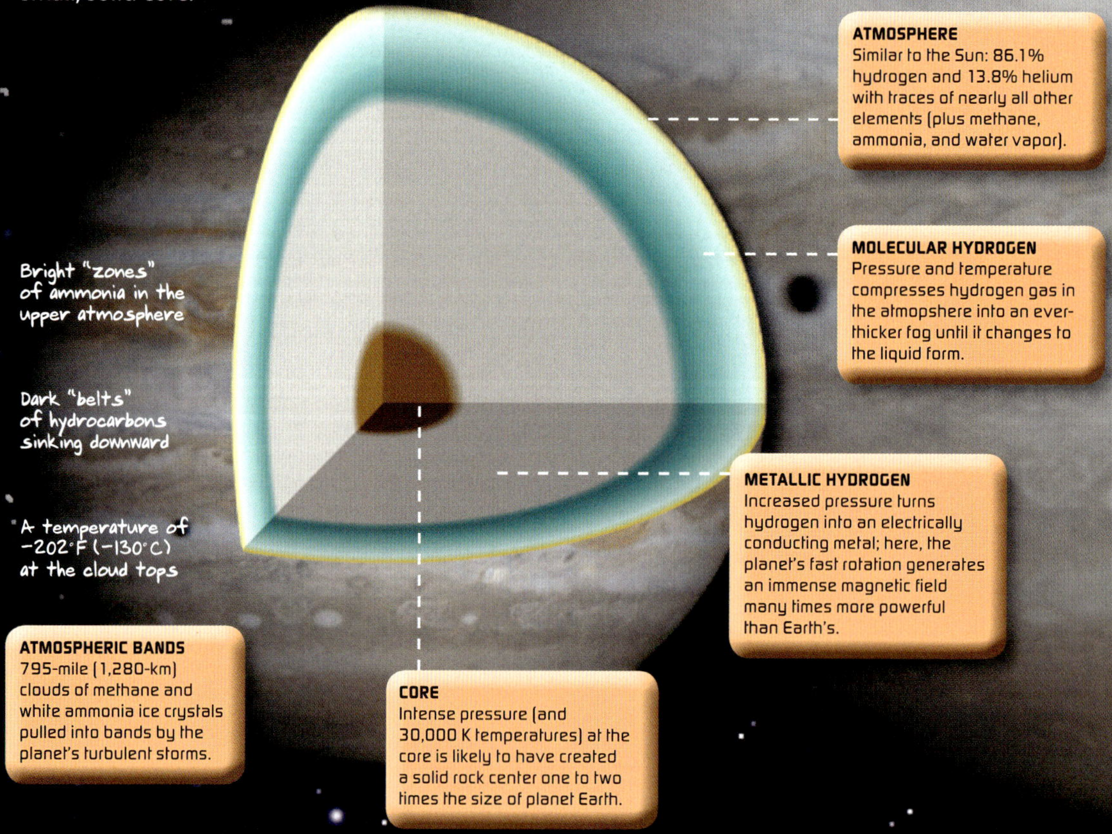

The **most expensive license plate** – the single digit "1" – was sold to Saeed Abdul Ghaffar Khouri (UAE) for Dh52.2 million ($14.2 million) during a special number plate auction in Abu Dhabi, UAE, on February 16, 2008.

DIZZYING HEIGHTS
Boosaule Montes, on the moon Io, reaches up to 52,493 ft (17,000 m) in height – taller than Earth's two biggest mountains, Everest and K2, put together.

MOST POWERFUL AURORAE IN THE SOLAR SYSTEM

The aurorae on Jupiter are around 1,000 times more powerful than Earth's. They are caused by energetic particles from the Sun being channeled on to the Jovian poles by Jupiter's magnetic field and causing atoms in its upper atmosphere to glow like the gas in a neon tube. They produce around 1 million megawatts (MW) of energy, enough to power 100 major cities on Earth. The bands and curtains of the Jovian aurorae can be as large as the Earth.

LARGEST PLANET IN THE SOLAR SYSTEM

With an equatorial diameter of 89,405 miles (143,884 km) and a polar diameter of 83,082 miles (133,708 km), Jupiter is the largest of the eight major planets. It has a mass 317.828 times, and a volume 1,323.3 times, that of the Earth. With its Sun-like composition, powerful magnetic field, and array of more than 60 moons, it is effectively a Solar System in miniature – indeed, it actually *would* be a star if it had sufficient mass to collapse in on itself and trigger a thermonuclear reaction.

LARGEST ANTICYCLONE IN THE SOLAR SYSTEM

Jupiter's Great Red Spot (right) is the largest known anticyclonic storm. Although it has varied in size since its discovery in 1664, it has been up to 24,800 miles (40,000 km) long and 8,700 miles (14,000 km) wide, and is as wide as three Earths. The storm rotates anticlockwise at around 270 mi/h (435 km/h) and its clouds tower some 5 miles (8 km) above the cloudscape.

FIRST DISCOVERY OF EXTRATERRESTRIAL VOLCANIC ACTIVITY

Shortly after *Voyager 1*'s 1979 encounter with Jupiter, navigation engineer Linda Morabito (USA) discovered in a black-and-white image an anomalous crescent protruding from the moon Io. Although initially thought to be a moon behind Io, the crescent was soon confirmed to be a part of Io itself. What Morabito had discovered was the first active volcano on a world other than Earth.

MOST POWERFUL OBSERVED ERUPTION

In February 2001, Io's Surt volcano erupted with an estimated power output of 78,000 gigawatts (GW) – a huge force by comparison with the 1992 eruption of Mount Etna in Sicily, Italy, which had an output of just 12 GW. The observations were made with the WM Keck II Telescope in Hawaii, USA, and published in the journal *Icarus* in November 2002.

HIGHEST VOLCANIC ERUPTION

On August 6, 2001, *Galileo* performed a flyby of Io at a distance of 120 miles (194 km) from the surface and passed through the top of a volcanic plume measuring around 310 miles (500 km) high. Originating at the Tvashtar volcano, near Io's North Pole, it is the highest volcanic eruption plume ever witnessed in the Solar System.

PLANET WITH THE MOST TROJAN ASTEROIDS

Trojan asteroids are clusters of small bodies that share the orbit of a planet, at positions 60° behind and ahead of the planet. As of January 2011, some 4,793 trojans have been discovered sharing Jupiter's orbit, with Neptune having seven and Mars four. The asteroids are named after figures from the Trojan Wars – the first being 588 Achilles, discovered in 1906 by the astronomer Max Wolf (Germany) – and designated one of two "camps": Greek (for those 60° ahead of Jupiter) or Trojan (60° behind).

JOVIAN MOONS

Jupiter has 63 confirmed moons, comprising eight "regular" moons (including the four "Galilean" moons detailed below) and 55 "irregular" moons. The Galilean moons – so called because they were discovered by the Italian astronomer Galileo – account for 99.997% of the mass of Jupiter's satellites and ring system.

IO
Jupiter's closest Galilean moon, Io is the **most volcanically active world in the Solar System**, pulled and squeezed by tidal interactions with Jupiter and Europa.

EUROPA
With prominences of just a few hundred yards, this ice-covered moon has the **smoothest surface in the Solar System**; believed to have a subsurface sea of saltwater.

GANYMEDE
At 3,273 miles (5,267 km) in diameter, Ganymede is the **largest satellite in the Solar System**, and bigger than the planet Mercury; it is also 2,017 times heavier than our own Moon.

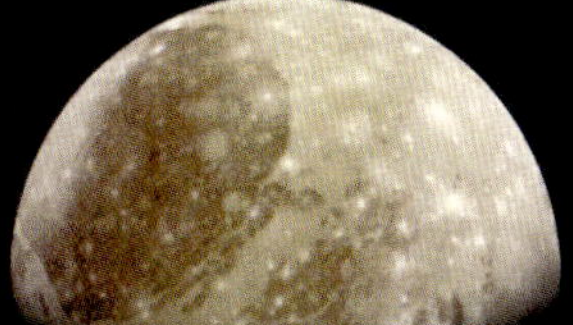

CALLISTO
The outermost of Jupiter's satellites, Callisto is the **most heavily cratered moon**, its surface entirely pitted with craters caused by meteorite impacts; its distance from Jupiter – and its geological stability – means that Callisto is a likely first target for future human exploration of the outer Solar System.

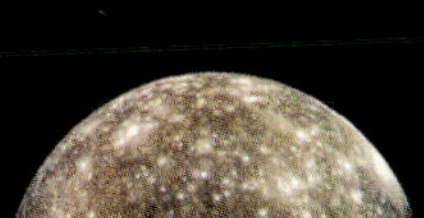

UPDATED RECORD
NEW RECORD

All vehicles need a license plate, even the VH Valiant that pulled off the **longest ramp jump**. Driven by Ray Baumann (Australia), the automobile covered 237 ft (72.23 m) at Ravenswood International Raceway in Perth, Australia, on August 23, 1998.

ASTEROIDS

LARGEST IMPACT CRATER ON EARTH

Of approximately 150 impact craters identified so far on Earth, the largest is the Vredefort crater, located near Johannesburg, South Africa, with an estimated diameter of 186 miles (300 km). This enormous, eroded structure was formed approximately 2 billion years ago, when an asteroid or comet collided with the Earth.

GREATEST IMPACT ON EARTH

Most astronomers now believe that 4.5 billion years ago, a planet the size of Mars collided with the young Earth. Some of the debris from this cataclysm went into orbit around the Earth and collected together under its own gravity to form the Moon. The effect of this impact would have been absolutely devastating to the Earth. The entire crust of the planet would probably have been blasted off into space, leaving behind an Earth whose entire surface was an ocean of molten magma.

FIRST TRIPLE ASTEROID

The potato-shaped asteroid 87 Sylvia was discovered in 1866 in the main asteroid belt. Its first moon was discovered in 2004; subsequently, in 2005, it became the first asteroid known to have two moons.

CLOSEST TRIPLE ASTEROID TO EARTH

Asteroid 2001 SN263 is a near-Earth asteroid – its orbit brings it close to the Earth, not to the main asteroid belt. Its closest approach to Earth is 6.9 million miles (11.2 million km). In 2008, astronomers at the Arecibo radio observatory, Puerto Rico, struck the asteroid with 500,000 watts of radar energy and discovered from the reflections that it consists of three small asteroids orbiting each other. They measure just 1.2 miles, 0.6 miles, and 0.2 miles (2 km, 1 km, and 0.4 km) across respectively.

FIRST MATERIALS RETURNED FROM AN ASTEROID

On June 13, 2010, the unmanned spacecraft *Hayabusa*, built and operated by the Japanese space agency JAXA, landed on Earth with around 1,500 tiny solid grains of material collected mostly from the surface of the asteroid Itokawa. *Hayabusa* was the **first spacecraft to lift off from an asteroid**.

LARGEST CONCENTRATION OF ASTEROIDS

Sitting between the orbits of Mars and Jupiter is the largest gathering of asteroids in the Solar System – the main asteroid belt. It contains between 700,000 and 1,700,000 asteroids that are at least 0.3 miles (1 km) across, and many millions of smaller bodies.

The **largest asteroid** within the main asteroid belt is 1 Ceres, which has an average diameter of 584.7 miles (941 km) and was discovered by Giuseppe Piazzi (Italy), a Catholic priest, on January 1, 1801.

First discovered in 1885, 253 Mathilde, like 1 Ceres, is found in the main asteroid belt. It measures 41 x 29 x 28 miles (66 x 48 x 46 km) and became the third and **largest asteroid visited by a spacecraft** in June 1997, when it was passed by NASA's *NEAR Shoemaker*.

FIRST ASTEROID WITH A MOON

While en route to Jupiter, NASA's *Galileo* spacecraft performed a flyby of the asteroid Ida in 1993. On February 17, 1994, scrutiny of the images from the flyby revealed that Ida, which is 33.3 miles (53.6 km) along its longest axis, has its own natural satellite. Dactyl measures just 0.9 x 0.8 x 0.7 miles (1.6 x 1.4 x 1.2 km) in diameter and orbits Ida once every 20 hours.

STAR STRUCK

The **first person injured by a meteorite** was Ann Hodges of Sylacauga, Alabama, USA, who suffered bruising when a 12-lb (5.5-kg) piece of chondrite crashed through the roof of her home on November 30, 1954.

FIRST ACCURATELY PREDICTED ASTEROID IMPACT

On October 6, 2008, astronomers discovered a small asteroid, later named 2008 TC3. Analysis of the asteroid's orbit indicated it would arrive at Earth just 21 hours later. At 2:46 a.m. (UTC) on October 7, 2008, it struck the atmosphere at high speed, causing it to explode some 23 miles (37 km) above Sudan. This main picture shows a NASA scientist with debris from the explosion; the smaller picture, right, shows the asteroid's trail, distorted by high-altitude winds.

The **most expensive cricket bat** was "The Don," used by Aussie cricket legend Sir Don Bradman in his debut Test in 1928. It sold for A$145,000 ($121,900) at Leski Auctions, Melbourne, Australia, on September 24, 2008.

700,000–1

The odds of you being killed by asteroid impact. In fact, asteroids with a diameter of up to 33 ft enter the Earth's atmosphere around once a year, but usually explode harmlessly almost immediately.

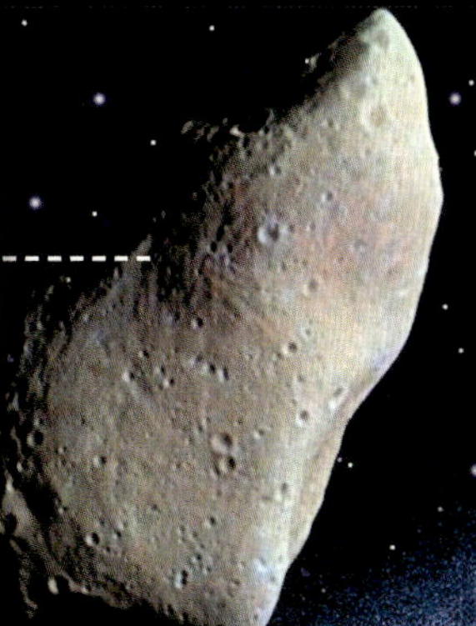

FIRST ASTEROID VISITED BY A SPACECRAFT
951 Gaspra, visited by NASA's *Galileo* on October 29, 1991

BRIGHTEST ASTEROID

Asteroid 4 Vesta was discovered on March 29, 1807 and is the only asteroid visible to the naked eye. This is due to a combination of the brightness of its surface, its size (357.9 miles, or 576 km across), and the fact that it approaches Earth to within 110 million miles (177 million km).

SMALLEST ASTEROID

There are several contenders for this record. Asteroid 1993KA2 was discovered on May 21, 1993 and has a diameter of around 16 ft (5 m); 2000LG6, discovered on June 4, 2000, appears to have a similar diameter. The other candidates are 1991BA, 1991TU, 1991VG, and 1994ES1.

FIRST ASTEROID LANDING

The *NEAR Shoemaker* spacecraft touched down on asteroid 433 Eros on February 12, 2001. The craft transmitted 69 images of the surface of Eros during its descent, showing details of small rocks just centimeters across. Eros measures around 20.5 miles (33 km) across.

LARGEST OBJECT CHAOTICALLY ROTATING

Saturn's moon Hyperion measures 254 x 161 x 136 miles (410 x 260 x 220 km) and is the largest highly irregularly shaped body in the Solar System. It is one of only two bodies in the Solar System discovered to have completely chaotic rotation, essentially randomly tumbling in its orbit around Saturn. The other is asteroid 4179 Toutatis, which has an area of 2.7 x 1.5 x 1.1 miles (4.5 x 2.4 x 1.9 km).

SLOWEST-ROTATING ASTEROID

The asteroid 288 Glauke was discovered by telescope in 1890. It measures around 20 miles (32 km) across but takes around 50 days to spin once on its axis. Of all the bodies in the Solar System, only the planets Mercury and Venus are known to spin more slowly.

SHORTEST-PERIOD ASTEROID

Asteroid 2004 JG6 orbits the Sun in 184.46 days. It was discovered by Brian Skiff (USA) at the Lowell Observatory, Flagstaff, Arizona, USA, and announced on May 13, 2004.

MOST ASTEROIDS DISCOVERED

The eminent astrogeologist Dr Eugene Shoemaker (USA, 1928–97) discovered 1,125 asteroids, many in partnership with his wife and fellow astronomer, Carolyn.

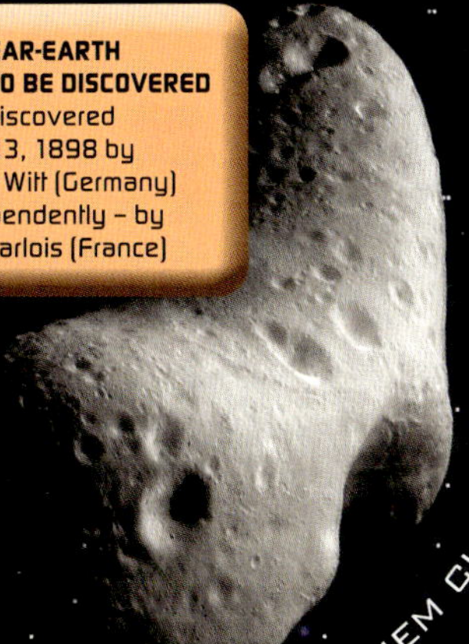

FIRST NEAR-EARTH ASTEROID TO BE DISCOVERED
433 Eros, discovered on August 13, 1898 by Carl Gustav Witt (Germany) and – independently – by Auguste Charlois (France)

FIRST ASTEROID WITH A TAIL
P/2010 A2, discovered in 2010 in the main asteroid belt between Mars and Jupiter

"NEAR-EARTH OBJECTS": SMALL OBJECTS WHOSE ORBITS BRING THEM CLOSE TO EARTH

OLDEST CONFIRMED IMPACT
Around 3.47 billion years ago, an asteroid 12–19 miles (20–30 km) across crashed into the Earth, leaving deposits in Australia and South Africa that were discovered by US scientists in 2002

TORINO SCALE

Professor Richard P Binzel of the Massachusetts Institute of Technology (MIT), USA, devised this scale, which ranks the chances of an object in space colliding with Earth.

0	No hazard	No prospect of a meteor or asteroid colliding with Earth
1	Normal	The body will pass near Earth, but there is little danger
2	Meriting attention from astronomers	Close but safe approach. No cause for concern
3		Extremely small chance of collision and local damage
4		Small chance of collision and regional damage
5	Threatening	Serious but uncertain danger of impact. Astronomers to investigate
6		Serious but uncertain danger of impact from large object. Astronomers to investigate
7		Prospect of an impact by a large object. International studies and contingency planning needed
8	Certain collisions	Local destruction
9		Large-scale regional destruction
10		Certain impact. Possible climatic catastrophe worldwide. Occurs perhaps once every 100,000 years on average

UPDATED RECORD
NEW RECORD

The **most valuable baseball bat** in the world once belonged to George Herman "Babe" Ruth. It was sold at an auction at Sotheby's, New York City, USA, for $1,265,000 on December 2, 2004.

INTERNATIONAL SPACE STATION

By 2012, assembly of the *International Space Station* – the most expensive object ever made by humans – will be complete. Join us in low Earth orbit as we survey the record-breaking research facility…

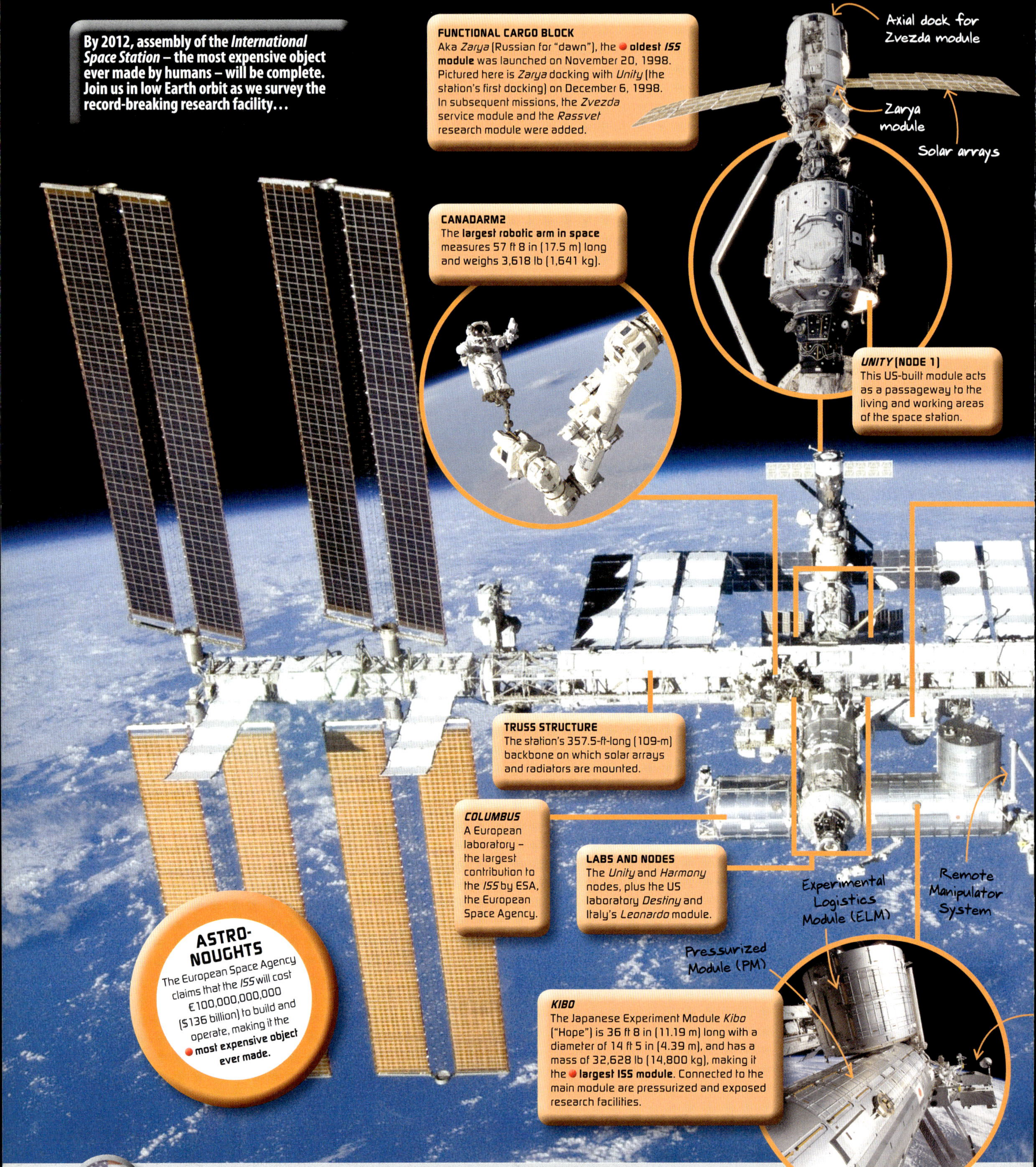

FUNCTIONAL CARGO BLOCK
Aka *Zarya* (Russian for "dawn"), the ● **oldest *ISS* module** was launched on November 20, 1998. Pictured here is *Zarya* docking with *Unity* (the station's first docking) on December 6, 1998. In subsequent missions, the *Zvezda* service module and the *Rassvet* research module were added.

CANADARM2
The **largest robotic arm in space** measures 57 ft 8 in (17.5 m) long and weighs 3,618 lb (1,641 kg).

***UNITY* (NODE 1)**
This US-built module acts as a passageway to the living and working areas of the space station.

TRUSS STRUCTURE
The station's 357.5-ft-long (109-m) backbone on which solar arrays and radiators are mounted.

COLUMBUS
A European laboratory – the largest contribution to the *ISS* by ESA, the European Space Agency.

LABS AND NODES
The *Unity* and *Harmony* nodes, plus the US laboratory *Destiny* and Italy's *Leonardo* module.

KIBO
The Japanese Experiment Module *Kibo* ("Hope") is 36 ft 8 in (11.19 m) long with a diameter of 14 ft 5 in (4.39 m), and has a mass of 32,628 lb (14,800 kg), making it the ● **largest ISS module**. Connected to the main module are pressurized and exposed research facilities.

ASTRO-NOUGHTS
The European Space Agency claims that the *ISS* will cost €100,000,000,000 ($136 billion) to build and operate, making it the ● **most expensive object ever made.**

According to the World Wealth Report's 2010 figures, the USA has 2,886,200 millionaires – making it the ● **country with the most millionaires.** The number has dropped from 3,028,000 in 2008.

$12.26 The average annual contribution you will pay as a taxpayer to fund the *International Space Station* once the total cost is shared between the citizens of participating nations.

PHOTOVOLTAIC ARRAYS
Four wing pairs of cells provide power to the main body of the station.

BLAST-OFF
To avoid a buildup of noxious flatulence on board space stations (where you can't open a window!), NASA once issued a "banned foods" list that included cabbages and beans!

LARGEST WINDOW IN SPACE
Cupola – a module attached to *Tranquility* – is a cluster of seven windows with an overall diameter of 9 ft 7 in (2.95 m). It was built by ESA and launched on February 8, 2010. Pictured is NASA's Tracy Caldwell Dyson (USA) looking down over Earth on September 11, 2010.

ELC
The ExPRESS Logistics Carrier (ExPRESS stands for "Expedites the Processing of Experiments to the Space Station") collects and handles experiment data.

LARGEST ARTIFICIAL SATELLITE
At 357 x 167 x 65 ft (109 x 51 x 20 m), the *ISS* is the largest manmade object to orbit the Earth, doing so once every 91 minutes. It can easily be seen from the ground with the naked eye during darkness.

MOST WOMEN IN ORBIT
On April 5, 2010, Dorothy Metcalf-Lindenburger, Stephanie Wilson, and Naoko Yamazaki joined Tracy Caldwell Dyson on board the *ISS* – the most females in orbit at once.

MOST VISITED SPACE STATION

As of December 2010, the *ISS* had received 297 visitors. This represents 196 different people, as many astronauts and cosmonauts have traveled to the station more than once. For comparison, the Russian *Mir* space station (in operation from 1986 to 2001) had 137 visitors over its lifetime, representing 104 different people.

MOST VISITS INTO SPACE BY A TOURIST

The Hungarian-born software billionaire Charles Simonyi (USA) paid $25 million for his first trip on a Russian *Soyuz* rocket on April 7, 2007, the first stage of a 12-day visit to the *ISS*.

Two years later, at the age of 60, Simonyi paid a further $35 million for a second voyage to the *ISS*, the **most expensive tourist trip**, departing March 26, 2009 and returning April 9, 2009.

THE ISS TOILET COST A RECORD $19 MILLION!

UPDATED RECORD
NEW RECORD

MOST TIME IN SPACE
Sergei Krikalev (Russia), commander of the *ISS* between April 14 and October 10 2005, has accumulated 803 days 9 hr 39 min in space.

FIRST RESIDENT CREW ON BOARD THE *ISS*
The crew of Expedition 1 – Russia's Sergei Krikalev (left) and Yuri Pavlovich Gidzenko (center), and the USA's William Shepherd – arrived at the *ISS* on November 2, 2000 and stayed for 136 days.

FASTEST MARATHON IN SPACE

The fastest time to complete a marathon in orbit was achieved by NASA astronaut Sunita Williams of Needham, Massachusetts, USA, above Earth on board the *ISS*. Ms Williams, who ran the 26.2-mile (42-km) race strapped to a treadmill with bungy cord, competed as an official entrant of the 111th Boston Marathon (USA) on April 16, 2007, finishing in a time of 4 hr 24 min.

The country with the **highest concentration of millionaires** (measured in US dollars) is not the USA but Singapore. Here, an astonishing 8.5% of households had $1 million in assets under management as of 2009.

SPACE DISASTERS

WORST DISASTER IN A MANNED SPACE FLIGHT

Of the nearly 300 attempted manned space flights as of February 2011, two missions have each seen a record seven fatalities. On January 28, 1986, an explosion occurred 73 seconds after liftoff of the space shuttle *Challenger*'s STS-51L mission from the Kennedy Space Center, Florida, USA, at a height of 46,000 ft (14,020 m). Five men and two women (below) died. In 2003, tragedy struck again (see opposite).

WORST UNCONTROLLED SPIN IN SPACE

In March 1968, during the first docking in space – between the *Gemini 8* craft flown by Neil Armstrong (right) and David Scott (both USA) and an unmanned *Agena* booster – the two spacecraft began an uncontrolled roll. After an emergency undocking, *Gemini 8* began to roll faster and the crew were close to g-forces that would have impaired their vision or made them black out. Armstrong stopped the roll using *Gemini 8*'s reentry thrusters and initiated a mission abort and emergency splashdown (below right).

FIRST FIRE ON A SPACE STATION

On February 23, 1997, a fire broke out on the Russian space station *Mir*, caused by lithium perchlorate "candles" that supplied oxygen to the station. The fire was put out, but the crew had come close to abandoning *Mir* in their *Soyuz* "lifeboat."

FAR OUT!

At 8:21 p.m. ET on April 14, 1970, the crew of *Apollo 13* were at apocynthion (the farthest point from the Moon), 248,655 miles (400,171 km) above our planet's surface, the **greatest distance from Earth reached by humans**.

FIRST FATALITIES AT A LAUNCH REHEARSAL

US astronauts Virgil Ivan "Gus" Grissom, Edward Higgins White II, and Roger Bruce Chaffee were killed in a fire inside their *Apollo 1* capsule on January 27, 1967 during a launch rehearsal at Cape Canaveral, Florida, USA. The fire was caused by a spark from an electrical fault in the capsule's artificial atmosphere of pure oxygen.

SPACE DEBRIS

Many thousands of pieces of manmade debris orbit Earth, from tiny particles to defunct satellites. Around 20,000 of them are tracked by radar. Here is a selection.

- A camera belonging to US astronaut Suni Williams drifted away in June 2007 while she was working on the *International Space Station*.
- In November 2007, a pair of needle-nosed pliers belonging to Scott Parazynski (USA) floated off while he was on a spacewalk to carry out work on a solar array.
- A glove belonging to the first US spacewalker, Ed White, waved goodbye in 1965. After orbiting the Earth for a month or so, it burned up in the atmosphere.
- In 2006, while testing material that could be used to repair damaged heat shields, astronaut Piers Sellers (US, b. UK) lost a spatula on *Discovery*'s STS-121 flight.
- A whole bag of tools belonging to Heide Stefanyshyn-Piper (USA) and worth about $100,000 drifted away while she was on a spacewalk in November 2008.

FOR EXPLORATIONS ON PLANET EARTH ITSELF, TAKE OFF FOR P.120.

Singapore is clearly a significant port of call for business. In 2009, a total of 1,040 billion lb (472 million tonnes) of cargo passed through, making it the world's **busiest port**.

SHORTEST MANNED MOON SHOT

An oxygen tank exploded on *Apollo 13*'s outward journey to the Moon in April 1970, forcing the US crew to evacuate the command module and use the attached lunar module as a lifeboat. *Apollo 13* used a "free return trajectory" to return home, relying on the Moon's gravity to slingshot the spacecraft around it and back to Earth. All three crew members survived their five-day, 22-hour ordeal.

WORST GROUND-BASED SPACE DISASTER

In the greatest space disaster on the ground, 91 people were killed when an R-16 rocket exploded during fueling at the Baikonur Space Center, Kazakhstan, on October 24, 1960.

MOST DAMAGING SPACECRAFT COLLISION

On June 25, 1997, an unmanned *Progress* supply vehicle, weighing 15,000 lb (7 tonnes), collided with the Russian *Mir* space station. Cosmonauts had to work quickly to seal a breach in the hull of *Mir's Spektr* module, while a US astronaut prepared *Mir's Soyuz* capsule for a possible evacuation. There were no fatalities, but *Mir* was left low on power and oxygen and temporarily tumbled out of control.

FIRST LIGHTNING STRIKE DURING A SPACE MISSION

Less than a minute after *Apollo 12* lifted off from Cape Canaveral, Florida, USA, on November 14, 1969, the spacecraft suffered severe electrical anomalies, including the loss of the fuel cells that provided power to the command module, leaving it on battery power alone. Mission control and the crew were able to overcome these problems and stay on course for Earth orbit. It was found that *Apollo 12* had been struck twice by lightning at 36 seconds and 52 seconds after launch.

FIRST DEATH IN ORBIT

A dog named Laika (meaning "barker") became the **first animal to orbit the Earth** when she launched into space aboard the Soviet *Sputnik 2* spacecraft on November 3, 1957. In October 2002, it was revealed that she had died just a few hours after launch from stress and overheating.

FIRST ASTRONAUT KILLED IN FLIGHT DURING TRAINING

Theodore ("Ted") Freeman (USA), pictured in training, died on October 31, 1964 when his T-38 trainer aircraft collided with a goose. Both engines flamed out and, while attempting an emergency landing away from buildings at Ellington Air Force Base, Freeman ejected too close to the ground to survive.

UPDATED RECORD
NEW RECORD

MOST FATALITIES DURING REENTRY

On February 1, 2003, the space shuttle *Columbia* was lost with all seven crew during reentry into Earth's atmosphere after a successful 15-day mission in orbit. The resulting investigation determined that a piece of insulating foam from the external fuel tank had impacted the leading edge of a wing during launch. This made a hole that allowed heat to build up during reentry, causing the left wing of the orbiter to break apart, and the rest of the spacecraft to disintegrate.

FIRST SPACE FLIGHT DEATH TOLL

By the end of the *Soyuz 11* mission, on June 30, 1971, Viktor Ivanovich Patsayev, Vladislav Nikolayevich Volkov (both Russia), and Georgy Timofeyevich Dobrovolsky (Ukraine) had spent three weeks on the Soviet *Salyut 1* space station. After undocking, a valve failed and exposed the crew, who were not wearing spacesuits, to the vacuum of space at an altitude of 104 miles (168 km). They were asphyxiated within seconds.

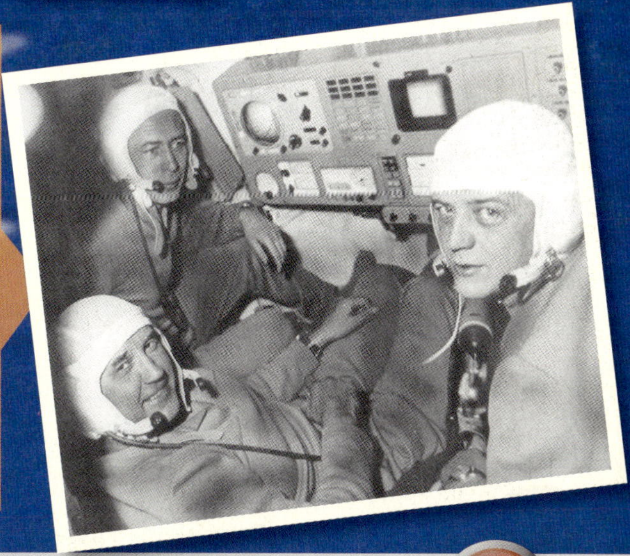

THE MOTHER OF ALL THUNDERSTORMS

Supercells are powerful thunderstorms that form around a mesocyclone (a deep, rotating updraft). They can be several miles across and may last several hours, making them both the **longest-lasting** and **largest thunderstorms**. They often occur on the Great Plains of the USA and can spawn tornadoes. This supercell occurred in July 2010 in Montana, USA, and was photographed by Sean Heavey. "It was around five-to-ten miles in diameter with hurling winds of around 85 miles an hour," he reported. "I'm not ashamed to admit that it scared the living daylights out of me."

As of 2006, China is the **largest producer of energy**, with 1,749 Mtoe (million metric tons of oil equivalent). A "toe" is a unit of measurement representing the amount of energy released when 1.1 tons (1 metric ton) of crude oil is burned.

The country with the **largest consumption of energy per head** is Qatar, with an average energy consumption of 48,627 lb (22,057 kg) of oil equivalent per person in 2006.

ANATOMY OF EARTH

OUR RECORD-BREAKING HOME

Earth is the **largest terrestrial planet**, the **densest**, the **most geologically active inner planet**, and the only body in the Solar System with significant liquid water on its surface. It is home to the only known life in the universe. We share the planet with at least 2 million species of animal that we know of, and maybe up to 100 million more. Our Moon – which is about as wide as Australia – is the **largest satellite relative to planet size**, and with it we revolve around our Sun at 18.5 mi/s (29.78 km/s). What an amazing world we live on!

WHAT A MOUTHFUL!

The Earth's total mass is given as 1.32×10^{25} lb, which can also be expressed as 13,200,000,000,000,000,000,000,000 lb, or 5.972 septillion kg.

EARTH FACT FINDER

Earth is a 4.6-billion-year-old oblate spheroid, meaning that its polar axis is shorter (by 26.7 miles) than its equatorial axis, giving it a bulge around the middle.

EARTH*	
Mass (total)	1.32×10^{25} lb
Mass (atmosphere)	1.1×10^{19} lb
Mass (hydrosphere)	3.09×10^{21} lb
Surface area (total)	196,939,900 miles^2
Surface area (water)	139,397,000 miles^2
Radius (equatorial)	3,963 miles
Radius (polar)	3,950 miles
Volume	2.6×10^{11} miles^3
Rotational period	23 hr 56 min 4.1 sec
Average temperature	59°F (15°C)
EXTREMES	
Highest point	29,029 ft (Mount Everest, Nepal)
Lowest point (on land)	1,371 ft (Dead Sea shore, Israel and Jordan)
Deepest point	35,797 ft (Challenger Deep in the Marianas Trench)
Highest temperature recorded	136°F (58°C) at Al'Aziziyah in the Sahara Desert, Libya
Lowest temperature recorded	-128.6°F (-89.2°C) at Vostok, Antarctica

Sources: NASA, National Geophysical Data Center; boundaries, and therefore data, vary depending upon agency.

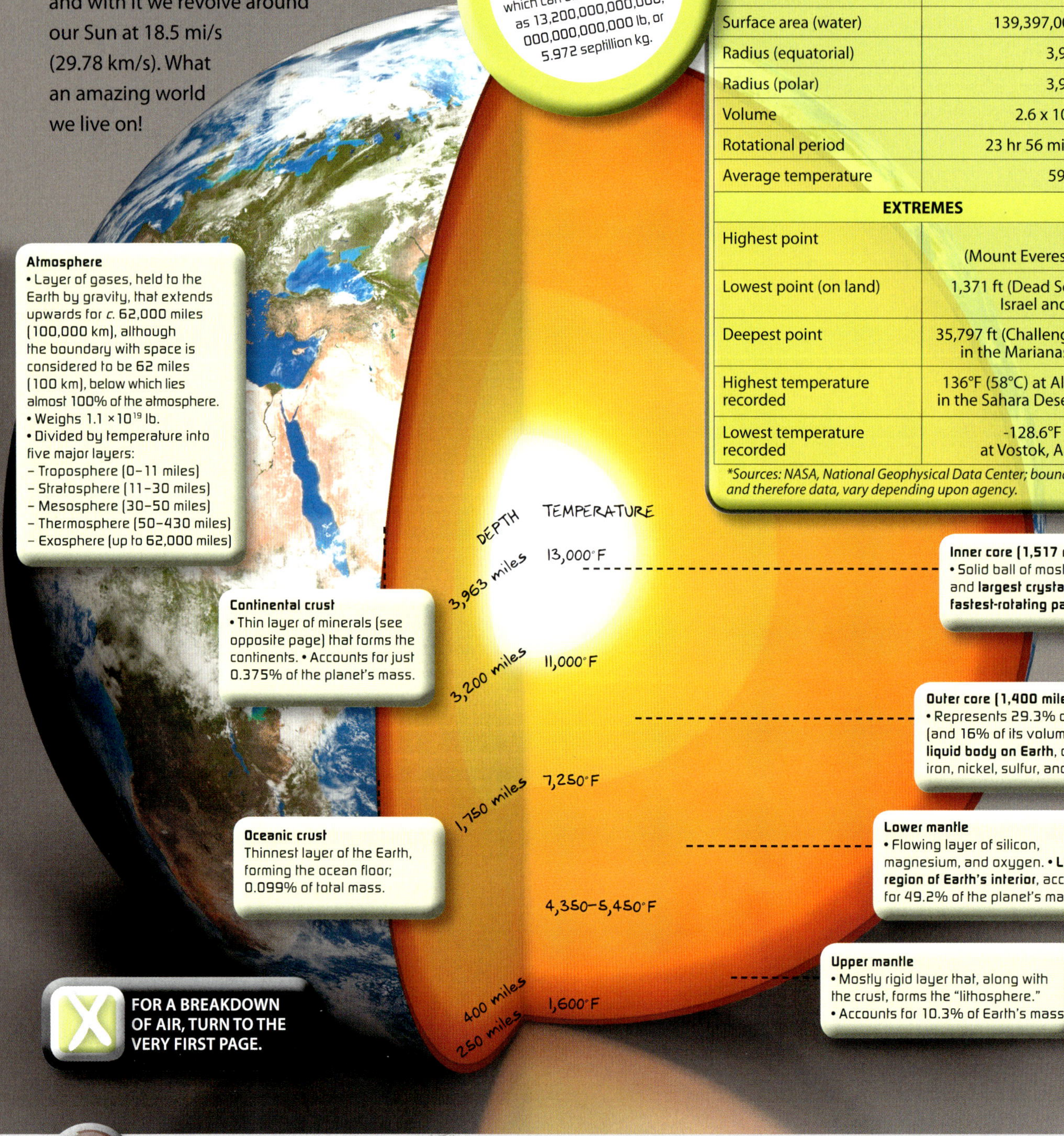

Atmosphere
- Layer of gases, held to the Earth by gravity, that extends upwards for *c.* 62,000 miles (100,000 km), although the boundary with space is considered to be 62 miles (100 km), below which lies almost 100% of the atmosphere.
- Weighs 1.1×10^{19} lb.
- Divided by temperature into five major layers:
  - Troposphere (0–11 miles)
  - Stratosphere (11–30 miles)
  - Mesosphere (30–50 miles)
  - Thermosphere (50–430 miles)
  - Exosphere (up to 62,000 miles)

Continental crust
- Thin layer of minerals (see opposite page) that forms the continents.
- Accounts for just 0.375% of the planet's mass.

Oceanic crust
Thinnest layer of the Earth, forming the ocean floor; 0.099% of total mass.

Inner core (1,517 miles wide)
- Solid ball of mostly nickel and iron and **largest crystal on Earth**.
- The **fastest-rotating part of the Earth**.

Outer core (1,400 miles thick)
- Represents 29.3% of Earth's mass (and 16% of its volume).
- **Largest liquid body on Earth**, comprising iron, nickel, sulfur, and oxygen.

Lower mantle
- Flowing layer of silicon, magnesium, and oxygen.
- **Largest region of Earth's interior**, accounting for 49.2% of the planet's mass.

Upper mantle
- Mostly rigid layer that, along with the crust, forms the "lithosphere."
- Accounts for 10.3% of Earth's mass.

FOR A BREAKDOWN OF AIR, TURN TO THE VERY FIRST PAGE.

UPDATED RECORD
NEW RECORD

The **most money paid for a cell phone number** is 10 million QAR ($2.75 million), by an anonymous Qatari bidder for the number 666-6666 on May 23, 2006.

2.01 Your share of the Earth in acres – i.e., the area of the world suitable for farming divided by the world's population. Barring fish, all your food comes from a piece of land the size of a soccer field.

COMPOSITION OF THE EARTH

The Earth was formed from the same cloud of gas and dust as the Sun and the other planets. But the chemical composition of the Earth is very different from that of the universe as a whole, where hydrogen is the **most abundant element** (accounting for at least 90% of all matter). The **most abundant element on Earth** is iron, at around 36%.

Like the other elemental building blocks of our planet, pictured here in their raw form, most of the oxygen (which is highly reactive) on Earth is locked away in minerals – the crystalline solids from which rocks are formed. The **most abundant minerals on Earth** are the silicates (formed with silicon and oxygen), which account for about 95% of the planet's crust. This explains why oxygen (a colorless gas indicated by the jar in the picture to the right) forms such a large part – around 46% – of the mass of the crust.

Land (29.1% of surface)
Area: *c.* 57,506,000 miles^2
(*c.* 148,940,000 km^2)
All the land on Earth combined would form a perfectly round island 8,556 miles wide – large enough to stretch across the Pacific Ocean from Mexico to China with 620 miles to spare at either end!

Water (70.9% of surface)
Area: *c.* 139.3 million miles^2
(*c.* 361.9 million km^2)
Of this, only 2.5% is fresh, comprising ice (1.6%), underground aquifers (0.6%), and lakes/rivers (0.36%). The rest is ocean and sea.

Q. What color is water?

A. It really *is* blue! But not because it reflects the blue sky. The main reason is because it absorbs light at the red end of the spectrum, so we see the opposite color: blue.

THE BLUE PLANET

Earth is known as the Blue Planet because its surface is covered mostly in water. Liquid water hasn't been found in significant quantities on the surface of any other planet in our Solar System. The word "hydrosphere" describes all the water on, over, and inside a planet, but although 70.9% of Earth's surface is covered in water, the hydrosphere accounts for just 0.023% of the planet's mass.

The average depth of the ocean is 12,430 ft (3,790 m) – roughly as deep as the Alps are tall – but the **deepest point in the ocean** is 35,797 ft (10,911 m). If Mount Everest was dropped into the ocean at this point, it would disappear 1.2 miles (2 km) below the surface.

THE OCEANS

About 97% of the surface water on Earth is ocean. We identify and name up to seven different oceans, but they are connected to form one continuous body of water covering an area of approximately 139 x 10^6 miles^2 (3.6 x 10^8 km^2). The droplets of water pictured here show the relative volumes of the five major oceans; in reality, the oceans combined would form a drop of water 852 miles (1,371 km) wide – about the same length as the British Isles.

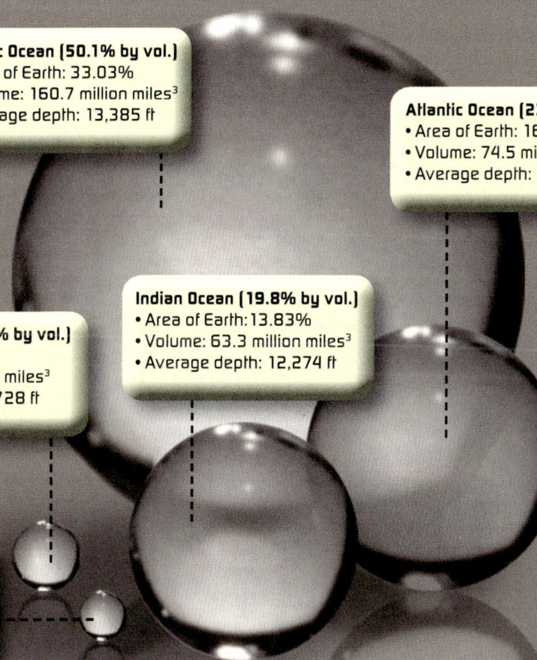

Pacific Ocean (50.1% by vol.)
- Area of Earth: 33.03%
- Volume: 160.7 million miles^3
- Average depth: 13,385 ft

Atlantic Ocean (23.3% by vol.)
- Area of Earth: 16.69%
- Volume: 74.5 million miles^3
- Average depth: 11,962 ft

Indian Ocean (19.8% by vol.)
- Area of Earth: 13.83%
- Volume: 63.3 million miles^3
- Average depth: 12,274 ft

Southern Ocean (5.4% by vol.)
- Area of Earth: 4.3%
- Volume: 17.2 million miles^3
- Average depth: 10,728 ft

Arctic Ocean (1.4% by vol.)
- Area of Earth: 3.05%
- Volume: 4.5 million miles^3
- Average depth: 3,953 ft

Source: NOAA National Geophysical Data Center

The **fastest completion of a prescribed 160-character text message** is 34.65 seconds by Frode Ness (Norway) at the Oslo City shopping mall in Oslo, Østlandet, Norway, on November 13, 2010.

POPULATIONS

LEAST COMMON LANGUAGE

Yaghan is an indigenous language of Tierra del Fuego, an archipelago on the southern tip of South America. The Yaghan numbered as many as 10,000 people before Argentina and Chile began exploring the islands in the late 19th century, but disease, relocation, and exploitation have since caused the population to collapse, to around 70 by 1930. Today, Cristina Calderón (born *c.* 1938), pictured, is the last native speaker.

MOST DENSELY POPULATED COUNTRY

With a disproportionately large population of 30,586 people and an area of just 0.75 miles² (1.95 km²), the tiny sovereign state of Monaco manages to squeeze in a world record 40,624 people per mile² (15,685 per km²).

MOST DENSELY POPULATED TERRITORY

The Chinese territory of Macau is just as crowded, with an estimated 567,957 people sharing a landmass of 11.3 miles² (29.2 km²) – that's a whopping 50,262 people for every mile² (19,450 per km²)!

LOWEST LIFE EXPECTANCY

Poor health care and a prevalence of diseases such as cholera mean that Angola's 13 million people can expect to live for an average of just 38.76 years. By 2011, females were living for 39.83 years, while males were surviving just 37.74 years.

HIGHEST LIFE EXPECTANCY

Monaco's wealthy inhabitants live for an average of 89.78 years, with males enjoying 85.81 years and females 93.9 years – 2.5 times the life of an Angolan man!

LARGEST URBAN POPULATION NORTH OF THE ARCTIC CIRCLE

Despite its inhospitable location 2° north of the Arctic Circle, the northwest Russian seaport of Murmansk has a healthy population of around 311,000 people.

MOST SOUTHERLY INHABITED PLACE

The hamlet of Puerto Toro on Navarino island, Chile, is the most southerly *permanent* human outpost, discounting Antarctic research stations. The 2002 census recorded a population of just 36 people.

LARGEST ANNUAL HUMAN MIGRATION

During the Lunar New Year celebrations in China, an estimated 1.3 billion city workers migrate back to their rural family homes. In 2010, *c.* 2.26 billion railroad journeys were made in China over this 40-day period.

HIGHEST SEASONAL POPULATION CHANGE

The human population of Antarctica is not permanent, but exists in research stations across the continent. In the course of a year, its population swells by a factor of five, from around 1,000 in the winter to around 5,000 during the more forgiving summer months.

Discover the largest populations on the planet, where elbow room comes at a premium...

City: Tokyo, Japan
36 million people, making Greater Tokyo home to 28% of Japan's 126.8 million citizens.

Island: Java, Indonesia
136 million people, or an incredible 57% of the Indonesian population!

Country: China
1.330 billion people, ahead of India's 1.148 billion and the USA's 303.8 million.

Continent: Asia
4 billion people, thanks largely to Chinese and Indian contributions.

LARGEST MAN-MADE FLOATING REED ISLANDS

Lake Titicaca (Peru/Bolivia) is famous for its unique population of several hundred Uros people, who live on its waters on a man-made archipelago of 42 islands. Knitted from mats of totora reed, the islands are constantly under construction, as they rot away over a three-month period.

UPDATED RECORD
NEW RECORD

Located in Longyearbyen on the island of Svalbard, Norway, the Radisson SAS Polar Hotel is the world's **most northerly full-service hotel**, with just 828 miles (1,333 km) separating it from the North Pole.

HIGHEST FERTILITY RATE: In Niger, 7.68 children are born to each woman on average. The West African state also has the highest population growth rate – 3.66% per year.

LITTLE AND LARGE

Nauru may be the smallest republic, but its citizens boast the largest waistlines in the world. With an average body mass index of 35, the South Pacific island has the **most obese population** on the planet.

SMALLEST REPUBLIC: The Pacific island of Nauru has an area of just 8.1 miles^2 (21 km^2) and a population of 9,267, making it the world's smallest independent republic.

HIGHEST-DWELLING ARBOREAL TRIBE: The remote Korowai of Papua, Indonesia, are a tree-dwelling people who live in tree-houses as high as 100 ft (30 m) above the ground.

HIGHEST CONCENTRATION OF UNCONTACTED TRIBES

According to the human rights organization Survival International, there are approximately 100 uncontacted tribes in the world today. More than half of these are believed to live in the Amazon rainforest (such as this tribe photographed in 2008 on the Peru–Brazil border), and many choose to have no contact with the outside world, sometimes exhibiting hostility to strangers.

Q. Which country has the **lowest population density** in the world?

A. Mongolia – which borders the world's most populous nation, China – is a lonely place, with just 5.11 people per mile^2 (1.97 people per km^2).

SOCIAL CLIMBERS

Discovered in the early 20th century, the 3,000-strong Korowai people originally took to the trees to escape the dangers of flooding, animals, and other tribes, building tree-homes with tools of stone or bone.

With an overall floor area of 570 ft^2 (53 m^2), the cosy Eh'hausl Hotel in Amberg, Germany, is the world's **smallest hotel**, capable of providing overnight accommodation for just two paying guests.

CONTINENTS

LARGEST CRATON
Cratons are large parts of continental crust that are stable and that have remained relatively unmodified by plate tectonics since the end of the Precambrian era, 542 million years ago. They are normally located in the interior of continents and contain some of the oldest rocks on Earth. The North American craton is the largest, covering around 70% of the continent. It was formed around 2 billion years ago by the collision of several smaller microcontinents. Pictured is the Adirondack Mountains, an exposed part of the craton.

LONGEST TRANSCONTINENTAL ISTHMUS
The country of Panama is 420 miles (676 km) long – and 31 miles (50 km) wide at its narrowest point – and provides the only land connection between North and South America. Shipping passes between the Atlantic Ocean and Pacific Ocean through the Panama Canal.

3

GREATEST DESERTIFICATION
Two-thirds of Africa is now desert or dryland. Deforestation, overintensive farming, and human migration have all contributed to this condition.

4

LONGEST CONTINENTAL MOUNTAIN RANGE
The Andes mountain range is 4,700 miles (7,600 km) long and spans seven countries. More than 50 of its peaks exceed 20,000 ft (6,000 m).

LARGEST CONTINENT EVER

Have you noticed that some of the coastlines of the continents seem to fit together, rather like a jigsaw puzzle? Geologists believe that around 250 million years ago, the world's landmasses formed one huge supercontinent, which they named Pangea (meaning "entire Earth").

THE CONTINENTS

The Earth has seven continents – although some authorities regard Europe and Asia as one landmass, termed Eurasia. In terms of their relative size, they are:

Ref.	Continent	Area
1	Asia	17,226,000 miles^2 (44,614,000 km^2)
2	Africa	11,667,000 miles^2 (30,216,000 km^2)
3	North America	9,355,000 miles^2 (24,230,000 km^2)
4	South America	6,878,000 miles^2 (17,814,000 km^2)
5	Antarctica	5,500,000 miles^2 (14,245,000 km^2)
6	Europe	4,056,000 miles^2 (10,505,000 km^2)
7	Oceania	3,283,000 miles^2 (8,503,000 km^2)

Karl Friedrich Benz of Karlsruhe, Germany, built the **first successful gasoline-driven automobile**, the three-wheeled Motorwagen. He tested it at Mannheim in late 1885.

0.12 Inches per month by which your fingernails grow – the same rate at which the continents of North America and Europe are moving apart. In a lifetime, that's 6 ft 8.7 in.

WIDEST CONTINENTAL SHELF
The world's widest continental shelf extends for 750 miles (1,210 km) off the coast of Siberia, Russia, into the Arctic Ocean.

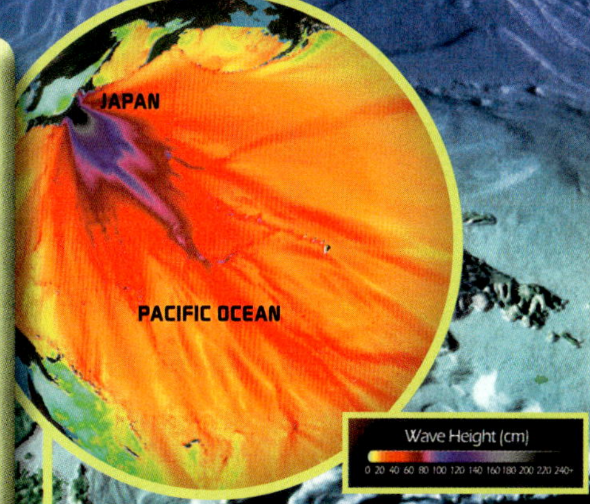

LARGEST VOLCANIC ZONE
The Pacific Ring of Fire is a huge arc of concentrated earthquake and volcanic activity about 24,800 miles (40,000 km) long, located in the Pacific Ocean. It contains some 452 volcanoes and more than 75% of the active and dormant volcanoes in the world. Japan, for example, experiences 1,500 earthquakes each year and is home to 10% of the planet's volcanoes. Pictured is a false-colored map showing the height of waves during the devastating quakes and tsunami that struck Japan on March 11, 2011.

FASTEST LANDMASS
Over time, Earth's continental plates move, relative to each other. The greatest movement occurs at the Tonga microplate, near Samoa, which is moving steadily into the Pacific Ocean at a rate of 9.4 in (24 cm) per year.

LAND FARTHEST FROM THE SEA
The point on the Earth's surface at latitude 46°15.8'N, longitude 86°40.2'E – in the Dzungarian Basin in China's Xinjiang Uygur region – is 1,645 miles (2,648 km) from the nearest open sea.

LEAST VOLCANICALLY ACTIVE CONTINENT
The continental landmass of mainland Australia has experienced no volcanic eruptions for more than 5,000 years. Geological processes other than recent volcanism therefore dominate the landscape. Wave Rock (pictured), more than 2.7 billion years old, is made from granite and has been shaped by chemical weathering. Australia has a mean elevation of just over 656 ft (200 m) above sea level, making it the **flattest continental landmass**. The highest point on the mainland is the tip of Mount Kosciuszko, at 7,312 ft (2,229 m) above sea level.

LEAST-EXPLORED CONTINENT
Antarctica's shoreline was first sighted in 1820 by sea captain William Smith (UK) and explorer Fabian Gottlieb von Bellingshausen (Russia). It was also the last continent to be discovered.

UPDATED RECORD
NEW RECORD

Nowadays, automobiles are commonplace and nowhere more so than in Luxembourg, which has the **highest rate of automobile ownership** in the world, with 647 automobiles per 1,000 people.

WORLD OF WONDERS

Over the next four pages, Guinness World Records focuses on the rich diversity of our planet, from deserts to ice fields, volcanoes to submarine mountains. The photographs on these pages show animals or places that the United Nations Educational, Scientific, and Cultural Organization (UNESCO) has designated World Heritage Sites because they have great cultural significance.

TREE-MENDOUS!
Trees such as the coast redwood (see below) are exceptionally long lived. Some of those redwoods standing today were saplings around 2,000 years ago!

TALLEST LIVING TREE

On August 25, 2006, a coast redwood (*Sequoia sempervirens*) was discovered by Chris Atkins and Michael Taylor (both USA) in the Redwood National Park in California, USA. Dubbed "Hyperion," it reached 379 ft 1 in (115.54 m) tall – more than twice the height of the Statue of Liberty – when measured in September 2006. The park is part of California's Redwood National and State Parks, home to thousands of redwoods, including the world's tallest trees.

● HIGHEST TROPICAL MOUNTAIN RANGE

Huascarán National Park in the Cordillera Blanca mountain range, Peru, has its highest point at 22,204 ft (6,768 m) above sea level. The protected area covers 840,158 acres (340,000 ha) and includes 33 peaks over 18,045 ft (5,500 m) in height.

LARGEST GEOGLYPHS

Peru is also home to the Nazca Lines – as many as 70 giant animals, lines, and shapes etched into the Nazca desert some time between 300 BC and AD 540. Remarkably, these shapes and animals can only be discerned when viewed from the sky – they are too huge to be perceived as shapes when viewed on the ground.

TALLEST MOUNTAIN FACE

The Rupal face of Nanga Parbat, in the western Himalayas, Pakistan, is a single rise of some 16,000 ft (5,000 m) from the valley floor to the summit. With a peak at 26,656 ft (8,125 m), Nanga Parbat is the world's eighth-highest mountain.

● HIGHEST DENSITY OF EOCENE WHALES: Since 1905, some 379 fossil whales from the Eocene era (56–34 million years ago) have been found in Wadi Al-Hitan in Egypt's Western Desert.

LARGEST BUDDHIST TEMPLE: Borobudur, near Yogyakarta in Java, Indonesia, was built between AD 750 and 842. It is 113 ft (34.5 m) tall, with a base measuring 403 x 403 ft (123 x 123 m).

● UPDATED RECORD
● NEW RECORD

The ● **largest restaurant wine list** is that of the Restaurant Chiggeri in Luxembourg City, Luxembourg. The list featured 1,746 wines when counted on December 31, 2008.

1,005 Weight in pounds of the butter you'll eat in your lifetime. Your personal butter mountain is the size of 1.5 refrigerators. If Mount Everest was made of butter, it could supply the whole world for 1,348 years.

FASTEST-RISING MOUNTAIN

Nanga Parbat, in Pakistan, is growing taller at a rate of 0.27 in (7 mm) per year. The mountain is part of the Himalayan Plateau, formed when India began colliding with the Eurasian continental plate between 30 and 50 million years ago.

LARGEST MUDFLOW FROM A VOLCANO

The Osceola Mudflow occurred some 5,600 years ago and began on top of Mount Rainier in the US Cascade Mountain range. The result of a volcanic eruption, it consisted of a debris flow of around 106,000 ft^3 (3 km^3) that hurtled down the mountain at around 56 mi/h (90 km/h). By the time it had reached the Puget Sound, more than 62 miles (100 km) away, the mudflow still had a thickness of around 98 ft (30 m). After it had subsided, it had created 177 $miles^2$ (460 km^2) of new land on the coast.

MOST ACTIVE VOLCANO

Kilauea, in Hawaii, USA, has been erupting continually since 1983. Lava is being discharged at a rate of 176 ft^3/s (5 m^3/s).

Mount Stromboli, in the Tyrrhenian Sea off the Italian coast, has given off mild emissions of gas and lava since at least the 7th century BC, making it the **longest continually erupting volcano**. The emissions – usually several every hour – have led it to be known as the "Lighthouse of the Mediterranean."

FIRST "DARK SKY" PARK

The International Dark Sky Association has named Utah's Natural Bridges National Monument as the first Dark Sky Park – that is, an area in which the night sky can be viewed clearly, without any "light pollution."

OLDEST WOODEN BUILDING

The Hōryū-ji temple in Ikaruga, Nara Prefecture, Japan, was built in AD 607 and is one of 48 ancient buildings protected by UNESCO in the area. The temple includes a five-story building known as the Gojunoto.

LONGEST STONE ARCH

The longest natural arches in the world are both in Utah, USA, and both span openings of equal width. Landscape Arch, in Arches National Park, and Kolob Arch, in Zion National Park, both stand over openings 310 ft (94.5 m) wide. Landscape Arch is the more dramatic as it spans an open gully and narrows to only 16 ft (5 m) thick, while Kolob Arch stands close to a high cliff face.

FIRST DISCOVERY OF PALEOLITHIC CAVE ART

In 1879, Don Marcelino Sanz de Sautuola, an amateur archeologist, and his daughter Maria (both Spain) discovered prehistoric paintings in the Altamira Cave, Cantabria, Spain. The artworks, which include animals and human handprints, have been dated to between 25,000 and 35,000 years old.

OLDEST REPTILE FOSSILS

The Joggins Fossil Cliffs are a 9.3-mile-long (15-km) stretch of cliffs on the Bay of Fundy, Canada, rich in fossils of the Carboniferous period (*c*. 354–290 million years ago). Fossil remains of 148 species have been found here, including those of *Hylonomus* – at *c*. 315 million years old, one of the oldest known reptiles.

LARGEST GIANT PANDA HABITAT

The Sichuan Giant Panda Sanctuaries in the Qionglai and Jiajin Mountains of Sichuan Province, China, represent the largest contiguous habitat of the giant panda (*Ailuropoda melanoleuca*). More than 30% of the world panda population lives in this 3,569-$mile^2$ (9,245-km^2) network of nature reserves and scenic parks.

BEARING UP!

The giant panda population was in decline for years, but now the numbers seem to be steadying. The latest available figures, from 2004, suggest a global population of 1,600.

The **largest wine cellars** belong to the Koöperatiewe Wijnbouwers Vereniging, at Paarl in Cape Province, South Africa. They cover an area of 54 acres (22 ha) and have a capacity of 27 million gal (121 million liters) of wine.

WATER WORLD

LARGEST HOT SPRING

The largest boiling river issues from alkaline hot springs at Deildartunguhver, north of Reykjavik, Iceland, at a rate of 65 gal (245 liters) of boiling water per second.

LONGEST RIVER

The Nile is credited as the longest river in the world. Its main source is Lake Victoria in east central Africa. From its farthest stream in Burundi, it extends 4,160 miles (6,695 km) in length. The **widest river**, however, is the Amazon River in South America. While not in flood, its main stretches (i.e., not its tidal reaches, where an estuary or delta can be much wider) can reach widths of up to 7 miles (11 km) at its widest points.

The Amazon also has the **greatest flow** of any river. It discharges an average of 7,100,000 ft^3/s (200,000 m^3/s) into the Atlantic Ocean, increasing to more than 12,000,000 ft^3/s (340,000 m^3/s) in full flood. The flow of the Amazon is 60 times greater than that of the Nile.

WIDEST RAPIDS

During the monsoon season, the Mekong River on the border between Cambodia and Laos increases in volume by a factor of 20, flooding the Sipandone wetlands and creating an area of turbulent rapids up to 8.5 miles (14 km) wide. The flow rate is twice that at Niagara Falls, with 2.2 million gal (10 million liters) of water thundering its way through a maze of channels between the area's many islands every second.

LARGEST SWAMP

Located principally in southwestern Brazil but encompassing small areas within neighboring Bolivia and Paraguay too, the Pantanal (which is Spanish for "marshland") covers a surface area of 57,915 $miles^2$ (150,000 km^2) – roughly that of the state of Georgia! During the rainy season (December–May), 80% of the Pantanal is flooded, and it contains the greatest diversity of water plants in the world.

LARGEST RIVER ISLAND

The island of Majuli in the Brahmaputra River in northeast India covers an area of around 340 $miles^2$ (880 km^2). Owing to the frequent flooding of the Brahmaputra, Majuli suffers heavy erosion, and in the last 30–40 years it is estimated that it has lost about one-third of its area. Majuli is currently home to some 160,000 people.

THICKEST ICE

On January 4, 1975, a team of seismologists measured the depth of ice in Wilkes Land, in eastern Antarctica, to be 2.96 miles (4.77 km) deep. That's the equivalent of 10 Empire State Buildings piled one on top of another!

The Antarctic ice cap is the largest single body of freshwater, holding *c.* 7.25 million $miles^3$ (30 million km^3) – or around 70% of the world's total.

LONGEST SUBMARINE MOUNTAIN RANGE

The Mid-Ocean Ridge extends 40,000 miles (65,000 km) from the Arctic

LARGEST CONCENTRATION OF GEYSERS: Located mostly in Wyoming, USA, Yellowstone National Park boasts at least 300 geysers, two-thirds of the planet's total; 250 are active.

STEAM POWER

Geysers are hot springs of boiling water that erupt periodically into the air as the underground steam expands up to 1,500 times its normal volume.

LARGEST SAND ISLAND: Fraser Island, off the coast of Queensland, Australia, has a sand dune 75 miles (120 km) long and covering approximately 402,750 acres (163,000 ha).

LARGEST NON-POLAR ICE FIELD

Located in Yukon Territory, Canada, the 8,490-$mile^2$ (21,980-km^2) Kluane National Park and Reserve is home to the largest ice field outside the Poles. Around 8,200–9,800 ft (2,500–3,000 m) high, it occupies more than half of the park and incorporates glaciers that stretch for 37 miles (60 km).

The Republic of South Africa is the **country with the most official languages**, with 11. The most widely spoken language is isiZulu, followed (in order) by isiXhosa, Afrikaans, Sepedi, Setswana, English, Sesotho, Xitsonga, siSwati, Tshivenda, and isiNdebele.

Other record-breaking World Heritage Sites identified by UNESCO:

Lake Baikal, Russia
Largest freshwater lake, with a volume of *c.* 5,500 miles³ (23,000 km³)

Shark Bay, Australia
Home to a living colony of stromatolites dating from 3.5 billion years ago – the longest known fossil record

Orinoco River, South America
Habitat of the pink, 9-ft-long (2.6-m) boto (*Inia geoffrensis*) – the largest river dolphin

Ocean to the Atlantic Ocean, around Africa, Asia, and Australia, and under the Pacific Ocean to the west coast of North America. It has a maximum height of 13,800 ft (4,200 m) above the base ocean depth – nearly eight times the height of the CN Tower in Toronto, Canada.

HIGHEST SUBMARINE MOUNTAIN

Mount Pico in the Azores Islands (Portugal) has a base-to-summit height of 27,719 ft (8,449 m) – just fractionally shorter than Mount Everest – but it has a prominence of just 7,711 ft (2,351 m) above the surface of the sea; beneath the waves, the mountain sinks 20,000 ft (6,098 m) to its submarine base – giving it the largest underwater mountain face.

HIGHEST WATERFALL

The Salto Angel, or "Angel Falls" – located in Venezuela, on a branch of the Carrao River – has a total drop of 3,212 ft (979 m). The longest single drop measures 2,648 ft (807 m).

On the basis of average annual flow, the **greatest waterfall** is the Boyoma Falls in the Democratic Republic of the Congo (former Zaire), at 600,000 ft³/sec (17,000 m³/sec).

LARGEST PROTECTED MARINE AREA

The Phoenix Islands Protected Area covers 157,630 miles² (408,250 km²) within the Republic of Kiribati. It is home to around 500 species of fish, 200 species of coral, and 44 bird and 18 marine mammal species.

LARGEST REEF IN THE NORTHERN HEMISPHERE

The Belize Barrier Reef Reserve is a 372-mile² (963-km²) coastal system of atolls, sand cays, mangrove forests, lagoons, and estuaries, and is home to the largest reef system in the northern hemisphere. The submarine shelf and barrier reef stretches from Mexico in the north to Guatemala in the south and is second in size only to the Great Barrier Reef of Australia. Pictured is the Great Blue Hole, a 407-ft-deep (124-m) submarine sinkhole located off the Belize coast.

LARGEST MANGROVE FORESTS: The Sundarbans stretches for nearly 6,000 miles² (15,540 km²) across India and Bangladesh. Its trees sometimes exceed 70 ft (21 m) in height.

UPDATED RECORD
NEW RECORD

The **most common language** is Chinese, which is spoken by more than 1.1 billion people. The "common speech" (Pûtônghuà) is the standard form of Chinese, with a pronunciation based on that of Beijing.

KILLER CLIMATE

LONGEST-LASTING TROPICAL CYCLONE

Hurricane/Typhoon John formed on August 11, 1994 in the eastern Pacific Ocean, lasted for 31 days, and covered the **farthest distance recorded for a tropical cyclone**: 8,250 miles (13,280 km). It traveled from the eastern to the western Pacific; as the two regions use different labels for tropical cyclones, it is known as both a hurricane and a typhoon.

LONGEST TORNADO PATH LENGTH

On March 18, 1925, a tornado traveled at least 218 miles (352 km) through the US states of Missouri, Illinois, and Indiana. It killed 695 people, more than any other tornado in US history. The tornado also lasted 3.5 hours, longer than any other in history.

LARGEST TROPICAL CYCLONE

At its maximum strength on October 12, 1979, Typhoon Tip had a diameter of around 1,370 miles (2,200 km) in the Pacific Ocean. During this period, Tip's gale-force winds covered an area of around 1.2 million miles^2 (3.8 million km^2). Typhoon Tip was studied in detail by the US Air Force, who flew some 60 research missions into the cyclone.

HIGHEST SEA-LEVEL RISE

Since detailed records began in the mid-19th century, the global average sea level has risen by 7.87 in (20 cm). The average rate for the 20th century was around 0.07 in (1.7 mm) per year. Satellite observations have shown that, since 1993, the global sea level has been rising by around 0.12 in (3 mm) per year.

GREATEST CLIMATIC DISRUPTION TO AIR TRAVEL

On April 14, 2010, the erupting Eyjafjallajökull volcano on Iceland began a highly explosive phase of activity, ejecting fine ash more than 5 miles (8 km) into the atmosphere. The ash cloud was carried by a jet stream (a fast-flowing air current) towards mainland Europe and – until April 21 – 313 airports were closed, about 100,000 flights were canceled, and 7 million people were stranded. The disruption is estimated to have cost the airline industry as much as $2.2 billion.

WIDEST TORNADO DAMAGE PATH: On May 22, 2004, 56 tornadoes hit the Midwestern USA. One, the Hallam Nebraska tornado, left a swathe of destruction up to 2.4 miles (4 km) wide.

STRIKING FACTS

Earth experiences around 40 lightning flashes per second. One bolt may comprise more than 100 million volts of electricity, and register a temperature of up to 50,000°F (27,700°C).

HIGHEST CONCENTRATION OF LIGHTNING: An area near Kifuka in the Democratic Republic of the Congo receives 409 bolts per mile^2 (158 lightning bolts per km^2) a year.

TRAVEL BY TWISTER

On March 12, 2006, Matt Suter (USA) was engulfed by a tornado while inside a mobile home in Missouri, USA. He woke up 1,307 ft (398 m) away – the **farthest distance to be moved in a tornado and survive.**

UPDATED RECORD
NEW RECORD

The **earliest recorded use of paper currency** can be traced back to China during the Song dynasty (AD 960–1279). It was utilized by a group of wealthy merchants and businessmen in Sichuan, China, where the art of printing was invented.

GREATEST MONTHLY RAINFALL

For a calendar month, the record for rainfall is 366 in (9,300 mm), at Cherrapunji, Meghalaya, India, in July 1861. Cherrapunji also saw the **greatest rainfall in 12 months**, with 1,041.75 in (26,461 mm) from August 1, 1860 to July 31, 1861.

WORST DAMAGE TO CORAL REEF BY A NATURAL EVENT

In 1998, around 16% of the world's coral reefs were destroyed or seriously damaged in a once-in-a-millennium event. The 1998 El Niño phenomenon may have triggered the disaster.

GREATEST RAINFALL IN 24 HOURS

A record 73 in (1,870 mm) of rain fell in 24 hours in Cilaos, Réunion, Indian Ocean, on March 15 and 16, 1952. This is equal to 8,327 tons (7,554 metric tons) of rain per acre.

For the **greatest number of rainy days**, you'd have to go to Hawaii. Located on the island of Kauai, Mount Wai'ale'ale has up to 350 rainy days per annum.

WORST DAMAGE TOLL FOR A SNOWSTORM

A total of $1.2 billion worth of damage was caused by a storm that traversed the entire east coast of the USA on March 12–13, 1993. In all, 500 people perished in this monumental winter storm, which has been described by one meteorologist as "a storm with the heart of a blizzard and the soul of a hurricane."

LOWEST TEMPERATURE FOR A PERMANENTLY INHABITED PLACE

The coldest inhabited place on Earth is the Siberian village of Oymyakon, which lies in the icy wastes of Russia at 63°16'N, 143°15'E. On February 6, 1933, the temperature there fell to -89.9°F (-67.7°C), which is the lowest ever seen outside Antarctica. Lying in second place is nearby Verkhoyansk (67°33'N, 133°23'E), which experienced -89.7°F (-67.6°C) on February 5 and 7, 1892.

GREATEST TEMPERATURE RANGE

Verkhoyansk is also subject to the world's greatest variations in temperature. Over the years, the temperature there has ranged an incredible 189°F (105°C) from the all-time low of -89.7°F (-67.6°C) in 1892 to a summer high of 99.1°F (37.3°C) in 1988.

On January 23–24, 1916, the town of Browning in Montana, USA, experienced the **greatest temperature range recorded in a day** when an Arctic cold front caused the temperature to plummet 100°F (56°C) from 44°F (7°C) to -56°F (-49°C).

HIGHEST RECORDED TEMPERATURE

The highest shade temperature ever recorded is 136°F (58°C), at Al'Aziziyah in the Sahara Desert, Libya, on September 13, 1922.

DEADLIEST HEATWAVE

In the summer of 2010, the northern hemisphere suffered from a series of freak heatwaves. The most devastating effects were felt in Russia, where as many as 56,000 people perished from overheating, droughts, forest fires, and smog. An estimated 11,000 people died in Moscow alone.

A RECORD 246 PEOPLE DIED IN A HAILSTORM IN INDIA IN APRIL 1888

HAILSTONES

Pictured here, at actual size, is an 8-in-wide (20.3-cm) hailstone that fell in Vivian, South Dakota, USA, on July 23, 2010 during a 85-mi/h (135-km/h) tornado. The largest on record in the USA, it pales somewhat when compared with the **largest ice fall** ever reported – a 20-ft-long (6-m) mass (technically known as a "megacryometeor") that fell in Ord in Scotland, UK, on August 13, 1849. In both cases, the hailstone was composed of smaller pieces of ice or hail fused together.

The **heaviest hailstones** accurately recorded weighed up to 2 lb (1 kg) and are reported to have killed 92 people in the Gopalganj area of Bangladesh on April 14, 1986.

100%

HAIL HERO

This Herculean hailstone was found by Vivian resident Les Scott, who stored it in his freezer until its size could be validated. Its weight – despite some melting – was a whopping 1 lb 15 oz (0.87 kg).

Canada is home to the **largest coin**, which weighs 220 lb 7 oz (100 kg) and measures 19.6 in (50 cm) in diameter and 1.1 in (3 cm) in thickness. It has a face value of CAN$1 million ($900,375).

LARGEST CAPTIVE CROCODILE

The Australian saltwater crocodile (*Crocodylus porosus*) is the largest present-day species of crocodile. Cassius, seen here, is the largest specimen in captivity, at 18 ft (5.5 m) in length, and the largest crocodile ever caught in Australia. He is currently housed in Marineland Melanesia wildlife zoo on Green Island, Australia.

SNAP!

Australian saltwater crocodiles can live to over 100 years of age and reach 23 ft (7 m) long, while mature specimens may weigh over 1.1 tons (1 metric ton). They are apex predators (see p.54) and can be very dangerous!

Canada is home to the world's **largest uninhabited island**. Devon Island is part of the Canadian archipelago in the Arctic Circle, to the north of Baffin Island, and has an area of 21,331 miles^2 (55,247 km^2).

Discounting Australia, which is usually regarded as a continental landmass, the **largest island** overall is Greenland, with an area of about 840,000 miles^2 (2,175,600 km^2).

CREEPY CRAWLIES

IT'S A BUG'S LIFE

Bugs are the most numerous – and diverse – forms of life on our planet. Here we present some of the titans of the bug world, and while some are gentle giants, others are ferocious predators, equipped with a lethal arsenal of stings, fangs, and even barbed hair. Each insect and arachnid here is shown actual size, so at least you'll know what you're up against should you come face to face with one in the wild!

MOST VENOMOUS SPIDER

Watch your step if you go walking in the rainforests of South America – venom from the aggressive Brazilian wandering spider (*Phoneutria* genus, which means "Murderess" in Greek) is so potent that just 0.00000021 oz (0.006 mg) will kill a mouse, while larger doses can be lethal to humans.

HEAVIEST INSECT

The goliath beetles (Scarabaeidae family) of Equatorial Africa are the heavyweights of the beetle world. The male, the larger of the two sexes, measures up to 4.33 in (11 cm) from the tips of the frontal horns to the end of the abdomen, and weighs a hefty 2.5–3.5 oz (70–100 g).

LONGEST BEETLE

South America's appropriately named titan beetle (*Titanus giganteus*) is a huge 6 in (15 cm) long, not including its antennae. Bizarrely, adult titans don't eat, but instead fly around in search of a mate until they die.

MOST VENOMOUS SCORPION

The Tunisian fat-tailed scorpion (*Androctonus australis*) has a very nasty surprise in its tail – it's responsible for 80% of all stings and 90% of all deaths from scorpion stings across the whole of North Africa.

With its northernmost two-thirds covered in permafrost, Greenland is the world's **least populated territory**, with a density of 0.43 people per mile^2 (0.16 per km^2).

100 trillion

Number of cells that you are made of. Although this sounds like a lot, your own cells are in fact outnumbered 10:1 by the hordes of bacteria – or microscopic creepy crawlies – hitching a ride on your body.

LARGEST WASP

Native to the mountains of Japan, the Asian giant hornet (*Vespa mandarinia*) can grow to 2.2 in (5.5 cm) in length, with a wingspan of 3 in (7.6 cm). Unfortunately, it also has a 0.25-in (0.6-cm) sting and can inject a venom so powerful that it dissolves human tissue. At least its size means you should see this angry critter coming...

LARGEST SPIDER

The male goliath bird-eater (*Theraphosa blondi*) weighs up to 6 oz (170 g) and has a legspan of 11 in (28 cm) – big enough to cover a dinner plate. This spider, however, is more predator than prey, and feeds on birds in the coastal rainforests of Suriname, Guyana, French Guiana, Brazil, and Venezuela.

ON THE DEFENSIVE

Given the considerable size of the goliath bird-eater's fangs, it may seem wise to stand behind, rather than in front, of it. However, the furry fiend has all angles covered, firing barbed hairs from its abdomen when threatened.

LARGEST CENTIPEDE

Measuring up to 10 in (26 cm) long, the giant centipede (*Scolopendra gigantea*) of Central and South America is a fearsome predator with huge jaws that are capable of killing mice, frogs, lizards, and even bats.

FOR CUDDLIER CREATURES, TURN TO P.148.

LARGEST WETA

With a length of 4.33 in (11 cm) and a legspan of 7 in (17.5 cm), there is nothing little about the Little Barrier Island giant weta (*Deinacrida heteracantha*). Hailing from New Zealand, this cockroach-like cricket also weighs as much as 2.5 oz (70 g) – three times the weight of a house mouse.

UPDATED RECORD
NEW RECORD

Because of its size, the Vatican City – an enclave within Rome, the Italian capital – has a relatively high population density. Even so, it is still the world's **least populated country**, with just 821 inhabitants in 2007.

NEW SPECIES

● NEWEST APE: Discovered by scientists from the German Primate Centre (DPZ) in Göttingen, Germany, the northern buff-cheeked gibbon (*Nomascus annamensis*) was formally described and named in September 2010.

● NEWEST MONITOR LIZARD

Over 6 ft 6 in (2 m) long, the northern Sierra Madre forest monitor (*Varanus bitatawa*) was formally described and named in spring 2010. This yellow-and-black species is very unusual in that it is a fruit eater, making it only the third known species of frugivorous lizard.

NEWEST...

● BIRD OF PREY

The most recently discovered bird of prey is the Socotra buzzard (*Buteo socotraensis*), which was first formally described and named in 2010. The bird is native only to the Socotra archipelago, a group of tiny islands forming part of Yemen in the Arabian peninsula.

BREED OF CAT

Although the Sphynx cat was first bred successfully in 1996, it was not until 2002 that the breed became officially recognized. This feline species appears to be hairless, but in fact it has a covering of short, fine down.

● NEWEST MONGOOSE

The semiaquatic Madagascan mongoose species Durrell's vontsira (*Salanoia durrelli*) first came to scientific attention in 2004, when a single specimen was encountered swimming in a remote lake. It was not formally recognized as a new, separate species until 2010. The mongoose shown here is being treated firmly but carefully by its handler. Mongooses can be aggressive.

CARNIVORE

Environmental researchers are hoping to capture what some believe may be a new species of carnivore on Borneo – which, if correct, would be the first such discovery on the island since that of the Borneo ferret-badger in 1895. The animal looks like a cross between a cat and a fox and was photographed in the mountainous rainforests of the Kayan Mentarang National Park in 2003, but was kept unpublished as research continued.

Some researchers have suggested that it might be a viverrid – a family of animals that includes the civets – but this potential new species has not yet been confirmed. Indeed, the latest theory is that it may not be a carnivore at all, but actually a specimen of an already known species of giant flying squirrel.

CETACEAN

The most recently recognized species of cetacean is the Australian snubfin dolphin (*Orcaella heinsohni*), formally reclassified as a separate species in its own right in 2005. This shy, tricolored dolphin, with a very rounded, bulbous brow and a very small, stubby dorsal fin, has been sighted regularly in the shallow waters off the Great Barrier Reef, Australia, for many years, but until DNA evidence and other studies confirmed its distinct status it had always been classified as belonging to the same species as the Irrawaddy dolphin (*O. brevirostris*).

CRUSTACEAN

In 1979, while diving in Lucayan Cavern, a water-filled cave beneath the island of Grand Bahama, American biologist Dr Jill Yager encountered some tiny, wormlike crustaceans. These proved to be not only a new species – dubbed *Speleonectes lucayensis* – but also one so different from all others that, in 1981, an entirely new taxonomic class of crustaceans (Remipedia) was created in order to accommodate it.

● HUMAN TYPE

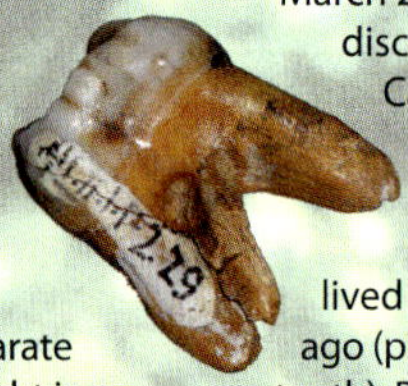

The newest type of fossil humans to have been discovered is Denisovan Man – a type whose existence was revealed in March 2010 following the discovery in Denisova Cave, Russia, of bone fragments from a juvenile human who had lived *c.* 41,000 years ago (pictured left is a tooth). Based upon mitochondrial DNA analysis, in December 2010 scientists revealed that this individual belonged to a previously unknown member of the hominin genus *Homo*, distinct from Neanderthals, with whom it coexisted, and modern humans.

● UPDATED RECORD
● NEW RECORD

Vatican City is the **smallest independent country**. The enclave, which has an area of 0.17 miles^2 (0.44 km^2), had its sovereignty recognized by the Italian government under the terms of the Lateran Treaty on February 11, 1929.

NEWEST AMPHIBIANS

On November 25, 2010, the discovery of three new amphibian species was announced. Native to the rainforests of Choco in western Colombia, and still awaiting formal scientific names and descriptions, they are a species of toad with ruby-colored eyes (above left), a species of rocket frog characterized by bright red flashes on its legs (below left), and a small toad with a long beak that hides in dead leaves.

IGUANA

Discoveries of large, conspicuously colored lizard species are very rare. In 2009, however, it was announced that a new species of iguana, rose-pink (rosada) in color and up to 5 ft 8.8 in (1.75 m) long, had been found living on a single volcanic mountain called Volcan Wolf on the island of Isabela in the Galápagos chain.

Genetic tests confirmed that it was a very distinctive species, dating back over 5 million years, and which had already branched off from the other, yellowish-brown species of iguana here while the Galápagos archipelago was still forming. Interestingly, park rangers first spotted the pink iguana, which has been named *Conolophus rosada*, on Isabela in 1986, although it was initially dismissed as nothing more than a freak color variety of the familiar yellow land iguana (*C. subcristatus*).

TREE

Discovered accidentally by a picnicking family in a remote, hilly, wooded area of northwestern Madagascar in 2006, but only recognized as a dramatically new species and genus following DNA analysis a year later, the Tahina palm tree (*Tahina spectabilis*) was not officially named and described until January 2008. What makes this species' belated scientific discovery so surprising is its size – standing more than 58 ft 6 in (18 m) tall, with fanlike leaves 16 ft (5 m) across – and its bizarre life cycle.

It takes decades for the tree to bloom, but when it does it produces an explosion of hundreds of nectar-rich flowers that tower above its crown, each of which develops into fruit. In doing so, however, the tree's nutrients become so depleted that once it has borne fruit it rapidly collapses and dies.

WILD CAT

The newest species of wild cat is the Bornean clouded leopard (*Neofelis diardi*). In 2006, scientists officially recognized this species as being significantly different enough from the clouded leopard (*N. nebulosa*) for it to be elevated to a species in its own right.

NEWEST MONKEY: The Caquetá titi (*Callicebus caquetensis*) was scientifically described and named in 2010. It inhabits the Colombian Amazon region near the borders with Peru and Ecuador.

NEWEST LEMUR

So new that it doesn't even have a formal zoological name yet, this species of fork-marked lemur (genus *Phaner*) is the size of a squirrel. It is distinguished behaviorally from all other lemurs by its unique head-bobbing movement.

NOW YOU SEE IT... Spotted by primate expert Dr Russell Mittermeier in 1995, this Madagascan lemur was not seen again until late 2010, when it was filmed by Dr Mittermeier's scientific team and a BBC TV crew.

The **largest landlocked country**, and the ninth largest overall, is Kazakhstan, which has an area of 1,052,100 miles^2 (2,724,900 km^2).

ENDANGERED SPECIES

RAREST BUMBLEBEE

Native to the USA, Franklin's bumblebee (*Bombus franklini*) is classed as Critically Endangered by the International Union for Conservation of Nature (IUCN). In a 1998 survey, 94 specimens were found, at eight separate sites. During 2006, however, only one was found during extensive surveys of its limited distribution range in southern Oregon and northern California. It has the most limited range of any bumblebee.

RAREST...

BOXWOOD

A shrub once found in Jamaica, Puerto Rico, and the US Virgin Islands, Vahl's boxwood (*Buxus vahlii*) is today threatened by habitat loss and is ranked as Critically Endangered by the IUCN. Two small populations survive in Puerto Rico, though these collectively number fewer than 50 specimens.

GALAGO

The Rondo dwarf galago (*Galagoides rondoensis*) is Critically Endangered and labeled as one of the world's 25 most endangered primates by the IUCN. First described as recently as 1996, it is entirely confined to eight small, discrete, highly threatened forest patches – a total area of under 38 miles² (100 km²) – in coastal Tanzania.

CIVET

Once a very common species, today the Malabar large-spotted civet (*Viverra civettina*) is categorized by the IUCN as Critically Endangered. It is possible that less than 250 of these small mammals still exist in the wild in South Malabar, southern India.

EGG-LAYING MAMMAL

The rarest species of monotreme (see above right) is Attenborough's long-beaked echidna (*Zaglossus attenboroughi*). Named after veteran British TV naturalist Sir David Attenborough, it is known from just a single specimen, found dead on a mountain peak in Irian Jaya, Indonesian New Guinea, in 1961. Local hunters claim to have seen living specimens, but none has been recorded to date.

OPOSSUM

Scientifically described in 1981, Handley's slender opossum (*Marmosops handleyi*) is categorized as Critically Endangered by the IUCN. It is known only from two specimens collected in a tiny area of rainforest in Antioquia, Colombia, at an altitude of 4,590 ft (1,400 m).

RAREST GROUP OF MAMMALS: The order Monotremata is a primitive group of mammals that lays eggs instead of producing live young. Its five living species include the platypus (above).

RAREST HERON

Native to the foothills of the eastern Himalayas, the world's rarest species of heron is the white-bellied heron (*Ardea insignis*). Critically Endangered, this large grey-and-white heron has a total population size estimated at between 50 and 249 individuals.

OUT OF FISH?

Herons love a fish dish, but probably won't come across the world's **most endangered fish**. There are between 200 and 500 Devil's Hole pupfish (*Cyprinodon diabolis*) left.

UPDATED RECORD
NEW RECORD

The **most powerful rocket** – the N-1 booster of the former USSR – was first launched from the Baikonur Cosmodrome at Tyuratam, Kazakhstan, on February 21, 1969. It exploded 70 seconds after takeoff.

27 Species that will become extinct on every single day of your life. This means that during the 28,745 days you will spend on Earth, 780,000 species will disappear forever.

RAREST CHAMELEON

Classed as Critically Endangered by the IUCN, Smith's dwarf chameleon (*Bradypodion taeniabronchum*) is limited to an area of occupancy estimated at 154 miles² (400 km²), near Algoa Bay in South Africa.

CHAMELEONS CHANGE COLOUR ACCORDING TO THEIR MOODS

RAREST SLOTH

Confined to Isla Escudo de Veraguas, a small island off the coast of Panama, the pygmy three-toed sloth (*Bradypus pygmaeus*) was scientifically described as a new species in 2001. Critically Endangered according to the IUCN, around 300 specimens are thought to exist. They live exclusively in red mangrove trees.

REPTILE

The Abingdon Island giant tortoise (*Geochelone elephantopus abingdoni*) is represented by a single living specimen, an aged male called Lonesome George, who is the world's rarest reptile. With little hope of discovering another specimen, this particular subspecies of Galápagos giant tortoise is effectively extinct while still alive, unless cloning techniques can generate future replicas of George.

Unsurprisingly, he also has the dubious distinction of being the world's **most endangered animal**.

SNAKE

There are thought to be fewer than 150 Antiguan racers (*Alsophis antiguae*) in existence, including those in captivity. The snake was once common in Antigua, but disappeared from the island following the introduction of nonindigenous predators – first black and brown rats (*Rattus rattus* and *R. norvegicus*) and then the Asian mongoose (*Herpestes javanicus*). Despite its recovering numbers, the species remains classified as Critically Endangered on the IUCN Red List.

STICKLEBACK

The world's rarest stickleback is the Greek stickleback (*Pungitius hellenicus*). Critically Endangered, it is entirely limited to three localities in the Sperchios Valley, central Greece, yielding a total area of less than 3.8 miles² (10 km²).

RAREST BIG CAT

The Critically Endangered Amur or Manchurian leopard (*Panthera pardus orientalis*) is native to the forests on the border of northeastern China and the Russian Far East. Fewer than 35 individuals are believed to exist.

SO WHAT CAN WE DO?

To find out more about the world's amazing animal and plant species – and how we can help them – visit the World Wide Fund for Nature (WWF) website at wwf.org.

For a taller and more successful rocket, you need to visit the USA. The *Saturn V* – the world's **largest rocket** – was 363 ft (110.6 m) tall with the *Apollo* spacecraft on top and weighed 6,400,000 lb (2,903 metric tons) on the launchpad.

APEX PREDATORS

LARGEST PREDATORY FISH

At the top of the ocean's food chain is the great white shark (*Carcharodon carcharias*). Adult specimens of this rare shark average 14–15 ft (4.3–4.6 m) in length – about three arm spans if you're a typical 10-year-old child – and can weigh up to 1,700 lb (770 kg). There are many claims of huge specimens up to 33 ft (10 m) in length, although – not surprisingly – few have been authenticated! Its prey includes fish (even other sharks) and marine mammals such as seals and sea lions.

AN APEX PREDATOR IS A CREATURE AT THE TOP OF ITS FOOD CHAIN – AS AN ADULT, IT HAS NO PREDATORS OF ITS OWN...

FIRST APEX PREDATOR

Anomalocaris – a large, superficially crustacean-like carnivorous invertebrate – inhabited shallow seas worldwide during the early to mid-Cambrian Period, 540–500 million years ago. Up to 3 ft 3 in (1 m) long, it was huge in size relative to all other animals alive at that time and is believed to have preyed upon trilobites and primitive shrimp-like organisms.

LARGEST SKUA

Skuas constitute a family of gull-related seabirds with no natural predators. They feed upon small mammals and fish, and often steal fish from other birds. The largest species is the 23-in-long (60-cm) brown skua (*Stercorarius antarctica*), which is broad-winged and heavy-bodied.

MOST SUCCESSFUL PREDATOR

African hunting dogs, also called Cape hunting dogs or hyena dogs (*Lycaon pictus*), are successful in 50–70% of their hunts, consistently the highest figure in the mammalian world.

LARGEST WILD DOG

Hayden's bone-crushing dog (*Epicyon haydeni*) was the largest wild dog of all time. Estimated to weigh up to 225 lb (170 kg) – nearly six times larger than the average pet labrador – it existed during the mid-to-late Miocene epoch (14–23 million years ago) in North America.

HIGHEST-LIVING PREDATOR ON LAND

The range of the snow leopard (*Uncia uncia*) extends across 12 countries in the mountainous regions of central and southern Asia. This rarely seen cat has been photographed by hidden cameras at an altitude of 19,000 ft (5,800 m).

MOST DANGEROUS SHARK

From 1900 to 1999, great white sharks (left) caused 251 out of the 1,860 confirmed unprovoked shark attacks on humans. Of these, 66 were fatal – the highest number for any shark. In the past four years, there has been an average of four fatal shark attacks per year.

LONGEST SNAKE FANGS: One specimen of the venomous gaboon viper of tropical Africa had fangs 2 in (50 mm) long – about as big as your thumb!

LARGEST CROCODILIAN: The saltwater (estuarine) crocodile of tropical Asia and the Pacific reach up to 33 ft (10 m) in length – the size of a stretch limo!

With an endowment of $26 billion, Harvard University in Cambridge, Massachusetts, USA, is the **richest university**.

2,222 Chickens you will eat in your lifetime, along with one sheep, six ducks, nine cows, and 63 turkeys – although you're unlikely to hunt, pounce on, and kill any of these creatures yourself!

LARGEST EAGLE

Commanding the skies over the coastal regions of Russia – and parts of Japan and Korea – is Steller's sea eagle (*Haliaeetus pelagicus*). This avian assassin weighs 11–20 lb (5–9 kg) and has a wingspan of 7 ft 2 in–8 ft (2.2–2.45 m). Its main prey? Salmon, cod, and trout, although it will happily snack on other birds such as geese and ducks, and even the odd seal has fallen prey to this beautiful but deadly creature.

GREATEST ECOLOGICAL DAMAGE CAUSED BY AN APEX PREDATOR

Since its accidental transportation shortly after World War II to the island of Guam, far from its normal South Pacific homelands, the brown tree snake (*Boiga irregularis*) has wreaked unprecedented devastation as an invasive apex predator.

Following a population explosion caused by a lack of predators, the snake has wiped out most of Guam's native vertebrate species (including birds). It has also caused thousands of residential, commercial, and military power breakdowns, and preyed extensively upon pets and livestock. It has even invaded human habitation, resulting in widespread panic.

LARGEST FELINE CARNIVORE: The male Siberian tiger (*Panthera tigris altaica*) averages 10 ft 4 in (3.15 m) from nose to tail. An adult male weighs the same as FOUR men!

UPDATED RECORD
NEW RECORD

LARGEST LAND CARNIVORE

The largest of all the carnivores is the polar bear (*Ursus maritimus*). Adult males typically weigh 880–1,320 lb (400–600 kg) and have a nose-to-tail length of 7 ft 10 in–8 ft 6 in (2.4–2.6 m).

The male Kodiak bear (*Ursus arctos middendorffi*) – a subspecies of brown bear found on Kodiak Island and the adjacent Afognak and Shuyak islands in the Gulf of Alaska, USA – is usually shorter in length than its northerly relation but more robustly built.

MOST EFFICIENT SCAVENGER

No animal makes such a meal of its prey as the spotted (aka laughing) hyena (*Crocuta crocuta*). Its jaw muscles and teeth are strong enough to crush the bones of large vertebrates such as zebras and wildebeest, and its powerful digestive system can break down the organic matter of bones, hooves, horns, and hides.

In one extreme example, a group of 38 hyenas was once seen to dismember an adult zebra in less than 15 minutes!

The title of **oldest university** belongs to the University of Karueein, founded in AD 859 in Fez, Morocco. It is the world's longest continually operating educational institution.

ANIMAL HOMES

LARGEST BOWERS
The male bowerbirds of Australia and New Guinea build and decorate courtship "bowers" in order to attract females. These elaborate, hutlike structures measure up to 5.25 ft (1.6 m) across and 3.28 ft (1 m) in height and include a "front lawn" several square yards in area. This "lawn" is cleared of forest debris then decorated with bright, shiny objects such as fruit, flowers, beetle wingcases, and colorful pieces of litter.

This satin bowerbird collects blue plastic garbage in an attempt to attract a mate!

LONGEST CHALK REEF
Stretching for over 20 miles (32 km) along the coast of Norfolk, England, UK, is a chalk reef consisting of a series of enormous arches and deep chasms. Approximately 300 million years old, it is home to numerous species of fish, sea slugs, sponges, and other marine life. It was discovered by diver Rob Spray and a team of 20 volunteer conservationists in 2010.

LARGEST SINGLE COBWEB
The world's largest cobwebs, measuring up to 30.13 ft² (2.8 m²), are woven by a newly discovered species of Madagascan spider known as Darwin's bark spider (*Caerostris darwini*). It weaves them over rivers so that they stretch from one bank to the other, using a mechanism as yet undocumented. These are also the world's **longest cobwebs**, at 82 ft (25 m), and the **strongest webs**, with a tensile strength of up to 520 MJ/m³ (megajoules per cubic meter) – twice as strong as any previously described silk and the **strongest known biomaterial**.

OLDEST COBWEB
Encased in amber formed approximately 140 million years ago during the Cretaceous Period, the oldest cobweb was found on a beach at Bexhill, East Sussex, UK, by amateur fossil hunters (and brothers) Jamie and Jonathan Hiscocks. Its silk is also the **oldest spider gossamer** (the fine, filamentous substance spun by spiders).

LARGEST BURROWING MAMMAL
The wombat (*Vombatus ursinus*) of Australia and Tasmania is a squat, bearlike creature that can measure up to 4 ft (1.2 m) and weigh up to 77 lb (35 kg). Their backward-opening pouch, large paws, and strong claws assist them in digging burrows that can be up to 65 ft (20 m) long and 6 ft (2 m) below ground, with interconnecting tunnels.

LARGEST BADGER SET
The European badger (*Meles meles*) spends more than half of its life underground, and builds the largest sets of any badger species. The largest set on record was estimated to contain a tunnel network measuring 2,883 ft (879 m) long, with 50 underground chambers and 178 entrances.

TOWERING ACHIEVEMENT
Termites are roughly 0.4 in (1 cm) long, so their mounds are the largest structures built relative to body size. The human equivalent would be a tower 4,600 ft (1,400 m) tall – nearly twice the size of the current tallest building.

GREATEST INSECT BUILDER
Mounds built by the termites (order Isoptera) in eastern Australia have measured up to 20 ft (6 m) tall and 100 ft (30.5 m) in circumference. These complex structures contain fungus gardens (for food), garrets, basements, and nurseries, and are honeycombed with ventilation shafts to regulate temperatures in the brooding chambers and in the royal palace, where the queen termite resides. Mounds are made by soldier termites mixing their saliva with particles of sand or clay.

UPDATED RECORD
NEW RECORD

The Great Hassan II Mosque in Casablanca, Morocco, has the **tallest minaret**, measuring 656 ft (200 m). The mosque can accommodate 105,000 worshippers and is the fifth largest in the world.

1,000 trillion

Number of bacteria living on your skin and in your gut. Your body's bacteria count is more than 160,000 times the human population of the planet. Worth pondering the next time (you think) you are alone.

LARGEST MAMMAL TO BUILD A NEST

Every day, gorillas (*Gorilla gorilla*) create a new ground nest from the surrounding vegetation. The nests are circular and measure about 3 ft 3 in (1 m) in diameter. This makes the gorilla – at 5 ft 6 in–6 ft (1.7–1.8 m) tall and weighing 300–500 lb (136–227 kg) – the largest of all the mammalian nest builders.

MASSIVE MOUNDS

Australia's mallee fowl (*Leipoa ocellata*) builds the ● **largest incubation mounds**, weighing in at 661,000 lb (300 metric tons) – as heavy as the average 747 jumbo jet plane!

DEEPEST BAT COLONY

A colony of approximately 1,000 little brown bats (*Myotis lucifugus*) – the most abundant bat in North America – spends each winter in a zinc mine in New York at a depth of 3,805 ft (1,160 m) – almost six times deeper than this species' normal roosting depth.

LARGEST BIRD NESTS

Bald eagles (*Haliaeetus leucocephalus*, pictured) build the largest single bird nests. A pair of bald eagles – and perhaps their successors – built a nest near St Petersburg, Florida, USA, that measured 9 ft 6 in (2.9 m) wide and 20 ft (6 m) deep. It was examined in 1963 and estimated to weigh 4,409 lb (2 metric tons).

LARGEST ARBOREAL MAMMAL

The largest tree-dwelling mammal is the orangutan, which lives in the canopy of tropical rainforests in Borneo and Sumatra. Bornean orangutan (*Pongo pygmaeus*) and Sumatran orangutan (*P. abelii*) males typically weigh 183 lb (83 kg) and measure 5 ft (1.5 m) tall. They have opposable toes on their feet and use their arm span of approximately 6 ft (2 m) to swing between branches and feed off fruit, small leaves, and tree bark. Being lighter (81 lb; 37 kg), females usually build nests in the trees, whereas the adult males sleep on the ground.

LARGEST COMMUNAL BIRD NESTS

The sociable weaver (*Philetairus socius*) of southwestern Africa builds a nest up to 26 ft (8 m) long and 6 ft 6 in (2 m) high. Resembling a giant haystack that hangs from a tree or utility pole, it contains up to 300 individual nests. Not surprisingly, these nests can get so heavy that the tree on which they are built collapses under the weight!

● MOST HOUSEBOUND ANIMAL

The wild animal that spends the longest time in an inactive state inside its home is the eastern chipmunk (*Tamias striatus*) of North America. When food is scarce, it will retreat inside its burrow and live off its stores of nuts for up to one year at a time.

LARGEST WASP NEST

A wasp nest found on a farm at Waimaukau, New Zealand, in April 1963 measured 12 ft 2 in (3.7 m) long and 5.25 ft (1.75 m) in diameter, and was approximately 18 ft (5.5 m) in circumference. It was so heavy that it had fallen from the tree in which it had been hanging and had then split into two. It had probably been constructed by introduced German wasps (*Vespula germanica*).

LARGEST STRUCTURE BUILT BY A TERRESTRIAL ANIMAL

Beavers (*Castor canadensis*, inset) of North America use mud, wood, vegetation, and stones to dam water and form a still pond in which they build a lodge for winter. The **largest beaver lodge** ever recorded was 40 ft (12.1 m) across and 16 ft (4.8 m) high, and the **longest beaver dam** ever measured stretched 0.9 miles (1.5 km).

EAGER BEAVERS

Beaver lodges typically take 20 days to build using 6,600 lb (3 metric tons) of materials. A family of four beavers can build 4 ft 11 in (1.5 m) of dam wall per day.

The Grand Mosque in Djenne, Mali, is the **largest mud building** in the world, measuring 328 ft (100 m) long and 131 ft (40 m) wide. The present structure was built in 1905, based on the design of an 11th-century mosque.

MIGRATIONS & MOVEMENTS

LONGEST INSECT MIGRATION

A tagged male monarch butterfly (*Danaus plexippus*), set free at Presqu'ile Provincial Park near Brighton, Ontario, Canada, on September 10, 1988, was recaptured in Austin, Texas, USA, on April 8, 1989. Assuming that it overwintered in Mexico, the insect traveled at least 2,880 miles (4,635 km) and possibly double this distance.

LONGEST AMPHIBIAN MIGRATION

Most amphibians do not migrate very far due to their reliance on water, but two species of European water frog – the pool frog (*Rana lessonae*) and the green frog (*R. esculenta*) – have been known to cover distances of up to 9 miles (15 km).

LONGEST TERRESTRIAL ANIMAL MIGRATION

Grant's caribou (*Rangifer tarandus*), which lives in Alaska and also Canada's Yukon Territory, migrates up to 2,982 miles (4,800 km) per year to more sheltered wintering grounds. That's more than 620 miles (1,000 km) greater than the distance from New York to Los Angeles!

LARGEST HERD OF MAMMALS

In the 19th century, vast herds of springbok (*Antidorcas marsupialis*) migrated across the plains of western parts of southern Africa. In 1849, John Fraser, the son of a local minister, observed a mass migration that took three days to pass through the town of Beaufort West, South Africa.

LONGEST REPTILE MIGRATION

The leatherback sea turtle (*Dermochelys coriacea*), the world's **largest living turtle**, also holds the record for the longest migration by any reptile. Between 2006 and early 2008, a leatherback was tracked by satellite on a 12,774-mile (20,558-km) journey from its nesting site on the beaches of Papua, Indonesia, to feeding grounds off the coast of Oregon, USA. The journey, to the other side of the planet, took 647 days.

LARGEST GATHERING OF MAMMALS

Each October, between 5 and 10 million straw-colored fruit bats (*Eidolon helvum*) converge from all over Africa on Kasanka in Zambia for a six-week binge on ripened mangoes.

GREATEST LAND MIGRATION

The last great land migration on Earth sees between 1 and 2 million wildebeest (*Connochaetus taurinus*) traveling a circuit between the Serengeti of Tanzania to Kenya and across the Mara River. Millions of other animals, such as zebras, impalas, and gazelles – plus their predators – join the wildebeest on their annual round trip in search of water.

Every 60 years or so, the Dogon peoples of Mali celebrate the Sigui, a festival marking the handover of secrets to the next generation. The last Sigui ran from 1967 to 1973. Unsurprisingly, it is the **longest religious ceremony**.

UPDATED RECORD
NEW RECORD

2,342 Days of your life you will spend on vacation. However, 1,186 of those will be school vacations, so by the time you leave school you'll already have had more than half your lifetime of days off.

WHY FLY?

Groups of mountain quail (*Oreortyx pictus*), native to western North America, often walk up to 5,000 ft (1,500 m) in winter to reach lower, warmer altitudes in the **longest bird migration on foot**.

LONGEST BIRD MIGRATION

The Arctic tern (*Sterna paradisaea*) breeds north of the Arctic Circle, then flies south to the Antarctic for the northern winter and back again. This represents a round trip of approximately 50,000 miles (80,467 km).

SHORTEST BIRD MIGRATION

During the winter, North America's blue grouse (*Dendragapus obscurus*) inhabits mountainous pine forests. When nesting time commences in spring, it descends just 984 ft (300 m) to deciduous woodlands in order to feed upon the early crop of seeds and fresh leaves.

FIRST HUMAN-LED BIRD MIGRATION

In 1993, two "artists turned naturalists," William Lishman and Joseph Duff (both USA), used two ultralight aircraft to guide 18 Canada geese 400 miles (644 km) from Ontario, Canada, to Virginia, USA. The flight confirmed that the birds could be "taught" to follow safe migratory routes.

LONGEST MAMMAL MIGRATION

The humpback whale (*Megaptera novaeangliae*) swims up to 5,100 miles (8,200 km) back and forth between its warm breeding waters near the Equator and the colder, food-rich waters of the Arctic and Antarctic regions.

On September 21, 2001, a female humpback seen off the coast of Brazil in August 1999 was photographed 6,089 miles (9,800 km) away near the island of Madagascar. The whale, known as Antarctic Humpback Whale Catalogue No.1363, had covered nearly a quarter of the globe in the **longest documented single journey ever undertaken by a mammal**.

SMALLEST MIGRANT

Copepods (subphylum Crustacea) are planktonic organisms measuring 0.04–0.08 in (1–2 mm) long on average and are the principal diet of many of the oceans' inhabitants, including whales. They live mainly at the bottom of the ocean to avoid predators, but make a nightly ascent to the surface to feed.

HIGHEST MIGRANT

The bar-headed goose (*Anser indicus*) migrates over the Himalayas to overwinter in India, Pakistan, and Burma, a journey of around 1,000 miles (1,600 km). Its migration sees it regularly reach altitudes of 29,000 ft (9,000 m), although it has been reported at 33,382 ft (10,175 m).

LARGEST MIGRANT

Up to 88 ft (27 m) long and weighing 352,000 lb (160 metric tons), the blue whale (*Balaenoptera musculus*) is the **largest animal** (by weight) and the largest to migrate, traveling thousands of kilometers from its Arctic or Antarctic feeding grounds to the warmer winter breeding grounds in the tropics. The calves – born with just a thin layer of blubber – need warm waters to survive.

MUNCHING EN MASSE

Each night, billions of tiny zooplankton make a return from the depths of the sea to the surface to feed on microscopic phytoplankton in the **largest animal migration in terms of numbers**.

BIG BOVINE

The **largest migrant on land – and the largest land animal in North America and Europe** – is the bison (genus *Bison*). It weighs nearly 2,200 lb (1 metric ton), and is as much as 6 ft 5 in (2 m) tall at the shoulder.

Speaking of big parties, the annual carnival in Rio de Janeiro, Brazil, normally held during the first week of March, is the **largest carnival** in the world. It attracts approximately 2 million people each day.

MICROSCOPIC LIFE

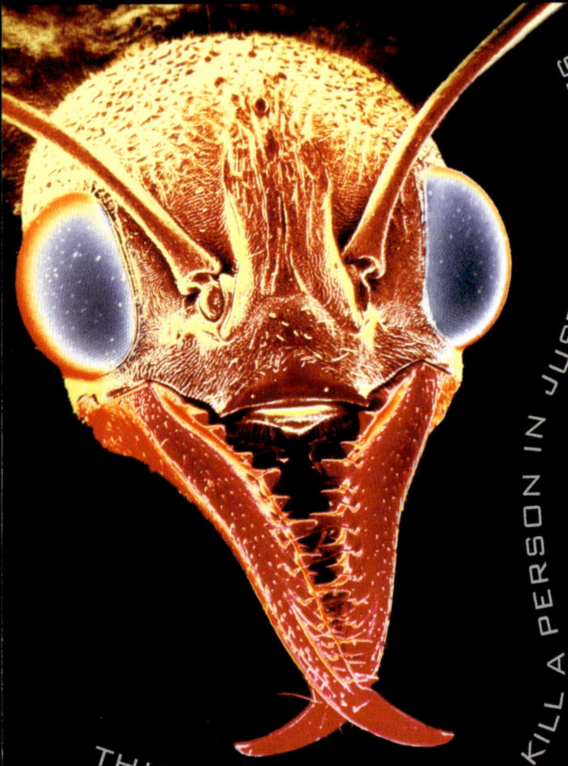

THIS ANT'S STING CAN KILL A PERSON IN JUST 15 MINUTES

MOST DANGEROUS ANT

The bulldog ant (*Myrmecia pyriformis*) – so called because of its ferocity and determination – is found in coastal regions of Australia. When attacking, the ant holds on to victims with its long mandibles while injecting deadly venom. Bulldog ants have caused at least three human fatalities since 1936, the latest a farmer in 1988.

HARDIEST ANIMALS IN OUTER SPACE

In 2007, scientists sent two species of tardigrade (microscopic eight-limbed creatures) into orbit, where they were exposed both to the vacuum of space and to sufficient radiation to incinerate a human. When they were brought back, a third of the total number were still alive, making them the only animals native to Earth that are known to have survived extraterrestrial conditions unassisted.

SMALLEST LIVING ORGANISM

The smallest entity universally recognized as a living organism (not all scientists consider the slightly smaller nanobes to be alive) is *Nanoarchaeum equitans*. This minuscule microbe was discovered only in 2002, in a hydrothermal vent on the seafloor off the coast of Iceland, and its cells are only 400 nanometers across. (One nanometer is a billionth of a meter.)

SMALLEST CELL

The brain cells in the cerebellum measure about 0.0001968 in (0.005 mm), or 5 microns.

SMALLEST PARASITE

Pneumocystis jirovecii, which causes pneumonia in humans, inhabits the lungs. It is 0.01–0.02 in (0.5–1 mm) long.

SMALLEST ORGANISM CAPABLE OF INDEPENDENT REPRODUCTION

Mycoplasma genitalium, a parasitic species of ultramicrobacterium that lives in the respiratory and genital tracts of primates, is the smallest creature that can reproduce independently and grow. It is approximately 200–300 nanometers in size.

LARGEST FAMILY OF SPIDERS

The largest zoological family of spiders is Salticidae, which includes jumping spiders. More than 4,400 species are known to science, and most live in the tropics. Jumping spiders hardly ever spin webs, catching their prey not by entrapment but by actively leaping at them.

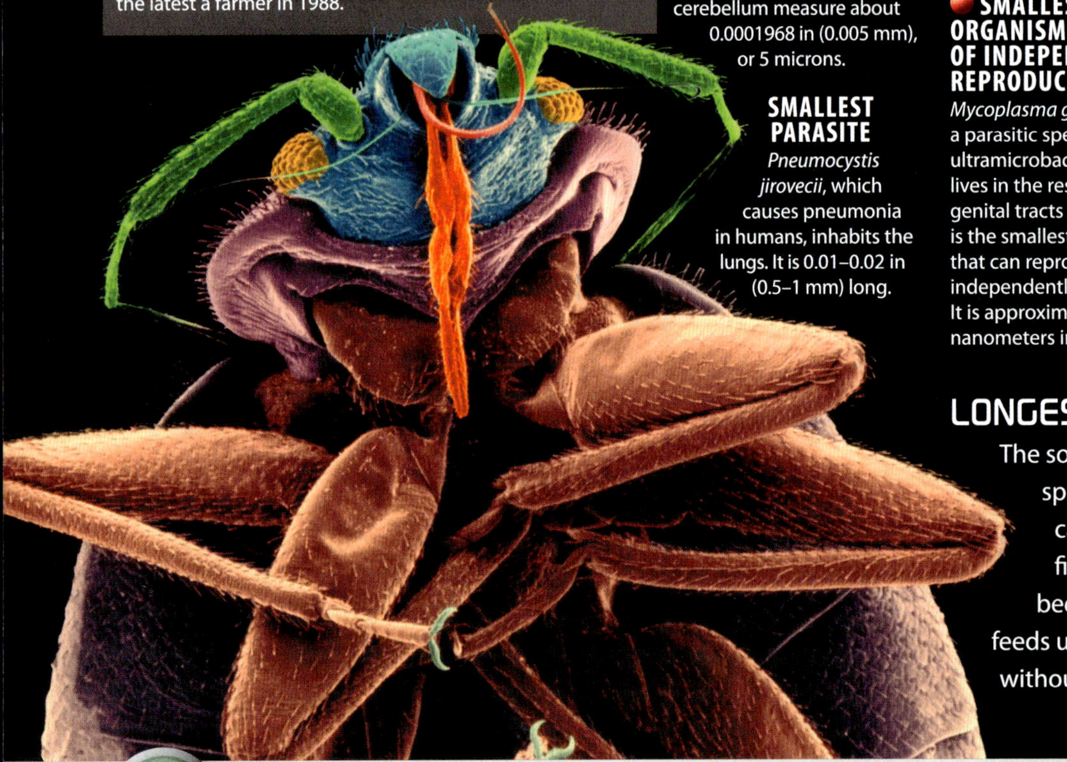

LONGEST PARASITIC FASTS

The soft tick (*Ornithodoros turicata*), which spreads the spirochaete bacteria that cause relapsing fever, can survive for five years without food. The common bedbug (*Cimex lectularius*, left), which feeds upon human blood, is able to survive without feeding for more than a year.

In 2005, Brazil had an estimated total forest cover of 1,844,400 miles^2 (477,698,000 ha), representing 57.2% of the state's total area, and making it the world's **most forested country**.

24 Ounces of insect parts that make it into your meals every year. It's impossible to stop insects getting into food somewhere along the line. During a lifetime, you'll swallow 117 lb of them.

UPDATED RECORD
NEW RECORD

LARGEST MICROBE
In terms of volume, the largest known protozoans are the extinct calcareous foraminifera (Foraminiferida) of the genus *Nummulites*. Samples 6 in (150 mm) wide were found in Middle Eocene Epoch rocks in Turkey. The Eocene Epoch was *c.* 55 million to 38 million years ago.

MOST DEADLY BUG
The bacterium *Yersinia pestis* caused the death of around 25 million people in mid-14th-century Europe. Named after French scientist Alexandre Yersin, who identified it in 1894, it causes bubonic plague, which is transmitted by fleas and rats.

EARLIEST FOSSIL CILIATE PROTOZOANS
Characterized by tiny hairlike structures (cilia) on their external surface, ciliate protozoans are microscopic single-celled organisms. Fossils of the species were formally documented in 2007. They were discovered within the Doushantuo Formation, a fossil-rich sedimentary deposit in China's Guizhou Province. Scientists have dated them to the Ediacaran Period, around 580 million years ago.

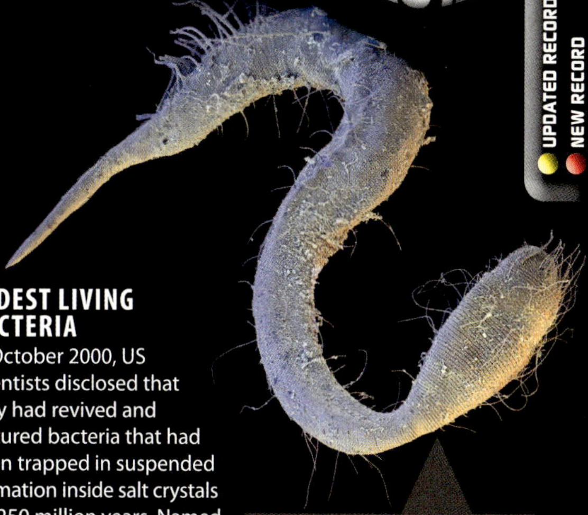

OLDEST LIVING BACTERIA
In October 2000, US scientists disclosed that they had revived and cultured bacteria that had been trapped in suspended animation inside salt crystals for 250 million years. Named Bacillus 2-9-3, it is 10 times older than the previous oldest revived bacteria.

SMALLEST NEMATODES
The world's smallest nematodes, or round worms, have no common names and live in marine sediments. They are only 80 micrometers long (one micrometer is a millionth of a meter) – roughly the same as the width of an average human hair. Nematodes are the most abundant multi-celled creatures on Earth.

MOST RADIATION-RESISTANT LIFE FORM
The red-colored bacterium *Deinococcus radiodurans* can resist 1.5 million rads of gamma radiation – about 3,000 times the amount that would kill a human.

LARGEST TARDIGRADE
Echiniscoides sigismundi, a marine Eurasian species of tardigrade, can reach 0.05 in (1.5 mm) long as a mature adult. Most other tardigrade species remain microscopic throughout their lives.

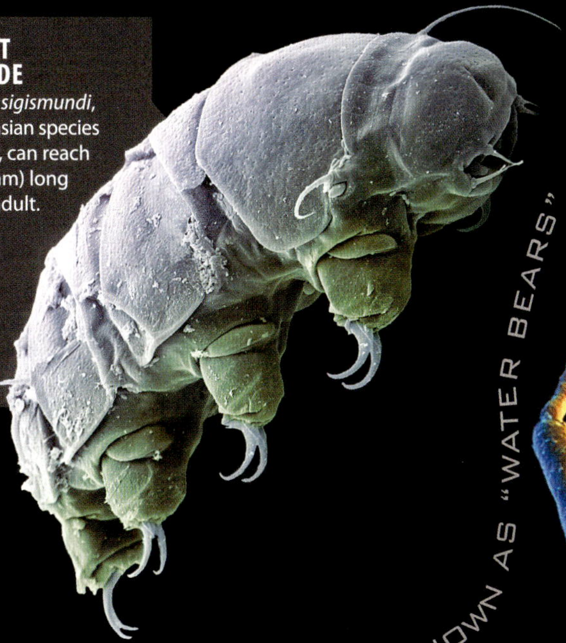

TARDIGRADES ARE ALSO KNOWN AS "WATER BEARS"

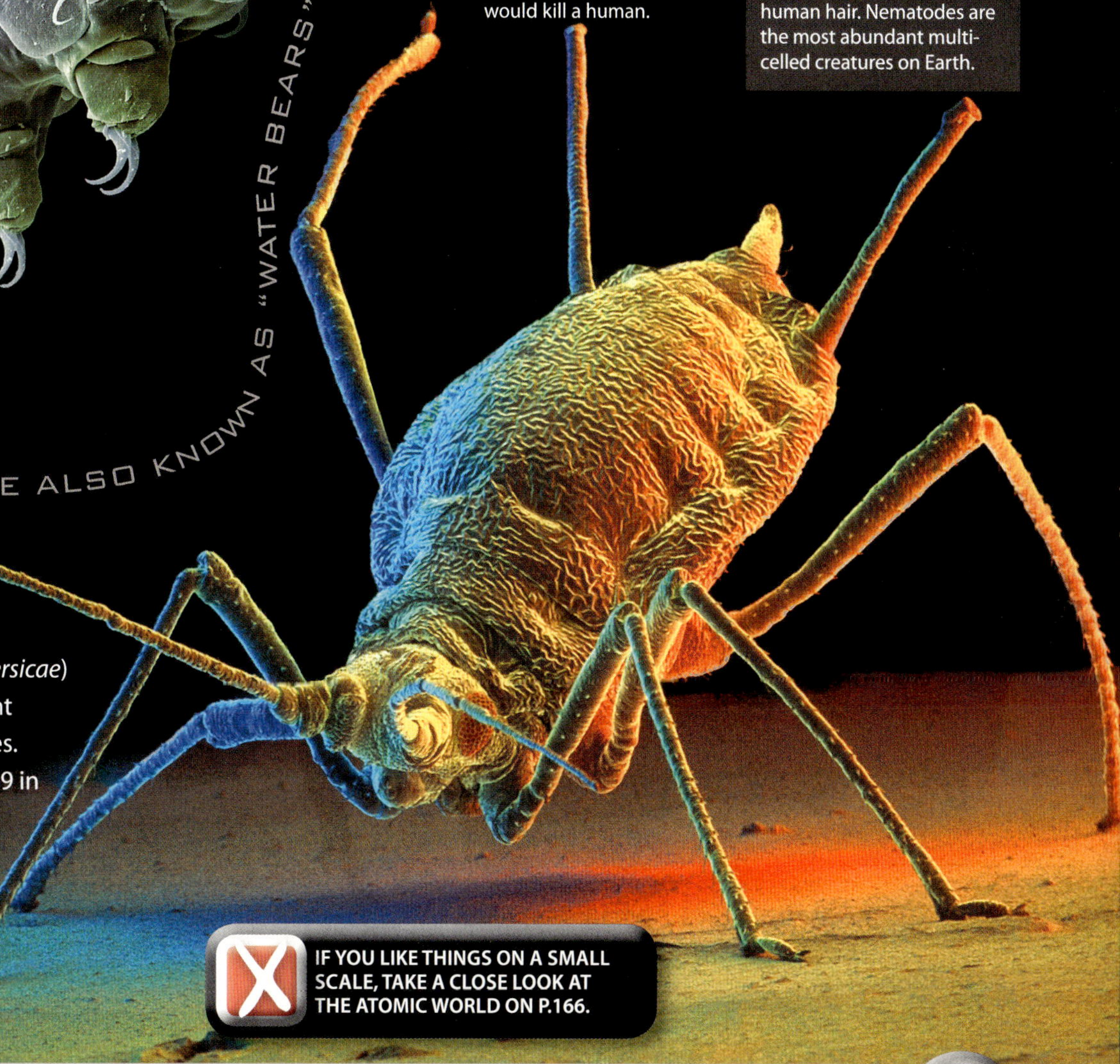

MOST INSECTICIDE-RESISTANT INSECT
The green peach aphid (*Myzus persicae*) has been documented as resistant to 71 different chemical pesticides. The aphids are approximately 0.09 in (2.3 mm) long when fully grown and vary in color from green to pale yellow or pink.

IF YOU LIKE THINGS ON A SMALL SCALE, TAKE A CLOSE LOOK AT THE ATOMIC WORLD ON P.166.

The **longest avenue of trees** is the 22-mile (35.41-km) Nikko Cryptomeria Avenue in Imaichi City, Tochigi Prefecture, Japan. Planted in 1628–48, more than 13,500 of its original 200,000 Japanese cedar (*Cryptomeria japonica*) trees survive.

AMAZING MENAGERIE

RAREST GORILLA

Little Snowflake was a unique male albino western lowland gorilla (*Gorilla gorilla gorilla*) who lived at Barcelona Zoo from 1966 until his death from age-related ill health on November 24, 2003. Unlike full albinos, Little Snowflake had blue eyes, suggesting that he was a chinchilla albino, caused by a recessive mutant gene form named chinchilla (also responsible for white tigers).

MOST TENTACLED OCTOPUS

In December 1998, an extraordinary specimen of common octopus (*Octopus vulgaris*) was captured alive in Matoya Bay, Japan. Each of its eight normal tentacles had branched to produce a profusion of additional ones, yielding an amazing 96 tentacles.

LARGEST COLLECTION OF TWO-HEADED ANIMALS

Todd Ray (USA) owns the world's most impressive collection of two-headed, or dicephalic, animals. He has spent over $157,824 on acquisitions and now owns 22 different specimens. These include a two-headed albino hog-nosed snake, a two-headed goat, a two-headed terrapin, a two-headed king snake, a two-headed bearded dragon (a species of lizard) named Pancho and Lefty, plus the world's only living three-headed creature: a turtle named Myrtle, Squirtle, and Thirdle.

LARGEST POPULATION OF WHITE TIGERS

Nandankanan Zoo, in the state of Orissa, India, is home to more than 34 white tigers. This zoo has bred many white tigers over the years, and has sent them to other zoos all over the world.

WHY WHITE?

Albinism affects all vertebrates, humans included. It is caused by the lack of a particular enzyme that is required to produce melanin – a pigment that provides color for eyes, hair, and skin.

OLDEST LIVING SPECIES

Tadpole shrimps (*Triops cancriformis*) are thought to be the oldest pedigree of any living creature. Fossil evidence suggests that they have hardly changed in the 200 million years they have existed.

SHORTEST COW

Diana, a seven-year-old Vechur cow who was born and bred at the Vechur Conservation Centre, Kerala, India, measured 30 in (77 cm) from the hoof to the withers (between the shoulder blades) on November 9, 2010.

LARGEST WATER WALKER

The South American basilisk lizard (*Basiliscus basiliscus*) can run bipedally at a velocity of 5 ft/s (1.5 m/s) for approximately 14 ft 9 in (4.5 m) before sinking. It can also "walk on water" on all fours, which extends the distance that it can travel on the surface by about 4 ft 3 in (1.3 m). Various small insects are also able to move across the surface of water in ponds and lakes without sinking.

Population figures for 2009 reveal that in Japan, the median age – that is, the age at which there are an equal number of people above and below – is a record high of 44.7, giving Japan the world's **oldest population**.

UPDATED RECORD
NEW RECORD

13,807 Hen eggs you will consume in a lifetime. That's enough eggs to make an omelette with a 164-ft diameter – the same distance as the length of an Olympic-sized swimming pool.

LARGEST HORN ON A BIRD: Also known as the unicorn bird, the South American horned screamer (*Anhima cornuta*) has a curved horn measuring up to 6 in (15 cm) in length.

BORN WITH A HORN
The unicorn bird's horn is actually a cartilaginous, unbranched feather shaft. Present in both sexes, it is too delicate to use as a weapon and has no clear purpose.

LARGEST EARDRUM

The eardrum of the gorilla (*Gorilla gorilla*) measures about 0.15 in² (97 mm²); our eardrums, by comparison, are just 0.096 in² (62 mm²).

FISH WITH MOST EYES

The six-eyed spookfish (*Bathylychnops exilis*) lives at depths of 300–3,000 ft (91–910 m) in the north-eastern Pacific. A slender 17-in-long (45-cm) pikelike species, it has a pair of large principal eyes, but also a second, smaller pair, known as secondary globes, within the lower half of its principal eyes and pointing down. Each globe possesses its own lens and retina, and may help to increase the spookfish's sensitivity to light in its shadowy surroundings.

Behind the secondary globes is a third pair of eyes. These lack retinas, but divert incoming light into the fish's large principal eyes.

LAZIEST FRESHWATER TURTLE

Native to the Mekong River in Cambodia, Cantor's giant soft-shelled turtle (*Pelochelys cantorii*) spends 95% of its life motionless in sand on the river bottom waiting for prey to approach. It comes up to the water surface to breathe air only twice each day.

CAMEL WITH MOST HUMPS

The Bactrian camel (*Camelus bactrianus*) normally has two humps, while the Arabian camel or dromedary (*C. dromedarius*) normally has just one. During the early 1970s, however, German zoologist Dr Bernhard Grzimek documented an apparently unique, freak dromedary that possessed no fewer than four distinct, fully formed humps.

LONGEST-SURVIVING JANUS CAT

Caused by a protein called sonic hedgehog homolog (SHH), diprosopia is an extremely rare congenital condition in which part or all of an individual's face is duplicated on its head. This condition has been recorded in the domestic cat (*Felis catus*) and some of the resulting two-faced kittens have survived into adulthood. Mindful of Janus, the two-faced Roman god of gates and doorways, British zoologist Dr Karl Shuker has dubbed these animals Janus cats. The longest-surviving Janus cat is Frank and Louie, from Millbury, Ohio, USA, which had reached six years of age by July 2006.

LARGEST CAT HYBRID

The liger (no scientific name) is the offspring of a male lion and a tigress. Ligers typically grow larger than either parent, reaching lengths of 10–12 ft (3–3.6 m). Although these hybrids could occur in the wild, such crossbreeding usually happens in zoos or private menageries.

FURRIEST CRUSTACEAN

The yeti lobster (*Kiwa hirsuta*) lives on hydrothermal vents on the seafloor in the South Pacific Ocean. Its long claws and shorter thoracic limbs are covered in long, silky, blond-colored filaments called setae. These very distinctive hairlike structures bear bacteria intertwined among them.

FASTEST MAMMALIAN EATER: Dr Kenneth Catania (USA) has recorded the average food "handling time" of the star-nosed mole (*Condylura cristata*) at 230 milliseconds.

From high age to lofty heights: the Dutch are the world's **tallest citizens**, with the average Dutch male measuring 6 ft (184 cm) tall.

PECULIAR PLANTS

LONGEST CONIFER CONES

The longest cones of any species of conifer belong to the sugar pine (*Pinus lambertiana*, see left and below), native to the western USA and to Baja California in northwestern Mexico. They range in size from 10–26 in (25–66 cm) and have a diameter of 4–5 in (10–13 cm).

FIRST BIOLUMINESCENT FLOWER

In December 1999, Professor Chia Tet Fatt from Singapore's National Institute of Education produced the world's first successful bioluminescent flowers, using a white-petaled Dendrobium White Fairy #5 orchid. He transferred biologically active DNA containing the luciferase gene from fireflies into the orchid tissues and then propagated them, yielding orchids that retain the firefly gene. These orchids emit a constant greenish-white light from their petals, roots, stem, and leaves for up to five hours at a time.

FASTEST-GROWING PLANT

Certain species of the 45 genera of bamboo have been found to grow at a rate of up to 35 in (91 cm) a day, or 0.00002 mi/h (0.00003 km/h). The **tallest bamboo** – the giant bamboo (*Dendrocalamus giganteus*) of tropical southeast Asia – can reach as high as 164 ft (50 m).

MOST ENDANGERED LOBELIA: Only eight plants of the species *Lobelia monostachya* are known to exist. They are confined to the southern leeward Koolau Mountains of Oahu, Hawaii.

FASTEST-GROWING TREE

The empress or foxglove tree (*Paulownia tomentosa*) can grow as much as 12 in (30 cm) over three weeks, and 19 ft 8 in (6 m) during its first year. It is native to central and west China, but is naturalized now in the USA.

The Netherlands has a total area of around 16,033 miles^2 (41,526 km^2), around 27% of which actually lies below sea level, making it the world's **lowest country**.

158,000 Number of new plant species that will be discovered during your lifetime. That works out at 2,000 new plants per year, or more than five every day.

GUINNESS WORLD RECORDS 2012

LARGEST INFLORESCENCE
The puya (*Puya raimondii*) is a rare species of giant bromeliad that lives high in the Bolivian mountains. When it blooms, the panicle (vertical stalk) it produces can grow to 35 ft (10.7 m) in height, with a diameter of up to 8 ft (2.4 m), and bears around 8,000 small white flowers. This enormous inflorescence (flowering) is strong enough to support a human.

MOST DANGEROUS TREE
The manchineel (*Hippomane mancinella*) of the Florida Everglades and the Caribbean coast exudes a sap that can blister human skin and, if it touches the eyes, can make a person blind. One bite of its small, apple-like fruit causes blistering and severe pain and can be fatal. If a manchineel is burned, the resulting smoke can cause blindness if it gets into the eyes.

LARGEST ALBINO PLANTS
There are between 25 and 60 albino coast redwood trees (*Sequoia sempervirens*) in California, USA, some up to 69 ft (21 m) tall. Lacking chlorophyll, they are a pale white color and are known as "everwhites."

TALLEST BLOOM
Louis Ricciardiello (USA) grew a Titan arum (*Amorphophallus titanum*) that measured 10 ft 2.25 in (3.1 m) tall on June 18, 2010. It was displayed at Winnipesaukee Orchids in Gilford, New Hampshire, USA.

MOST LEAVES ON A CLOVER
Shigeo Obara of Hanamaki City, Iwate, Japan, found a 56-leaf white clover (*Trifolium repens L.*) on May 10, 2009.

SMALLEST SPECIES OF WATER LILY
Nymphaea thermarum, also known as the thermal lily, has pads that measure 0.3–0.6 in (10–20 mm) across.

The world's **largest water lily** is *Victoria amazonica*: its gigantic floating leaves measure up to 10 ft (3 m) across, and are held in place by an underwater stalk 23–26 ft (7–8 m) long.

OLDEST-KNOWN HUMAN-PLANTED TREE
A 2,300-year-old sacred fig or bo-tree (*Ficus religiosa*) given the name Sri Maha Bodhiya stands in Anuradhapura, Sri Lanka. It was planted in 288 BC. The mother tree from which this specimen was propagated was the famous Bodhi tree, under which the Lord Buddha, Siddhartha Gautama, was sitting for three days and three nights when he gained enlightenment.

LARGEST LIVING TREE
In the Sequoia National Park in California, USA, there is a giant sequoia (*Sequoiadendron giganteum*) known as General Sherman. An estimated 2,100 years old, it stands 271 ft (82.6 m) tall and has a circumference of approximately 85 ft (26 m). The trunk had a volume of 52,508 ft^3 (1,487 m^3) in 1980, when it was last measured accurately, but by 2004 it was thought to be almost 54,000 ft^3 (1,530 m^3) – that's enough wood to provide timber for building as many as 35 five-room houses.

UPDATED RECORD
NEW RECORD

LIVING HISTORY
This bizarre, exceptionally resilient ancient species is classed as a living fossil as it has no close modern-day relatives. It has a 400–1,500-year life span.

DESERT PLANT WITH THE LONGEST LEAVES
The wonder plant (*Welwitschia mirabilis*) of the Namib Desert in Namibia and Angola produces only two leaves, but each grows 6 ft 6 in–13 ft 1 in (2–4 m) long. The leaves eventually split, or at least become shredded at their tips, owing to the arid desert winds and harsh living conditions.

Rising above the Netherlands, but only just, comes the Maldives, with a maximum elevation above sea level of 8 ft (2.4 m). As the world's **flattest country**, the Maldives is now under threat from rising sea levels and coastal erosion.

TIME TALES

The country may be flat but the divorce rate in the Maldives is anything but – this beautiful island nation has the **highest divorce rate** in the world, with 10.97 divorces per 1,000 inhabitants per year.

OLDEST PRE-COLUMBIAN CALENDAR STILL IN USE

Sacred round Mesoamerican calendars – that is, those devised by the pre-Columbian cultures of present-day Mexico and Central America – continue to be used in one form or another to the present day, having passed from the Olmecs (1500–400 BC) to the Maya (up to AD 900) and then to the Aztecs (up to the 1500s; pictured is an Aztec calendar at the Mexico Museum of Anthropology in Mexico City).

The **oldest calendar still in use** is the Jewish calendar, which has been in popular use since the 9th century BC. It is based on biblical calculations that place the creation at 3761 BC.

IS THE END NIGH?

The Maya used three interlocking calendars that created "Great Cycles" of time. The present cycle is due to end on December 23, 2012, at which time the Maya would expect not the end of the world but a spiritual "rebirth."

Of course, not everyone gets married. According to the latest year for which data is available, the Dominican Republic has the **lowest marriage rate** in the world, with just two marriages per 1,000 population in 1994.

BRIEF HISTORY OF TIME

KEEPING TRACK OF TIME

Time is the measure by which we live our lives, and over the last 5,000 years we have developed ever more accurate ways of keeping track of it. Starting at 1 o'clock, work your way round the clock face to discover how we have harnessed the power of sunlight, water, fire, gravity, electricity, and even atoms, all just to tell the time...

11 QUARTZ CLOCK

In *c.* 1880, scientists discovered that when an electric current passes through quartz crystals, it made the crystals vibrate with a regularity that was ideal for timekeeping. The first quartz clocks arrived in the 1920s, but were so large that they were confined to laboratories. By the late 1960s, technological refinements led to smaller, domestic models such as the popular Astro-Chron (below) as well as the first ever analog quartz wristwatches.

10 ELECTRIC CLOCK

The **first electric clock** was designed by the Scottish inventor Alexander Bain (1811–77) and patented in 1841. Although Bain employed a pendulum to measure time, he took the revolutionary step of powering it with an electric current rather than the traditional method of springs or weights. The clock pictured was a refinement of Bain's design, built by Frenchmen Marcel Moulin (1881–1914) and Maurice Favre-Bulle (1870–1954), who claimed it could run for 800 days on one battery.

9 HARRISON'S H4 SEA CLOCK

John Harrison (UK, 1693–1776) built the **first marine clock**, the H4, in response to a UK Government challenge to create a timekeeping device capable of calculating a ship's longitude to within 0.5° (two minutes of time). No bigger than a large pocket watch, the H4 was 5.11 in (13 cm) across and weighed 3 lb 3 oz (1.45 kg). On its first trial, sailing to Jamaica on HMS *Deptford* from November 18, 1761 to January 9, 1762, the clock was found to be just 5.1 seconds slow, thus solving the "longitude problem" and revolutionizing long-distance navigation at sea.

TIME ON YOUR HANDS

Wristwatches were a natural progression from pocket watches, but men initially refused to wear them, preferring the more traditional timepiece. The **first wristwatch** was made for a woman, Countess Koscowicz of Hungary, by Patek Philippe (Switzerland) in 1868.

8 PENDULUM CLOCK

The Italian scientist Galileo Galilei (1564–1642) was among the first to observe that the steady, predictable rate of a pendulum's swing made it ideal for use in timekeeping. Soon afterwards, in 1656, the Dutch horologist Christiaan Huygens (1629–95) built the **first operational pendulum clock**, which was accurate to within a minute per day and represented a huge leap forward in timekeeping. Toward the end of the century, this margin of error had been reduced to just 0.5 seconds – accurate enough to warrant the introduction in the late 1690s of the first-ever second hand.

FIRST PENDULUM CLOCK DESIGN

Galileo began building a pendulum clock in the late 1630s, although he died before he could finish it. A reconstruction based on a drawing of his design (pictured) was built in the 1800s.

7 HOURGLASS

The **first hourglass**, or sand clock, measured time by the descent of sand from one glass bulb to another. It may have been invented by a French monk named Liutprand in the 8th century. However, concrete evidence of the device first appeared in European ship inventories from the 14th century. Arriving just in time for the "Age of Discovery," the hourglass was ideal for ocean travel because the bobbing waves didn't affect its accuracy.

LARGEST HOURGLASS

In 2000, Bob Ciscell (USA) built the world's largest hourglass. Standing 42 in (1.06 m) tall and 15 in (38 cm) across, it contains 65 lb (29.4 kg) of sand, which takes eight hours to run through.

Joaquín Balaguer (1907–2002) was president of the Dominican Republic three times, from 1960 to 1962, 1966 to 1978, and 1986 to 1996, by which time he was the world's **oldest president** at the age of 89.

78 Orbits you will make of the Sun in your lifetime – one for every year of your life. In celebration, you will receive a total of 1,450 birthday cards – 18 per orbit.

12 ATOMIC CLOCK

Today, we live on atomic time, which is measured through the vibration of atoms to produce an unprecedented level of accuracy – 1 second in millions of years. Although atomic clocks have existed since the 1930s, Louis Essen's (1908–97) Caesium I clock, built in 1955, was the first to keep time more precisely than pendulum and electric clocks. Since the 1980s invention of radio-controlled clocks such as the Space Timer (left), which synchronize with atomic clocks over the airwaves, we no longer have any excuse to be late.

FASTEST ATOMIC CLOCK

Physicists at the National Institute of Standards and Technology in Colorado, USA, have built an atomic clock that "ticks" about a quadrillion times per second and may eventually be accurate to 1 second in 30 billion years.

1 TIME STICK

First used in Mesopotamia in *c.* 3500 BC, the time (or shadow) stick was the **earliest form of clock**. Planted in the earth, it told the time by casting a shadow on the ground that changed length and position as the Sun "moved" overhead. Later, more sophisticated versions such as this 19th-century Tibetan example were created with multiple sides featuring timescales for different months.

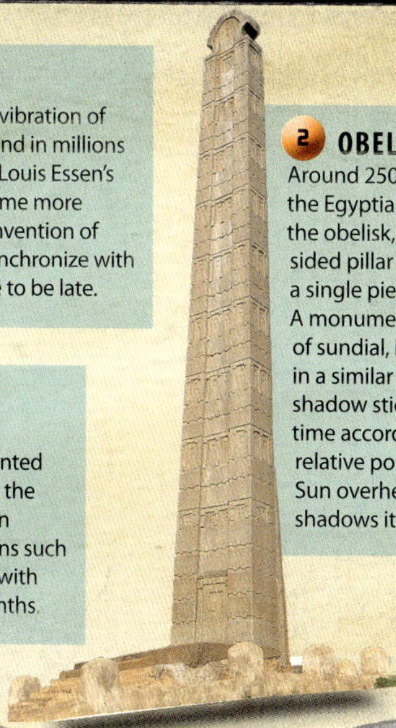

2 OBELISK

Around 2500–2000 BC, the Egyptians developed the obelisk, a tall, four-sided pillar made from a single piece of stone. A monumental form of sundial, it worked in a similar way to the shadow stick, measuring time according to the relative position of the Sun overhead and the shadows it cast.

TURN TO P.86 FOR MORE OLD TIMERS...

MOST VALUABLE SUNDIAL

The golden sundial in Yanggu, South Korea, is made from 4 lb 6 oz (2 kg) of gold, 5 lb (2.3 kg) of gold-plating, and 9.4 tons (8.5 metric tons) of bronze. It is valued at 811.7 million won ($667,225).

3 WATER CLOCK

As sundials depended on light, the Egyptians created water clocks in the 15th century BC to tell the time in all conditions, 24 hours a day. Essentially the **first all-weather clock**, the device, called a *clepsydra* ("water thief"), was a large pot that leaked water through a hole in the bottom at a steady, measurable rate.

OLDEST SURVIVING CLOCK

The faceless mechanical clock at Salisbury Cathedral, Wiltshire, UK, was built in around 1386. It was restored in 1956, having struck the hours for 498 years and ticked more than 500 million times.

5 CANDLE CLOCK

Invented in *c.* AD 800, the candle clock was the **first practical indoor clock**. Markers on the stem indicated the passing of time as the candle burned down. In the late 9th century, King Alfred the Great of England created an intricate 24-hour clock made from six large candles, each of which was designed to burn for four hours.

4 SUNDIAL

Sundials such as the one shown left were first developed in *c.* 300 BC. A vertical pointer – called a *gnomon* (Greek for "one who knows") – cast a shadow on to a dial marked with the hours of the day. Special devices called "merkhets" could be placed over the sundial at night to measure the time by the stars.

6 WATER WHEEL CLOCK

In *c.* 1088, the astronomer Su Sung (China) built a vast water clock for the Emperor, powered by an 11-ft (3.3-m) water wheel (model, left). The complex device featured one of the earliest escapements – the mechanism by which continuous motion is converted into the uniform "tick-tick" of a mechanical clock.

FIRST MECHANICAL CLOCK

The earliest mechanical clock – that is, one that features an escapement – was built in China in AD 725 by Yi Xing and Liang Lingzan (China).

When it comes to staying power, few can compare to Fidel Castro (Cuba, b. August 13, 1927), who led Cuba from July 26, 1959 until his retirement on February 19, 2008 – in total, 48 years 208 days – making him the world's **longest-serving nonroyal head of state**.

MAPS

OLDEST SURVIVING MAP

In the 1920s, archeological excavations at Nuzi in northern Iraq turned up a series of clay tablets dating to 2300 BC that depict the Euphrates river and nearby hills, streams, and settlements. These ancient clay "maps" represent the earliest direct evidence of cartography.

OLDEST SURVIVING MAP WITH DISTANCE MEASUREMENTS

A brass map dating to the 4th century BC was discovered in Hebei, China, in the 1970s. Engraved with the words *Zhao Yu Tu* ("Map of the Mausoleum"), it maps the five mausoleums of Emperor Wang Cuo and is marked with numerals indicating distances.

MOST EXPENSIVE ATLAS

A version of Ptolemy's *Cosmographia* dating from 1477 went under the hammer for a record £2,136,000 ($3,990,010) at Sotheby's auction rooms in London, UK, on October 10, 2006.

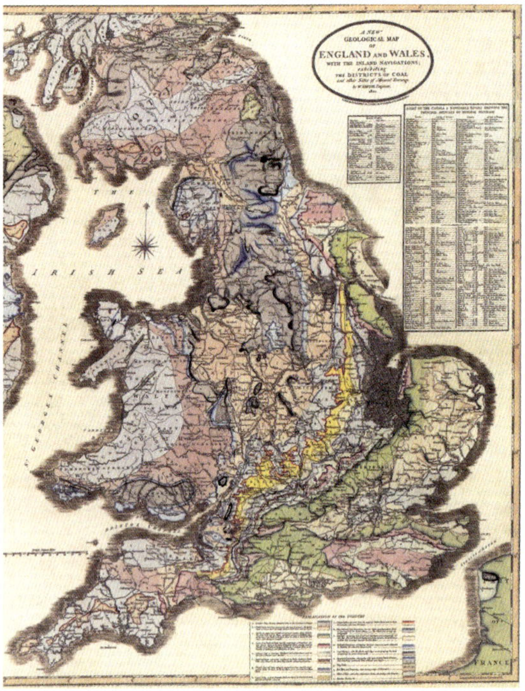

MOST EXPENSIVE MAP

On December 3, 2010, a map of the USA, the first to be printed in that country, sold at auction at Christie's, New York, USA, for $2,098,500 including commissions. Created in 1784, the map came from the collection of the New Jersey Historical Society and is one of only seven such prints known to exist. It is also the first map printed in the USA to show the national flag and the first map to be copyrighted in the USA.

FIRST PUBLISHED WORLD ATLAS

Created by the Flemish cartographer Abraham Ortelius, the *Theatrum Orbis Terrarum* ("Theater of the World") was published in 1570 by the notable Antwerp printer Gilles Coppens van Diest. The original was in Latin and featured 70 maps on 53 pages, but between 1570 and 1612, numerous updated editions followed, including versions in German, Dutch, French, Spanish, English, and Italian.

FIRST MAP OF THE NEW WORLD

The first cartographer to compile a map of the New World was Martin Waldseemüller (Germany). His map, created in 1507, showed for the first time the new lands explored by Christopher Columbus and Amerigo Vespucci, while it also marked the first use of the name "America," which Waldseemüller coined in honor of Vespucci.

FIRST GEOLOGICAL COUNTRY MAP

William Smith's (UK) 1801 *Delineation of the Strata of England and Wales with part of Scotland* was the first countrywide map to illustrate the different rock layers found across the land. The "Father of English Geology," Smith had earlier created the **first geological map**, of the area around Bath, UK, in 1799.

FIRST SILK MAPS

In 1973–74, archaeologists exploring a 2nd-century-BC tomb in Hunan, China, found a series of detailed silk maps depicting the topography of Hunan Province all the way down to the South China Sea.

FIRST ROAD MAP

Prolific road-builders, the Romans were also the first to map them, creating a huge circular map of the Empire's network engraved in stone near the Forum in Rome, Italy. Marcus Agrippa (63–12 BC), the son of Emperor Augustus Caesar, was the man charged with driving this mammoth project. In the course of 20 years, he oversaw the charting of the Empire's *cursus publicus* ("roads") for thousands of miles across Europe and as far afield as the Middle East. The finished map, known as the "Itinerarium," was used primarily to help administer the vast Empire, but it also stood as a symbol of Roman power.

The **smallest bird** is the bee hummingbird (*Mellisuga helenae*) of Cuba's Isle of Youth. The male weighs 0.056 oz (1.6 g) and measures 2.24 in (57 mm) in length, half of which is taken up by the bill and tail.

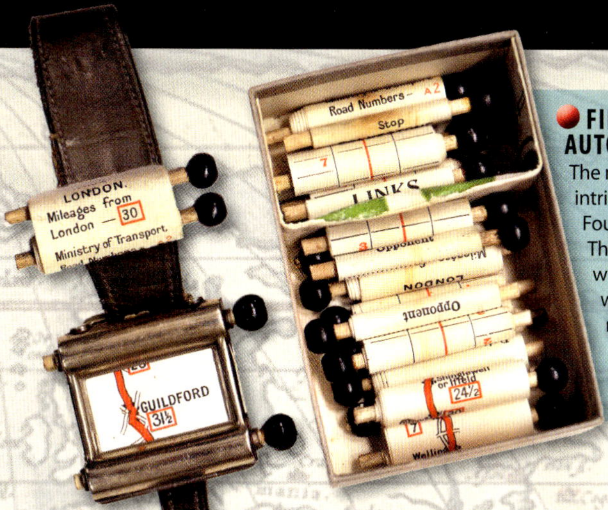

FIRST INTERACTIVE AUTOMOTIVE ROUTE PLANNER

The modern sat-nav had an intriguing precedent in the Plus Fours Routefinder, created in 1920. This device took the form of a wristband that could be loaded with small scrolls featuring UK road maps. By rotating the rollers, the map on the scroll could be advanced, enabling a driver to navigate the route.

FIRST MAP FOR AUTOMOBILE DRIVERS

For an automobile race held in the USA on Thanksgiving Day in 1895, the *Chicago Sun Herald* published a map of the 53.4-mile (86-km) course from Jackson Park, Illinois, to Waukegan, Illinois, and back again. Competitor Frank Duryea – the first American to build a successful commercial automobile – tore the map out of the newspaper and used it to drive to victory.

PILGRIM'S PROGRESS

In AD 330, a French pilgrim wrote the **first tourist guide** – the *Itinerarium Burdigalense*. In it, he described his route to Jerusalem, Israel, and gave details of hostels and watering points.

LARGEST MAP COLLECTION

The Geography and Map Division of the US Library of Congress, Washington, DC, USA, has custody of the largest and most comprehensive cartographic collection in the world. In total, it holds over 4.5 million maps, including 60,000 atlases, 6,000 reference works, numerous globes and plastic relief models, and a large variety of cartographic material in other formats, including digital.

LARGEST ONLINE MAP

Google Earth, owned by search engine Google, is a virtual 3D globe of the entire planet comprised of satellite data that can be browsed by home internet users.

SMALLEST MAP

In 1992, Dr H Jonathon Mamin of IBM's laboratory in Zürich, Switzerland, used sudden electrical pulses to create a map of the Western Hemisphere from atoms. It has a diameter of 1 micron – just 100th of the diameter of a human hair.

MOST POPULAR SAT-NAV VOICE

According to TomTom, the market-leading manufacturer of automobile satellite navigation systems, Homer Simpson, voiced by US actor Dan Castellaneta, has been downloaded a record 128,500 times since 2009.

OLDEST SURVIVING TERRESTRIAL GLOBE

In 1491–92, Martin Behaim – a German cosmographer and explorer working for the Portuguese court – created the *Erdapfel* ("Earth Apple"), a metal sphere on which a world map was painted by Georg Glockendon (Germany). The map does not include the Americas as their discoverer, Christopher Columbus, did not return from his famous journey until 1493.

LARGEST ATLAS

The huge Klencke atlas measures 5 ft 10 in (1.78 m) high, 3 ft 5 in (1.05 m) wide, and 4 in (11 cm) thick. Presented to Charles II, King of England, by a Dutch merchant in around 1660, it contains 39 pages with 41 maps all dating from the first half of the 17th century.

LARGEST REVOLVING GLOBE

Old as it is, the *Erdapfel* (left) is tiny compared to the world's largest revolving globe, *Eartha*, which was built by GPS and digital map manufacturer DeLorme (USA) in 1998. The vast globe, which has a diameter of 41 ft 18 in (12.52 m) and weighs 5,600 lb (2,540 kg), occupies a three-story glass atrium at the company's headquarters in Maine, USA. Powered by two computer-controlled electric motors, it revolves on a specially designed cantilever arm.

SMALLEST-SCALE 3D MAP

A representation of the 2dF survey of galaxies – the most detailed available – was created by Crystal Nebulae (UK) on a scale of 1 cm (0.39 in): 1 billion light years. Around 200,000 galaxies were laser-etched into a cube of just 0.37 in³ (6 cm³).

OLDEST MOON MAP

A series of 5,000-year-old carvings on a rock at Knowth in Ireland have been identified as the world's most ancient Moon map.

OLDEST SURVIVING STAR CHART ON MANUSCRIPT

Dating to AD 649–684, the Dunhuang Chinese Sky star chart comprises a sequence of drawings of sky maps on rolls of manuscript. Discovered in 1907, it depicts the constellations visible from the Northern Hemisphere and includes 1,300 stars.

UPDATED RECORD
NEW RECORD

EARLY CIVILIZATIONS

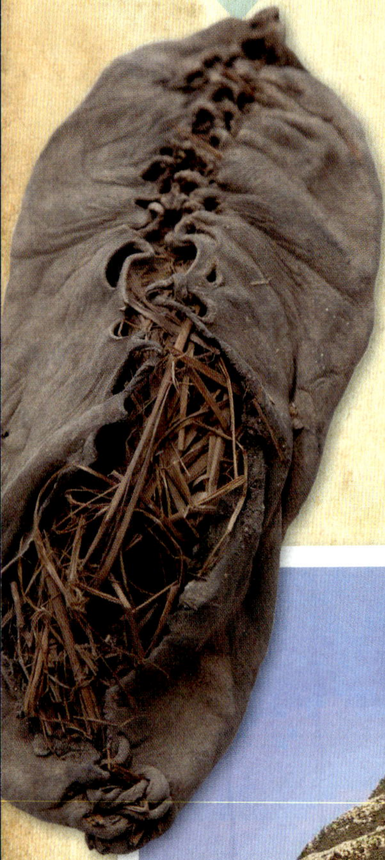

OLDEST LEATHER SHOE

In 2008, archaeologists found a 5,500-year-old leather shoe in the Areni-1 cave in the southeastern Vayotoz Dzor province of Armenia.

FIRST ZOO

Archaeological discoveries made south of Luxor in Egypt in 2009 suggest the existence of a vast menagerie of animals – 112 creatures in total, including elephants, wildcats, baboons, and hippos – dating back to 3500 BC. The zoo – likely to have been privately owned, as the animals were buried in an elite cemetery – was unearthed during excavations of the ancient settlement of Hierakonpolis.

FIRST CITY

Dating back to *c.* 3200 BC, Uruk, located in southern Mesopotamia (modern Iraq), was home to some 50,000 people. It was the largest settlement of its time, covering 1,112 acres (450 ha) and encircled by a 5.9-mile (9.5-km) city wall. Uruk thrived as a result of trade and agriculture and became a great artistic center.

FIRST DOMESTICATION OF DOGS

The oldest verifiable domestication of dogs (*Canis familiaris*) is thought to have been carried out by Paleolithic humans in east Asia, approximately 15,000 years ago, as they successfully bred aggression out of wolves (*Canis lupus*).

OLDEST ROYAL CEMETERY

In 1922, British archaeologist Leonard Woolley excavated what is believed to be the first royal cemetery, at Ur in ancient Mesopotamia. He uncovered some 1,800 graves dating back as far as 2600 BC, 16 of which were elaborate tombs with several rooms with spectacular artefacts. The tombs also included the remains of servants and members of the court.

OLDEST MUMMY

Mummification dates from 2600 BC or the 4th dynasty of the Egyptian pharaohs. The oldest complete mummy is of Wati, a court musician of *c.* 2400 BC from the tomb of Nefer in Saqqâra, Egypt.

FIRST HORSE RACE

Horsemanship was an important part of the Hittite culture of Anatolia, Turkey, dating from 1400 BC. The 33rd ancient Olympic Games of 648 BC in Greece featured horse racing as an event.

FIRST ACTOR

Dionysian priest Thespis of ancient Greece was part of a chorus group that performed songs and dances based on Greek myths. In 534 BC, at a performance in Athens, he is said to have leapt from the chorus to act out the roles of the characters that the group were singing about.

OLDEST PYRAMIDS

The Djoser Step Pyramid (left) at Saqqâra, Egypt, was built *c.* 2750 BC and rose to a height of 204 ft (62 m) and is the **first cut-stone pyramid**. Archaeologists later found that, *c.* 2700–2600 BC, similar structures were built in the Peruvian city of Caral (below), which featured up to 20 pyramids. It is impossible to say for certain which pyramids are the oldest.

KEY STAGES IN THE HISTORY OF MANKIND, FROM THE BEGINNING OF AGRICULTURE IN 8000 BC TO THE FOUNDING OF ISLAM IN *c.* AD 600.

8000 BC Agriculture begins; wheat, oats, rye, and barley grown along the Tigris and Euphrates Rivers in Mesopotamia and in Egypt by the Nile River

5000 BC Mesopotamia, "the cradle of civilization," comes into being; earliest system of laws, mathematics, and astronomy developed

3200 BC World's **first city**, Uruk, established in southern Mesopotamia

c. 3000 BC

ASTROLOGICAL TABLET Clay tablet, *c.* 3000 BC, inscribed in cuneiform with astrological data

1800 BC According to Jewish tradition, Abraham, the first Jewish Patriarch, born in the city of Ur in Babylonia

1100 BC Mesoamerican civilization begins with settlements in Mexico built by the Olmecs

1200–800 BC

OLMEC SCULPTURE Green jadeite ceremonial ax with "flaming eyebrows"

Madagascar is the world's **oldest island**. It split off from the Indian subcontinent around 80–100 million years ago and is now closer to the coast of Africa than it is to India.

28 Average life expectancy of a person living in ancient Greece or ancient Rome. Richer citizens often lived longer, unsurprisingly, while slaves often died at a younger age.

LARGEST BATTLE AT SEA IN ANCIENT TIMES

The largest ancient naval battle was the Battle of Salamis, Greece, which took place in autumn 480 BC. There were thought to be 800 vessels in the defeated Persian fleet and 380 in the victorious fleet of the Athenians and their allies. It is estimated that as many as 200,000 men were involved in the conflict.

FIRST PERMANENT THEATER

Constructed in ancient Athens *c.* 500 BC, the outdoor Theater of Dionysius was the world's first theater. It had an estimated capacity of up to 17,000 people.

OLDEST SEED GERMINATED

A 2,000-year-old date-palm seed found in Masada, Israel, in the 1960s and replanted in 2005 by Dr Sarah Sallon (Israel) and Dr Elaine Soloway (USA) germinated after eight weeks. The seed was carbon-dated to the infamous siege of Masada by the Romans in AD 73, during which hundreds of Jewish zealots committed suicide.

OLDEST NOVEL

Chariton's (Greece) *Chaireas and Callirhoe*, written in the 1st century AD, narrates the adventures of a beautiful bride named Callirhoe.

OLDEST CASTLE

The earliest known castle is in the old city of Sana'a, Yemen. Known as Gomdan or Gumdan Castle, it dates from before AD 200 and originally had 20 stories.

FIRST PEOPLE TO RECORD HISTORY IN THE AMERICAS

The Maya were the first people in the Americas to keep historical records. Their writing (although not the first produced in the New World) used ideographic and phonetic elements on stone monuments. The Maya were also responsible for the **first written record of tobacco use**.

LARGEST GLADIATOR SCHOOL

Protected only by basic armor, such as the helmet seen below, gladiators were armed combatants who provided entertainment by fighting each other. The Ludus Magnus – the Great Gladiator School – was the largest of the four gladiator schools in ancient Rome; its arena could accommodate up to 3,000 spectators.

The **first gladiatorial games** took place in Rome in 264 BC and were staged by the sons of Junius Brutus Pera to mark his death. Other citizens were swift to offer their own (increasingly large) gladiatorial contests.

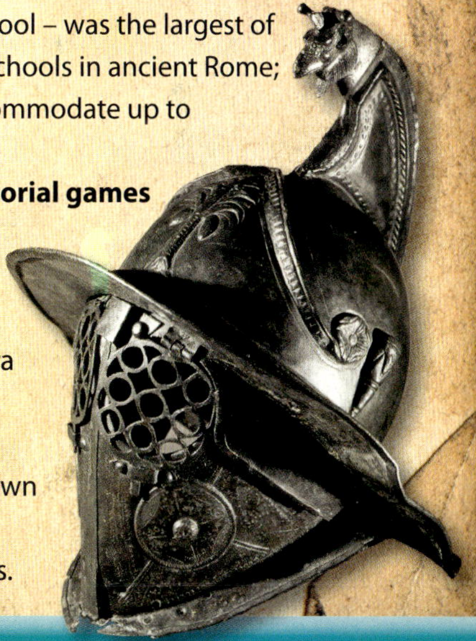

776 BC First Olympic Games

c. 753 BC Rome founded

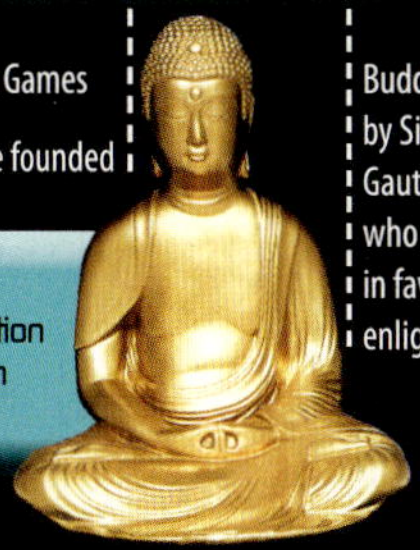

BUDDHA Representation of Buddha in pure gold

600 BC Buddhism started by Siddhartha Gautama, a prince who spurns wealth in favor of spiritual enlightenment

THEATER MASK Life-size terracotta mask from the Hellenistic period (5th century)

500 BC Western theater originates in Greece

214 BC Great Wall of China completed

4 BC Jesus Christ is born, leading to founding of Christianity

AD 80 The Colosseum – the **largest Roman amphitheater** – first used for gladiator games

COLOSSEUM Amphitheater in Rome, Italy, capable of seating 50,000 spectators

AD 476 The Western Roman Empire falls as Germanic leader Odoacer deposes Romulus Augustus

AD 570 Mohammad, founder of Islam, born in the Arabian city of Mecca

The **largest volcanic island** is Iceland, formed from eruptions from the Mid-Atlantic Ridge. Measuring 39,768 miles^2 (103,000 km^2) in area, Iceland is essentially ocean floor exposed above the ocean surface.

GREATEST EMPIRES

UPDATED RECORD
NEW RECORD

FIRST EMPIRE

The Neo-Assyrian Empire originated in the late 10th century BC in Mesopotamia (modern Iraq). It reached the height of its power and influence in the 8th century BC, when the territories under its control stretched from the Persian Gulf in the Near East to the Mediterranean Sea to the west. The empire fell in 612 BC, when the capital city of Nineveh (modern Mosul) was destroyed by the Babylonians and their allies. Pictured is a relief of an Assyrian priest c. 721–705 BC.

LARGEST EMPIRE BY PERCENTAGE OF WORLD POPULATION

By share of population, the largest empire was the Achaemenid Empire, better known as the Persian Empire, which accounted for approximately 49.4 million of the world's 112.4 million people in around 480 BC – an astonishing 44%. Originating in modern-day Iran, the empire was first established by Cyrus the Great and included parts of Central Asia, the Mediterranean, North Africa, and European territories such as ancient Thrace and Macedonia.

LARGEST NEW WORLD CIVILIZATION

The most successful and largest empire in the New World, before its discovery by European explorers, was that of the Inca, a tribe who founded the city of Cuzco around the year 1200. At their height, *c.* 1460, they ruled over 10 million people across an area of western South America similar in size to the Roman Empire.

LARGEST EMPIRE (CONTIGUOUS)

The Mongol Empire (1206–1367) was run by the Khan Dynasty. At its height in 1279 under Khubilai Khan (pictured), it encompassed 100 million people and 13.8 million miles^2 (35.7 million km^2), including the present-day territories of China, Russia, Mongolia, Central Asia, the Middle East, and the Korean Peninsula.

FIRST SENATE

The term "senate" comes from the Latin word "senex," meaning elder, old man, or council of elders. The Roman Senate dates back to the earliest days of Rome in the 8th century BC. The early Senate was a deliberative body – it did not propose laws or vote on them. The Roman historian Livy said that it comprised 100 senators, whose duty was to advise the King of Rome.

KEY STAGES IN THE HISTORY OF MANKIND, FROM THE RISE OF THE TANG DYNASTY IN AD 618 TO COLUMBUS'S VOYAGE TO THE AMERICAS IN 1492.

AD 618 – The rule of the Tang Dynasty begins. For nearly 300 years it will preside over the unification of China

AD 712 – Muslim conquest of Spain is completed, after an eight-year campaign

c. AD 797 – Irish monks create the Book of Kells, a masterfully illustrated version of the four Gospels of the Bible

AD 800

BRONZE SCULPTURE
Sculpture from AD 814 depicting Charlemagne, who became Emperor of the Romans in AD 800

AD 871 – Saxon king Alfred the Great begins his reign in England

1066

TAPESTRY
William of Normandy becomes ruler of England, defeating Harold. Later celebrated in the Bayeux Tapestry

The **largest recorder,** constructed of specially treated stone pine and measuring 16 ft 5 in (5 m) long, was made in Iceland by Stefan Geir Karlsson in 1994. Each hole has a diameter of 3.3 in (8.5 cm).

LARGEST EMPIRE (ABSOLUTE)

Geographically, the British Empire was the largest in history. In 1922, it covered over 13 million miles² (34 million km²), about a quarter of the world's landmass, and boasted territories on every continent except Antarctica. Pictured is a British soldier in India, and the stamp shows Britain's reach (red), giving credence to the saying, "The Sun never sets on the British Empire."

GREATEST HISTORICAL RANSOM

Historically, the greatest ransom paid was that raised for Atahualpa, the last emperor of the Inca, and given to the Spanish conquistador Francisco Pizarro in 1532–33 at Cajamarca, Peru. The payment constituted a hall full of gold and silver, worth some $1.5 billion in today's terms. Atahualpa was later executed.

LONGEST EMPIRE

Most historians agree that the Roman Empire began in 27 BC, when Octavian overthrew the Roman Republic to become Emperor Augustus. Rome later fell to the Barbarians in AD 476, but the ensuing Eastern (Byzantine) Empire based at Constantinople (modern-day Istanbul in Turkey) is widely regarded as a continuation. The fall of Constantinople in 1453 finally ended a period of dominance that had lasted for almost 1,500 years.

LARGEST PALACE

The Imperial Palace in the center of Beijing, China, covers 3,150 x 2,460 ft (960 x 750 m) over an area of 178 acres (72 ha). The outline survives from the construction under the third Ming Emperor, Yongle (1402–24), but owing to constant reconstruction most of the internal buildings are from the 18th century. By way of comparison, the Palace of Versailles, completed for Louis XIV in 1682, is 1,902 ft (580 m) long.

LARGEST EMPIRE BY POPULATION

At the outbreak of World War I in 1914, the population of the British Empire stood at an estimated 400 million. By 1922, however, following the acquisition of additional territories in the wake of that war, this figure had grown to some 458 million. The population eventually peaked in 1938, on the eve of World War II, by which time the British Empire accounted for an incredible 531 million people, making it history's largest empire by population. Today, it is estimated that the British Commonwealth includes as many as 2 billion people within its 54 member states.

FIRST GLOBAL EMPIRE

In the 15th century, Portugal established the first global maritime and commercial empire, under Henry the Navigator. In the 1440s, he sent key expeditions to Africa and Asia, and in the 16th and 17th centuries, Portugal set up colonies in Brazil, Africa, East Timor, India, and Macau. This 16th-century map shows two Portuguese claims in Africa – "Guine" (Guinea) and "Amina," meaning the Mina Coast, which was also known as the Portuguese Gold Coast and later just the Gold Coast (modern-day Ghana).

BRAVE NEW WORLD

OLDEST MECHANICALLY PRINTED BOOK

It is widely accepted that the first mechanically printed full-length book was the Gutenberg Bible, printed in Mainz, Germany, *c.* 1455 by Johann Henne zum Gensfleisch zur Laden, called zu Gutenberg (*c.* 1398–1468). The Chinese, however, may have invented movable type 600–700 years earlier.

FIRST WATCH

The invention of a portable timekeeping device *c.* 1509 is attributed to Peter Henlein (Germany), designer of the "Nuremberg Egg" – a small, drum-shaped clock (with only an hour hand) that could be carried. References to a "pocket clock" have since been discovered that predate this invention by 40 years, but Henlein is credited with being the first person to manufacture such devices and introduce the concept of regular timekeeping – an essential tool for the "modern" world.

FIRST SETTLEMENT IN THE NEW WORLD

La Isabela, on the island of Hispaniola (in the present-day Dominican Republic), was built in 1493 by Christopher Columbus's crew on his second voyage to the Americas. The area – the first permanent European settlement in the New World – was created in order to exploit local reserves of precious metals, but was abandoned within five years following hurricanes, hunger, disease, mutiny, and constant clashes with the native Taíno people.

OLDEST MUSEUM

The British Museum in London, UK, has stood on the same site since it was established in 1753; it opened for free entry to the public on January 15, 1759. The original set of exhibits was based on scientist Sir Hans Sloane's collection.

FIRST MANNED FLIGHT

Frenchman François Pilâtre de Rozier is regarded as the first human to have flown. On October 15, 1783, he rose 84 ft (26 m) into the air in a tethered hot-air balloon built by French inventors Joseph and Jacques Montgolfier.

FIRST HELIOCENTRIC SOLAR-SYSTEM MODEL

Just before his death in 1543, Nicolaus Copernicus (Poland) published *On the Revolutions of the Celestial Spheres*, in which he outlined his revolutionary notion of heliocentrism – the idea that planets travel around the Sun. It took at least another 150 years for his idea to become widely accepted.

MOST EXPENSIVE MANUSCRIPT

The *Codex Leicester*, written by Leonardo da Vinci (Italy) in 1508–10, was bought by Bill Gates (USA) for a record $30,802,500 at Christie's, New York City, USA, on November 11, 1994. This working journal was used by da Vinci to document his sketches of the submarine and the steam engine.

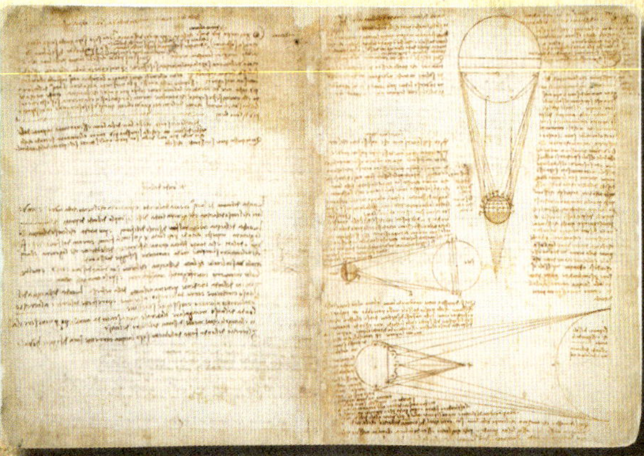

KEY STAGES IN THE HISTORY OF MANKIND, FROM MICHELANGELO'S PAINTINGS IN THE SISTINE CHAPEL TO THE BIRTH OF THE WORLD WIDE WEB.

1512 Michelangelo completes his epic frescoes for the ceiling of the Sistine Chapel in Vatican City

1588 An attempt to invade England by the Spanish Armada is foiled by the British fleet – and storms

SHAKESPEARE Print taken from a painting of the writer (1564–1616)

1620 Puritan pilgrims set sail on the *Mayflower* from Plymouth, England, for the Americas

1682 Peter I ("the Great") becomes ruler of Russia, ushering in a period of major reform and modernization

1776 American colonies formally declare their secession from Britain, prompting the American War of Independence

NAPOLEON Watercolor of the French emperor by Jean-Baptiste Isabey, dated 1812

Pablo Picasso (Spain) was the **most prolific professional painter**. He produced an estimated 13,500 paintings and designs, 100,000 prints and engravings, 34,000 book illustrations, and 300 sculptures and ceramics.

UPDATED RECORD
NEW RECORD

8.3 Weight in tons of all the potatoes you will eat. The world's favorite vegetable was discovered in the New World and is mildly poisonous: 8.3 tons contains enough neurotoxin to kill 3,750 people.

HIGHEST DEATH TOLL
There are thought to have been 56.4 million fatalities in World War II (1939–45), including battle deaths and civilians of all countries.

World War II was also the **costliest war**. Its overall expense of $1.5 trillion exceeds the cost of the rest of history's wars put together.

FIRST PHONOGRAPH
Thomas Alva Edison (USA) invented the "Tinfoil Phonograph" in 1877, initially to record and play back messages from another new communications device – the telephone. To record sound, Edison used some tinfoil that was wrapped around a cylinder.

FIRST TELEPHONE CALL
On February 14, 1876, Alexander Graham Bell (UK) filed a patent for the telephone. In March 1876, in Boston, Massachusetts, USA, Bell phoned his assistant in a nearby room to say, "Come here, Watson, I want you."

FIRST HUMANS ON THE MOON
Neil Alden Armstrong and Edwin Eugene "Buzz" Aldrin (both USA) became the first people to set foot on the Moon when they stepped out of the *Eagle* lunar module on to the Sea of Tranquillity on July 21, 1969.

FIRST COUNTRY TO PASS WOMEN'S SUFFRAGE
The 1893 Women's Suffrage Petition led to New Zealand becoming the first self-governing nation in the developing world to grant women the right to vote.

FIRST INDUSTRIAL MOVING ASSEMBLY LINE
In 1913, the Ford Motor Company introduced a moving assembly line in Highland Park near Michigan, Detroit, USA. Assembly time for vehicles was cut from 12.5 hours to 1 hr 33 min. Manufacture soared from 200,000 automobiles in 1913 to well over a million by 1920.

FIRST SKYSCRAPER
The Home Insurance Building in Chicago, USA, was erected in 1884–85. It was 10 stories high, peaking at 138 ft (42 m).

FIRST HYPERTEXT BROWSER
In October 1990, Tim Berners-Lee (UK) started work on a global hypertext browser. The finished result – the world wide web – was made available on the internet for the first time in the summer of 1991.

FIRST CELL PHONE
Martin Cooper (USA) of Motorola invented the first portable telephone handset, making the first call on April 3, 1973 to his rival, Joel Engel, head of research at Bell Labs. The first commercial cell phone network launched in Japan in 1979.

MOST TATTOOED PERSON

Having adorned his body with colorful designs from around the world, Lucky Diamond Rich (Australia, b. New Zealand) opted next for a 100% covering of black ink. He is now adding white designs over the black... and colored designs on top of those. With this layering of tattoos, he has over 200% skin coverage!

"My first tattoo was like a little juggling club on my hip, but that was when I was nervous about what my Mom thought..."

The **longest railroad platform** is located at Kharagpur Station in West Bengal, India, and measures 2,733 ft (833 m) in length – as long as 12 jumbo jet planes end to end.

Sticking with rail records, the National Belgian Railroad Company (NMBS) built the **longest passenger train**. It measured 5,685 ft 4 in (1,732.9 m) and consisted of 70 cars pulled by one electric locomotive.

BODY MODIFICATIONS

PUNCTURES, PIERCINGS, IMPLANTS, AND TATTOOS

Human beings have always sought to alter their looks. Ötzi the iceman, who lived c. 5,300 years ago and was discovered preserved in ice in 1991, has at least 57 tattoos – the **oldest known tattoos** in the world. And even our Neanderthal cousins wore makeup. Here, then, is our selection of the most striking record-breaking transformations.

PIERCING

The practice of puncturing the skin with metal rings, studs, and other items of jewelry dates back at least 5,000 years – as confirmed by ancient mummified remains found wearing earrings. Piercings are no longer limited to ears – anything can be, and is, skewered and studded in the name of fashion. The **most pierced man**, for example, Rolf Buchholz, has 453 studs and rings all over his body.

SCARIFICATION

This permanent procedure involves taking a knife – or, more traditionally, stone or shards of glass or coconut shell – and etching or cutting the skin with a design. The deep wounds are often rubbed with toxic plant juices to promote (or encourage) raised scars or "keloids." This form of modification is still carried out by some Sudanese women belonging to the Nuer and Nubia-Kush tribes.

HUMAN PINCUSHION

Since having her first piercing in 1997, Elaine Davidson (UK) – the **most pierced woman** – has had a record 4,225 pieces of metal attached to, and inside, her body.

NECK STRETCHING

The wearing of an increasingly long brass coil around the neck – as carried out by women of Burma's Padaung and Karenni tribes – results in a neck extension of up to 15.75 in (40 cm). Only initial discomfort is reported after the coils are set, yet the distance from earlobe to collarbone lengthens to more than double the average.

WHAT A STUD!

Rolf Buchholz, from Dortmund, Germany, has – among others – 94 piercings in and around his lips, 25 in his eyebrows, 16 in his right ear and eight in his nose.

The Nemo 33 diving pool in Brussels, Belgium, is the world's **deepest pool**, sinking to 108 ft (33 m) at its greatest depth.

2 Number of weeks it takes your body to completely renew your skin. Your bones replace themselves more slowly – every 10 years. In a lifetime, your seven skeletons will wear out 2,064 suits of skin!

TATTOOING

A tattoo is a permanent marking of the skin using pigments that are injected by needles deep into the dermis. In the healing process, the top layer of skin flakes away, leaving the deeper marks trapped beneath the surface. Here, illustrating the beauty of tattoos, is Isobel Varley (UK) – at 72 years old, the **most tattooed female senior citizen.**

LATE STARTER

Isobel caught the tattooing bug at the age of 49 when she first visited a tattoo convention in London, UK. Her first tattoo followed shortly afterwards, and today, 93% of her body is covered in ink!

LIP PLATING

Necks are not the only body parts that can be stretched – earlobes are commonly elongated beyond their natural length, for example – but the most arresting example of this body art is lip stretching. Pictured is a female from Ethiopia's Mursi ethnic group, which practices the wearing of clay plates in the lower lip. Plates can reach 6 in (15 cm) in diameter.

TAT'S THE WAY TO DO IT!

The **most tattooed senior citizen** is former most-tattooed man Tom Leppard. His body is 99.9% covered in a leopard-print pattern.

UPDATED RECORD
NEW RECORD

CORSETING

Get that Victorian wasp-waisted look with years of perseverance in ever-tightening corsets. Epitomizing this retro look is Cathie Jung (USA), proud owner of the **smallest waist on a living person** – 15 in (38.1 cm).

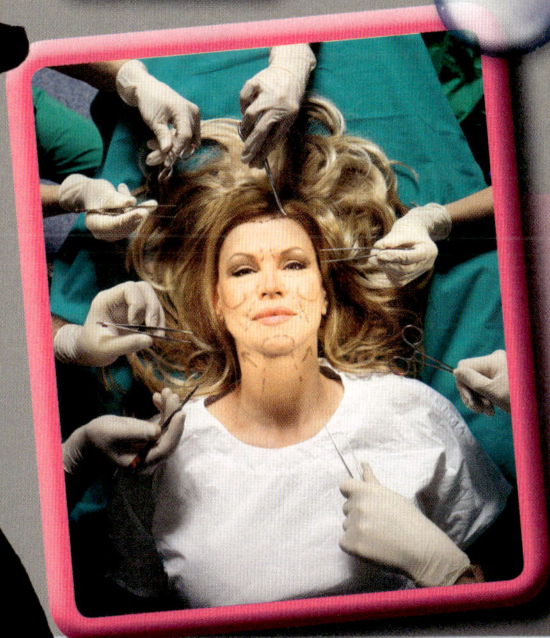

COSMETIC SURGERY

Going under the surgeon's knife remains a popular option for body modders, although figures are dropping as the economy falters – more than 1.5 million procedures took place in the USA in 2009, down 20% on 2000 figures. Continuing to lead the way with the **most cosmetic surgeries** is Cindy Jackson (USA), who has had 47 cosmetic procedures, including nine full-scale surgical operations, since 1988.

The **largest swimming pool** in the world is the San Alfonso del Mar seawater pool in Algarrobo, Chile. Completed in December 2006, it is 3,324 ft (1,013 m) long and has an area of 19.77 acres (8 ha).

BODY PARTS

WIDEST TONGUE

Measuring an amazing 3.1 in (7.9 cm) across at its maximum is the tongue of Jay Sloot (Australia) – the widest in the world. The massive, mobile muscle was measured on the set of *Lo Show dei Record* in Rome, Italy, on March 18, 2010.

FOR THE RECORD

The Dutchess hasn't let 18 years of nail-growing get in the way of her other interests – a talented musician, she has already recorded her first studio album, *Live and Let Live*.

LONGEST FINGERNAILS

No woman has a longer set of fingernails than Chris "The Dutchess" Walton (USA). They come in at 10 ft 2 in (309.8 cm) for her left hand and 9 ft 7 in (292.1 cm) for her right – a total of 19 ft 9 in (601.9 cm). A rock singer and recording artist, The Dutchess had her record-breaking nails measured by Guinness World Records in Las Vegas, Nevada, USA, on February 21, 2011.

NAIL-BITING COMPETITION

The Dutchess inherits the fingernail record from Lee Redmond (USA), who grew her nails for 30 years before losing them in unfortunate circumstances (see main text).

LONGEST FINGERNAILS EVER (FEMALE)

The longest set of fingernails ever recorded belonged to Lee Redmond (USA), who started to grow them in 1979 and carefully manicured them to reach a total length of 28 ft 4.5 in (8.65 m), as confirmed on the set of *Lo Show dei Record* in Madrid, Spain, on February 23, 2008. Unfortunately, Lee lost her nails in an automobile accident in early 2009.

The **longest fingernails for a man** belonged to Melvin Boothe (USA), whose nails had a combined length of 32 ft 3.8 in (9.85 m) when they were measured on May 30, 2009 in Troy, Michigan, USA. Sadly, Melvin passed on in December 2009.

LARGEST HANDS ON A LIVING PERSON

Sultan Kösen (Turkey) – the **tallest living man** – had hands measuring 11.22 in (28.5 cm) from the wrist to the tip of the middle finger when last measured on February 8, 2011. He also has the **widest handspan** at 12 in (30.48 cm).

The **largest hands ever**, though, still belong to Robert Pershing Wadlow (USA, 1918–40), the **tallest man ever**, whose hands measured 12.75 in (32.3 cm) from the wrist to the tip of his middle finger.

The Atacama Desert in Chile covers only 40,600 miles^2 (105,200 km^2) and is the world's **smallest desert**.

0.57 Gallons of hydrochloric acid your stomach produces every day. Enough to fill a bathtub every two months. In a lifetime, that's enough to dissolve yourself in your own stomach acid 440 times.

LONGEST TONGUE (FEMALE)

Chanel Tapper (USA, above left) has a tongue that measured 3.8 in (9.75 cm), from tip to top lip, in California, USA, on September 29, 2010. The outright **longest tongue** record, though, is held by Stephen Taylor (UK) – his lengthy licker measured 3.86 in (9.8 cm) from tip to lip on February 11, 2009.

LARGEST FEET ON A LIVING PERSON

Excluding sufferers of elephantiasis, Sultan Kösen (Turkey) has the biggest feet. His 1-ft 2-in (36.5-cm) left foot and 1-ft 1.98-in (35.5-cm) right foot were measured in Ankara, Turkey, in 2009.

And the **largest feet ever**? You guessed it: the tallest man ever, Robert Pershing Wadlow, wore US size 37AA shoes, equivalent to 18.5 in (47 cm) long.

LARGEST ARTERY

The aorta has a 1.18-in (3-cm) diameter at the point where it leaves the heart. It ends with a diameter of 0.68 in (1.75 cm) at the level of the fourth lumbar vertebra.

Slightly larger than the aorta is the inferior vena cava, which returns the blood from the lower half of the body to the heart. It is the **largest vein**.

LARGEST INTERNAL ORGAN

The adult liver can weigh 2 lb 10 oz–3 lb 5 oz (1.2–1.5 kg) and measure 8.6 in (22 cm) long and 3.9 in (10 cm) wide.

LONGEST NOSE ON A LIVING PERSON

Mehmet Ozyurek (Turkey) has a remarkable nose that measured 3.46 in (8.8 cm) long from the bridge to the tip on the set of *Lo Show dei Record* in Rome, Italy, on March 18, 2010.

LARGEST KIDNEY

On January 26, 2010, Dr Abdul Rasheed Shaikh removed a kidney weighing 3 lb 15 oz (1.8 kg) and measuring 12 x 5 x 4 in (30 x 13 x 10 cm) at the Chandka Medical College Hospital, Larkana Sindh, Pakistan. His patient was Waziran Malah (Pakistan).

LARGEST MUSCLE

The bulkiest of the body's 639 named muscles is usually the *gluteus maximus*, or buttock muscle, which extends to the thigh. However, in pregnancy the uterus (womb) can increase from about 1 oz (30 g) to over 2 lb 3 oz (1 kg) in weight.

The **smallest muscle** in the body is the stapedius, which controls the stapes – the **smallest bone**, located in the ear. The muscle is less than 0.05 in (0.127 cm) long.

Eye muscles move more than 100,000 times a day, making them the **most active muscles**.

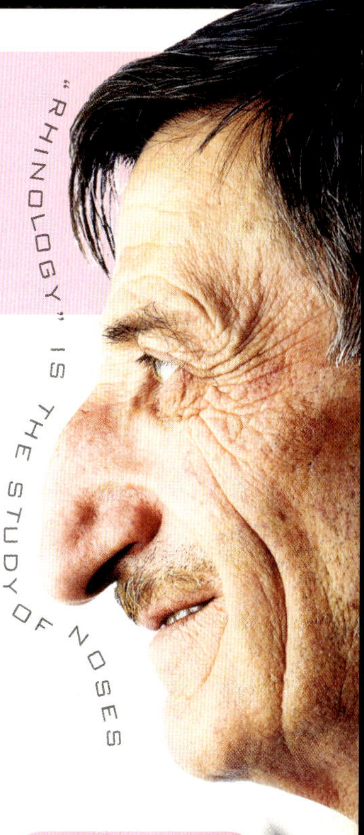

"RHINOLOGY" IS THE STUDY OF NOSES

Longest tooth extracted: 1.26 in (3.2 cm) – Loo Hui Jing (Singapore).

Widest tooth extracted: 0.6 in (1.67 cm) – nine-year-old Shane Russell (Canada).

Most teeth at birth: 12 – Sean Keaney (UK) on April 10, 1990.

Oldest person to grow a new tooth: Australian Brian Titford, 76, had two upper wisdom teeth erupt in March 2009.

LONGEST LEGS (FEMALE)

On July 8, 2003, the long, long legs of Svetlana Pankratova (Russia) were measured at 51.9 in (132 cm) in Torremolinos, Spain.

LEGWORK
Being a record breaker can present its own challenges! Svetlana has to have some clothes made for her, ducks through most doorways, and needs lots of legroom in automobiles and airplanes.

Egypt's Nile Valley and Delta is the **largest oasis** on Earth, covering approximately 8,500 miles^2 (22,000 km^2). Without the Nile, Egypt would be entirely composed of desert.

LITTLE & LARGE

HEAVIEST MEN

Ever: Jon Brower Minnoch (USA, 1941–83) suffered from obesity since childhood. He reached his peak weight in March 1978 – he was admitted to University Hospital in Seattle, USA, where it was calculated that he must have weighed more than 1,400 lb (100 st; 635 kg).

Living: Manuel Uribe Garza (Mexico) weighed 917 lb (65.5 st; 416 kg) during a weigh-in in December 2009.

Twins (ever): Billy Leon and Benny Loyd McCrary, alias McGuire (both USA), were normal in size until the age of six. By November 1978, however, Billy and Benny weighed 743 lb (53 st 1 lb; 337 kg) and 723 lb; 51 st 9 lb; 328 kg) respectively, and each had a waist of 84 in (2.13 m).

SHORTEST WOMEN

Ever: "Princess" Pauline Musters (Netherlands, 1876–95) measured exactly 24 in (61 cm) at the time of her death from pneumonia aged 19 years.

Living: Madge Bester (South Africa) is 2 ft 1.5 in (65 cm) tall; she is confined to a wheelchair as a result of the skeletal disorder osteogenesis imperfecta.

Living (mobile): Bridgette Jordan (see right).

Living (teenager): Jyoti Amge (India, b. December 16, 1993) was measured by a team of physicians in Tokyo, Japan, for *Bikkuri Chojin 100 Special #2* (Fuji TV) and found to be 2 ft (61.95 cm) tall on September 6, 2009. She is destined to become the new **shortest living woman (mobile)** if she remains this height on her 18th birthday in 2011.

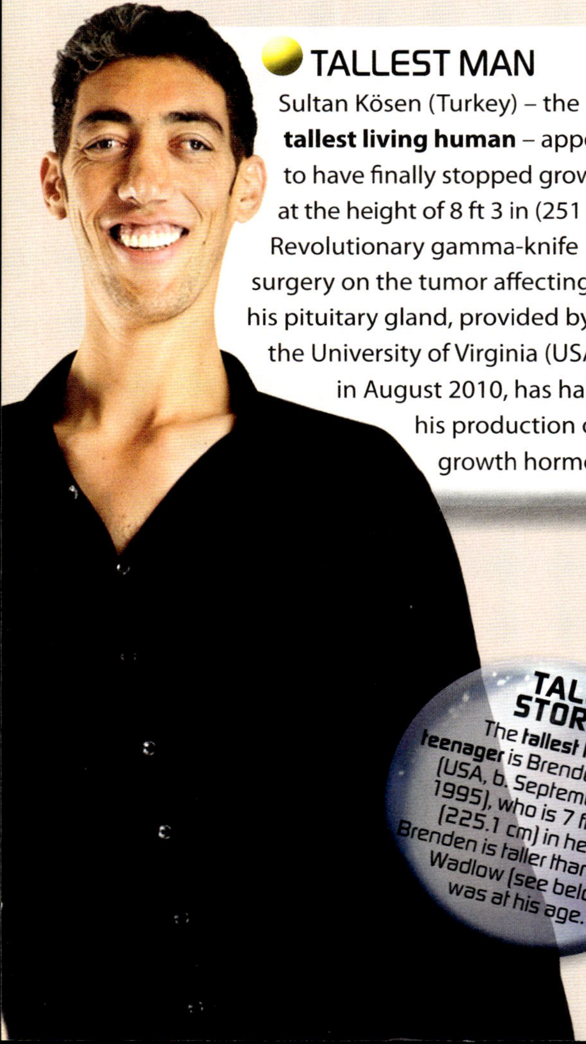

TALLEST MAN

Sultan Kösen (Turkey) – the **tallest living human** – appears to have finally stopped growing at the height of 8 ft 3 in (251 cm). Revolutionary gamma-knife surgery on the tumor affecting his pituitary gland, provided by the University of Virginia (USA) in August 2010, has halted his production of growth hormone.

TALL STORY

The **tallest living teenager** is Brenden Adams (USA, b. September 20, 1995), who is 7 ft 4.6 in (225.1 cm) in height. Brenden is taller than Robert Wadlow (see below) was at his age.

SHORTEST MEN

At the time of going to press, the **shortest living man** was Khagendra Thapa Magar (Nepal, b. October 14, 1992, below left), who was measured by Guinness World Records at Fewa City Hospital in Pokhara, Nepal, on October 14, 2010 and found to be 2 ft 2.41 in (67.08 cm) tall.

In April 2011, however, an even shorter male came to our attention.

Although Junrey Balawing (below right) of Zamboanga del Norte in the Philippines has yet to be measured by Guinness World Records, he is reportedly just 22 in (55.8 cm) and, at the age of 17, unofficially the **shortest living teenager**. Once he turns 18, he will qualify as the **shortest living man**.

If the figures are confirmed, it would make Junrey shorter than Gul Mohammed (India, 1957–97), the **shortest adult ever** at 22.5 in (57 cm).

SHORTEST SIBLINGS

Bridgette and Brad Jordan (both USA) are 28 in (71.1 cm) and 38 in (96.5 cm) tall respectively. Their reduced height is caused by the condition Majewski osteodysplastic primordial dwarfism type II. Undeterred, they both have full and active lives – and Bridgette wants to become a model.

Bridgette's height makes her the **shortest living woman (mobile)** – a record she may only hold on to until December 2011, when Jyoti Amge (see main text) turns 18.

LIGHTEST BIRTH

The lowest birth weight for a surviving infant of which there is evidence is 9.17 oz (260 g). Rumaisa Rahman (USA) was born at Loyola University Medical Center, Maywood, Illinois, USA, on September 19, 2004 after a gestation period of just 25 weeks 6 days.

TALLEST LIVING MARRIED COUPLE

Wayne (6 ft 10 in; 209.3 cm) and Laurie (6 ft 6 in; 198 cm) Hallquist (USA) have a combined height of 13 ft 4 in (407.3 cm).

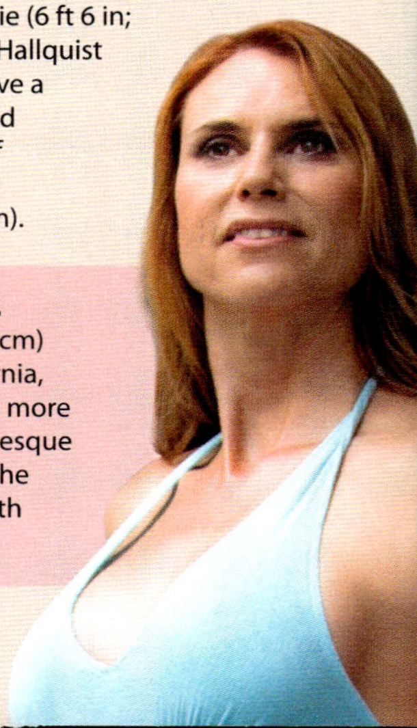

TALLEST PROFESSIONAL MODEL

Amazon Eve (USA) was 6 ft 7.39 in (201.66 cm) tall when measured in Beverly Hills, California, USA, on February 25, 2011. Seen here with more diminutive model Qeyda Penate, the statuesque Amazon is also a wrestler and an actress. She credits her Dutch and German heritage with providing her record-breaking stature.

FOR GIANTS OF THE GARDEN, SEE P.140.

Tallest man ever: Robert Pershing Wadlow (USA): 8 ft 11.1 in (272 cm)

Tallest woman ever: Zeng Jinlian (China): 8 ft 1.75 in (248 cm)

Tallest living woman: Yao Defen (China): 7 ft 7 in (233.3 cm)

Tallest married couple ever: Anna Hanen Swan (Canada): 7 ft 5.5 in (227 cm); Martin van Buren Bates (USA): 7 ft 2.5 in (220 cm). Combined height: 14 ft 8 in (447 cm).

TITANIC TOT

Anna Bates (Canada, 1846–88), a giantess who was 7 ft 5.5 in (2.27 m) tall, gave birth to a boy weighing 23 lb 12 oz (10.8 kg) at her home in Seville, Ohio, USA, on January 19, 1879 – the **heaviest birth ever.**

HEAVIEST LIVING WOMAN

Pauline Potter of Sacramento, California, USA, weighed 643 lb (291.6 kg) on May 13, 2010. Pauline leads the way in terms of large ladies, but she would be dwarfed by Rosalie Bradford (USA) – the **heaviest woman ever** – who peaked at 1,200 lb (85 st; 544 kg) in January 1987.

UPDATED RECORD
NEW RECORD

The **earliest known example of an alphabet** dates back to around 1900 BC and was found carved into limestone in Wadi el Hol near Luxor in Egypt.

The **language with the most letters** is Khmer (Cambodian), which has a total of 74 characters, including some that lack any current use.

LONG LIVES

OLDEST LIVING PERSON

On May 13, 2011, Maria Gomez Valentim (b. July 9, 1896, right) of Carangola, Brazil, was – at the age of 114 years 308 days – confirmed as the world's oldest living person.

Jeanne Louise Calment (February 21, 1875–August 4, 1997) of Arles, France, lived to be 122 years 164 days old, the **greatest age ever verified for a human being**.

OLDEST LIVING MAN

Jiroemon Kimura (Japan, b. April 19, 1897, pictured right) became the oldest living man just five days before his 114th birthday. He is also the last living man born in the 19th century.

OLDEST LIVING TWINS (MIXED)

Benjamin Franklin Colvett and Rose Frances Bruce (both USA) were born near Alamo, Tennessee, USA, on August 23, 1912.

Twins Glen and Dale Moyer (USA) each reached the age of 105, making them the **oldest male twins ever**. Born on June 20, 1895, they became the oldest living twins on January 23, 2000.

OLDEST SINGLETON TWIN EVER

Mary Belle Murphy Crombie (USA, 1890–2003) lived to the age of 113 years 78 days, while her twin sister Mabel Jean died in 1984 aged 94.

HIGHEST COMBINED AGE FOR FOUR SIBLINGS

As of March 14, 2011, the four siblings of the Stepham family (UK) totaled 390 years 81 days: Clara Goldsmith (100 years 37 days), Belle Dell (98 years 344 days), Anne Goldsmith (96 years 119 days), and Jack Stepham (94 years 311 days).

Sadly, Jack passed away on March 14, 2011.

OLDEST LIVING PEOPLE

As of May 13, 2011, these are the world's 10 oldest people. When they were born, Queen Victoria was still alive and the Ford Motor Company did not yet exist.

	Holder	Age	Sex	Born
1	Maria Gomez Valentim (Brazil, right)	114	Female	Jul 9, 1896
2	Besse Cooper (USA)	114	Female	Aug 26, 1896
3	Chiyono Hasegawa (Japan)	114	Female	Nov 20, 1896
4	Venere Pizzinato-Papo (Italy)	114	Female	Nov 23, 1896
5	Shige Hirooka (Japan)	114	Female	Jan 16, 1897
6	Dina Manfredini (Italy/USA)	114	Female	Apr 4, 1897
7	Jiroemon Kimura (Japan, right)	114	Male	Apr 19, 1897
9	Delma Kollar (USA)	113	Female	Oct 31, 1897
10	Toshi Horiya (Japan)	113	Female	Nov 8, 1897
10	Leila Denmark (USA)	113	Female	Feb 1, 1898

LONG LIVE LADIES!

Evidence suggests that if you plan to live to a ripe old age, it helps to be female! Of more than 75 people in history known to have reached the age of 114, only five have been men.

TRAVEL BACK IN TIME WITH OUR HISTORY FEATURES, FROM P.72.

OLDEST MAN EVER

Despite his fondness for smoking – a habit not generally associated with longevity – Thomas Peter Thorvald Kristian Ferdinand "Christian" Mortensen (Denmark, b. August 16, 1882) of San Ramon, California, USA, lived to be the oldest man whose age has been satisfactorily verified. He died on April 25, 1998, aged 115 years 252 days.

UPDATED RECORD
NEW RECORD

The **largest religious structure ever built** is Angkor Wat (City Temple), enclosing 401 acres (162.6 ha) in Cambodia. Dedicated to the Hindu god Vishnu, it was built by the Khmer king Suryavarman II between 1113 and 1150.

OLDEST LIVING TWINS (FEMALE)

At 101 years old, sisters Lily Millward (left) and Ena Pugh (née Thomas, right; both UK) are the oldest living twins. Farmers' daughters, they were born on January 4, 1910 in Llechach, Wales, UK.

OLDEST DEBUT AS A FEATURE FILM DIRECTOR

Takeo Kimura (Japan, b. April 1, 1918) was aged 90 years 207 days when he made his directorial debut with *Dreaming Awake*, released on October 18, 2008.

OLDEST BALLERINA

The oldest performing ballerina is Grete Brunvoll (Norway, b. July 27, 1930). She began dancing at the age of six and her first professional performance was at the Nathionalteater in 1945, when she was aged 15.

OLDEST PRACTICING PHYSICIAN

Dr Walter "Papa Doc" Watson (USA), an obstetrician born in 1910, was still practicing at University Hospital in Augusta, Georgia, USA, in May 2010 at the age of 100.

OLDEST PERSON TO RECEIVE A DOCTORATE

Emeritus Professor Dr Heinz Wenderoth (Germany) was awarded the degree of Doctor of Science by the Gottfried Wilhelm Leibniz University of Hannover on September 29, 2008 at the age of 97 years 8 months 18 days. His dissertation was titled: *Cell Biological Studies in the Morphology and Physiology of Primitive Marine Placozoons Trichoplax Adhaerens.*

OLDEST YOGA TEACHER

The world's oldest yoga teacher was Gladys Morris (UK, b. January 31, 1921). At the age of 90, she was still teaching regular yoga classes at the Shaw Lifelong Learning Centre, Oldham, UK. She died in March 2011.

OLDEST IN THEIR FIELD

If you're lucky enough to enjoy good health into your old age, there's no reason why you can't stay active and even keep working. These people did just that…

Oldest…	Name	Age/date achieved
Abseiler	Doris Cicely Long (UK)	96 years 11 days; May 29, 2010
Bungee jumper	Mohr Keet (South Africa)	96 years; April 10, 2010
Doctor	Leila Denmark (USA)	Retired May 2001; 103 years
Scuba diver (from shore)	Saul Moss (Australia)	85 years 14 days; August 1, 2009
Appointed prime minister	Morarji Ranchhodji Desai (India)	81 years; March 1977
Oscar winner (Best Actress)	Jessica Tandy (UK)	80 years 295 days; March 29, 1990
Oscar winner (Best Actor)	Henry Fonda (USA)	76 years 317 days; March 29, 1982
Ballet dancer	Frank Russell Galey (USA)	74 years 101 days; December 17, 2006

MOVIE MEMORIES

Jeanne Calment, the **oldest woman ever**, was the last living person to have known the artist Vincent van Gogh. Aged 114, she played herself in the film *Vincent and Me* (Canada, 1990), making her the **oldest actress**.

OLDEST CURLING PLAYER

Centenarian Stephen Gittus (Canada, b. February 17, 1910) continued to play in competitions on a regular basis at the Kamloops Curling Club in Kamloops, British Columbia, Canada, as of November 18, 2010. He first took up the sport when he turned 43.

A more modern construction, the **largest ice structure** is the Ice Hotel in Jukkasjärvi, Sweden, which has been rebuilt each December since 1990 and has a total floor area of 43,000–54,000 ft^2 (4,000–5,000 m^2).

HAIR

LONGEST MUSTACHE

Ram Singh Chauhan (India) is the owner of the world's longest mustache, which he has been growing since 1982. The phenomenal facial hair measured 14 ft (4.29 m) in length on the set of *Lo Show dei Record* in Rome, Italy, on March 4, 2010. Ram was inspired by a previous GWR record-holder for the longest mustache – Karna Bheel – who, like Ram, came from Rajasthan.

LONGEST BEARD ON A LIVING PERSON (FEMALE)

Vivian Wheeler of Wood River, Illinois, USA, started shaving at the age of seven and grew a full beard in 1990. The longest strand, from the follicle to the tip of hair, was measured at 11 in (27.9 cm) in 2000. She is seen here with her son – who clearly likes beards too.

TALLEST MOHICAN

It took four hours for stylists to erect Kazuhiro Watanabe's (Japan) 41.3-in-tall (105-cm) mohican. The length was verified at the MACRO hair salon in Sapporo, Hokkaido, Japan, on January 10, 2011. The mohawk was an incredible 9.8 in (25 cm) taller than that of the previous record-holder from Germany.

HAIRIEST FAMILY

Jesus Manuel Fajardo Aceves and Luisa Lilia De Lira Aceves (both Mexico) come from a family with the rare condition of Congenital Generalized Hypertrichosis, giving rise to excessive facial and torso hair. They are seen here with the **hairiest car**, a Fiat 500 owned by Maria Lucia Mugno (Italy), which is covered with 220 lb (100 kg) of human hair.

HAIRIEST CHILD

According to the Ferriman Gallwey score – which grades hair density on nine areas of the body from 0 (little) to 4 (heavy coverage) – the most hirsute child is Supatra Sasuphan (Thailand). She was assessed during a trip to Rome, Italy, on March 4, 2010.

LARGEST GATHERING OF NATURAL REDHEADS

On July 17, 2010, Anne Lindsay (USA) organized for 890 redheads to meet at Skyline High School in Sammamish, Washington, USA.

LARGEST GATHERING OF MUSTACHIOED MEN

An event organized by KARE-1 TV at the Xcel Energy Center in St Paul, Minnesota, USA, on November 26, 2010, drew 1,131 men with 'taches.

MOST HIGHLY INSURED HAIR

The iconic locks of American footballer Troy Polamalu (USA) of the Pittsburgh Steelers (USA) were insured for $1 million with Lloyd's of London by shampoo brand Head & Shoulders on August 30, 2010.

LONGEST HAIR EXTENSIONS

Sarina Russo (Australia) unveiled pink and blonde hair extensions measuring 966 ft 2 in (294.49 m) long at the Sydney Convention and Exhibitions Centre in Sydney, Australia, on June 13, 2010.

HIGHEST HAIRSTYLE

A hairdo measuring 8 ft 8 in (2.66 m) high was created by hairdressers from KLIPP unser Frisör in Wels, Austria, on June 21, 2009.

The world's **oldest surviving banknote** (banco-sedlar) is a five-daler note issued in Stockholm, Sweden, on December 6, 1662.

HAIR TODAY… We lose between 50 and 100 hairs every day. But don't worry! Replacement hairs are growing all the time.

Longest arm hair: 5.75 in (461 cm) – Justin Shaw (USA)

Longest beard (ever): 17 ft 6 in (5.33 m) – Hans N Langseth (Norway)

Longest chest hair: 9 in (22.8 cm) – Richard Condo (USA)

Longest ear hair: 7.12 in (18.1 cm) – Anthony Victor (India)

Longest eyebrow hair: 7.01 in (17.8 cm) – Toshie Kawakami (Japan)

Longest leg hair: 6.5 in (16.51 cm) – Wesley Pemberton (USA)

Longest nipple hair: 5.07 in (12.9 cm) – Douglas Williams (USA)

HAIRCUTTING

MOST CONSECUTIVE CUTS IN 24 HOURS (TEAM)

Ten stylists from Pump Salon carried out 618 consecutive haircuts in 24 hours at Rookwood Commons & Pavilion in Cincinnati, Ohio, USA, from September 24 to 25, 2010.

MOST CONSECUTIVE CUTS IN 24 HOURS (INDIVIDUAL)

On May 20, 2009, Bharat L Galoriya (India) cut 465 heads of hair in 24 hours at an event organized by Sunil Surani in Rajkot, India.

MOST CONSECUTIVE CUTS IN 12 HOURS (TEAM)

Sport Clips Haircuts (USA) performed 329 consecutive haircuts in 12 hours in Nottingham, Maryland, USA, on July 22, 2010.

FASTEST HAIRCUT

Ivan Zoot (USA) cut a full head of hair in 55 seconds at the Men's Grooming Center in Austin, Texas, USA, on August 22, 2008.

Those not in a rush could try the **most expensive haircut** – one customer paid Stuart Phillips (UK) £8,000 ($16,420) for a cut at his London, UK, salon on October 29, 2007.

MOST PEOPLE CUTTING HAIR

On November 9, 2010, 1,155 stylists cut hair at an event organized by United Dansk in Yokohama, Japan.

UPDATED RECORD
NEW RECORD

LONGEST BEARD ON A LIVING PERSON (MALE)

Sarwan Singh (Canada) has a world-beating beard that measured 7 ft 9 in (2.37 m) on the set of *Lo Show dei Record* in Rome, Italy, on March 4, 2010.

LARGEST AFRO

Aevin Dugas (USA) is the proud owner of a record-breaking afro. When measured in New Orleans, USA, on October 4, 2010, it had a circumference of 4 ft 4 in (1.32 m). She trims her afro two or three times a year, and uses up to five conditioners at once when she washes it.

GO AFRO! Also known as the "natural," the afro was a defining fashion in the 1960s and early 1970s, though its origins lie in the mid-19th century.

The **smallest national bill ever issued** was the 10-bani note of the Ministry of Finance of Romania, which entered circulation in 1917. Its printed area measured 1.08 x 1.49 in (27.5 x 38 mm).

URBAN ACROBATS

3RUN is the UK's leading Parkour and Freerunning team. Parkour and Freerunning is a combination of disciplines and movement art forms in which practitioners adapt and overcome obstacles as they traverse their environment.

BREAKING RECORDS WITH 3RUN

On September 8, 2010, GWR spent a day record-breaking with 3RUN – the UK-based freerunning team. As well as setting individual records (see right), a 3RUN team comprising Cane and Cole Armitage, Adam Brashaw, Scott Fidgett, Sam Parham, and James Stokes (all UK) completed the **most backflips off a wall in one minute**, with 55.

The **heaviest building** is the Palace of the Parliament in Bucharest, Romania. It is constructed from 1.5 billion lb (700,000 metric tons) of steel and bronze, 35.3 million ft^2 (1 million m^2) of marble, 7.7 million lb (3,500 metric tons) of crystal glass, and 31.7 million ft^2 (900,000 m^2) of wood.

NY

11 Pairs of running shoes you'll get through. It's recommended that you replace running shoes every 300 miles, meaning that you'll cover 3,300 miles in those shoes in a lifetime, or 127 marathons' worth.

"It's about utilizing your environment as an obstacle course – tackling any objects that come in your way, both physical and psychological."

Sam Parham

ADAM
UK, b. 10/15/84
Longest sideflip
14 ft 8 in (4.48 m)
September 8, 2010

CANE
UK, b. 02/20/91
Longest standing jump between two objects
9 ft 4 in (2.85 m)
September 8, 2010

CHASE
UK, b. 08/02/85
Farthest backflip off a wall
11 ft 5 in (3.48 m)
May 24, 2010

COLE
UK, b. 10/07/87
Longest standing jump from vault-to-handstand
7 ft 9 in (2.37 m)
September 8, 2010

MICHAEL
UK, b. 02/02/82
Farthest distance wall running
8 ft 9 in (2.69 m)
September 8, 2010

SAM
UK, b. 02/03/87
Longest distance vaulted between two objects
7 ft 8 in (2.35 m)
September 8, 2010

SCOTT
UK, b. 09/17/88
Longest running vault-to-vaulted handstand
7 ft 3 in (2.22 m)
September 8, 2010

Made by Kwang Hua Industries, the **largest building made from paper** had a base measuring 49 ft 9 in x 58 ft 8 in (15.2 x 17.9 m) and was 21 ft (6.4 m) tall. Unveiled in Bangkok, Thailand, in October 2003, it took the form of a traditional Thai house.

MOST DANGEROUS

WHO DARES WINS

One of the questions most commonly asked of a GWR adjudicator is "What's the most dangerous record attempt you've ever witnessed?" As revealed here, we do monitor some records that are considered hazardous, even by the well-trained professionals who attempt them. Of course, these record attempts are strictly for professionals who plan carefully and have years of experience.

MOST CHAINSAWS JUGGLED

Aaron Gregg (Canada) juggled three chainsaws, catching them 88 times, on the set of *El Show Olímpico* in Mexico City, Mexico, on July 28, 2008.

LONGEST MOTORCYCLE RIDE THROUGH A TUNNEL OF FIRE

On January 27, 2008, professional stunt rider Clint Ewing (USA) sped down a tunnel of fire 200 ft (60.96 m) long on a motorcycle at Universal City, Los Angeles, USA. The record was being attempted for the NBC TV Special *Guinness World Records Live – The Top 100.*

MOST SIMULTANEOUS FULL-BODY BURNS

The greatest number of individuals carrying out full-body burns at one time is 17. The fiery feat was achieved during an event organized by Ted Batchelor and the Ohio Burn Unit (both USA) in South Russell, Ohio, USA, on September 19, 2009. All participants remained alight for at least 43.9 seconds.

SEE CHAPTER 7 FOR MORE FOLKS WHO THRIVE ON DANGER.

The **largest animal orchestra** is the 12-piece Thai Elephant Orchestra at the Thai Elephant Conservation Centre, Lampang, Thailand. The percussion- and wind-based orchestra was founded in 2000 to help conserve the Asiatic elephant species.

314 Number of visits you'll make to a physician in a lifetime. The average visit is 11.7 minutes – making a total of 61 hours, or 2.5 days. During your life, you will spend the equivalent of a long weekend with your physician.

UPDATED RECORD
NEW RECORD

MOST BUILDINGS CLIMBED UNASSISTED

As of 2011, urban climber Alain "Spiderman" Robert (France) had climbed more than 100 towers, monuments, and skyscrapers without ropes, suction devices, or safety equipment. Amazingly, Alain suffers from vertigo.

BREAKING BONES

Motorcycle daredevil Evel Knievel (USA, born Robert Craig Knievel) doesn't hold any records for his death-defying leaps, but he did set one record: **most bones broken in a lifetime**! Until his retirement in 1975, he endured a record 433 fractures (of the same 35 bones, including all of his ribs), plus 14 open surgeries and a total of 36 months in hospital.

BANZAI!

Heard of Banzai Skydiving? In this most extreme of sports, which originated in Japan, you fly to 10,000 ft (3,000 m), throw your parachute out of the plane, wait two seconds, then throw yourself out. The aim? Grab that 'chute!

SWORD SWALLOWING

There are many dangers associated with swords before you even *think* about sliding them into your throat! For years GWR declined to monitor such feats as world records, but following careful discussion with the sword-swallowing community we reconsidered our position and now accept claims from trained swallowers in conjunction with the Sword Swallowers Association International. Matt Henshaw (Australia, right), for example, has trained for years to achieve the record for the **most swords swallowed at once**: 21.

LOWEST DEATH-DIVE ESCAPE

Robert Gallup (Australia) was leg-manacled, handcuffed, chained, tied into a secured mailbag, and then locked in a cage before being thrown from a C-123 plane 18,000 ft (5,485 m) above the Mojave Desert in California, USA. Less than a minute before impact – and traveling at 150 mi/h (240 km/h) – he escaped, deployed his parachute, and landed safely.

READ ME FIRST
Before embarking upon any record attempt, please contact us first at www.guinnessworldrecords.com. We need to approve your idea and send you all the rules.

The **smallest elephant** is the Borneo pygmy, which grows to 5 ft 6 in–8 ft 6 in (1.7–2.6 m) tall. It lives in the Malaysian states of Borneo.

IN A MINUTE

MOST HANDCUFFS UNLOCKED

Merlin Cadogan (UK) unlocked six separate sets of handcuffs in a minute before a live studio audience on the set of ITV's *Magic Numbers* TV show in London, UK, on August 28, 2010.

MOST GLOVES WORN ON ONE HAND

On November 12, 2009, Alastair Galpin (NZ) pulled 10 gloves on to one hand in a minute at the Britomart Transport Centre, Auckland, New Zealand.

MOST JOKES TOLD

The greatest number of jokes told in one minute is 17 and was achieved by Ted Robbins (UK) from BBC Radio Lancashire and Ben Day (UK) from Touch FM radio station on November 18, 2010 in celebration of Guinness World Records Day.

MOST CHAMPAGNE BOTTLES SABERED

On February 14, 2010, Andrew Duminy (South Africa) sabered 27 champagne bottles in one minute at the Bull Run Restaurant, Sandton, South Africa. The practice of using a saber to open a champagne bottle became popular during the reign of Napoleon Bonaparte.

MOST PUSH-UPS ON THE BACKS OF HANDS WITH A 40-LB PACK

Andre Turan (USA) carried out 40 push-ups using the back of his hands in one minute, while carrying a 40-lb (18.2-kg) backpack, at Catskill Mountain Boot Camp in Sullivan County, New York, USA, on November 15, 2008.

MOST COINS BALANCED ON THE FACE

The most coins balanced on the face is 27. Marica Rosengård (Finland) achieved the feat in Stockholm, Sweden, on November 20, 2010.

FEWEST POGO-STICK JUMPS

A record sanctioned by the international governing body Pogopalooza, this feat requires that the participant not stall and not step off the stick at any time. As such, height per jump is optimal in achieving the best results. The fewest pogo-stick jumps in one minute is 39 by Biff Hutchison (USA) at Redstone Center in Park City, Utah, USA, on August 20, 2010.

MOST JUICE TRODDEN FROM GRAPES

Martina Servaty (Germany) extracted an impressive 1.19 gallons (5.4 liters) of juice from grapes in one minute by treading on them in Mesenich, Germany, on November 9, 2008. The feat took place in celebration of Guinness World Records Day.

MOST MARTIAL ARTS THROWS

Karipidis Konstantinos (Greece) carried out 51 martial arts throws in one minute at the indoor Central Stadium in Alexandroupolis, Greece, on June 26, 2010.

DID YOU KNOW?

In a minute: the Earth rotates 17.3 miles (28 km) and is struck by lightning 6,000 times; light travels 11,176,943.82 miles (17,987,547.48 km); our hairs grow 0.00027 in (0.00068 cm).

IN A MINUTE, 267 PEOPLE ARE BORN AND 108 DIE

MOST WATERMELONS CHOPPED ON THE STOMACH

Jim Hunter chopped 25 watermelons on the stomach of Celia Curtis (both Australia) in one minute, using a machete, on the set of *Australia Smashes Guinness World Records* at Seven Network Studios, Sydney, New South Wales, Australia, on August 16, 2005.

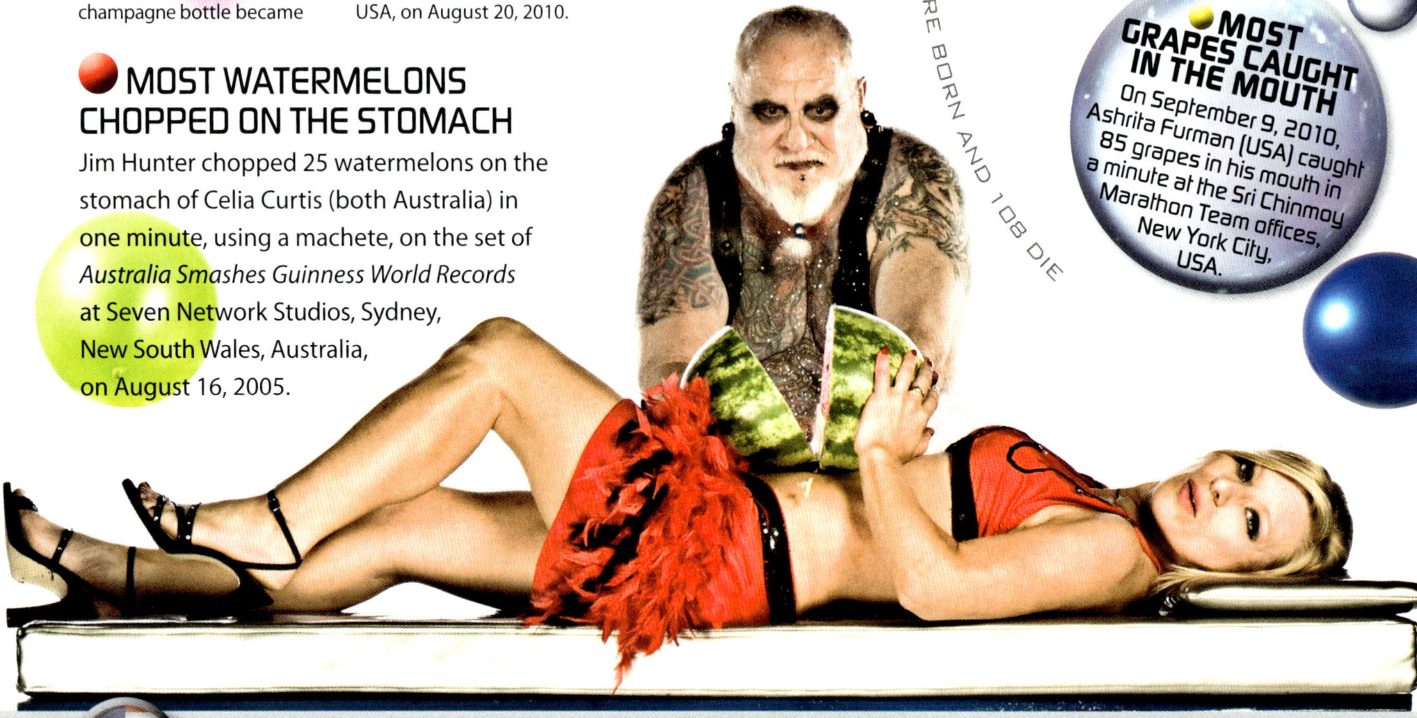

MOST GRAPES CAUGHT IN THE MOUTH

On September 9, 2010, Ashrita Furman (USA) caught 85 grapes in his mouth in a minute at the Sri Chinmoy Marathon Team offices, New York City, USA.

With a population of more than 22.5 million and a total of 336,000 admissions in 2003, Malaysia had the **lowest movie-theater attendance per capita** with 14.83 visits per 1,000 people (0.01483 visits per person).

11,520 Number of times you will blink in a waking day – that's 12 every minute. With each blink lasting 0.1 seconds, you will spend 383 days of your life wide awake with your eyes closed. A life gone by in 331,148,160 blinks of an eye.

MOST CUSTARD PIES THROWN BY A PAIR
Ashrita Furman received 56 custard pies in the face from Bipin Larkin (both USA) at the Sri Chinmoy Center in New York City, USA, on April 7, 2010. Although 59 pies hit Ashrita, only 56 were full in the face as required.

MOST BEERMATS FLIPPED AND CAUGHT
David Cowling-Cass (UK) flipped and caught a total of 70 beermats in a minute at the World Trade Centre, Barcelona, Spain, on May 14, 2010.

MOST LASSO TEXAS SKIPS IN ONE MINUTE
The most lasso Texas skips in a minute is 80 by Daniel Ledda (Spain) on the set of *Guinness World Records – El Show de los Records* in Madrid, Spain, on June 11, 2006. A Texas skip involves twirling a lasso in a vertical loop on one side of the body, then jumping sideways back and forth through the loop.

MOST SOCCER PASSES BY A PAIR
On May 4, 2010, Shunsuke and Ryosuke Kaketani (both Japan) executed 79 soccer passes between them in a minute at Park Challenge/GWR Live! in Tokyo Midtown, Tokyo, Japan.

MOST KISSES GIVEN
As part of World Aids Day, Rohit Timilsina (Nepal) set a new record for the most kisses given in one minute – 116 – in Kathmandu, Nepal, on December 1, 2009.

MOST STAIRS CLIMBED WITH BOOKS BALANCED ON THE HEAD
On October 25, 2009, Ashrita Furman (USA) climbed 122 stairs while balancing books weighing 7 lb 11.4 oz (3.5 kg) on his head at the subway at Lexington Avenue and 63rd Street, New York City, USA.

MOST BALLOONS POPPED USING A POGO STICK
The most balloons popped using a pogo stick in one minute is 57 and was achieved by Mark Aldridge (UK) on the set of *Lo Show dei Record* in Rome, Italy, on April 1, 2010. Mark burst the balloons at a rate of nearly one per second.

MOST EGGS CRUSHED WITH THE HEAD
Leo Mondello (Italy) crushed 130 eggs with his head in one minute in Patti, Messina, Italy, on April 24, 2010.

MOST CONSECUTIVE YO-YO INSIDE LOOPS
On July 6, 2010, Arron Sparks (UK) performed 151 consecutive yo-yo inside loops at Camden Town Hall, London, UK.

MOST WHIP CRACKS WITH TWO WHIPS
On August 7, 2010, Adam Winrich (USA) performed 513 whip cracks, using two whips, in one minute at the Bristol Renaissance Faire in Kenosha, Washington, USA.

MOST TAP-DANCING TAPS
Tony Adams (New Zealand) performed 1,056 tap-dancing taps in one minute live on Television New Zealand's *Good Morning Show* at Avalon TV Studios, Wellington, New Zealand, on June 19, 2009.

MOST KICKS TO THE HEAD
Walt Saine (Switzerland) administered 110 kicks to his own head in one minute in Lausanne, Switzerland, on October 30, 2010. Saine used both his left and right legs to kick himself in the forehead an average of 1.8 times per second.

THE FIRST POGO STICKS, PATENTED IN 1919, WERE MADE OF WOOD

Q. What was the first manmade object to break the sound barrier?

A. Probably the whip. The "crack" is a mini sonic boom made by the end of the whip when it exceeds the speed of sound.

UPDATED RECORD
NEW RECORD

A far bigger number for the big screen is The Panasonic IMAX Theatre at Darling Harbour, Sydney, Australia. Measuring 117 x 97 ft (35.72 x 29.57 m), it is the **largest IMAX screen in the world**.

IN AN HOUR

MOST POTS THROWN

Master potter Mark Byles (UK) came out on top in the pot-throwing contest held at the Ceramics South East Potters Market at The Friars, Aylesford, UK, on June 28, 2009. Mark made 150 clay flowerpots in an hour, seeing off the challenge of nearest rival Mary Chapellhow (UK), who managed 118 pots of her own in the allotted time.

MOST VAULTS: On September 5, 2009, the Blue Falcons Gymnastic Display Team leaped into the record books by performing 6,250 vaults at the Meadows Shopping Centre in Chelmsford, UK.

MOST CUPS OF TEA MADE (12-MAN TEAM)

A team of 12 tea-lovers, led by Alex Loughlin (UK) and *X Factor* singer Olly Murs (UK, pictured left with Channel 4 TV host Miquita Oliver), brewed a record 491 cups of tea in 60 minutes on the set of *T4: Battlefront* at Witham Hall, Essex, UK, on January 17, 2010.

MOST COCKTAILS MIXED

Brilliant bartender Matthias Knorr (Germany) mixed 937 cocktails in an hour on the set of the television show *ZDF Fernsehgarten* in Mainz, Germany, on July 25, 2010.

MOST PIZZAS MADE

Prolific pizzaiolo Brian Edler (USA) prepared 206 pizzas at the Domino's Pizza store on North Main Street, Findlay, Ohio, USA, on December 9, 2010.

MOST BASKETBALL FREE THROWS

Perry Dissmore (USA) sank a record 1,968 free throws on *Live! with Regis and Kelly* in New York, USA, on September 14, 2010.

MOST BALLOONS BLOWN UP

On June 20, 2010, Brian Jackson (USA) inflated a lung-busting 335 balloons in an hour at Three Forks Harbor in Muskogee, Oklahoma, USA.

MOST LEGS WAXED

Susanne Baird (UK) waxed 40 pairs of legs in the name of beauty at Grange Cricket Club in Stockbridge, Edinburgh, Scotland, UK, on April 14, 2008.

MOST HAIRCUTS

On August 22, 2008, Ivan Zoot (USA), the world's quickest clipper, treated 34 customers to new haircuts at the Men's Grooming Center in Austin, Texas, USA.

FLIGHT OF FANCY

An hour was more than enough time for pilot Steve Slade (UK) to perform a record 102 successive takeoffs and landings in his RANS S6 light aircraft at Kemble Airfield, UK, on July 27, 2002.

MOST ESCAPES FROM HANDCUFFS

On his way to a landmark 10,625 handcuff escapes in 24 hours, Zdeněk Bradáč (Czech Republic) set a new record of 627 escapes in an hour at the Liberec Film Club in Liberec, Czech Republic, on February 12, 2010.

MOST BUNGEE JUMPS (CORD OF 5–10 M)

Using a 19-ft 8-in (6-m) bungee cord, James Field (UK) completed 42 bungee jumps in 60 minutes at an event organized by Extreme Element & UK Bungee Club at the London Rat Race (UK) on September 26, 2010.

MOST SANDCASTLES BUILT

On July 12, 2010, the staff, friends, family, and volunteers of Lewis-Manning Hospice (UK) built a miniature sand city on Southbanks Beach in Poole, UK, erecting 539 sandcastles in an hour and breaking the previous record of 520 set in 2007.

The Kalgoorlie Australian federal parliamentary constituency in Western Australia covers more than 1 million miles^2 (2.6 million km^2) – an area greater than Western Europe – and is the world's **largest political constituency**.

GREATEST DISTANCE CYCLED WITHOUT USING HANDS: Perfectly balanced Erik Skramstad (USA) cycled 23.25 miles (37.41 km) without the use of his hands in Las Vegas, USA, on June 23, 2009.

MOST BLUNT-TO-FAKIES

On September 18, 2010, 14-year-old Cohl Orebaugh (USA) performed a record 794 blunt-to-fakies (ollie blunts) in an hour at Liberty Lake, Washington, USA, exceeding his own prediction of 500. The trick is carried out on a half-pipe and involves riding up and down each side and balancing the board on the lip of the ramp at the end of each run.

GREATEST DISTANCE CARRYING A CAR

In 60 breathless minutes, Mark Anglesea (UK) carried an 837-lb (380-kg) automobile a record 1,337 ft (407.7 m) at Herringthorpe Running Track, Rotherham, UK, on October 2, 2010.

GREATEST DISTANCE ON A UNICYCLE

Ken Looi (NZ) took an hour to cover 18.63 miles (29.993 km) on his unicycle at Victoria Park Oval, New South Wales, Australia, on August 18, 2009.

GREATEST DISTANCE MOONWALKING

Krunoslav Budiselic (Croatia) performed a sole-destroying 3.54-mile (5.7-km) moonwalk in Zagreb, Croatia, on October 12, 2009.

GREATEST DISTANCE PUSHING A MINI SCOOTER

Harald Hel (Austria) pushed a scooter 16.57 miles (26.66 km) in Vienna, Austria, on September 30, 2007.

GREATEST DISTANCE STATIC CYCLING

Literally going nowhere fast, Miguel Angel Castro (Spain) cycled 57.54 miles (92.6 km) at a sports center in Tenerife, Spain, on March 20, 2010.

IF SHOWS OF STRENGTH ARE YOUR THING, TURN TO "TOUGH GUYS" ON P.104.

GIVE US A LIFT

Mark Anglesea is also the proud holder of the record for the **most lifts of an automobile in an hour**, upending the rear end of a 1,785-lb (810-kg) Mini Metro 580 times on October 3, 1998.

UPDATED RECORD
NEW RECORD

PLANET DANCE

MOST BALLET DANCERS *EN POINTE*

On August 2, 2010, in an event organized by Ellen and Gene Schiavone (both USA), 230 ballet dancers stood *en pointe* (i.e. on the tips of their toes) in Central Park, New York City, USA.

Staying with the ballet, the **most *grandes pirouettes à la seconde* in 30 seconds by a woman** is 50 and was achieved by Alicia Clifton (USA) on the set of *Zheng Da Zong Yi – Guinness World Records Special* in Beijing, China, on December 19, 2010.

The **largest ballet class** involved 1,055 dancers in an event staged by Staatsoper Hannover (Germany) in Hanover, Germany, on June 13, 2010.

MOST DANCE PARTNERS IN 24 HOURS

On November 23–24, 2007, Michael Hull (Germany) danced with 1,068 partners in Osnabrück, Germany.

MOST SPINS IN A MINUTE BY A COUPLE

Marina Femia (Italy) and Alexander Caicedo Sastoque (Colombia) made 195 dance spins in a minute for *Lo Show dei Record* in Rome, Italy, on March 27, 2010.

LARGEST UMBRELLA DANCE: On August 5, 2010, 322 dancers performed an umbrella dance in an event staged by Achariya World Class Educational Institutions (India) in Puducherry, India.

LARGEST TUCA TUCA DANCE: A group of 494 participants danced the Tuca Tuca at an event organized by (and staged in) the city of Bellaria Igea Marina, Italy, on August 7, 2010.

IF YOU'RE MAD FOR MUSIC, JUMP TO P.214.

LONGEST DANCE BY AN INDIVIDUAL

Kalamandalam Hemaletha (India) danced the traditional Indian Mohiniyattam for 123 hr 15 min, from September 20 to 26, 2010, at the Kerala Sangeetha Nadaka Academy in Thrissur, Kerala, India.

DANCE GAMING

FIRST FULL-BODY-MOTION DANCE GAME

Released on September 25, 2007 for the Nintendo Wii, *Dance Dance Revolution Hottest Party* (Konami, 2007) was the first dance game to track players' upper and lower body movements.

LONGEST-RUNNING DANCE MAT GAME SERIES

A total of 11 years and 227 days elapsed between the release of *Dance Dance Revolution* (Konami, 1998) and the most recent game in the hit series, *Dance Dance Revolution X2* (Konami, 2010), which was released on July 7, 2010.

LARGEST DANCE MAT ROUTINE

On July 2, 2010, a group of 120 dancers performed a dance mat routine together at an event staged by West Sussex West School Sport Partnership and Cyber Coach (both UK) at the Arena Sports Centre in Bognor Regis, UK. They danced to the "Disco Disco" game on the Webskape platform.

LONGEST MARATHON ON A DANCE GAME

On October 23, 2010, Chris McGivern (UK) played *Dance Dance Revolution* for 13 hr 33 min 56 sec at Funland in London, UK.

THE INVENTION OF THE WINDMILL IS CREDITED TO "CRAZY LEGS" OF NEW YORK GROUP THE ROCK STEADY CREW

50 WINDMILLS

MOST WINDMILLS IN 30 SECONDS

Mauro Peruzzi (Italy), also known as Cico, performed a total of 50 windmills in a break-dancing style in 30 seconds at the world finals of the Sony Ericsson UK B-Boy Championships in London, UK, on October 10, 2010.

UPDATED RECORD
NEW RECORD

The **cheapest production automobile** is India's Tata Nano, a four-door, five-seater family automobile with a top speed of 43 mi/h (70 km/h). It went on sale in March 2009 for Rs 100,000 ($2,500).

LARGEST DANCES

CANCAN
On September 13, 2009, 1,503 dancers did the cancan at Glasgow Green, Glasgow, UK, at an event organized by IRN-BRU.

CLOG
A group of 2,605 people danced with clogs at an event staged by the Pella Historical Society (USA) in Pella, Iowa, USA, on May 8, 2010.

DANCE ON! AND ON...
Fred Salter (UK, b. February 13, 1911) is the **oldest competitive ballroom dancer.** He passed his gold bar exams aged 99 years 3 months and 2 days on May 15, 2010.

LARGEST BAMBOO DANCE
The government of Mizoram, in Aizawl, Mizoram, India, organized the largest bamboo dance (or Cheraw) on March 12, 2010. The event featured 10,736 dancers.

FANDANGO
On November 30, 2009, a total of 1,146 people danced a fandango – originally an Andalusian folk dance – in an event organized by FUNDEV (Colombia) in Cereté, Cordoba, Colombia.

HOKEY COKEY
On September 3, 2010, 7,384 participants performed the hokey cokey at an event organized by FRY Fest (USA) at FRY Fest in Coralville, Iowa, USA.

MACARENA
On November 12, 2010, in celebration of Guinness World Records Day 2010, 1,861 people danced the Macarena in an event staged by Ancaster High School in Ancaster, Ontario, Canada. The dance was inspired by the 1995 Los del Rio hit "Macarena."

POLONAISE
On September 12, 2010, at an event staged by the Polish Tourist Organization, 300 participants danced the polonaise in London, UK.

SWING
On July 11, 2009, a group of 291 people danced to swing music at an event organized by Øystein Ulen (Norway) and Dansefestivalen at Dansefestivalen, Norway. Swing, a type of jazz, emerged in the 1920s. The best-known style of swing dance is the energetic Lindy Hop.

LOWEST LIMBO (FEMALE)
Shemika Charles (USA) passed under a bar set at just 8.5 in (21.59 cm) off the floor on the set of *Live! with Regis and Kelly* in New York City, USA, on September 16, 2010.

TEA DANCE
A total of 306 couples took part in a tea dance in Glasgow, Scotland, UK, on September 12, 2010. To qualify as a tea dance, tea, cakes, and sandwiches must be served, and the music must be live; in this attempt, the Swing Sensation Big Band supplied the tunes.

LARGEST BHANGRA
On November 11, 2010, 2,100 participants from the Art of Living Foundation (UK) danced a bhangra at the Punjab Agricultural University Campus, Ludhiana, India, in traditional bhangra costumes.

SHE'S NOW BEST KNOWN FOR HER BREAK-DANCING SKILLS, BUT B-GIRL ROXY USED TO BE A TRAMPOLINIST

MOST VIRGIN AIR FLARES IN A MINUTE
B-Boy Junior (France) made 39 break-dance virgin air flares in a minute at the world finals of the Sony Ericsson UK B-Boy Championships on October 10, 2010. At the same event, B-Girl Roxy (UK), aka Roxanna Milliner, performed the **most consecutive headspins by a woman** – 25.

INCREDIBLE CLOTHING

245

MOST T-SHIRTS WORN AT ONCE

Krunoslav Budiselić (Croatia) successfully struggled into a phenomenal 245 T-shirts in Utrine, Zagreb, Croatia, on May 22, 2010. T-shirts ranging from size M to size 10XL were used for the attempt.

BEST-SELLING FASHION BRAND

Nike had sales of $19 billion in the fiscal year ending May 31, 2010.

BEST-SELLING DESIGNER LABEL

Designer clothing brand Ralph Lauren announced an annual revenue of over $4.9 billion as of April 3, 2010.

LARGEST FASHION FRANCHISE

The Benetton Group is present in more than 120 countries via 6,000 franchised stores and company-owned megastores. The group sells around 150 million garments annually, most under the casual "United Colors of Benetton" brand.

MOST VALUABLE TIARA

Decorated with 100-carat diamonds and set in yellow gold, a tiara designed by Gianni Versace (Italy) had an estimated retail value of $5 million.

MODELS AND SHOWS

MOST BRITISH *VOGUE* COVERS

Kate Moss (UK) has appeared on the cover of British *Vogue* magazine 30 times. Her first cover was in March 1993 and her latest to date was for the September 2010 issue.

OLDEST FASHION MODEL

Professional model Daphne Selfe (UK) celebrated her 82nd birthday in July 2010. Her career spans more than 60 years.

MOST MODELS ON A RUNWAY

A total of 521 models paraded from end to end of a 492-ft-long (150-m) runway at Galeries Lafayette in Paris, France, on September 30, 2010.

HIGHEST ANNUAL EARNINGS FOR A MODEL

Gisele Bündchen (Brazil) earned $25 million in 2010, placing her at the top of the list of highest-paid supermodels. She has worked for famous brands such as Ralph Lauren, Dolce & Gabbana, and Versace.

HEAVIEST MODEL

American model Teighlor (b. Debra Perkins) weighed 718 lb 11 oz (326.14 kg) in the early 1990s. She forged a successful career, appearing on greeting cards and in movies and advertisements.

HIGHEST EVER ANNUAL EARNINGS FOR A FASHION DESIGNER

Giorgio Armani (Italy) earned $135 million in 1999, according to *Forbes* magazine.

LARGEST T-SHIRT

The Qatar PetroChemical Company (QAPCO) unveiled a T-shirt 236 ft 10.5 in (72.2 m) long and 159 ft 9 in (48.7 m) wide at ASPIRE Park, Doha, Qatar, on November 23, 2010.

LONGEST LINE OF SOCKS

A line of socks measuring 7,624 ft 11 in (2,324.08 m) was created by the Erlebnispark Tripsdrill (Germany) in Cleebronn, Germany, on May 23, 2010.

DESIGN OF THE TIMES

Charles Frederick Worth, who died in 1895, was the first designer to sign his work with a label and show clothes on live models, thereby creating the **first designer label**.

LARGEST TURBAN

Major Singh (India), a Nihang Sikh, wears a turban made from 1,312 ft (400 m) of cloth and featuring more than 100 hairpins and 51 religious symbols made out of metal. This style of round turban is known as a "dumaala" and is common to Nihang Sikhs.

"The Old Gentleman of Raahe," at the Museum of Raahe in Finland, is the **oldest surviving diving suit.** It was made from stitched calfskin and dates from the 18th century.

LARGEST SHOE
The Nationaal Fonds Kinderhulp (Netherlands) unveiled a titanic shoe measuring 18 ft (5.5 m) x 6 ft 11 in (2.11 m), and with a height of 9 ft 6 in (2.9 m), in Amsterdam, the Netherlands, on November 17, 2010, in celebration of Guinness World Records Day 2010. The shoe is an exact replica of a Converse Chuck Taylor All Star and is the equivalent of a US size 846!

SMALLEST TAILORED EVENING SUIT
Designed by John Richmond (UK), the smallest tailored evening suit comprised a jacket 8 in (21 cm) long and trousers 1 ft 6 in (46 cm) in length. He Pingping (China) – then the world's **shortest man** – wore it on *Lo Show dei Record* on April 26, 2009.

LARGEST LEDERHOSEN
The world's largest lederhosen measure 16 ft 4 in (5 m) tall and 12 ft 3 in (3.75 m) wide. They were created by Walter Sinnhofer (Austria) in Henndorf am Wallersee, Austria, on August 5, 2010.

A total of 828.82 ft^2 (77 m^2) of cow suede was used to create the huge pants, which weigh 101 lb 6.5 oz (46 kg).

THE FIRST LEDERHOSEN WERE MADE IN THE 6TH CENTURY AD

THAT'S RICH! Former medical school dropout Giorgio Armani (Italy) is now worth a record $5.3 billion, making him the world's **richest fashion designer!**

FASHION ITEMS

MOST EXPENSIVE BRA
The Heavenly Star Bra, by US lingerie retailer Victoria's Secret, was made in 2001 and has a $12.5-million price tag. It features 1,200 Sri Lankan pink sapphires and a 90-carat emerald-cut diamond worth $10.6 million.

LARGEST DIRNDL
The dirndl is a traditional Alpine peasant dress, the largest of which is 16 ft (4.9 m) long and 12 ft 4 in (3.8 m) wide. It was presented by GDL-Handels- und Dienstleistungs GmbH in Bad Ischl, Austria, on July 17, 2010.

LARGEST KNITTED HAT
The largest knitted hat measures 22 ft 7 in (6.9 m) high and 49 ft 4 in (15.05 m) in circumference. It was assembled by volunteers and presented in Puchheim, Germany, on October 5, 2008.

LARGEST STRAW HAT
Created by Atalia Bis & Partners Company in Kozieglowy, Poland, the largest straw hat is 21 ft 9 in (6.65 m) in diameter and 8 ft 6 in (2.6 m) high. It was measured in August 2006.

UPDATED RECORD
NEW RECORD

MASS PARTICIPATION

LARGEST GATHERING OF PEOPLE DRESSED AS SUMO WRESTLERS

On June 19, 2010, 205 people donned inflatable sumo suits to take part in the 3-mile (5-km) Sumo Run, a fancy-dress fun run organized annually by Gemin-i.org at Battersea Park in London, UK.

UP IN THE AIR

Talking of balls in the air, 1,062 students and footy fans played "keepy uppy" together in Yangi City, China, on July 10, 2010, breaking the record for the **most people keeping a soccer ball in the air.**

DRESS TO EXCESS

In the bustling world of mass participation, there's nothing like a good costume for bringing people together in their hundreds and thousands! Check out this year's eclectic mix of fancy-dress get-togethers from all over the globe.

Category	People	Organizer	Location	Event date
Pirates	6,166	Roger Crouch (UK)	Hastings, East Sussex, UK	Aug 6, 2010
Peter Pan	5,206	Great Ormond Street Hospital Children's Charity (UK)	Schools across the UK	Apr 30, 2010
Wearing singlets	3,500	Deniliquin Ute Muster (Australia)	Deniliquin, NSW, Australia	Oct 2, 2010
Gorillas	1,061	Mountain Gorilla Conservation Fund (USA)	Denver, Colorado, USA	Oct 31, 2009
Angels	1,039	Hauzenberg aktiv (Germany)	Hauzenberg, Lower Bavaria, Germany	Dec 13, 2009
Flintstones characters	905	Muckno Mania Festival (Ireland)	Co. Monaghan, Ireland	Jul 16, 2010
Wearing bobble hats	764	St Anne's Primary School (UK)	Belfast, Northern Ireland, UK	Nov 18, 2010
Elvis	645	Nike Western Europe (USA)	Aria Hotel, Las Vegas, Nevada, USA	Nov 23, 2010
Star Trek characters	543	Creation Entertainment (USA)	Hilton Hotel, Las Vegas, Nevada, USA	Aug 7, 2010
Regency costume	409	Jane Austen Festival (UK)	Bath, Somerset, UK	Sep 19, 2009
Storybook characters	359	Higham Ferrers Junior School (UK)	Rushden, Northants., UK	Nov 18, 2010
Vampires	354	Loveland Road Runners (USA)	Loveland, Colorado, USA	Oct 17, 2009
Superman	288	Cuchulainn Gaels (Ireland)	Omeath, County Louth, Ireland	Aug 21, 2010
Gandhi	255	AVB Matriculation Higher Secondary School (India)	Coimbatore, India	Jun 13, 2010

LARGEST SIMULTANEOUS BASKETBALL BOUNCE

On July 22, 2010, a total of 7,556 people bounced basketballs in the air at the same time during an event organized by the United Nations Relief and Works Agency (UNRWA) in Rafah, Gaza Strip, Palestine.

LARGEST CYCLING RACE

Other sports-related mass gatherings include the Cape Argus Pick 'n Pay Cycle Tour, a grueling 68-mile (109-km) bike race in Cape Town, South Africa, that drew 42,614 entrants in 2004, including the five-times Tour de France winner Miguel Indurain (Spain).

LARGEST GAME OF DODGEBALL

On February 4, 2011, a record 2,012 competitors played the largest ever game of dodgeball, a sport made famous by the 2004 film of the same name. The game was organized by the University of Alberta at the Universiade Pavilion (Butterdome), in Edmonton, Alberta, Canada.

UPDATED RECORD
NEW RECORD

The Salt River Morgue in Cape Town, South Africa, handled more than 30,000 cadavers in 1998, making it the **busiest morgue**. Almost 4,000 of these bodies had untraceable identities and were likely to have been the victims of violent crime.

159,635 Number of people who will die on the same day as you. It might be more cheering to think of the 18,562,289 people around the world who share your birthday.

TIGHT SQUEEZE
Green Scream can only take 40 people per ride, but that would still have been enough to break the previous record of 32 naked roller-coaster riders, held by *Nemesis* at Alton Towers, Staffordshire, UK.

GREEN SCREAM HAD TO RUN THREE TIMES TO ALLOW EVERYONE TO TAKE PART!

MOST NAKED RIDERS ON A THEME PARK RIDE
The greatest number of people to bare all on a theme park ride is 102, a record set by enthusiastic members of the public on the *Green Scream* roller-coaster at Adventure Island, Southend-on-Sea, Essex, UK, on August 8, 2010.

LONGEST HUMAN CENTIPEDE
Staged by the Thai Beverage Marketing Co. and Have a Good Dream Co., a human centipede of 2,961 people linked up at Ratchaburi, Thailand, on June 16, 2010.

LONGEST HUMAN DOMINO LINE
Sat in a line, 10,267 "human dominoes" formed a 4.5-mile (7.2-km) chain in Ordos City, China, on August 12, 2010.

MOST PEOPLE SKIPPING
On February 1, 2010, 70,880 people from 294 schools skipped at an event staged by California Association for Health, Physical Education, Recreation & Dance (CAHPERD) and Jamba Juice in California, USA.

LARGEST HUMAN CROSS
A group of 935 red-robed people formed a human cross under the guidance of the Oslo Red Cross (Norway) at the Oslo Opera House in Oslo, Norway, on May 7, 2010.

LARGEST HUMAN SMILEY
On September 22, 2010, 551 people formed a smiley face in a stunt orchestrated by Igors Puntuss (Latvia) in Riga, Latvia.

MOST PEOPLE DRESSED AS SUPERHEROES
To promote the Dreamworks movie *Megamind*, 1,580 people donned superhero costumes in Los Angeles, USA, on October 2, 2010, in an event staged by Paramount Studios (USA).

MOST PEOPLE WEARING RED NOSES
On June 5, 2010, 15,956 people sported red noses at the Mega Pic-Nic 2010, arranged by Realizar Eventos Especiais and Modelo in Lisbon, Portugal.

MOST ENTRIES IN A TWO-PERSON PANTOMIME ANIMAL RACE
In a contest organized by RSA, Have a Heart, and Action on Addiction, 37 two-man teams dressed as pantomime animals and raced one another at Goodwood Racecourse, UK, on June 24, 2010.

An estimated 10.2 million people filled the 20-mile (32-km) route to Tehran's Behesht-e Zahra cemetery, Iran, for the funeral of Ayatollah Ruhollah Khomeini, the Iranian religious leader, on June 11, 1989, making it the world's **largest funeral**.

TOUGH GUYS

(Yellow) UPDATED RECORD
(Red) NEW RECORD

(New record) MOST AUTOMOBILE WINDOWS SMASHED

Kevin Taylor (USA) smashed 20 automobile door windows using only his fists on the set of *Lo Show dei Record* in Rome, Italy, on February 25, 2010. The task took him just 1 min 35 sec.

(Updated record) MOST PUSH-UPS IN 24 HOURS

On April 24–25, 1993, Charles Servizio (USA) completed 46,001 push-ups in 24 hours at Fontana City Hall in Fontana, California, USA.

(Updated record) MOST CONSECUTIVE MARTIAL ARTS BOUTS

Paddy Doyle (UK) carried out 141 consecutive martial arts bouts at St Benedict's School Sports Centre, Cheltenham, UK, on November 19, 2005.

(Updated record) MOST CHIN-UPS IN ONE HOUR

On June 2, 2010, Stephen Hyland (UK) performed 968 chin-ups in an hour in Stoneleigh, Surrey, UK.

(New record) HEAVIEST HOUSE PULLED

Kevin Fast (Canada) pulled a 79,145-lb (35.9-tonne) house for 39 ft 2.47 in (11.95 m) in Cobourg, Ontario, Canada, on September 18, 2010.

A minute may not sound like a very long time, but it's enough to…

- (New record) **Smash 11 pumpkins (Ben Shephard, UK)**
- (New record) **Smash 88 alarm clocks using only your feet (Jay Wheddon, UK)**
- (New record) **Break 55 baseball bats or (Updated record) 111 coconuts using only your hands (both Muhamed Kahrimanovic, Germany)**
- (Updated record) **Smash 40 watermelons with your head (John Allwood, Australia)**
- (Updated record) **Perform 805 full-contact punch strikes (Robert Ardito, Australia)**
- (New record) **Deadlift 3,864 lb (1,752.68 kg) (Thienna Ho, Vietnam)**

RUN FOR IT! Cristina Borra (Italy) ran a lung-bursting 13 marathons from February 16 to 28, 2010 in Turin, Italy – the (Updated record) **most marathons run on consecutive days by a woman.**

THAT'S TORN IT! The (New record) **most telephone directories torn behind the back in three minutes** is six, by Alexander Muromskiy (Russia) on October 17, 2009 at the Moscow Center of Martial Arts, Russia.

The Iranian/American businesswoman Anousheh Ansari became the **first female space tourist** on September 18, 2006.

296 Gallons of blood you'll lose in a lifetime, along with 557 gallons of sweat and 16 gallons of tears – enough blood for 10 baths, enough sweat for a five-hour shower, and enough tears to wash eight tracksuits!

MOST WATERMELONS SMASHED WITH A PUNCH IN ONE MINUTE

Davide Cenciarelli (Italy) smashed 70 watermelons with his fist in one minute for *Lo Show dei Record* in Rome, Italy, on March 18, 2010.

The **fastest time to crush 10 watermelons with the head** is 16 seconds, by Leonardo D'Andrea (Italy) on the set of *Zheng Da Zong Yi – Guinness World Records Special* in Beijing, China, on December 17, 2006.

LONGEST DURATION HOLDING WEIGHT WITH OUTSTRETCHED ARMS

On March 4, 2010, Tomi Lotta (Finland) held a weight (minimum 44 lb; 20 kg) suspended with outstretched arms for 1 min 16.63 sec on the set of *Lo Show dei Record* in Rome, Italy.

FASTEST TIME TO BEND AN IRON BAR INTO A SUITCASE

Alexander Muromskiy (Russia) bent a 19-ft 7-in-long (6-m) iron bar and fitted it into a suitcase in 25 seconds in St Petersburg, Russia, on November 9, 2008.

MOST CONCRETE BLOCKS BROKEN IN ONE MINUTE

Ali Bahçetepe (Turkey) broke 1,145 concrete blocks in one minute at the Taekwondo Sport Centre in Datça, Turkey, on November 17, 2010.

LONGEST TIME TO HOLD ONE'S BREATH VOLUNTARILY (MALE)

On April 1, 2010, Stig Åvall Severinsen (Denmark) held his breath for 20 min 10 sec in the shark tank at Kattegat Centre, Grenaa, Denmark.

LONGEST TIME IN FULL-BODY CONTACT WITH SNOW

Jin Songhao (China) was immersed in a pile of snow for 46 min 7 sec at the Center Square, A'ershan City, Inner Mongolian Autonomous Region, China, on January 17, 2011. During the attempt, the temperature was -34.6°F (-37°C). The snow pile had a diameter of approximately 5 ft 6 in (1.7 m) at the base and was 2 ft 3 in (0.7 m) tall.

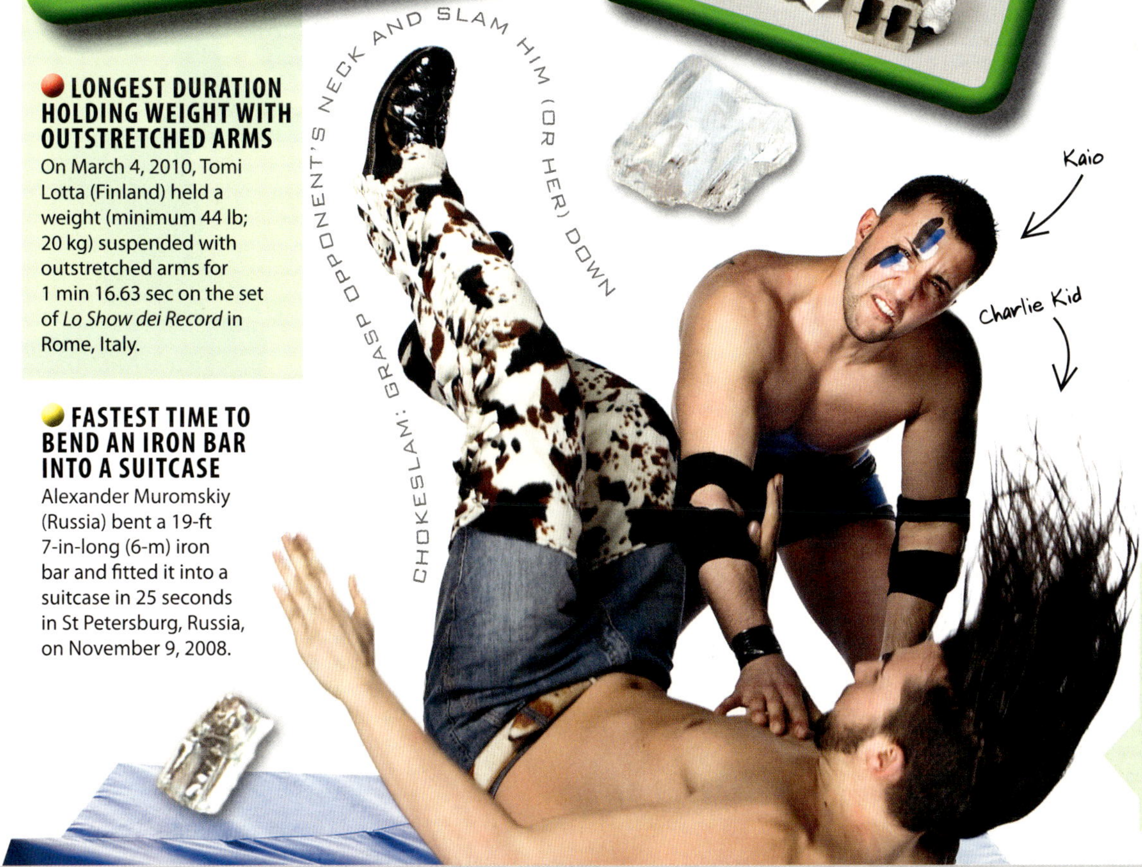

MOST CHOKESLAMS IN ONE MINUTE

Nury Ayachi (aka Kaio), Carlo Lenzoni (aka Charlie Kid), and Mariel Shehi (all Italy) performed 34 chokeslams in one minute on the set of *Lo Show dei Record* in Rome, Italy, on February 25, 2010.

Tourists visiting Planet Earth might like to use the world's **first official UFO landing pad**, built in the small Canadian prairie town of St Paul in Alberta, Canada, and formally opened on 3 June 1967.

IN THE HOME

THE CRYING GAME

Bob Blumer (Canada) fought back the tears to peel 31 onions in 2 min 39 sec on July 18, 2010, slicing his way to the record for the **fastest time to peel 50 lb (22 kg) of onions.**

FASTEST TIME TO PLACE SIX EGGS IN EGG CUPS USING ONE'S FEET

On February 16, 2008, nimble-toed Tatiana Dudzan (Ukraine) slotted half a dozen eggs into egg cups using only her feet in a time of 42.60 seconds on the set of *Lo Show dei Record*, in Madrid, Spain.

FASTEST WINDOW CLEANER

Terry Burrows (UK) took just 9.14 seconds to clean three standard office windows (45 x 45 in; 114.3 x 114.3 cm) with an 11.75-in (300-mm) squeegee and 2 gal (9 liters) of water at the National Window Cleaning Competition held in Blackpool, UK, on October 9, 2009.

FASTEST TIME TO BALANCE A DOZEN EGGS

Prolific record-breaker Ashrita Furman (USA) turned his talents to eggs on September 22, 2009, when he balanced 12 of them upright on a table in a record 1 min 36 sec in the kitchen of the Sri Chinmoy Centre, Jamaica, New York, USA.

FASTEST TIME TO BUTTER 10 SLICES OF BREAD

Hungry New Zealander Alastair Galpin buttered 10 slices of bread in a swift 52.42 seconds in Pt Chevalier, Auckland, New Zealand, on December 3, 2009.

FASTEST TIME TO BOIL WATER WITH ELECTRICITY CONDUCTED THROUGH THE BODY

With electricity passing through his body, Slavisa Pajkic "Biba" (Yugoslavia) heated a 0.5-fl-oz (15-ml) cup of water from 77°F to 206°F (25°C to 97°C) in 1 min 37 sec on the set of *Guinness Rekord TV*, Stockholm, Sweden, on November 24, 2001.

FASTEST TIME LAYING CARPET

On August 7, 2008, on the set of ITV's *60 Minute Makeover* (UK), Stephen Dineley (UK) took a record 6 min 20.18 sec to lay a carpet measuring 129.2 ft² (12 m²).

FASTEST TIME TO MAKE A BED (TEAM)

Since November 26, 1993, nobody has managed to beat the bed-making masterclass performed by Charge Nurse Sharon Stringer and Nurse Michelle Benkel of the Royal Masonic Hospital, London, UK. The duo dressed a bed with a blanket, two sheets, an undersheet, an uncased pillow, a pillowcase, and a bedspread in just 14 seconds – and still had time for the hospital corners!

FASTEST TIME TO BURST THREE HOT WATER BOTTLES

Brian Jackson (USA) blew up three standard hot water bottles to bursting point in a record- and lung-busting 1 min 8 sec on the set of *Lo Show dei Record*, in Milan, Italy, on April 19, 2009.

DO TRY THIS AT HOME!

Damiano Falcioni (Italy) holds the record for the **longest time to spin a fry pan on one finger**, notching up 17 min 47 sec with his dynamic digit on March 24, 2010.

MOST ITEMS WASHED UP IN EIGHT HOURS

On January 10, 2011, the soap suds flew as Louise Dooey (UK) donned her rubber gloves and embarked on an eight-hour washing-up marathon that left an incredible 2,250 plates, bowls, pans, and cutlery items sparkling! Louise achieved the feat at the Guinness World Records head office in London, UK.

Trever McGhee (Canada) completed the **longest firewalk** when he hotfooted it 597 ft (181.9 m) over embers with a temperature of up to 1,307°F (853.33°C) at Symons Valley Rodeo Grounds in Calgary, Canada, on November 9, 2007.

LONGEST IRONING MARATHON

In return for a small charity donation, Daniel Peetz (Germany) ironed the clothes of strangers nonstop for a record 58 hours exactly in Rheinberg, Germany, on June 17–19, 2010.

The most fun you can have with a pair of underpants – or two...

- **Most underpants worn at once:** 231, by Taro Yabe (Japan) on August 29, 2010.
- **Most underpants pulled on in a minute:** 22, by Sheena Reyes (Australia) on March 27, 2010.
- **Most underpants jumped into in an hour:** 234, by Kevin Velaiden (UK) on March 27, 2009.
- **Most underpants somersaulted into in 90 seconds:** 94, by Team Spektaculer (Germany), a troupe of 12 gymnasts, on January 20, 2000.

MOST SOCKS WORN ON ONE FOOT

On November 13, 2010, Croatian Krunoslav Budiselic adorned his right foot with a record-breaking 150 socks at City Centar One in Zagreb, Croatia. Budiselic used socks provided by local supplier Jadran Hosiery and needed 45 minutes to pull them all on to his foot.

MOST SOCKS SORTED IN ONE MINUTE

Super-quick sock-sorter John Harrold (UK) managed to ball a world record 34 socks into 17 pairs in the space of a minute. John claimed his new sock-sorting record at a GWR Live! event held at the World Trade Centre in Barcelona, Spain, on May 14, 2010.

MOST CLOTHES RETRIEVED FROM A WASHING LINE BY A DOG

On November 29, 2009, Gustl, a terrier cross owned by Heidi Deml (Germany), fetched 13 laundry items from a washing line in a minute at the Vienna Congress Centre, Vienna, Austria. The clever canine can perform more than 50 commands.

MOST EGGS CRACKED IN ONE HOUR

Proving that you can't make an omelette without cracking some eggs, Canadian Bob Blumer broke open 2,069 eggs one-handed in an hour at the Festival de l'Omelette Géante in Granby, Québec, Canada, on June 24, 2010.

MOST ORANGE JUICE EXTRACTED IN A MINUTE

Ulaş Baş (Turkey) squeezed into the record books by extracting 0.19 gal (880 ml) of juice from oranges at the GWR Live! Roadshow at Forum Mersin, in Mersin, Turkey, on June 20, 2010.

UPDATED RECORD
NEW RECORD

DON'T TRY THIS AT HOME!
Unlike Daniel Peetz, Jonathan Macfarlane (NZ) is no laundry fan, expressing his distaste on August 23, 2009 with the **farthest washing machine throw** – 13 ft 2 in (4.01 m)!

OUT OF THE ORDINARY

FASTEST MILE BALANCING A SOCCER BALL ON THE HEAD

Yee Ming Low (Malaysia) completed a mile in 8 min 35 sec, while balancing a soccer ball on his head, at MPSJ Athletics Stadium in Selangor, Malaysia, on March 20, 2010.

MOST SPEARS CAUGHT FROM A SPEARGUN IN ONE MINUTE

Joe Alexander (Germany) caught seven spears shot from a speargun underwater from a distance of 6 ft 6 in (2 m) in one minute on the live TV show *ZDF Fernsehgarten* in Mainz, Germany, on September 6, 2009.

MOST...

TOPS SPUN AT THE SAME TIME

Steve Faulkner (UK) spun 22 tops simultaneously at the Substance offices in London, UK, on November 30, 2010.

GOLF BALLS HELD IN ONE HAND

Guillaume Doyon (Canada) held 24 golf balls in one hand for 10 seconds at Collège Saint-Alexandre in Gatineau, Quebec, Canada, on November 30, 2009. This record was equaled by Rohit Timilsina (Nepal) in Dharmasthali, Kathmandu, Nepal, on May 15, 2010.

LEAPFROG JUMPS IN 30 SECONDS BY A PAIR

Haruka Nakano and Asuka Ogawa (both Japan) performed 25 leapfrog jumps in 30 seconds at Park Challenge GWR Live! in Tokyo Midtown, Tokyo, Japan, on May 5, 2010.

MOUSETRAPS RELEASED ON THE TONGUE IN ONE MINUTE

Joshuah Hoover, aka "Sweet Pepper Klopek" (Canada), became a record breaker by releasing 40 mousetraps on his tongue in one minute on the set of *Lo Show dei Record* in Milan, Italy, on April 14, 2011.

RUBBER BANDS STRETCHED ON THE FACE

Shay Horay, better known as "Rubberband Boy" (NZ), had 78 rubber bands stretched over his face on the set of *Lo Show dei Record* in Milan, Italy, on April 8, 2011.

EGGS THROWN AND CAUGHT IN ONE MINUTE BY A PAIR

Ashrita Furman and Bipin Larkin (both USA) threw and caught 75 eggs across 16 ft 4 in (5 m) in Felvonulasi Square in Budapest, Hungary, on May 14, 2010.

CONSECUTIVE ONE-HANDED CLAPS

The greatest number of consecutive one-handed claps performed by an individual is 310, by Abhinav Upadhyaya (India) at Pranav Studios in Bangalore, Karnataka, India, on May 16, 2010.

HANDCUFF ESCAPES IN 24 HOURS

Zdeněk Bradáč (Czech Republic) made 10,625 handcuff escapes in Liberec, Czech Republic, on February 12–13, 2010.

On September 9, 2009, he also set the **fastest time to escape from three sets of handcuffs underwater**: 38.69 seconds, in Jablonec nad Nisou, Czech Republic.

MOST TIMES TO PASS THROUGH A TENNIS RACKET IN THREE MINUTES

Skye Broberg (Australia) passed her body through a tennis racket seven times in three minutes on the set of *Lo Show dei Record* in Rome, Italy, on February 25, 2010. Skye honed her serpentine skills as a circus act and street theater artist: as well as contortion, her acts include performing with the hula hoop, aerial hoop, and neck hoop. One of her trademark specialities involves cramming her entire body into a small glass box!

Vrtoglavica (meaning "vertigo") is an unbroken vertical shaft 1,978 ft 4 in (603 m) deep in Monte Kanin, Slovenia. The **deepest naturally occurring shaft**, it could comfortably accommodate two Eiffel Towers (984 ft; 300 m).

FASTEST 100 M HURDLES WEARING FLIPPERS

Christopher Irmscher (Germany) completed the 100 m hurdles wearing flippers in 14.82 seconds on the set of *Guinness World Records: Die Größten Weltrekorde* in Cologne, Germany, on September 13, 2008.

Veronica Torr (New Zealand) achieved the same feat in 18.523 seconds for *Zheng Da Zong Yi – Guinness World Records Special* in Beijing, China, on December 8, 2010, the **fastest 100 m hurdles wearing flippers by a woman.**

Farthest distance to…

Flick a coin
39 ft 8 in (12.11 m), by Alastair Galpin (New Zealand), at the Britomart Transport Centre, Auckland, New Zealand, on November 12, 2009.

Blow a coin
16 ft 2.76 in (4.947 m), by Ashrita Furman (USA), at the Jamaica YMCA in Jamaica, New York City, USA, on October 9, 2010.

Throw a dry cowpat
266 ft (81.1 m), by Steve Urner (USA), at the Mountain Festival, Tehachapi, California, USA, on August 14, 1981.

FASTEST TIME TO…

HALVE 10 MATCHES WITH AN AX

Bipin Larkin (USA) took just 3.59 seconds to halve 10 matches with an ax at the Sri Chinmoy Center in New York, USA, on October 20, 2010.

TYPE THE ALPHABET

Sudhakar Raju (India) typed the alphabet in 3.52 seconds at Press Club in Anantapur, India, on February 13, 2011.

ESCAPE A STRAITJACKET

Jackson Rayne (USA) escaped a straitjacket in 7.26 seconds at the Las Vegas Convention Center, Las Vegas, Nevada, USA, on November 17, 2009.

PASS THROUGH A TOILET SEAT THREE TIMES

Ilker Çevik (Turkey) wriggled his entire body through a toilet seat three times in just 28.14 seconds at the GWR Live! Roadshow at Forum Bornova in Izmir, Turkey, on May 25, 2010.

DRESS A FEMALE MANNEQUIN

Nuran Ozdemir (Turkey) dressed a female dummy in 28.57 seconds at the GWR Live! Roadshow at Forum Trabzon in Trabzon, Turkey, on June 4, 2010.

DUCT-TAPE A PERSON TO A WALL

Hendrik Leschke duct-taped Kai Otte (both Germany) to a wall on the set of *Guinness World Records – Wir holen den Rekord nach Deutschland* in 55.03 seconds in Berlin, Germany, on April 2, 2011.

FASTEST 4 X 100 M RELAY IN HIGH HEELS

The Pinkettes – Brittney McGlone, Jessica Penney, Laura Juliff, and Casey Case (all Australia) – ran a 4 x 100 m relay in 1 min 4.19 sec in Sydney, Australia, on September 28, 2010.

COMPLETE A GAME OF HOPSCOTCH

On November 9, 2010, Ashrita Furman (USA) finished a hopscotch game in 1 min 1.97 sec in New York City, USA. Furman made just one errant throw, needing two slides of the rock to land it in the "3" square.

BLOW UP A BALLOON WITH A 100-M FIRE HOSE

Ding Zhaohai (China) inflated a balloon using a 100-m-long (328-ft) fire hose in 7 min 49 sec in Xitai City, Shandong Province, China, on November 21, 2010 for the TV show *Zheng Da Zong Yi*.

UPDATED RECORD
NEW RECORD

MOST SUGAR-GLASS BOTTLES BROKEN ON THE HEAD IN 30 SECONDS

Mariana Arnaut (Moldavia) broke 56 sugar-glass bottles on her head in 30 seconds for *Lo Show dei Record* in Rome, Italy, on March 4, 2010. Sugar glass is a fake glass used in movies and on television.

COOL HEADED

The **longest journey with a refrigerator** covered 1,025.26 miles (1,650 km) and was achieved by comedian Tony Hawks (UK), who hitchhiked across Ireland between May 6 and 30, 1997.

From great depths to soaring heights, the **highest cell phone call** was made from the summit of Mount Everest, Nepal – 29,029 ft (8,848 m), or 29.5 Eiffel Towers, above sea level – by Rod Baber (UK) on May 21, 2007.

AT THE CIRCUS

FIRST FLYING-RETURN TRAPEZE ACT: Jules Léotard (France) in Paris, France, on November 12, 1859.

FIRST HUMAN CANNONBALL: "Zazel," whose debut came in 1877 when she was shot about 30 ft (6.1 m) at Westminster Aquarium, London, UK.

OLDEST TOURING CIRCUS

The celebrated Circo Atayde opened on August 26, 1888 in the Plaza de Toros, Mazatlán, Mexico. It has been run continuously by the Atayde family ever since.

FARTHEST DISTANCE ON A TIGHTROPE IN 24 HOURS

Joey Kelly (Germany) walked 9.74 miles (15.68 km) along a tightrope over a period of 24 hours on the set of *RTL Spendenmarathon* at MMC studios in Hürth, Germany, on November 18–19, 2010 in celebration of Guinness World Records Day 2010. The wire was 36 ft 1.07 in (11 m) long and hung 36 ft 1.07 in (11 m) above the ground.

FASTEST MOTORCYCLE WHEELIE ON A TIGHTROPE

Johann Traber (Germany) pulled off a daring 33-mi/h (53-km/h) motorcycle wheelie while riding along a tightrope at the Tummelum Festival in Flensburg, Germany on August 13, 2005.

HEAVIEST STILTS WALKED WITH

Doug Hunt (Canada) took an amazing 29 steps unaided on a pair of stilts with a collective weight of 137 lb (62.1 kg), and 50 ft 9 in (15.56 m) tall, on September 14, 2002.

FASTEST MILE ON STILTS

Ashrita Furman (USA) covered a mile (1.6 km) on stilts in 12 min 23 sec at the Queens College running track in Flushing, New York City, USA, on August 29, 2008.

Ashrita also ran the **fastest 100 m on spring-loaded stilts**, in a time of 19.78 seconds, at the Piazza dei Miracoli, Pisa, Italy, on March 27, 2010.

Finally, he also recorded the **greatest vertical height walked on stilts** – 2,848 ft (868 m) – when he climbed to the summit of Mount Equinox in Manchester, Vermont, USA, on September 23, 2008.

MOST DOGS SKIPPING ON THE SAME ROPE

A total of 13 dogs from Uchida Geinousha's Super Wan Wan Circus (Japan) skipped on one rope in Tochigi, Japan, on October 27, 2009 for *Bikkuri Chojin Special #3* (Fuji TV).

UPDATED RECORD
NEW RECORD

Deepak Sharma Bajagain (Nepal) licked 70 postage stamps in one minute at Hindu Vidya Peeth-Nepal in Balkumari, Lalitpur, Nepal, on August 6, 2010, giving him the record for the **most stamps licked in a minute**.

1,344,290 Number of times you will laugh throughout your life. According to German psychologist Dr Michael Titze, the average person spends six minutes a day laughing – 12 minutes less than we did in the 1960s.

HIGHEST FLAME BLOWN BY A FIRE BREATHER

Antonio Restivo (USA) blew a flame 26 ft 5 in (8.05 m) into the air at a warehouse in Las Vegas, Nevada, USA, on January 11, 2011.

MOST CANDLES EXTINGUISHED BY A WHIP IN ONE MINUTE

On November 11, 2008, Adam Winrich (USA) extinguished 50 candles in one minute by cracking a whip – without touching the candle wax – on the set of *Zheng Da Zong Yi – Guinness World Records Special* in Beijing, China.

MOST AXES THROWN AROUND A HUMAN TARGET IN 30 SECONDS

Wang Shengli (China) hurled a total of 12 axes at a revolving human target in 30 seconds on the set of *Zheng Da Zong Yi – Guinness World Records Special* in Beijing, China, on December 20, 2010.

MOST RABBITS PULLED OUT OF A HAT

Piero Ustignani, aka Jabba, and Walter Rolfo (both Italy) pulled 300 rabbits out of a magician's hat in less than 30 minutes. This variation on a classic magic trick took place during the Magic Congress in Saint-Vincent, Aosta, Italy, on May 17, 2008.

FASTEST THROWING OF 10 KNIVES AROUND A HUMAN TARGET

Dr David R Adamovich, aka "The Great Throwdini" (USA), threw ten 14-in (35.5-cm) throwing knives around his partner, "Target Girl" Tina Nagy, in 4.29 seconds on 29 July 2008.

MOST SWORDS SWALLOWED UNDERWATER

On March 24, 2010, Dan Meyer (USA) swallowed two swords underwater on the set of *Lo Show dei Record* in Rome, Italy.

HEAVIEST WEIGHT DANGLED FROM A SWORD

Thomas Blackthorne (UK) dangled a weight of 55 lb 1 oz (25 kg) from a swallowed sword on the set of *Lo Show dei Record* in Italy on April 19, 2009.

MOST OPEN UMBRELLAS BALANCED SIMULTANEOUSLY

Liu Lina (China) balanced eight open umbrellas at the same time on the set of *Zheng Da Zong Yi – Guinness World Records Special* in Beijing, China, on June 21, 2009.

LARGEST CURVE FOR A SWALLOWED SWORD

On September 12, 2009, Dai Andrews (USA) successfully swallowed a sword with a curvature of 120° at the Blue Thunder Festival at Pimlico Racetrack, Baltimore, Maryland, USA.

HIGHEST JUMP THROUGH A HOOP

Qiu Jiangning (China), of the China National Acrobatic Troupe, jumped 10 ft 2 in (3.12 m) through a hoop on the set of *Zheng Da Zong Yi – Guinness World Records Special* in Beijing, China, on June 17, 2009.

Milestones at the circus:

First three-ring circus
Presented by "Lord" George Sanger (UK), 1860

First human arrow
Tony Zedoras (USA), aka "Alar," Barnum & Bailey Circus, 1896

First loop-the-loop trick cycling
A member of the Ancillotti Troupe, Barnum & Bailey Circus, 1904

Stamping his name into our record book, Christian Schäfer (Germany) claimed the **fastest time to blow a stamp 100 m**, with a time of 3 min 3 sec at ASV Dachau in Dachau, Germany, on October 3, 2010.

JUGGLING

MOST OBJECTS JUGGLED

Balls: In the early 1900s, three performers were said to have succeeded in juggling a record 10 balls: Frank Le Dent (USA), Jenny Jaeger (Russia/Germany), and Enrico Rastelli (Italy), who is still acclaimed as one of the world's greatest jugglers. Yet history does not accurately record whether they were able to do what is now called a "qualifying" run of at least 20 catches, or only managed a "flash" – that is, making a single cycle of the objects, attaining 10 catches. The only person to succeed in qualifying 10-ball juggling has been Bruce Sarafian (USA), who, in 1996, was documented making 23 catches.

● **Clubs**: Anthony Gatto (USA, b. Anthony Commarota) juggled a record eight clubs on August 30, 2006, making 16 catches.

• **Flaming torches**: Anthony Gatto (USA) juggled seven flaming torches in 1989.

● LONGEST TIME TO JUGGLE THREE OBJECTS UNDERWATER (NO AIR SUPPLY)

A submerged Merlin Cadogan (UK) juggled three objects underwater while holding his breath for 1 min 20 sec in Potters Fields Park, London, UK, on November 18, 2010.

5 MIN 45 SEC

MOST JUGGLING CATCHES IN ONE MINUTE (THREE BALLS)

Zdeněk Bradáč (Czech Republic) achieved a record 339 catches of three balls in one minute at the Prinzenraub Festival in Altenburg, Germany, on July 12, 2009.

FIVE SOCCER BALLS

MOST SOCCER BALLS JUGGLED

Professional soccer freestyler Victor Rubilar (Argentina) juggled five regulation-size soccer balls for the required minimum of 10 seconds at the Gallerian shopping mall in Stockholm, Sweden, on November 4, 2006.

• **Plates**: Enrico Rastelli reputedly kept eight plates aloft in the 1920s.

• **Rings**: At least three people have each been reported to have juggled 11 rings – Albert Petrovski in 1963, Eugene Belaur in 1968, and Sergei Ignatov in 1973 (all USSR) – but there is no verification that the attempts qualified with the required 22 catches. The highest number of rings to be authenticated is 10 by Anthony Gatto (USA), who made 47 catches in 2005.

GREATEST COMBINED WEIGHT JUGGLED

Milan Roskopf (Slovakia) juggled three shot puts weighing a total of 57 lb (25.86 kg) for 40.44 seconds in Starnberg, Germany, on November 7, 2004.

● LONGEST TIME TO JUGGLE THREE OBJECTS WHILE SUSPENDED

Hanging from gravity boots, Erik Kloeker (USA) juggled three objects for 5 min 45 sec in Beijing, China, on May 23, 2010.

● LONGEST TIME TO JUGGLE THREE OBJECTS BLINDFOLDED

Zdeněk Bradáč (Czech Republic) juggled three balls blindfolded for 25.30 seconds at the Flying Teapots Circus Club in Sheffield, UK, on February 25, 2009.

FASTEST 100 M JOGGLING WITH FIVE OBJECTS

Owen Morse (US) ran 100 m while juggling five objects in a time of 13.8 seconds in 1988.

● UPDATED RECORD
● NEW RECORD

In 2009, Germans spent $81 billion while on holiday in foreign countries according to the World Tourism Organization (UNWTO), giving them the record for the ● **highest-spending tourists**.

MOST CONSECUTIVE FOOT-JUGGLING FLIPS

Hou Yanan and Jiang Tiantian (both China), from the Wuqiao County Acrobatic Group, performed 90 foot-juggling flips in a row in Beijing, China, on September 19, 2007.

MOST CLUBS PASSED BY A DUO

Wes Peden (USA) and Patrik Elmnert (Sweden) passed 13 clubs between them in 2009 – a total of 26 catches. The **most clubs flashed** by a duo is 14, when Peter Kaseman and Darin Marriott (both USA) attempted a flash of 14-club passing in 2004.

FLASHING

A "flash" is a single cycle of juggling in which you make one catch for each object; a true "juggle" involves at least two catches. The **most balls or beanbags flashed** is 12, achieved by Alex Barron (UK) with 13 beanbags in 2010.

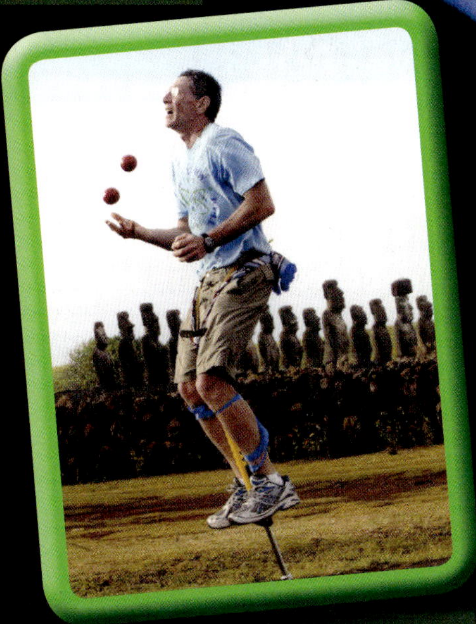

LONGEST TIME TO JUGGLE FIVE BASKETBALLS

Pedro Elis (Spain) was filmed juggling five basketballs for 37.46 seconds on the *Guinness World Records* TV show in Madrid, Spain, on January 30, 2009.

MOST BALLS BOUNCE-JUGGLED

Bounce juggling allows for balls to be bounced off the ground before returning to the hands. The most balls bounce-juggled at any one time is 11, by Tim Nolan (USA) at the Old Dominion University Fieldhouse in Norfolk, Virginia, USA, on March 11, 2006.

FASTEST MILE BOUNCE-JUGGLING

Ashrita Furman (USA) took just 7 min 42 sec to cover the distance of 1 mile (1.6 km) while bounce-juggling three objects at Jamaica High School in New York, USA, on October 21, 2009.

WHY "JOGGLING"?

Bill Giduz (USA) devised this hybrid of juggling and jogging in 1979. As a runner and a juggler, he saw that the two activities fitted well together: a runner's arms naturally make a juggling motion.

GREATEST DISTANCE JUGGLING ON A POGO STICK

The greatest distance over which anyone has traveled on a pogo stick while simultaneously juggling is 4 miles (6 km) by Ashrita Furman (USA), while visiting Easter Island, Chile, on January 28, 2010.

THREE-BALL JOGGLING

Juggling + jogging = joggling! Sounds easy enough, but not when taken to these extremes…

Distance	Time	Holder	Date
100 m (male)	11.68	Owen Morse (USA)	1989
100 m (female)	17.20	Sandy Brown (USA)	Jul 22, 1990
1 mile (male)	4:43	Kirk Swenson (USA)	1986
1 mile (female)	6:17	Kathy Glynn (USA)	Jul 22, 1989
10 km (6.2 miles)	36:27	Michal Kapral (Canada)	Sep 10, 2006
Marathon (26 miles; 42 km)	2:50.12	Michal Kapral (Canada)	Sep 30, 2007
50 miles (80.5 km)	8:23.52	Perry Romanowski (USA)	Oct 27, 2007

MOST BATONS JUGGLED

Françoise Rochais of Les Sables-d'Olonne, France, juggled seven batons at once while performing with the After Cloudy Company in Japan in 1999.

FLIP TO P.262 FOR MORE AERIAL ARTISTRY.

Skills & Talents

WHEEL SKILLS

BICYCLE

MOST CANDLES EXTINGUISHED WITH A TRIAL BICYCLE IN ONE MINUTE

Benito Ros Charral (Spain) managed to put out 22 candles with a trial bicycle in just a minute in Beijing, China, on December 18, 2010.

HIGHEST BACKFLIP

Ben Wallace (UK) performed a bicycle backflip 9 ft 2.23 in (2.8 m) high on *Zheng Da Zong Yi – Guinness World Records Special* in Beijing, China, on December 9, 2010.

LONGEST 180 FLIP

On November 18, 2008, Jim Dechamp (USA) carried out a 10-ft (3-m) 180° flip on a mountain bike at Miller Motorsports Park in Tooele, Utah, USA, for the MTV show *Nitro Circus*. Jim also holds 10 other GWR cycling records.

FASTEST 100-M WHEELIE

Austen Nunes (USA) covered 100 m on the back wheel of his bicycle in 14.05 seconds in Manteca, California, USA, on March 15, 2010.

LONGEST WHEELIE IN ONE HOUR

Aaron Stannage (UK) rode a sustained bicycle wheelie for a cumulative distance of 8.17 miles (13.15 km) in an hour at the John Charles Sport Stadium in Leeds, UK, on January 17, 2010. The course measured 454 ft 8.6 in (138.6 m) long and at no time did his front wheel touch the ground.

MOST ARTISTIC CYCLING ROUNDS WITH A PERSON ON THE SHOULDERS

Carla and Henriette Hochdorfer (both Germany) carried out four consecutive artistic cycling rounds in the raiser head tube reverse/shoulder stand position on the set of *Lo Show dei Record* in Rome, Italy, on March 18, 2010.

MOST STEPS CLIMBED BY BICYCLE

On December 31, 2007, Zhang Jincheng (China), Xavi Casas (Andorra), and Javier Zapata (Colombia) climbed all 88 stories of the Jin Mao Tower in Shanghai, China, by bicycle, covering 2,008 steps in all. The number 2,008 was symbolic: the feat took place on New Year's Eve and was in recognition of the 2008 Beijing Olympic Games.

MOST WHEELIES IN ONE MINUTE

On August 1, 2010, at X Games 16 in Los Angeles, California, USA, Guadalupe Alvarez (USA) did 167 wheelies in a minute.

LONGEST JUMP WITH BACKFLIP ON A MINIMOTO

Spain's Ricardo Piedras produced a 41-ft 9-in (12.72-m) backflip on a minimoto bike on the set of *Lo Show dei Record* in Milan, Italy, on April 11, 2009.

UPDATED RECORD
NEW RECORD

To achieve the **fastest circumnavigational flight** under the Fédération Aéronautique Internationale (FAI) rules, Air France Concorde flight AF1995 traveled from JFK airport in New York, USA, eastbound on August 15 and 16, 1995, in 31 hr 27 min 49 sec.

1.9 Average number of legs per person. Why? Average = number of legs ÷ number of people. If just one person has one leg, the average is less than two. Because of unicycles, the average cycle has 1.9 wheels.

HIGHEST TIGHTROPE CROSSING BY BICYCLE

Nik Wallenda (USA) rode a bicycle across a tightrope suspended at a height of 238 ft (72.5 m) between the Royal Towers of the Atlantis Paradise Island hotel in Nassau, The Bahamas, on August 28, 2010.

SKATEBOARD

MOST KICK FLIPS IN ONE MINUTE

On May 15, 2010, Zach Kral (USA) performed a total of 29 skateboard kick flips in one minute in Waterford, Wisconsin, USA.

FASTEST TIME TO SLALOM 100 CONES

Janis Kuzmins (Latvia) slalomed through 100 cones in 20.77 seconds at Meza Park in Riga, Latvia, on September 12, 2010. Each cone was placed 5 ft 3 in (1.6 m) apart from the next.

MOST AXLE STALLS IN 30 SECONDS

Alex Sorgente (USA) made 15 axle stalls on a skateboard in 30 seconds at X Games 16 in Los Angeles, California, USA, on July 30, 2010.

MOST BACKSIDE GRINDS IN ONE MINUTE

On August 1, 2010, Annika Vrklan (USA) produced 31 backside grinds on a skateboard in one minute at X Games 16 in Los Angeles, California, USA.

MOST OLLIE 180s IN ONE MINUTE

Gray Mesa (USA) racked up 17 ollie 180s on a skateboard in a minute at X Games 16 in Los Angeles, California, USA, on July 30, 2010.

LONGEST WHEELIE ON FRONT WHEEL WITH FEET OFF PEDALS

On January 28, 2010, Shane Badman (Australia) performed a wheelie over 617 ft 9 in (188.3 m) on the front wheel of a BMX without touching the pedals. The feat took place on the set of *Australia Smashes Guinness World Records*, in Sydney, Australia.

HIGHEST INLINE SKATE DROP INTO A HALF PIPE

The record for the highest inline skate drop into a half pipe was 41 ft (12.5 m), achieved by Taïg Khris (France) during the M6 Mobile Mega Jump event in Paris, France, on May 29, 2010.

Frederick W Finn (UK) made an incredible 718 Atlantic crossings by Concorde – the **most supersonic journeys by a passenger** – before the aircraft was retired in 2003.

The **first female Beefeater** was Moira Cameron (UK), who was appointed as Yeoman Warder of Her Majesty's Royal Palace and Fortress, the Tower of London, UK, in January 2007. Beefeaters are all retired members of the armed forces.

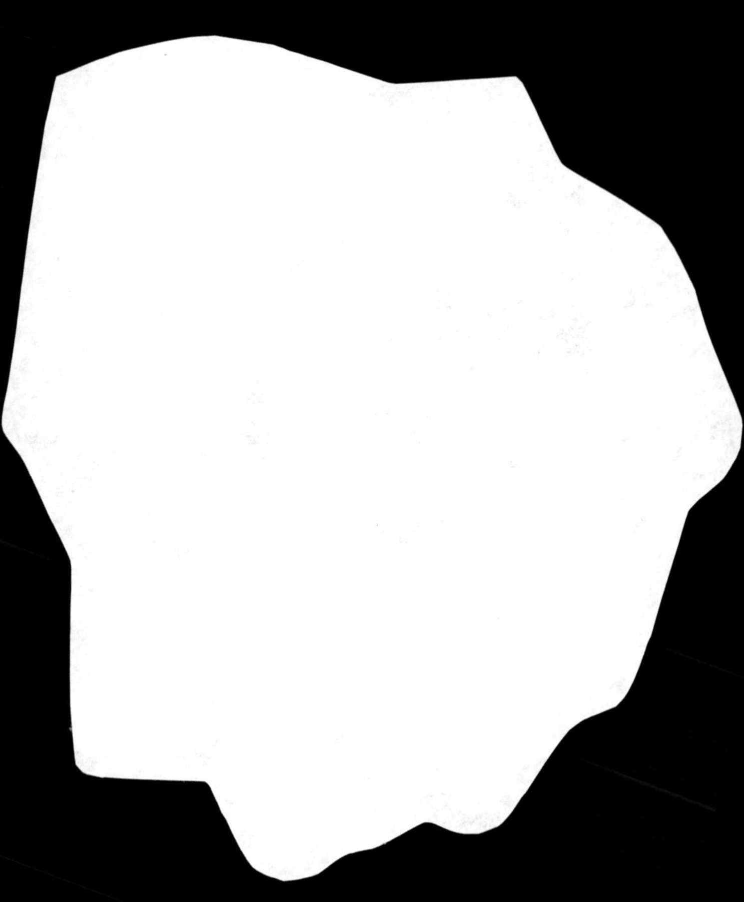

HIGHEST CABLE WALK

On January 29, 2011, Swiss high-wire artist Freddy Nock braved high winds and temperatures of 5°F (-15°C) to perform a death-defying aerial walk 10,836 ft (3,303 m) above the Silvaplana ski resort near St Moritz, Switzerland. Despite the harsh conditions, Freddy performed his stunt without a harness or safety net and covered a distance of 1,876 ft (572 m) under the watchful eyes of Guinness World Records adjudicators and photographers.

Another first for a fighting female, Sabiha Gökçen, an adopted daughter of the first President of Turkey, enrolled in the Military Aviation Academy in Eskişehir in 1936. She flew fighter and bomber planes, becoming the world's **first female combat pilot**.

Spirit of Adventure: Fact File

MOUNT EVEREST

THE FIVE-MILE-HIGH CLUB

Illustrated here is a typical route – one of many – to the top of the **highest mountain** on Earth. If you take this route via the southeast ridge, put aside about 60 days – and around $62,000. You could be on your way to the top of the world!

GODDESS OF THE SKY

STATS	
Name	English: Mount Everest; Tibetan: Chomolungma ("Goddess Mother of Mountains"); Nepalese: Sagarmatha ("Goddess of the Sky")
Elevation	29,029 ft (8,848 m) above sea level
Location	Himalayas, Nepal–China border
Coordinates	27°58'60N, 86°55'60E
Summit temperature	-4°F to -31°F (-20°C to -35°C)
Summit wind speed	Up to 174 mi/h (280 km/h); average of one hurricane every four days

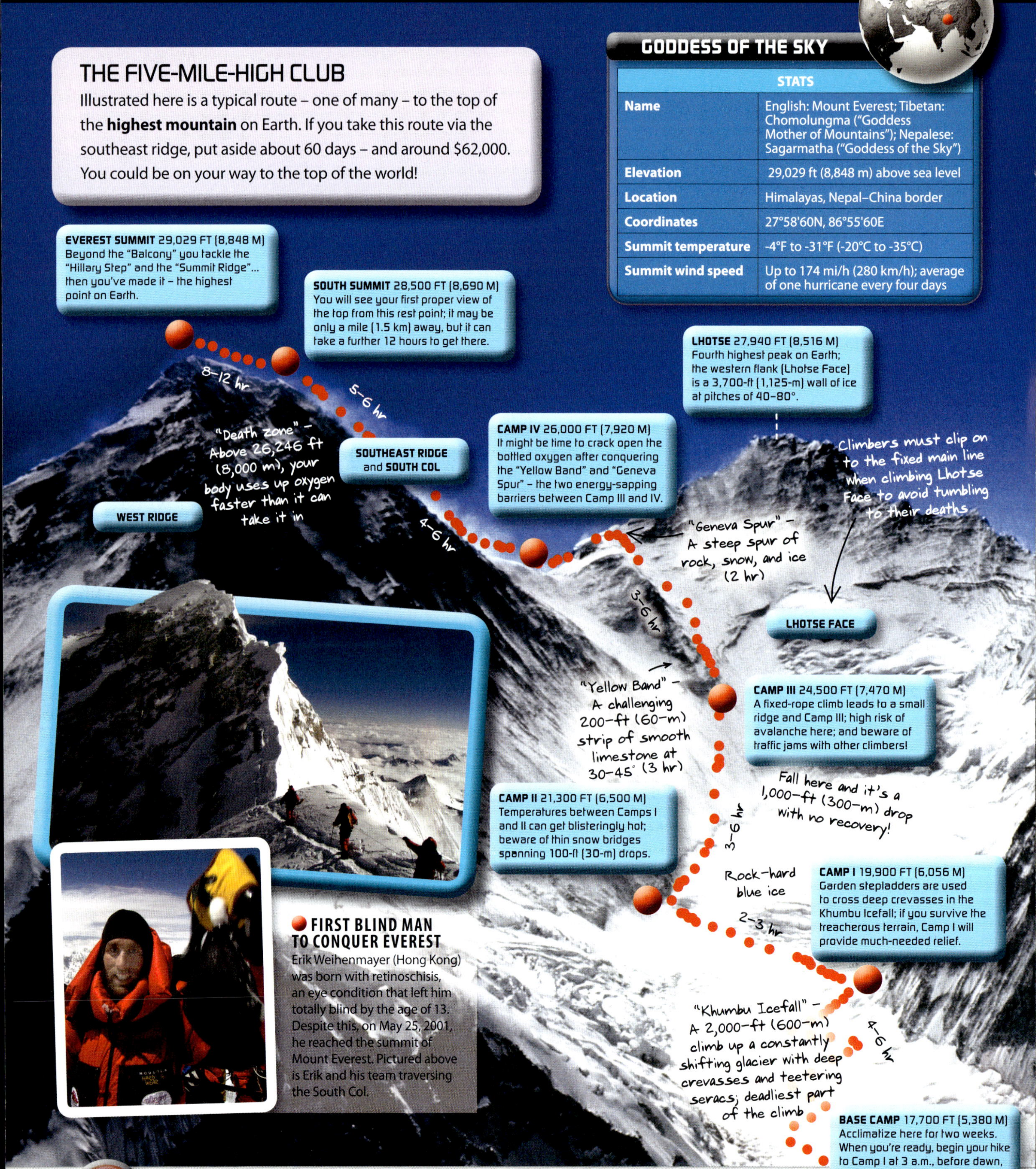

EVEREST SUMMIT 29,029 FT (8,848 M)
Beyond the "Balcony" you tackle the "Hillary Step" and the "Summit Ridge"... then you've made it – the highest point on Earth.

SOUTH SUMMIT 28,500 FT (8,690 M)
You will see your first proper view of the top from this rest point; it may be only a mile (1.5 km) away, but it can take a further 12 hours to get there.

LHOTSE 27,940 FT (8,516 M)
Fourth highest peak on Earth; the western flank (Lhotse Face) is a 3,700-ft (1,125-m) wall of ice at pitches of 40–80°.

CAMP IV 26,000 FT (7,920 M)
It might be time to crack open the bottled oxygen after conquering the "Yellow Band" and "Geneva Spur" – the two energy-sapping barriers between Camp III and IV.

CAMP III 24,500 FT (7,470 M)
A fixed-rope climb leads to a small ridge and Camp III; high risk of avalanche here; and beware of traffic jams with other climbers!

CAMP II 21,300 FT (6,500 M)
Temperatures between Camps I and II can get blisteringly hot; beware of thin snow bridges spanning 100-ft (30-m) drops.

CAMP I 19,900 FT (6,056 M)
Garden stepladders are used to cross deep crevasses in the Khumbu Icefall; if you survive the treacherous terrain, Camp I will provide much-needed relief.

BASE CAMP 17,700 FT (5,380 M)
Acclimatize here for two weeks. When you're ready, begin your hike to Camp I at 3 a.m., before dawn, when the ice is at its most solid.

FIRST BLIND MAN TO CONQUER EVEREST

Erik Weihenmayer (Hong Kong) was born with retinoschisis, an eye condition that left him totally blind by the age of 13. Despite this, on May 25, 2001, he reached the summit of Mount Everest. Pictured above is Erik and his team traversing the South Col.

The **largest consumers of bread per capita** are the Turks, who eat 440 lb (199.6 kg) of it each year – more than three times their own body weight.

MOST DEATHS ON EVEREST IN A DAY

On May 10, 1996, a severe blizzard on Mount Everest claimed the lives of eight climbers and caused serious injuries to more than 20 others. The climbers, from the USA, India, Japan, and New Zealand, were surprised by 90 mi/h (145 km/h) winds that sent temperatures plummeting to -40°F (-40°C).

Pictured right is Dr Seaborn "Beck" Weathers (USA), who was trapped on the South Col for 16 hours and who lost his right hand, part of his left hand, and his nose to frostbite.

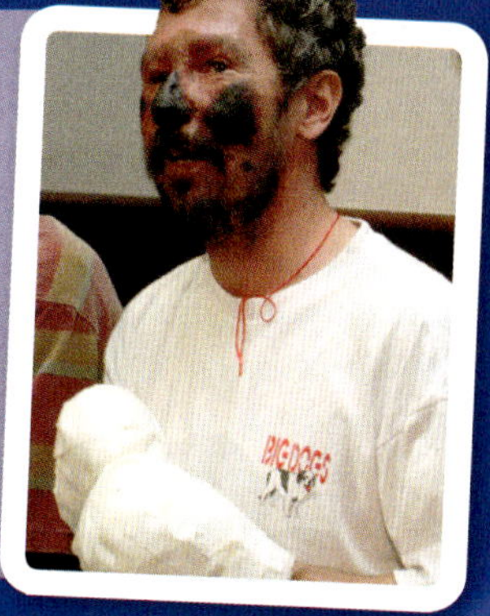

NUPTSE 25,790 FT (7,861 M)
Seven-peaked ridge along the Lhotse-Nuptse massif to the west-southwest of Everest.

UPDATED RECORD
NEW RECORD

GLOBAL WARNING

Apa Sherpa (see below) has talked passionately about how Everest has changed over the past 20 years – the warming planet has made the peak increasingly difficult to climb, he believes.

MOST CONQUESTS OF MOUNT EVEREST

Apa Sherpa (Nepal, b. Lhakpa Tenzing Sherpa) reached the summit of Everest for the 20th time on May 21, 2010, the most times anyone has ever successfully climbed the world's highest mountain. His first successful ascent was on May 10, 1990 as part of an international expedition alongside Peter and Edmund Hillary, sons of the mountain's first conqueror, Edmund Hillary (see right).

COLONEL SIR GEORGE EVEREST (UK, 1790–1866): Surveyor-General of India after whom the mountain is named (pronounced EVE-rest). Prior to this, the peak was known to the Brits simply as PEAK XV.

THEODOLITE: This large, unwieldy measuring device was used to assess Everest's height in 1856. It gave a reading documented as 29,002 ft (8,840 m).

EDMUND HILLARY & TENZING NORGAY: The New Zealand climber and Nepalese Sherpa were confirmed as the first people to reach the summit of Everest, on May 29, 1953. The expedition was led by Colonel Henry Cecil John Hunt (UK).

JUNKO TABEI (Japan, b. Sep 22, 1939): The first woman to summit Everest, on May 16, 1975, and the first female to reach the peak of the highest points on each continent (the Seven Summits). See p.122–23 for more Seven Summits achievements.

GEORGE MALLORY (UK, 1886–1924): Why climb Mount Everest? "Because it's there," said this English mountaineer famously. Part of the first three British attempts to scale Everest in the 1920s, Mallory was last seen alive close to the summit. Did he make it and die on the descent? We may never know...

FANTASTIC VOYAGES

FIRST PERSON TO WALK THE LENGTH OF THE AMAZON

On August 9, 2010, Edward Stafford (UK) finished his walk along the length of the Amazon river in South America. The trip took him 2 years, 4 months, and 8 days (860 days in total).

FARTHEST DISTANCE NORDIC WALKING IN 24 HOURS

Walter Geckle (Austria) covered 108 miles (175 km) while Nordic walking in Unzmarkt, Austria, on August 14–15, 2010. Helpfully, he is a former world champion in the sport.

MOST COMPLETED JOURNEYS FROM LAND'S END TO JOHN O'GROATS

The greatest number of journeys from Land's End to John o'Groats (and vice versa) is 20, by John Taylor (Australia) – cycling, driving, or on foot – from January 14, 1980 to May 18, 2009.

FASTEST JOURNEYS

JOHN O'GROATS TO LAND'S END ON FOOT

Andrew Rivett (UK) ran between Great Britain's most extreme points in 9 days 2 hr 26 min from May 4 to 13, 2002.

The **fastest confirmed journey from Land's End to John o'Groats on foot by a woman** is 12 days 15 hr 46 min 35 sec, by Marina Anderson (UK) from July 16 to 28, 2008.

CROSSING AMERICA ON FOOT

Frank Giannino, Jr (USA) ran 3,100 miles (4,989 km) from San Francisco to New York City (both USA) in 46 days 8 hr 36 min from September 1 to October 17, 1980.

The **fastest time to cross America on foot by a woman** is 69 days 2 hr 40 min, by Mavis Hutchinson (South Africa) from March 12 to May 21, 1978.

CYCLING THE LENGTH OF SOUTH AMERICA

Giampietro Marion (Italy) cycled the South American portion of the Pan-American Highway, from Chigorodo, Colombia, to Ushuaia, Argentina, in 59 days between September 17 and November 15, 2000.

CROSSING CANADA ON FOOT

From June 21 to September 1, 1991, Al Howie (UK) ran from St John's, Newfoundland, to Victoria, British Columbia – 4,533.2 miles (7,295.5 km) – in 72 days 10 hr 23 min.

FASTEST TIME FROM PERTH TO SYDNEY BY HANDCYCLE (RELAY)

Thomas Bechter, Philipp Bonadimann, Jürgen Egle, and Wolfgang Wimmer (all Austria) traveled across Australia by handcycle, in relay, from Perth to Sydney in 6 days 10 hr 42 min. The feat took place between October 16 and 23, 2010, in the Race Across Australia (RAAUS) charity event.

ROYAL LAUNCH

The **first royal in space** was Prince Abdulaziz al-Saud, a nephew of King Fahd of Saudi Arabia. The Prince flew as part of the crew of the *Discovery* on flight STS 51G in 1985.

THE FOUR CYCLISTS COVERED 2,505 MILES (4,031 KM) IN ALL

The **largest ceramic mosaic** has an area of 16,901 ft² (1,570.2 m²) and was constructed by Nguyen Thu Thuy (Vietnam), with the help of 35 artists, on the walls of the Red River Dyke in Hanoi, Vietnam, on October 5, 2010.

Ann Keane (Canada) ran across Canada from St John's, Newfoundland, to Tofino, British Columbia, in 143 days from April 17 to September 8, 2002, the **fastest crossing of Canada on foot by a woman**. She covered 4,866 miles (7,831 km) and ran for all but three of the days.

CROSSING AUSTRALIA ON FOOT

Donnie Maclurcan (Australia) ran across the Australian continental mainland from Cottesloe Beach, Perth, Western Australia, to Bondi Beach, Sydney, New South Wales, in 67 days 2 hr 57 min between January 5 and March 13, 2002.

FARTHEST JOURNEYS

BY BUS

Between November 6, 1988 and December 3, 1989, Hughie Thompson, John Weston, and Richard Steel (all UK) covered 54,289 miles (87,367 km) and a total of 18 countries in the "World Bus," a red London Routemaster double-decker.

BY AUTOMOBILE

Emil and Liliana Schmid (Switzerland) have covered 407,618 miles (656,000 km) in their Toyota Land Cruiser since October 16, 1984, crossing 169 countries and territories in the process.

BY AIRBOAT

Bill Fadeley and Eugene Hajtovik (both USA) completed a 1,100-mile (1,770.28-km), 13-day trip by airboat along the Intracoastal Waterway from Jacksonville, Florida, to the Statue of Liberty in New York, USA, on July 3, 1986. They made their "Ride to Liberty" on the 16-ft (5-m), 350-hp *Miss Jacksonville* and reached the iconic statue in time to celebrate its restoration and centennial.

BY DRAGON BOAT

Team Beauties & Barnacles (USA) sailed 294 nautical miles (339 miles; 545 km) down the Missouri river by Chinese dragon boat, starting at Kaw Point, Kansas City, and ending in St Charles, Missouri, USA, on August 24–25, 2010.

BY KITE-SKI (24 HOURS)

On June 5, 2010, Eric McNair-Landry (Canada) and Sebastian Copeland (USA/France) kite-skied 370 miles (595 km) in 24 hours during their 43-day expedition to cross the 1,429-mile-long (2,300-km) Greenland icecap from Narsarsuaq in the south to Qaanaaq in the north. They reached speeds of 46 mi/h (60 km/h), beating the previous record of 315 miles (507.5 km) by Hugo Rolf Hansen and Bjørn Einar Bjartnes (both Norway), set on July 2, 2009.

BY LAWNMOWER

Gary Hatter (USA) covered 14,594.5 miles (23,487.5 km) in 260 consecutive days on the back of his Kubota BX2200-60 lawnmower. He started in Portland, Maine, on May 31, 2000 and passed through all 48 contiguous US states, as well as Canada and Mexico, before arriving in Daytona Beach, Florida, on February 14, 2001.

GREATEST DISTANCE BY CANOE/KAYAK IN 24 HOURS ON FLOWING WATER (FEMALE)

Katherine Pfefferkorn (USA) paddled 192.1 miles (309.1 km) down the Missouri river, USA, in 24 hours on May 29–30, 2010. It took Katherine just 9.5 hours to beat the previous record.

BY MOTORCYCLE

Between 1985 and 1995, Emilio Scotto (Argentina) made a 457,000-mile (735,000-km) trip by motorcycle, taking in 214 countries.

BY MOTORCYCLE IN A SINGLE COUNTRY

The longest continual motorbike ride within one country is 10,095 miles (16,240 km) by Ryan and Colin Pyle (both Canada), who toured China between August 16 and October 17, 2010. The brothers started and finished their expedition in Shanghai.

BY PADDLEBOARD

From May 19 to 27, 2007, Wyatt Werneth (USA) traveled up the coast of Florida, USA, on a paddleboard for a distance of 345 miles (555 km).

RIDE OF A LIFETIME
Rob's record-breaking skate was just a small part of a 12,427-mile (20,000-km) multi-leg trip he made from Switzerland to China by bike, raft, sailboat, and train!

LONGEST JOURNEY BY SKATEBOARD

Rob Thomson (New Zealand) traveled 7,555 miles (12,159 km) on his skateboard, starting in Leysin, Switzerland, on June 24, 2007 and finishing in Shanghai, China, on September 28, 2008.

UPDATED RECORD
NEW RECORD

The **largest marble mosaic** measured 27 ft 2.77 in (8.3 m) high and 17 ft 4.66 in (5.3 m) wide. It was an image of His Majesty Sultan Qaboos bin Said of Oman, produced by Sablat Oman (Oman) in collaboration with more than 40 artists.

CLIMBING MOUNTAINS

OLDEST PERSON TO CLIMB THE SEVEN SUMMITS

On 22 April 2007, at the age of 73 years 357 days, Ramón Blanco (Spain) reached the tip of the Carstensz Pyramid in Indonesia, making him the oldest person to climb the highest peaks on each of the seven continents. The project took Ramón 31 years 114 days to complete.

FASTEST TIME TO CLIMB THE HIGHEST PEAKS IN ALL AFRICAN COUNTRIES

Five years after he set out to climb the greatest peaks in each African country, Eamon "Ginge" Fullen (UK) completed his feat when he reached the Bikku Bitti Peak, Libya, on 25 December 2005.

OLDEST MAN TO CLIMB MOUNT KILIMANJARO

On 14 July 2010, George Solt (UK, b. 28 September 1927) reached the summit of Mount Kilimanjaro, Tanzania, aged 82 years 289 days. He made the journey with his son, daughter-in-law and three grandchildren. It took him from 9 to 14 July to reach the summit, after which he descended to the starting gate on 16 July.

FIRST ASCENT OF K2

On 31 July 1954, Italians Achille Compagnoni and Lino Lacedelli completed the earliest ascent of K2, which at 8,611 m (28,251 ft) is the world's second-highest mountain. They were part of an Italian expedition led by Ardito Desio. K2 is situated in the Karakoram range on the border between Pakistan and China.

Wanda Rutkiewicz (Poland) became the **first woman to climb K2**, on 23 June 1986.

UP UNDER

The Seven Summits are the highest points on each continent (see list opposite). If Australia is considered a continent, Mount Kosciuszko is listed instead of Carstensz – despite being only 2,228 m (7,310 ft).

DEADLIEST MOUNTAIN TO CLIMB

Annapurna I (pictured), in the 55-km-long (34-mile) Annapurna massif, has been climbed by 130 people, 53 of whom died along the way, giving the peak a 41% mortality rate. On 28 October 2007, Tomaz Humar (Slovenia) became the **first person to climb Annapurna I solo**. He climbed a new route along the right side of the south face in pure "alpine" style – i.e., he carried all his equipment and food with him.

FIRST PERSON TO CLIMB ALL 8,000-M PEAKS

Reinhold Messner (Italy) became the first person to climb the world's 14 peaks above 8,000 m (26,246 ft) when he summitted Lhotse (8,501 m; 27,890 ft), on the Nepal/Tibet border, on 16 October 1986. His quest had started in June 1970, and the difficulty of his achievement is illustrated by the fact that, 20 years later, only 12 people had achieved it.

Messner was also the **first person to climb Mount Everest solo**, reaching the summit on 20 August 1980. It took him three days to make the ascent from his base camp at 6,500 m (21,325 ft). The climb was made all the more difficult by the fact that he did not use bottled oxygen.

Accompanied by Peter Habeler (Austria), Messner also completed the **first oxygen-less ascent of Mount Everest**, on 8 May 1978.

OLDEST PERSON TO CLIMB MOUNT EVEREST

According to the Senior Citizen Mount Everest Expedition (SECEE), Min Bahadur Sherchan (Nepal, b. 20 June 1931) reached the highest point on Earth on 25 May 2008 at the age of 76 years 340 days.

FIRST MARRIED COUPLE TO CLIMB MOUNT EVEREST

Phil and Susan Ershler (USA) reached the summit of Mount Everest on 16 May 2002 – the same day that a record 54 people (including the Ershlers) reached the top. The couple have also scaled the highest peaks on every one of the world's seven continents.

FIRST EXPLORERS' GRAND SLAM

Young-Seok Park (South Korea) reached the North Pole on foot on 30 April 2005, becoming the first person to achieve the explorers' grand slam. This feat involves climbing the highest peaks on all seven continents (the Seven Summits), the 14 peaks over 8,000 m (26,246 ft), and reaching the North and South Poles on foot. His quest began when he summitted Mount Everest on 16 May 1993.

FIRST ADVENTURERS' GRAND SLAM

The adventurers' grand slam involves climbing the highest peak on every continent and trekking to all four poles (magnetic and geographical). David Hempleman-Adams (UK) began this challenge in 1980 by climbing Mount McKinley in Alaska, USA. He completed the feat 18 years later when he and Rune Gjeldnes (Norway) walked to the North Pole from March to May 1998.

FASTEST TIME TO CLIMB THE SEVEN SUMMITS

Henrik Kristiansen (Denmark) climbed the highest peak on each of the seven continents in a record time of 136 days, between 21 January 2008, when he ascended Mount Vinson in Antarctica, and 5 June 2008, when he conquered Mount McKinley in Alaska, USA.

The **longest distance driven on a motorcycle in 24 hours** is 2,127 km (1,321 miles), by Omar Hilal Al-Mamari (Oman) on a sealed-off road between Marmool and Thamrait in Oman between 18 and 19 August 2009.

LARGEST CLEAR-UP ON MOUNT EVEREST

Since 2008, the Nepali Eco Everest Expeditions have seen annual trips to the world's highest mountain to clear away rubbish from previous climbs, removing 12,000 kg (26,450 lb) of ropes, tents, food packaging, oxygen bottles, gas canisters and other discarded gear. The 2008 expedition saw the removal of 965 kg (2,120 lb) of refuse. A record 6,000 kg (13,225 lb) – including 700 kg (1,540 lb) of debris from a helicopter that had crashed in 1973 and 115 kg (253 lb) of human waste – was cleared in 2009, and 5,000 kg (11,020 lb) of rubbish was removed in 2010. This latest clean-up expedition was led by Apa Sherpa (Nepal).

THE SEVEN SUMMITS

The highest peak on each of the seven continents according to alpinist Reinhold Messner...

Africa: Mount Kilimanjaro, Tanzania – 5,894 m (19,340 ft)

Antarctica: Vinson Massif, Ellsworth Land – 5,140 m (16,863 ft)

Asia: Mount Everest, Nepal/China – 8,848 m (29,029 ft)

Europe: Mount Elbrus, Russia – 5,642 m (18,510 ft)

North/Central America: Mount McKinley, USA – 6,194 m (20,320 ft)

Oceania: Carstensz Pyramid (Puncak Jaya), Indonesia – 4,884 m (16,024 ft)

South America: Cerro Aconcagua, Argentina – 6,960 m (22,834 ft)

MOST ASCENTS OF MOUNT EVEREST BY A WOMAN

Lakpa Sherpa (Nepal) reached the summit of Everest for a record fifth time on 2 June 2005, completing the climb alongside her husband, George Demarescu (USA), who was making his seventh ascent of the world's **highest mountain**. Lakpa made her first ascent in 2000, and her second in 2001. In 2003, she climbed with her sister Ming Kipa Sherpa, who was just 15 at the time. Her 2004 summit was her first with her husband.

FASTEST ASCENTS OF MOUNT EVEREST

Hans Kammerlander (Italy) completed the **fastest ascent of Mount Everest on the north side**, making the climb from base camp to the summit in 16 hr 45 min on 23–24 May 1996.

Pemba Dorje Sherpa (Nepal) climbed from base camp to the summit of Everest on the south side in 8 hr 10 min on 21 May 2004. This is the **fastest ascent of Mount Everest** by any route.

FIRST PERSON TO CLIMB THE SEVEN SUMMITS

The first person to reach the highest points on each of the seven continents was Richard "Dick" Bass (USA), who did so on 30 April 1985. The "Bass List", as it is known, counts Mount Kosciuszko as the highest point in Australasia; however, Reinhold Messner suggested that Puncak Jaya (aka the Carstensz Pyramid) in Indonesia should be climbed, in which case the "first" record goes to Patrick Morrow (Canada), who completed Messner's list on 5 August 1986.

OLDEST FEMALE TO CLIMB THE SEVEN SUMMITS

Caroline (Kay) LeClaire (USA, b. 8 March 1949) completed her last Seven Summit climb when she reached the summit of Mount Everest on 23 May 2009, aged 60 years 77 days. A nurse, competitive ballroom dancer and mother, Kay did not take up climbing until she was 51 years old.

YOUNGEST PERSON TO CLIMB THE SEVEN SUMMITS

John Carl "Johnny" Collison (USA, b. 29 March 1992) took exactly one year to climb the Seven Summits, reaching his seventh peak – the Vinson Massif in Antarctica – on 18 January 2010 at the age of just 17 years 295 days.

The youngest person to climb the Seven Summits *plus* Mount Kosciuszko in Australia is Robert "R C" Scull II (USA, b. 16 March 1987), who was 21 years 292 days old when he summitted the Carstensz Pyramid.

YOUNGEST FEMALE TO CLIMB THE SEVEN SUMMITS

Samantha Larson (USA, b. 7 October 1988) is the youngest female to have climbed all seven summits (see above right). She reached the seventh and final peak, the Carstensz Pyramid, on 4 August 2007, aged 18 years 301 days.

TIP-TOP POP

Samantha climbed the Seven Summits alongside her dad David, which makes them the first father-and-daughter team to do so. Samantha also became the youngest non-Nepalese female to conquer Everest.

UPDATED RECORD
NEW RECORD

Manrique Saenz Cruz (Colombia) performed the **longest non-stop motorcycle ride with no hands**, driving his Honda 125 XL – without a break and without touching the handlebars – for 213 km (132 miles) on 25 February 2001.

EXPLORING THE POLES

FIRST UNDISPUTED OVERLAND JOURNEY TO THE NORTH POLE

The earliest indisputable attainment of the North Pole over the sea ice took place at 3 p.m. (Central Standard Time) on April 19, 1968. Ralph Plaisted (USA) led an expedition that reached the Pole after a 42-day trek in snowmobiles.

Why "undisputed"? The issue of the first person to reach the North Pole has long been a matter of controversy and debate between two American explorers and their supporters. Robert Peary, traveling with Matt Henson, indicated he had reached the North Pole on April 6, 1909; however, Frederick Cook claimed that he had done so a year earlier, on April 21, 1908. Despite investigations into the claims, neither can be unquestionably proven.

FASTEST SOLO JOURNEY TO THE SOUTH POLE (UNSUPPORTED AND UNASSISTED)

On January 13, 2011, Christian Eide (Norway) completed a solo unsupported trek to the South Pole in 24 days 1 hr 13 min. He skied an average of 29 miles (47 km) per day – although managed 56 miles (90 km) on the last day – smashing Todd Carmichael's (USA) 39-day record and setting a benchmark that many polar explorers consider near-impossible to beat. Pictured is Eide's self-portrait, reflected in the sphere of the Ceremonial South Pole.

LONGEST ARCTIC SNOW-KITING EXPEDITION (UNSUPPORTED)

UAE-based adventurer Adrian Hayes (UK) and adventurers Devon McDiarmid and Derek Crowe (both Canada) achieved a straight-line vertical crossing of the Greenland ice cap by snow kite – a distance of 1,938.67 miles (3,120 km) – in 67 days from May 20 to July 25, 2009.

FIRST SOLO EXPEDITION TO THE NORTH POLE

Naomi Uemura (Japan) became the first person to reach the North Pole solo at 4:45 a.m. GMT on May 1, 1978 after a trek across the Arctic sea ice. He had traveled 450 miles (725 km), setting out on March 7 from Cape Edward on Ellesmere Island in northern Canada.

Erling Kagge (Norway) completed the **first solo expedition to the South Pole** on January 7, 1993. His 870-mile (1,400-km) journey from Berkner Island took 50 days.

FASTEST SOLO UNSUPPORTED TREK TO THE NORTH POLE

Børge Ousland (Norway) skied his way to the North Pole from the Severnaya Zemlya archipelago in the Russian Federation without any external assistance, motorized transport, or parafoil kites in a time of 52 days, from March 2 to April 23, 1994.

FIRST PERSON TO VISIT BOTH POLES

Dr Albert Paddock Crary (USA) reached the North Pole in a Dakota aircraft on May 3, 1952. He arrived at the South Pole by Sno-Cat as part of a scientific traverse party on February 12, 1961.

The **first person to walk to both the North and the South Poles**, however, was Robert Swan (UK). He led the three-man "In the Footsteps of Scott" expedition, which reached the South Pole on January 11, 1986. Three years later, he headed the eight-man "Icewalk" trip, which arrived at the North Pole on May 14, 1989.

FASTEST TIME TO REACH BOTH POLES UNSUPPORTED

Married couple Thomas and Tina Sjögren (both Sweden) reached the South Pole on February 1, 2002, and the North Pole 117 days later, on May 29, 2002 – the shortest time taken to walk between Poles.

FIRST FEMALE TO COMPLETE THE THREE POLES CHALLENGE

Tina Sjögren's success at the Poles (above) also constitutes the first completion by a female of the Three Poles Challenge – the conquest of the North and South Poles plus Mount Everest (regarded as a "pole" owing to its inaccessibility). Prior to her polar expeditions, Tina had summited Everest on May 26, 1999.

FASTEST COMPLETION OF THE THREE POLES CHALLENGE

Adrian Hayes (UK) summited Mount Everest on May 25, 2006, reached the North Pole on April 25, 2007 (from Ward Hunt Island, Canada), and made it to the South Pole on December 28, 2007 (from the Hercules Inlet). The feat took 1 year 217 days to complete.

HEADING SOUTH

At 11 a.m. on December 14, 1911, Captain Roald Amundsen (Norway), leading a five-man party, became the **first person to reach the South Pole** after a 53-day march with dog sleds.

OLDEST PERSON TO TREK TO THE SOUTH POLE UNSUPPORTED

At the age of 63 years 309 days, Simon Murray (UK, b. March 25, 1940) completed a trek to the South Pole. He left from the Antarctic coastline near Hercules Inlet on December 2, 2003 and arrived at the Pole with his trekking partner, Pen Hadow, on January 28, 2004.

OLDEST PERSON TO VISIT THE NORTH POLE

Dorothy Davenhill Hirsch (USA, b. May 11, 1915) reached the North Pole aboard the Russian nuclear icebreaker *Yamal* on August 28, 2004 aged 89 years and 109 days.

UPDATED RECORD
NEW RECORD

Created in December 2003 by Nelson Jimenez Florez (Colombia), the **largest sandal** measures 21 ft 7 in (6.6 m) long, 6 ft 6 in (2 m) wide, and 11 ft 5 in (3.5 m) high and was designed for Diseños Ruddy of Bucaramanga, Colombia.

4.4 Weight in tons of the frozen food you'll eat during your life. Freezers keep food at 1.4°F, the point where the natural processes of ripening and rotting are put on hold. It's also the average temperature of the North Pole.

FASTEST OVERLAND JOURNEY TO THE SOUTH POLE

Using a modified 6x6 vehicle, a team of five drivers – Jason De Carteret, Andrew Regan, Richard Griffiths, Andrew Moon (all UK), and Gunni Eglisson (Iceland) – completed an overland journey to the South Pole from Patriot Hills on the Antarctic coastline in 69 hr 21 min, from December 9 to 12, 2005.

OLDEST PERSON TO SKI TO BOTH POLES

On January 18, 2007, Norbert H Kern (Germany, b. July 26, 1940) skied to the South Pole. On April 27, 2007, he also skied to the North Pole, which he reached when he was 66 years 275 days old.

OLDEST PERSON TO VISIT BOTH POLES

On April 9, 1990, Major Will Lacy (b. July 17, 1907) of Whitby, UK, journeyed to the North Pole at the age of 82 and, on December 20, 1991, the South Pole at the age of 84. On both trips, he arrived and left by light aircraft.

YOUNGEST PERSON TO VISIT BOTH POLES

Jonathan Silverman (USA, b. June 13, 1990) reached the North Pole on July 25, 1999 and the South Pole on January 10, 2002, aged 11 years 211 days.

YOUNGEST PERSON TO VISIT THE NORTH POLE

Alicia Hempleman-Adams (UK, b. November 8, 1989) stood at the geographic North Pole at the age of 8 years 173 days on May 1, 1998, the youngest person ever to have done so. She flew to the Pole to meet her father, the well-known adventurer David Hempleman-Adams (UK), at the end of his successful trek to the Pole.

YOUNGEST PERSON TO TREK TO THE SOUTH POLE

The youngest person to trek overland to the South Pole without the use of dogs or motorized vehicles is Sarah Ann McNair-Landry (Canada, b. May 9, 1986), who was 18 when she arrived at the Pole on January 11, 2005. Remarkably, she had made the 684-mile (1,100-km) kite-assisted trip as part of an unsupported expedition led by her mother Matty McNair, a professional polar-trekking guide. The expedition also featured her brother Eric (USA/Canada), who was 20 years old at the time.

Q. How many Poles does Earth have?

A. More than you'd think! As well as the geographic North and South Poles, there are also the magnetic and geomagnetic North and South Poles, which move around as the Earth's magnetic field varies, and the "Poles of Inaccessibility" – those points on land or sea farthest from geographical features.

HEADING NORTH

The **fastest unsupported trek to the North Pole by a female** is 48 days 22 hr, by Cecilie Skog (see below) with Rolf Bae and Per Henry Borch (all Norway). They reached the Pole on April 24, 2006.

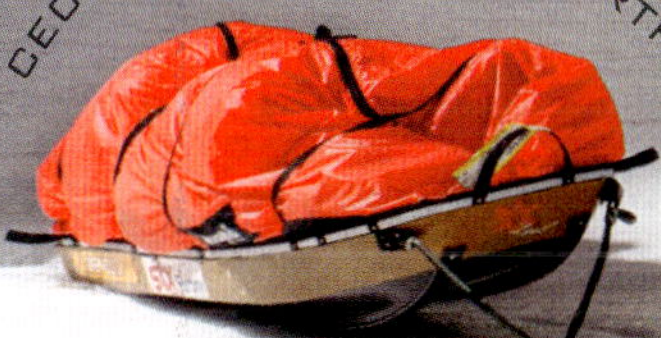

CECILIE REACHED THE NORTH POLE IN A RECORD TIME OF 48 DAYS 22 HR

FASTEST COMPLETION OF THE THREE POLES CHALLENGE (FEMALE)

Cecilie Skog (Norway) conquered Mount Everest, the North Pole, and the South Pole in 1 year 336 days. She topped Mount Everest on May 23, 2004, reached the South Pole on December 27, 2005, and finally claimed the North Pole on April 24, 2006.

No sandals for Wim Hof (Netherlands), who completed the **fastest half marathon while barefoot on ice or snow** in Oulu, Finland, in 2 hr 16 min 34 sec on January 26, 2007.

CROSSING THE OCEANS

LONGEST DISTANCE ROWED IN AN OCEAN-ROWING CAREER
Between 1974 and 1996, ocean rower Peter Bird (UK) racked up a cumulative total of 18,487 nautical miles (21,275 miles; 34,238 km) rowing the Atlantic east to west, the Pacific east to west, and the Pacific west to east.

FIRST FEMALE TO ROW OCEANS THREE TIMES
US Paralympic rower Angela Madsen crossed her first ocean with Frenchman Franck Festor during the 2007 Atlantic Rowing Race from the Canary Islands to Antigua. Following this, she became the **first woman to row the Indian Ocean**, alongside Helen Taylor (UK) in the eight-man *Aud Eamus*, crossing from Australia to Mauritius between April 28 and June 25, 2009. For her third crossing, she returned to the Atlantic in the 16-man *Big Blue*, traveling from Morocco to Barbados in the West Indies from January 15 to March 4, 2011.

FIRST PERSON TO ROW THREE OCEANS
Erden Eruç (Turkey) became the first oarsman to conquer three different oceans when he completed his crossing of the Indian Ocean from Australia to Madagascar on November 26, 2010 after 136 days 12 hr at sea. Erden had previously crossed the Atlantic from the Canary Islands to Guadeloupe (January 29 to May 5, 2006) and the Pacific from California, USA, to New Guinea (July 10, 2007 to May 17, 2008).

FIRST FEMALE TO ROW THE INDIAN OCEAN SOLO
In 2009, Sarah Outen (UK, b. May 6, 1985) became the first woman to row the Indian Ocean single-handed, making her journey on the *Serendipity* from Fremantle, Australia, to Mauritius in 124 days 14 hr 9 min from April 1 to August 3, 2009. Aged 23 years 310 days at the outset, Sarah is also the **youngest person to row the Indian Ocean solo**.

YOUNGEST PERSON TO ROW ANY OCEAN SOLO
On March 14, 2010, Katie Spotz (USA, b. April 18, 1987) rowed across the Atlantic from Senegal to Guyana. She had set off on January 3, 2010, aged just 22 years 260 days.

LONGEST OCEAN SWIM
The farthest distance ever swum in the open sea without flippers is 139.8 miles (225 km) by Veljko Rogošić (Croatia), who swam across the Adriatic Sea from Grado to Riccinoe (both Italy) in 50 hr 10 min between August 29 and 31, 2006.

FASTEST ATLANTIC ROW IN A MULTIHULL
On board the trimaran *Hallin Marine*, David Hosking, Chris Covey, Paddy Thomas, Naomi Hoogesteger, Justin Johanneson, and Jack Stonehouse (all UK) rowed the Atlantic east to west on the "Trade Winds I" route from San Miguel, Tenerife, to Barbados, West Indies, in a record 31 days 23 hr 31 min between January 6 and February 7, 2011. The crew covered 2,563 nautical miles (2,949.45 miles; 4,746.67 km) at an average overall speed of 3.34 knots (3.84 mi/h; 6.19 km/h).

DURING HER TWO CROSSINGS, ROZ COMPLETED AROUND 3.8 MILLION OARSTROKES

UPDATED RECORD
NEW RECORD

FIRST FEMALE TO ROW TWO OCEANS SOLO
British rower Roz Savage is the first woman to cross two oceans – the Atlantic and the Pacific – under her own power. On November 30, 2005, she set out across the Atlantic from the Canary Islands, arriving in Antigua, West Indies, on March 13, 2006. She started the longer Pacific crossing on May 25, 2008 and rowed in three stages from California, USA, to Madang, Papua New Guinea, arriving on June 3, 2010 after nearly 250 days at sea.

SAVAGE SEAS
Roz Savage's transpacific journey, via Hawaii and Kiribati, made her the **first solo female to row the Pacific**. However, Roz was no stranger to the ocean – her first attempt to cross it, in 2007, ended when storms capsized her three times in 24 hours.

Dennis Storm (Netherlands) holds the record for the **most bras unhooked in one minute using one hand**. Dennis detached 69 bras on the set of *Try Before You Die* in Amsterdam, the Netherlands, on August 17, 2008.

FASTEST ATLANTIC ROW IN A MONOHULL

The fastest east–west transatlantic crossing via the "Trade Winds I" route was achieved by the six crew of the *Sara G* – Matt Craughwell, Graham Carlin (both UK), Thomas Cremona (Malta), Rob Byrne, Adam Burke (both Ireland), and Fiann Paul (Iceland) – who rowed 2,753 nautical miles (3,168 miles; 5,099 km) from Tarfaya, Morocco, to Barbados, West Indies, in 33 days 21 hr 46 min from January 5 to February 8, 2011, at an average overall speed of 3.38 knots (3.9 mi/h; 6.3 km/h).

FASTEST TEAM TO ROW THE ATLANTIC WEST TO EAST ("FROM USA, NEW YORK AREA")

After 114 years, the longest-standing record in the history of ocean rowing finally fell in 2010, when Leven Brown, Don Lennox (both UK), Ray Carroll (Ireland), and Livar Nysted (Faroe Islands) rowed *Artemis Investments* from New York, USA, to St Mary's, Scilly Isles, UK, in 43 days 21 hr 26 min 48 sec. Traveling from June 17 to July 31, 2010, they beat the previous record, set in 1896, by over 11 days.

OLDEST FEMALE TO ROW ANY OCEAN

Suzanne Pinto (USA, b. February 3, 1954) was 57 years 325 days old when she helped row the $126,800 12-man vessel *Britannia III* across the Atlantic east to west from Gran Canaria in the Canary Islands to Barbados in the West Indies between January 31 and March 15, 2011.

OLDEST PERSON TO ROW ANY OCEAN

Suzanne Pinto's senior by nearly a decade, Swiss/Canadian oarsman Thomas Butscher (b. June 11, 1944) was 67 years 210 days old when he joined the 16-man crew of the ocean catamaran *Big Blue* and successfully rowed the Atlantic east to west from Tarfaya in Morocco to Barbados, West Indies, in 52 days between January 15 and March 4, 2011.

FIRST TEAM OF 16 TO ROW ANY OCEAN

Thomas Butscher and Angela Madsen were joined on board *Big Blue* by skipper David Davlianidze (Georgia), Ernst Fiby (Austria), Ryan Worth, Elizabeth Koenig, Aleksandra Klimas-Mikalauskas, Louise Graff (all USA), Liam Flynn (UK), Steve Roedde, Nigel Roedde, Dylan White, Zach Scher, Charles Wilkins, Sylvain Croteau (all Canada), and Margaret Bowling (Australia). The largest crew to cross the Atlantic, they completed the trip in a speedy 47 days 18 hr.

FASTEST CROSSING OF THE PACIFIC OCEAN BY SOLAR POWER

In his solar-powered boat, *Malt's Mermaid*, Kenichi Horie (Japan) traveled 10,000 miles (16,092 km) from Salinas, Ecuador, to Tokyo, Japan, in a record time of 148 days between March 20 and August 5, 1996. The boat was built from recycled aluminum and powered by 130 ft^2 (12 m^2) of solar panels.

YOUNGEST MALE TO ROW ANY OCEAN SOLO

Aged just 23 years 175 days at the outset, Oliver Hicks (UK, b. December 3, 1981) rowed *Miss Olive, Virgin Atlantic* across the Atlantic Ocean west to east solo and unsupported between May 27 and September 28, 2005. His journey took 123 days 22 hr 8 min and covered 3,967 miles (6,384 km) from Atlantic Highlands, New Jersey, USA, to St Mary's, Scilly Isles, UK.

BORN ADVENTURER
Following his Atlantic exploits, Oliver Hicks aimed to become the first oarsman to row round Antarctica, on his custom vessel *The Flying Carrot* (pictured), but treacherous conditions in the Southern Ocean forced him to abort the journey after 95 days at sea, on April 30, 2009.

The **longest bra chain** consisted of 166,625 bras and measured 101.7 miles (163.77 km). It was created by volunteers raising money for the breast cancer charity Citizens Who Care (Australia) at the Bundaberg Show Grounds, Australia, on August 9, 2009.

CIRCUMNAVIGATION

BY AIR

FASTEST BY SCHEDULED FLIGHTS, SIX CONTINENTS

Michael Quandt (Germany), travel editor of the *Bild am Sonntag* newspaper, flew around the world aboard scheduled flights in 66 hr 31 min from July 6 to 8, 2004. The speedy journey began and ended in Singapore and went via Sydney (Australia), Los Angeles (USA), Houston (USA), Caracas (Venezuela), London (UK), Cairo (Egypt), and Kuala Lumpur (Malaysia).

Quandt's journey was five days faster than the **first solo circumnavigation by aircraft**, in a Lockheed Vega named *Winnie Mae* piloted by Wiley Post (USA) from July 15 to 22, 1933.

FIRST BY HELICOPTER VIA BOTH POLES

Flying out of Fort Worth, Texas, USA, Jennifer Murray and Colin Bodill (both UK) piloted a Bell 407 helicopter around the globe, taking in the spectacle of the North and South Poles, in 170 days 22 hr 47 min 17 sec from December 5, 2006 to May 23, 2007. In doing so, Murray added to her record for the **fastest helicopter circumnavigation by a solo female** – 99 days from May 31 to September 6, 2000.

FASTEST BY MICROLIGHT

In 2000, Colin Bodill rounded the globe in his Mainair Blade 912 Flexwing microlight, flying alongside Jennifer Murray, who was making a solo helicopter circumnavigation attempt (see left). The pair covered approximately 21,750 miles (35,000 km), starting and finishing together at Brooklands Airfield, Surrey, UK.

FIRST BY AIRCRAFT

Two US Army Douglas DWC seaplanes – the *Chicago*, piloted by Lt Lowell H Smith, and the *New Orleans* (left), flown by Leslie P Arnold – flew around the world in 57 "hops" from April 6 to September 28, 1924, beginning and ending in Seattle, Washington, USA.

FIRST BY BALLOON

Brian Jones (UK) and Bertrand Piccard (Switzerland) completed a nonstop circuit of the globe in March 1999, piloting their *Breitling Orbiter 3* balloon from Château d'Oex, Switzerland, to Mauritania in North Africa. The **first solo circumnavigation by balloon** was by Steve Fossett (USA), who flew his *Bud Light Spirit of Freedom* from Western Australia to Queensland, Australia, in 13 days 8 hr 33 min from June 19 to July 2, 2002.

BY SEA

MOST CONSECUTIVELY

Jon Sanders (Australia) completed a series of three consecutive nonstop solo circumnavigations in his 44 ft (13.9 m) sloop *Parry Endeavour* in 657 days from May 25, 1986 to March 13, 1988. Starting and finishing in Fremantle, Western Australia, he made one journey west and two east, covering 81,732 miles (131,535 km) – the **longest distance sailed nonstop by any vessel**.

LONGEST JOURNEY BY FIRE ENGINE

Between July 18, 2010 and April 10, 2011, Stephen Moore (UK) traveled 31,663 miles (50,957 km) around the globe in a 16-year-old Mercedes 1124 AF fire engine nicknamed "Martha" and donated by Dorset Fire and Rescue (UK). Accompanied by volunteers, Stephen visited 28 countries on five continents, beginning and ending his journey in London, UK. He received his certificate at GWR's London offices (inset).

UPDATED RECORD
NEW RECORD

The **most livestock killed by a single bolt of lightning** is 68 Jersey cows zapped at Warwick Marks's (Australia) dairy farm near Dorrigo, New South Wales, Australia, on October 31, 2005.

74,565 Length in miles of all the blood vessels in your body. If you connected all your veins, arteries, and capillaries end to end, you'd be long enough to travel round the world three times.

GUINNESS WORLD RECORDS 2012

FASTEST SOLO

Francis Joyon (France) sailed solo and nonstop around the world in 57 days 13 hr 34 min 6 sec from November 23, 2007 to January 20, 2008, in the 97-ft (29.5-m) maxi-trimaran *IDEC II*. Joyon, who began and ended his 24,170-mile (38,900-km) journey in Brest, France, beat the previous record, set by Ellen MacArthur (UK), by around 14 days.

BY LAND

FIRST ON FOOT

The first man reputed to have walked around the planet was George Matthew Schilling (USA), from 1897 to 1904. However, the first verified effort was David Kunst's (USA) 14,450-mile (23,250-km) trek across four continents between June 20, 1970 and October 5, 1974.

FIRST OVER LAND VIA BOTH POLES

Relying only on land and sea transport, Charles Burton and Ranulph Fiennes (UK) circled the world on its polar axis in three years from September 2, 1979 to August 29, 1982. Traveling southward from London, UK, the pair covered 35,000 miles (56,000 km) and twice had to brave the dangers of polar exploration.

FASTEST BY CAR

The record for the first and fastest man and woman to have circumnavigated the Earth by car covering six continents under the rules applicable in 1989 and 1991 embracing more than an equator's length of driving (24,901 road miles; 40,075 km), is held by Saloo Choudhury and his wife Neena Choudhury (both India). The journey took 69 days 19 hours 5 minutes from September 9 to November 17, 1989. The couple drove a 1989 Hindustan "Contessa Classic" starting and finishing in Delhi, India.

FASTEST POWERED-BOAT CIRCUMNAVIGATION: Crewed by volunteers, *Earthrace* circled the world in 60 days 23 hr 49 min from April 27 to June 27, 2008, starting out from Sagunto, Spain.

TURN TO P.120 FOR MORE EPIC ADVENTURES.

VINCENT CYCLED THROUGH OVER 20 COUNTRIES ON SIX CONTINENTS

ROUGH RIDE

Vincent's record ride was no picnic. Along the way, he braved floods, storms, snowdrifts, and earthquakes as well as 13 punctures, dysentry in Libya, and two arrests, in Egypt and Indonesia.

FASTEST CIRCUMNAVIGATION BY BICYCLE (MALE)

Vincent Cox (UK) completed the fastest round-the-world trip by pedal power in 163 days 6 hr 58 min from February 7 to August 1, 2010. Starting and finishing in London, UK, he cycled a distance of 18,226 miles (29,331 km) and traveled a total of 36,860 miles (59,321 km) including transfers.

The **worst lightning strike disaster** killed 91 people when LANSA Flight 508 was struck over Peru by a lightning bolt and then smashed into the Amazon rainforest on December 24, 1971. Incredibly, one passenger survived.

FLIGHTS OF FANCY

FASTEST SPEED IN A NON-SPACESHIP AIRCRAFT

On October 3, 1967, US Air Force pilot Major William J Knight (USA) hit Mach 6.7 (4,520 mi/h; 7,270 km/h) in the North American Aviation X-15A-2 over the Mojave Desert, USA. In doing so, he set an absolute human speed record that stood unbroken until exceeded by the Space Shuttle in the 1980s.

LONGEST HUMAN-POWERED FLIGHT

Kanellos Kanellopoulos (Greece) pedaled his *Daedalus 88* aircraft 71.52 miles (115.11 km) from Heraklion, Crete, to the Greek island of Santorini on April 23, 1988. His heroic flight lasted 3 hr 54 min 59 sec before strong winds broke off the plane's tail and caused it to crash into the sea just a short distance from the shore.

LONGEST FLIGHT IN A HANG GLIDER

On July 17, 2001, pilot Manfred Ruhmer (Austria) steered his hang glider a record distance of 435.33 miles (700.6 km) from Zapata to Lamesa, Texas, USA, powered by nothing but the wind.

OLDEST WING WALKER

At the spritely age of 90 years 177 days, fearless Thomas Lackey (UK, b. May 22, 1920) donned his goggles to complete a wing walk over Cirencester, Gloucestershire, UK, on November 15, 2010, for Guinness World Records Day.

CLOSEST CALYPSO PASS

A "Calypso Pass" is an aerial maneuver in which two planes fly back-to-back at high speeds. The closest pass was performed by two 71,000-hp Lockheed-Martin F-16 Falcons from the US Air Force Thunderbirds display team at the Aviation Nation Air Show 2005 held in Las Vegas, USA. Flying at a speed of 760 mi/h (1,223 km/h), the planes closed to within 18 in (45 cm) of each other – just over the height of this book.

HIGHEST FLIGHT BY A HOT-AIR BALLOON

On November 26, 2005, Vijaypat Singhania (India), a 67-year-old business tycoon and part-time adventurer, achieved the hot-air balloon altitude record in a Cameron Z-1600. In a pressurized cabin attached to a balloon the height of a 22-story building, he rose 68,986 ft (21,027 m) over Mumbai, India – twice the cruising altitude of a commercial airliner.

FIRST HOT-AIR BALLOON FLIGHTS OVER THE POLES

Ivan André Trifonov (Austria) flew a one-man Thunder and Colt Cloudhopper balloon 0.6 miles (1 km) over the geographic North Pole on April 20, 1996. Four years later, he followed this feat with the first balloon flight over the geographic South Pole, piloting a Cameron AX-60 EC-HDB into the record books alongside his two Spanish crew members.

FASTEST SPEED IN A HOT-AIR BALLOON

The greatest speed ever reached in a manned balloon is 200.23 mi/h (322.25 km/h), by Steve Fossett (USA) in his *Bud Light Spirit of Freedom* on July 1, 2002. Fossett achieved the record during his successful solo circumnavigation of the world, a feat that also saw him claim the record for the **longest solo balloon flight**, with a distance of 20,627 miles (33,195.1 km).

THE BALLOON OF THE BREITLING ORBITER 3 STOOD 180 FT (55 M) TALL WHEN FULLY INFLATED

SKY'S THE LIMIT

On April 3, 1933, RAF pilots in two aircraft – one Houston-Westland and one Westland-Wallace – completed the **first flights over Mount Everest** (29,029 ft, 8,848 m), the highest mountain in the world, scraping over it by just 100 ft (30.5 m).

LONGEST FLIGHT IN A HOT-AIR BALLOON

Between March 1 and 23, 1999, Brian Jones (UK) and Bertrand Piccard (Switzerland) undertook the longest balloon flight in history, in terms of both distance and duration. Lifting off from Chateau d'Oex, Switzerland, aboard the *Breitling Orbiter 3*, they traveled nonstop for 477 hr 47 min and covered 25,361 miles (40,814 km) on an epic journey that saw them circumnavigate the globe.

The **largest roll of toilet paper** was 5 ft 7 in (1.7 m) in diameter and was created by Kimberly-Clark Perú, in Lima, Peru, on June 7, 2008. With its 602,779 ft^2 (56,000 m^2) of surface area, it had enough paper to last the average human 100 years.

129,354 The number of dreams you'll dream in a lifetime. Although many of these will be about flying – one of the most common and exhilarating types of dream – just as many will be about falling, so brace yourself!

FIRST SUPERSONIC FLIGHT

On October 14, 1947, Captain (later Brigadier General) Charles "Chuck" Elwood Yeager (USA) became the first man to fly faster than the speed of sound, reaching Mach 1.015 (670 mi/h; 1,078 km/h) in his Bell XS-1 rocket aircraft at an altitude of 42,000 ft (12,800 m) over Lake Muroc, California, USA.

FIRST SOLO CIRCUMNAVIGATION BY AIRCRAFT WITHOUT REFUELING

From March 1 to 3, 2005, Steve Fossett (USA) flew around the world nonstop without refueling in 67 hr 1 min in the Virgin Atlantic *GlobalFlyer*, starting and finishing at Salina, Kansas, USA. The aircraft, built by Scaled Composites (USA), carried nearly 5.5 tons (5 metric tons) of fuel.

FIRST AIRCRAFT CIRCUMNAVIGATION BY AIRCRAFT WITHOUT REFUELING

Richard G Rutan and Jeana Yeager (both USA) traveled westward around the world from Edwards Air Force Base in California, USA, in 9 days 3 min 44 sec, from December 14 to 23, 1986. The duo's plane, *Voyager*, was designed and built by the same man behind Virgin's *GlobalFlyer*: Rutan's brother Burt, of Scaled Composites.

FIRST JET WING FLIGHT ACROSS THE ENGLISH CHANNEL

On September 26, 2008, Yves Rossy, a Swiss pilot and inventor known as "Jet Man," became the first person to fly across the English Channel using a jet-powered fixed wing strapped to his back. He completed the flight in 9 min 7 sec, reaching a top speed of 186 mi/h (300 km/h) propelled by four kerosene-burning jet turbines.

FIRST FLIGHT ACROSS ANTARCTICA BY SINGLE-ENGINE AIRCRAFT

RAF Squadron Leader John Lewis (UK) and three crew flew a single-engined Otter XL 710 from South Ice to Scott Base in 10 hr 58 min on January 6–7, 1958.

FIRST FLIGHT OVER THE NORTH POLE

On May 12, 1926, Arctic explorers Roald Amundsen (Norway) and Umberto Nobile (Italy) led a crew of 16 men in the world's first flight over the North Pole, achieving the feat in three days aboard a 348-ft (106-m) airship designed by Nobile himself.

FIRST MIDAIR RESCUE

Dolly Shepherd and Louie May (both UK) were part of a performing troupe who leapt from hot-air balloons wearing parachutes. However, on June 9, 1908, Louie's ripcord jammed during a jump 11,000 ft (3,352 m) above Longton, UK, and Dolly had to save her by sharing her own parachute.

YOUNGEST PERSON TO FLY SOLO AROUND THE WORLD

From March 23 to June 27, 2007, 23-year-old Barrington Irving (Jamaica/USA, b. November 11, 1983) braved snow, storms, and monsoon rains to circumnavigate the globe in his single-engine plane *Inspiration*, becoming the youngest person, and first black pilot, to achieve the feat.

INSPIRATION

When Barrington found that nobody would lend him an aircraft for his journey, he had one built instead. The Columbia 400 he flew was made entirely from donated parts and assembled for free by the Columbia Aircraft Manufacturing Company.

UPDATED RECORD
NEW RECORD

Created by jeweler Lam Sai-wing in 2001, the world's **most expensive bathroom** is located in his store in Hong Kong, China – it is made out of 24-karat gold and jewels worth HK$27 million ($3.5 million).

LARGEST POOL PARTY?

On July 4, 2010, hundreds of residents of Suining, Sichuan province, China, enjoyed perhaps the largest pool party ever, when they crowded into the local pool to escape scorching summer temperatures of over 95°F (35°C).

On June 28, 2008, Zhao Danyang (Hong Kong) paid $2.1 million for the world's **most expensive lunch date sold at auction**, with the famous US investor Warren Buffett at Smith & Wollensky's steakhouse in New York, USA.

COUNTRY WITH THE HIGHEST POPULATION

China has the world's largest population, with 1.33 billion people and counting by 2010. As global population numbers continue to rise, our planet is set to become more crowded than ever. The UN estimates that by the end of 2011, there will be 7 billion of us, rising to 9 billion by 2045 – a far cry from the 2 billion people who walked the Earth in 1930, just eight decades ago.

On November 14, 2003, another kind of buffet lunch was held in Surin Province, Thailand. During the annual elephant parade, 269 Asian elephants chomped through 110,000 lb (50 metric tons) of fruits and vegetables, making it the **largest elephant buffet**.

VILLAGE EARTH

CROWDED PLANET

According to the United Nations, the world's population will reach 7 billion on August 26, 2011 – just 12 years after the 6-billion mark was passed in 1999. Although slowing down, population growth is still heading upward, and is estimated to reach 8 billion by 2030.

Below is a map projection showing the actual landmass (top), then the same map distorted to show where the population is distributed – if we all had a fair share of the Earth, this is how our nations would have to change to accommodate us. The largest area on the map is China, which currently has the **largest population** at 1.33 billion.

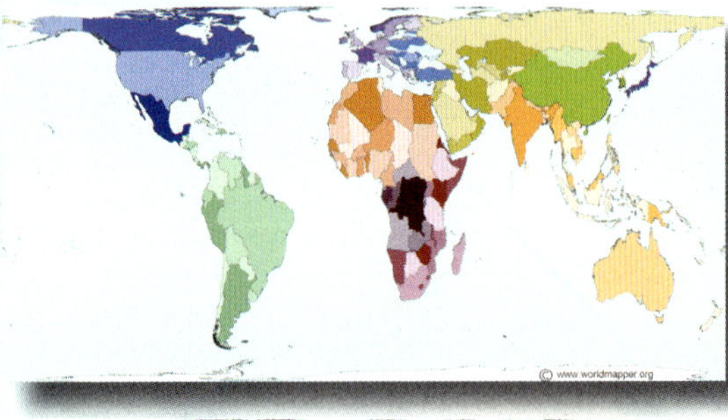

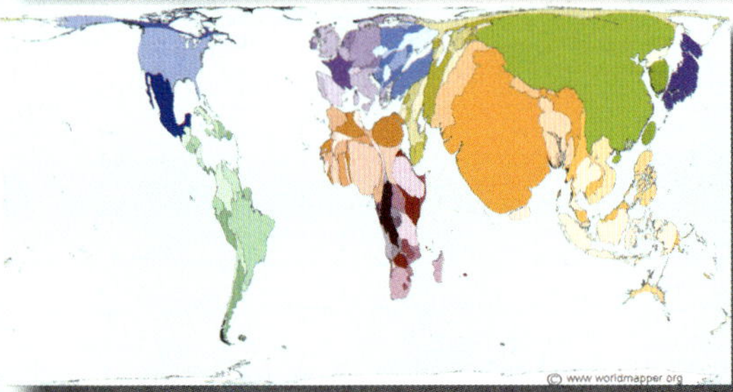

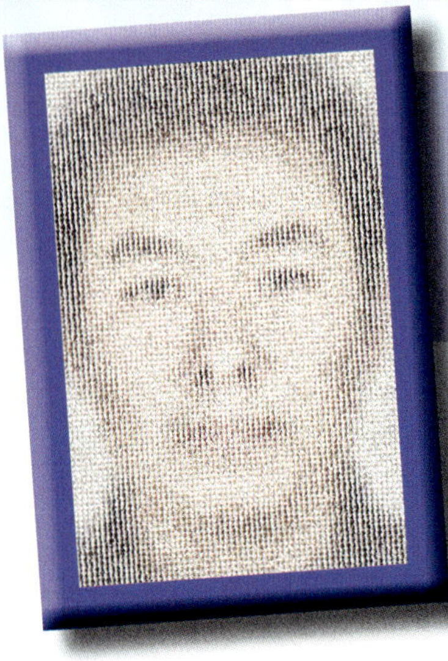

Demographics can be used to paint a picture of the ● **most typical human being**: a 28-year-old, right-handed, urban, Han Chinese male earning less than $12,000 (£7,480) a year. Pictured is a composite of 200,000 photographs of men who fit this profile, giving a face to the average human being.

100-1

This gathering of 100 people mirrors – as closely as possible – the demographics (age, sex, ethnicity, etc.) of the world today. It is only representative, however, given that half of the world lives in poverty. The real image would be somewhat different.

A HUNDRED HUMANS

Demographics is the study of human populations. Attempting to comprehend numbers – and populations – in their billions can be difficult, so here we've reduced the planet to a village of just 100 people that best represent the mix of human life on Earth. This makes the demographics easier to grasp and helps paint a picture of how our population is composed.

Sources: UN, CIA, World Bank, Population Media Center

SEX
51 are men
49 are women

EMPLOYMENT
63 work in the service sector
30 work in industry
5 work in farming
2 are unemployed

EDUCATION
17 cannot read or write

ISLE OF MANKIND

The average plot of land available to each of the 7 billion people on Earth – if surface land area is shared out equally – is 226 ft² (21,500 m²)… about the size of 82 tennis courts.

But what's the smallest space we'd need to fit us all in? Assuming 2.5 ft² (0.23 m²) per person – the typical space you're allocated in an elevator – you could squeeze all 7 billion of us on to the Isle of Skye in Scotland with a tiny bit of elbow room too! Everybody breathe in!

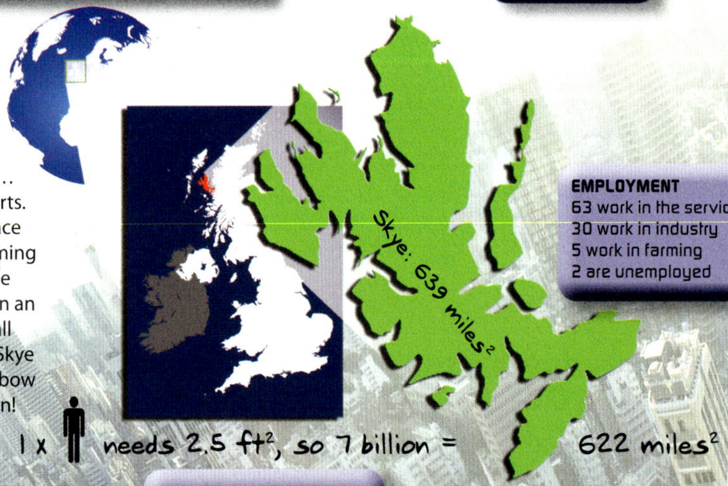

1000 BC: POP. 50 MILLION

500 BC: 100 MILLION

In October 2008, the world's **longest tunnel aquarium** opened in Chiang Mai, in northern Thailand. It measures 436 ft (133 m) long, 218 ft (66.5 m) wide and houses 8,000 aquatic animals belonging to 250 different species.

1,465 Number of gallons of milk you'll drink. And to produce it, you'd need at least one cow eating 88 lb of grass a day for the whole of your life.

MOST POPULATED CITY

While it's difficult to get global agreement on the populations (and even definitions) of cities, Tokyo (left) currently tops most lists. According to the *CIA Factbook*, 36.5 million people live in Tokyo's metropolitan area.

In terms of the population of a city's core and inner districts, the most populous is Shanghai, with 13.831 million urbanites.

BOOMING POPULATION

The graph creeping up the page charts world population against time. There are now more than twice as many people on Earth as there were 50 years ago. There's room on our planet for all these people (see below left), but we tend to concentrate ourselves into relatively small areas: there are 21 cities with more than 10 million inhabitants, and some cities are 40 times more populated today than they were 50 years ago.

2011: 7 BILLION

1999: 6 BILLION

1987: 5 BILLION

1974: 4 BILLION

1960: 3 BILLION

1930: 2 BILLION

1800: 1 BILLION

1700: 600 MILLION

1100: 300 MILLION

AD 600: POP. 200 MILLION

HIGHEST POPULATION DENSITY

The densest territory is Macau, a Special Administrative Region of China, with 50,262 people per mile² (19,450 per km²). But it's a small region – the true extent of Earth's overcrowding is told by looking at the top 10 most densely packed countries with a population over 50 million:

Country	Population	Area (miles²)	Density (per miles²)
Bangladesh	162,221,000	55,600	2,918
India	1,210,193,422	1,269,210	954
Japan	127,387,000	145,900	873
Philippines	92,226,600	115,860	796
Vietnam	85,789,573	128,066	670
UK	62,041,708	94,058	660
Germany	81,757,600	137,846	593
Pakistan	175,730,000	310,403	566
Italy	60,200,060	116,340	518
Nigeria	154,729,000	356,669	433

FIRST LANGUAGES
13 speak Chinese
5 speak Spanish
5 speak English
3 speak Arabic
3 speak Hindi
3 speak Bengali
3 speak Portuguese
2 speak Russian
2 speak Japanese
2 speak German
2 speak Javanese

TELEPHONES
18 have a telephone line
59 have a cell phone

AGES
29 are under 15
11 are over 60

RELIGION
30 are Christian
21 are Muslim
15 are nonreligious
14 are Buddhist/Eastern
12 are Hindu

INTERNET
15 have a computer
30 have internet access

HEAD COUNT

It took from the dawn of mankind until c. 1800 for the population to reach 1 billion; to reach 2 billion took just over 100 years, and 3 billion took about 90 years. To go from 6 to 7 billion took a mere 13 years.

A truly towering architectural achievement, the Burj Khalifa in Dubai, UAE, holds the record for the **building with the most floors**, with a staggering 160 stories. Make sure you use the elevator!

CRIME & PUNISHMENT

MOST HOMICIDES PER CAPITA
According to figures from the United Nations Office on Drugs and Crime, Honduras is the most dangerous country on the planet, with 60.87 homicides per 100,000 people in 2008.

MOST JUVENILE EXECUTIONS
Amnesty International has reported that in Iran in 2009 there were seven executions of juveniles – a person under the age of 18 at the time of their crime. This followed eight such executions in 2008, while today a further 133 juveniles remain at risk.

LARGEST DNA DATABASE
Between 1994 and April 2010, the FBI's (USA) National DNA Index System collected over 8.2 million offender profiles.

LARGEST DRUGS HAUL BY WEIGHT
On June 9, 2008, coalition forces in Afghanistan turned up a cannabis cache worth $443.2 million and weighing 261 tons (237 metric tons) – the equivalent of 30 double-decker buses. Found in trenches covering an area the size of two soccer pitches, the drugs were destroyed by Harrier fighter jets. In 2010, coalition forces went on to make the **largest seizure of heroin**, which weighed 6.28 tons (5.7 metric tons).

LARGEST SUPPLIER OF CANNABIS
Afghanistan produces up to 3,850 tons (3,500 metric tons) of cannabis each year, with up to 59,300 acres (24,000 ha) of land devoted to its production across 17 of the country's 34 provinces.

HIGHEST NUMBER OF POLICE OFFICERS PER CAPITA
According to the British news and international affairs publication *The Economist*, the State of Brunei has more police officers per capita than any other country in the world. For every 100,000 citizens, it has 1,074 policemen.

LARGEST SUPPLIER OF COCAINE
Colombia produces 70% of the global cocaine supply, with much coming through the Revolutionary Armed Forces of Colombia (FARC), one of the world's most powerful guerrilla armies. By 2007, Colombia had 412,666 acres (167,000 ha) in coca production, producing a potential 590 tons (535 metric tons) of pure cocaine.

MOST WANTED MAN: Following the death of Osama bin Laden in May 2011, *Forbes* identifies Mexican drug lord Joaquín 'El Chapo' Guzmán as the new most wanted man.

FIRST CAPTURED "NARCO SUB"
On July 2, 2010, Ecuadorian police seized a 102-ft-long (31-m) diesel-electric submarine from drug smugglers in a mangrove swamp just south of the Colombian border. Although smugglers had been using semisubmersible subs for 17 years, this was the first time a long-range, fully submersible vessel had been captured. It was capable of transporting 7.7–11 tons (7–10 metric tons) of cocaine with an estimated value of $100 million.

Opened in 2008, the **largest shopping mall** is the Dubai Mall, located within Downtown Dubai, UAE. Consisting of four levels with over 1,360 retail, food, and drink outlets, it has an internal floor area of 5.9 million ft^2 (548,127 m^2).

38,710,000 Homicides that will occur in the world during your lifetime. That's 490,000 every year or one every minute and is the equivalent of nearly the entire population of Kenya.

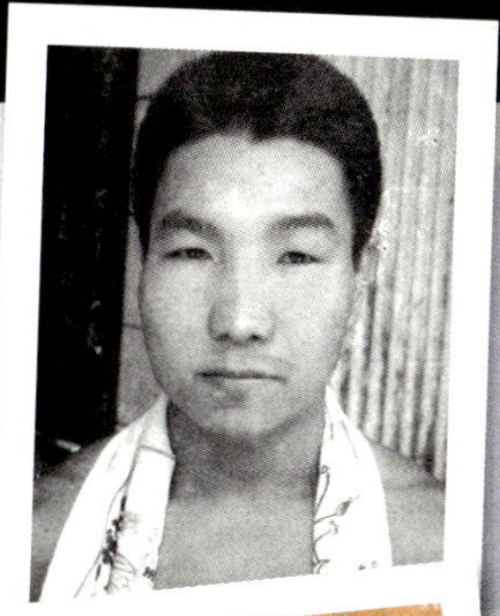

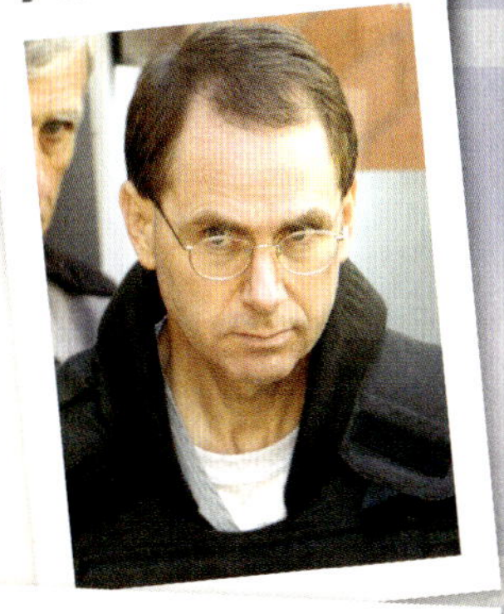

LONGEST-SERVING PRISONER ON DEATH ROW

Now 75, Iwao Hakamada (Japan) has been on death row in Japan for 42 years, convicted of murdering a family in Shizuoka in 1968.

MOST LIFE SENTENCES

Terry Lynn Nichols (USA) is serving 161 consecutive life terms without the possibility of parole for his part in the 1995 bombing of a federal building in Oklahoma, USA, in which 168 people, including 19 children, were killed.

WORST KLEPTOCRAT

President Suharto, President of Indonesia from 1967 until his regime was overthrown in 1998, looted more riches from his own country than any other government official in history, making him the world's biggest kleptocrat. In a 2004 report, Transparency International estimated that during his three decades in power he had stolen up to $35 billion. Suharto died in 2008, having never been brought to justice.

LONGEST-SERVING POLITICAL PRISONER

On May 1, 2009, Nael Barghouthi, a Palestinian sentenced to life in jail, became the longest-serving political prisoner. He began his sentence on April 4, 1978 and has now served more than 32 years in an Israeli jail. Incarcerated at the age of 21, Barghouthi has now been in jail for a decade longer than he was previously free.

LONGEST JAIL TERM

On December 23, 1994, American Charles Scott Robinson was sentenced in Oklahoma City, USA, to 30,000 years, the jury having recommended 5,000 years for each of the six counts against him.

LOWEST PRISON RATE

According to the current edition of the World Prison Population List, San Marino's 12-man prison had just a single occupier as of 2008.

OLDEST LIVING JUDGE

Born on June 22, 1907 in Kansas, USA, Judge Wesley E Brown is still presiding over courtrooms at the age of 103. If he continues for another year, he'll become the oldest federal judge in US history.

LONGEST-SERVING EXECUTIONER

William Calcraft (UK) presided over nearly every hanging carried out at Newgate Prison in London, UK, for 45 years between 1829 and 1874.

FASTEST POLICE CAR

On the road at least, the Italian police has the edge over most criminals, with a fleet of 192-mi/h (309-km/h) Lamborghini Gallardos.

FIRST COUNTRY TO USE IRIS SCANS ON ID CARDS

Mexico introduced iris-scanning to ID cards on January 24, 2011. The government says the system, which identifies a person by their unique iris pattern using a camera, is 99% reliable and is slated for full rollout by 2013. The ID card will include fingerprints and an image of the cardholder's eye.

HIGHEST RANSOM PAID FOR A SHIP

In November 2010, a ransom of $9.5 million was paid to release the *Samho Dream*, a South Korean tanker hijacked near the Gulf of Aden on April 4, 2010 carrying $170 million of crude oil.

MOST HOSTAGES TAKEN BY PIRATES

According to the International Maritime Bureau, there were 445 pirate attacks globally in 2010, with 53 vessels and a record 1,181 hostages taken. Of these hostages, 638 were the crews of the 28 vessels remaining in Somali hands at the close of the year, representing ransoms of more than $10 million.

DOUBLE TROUBLE

In 2010, policeman Andy Filton (UK) handed out a traffic ticket to a motorist in his adopted New Zealand only to discover that the offender was the same man he had fined in 2008 while still living in the UK.

UPDATED RECORD

NEW RECORD

Still with shopping, the **largest department store** is the Shinsegae Centumcity in Busan, South Korea. The store covers an area of 3.16 million ft^2 (293,905 m^2) and even contains an impressive 60-tee golf driving range!

MODERN CONFLICT

MOST SOPHISTICATED CYBER WEAPON ATTACK

In 2010, a software "worm" named Stuxnet attacked computers running software called WinCC, which runs on Microsoft Windows. Because of its complexity, experts suspect it was the work of a government agency. Around 60% of the attacks centered on Iran and its nuclear facilities (below).

LARGEST MILITARY BUDGET

According to the Stockholm International Peace Research Institute, the world spent $1,531 billion in total on defense in 2009, with the USA alone accounting for $661 billion – over 43%. The US figure is set to rise to some $739 billion by 2012.

LARGEST MILITARY BUDGET BY GDP

Although China has the most troops and the USA has the biggest defense budget, the country that spends the most on its armed forces as a proportion of gross domestic product is the Middle East state of Oman – it invests 11.4% in its military might.

LONGEST-RUNNING REPARATIONS BILL

On October 3, 2010, nearly 92 years after the end of World War I (1914–1918), Germany paid the final $94-million portion of its war reparations, compensation for the costs incurred by the Allies and the damage suffered by France and Belgium.

FIRST MODERN-DAY CLIMATE-CHANGE WAR

In Darfur, Sudan, the dramatic reduction in rainfall in the last 50 years and the southward advance of the Sahara Desert have caused the province's northern Muslims and its southern Christian/Animists to arm themselves and begin fighting for land and water.

LARGEST SUPPLIER OF FIGHTER AIRCRAFT

The USA and Russia are the largest providers of combat aircraft to the world's air forces, with the USA supplying 341 planes, and Russia 219, between 2005 and 2009. India, Israel, and the UAE were the main customers.

MOST DEATHS IN THE WAR ON DRUGS

In 2006, Mexican president Felipe Calderón initiated a military crackdown on the drugs trade. According to the Attorney General, Arturo Chavez, over 30,000 soldiers, police, civilians, and gangsters have been killed since.

MOST ENDANGERED FOOD SUPPLY

According to the Food Security Risk Index 2010, Afghanistan's ability to feed itself is threatened by war, poverty, poor infrastructure, drought, and flooding. All of the other nine nations in the top 10 are in Africa.

LONGEST AFGHAN WAR

On November 27, 2010, NATO forces exceeded the nine years and 51 days the Russians spent in Afghanistan during the 1980s. NATO forces arrived on October 7, 2001 and have now been there for nine years and 236 days to the end of May 2011. The Russians sought to prop up a communist regime facing an uprising, whereas the US and its allies entered Afghanistan to subdue the Taliban and destroy the terrorist organization Al Qaeda.

Q. Which is the world's **most landmined country?**

A. Iraq and Afghanistan each have 10 million landmines, but Egypt is blighted by 23 million, planted in World War II and the wars with Israel in 1956, 1967, and 1973.

The **largest snowball fight** involved 5,387 participants at the 17th Mount Taebaek Snow Festival, Gangwon-do, South Korea, on January 22, 2010.

UPDATED RECORD
NEW RECORD

12,646 Gallons of water you need to drink in a lifetime to stay alive. Water covers 70% of our planet, but drinking water is scarce in some parts of the world and it is likely that the wars of the future will be fought over it.

OLDEST CONTINUOUSLY OPERATING INTELLIGENCE AGENCY

Publicly acknowledged for the first time in 1994, the British Secret Intelligence Service was founded in 1909. Headquartered in London (left), it is popularly referred to as MI6 – Military Intelligence 6 – a cover name used in World War II.

NEWEST SPY AGENCY

As head of the Coalition Provisional Authority in Iraq, US diplomat Paul Bremer signed Authority No.69 in April 2004, which brought into existence the Iraqi National Intelligence Agency with the aim of preventing terrorism and protecting the country's national security.

LARGEST SPY-SWAP SINCE THE COLD WAR

On June 27, 2010, a group of 10 Russian "sleeper" agents were arrested in New York, USA, put on trial and later deported to Russia on July 8, 2010. The most notable agent, Anna Chapman (above), has subsequently gone on to become a TV celebrity in Russia.

MOST FOREIGN TROOPS DEPLOYED IN ONE COUNTRY

By December 2010, there were 131,730 troops from 48 different nations deployed under the auspices of NATO's International Security Assistance Force (ISAF) in Afghanistan to deal with the Taliban insurgency and other problems in that country. The top contributor is the USA with 90,000 personnel, which represents just over 68% of the total force.

LONGEST SNIPER KILL

British sniper Craig Harrison killed two Taliban fighters from a distance of 8,120 ft (2,474 m) in November 2009. The bullets took nearly three seconds to hit their targets.

MOST IEDS DEFUSED

During a six-month tour in Afghanistan in 2010, bomb-disposal expert Sergeant Major Karl Ley (UK) made safe 139 improvised explosive devices (IEDs) planted by the Taliban – including 42 in one day. He was awarded the George Medal on his return.

The **worst year for IED attacks in Afghanistan** was 2009, with 7,228 incidents – up 120% over 2008.

FIRST USE OF MILITARY ROBOTS IN COMBAT

Robots were first deployed in combat in Afghanistan in July 2002. "Hermes," a wheeled robot fitted with cameras, a grenade launcher, and a shotgun, was used by US troops to search a network of caves in Qiqay for enemy personnel and weaponry.

LUCKIEST SOLDIER?

In Afghanistan in 2010, Guardsman Ben Ralph (UK) was shot five times in one battle. His armor stopped two rounds, his ammo pouches stopped two more, and the fifth tore through his pants!

DEADLIEST YEAR IN THE WAR IN AFGHANISTAN

Of the 2,228 deaths among coalition forces in Afghanistan between October 2001 and January 2011, a record 711, or 32%, were killed in 2010 alone. Added to the 2,412 civilian deaths, this makes 2010 the deadliest year of the war so far.

LONGEST CEASEFIRE WITHOUT A PEACE TREATY

The Korean War between the communist North and democratic South started with the invasion of the South on June 25, 1950. After three years of fighting, a ceasefire was agreed on July 27, 1953. However, with relations worsening and no treaty in sight, the two sides are technically still at war.

The snow petrel is the **most southerly bird**, nesting up to 150 miles (240 km) inland on the continent of Antarctica.

GARDEN GIANTS

HEAVIEST FRUIT & VEG

This selection of garden produce illustrates the heaviest specimens ever grown. The actual produce is, of course, *much* bigger than what you see here – the **heaviest pumpkin** ever recorded, for example, which was grown in 2010 by Chris Stevens (USA), weighed a whopping 1,810 lb 8 oz (821.23 kg) and measured 15 ft 6 in (4.73 m) around the middle – but we'd never fit them all on one page!

MOST TOMATOES FROM ONE PLANT

Graham Tranter of Bridgnorth in Shropshire, UK, grew a single tomato stem (or "truss") that yielded a record 488 tomatoes when counted during the October 2010 harvest. Green-fingered Graham beat his own record, set the previous year at 304 tomatoes.

The **fastest, first, solo, and unaided crossing of the Antarctic continent** was made by the Norwegian Børge Ousland, who completed the 1,675-mile (2,690-km) trek on January 18, 1997, after 64 days.

13.5 Tons of vegetables you will eat – equal in weight to five medium-sized carrots a day. If all 13.5 tons were made into five giant carrots, each would be the size of a stretch limousine!

OH MY GOURD!

Chris Stevens's **heaviest pumpkin** or "gourd" (see left) weighed almost the same as an entire Premier League soccer team! It was later carved into the world's **largest jack o'-lantern**.

HEAVIEST POTATO

Peter Glazebrook (UK) is a 10-time Guinness World Record-breaker and the current holder of three giant vegetable records. In 2010, he presented a potato at the Shepton Mallet big veg competition in Somerset, UK, that tipped the scales at 8 lb 4 oz (3.76 kg) – the weight of a newborn baby!

The **first person to walk on skis to both Poles solo and unsupported** was Marek Kaminski (Poland), who reached the North Pole from Ward Hunt Island on May 23, 1995 (in 72 days) and the South Pole from Berkner Island on December 27, 1995 (in 53 days).

BIG FOOD

LARGEST SERVING OF CURRYWURST

A currywurst – a pork sausage flavored with curry powder – weighing 386 lb 4 oz (175.2 kg) and 1,049 ft 10 in (320 m) in length was made by kitchen technologists MKN (Germany) in Wolfenbüttel, Germany, on April 30, 2010.

FAST FOOD!

It would take Usain Bolt (Jamaica) – the world's **fastest man** – about 30 seconds to run the entire length of the **largest currywurst** (left).

LARGEST ICE-CREAM CONE

An ice-cream cone measuring 9 ft 2.6 in (2.81 m) tall was created over a period of 30 hours by Mirco Della Vecchia and Andrea Andrighetti (both Italy) at the Rimini Fair in Rimini, Italy, on January 21–22, 2011.

LARGEST...

BOWL OF PORRIDGE

A bowl containing 1,388 lb 14 oz (630 kg) of porridge was prepared by Cupar Round Table in association with Scott's Porage Oats (both UK) during the Cupar Highland Games in Cupar, Scotland, UK, on July 4, 2010.

BURRITO

A vast burrito prepared by CANIRAC La Paz in Baja California Sur, Mexico, on November 3, 2010, measured 1.5 miles (2.4 km) long and weighed a record 12,785 lb (5,799 kg). Despite translating from the Spanish as "little donkey," the burrito contained the typical ingredients of fish, onions, chilis, and beans.

CHOCOLATE BAR

On September 10, 2010, the Grand Candy Company of Yerevan, Armenia, unveiled a 9,722-lb (4,410-kg) chocolate bar – enough chocolate to make a solid cube with sides 5 ft (1.5 m) long!

COCKTAIL

Imagine a cocktail large enough to swim in. This is what Ricardo's Mexican

HAVE A PIZZA THAT!

Too vast even for Big Mama's and Papa's Pizzeria, the **largest pizza** ever baked was 122 ft 8 in (37.4 m) across and weighed over 13 tons (12 tonnes). It was made at Norwood Hypermarket in Norwood, South Africa, on December 8, 1990.

LARGEST PIZZA COMMERCIALLY AVAILABLE

Available on the menu at Big Mama's and Papa's Pizzeria in Los Angeles, California, USA, is an enormous 4-ft 6-in-wide (1.37-m) square pizza. Retailing at $199.99 plus tax, this mammoth meal can feed up to 100 people and can be ordered for delivery – as long as you give the pizzeria 24 hours' notice!

UPDATED RECORD
NEW RECORD

Measuring 3,314 ft 6.7 in (1,010.28 m) in length, the **longest pizza** was cooked by a team of chefs organized by MAKRO Cash and Carry Polska S.A. and Magillo restaurant (both Poland) in Krakow, Poland, on August 29, 2010.

750 Milliliters of saliva you produce every day – enough to fill a wine bottle. You need saliva to lubricate the swallowing process. A lifetime's worth of food will be accompanied by 25,348 bottles of spit!

Restaurant and Rosangel Tequila (both USA) created in Las Vegas, Nevada, USA, with their 6,350-gal (28,871-liter) margarita on October 15, 2010 – enough to fill a bathtub every day for a year.

HAMBURGER

The largest commercially available hamburger weighs 300 lb 4 oz (136.2 kg). It was available for 150,000 yen ($1,780.59) at the Phoenix Seagaia Resort in Miyazaki, Japan, as of July 4, 2009. This is the cooked-weight equivalent of a gut-busting 796 quarterpounders!

MEATBALL

A meatball weighing 749 lb 9 oz (340 kg) and with a diameter of 5 ft 3 in (1.6 m) was prepared by Spieckermann BAU GmbH (Germany) during a staff picnic at their premises in Essen-Dellwig, Germany, on May 29, 2010.

OPEN SANDWICH

A bun weighing 1,337 lb (606.45 kg) was prepared by Moore's BBQ (USA) in New Bern, North Carolina, USA, on July 4, 2010. The sandwich, made to celebrate Moore's 300th anniversary, measured 8 ft 9 in (2.6 m) x 7 ft 9 in (2.37 m) and contained 586 lb (265.81 kg) of pork.

POT OF BEANS

A pot filled with 841 gal (3,825.7 liters) of baked beans – or more than 9,000 regular cans – was prepared at the Alabama Butterbean Festival in Pinson, Alabama, USA, on September 4, 2010.

SALAD

A serving of Greek salad measuring 82 ft (25 m) in length was prepared by KEDI, the Public Benefit Municipal Enterprise of Ierapetra, on the Greek island of Crete on June 19, 2010. This super-sized salad weighed a record 29,579 lb (13,417 kg).

FALAFEL

Chef Ramzi Choueiri (pictured) and students of Al-Kafaat University (all Lebanon) produced the **largest serving of falafel** – a total weight of 11,404 lb 8 oz (5,173 kg) – in Beirut, Lebanon, on May 9, 2010.

The **largest falafel ball**, however, was prepared two weeks later by the Jewish Community Relations Council of New York and the Olympic Pita Restaurant (both USA) and weighed 24 lb (10.89 kg)!

SMOOTHIE

To celebrate the quality of their home-grown produce, the Dairy Farmers of Canada blended a 219.9-gal (1,000-liter) smoothie at the Bust-A-Record Dairy Day in Toronto, Ontario, Canada, on July 8, 2010. The ingredients included 661 lb (300 kg) of blueberries.

LARGEST OMELETTE

A 9,702-lb 8-oz (4.4–ton) omelette made from 110,000 eggs was served by Yum-Bir (the Turkish Egg Producers Association) and the Pruva Neta tourist agency (both Turkey) at the Cepa shopping mall in Ankara, Turkey, on October 8, 2010.

CUSTARD CREAMS ARE THE MOST DANGEROUS COOKIES, SAY INSURANCE COMPANIES

LARGEST CREAM-FILLED BISCUIT

The largest cream-filled biscuit (aka Custard Cream) measures 1 ft 11 in x 1 ft 3 in x 2.5 in (59 x 39 x 6.5 cm) and weighs 34 lb 10.8 oz (15.7 kg). It was crafted by Executive Chef Paul Thacker (left) and amateur biscuit master Simon Morgan (both UK) in the Chino Latino's restaurant in Park Plaza, Nottingham, UK, on November 18, 2010 for Guinness World Records Day 2010.

COOKIE AUCTION

The colossal Custard Cream took 11 hours to make and was inspired by Simon's cookie-loving children Jack, Sam, and Olivia. It was auctioned for charity, raising £410 ($646) for Children in Need.

TURN THE PAGE FOR MORE RECORD-BREAKING FOOD FUN.

New Zealander Josh Anderson ate a 12-inch (30-cm) pizza in 1 min 45.37 sec in Wellington, New Zealand, on March 22, 2008 – the **fastest time to eat a 12" pizza.**

FOOD FEATS

MOST...

COCKTAILS AVAILABLE

The menu of Pench's Cocktail Bar in Varna, Bulgaria, listed 1,244 separate cocktails as of September 23, 2010. Also on the list, but not included in the record count, are 44 nonalcoholic cocktails.

EGGS BALANCED

Ashrita Furman (USA) balanced 888 eggs on their ends at York College in New York City, USA, on June 12, 2010.

PEOPLE IN A PIE FIGHT

On November 11, 2010, 1,541 chocolate mousse pies were thrown in a fight between 671 people on the grounds of Lawrenceville School in New Jersey, USA.

LARGEST CHEESE PLATTER

On November 24, 2010, a 40-cheese platter weighing 2,474 lb 11 oz (1,122.5 kg) was prepared at the World Cheese Awards at the NEC in Birmingham, UK.

PIZZAS MADE IN 24 HOURS (TEAM)

A team from Domino's Pizza #8209, including owners Bob and Tina Leikam (all USA), made 6,838 pizzas in a day in Taft, California, USA, on October 22–23, 2010.

MOST EXPENSIVE HOT DOG

The Foot-Long Haute Dog sells for $69 at Serendipity 3 in New York City, USA. Introduced on July 23, 2010 – US National Hot Dog Day – this fantastic frankfurter is served in a pretzel bun topped with foie gras and black truffles. The record-breaking snack also comes with specially prepared premium condiments.

FAST FEEDERS

Hamburgers (3 min): Takeru Kobayashi (Japan) scoffed 10 burgers in three minutes in Madison Square, New York City, USA, on August 29, 2010.

Rice grains (3 min): Bob Blumer (Canada) ate 134 rice grains – one at a time, with chopsticks – in three minutes in Taipei, Taiwan, on August 30, 2010.

Chicken nuggets (3 min): Jordan Ryan (UK) ate 10.16 oz (287.9 g, or 17 pieces) of McDonald's chicken nuggets in three minutes at Barclay House in Manchester, UK, on November 19, 2010.

Mars bars (1 min): Pat Bertoletti and Joe Chestnut (both USA) each ate three Mars bars in a minute at the Tin Fish Restaurant in San Diego, California, USA, on July 22, 2010.

After Eights (1 min): Jim Lyngvilds (Denmark) ate nine After Eight thin mint chocolates – without using his hands – on the set of the TV show *Go'aften Danmark* in Copenhagen, Denmark, on October 1, 2010.

EXTREME BARTENDING

Flair bartending – aka "extreme bartending" or "flairtending" – was first contested in the TGI Friday's in Marina del Rey, California, USA, in the mid-1980s.

OLD-FASHIONED

The **earliest known cocktail** was a concoction of honey, apple juice, tartaric acid, and barley found in a 5,000-year-old earthenware jug on the banks of the Tigris between Iran and Iraq in 2005.

COCKTAIL FLAIRING

When it comes to cocktail flairing – in which bartenders prepare drinks with dynamic, quickfire actions to entertain customers – world champion Tom Dyer (UK) is a real mover and shaker. On January 25, 2011, Tom performed the **most consecutive bottle bumps on the elbow** – 29 – and the **most hand stalls in one minute** – 108 – both in London, UK. He even has his own bartending school.

UPDATED RECORD
NEW RECORD

The **largest game of leapfrog** involved 1,348 schoolchildren in an event organized at the Canterbury A&P Show (New Zealand) in Christchurch, New Zealand, on November 11, 2010.

FOR ART OF A MORE CONVENTIONAL NATURE, SEE P.226.

75 Tons of food you will eat in a lifetime. If you bought it all in one mammoth shopping trip, it would fill 1,511 shopping carts, forming a line 0.7 miles long at the checkout.

FASTEST TIME TO...

CARVE A FACE INTO A PUMPKIN

David Finkle (UK) cut the likeness of a face into a pumpkin in 20.1 seconds for the BBC's *Countryfile* program, in Colchester, UK, on October 7, 2010.

The **fastest time to carve one metric ton (1.1 tons) of pumpkins** is 3 hr 33 min 49 sec, achieved by Stephen Clarke (USA) at Harrah's Casino Resort, Atlantic City, New Jersey, USA, on October 29, 2008.

MAKE ONE LITER OF ICE CREAM

On June 6, 2010, Andrew Ross (UK) made a liter (just over one quart) of ice-cream in 10.34 seconds in Sheffield, South Yorkshire, UK. The ingredients included cream, vanilla, sugar, and liquid nitrogen.

PEEL AND EAT THREE ORANGES

In just 1 min 16 sec, Tekiner Sonkurt (Turkey) peeled and ate three oranges at the GWR Live! Roadshow at Forum Mersin, in Mersin, Turkey, on June 20, 2010.

SHELL A BOILED EGG

Serial record-breaker Alastair Galpin (New Zealand) took 18.95 seconds to shell one unpricked boiled egg at the Trusts Stadium in Waitakere, Auckland, New Zealand, on November 14, 2009.

LARGEST...

MENTOS AND SODA FOUNTAIN

Perfetti Van Melle (Philippines) organized for 2,865 Mentos and soda fountains to be launched at the SM Mall of Asia Complex in Manila, the Philippines, on October 17, 2010.

SERVING OF FRIED CHICKEN

The Canoefest Fryers Club (USA) dished up 1,645 lb (746.16 kg) of fried chicken in Brookville, Indiana, USA, on July 2, 2010.

SERVING OF PARMIGIANA

On August 7, 2010, Nuova Solidarietà (Italy) served up 833 lb 5 oz (378 kg) of the Italian dish parmigiana in Reggio Calabria, Italy.

SUSHI MOSAIC

Featuring 8,374 pieces of sushi, and using 264 lb 8 oz (120 kg) of rice and 143 lb 4 oz (65 kg) of salmon, cod, mackerel, and prawns, the largest sushi mosaic is 216.67 ft^2 (20.13 m^2) in area. It was created by the Norwegian Seafood Export Council (Norway) with the help of the student chefs from Zhonghua Vocational School in Shanghai (China) at the 2010 World Expo Shanghai China, on October 15, 2010.

FASTEST TIME TO EAT TWO BAGS OF WATERCRESS

Sam Batho (UK) scoffed two 3-oz (85-g) bags of watercress in 49.69 seconds at the Watercress Festival 2010 in Alresford, UK, on May 16, 2010. His winning technique? Swallowing one bag at a time, with large gulps of water.

HIGH-FLYING FOOD

The **highest pancake toss** measured 30 ft 1 in (9.17 m) and was thrown by Dominic Cuzzacrea (USA) at the Palace Theater in Lockport, New York, USA, on June 22, 2010.

GWR presents the world of crazy cookery:

Longest cooking marathon (individual)
24 hr 30 min 12 sec, by Dr Chef K Damodaran (India) at the Savera hotel in Chennai, India, on December 22, 2010.

Largest cookery lesson
440 participants, organized by Stichting Helioskoop in Beverijk, the Netherlands, on March 30, 2009.

Most people cooking simultaneously
105, by Maison Malesan (France) in Salon de l'Escale, Yachts de Paris, Paris, France, on September 25, 2010.

LARGEST TOAST MOSAIC

Laura Hadland (UK) and 27 friends made a 1,387.31-ft^2 (121.05-m^2) mosaic from toast at Parr Hall in The Pyramid Centre, Warrington, UK, on October 17, 2010. It depicts Sandra Whitfield, Laura's mother-in-law.

From leapfrog to real frogs. The **smelliest species of frog** is the Venezuelan skunk frog (*Aromobates nocturnus*); its vile-smelling skin secretion is released as a defense.

DOGS

Breaking records was a walk in the park for these furry friends:

- **Largest dog walk:** 18,113 dogs (178 breeds), in the Great North Dog Walk in South Shields, UK, on June 13, 2010.
- **Largest dog walk (single breed):** 700 labradors, in a 3-mile (5-km) charity walk in Warsaw, Poland, on August 29, 2010.
- **Most dogs walked by an individual:** 27 dogs, by Melissa Crispin Piche (Canada) in Alberta, Canada, on September 31, 2008. Although 31 dogs began the walk, one escaped and three retired!

LARGEST LITTER

On November 29, 2004, Tia, a Neopolitan mastiff owned by Damian Ward (UK) and Anne Kellegher (Ireland), gave birth to a record litter of 24 puppies. Most survived, but one puppy was stillborn and three others died in the first week.

OLDEST DOG (LIVING)

Pusuke, a male cross owned by Shigeo Nagai (Japan), was born on April 1, 1985 and is still enjoying life today at over 25 years of age. The **oldest dog ever** was an Australian cattle-dog named Bluey, who was obtained as a pup in 1910 and worked with cattle and sheep for almost 20 years before his death on November 14, 1939 at the ripe old age of 29 years 5 months.

LONGEST DOG (LIVING)

At a whopping 7 ft 9 in (2.37 m) from nose to tail, the longest dog alive is Farrell, an Irish wolfhound owned by Robert and Kate Fandetti (USA).

SMALLEST DOG BY HEIGHT (LIVING)

Measuring just 4 in (10.16 cm) tall on May 12, 2007, a female long-haired chihuahua called Boo Boo is the world's most vertically challenged dog. Owned by Lana Elswick of Kentucky, USA, she is tiny enough to fit in the palm of a hand.

SMALLEST DOG BY LENGTH (LIVING)

At 6 in (15.2 cm) long – just half the length of a standard ruler – Paulette Keller's (USA) diminutive dog Brandy is, from nose to tail tip, the shortest canine on the planet.

SMALLEST WORKING DOG

Momo, a seven-year-old chihuahua weighing 6.6 lb (3 kg), saw off competition from German shepherds to win a place in the search-and-rescue team of the Japanese police force in November 2010. Her size allows her to reach places other dogs can't.

LOUDEST BARK

On June 15, 2009, Daz, a German shepherd belonging to Peter Lucken (UK), produced a "woof" measuring 108 dB – the most deafening ever registered by one dog.

Not to be outdone, a chorus of 76 hounds on the other side of the Atlantic produced the **loudest bark by a group**, hitting a record 124 dB in an event staged by Petmate in Colorado, USA, on November 7, 2009.

LONGEST SOLID OBJECT SWALLOWED BY A DOG

Kyle, a collie–Staffordshire bull terrier cross, who was 18 in (45.7 cm) long at the time, had to have a 15-in (38.1-cm) bread knife removed from his stomach after swallowing it handle-first in December 2000.

LONGEST DOG EARS (LIVING)

A black and tan coonhound named Harbor has the longest ears of any living dog, with measurements of 12.25 in (31.1 cm) for the left ear and 13.5 in (34.3 cm) for the right, as of June 8, 2010. Traditionally a hunting dog, the breed is well known for its droopy ears, which it uses to sweep up scents from the ground, but Harbor, owned by Jennifer Wert of Colorado, USA, is way ahead of the pack!

DOG-EARED

Harbor is only beaten in the ear stakes by Tigger the bloodhound. Prior to his death in October 2009, Tigger sported a left ear of 13.5 in (34.2 cm) and a right ear of 13.75 in (34.9 cm) – the **longest dog ears ever!**

The **longest bird beak** in relation to overall body length is that of the sword-billed hummingbird, found in the Andes from Venezuela to Bolivia. The beak measures 4 in (10.2 cm) – longer than the bird's actual body.

3,326 Hours you will spend walking your dog in its lifetime. Regular walkies make dog owners slightly healthier than average. On the downside, there will be 15,308 separate pieces of dog poop to deal with.

LONGEST JOURNEY HOME BY A LOST DOG

In 1979, a labrador–boxer cross named Jimpa turned up at his old home in Victoria, Australia, after walking 2,000 miles (3,218 km) across the country from Nyabing, Western Australia. His owner, Warren Dumesney (Australia), had moved to Nyabing 14 months earlier for work, but had later lost his pet. During the epic trek, Jimpa negotiated the almost waterless Nullarbor Plain, which stretches 684 miles (1,100 km) east to west.

FASTEST TIME TO POP 100 BALLOONS

Under the watchful eye of owner Doree Sitterly (USA), determined Jack Russell terrier Anastasia popped 100 balloons in just 44.49 sec on the set of *Live! with Regis and Kelly* in Los Angeles, USA, on February 24, 2008.

MOST KNOTS UNTIED BY A DOG IN THREE MINUTES

Ben, a pug–springer spaniel cross owned by Claudia Neumann (Germany), managed to untie a record 14 knots in three minutes at the Vienna Recordia event in Vienna, Austria, on September 26, 2010.

HARDIEST DOG

On April 15, 2003, 10-month-old mongrel Dosha escaped from her home in California, USA, only to be run over by a car and then shot in the head by police, who were trying to put her out of her misery. Subsequently sealed in a bag and placed in a freezer at an animal center, she was discovered by staff two hours later, alive and sitting upright! All three potentially fatal events occurred in a 24-hour period, making Dosha the world's most resilient dog.

HIGHEST MAN-AND-DOG PARACHUTE DEPLOYMENT

Mike Forsythe (USA) and his working dog Cara dived from an aircraft and deployed a parachute at a record altitude of 30,100 ft (9,174 m). Cara was strapped to Forsythe, a trainer for US Special Operations Units, in a K9 Storm aerial insertion vest, a harness specially designed for dogs of war deployed on aerial missions.

MOST CATCHES OF A FRISBEE BY A DOG IN THREE MINUTES

Ciaki caught a frisbee thrown by owner Nicola Ratti (Italy) 11 times on the set of *Lo Show dei Record* in Rome, Italy, on February 25, 2010.

MOST EXPENSIVE DOG

With a price tag of 10 million Chinese yuan or $1,513,417 (£945,000), an 11-month-old red Tibetan mastiff became the world's costliest canine when sold by breeder Lu Liang to a Chinese multi-millionaire in March 2011. Weighing 180 lb (82 kg), Big Splash enjoys a diet of chicken and beef.

TALLEST DOG

The aptly named Giant George is not only the tallest dog alive, but also the **tallest dog ever**. Owned by David Nasser of Tucson, Arizona, USA, the huge great dane registered a height of 43 in (1.092 m) on February 15, 2010.

UPDATED RECORD
NEW RECORD

During Birdwatch Kenya 86, held on November 29–30, 1986, twitchers Terry Stevenson, John Fanshawe, and Andy Roberts (all Kenya) claimed the record for the **most bird species spotted in 24 hours**, sighting 342 different types of bird.

CATS

PAWS FOR THOUGHT

The cat with the most toes is Jake, a male ginger tabby from Bonfield in Ontario, Canada, who has 28 toes – seven on each paw. Each toe has its own claw, pad, and bone structure.

SMALLEST LIVING DOMESTIC CAT

The shortest living cat is Fizz Girl, a two-year-old female munchkin cat who measured 6 in (12.24 cm) from the floor to the shoulder on July 23, 2010. The pint-sized puss weighs just 4 lb 2.3 oz (2.09 kg) and is owned by Tiffani Kjeldergaard (USA).

FIRST DOMESTICATED CATS

The oldest evidence of the domestication of the cat dates back 9,500 years. The bones of a cat were discovered in the neolithic village of Shillourokambos in Cyprus by a team of French scientists, and the find announced in the journal *Science* in April 2004.

OLDEST CAT EVER

Creme Puff was born on August 3, 1967 and lived until August 6, 2005, a total of 38 years 3 days. She lived with her owner, Jake Perry, in Austin, Texas, USA.

SMALLEST CAT EVER

A male blue point Himalayan-Persian named Tinker Toy measured only 2.75 in (7 cm) tall and 7.5 in (19 cm) long when full-grown (aged 2.5 years). The unusually tiny cat was owned by Katrina and Scott Forbes (USA).

LARGEST LITTER BY A DOMESTIC CAT

On August 7, 1970, a Burmese/Siamese cat belonging to V Gane of Kingham, Oxfordshire, UK, gave birth to 19 kittens. Four of the kittens in the litter were stillborn.

LONGEST DOMESTIC CAT

At 48.5 in (123 cm) long, Mymains Stewart Gilligan (aka Stewie) is the world's longest domestic cat. The five-year-old feline is owned by Robin Hendrickson and Erik Brandsness (USA) and was measured on August 28, 2010. He also has the **longest domestic cat tail** at 16.34 in (41.5 cm).

HOUSE CAT

Cats may have been the first (and perhaps only) animals to have *chosen* to be domesticated. They preyed on the rodents found in human communities, but also thrived on the food and company provided by people.

Lake Turkana in Kenya has a surface area of 2,472 $miles^2$ (6,405 km^2), making it the **largest desert lake** in the world.

0.44 Number of pets you can expect to own at any one time. It's most likely to be 0.44 of a cat or a dog. In its lifetime, the average dog will cost its owners $10,943, the average cat $8,029.

UPDATED RECORD
NEW RECORD

FIRST ORCHESTRAL WORK WRITTEN FOR CAT AND PIANO

"Catcerto" is a four-minute piano concerto for chamber orchestra and cat composed by Mindaugas Piečaitis (Lithuania). The piece – in which an orchestra accompanies a video of a cat pawing at notes on a piano – debuted at the Klaipeda Concert Hall in Klaipeda, Lithuania, on June 5, 2009, with Nora the cat at the piano.

FIRST ANIMAL WITH TWO BIONIC LEG IMPLANTS

Oscar the cat lost his legs in an accident in late 2009 and was not expected to survive. In June 2010, vet Noel Fitzpatrick and his team drilled holes into what remained of Oscar's legs and inserted metal implants into his ankle bones – making him the **first animal to receive implants into moving joints**. Skin and bone have grown over the implants, which have now become part of his body.

CATWALK
Oscar first road-tested a series of round pegs as replacement feet, but has since upgraded to "blades," on which he is able to walk normally. Noel hopes that this surgery will be a step forward in animal and human rehabilitation.

MOST PROLIFIC CAT

A tabby cat named Dusty, born in 1935, who lived in Bonham, Texas, USA, produced a total of 420 kittens during her breeding life. She gave birth to her last litter, a single kitten, on June 12, 1952.

LONGEST CAT WHISKERS

The longest recorded whiskers on a cat measured 7.5 in (19 cm) and belong to Missi, a Maine coon who lives with her owner, Kaija Kyllönen (Finland). The world-beating whiskers were measured in Iisvesi, Finland, on December 22, 2005.

MOST AIR FLIGHTS BY A PET

A domestic cat called Smarty made her 79th flight on June 28, 2005. All the flights were trips between Cairo, Egypt, and Larnaca, Cyprus, with her owners Peter and Carole Godfrey (UK).

LARGEST CAT SANCTUARY

The 30-acre (12-ha) Caboodle Ranch houses 500 cats in a sanctuary the size of 22 American football fields. It was founded in Lee, Florida, USA, in 2003 by Craig Grant (USA), who has erected scale buildings for his feline guests.

WEALTHIEST CAT

When Ben Rea (UK) died in May 1988, he bequeathed his $12.5-million (£7-million) fortune to Blackie, the last surviving of 15 cats.

MOST EXPENSIVE CAT

A Californian spangled cat was bought for $24,000 in January 1987.

GREATEST MOUSER

Towser (b. April 21, 1963), a female tortoiseshell cat owned by Glenturret Distillery near Crieff in Perth and Kinross, Scotland, UK, notched up an estimated 28,900 murine victims (i.e., dead mice). She averaged 3.3 rodents a day until her death on March 20, 1987.

At around 60 miles (100 km) by 18 miles (30 km) in extent, and 1,656 ft (505 m) deep at its deepest point, Lake Toba in the Indonesian island of Sumatra is the **largest crater lake**.

COLLECTIONS 1

Q. Where do penguins live in the wild?

A. Penguins are largely associated with Antarctica, of course, but they also live wild in Australia, New Zealand, Africa, and South America. Even the Equator is home to penguins – the Galápagos penguin can be found living in Ecuador!

PENGUINS

As of March 14, 2011, Birgit Berends (Germany) had amassed a collection of 11,062 different penguin-related items. Birgit started her collection at the age of 18, inspired by the animated series *Pingu*, although her very first penguin dates back to her days in elementary school.

CRABS

As of March 9, 2011, Darren Martin (UK) had created a collection of 441 crab-related items, which he had been putting together for over 10 years.

CATS

Carmen de Aldana (Guatemala) has 21,321 cat-related items, as of March 14, 2011. She has been collecting them since 1954.

CHICKENS

As of June 2006, Cecil and Joann Dixon (both USA) had 6,505 chicken-themed items.

DALMATIANS

Karen Ferrier (UK) had 1,117 different Dalmatian-related objects as of February 3, 2009, including a car and items that had belonged to Dodie Smith, author of *The Hundred and One Dalmatians*.

DONALD DUCK MEMORABILIA

As of March 2011, Mary Brooks (USA) had 1,411 objects relating to Donald Duck. Oddly, her husband's name was Donald and his school nickname was "Duck".

DONKEYS

Since 1976, Delores DeJohn (USA) has amassed 690 donkey-related items.

DRAGONS

Charlene Leatherman (USA) has a 793-strong dragon collection. European dragons are usually depicted with wings and most often pictured fighting knights, while Chinese dragons are usually shown as long and lean, holding a pearl jewel.

ELEPHANTS

As of April 8, 2008, Janet Mallernee-Briley (USA) had 5,779 items relating to elephants. She received her first elephant from an uncle when she was 16.

FROGS

Sheila Crown (UK) has 10,502 frog items that she has been collecting since 1979. Her collection was displayed at the FrogsGalore Museum, Malborough, UK, on May 12, 2002.

The **longest open saltwater scuba-dive** lasted 48 hr 8 min 17 sec and was performed by William Goodman (UK) at Blue Marlin Dive, Lombok, Indonesia, from January 7 to 9, 2010.

954 Christmas presents you'll receive in a lifetime. According to a survey by charity shops, 10% of gifts are unwanted. This means you are going to receive about 100 gifts you don't like or need.

UPDATED RECORD
NEW RECORD

COWS

Denise Tubangui (USA) had a collection of 2,429 cow-related items as of March 2011. Denise started collecting in 1990, when she saw a cow figurine in her mother's kitchen. Her favorite item is the life-sized calf that her neighbors gave her as a present.

GIRAFFES

Susa Forster (Germany) has collected 2,443 separate giraffe items since 1974. These include a 15-ft 1-in-tall (4.6-m) giraffe that stands in her living room.

HEDGEHOGS

Bengt W Johansson (Sweden) had 495 different hedgehog-related items as of March 2011, including a hedgehog clock from his wife.

LADYBIRDS

Carine Roosen (Belgium) has amassed 3,531 ladybird items over a period of more than 10 years. One of her favorite items is a ladybird toilet seat.

MICE AND RATS

Christa Behmenburg (Germany) has a total of 27,623 objects related to mice and rats, including cigarette cards and money.

MICKEY MOUSE MEMORABILIA

As of December 2008, Janet Esteves (USA) had amassed 2,760 different Mickey Mouse items.

MONKEYS

Since 1970, Wang Lingxian (China) has collected 5,680 monkey-themed items. Fittingly, both she and her husband were born in the Chinese Year of the Monkey.

OWLS

Dianne Turner (USA) owned a collection of 18,055 owl-themed objects, which she completed in 2002, aged 55.

PANDAS

As of March 2011, Miranda Kessler (USA) had a collection of 1,225 different panda items. She was given her first stuffed panda bear from her father when she was three years old.

PIGS

Anne Langton of Alfreton, Derbyshire, UK, has amassed a total of 11,505 pig items, which she has been collecting for over 20 years.

RABBITS

Husband and wife Steve Lubanski and Candace Frazee, (both USA) had 28,423 bunny-themed collectibles as of March 2011, displayed in their own Bunny Museum in Pasadena, California.

RUBBER DUCKS

As of February 10, 2010, Charlotte Lee (USA) had 5,249 different rubber ducks, which she has been collecting since 1996. All her rubber ducks are kept in glass showcases on the four walls of her dedicated duck room.

SNAILS

A G Straver (Netherlands) has 457 items relating to snails. In his village, many people share the same name, and each family has a nickname; that of his wife's family was "the snail." In 1993, he gave her a ceramic snail for her birthday, and then began his collection.

TEDDY BEARS

Jackie Miley (USA) had 7,106 different teddy bears as of March 11, 2011, having begun collecting in 2002. She now keeps the bears in a little house of their own, called Teddy Bear Town, located across the street from her own apartment.

LIONS

Reinhard Stöckl (Austria) had 1,761 different lion-related items as of March 27, 2010, a collection that he has been building since 1998.

TORTOISES AND TURTLES

Connie and Danny Tan (both Singapore) have built up a collection of 3,456 items relating to tortoises and turtles, including more than 1,000 live specimens. They keep their collection in the Live Turtle and Tortoise Museum, Singapore.

COLLECT A RECORD!

If you've got a record-worthy collection of animal-related items – or a colossal collection of any kind – tell us about it by visiting the website: www.guinnessworldrecords.com.

For the **longest open saltwater scuba-dive in cold water** you have to go to the Republic of Ireland, where Declan Devane (Ireland) performed an 11-hr 42-min dive in Little Killary, Co. Galway, Ireland, on October 10, 2009.

COLLECTIONS 2

CHOCOLATE BARS
Chocolate-lover Bob Brown (USA) has the world's largest personal collection of chocolate bars, with 770 unique items. His tempting cache was put on display at the Castleton Square Mall in Indianapolis, USA, on October 29, 2010.

OLIVE OIL BOTTLES
By April 2010, Ronald Popeil (USA) had collected 1,221 different olive oil bottles. Ronald started the unusual collection the year he began working on his invention, an electric automatic pasta maker, a device that requires a healthy supply of olive oil.

UPDATED RECORD
NEW RECORD

MUSHROOM-RELATED ITEMS
If it features a mushroom, Shara Hoffman (USA) will buy it – since 2000, she has accumulated 263 mushroom-related items, ranging from clocks, pots, and pans to fabrics and even furniture.

SALT AND PEPPER SHAKERS
LaVerne Tish (USA) owns 6,971 pairs of salt and pepper shakers, collected between 1984 and January 2011.

SUGAR PACKETS
By June 11, 2010, sweet-toothed Ralf Schröder (Germany) had collected 6,991 different sugar packets.

COCA-COLA MEMORABILIA
Since 2005, Rebecca Flores (USA) has put together a colorful array of 945 Coke-related collectibles.

STAMPS FEATURING IMAGES OF POPES
Magnus Andersson (Sweden) has a philatelic collection with a twist, boasting 1,119 postage stamps featuring the faces of various pontiffs from over the years.

POOH AND FRIENDS MEMORABILIA
At the last count on May 1, 2010, Pooh Bear fan Deb Hoffman (USA) had accumulated a record 4,805 different pieces of memorabilia from the popular children's story about a toy bear and his many animal friends.

MR MEN MEMORABILIA
Despite only beginning her collection in 2001, Joanne Black (UK) has wasted no time in putting together a collection of 2,225 Mr Men toys, books, and other items.

SUPER MARIO MEMORABILIA
Mitsugu Kikai (Japan) is the proud owner of the world's largest collection of Super Mario memorabilia. Counted in Tokyo, Japan, on July 15, 2010, the collection contains 5,400 unique items relating to the famous Italian plumber from the popular Nintendo video game series.

POKÉMON MEMORABILIA
As of October 14, 2010, Lisa Courtney (UK) had amassed a record 14,410 Pokémon items, picked up in the UK, USA, France, and Japan.

CHARLIE'S ANGELS MEMORABILIA
Since 1976, Jack Condon (USA) has collected 1,460 items related to the hit 1970s TV crime show.

COOKING UP A STORM
Maria Coyne (USA) isn't short of a recipe or two, being the owner of the **largest collection of cookbooks**. With 1,070 collected since 1965, the only problem is finding a kitchen large enough to store them all.

DALEKS
Although not a fan of the sci-fi show *Doctor Who* (BBC, UK), Rob Hull (UK) is nevertheless the world's biggest fan of the Doctor's arch nemeses, the Daleks. As of March 25, 2011, Rob's Dalek collection runs to over 571 examples and includes several rare pieces as well as a full-size working model, which, at the press of a button, issues the famously menacing war cry: "Exterminate!"

The **longest dance party** was staged by Unique Events Limited (Ireland). It began on October 27, 2006 at 12:00 p.m. with 40 dancers, 31 of whom completed the marathon after 55 hours, at the Quay Front, Wexford, Ireland, on October 29, 2006.

NO PLACE LIKE GNOME
Like Ortrud, another collector forced to set up a special home for her growing collection is Ann Atkin (UK), whose record 2,042 gnomes and pixies live at her Gnome Reserve in Devon, UK.

CLOWNS

Clown-lover Ortrud Kastaun (Germany) has been collecting clown-related items since 1995 and had amassed a record 1,610 different pieces up to June 3, 2010. Over the years, Ortrud's flat became too small to accommodate her growing collection, so in 2001 she moved to a larger place and set up her own private clown museum, located in Essen, Germany.

"DO NOT DISTURB" SIGNS

Since 1985, Jean-François Vernetti (Switzerland), a frequent business traveler, has collected an extraordinary 11,111 different "Do Not Disturb" signs during his visits to hotels in 189 countries across the globe. Sssshhh…

MAGIC ARTIFACTS

David Copperfield's (USA) International Museum and Library of the Conjuring Arts, founded in 1991 in Nevada, USA, contains 150,000 props, books, posters, and other historical ephemera related to magic and conjuring, of which 90,000 are on display.

PLAYING CARDS

Liu Fuchang (China) is the real deal when it comes to collecting playing cards. His record-breaking collection, verified in 2007, features 11,087 different sets, themed on subjects ranging from art and literature to travel, television, and the military.

MODEL AIRPLANES

The largest collection of handmade aircraft belongs to John Kalusa (USA), who has created 5,737 wooden planes since 1936. The collection is currently housed in the library of Embry-Riddle Aeronautical University in Arizona, USA.

MODEL BUSES

Classic car fan Geoff Price (UK) also has a passion for model four-wheelers. Among his vast collection of 10,955 buses, as of April 2011, he also has the **largest model tram collection**, with 830 amassed since 1959.

TELEPHONES

Rita Zimmermann (Switzerland) must have ringing in her ears, due to her 771-strong collection of telephones, amassed from 1990 to July 10, 2010.

MEN'S NECKTIES

Derryl Ogden (USA) is the undisputed king of grabatology – the collecting of neckties – with 16,055 accumulated since 1934.

BROOCHES

As of May 2011, Adam Wide (UK) has 4,061 brooches. Each one is themed on the festive season, making this also the **largest collection of Christmas brooches**.

PERSONAL SCRAPBOOKS

US media mogul Hugh Hefner has put together a record 2,396 personal scrapbooks during his colorful 85-year life.

From dance marathons to video games marathons, the **longest nonstop LAN party** lasted 40 hours and was completed by 274 gamers during Cyber Fusion 2009 at the Multimedia University in Cyberjaya, Malaysia, on April 11–12, 2009.

TOYS & GAMES

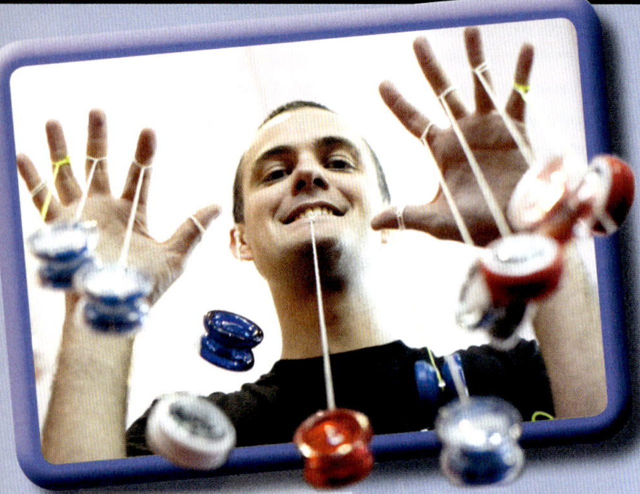

LARGEST TREASURE HUNT GAME

To mark the relaunch of the Kinder Surprise egg, 250 children took part in the world's largest treasure hunt in Bucharest, Romania, on September 4, 2010.

MOST PEOPLE PLAYING MONOPOLY SIMULTANEOUSLY

On August 27, 2008, a record 2,918 people at 21 locations worldwide and online played Monopoly® at the same time in an event organized by the manufacturer Hasbro (USA).

MOST YO-YOS SPUN SIMULTANEOUSLY

Australian yo-yo champion Ben McPhee got 16 yo-yos spinning at the same time at the Toy Fair, held in London, UK, on January 26, 2010. Ben mounted 10 spinning yo-yos on hooks, then hung two from his ears, two from his mouth, and a final pair, somewhat more conventionally, from his fingers.

LONGEST PLASTIC TOY TRAIN TRACK

Built by Mattel Inc. and Hit Entertainment (both Australia), a toy train track measuring 6,902 ft (2,104 m) was laid at the Workshops Rail Museum in Queensland, Australia, on November 4, 2010. A toy train took 2 hr 52 min 23 sec to complete the epic journey.

FASTEST GAME OF OPERATION

With nerves of steel and a steady hand, Maharoof Decibels (India) took just 21.87 seconds to extract every troublesome body part in the electronic surgery game Operation on November 28, 2008.

MOST DOMINOES TOPPLED IN A MINUTE

On August 7, 2010, Gemma Hansen (UK) stacked then toppled a line of 75 dominoes in the space of one minute at Butlins holiday park in Minehead, Somerset, UK.

LARGEST TETRIS GAME

On September 15, 2010, *The Gadget Show* (UK) created a fully working Tetris® game of 1,138.71 ft² (105.79 m²) by projecting LED lights on to a grid of cardboard boxes.

MOST SIMULTANEOUS GAMES OF INTERNATIONAL CHECKERS (INDIVIDUAL)

Dutch international checkers player Jos Stokkel took on 251 opponents at the same time in Hengelo, the Netherlands, on November 6–7, 2010. He won 174 games, drew 62, and lost just 15 in 18 hours of play.

MOST GAMES OF CHESS PLAYED SIMULTANEOUSLY IN ONE LOCATION

On December 24, 2010, an incredible 20,017 budding chess players from schools across the state of Gujarat, India, competed against 1,024 chess masters in 20,480 games of chess. Well prepared for their clash with the experts, the school children had been coached in preparation for the record attempt by the reigning World Chess Champion, Viswanathan Anand (India).

UP, UP, AND AWAY

On May 3, 2008, a squadron of 99 remote-control planes took to the skies over Georgia, USA, and flew into the record books as the **most model aircraft airborne simultaneously.**

FASTEST REMOTE-CONTROL JET-POWERED MODEL AIRCRAFT

Axel Haché (Dominican Republic) and David Shulman's (USA) jet reached a speed of 293 knots (337.24 mi/h or 542.64 km/h) at Hobbyland Airfield in the Dominican Republic on January 18, 2010.

UPDATED RECORD
NEW RECORD

The world's **largest butterfly farm** is on the Malaysian island of Penang. Opened in March 1986, and occupying 1.98 acres (0.8 ha), it contains over 4,000 living specimens belonging to more than 50 different species.

$540,864 Your spending on houses in a lifetime. If Monopoly money was real, you would need the cash from 16 sets of the game to buy, rent, and constantly repair the roof over your head.

LONGEST RAMP JUMP BY A REMOTE-CONTROL CAR

An HPI Vorza, controlled by Jason Bradbury (UK), completed a record leap of 85 ft 10.7 in (26.18 m) on the set of *The Gadget Show* in Birmingham, UK, on March 25, 2010.

SMALLEST REMOTE-CONTROL HELICOPTER

The Air Hogs Pocket Copter by Spin Master Ltd (Canada) is in fact pocket-sized, measuring just 3.94 in (10 cm) from nose to tail on July 28, 2010. The mini-copter, which flies beautifully, achieved a flight of 3 min 50 sec on the day.

TALLEST STRUCTURE MADE WITH CONNECTING PLASTIC BRICKS

In an event organized by LEGO® Norway, children and adults joined forces to build a LEGO tower 99 ft 1 in (30.22 m) high in Oslo, Norway, on April 24, 2010.

LARGEST PUBLISHED CROSSWORD

It took Ara Hovhannisian of Armenia almost a year, from November 2007 to October 2008, to compile an enormous crossword consisting of 132,020 squares and featuring 12,842 clues across and 13,128 clues down. Measuring 61.14 ft^2 (5.68 m^2), it was published in a special edition of *Russiky Crossword*.

LARGEST COMMERCIALLY AVAILABLE JIGSAW

Fans of the jigsaw will have their work cut out with this September 2010 offering from German manufacturer Ravensburger AG. Players must puzzle out a mind-boggling 32,256 pieces to complete the image, which measures 17 ft 8 in x 6 ft 3 in (5.4 x 1.9 m).

RUBIK'S REKORDS!

From Cubes to Clocks and everything in between, discover who has the fastest fingers in Rubik history. *Correct at March 31, 2011.*

Category	Holder	Time	Competition	Date
3x3 Cube	Feliks Zemdegs (Australia)	0:06.65	Melbourne Summer 11	Jan 29, 2011
4x4 Cube	Feliks Zemdegs (Australia)	0:31.97	Melbourne Cube Day	Nov 13, 2010
5x5 Cube	Feliks Zemdegs (Australia)	1:01.59	Melbourne Summer 11	Sep 19, 2010
7x7 Cube	Michal Halczuk (Poland)	3:25.91	Pabianice Open	Sep 26, 2010
Rubik's Clock	Sebastián Pino Castillo (Chile)	0:05.05	Bicentenario Open	Aug 29, 2010
3x3 (one hand)	Piotr Alexandrowicz (Poland)	0:11.19	Polish Nationals	Nov 7, 2009
Rubik's Magic	Yuxuan Wang (China)	0:00.71	Beijing No Cubes	Nov 28, 2010
Megaminx	Simon Westlund (Sweden)	0:46.81	Helsinki Open	Jan 23, 2011
Pyraminx	Oscar Roth Andersen (Denmark)	0:02.40	Fredericia Open	Jan 30, 2011

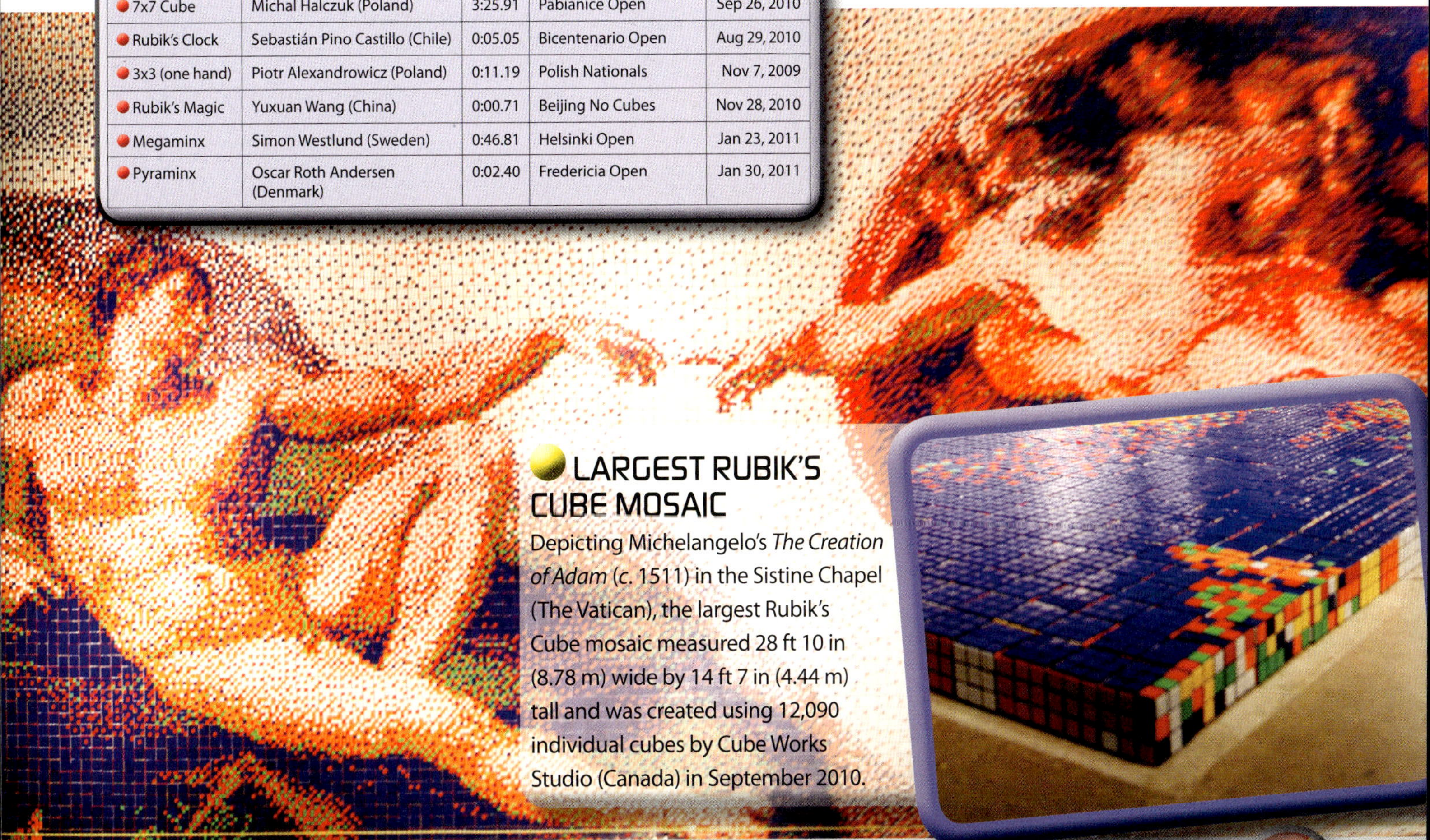

LARGEST RUBIK'S CUBE MOSAIC

Depicting Michelangelo's *The Creation of Adam* (*c.* 1511) in the Sistine Chapel (The Vatican), the largest Rubik's Cube mosaic measured 28 ft 10 in (8.78 m) wide by 14 ft 7 in (4.44 m) tall and was created using 12,090 individual cubes by Cube Works Studio (Canada) in September 2010.

A prize catch for any butterfly farm would be the Queen Alexandra's birdwing (*Ornithoptera alexandrae*) of Papua New Guinea – the **largest known butterfly**. Females can weigh more than 0.9 oz (25 g) and have a wingspan exceeding 11 in (28 cm).

ROYALTY & MONARCHIES

YOUNGEST REIGNING MONARCH OF A SOVEREIGN NATION

Born on February 21, 1980, Jigme Khesar Namgyel Wangchuck became the 5th King of Bhutan on December 14, 2006 and, at 31 years old, he is the youngest monarch of a sovereign nation. The Oxford-educated King presides over one of the world's most isolated countries, a tiny realm in the Himalaya Mountains where progress is measured in terms of "Gross Domestic Happiness."

SHORTEST REIGN OF A MONARCH

In 1830, Louis XIX of France abdicated within 20 minutes of being crowned, making his reign the joint shortest in history. He shares the record with the unfortunate Prince Luis Filipe of Portugal, who technically became king for the same brief period on February 1, 1908, following the assassination of his father, Dom Carlos I. Luis Filipe was himself mortally wounded in the attack, but survived his father by 20 minutes.

OLDEST REIGNING MONARCH

Born in 1924, King Abdullah bin Abdulaziz Al-Saud of Saudi Arabia became the world's oldest monarch, at the age of 82 years 253 days, after the death of the previous holder, Malietoa Tanumafili II of Samoa, on May 11, 2007. He was crowned in 2005.

YOUNGEST REIGNING MONARCH

King Oyo – aka Rukirabasaija Oyo Nyimba Kabamba Iguru Rukidi IV – is the 19-year-old ruler of Toro, a kingdom in Uganda. Born on April 16, 1992, he came to power at the age of three (pictured) and now rules over 3% of Uganda's 33-million-strong population. Despite his title, the King's influence is largely symbolic, as the country is governed by an elected president.

ROYAL ROCKER

Princess Stéphanie of Monaco is the only royal in the world to have had hit records in Europe. Her debut album, *Besoin*, has sold more than a million copies since its release in 1986.

RICHEST MONARCH

According to Forbes.com, the richest monarch in the world is Thailand's King Bhumibol Adulyadej, King Rama IX of the Chakri Dynasty. In July 2010, the popular ruler's wealth was estimated to be around $30 billion.

LARGEST ROYAL FAMILY

The royal House of Saud of Saudi Arabia, currently presided over by King Abdullah bin Abdulaziz Al-Saud, has royal relatives numbering in the tens of thousands. The kingdom was established by King Abdul Aziz in 1932. With his 17 wives, he fathered a total of 44 sons, four of whom have gone on to rule the kingdom since his death in 1953.

Being a monarch can be a job for life – check out the record reigns of history's most resilient rulers:

Longest ever reign: 94 years, by Phiops II, an Egyptian pharaoh whose reign began in 2281 BC when he was just six years old.

Longest reigning monarch – living: 64 years, by King Bhumibol Adulyadej of Thailand, who was crowned King on June 9, 1946.

Longest reign in Europe: 73 years 220 days, by Afonso I Henrique of Portugal, who ruled as count and then king from 1112 until 1185.

TALLEST CROWN PRINCE

The heir to the Spanish throne, Príncipe de Asturias, Don Felipe de Borbón y Grecia, stands 6 ft 5 in (1.97 m) tall. The Crown Prince was a member of the Spanish Olympic sailing team that competed at the Barcelona Games in 1992.

FOR MORE ON KINGS AND QUEENS, DISCOVER THE AGE OF EMPIRES ON P.74.

Native to Papua New Guinea, Bulmer's fruit bat (*Aproteles bulmerae*) is the **largest cave-dwelling bat**. Adult females have a wingspan of 3 ft 3 in (1 m).

MOST PHOTOGRAPHED QUEEN

One of the most popular monarchs in history, Queen Elizabeth II (UK) is the most photographed queen, pictured here accepting a golden anniversary edition of *Guinness World Records* from Managing Director Alistair Richards.

MOST PORTRAYED LIVING MONARCH

Queen Elizabeth II has been portrayed on stage and screen more than any other living monarch. Memorable portrayals include (clockwise from top left): Prunella Scales (UK) in the play *A Question of Attribution* (1988), Helen Mirren (UK) in the movie *The Queen* (2006), a cartoon cameo in *The Simpsons* (2003), and numerous stage, screen, and public appearances by Jeanette Charles (UK).

MOST COUNTRIES RULED AS HEAD OF STATE SIMULTANEOUSLY

The most powerful woman in the world, Queen Elizabeth II is the lawful head of state of 16 independent nations. While the Queen's role is nominal and ceremonial (exercising no political powers), 128 million people in 15 Commonwealth states, plus the UK, recognize her as monarch.

During her long reign, Her Majesty, Queen Elizabeth II has broken numerous royal records:

Longest reigning queen – living: 59 years 95 days from February 6, 1952 to May 12, 2011.

Oldest British monarch: 85 years 21 days as of May 12, 2011.

Wealthiest queen: $682 million, including fine art, jewelry, and property.

Most depicted person on international currencies: 35 countries feature Queen Elizabeth II on their national coinage.

MOST LIVE STREAMS FOR A SINGLE EVENT

The YouTube broadcast of Prince William's marriage to Catherine Middleton (both UK) in London, UK, on April 29, 2011 achieved a record 72 million live views, as people from 188 countries around the world tuned in to watch the event on the company's official Royal Channel. Although this figure alone was enough to beat the 70 million streams achieved during the inauguration of US President Barack Obama in 2009, the wedding's overall tally is likely to have been significantly higher when taking into account the millions watching via other live streaming services.

UPDATED RECORD
NEW RECORD

A treat for a hungry fruit bat would be a juicy fig. In 2006, nine carbonized figs up to 11,400 years old were found in a Neolithic village in Israel. A variety that could only have been produced through human intervention, they are the **oldest examples of fruit cultivation**.

CODES & CRYPTOGRAPHY

FIRST USE OF AN ENCRYPTION TECHNIQUE

The Caesar Cipher was first used during the Gallic War *c.* 50 BC. According to Roman historian Suetonius, Julius Caesar employed this cipher in his military campaigns, the earliest known use of an encryption technique. The cipher is fairly simple, and in this instance involved shifting each letter of the alphabet three places to the left to produce apparently meaningless groups of letters. The recipient of the cipher had merely to move each letter three places to the right to reveal the message from Caesar.

FIRST USE OF POSTAL CODES

Sir Rowland Hill (UK) introduced a code for the postal system in London, UK, in 1857. The code divided the city into postal districts based on compass points. The present form of the postcode – a mix of letters and numbers that can be decoded by machine for faster sorting – was first used in Norwich, UK, in October 1959. The similar US zip code arrived in July 1963.

FIRST CRYPTIC CROSSWORD

The earliest crossword comprising only cryptic clues appeared in 1925 in the *Saturday Westminster Gazette*. There had been cryptic elements within crosswords before, but Edward Powys Mathers (UK), who set crosswords for this newspaper under the name "Torquemada," and for *The Observer* from 1926, was the first compiler to use cryptic clues only.

MOST ENDURING ELECTRICAL CODING SYSTEM

On May 24, 1844, Samuel Morse (USA) transmitted a line of code ("What hath God wrought?") by telegraph from Washington, DC, to a partner in Baltimore, Maryland (both USA) – the **first instant telecommunication.** It hailed the dawn of modern telecommunications. More than 160 years later, Morse code is still in use.

FIRST COMPUTER VIRUS

The earliest computer program that replicates itself surreptitiously was demonstrated by Fred Cohen (USA), a student at the University of Southern California, USA, on November 11, 1983. Cohen described his creation as "a program that can 'infect' other programs by modifying them to include a… version of itself." Although computer viruses had been theorized previous to this, Cohen was the first to write and execute a working code. Today, more than a million such viruses exist, according to security firm Symantec.

SPEEDY CIPHER

The Navajo-based code could be used to communicate, within 20 seconds, information that would take around 30 minutes to convey using traditional coding machines.

	A	B	C	D	E	F	G	H	I	J	K	L	M	N	O	P	Q	R	S	T	U	V	W	X	Y	Z
A	A	B	C	D	E	F	G	H	I	J	K	L	M	N	O	P	Q	R	S	T	U	V	W	X	Y	Z
B	B	C	D	E	F	G	H	I	J	K	L	M	N	O	P	Q	R	S	T	U	V	W	X	Y	Z	A
C	C	D	E	F	G	H	I	J	K	L	M	N	O	P	Q	R	S	T	U	V	W	X	Y	Z	A	B
D	D	E	F	G	H	I	J	K	L	M	N	O	P	Q	R	S	T	U	V	W	X	Y	Z	A	B	C
E	E	F	G	H	I	J	K	L	M	N	O	P	Q	R	S	T	U	V	W	X	Y	Z	A	B	C	D
F	F	G	H	I	J	K	L	M	N	O	P	Q	R	S	T	U	V	W	X	Y	Z	A	B	C	D	E
G	G	H	I	J	K	L	M	N	O	P	Q	R	S	T	U	V	W	X	Y	Z	A	B	C	D	E	F
H	H	I	J	K	L	M	N	O	P	Q	R	S	T	U	V	W	X	Y	Z	A	B	C	D	E	F	G
I	I	J	K	L	M	N	O	P	Q	R	S	T	U	V	W	X	Y	Z	A	B	C	D	E	F	G	H
J	J	K	L	M	N	O	P	Q	R	S	T	U	V	W	X	Y	Z	A	B	C	D	E	F	G	H	I
K	K	L	M	N	O	P	Q	R	S	T	U	V	W	X	Y	Z	A	B	C	D	E	F	G	H	I	J
L	L	M	N	O	P	Q	R	S	T	U	V	W	X	Y	Z	A	B	C	D	E	F	G	H	I	J	K
M	M	N	O	P	Q	R	S	T	U	V	W	X	Y	Z	A	B	C	D	E	F	G	H	I	J	K	L
N	N	O	P	Q	R	S	T	U	V	W	X	Y	Z	A	B	C	D	E	F	G	H	I	J	K	L	M
O	O	P	Q	R	S	T	U	V	W	X	Y	Z	A	B	C	D	E	F	G	H	I	J	K	L	M	N
P	P	Q	R	S	T	U	V	W	X	Y	Z	A	B	C	D	E	F	G	H	I	J	K	L	M	N	O
Q	Q	R	S	T	U	V	W	X	Y	Z	A	B	C	D	E	F	G	H	I	J	K	L	M	N	O	P
R	R	S	T	U	V	W	X	Y	Z	A	B	C	D	E	F	G	H	I	J	K	L	M	N	O	P	Q
S	S	T	U	V	W	X	Y	Z	A	B	C	D	E	F	G	H	I	J	K	L	M	N	O	P	Q	R
T	T	U	V	W	X	Y	Z	A	B	C	D	E	F	G	H	I	J	K	L	M	N	O	P	Q	R	S
U	U	V	W	X	Y	Z	A	B	C	D	E	F	G	H	I	J	K	L	M	N	O	P	Q	R	S	T
V	V	W	X	Y	Z	A	B	C	D	E	F	G	H	I	J	K	L	M	N	O	P	Q	R	S	T	U
W	W	X	Y	Z	A	B	C	D	E	F	G	H	I	J	K	L	M	N	O	P	Q	R	S	T	U	V
X	X	Y	Z	A	B	C	D	E	F	G	H	I	J	K	L	M	N	O	P	Q	R	S	T	U	V	W
Y	Y	Z	A	B	C	D	E	F	G	H	I	J	K	L	M	N	O	P	Q	R	S	T	U	V	W	X
Z	Z	A	B	C	D	E	F	G	H	I	J	K	L	M	N	O	P	Q	R	S	T	U	V	W	X	Y

cipher	VVVRBACP
key	COVERCOVER…
plaintext	THANKYOU

LONGEST TIME TO CRACK A CODE

The Vigenère Cipher, which uses a polyalphabetic system of encryption (left), was so effective that it was not broken for over 300 years. Invented by cryptographer Giovan Battista Bellaso (Italy) in 1553, it was finally cracked by mathematician and computer pioneer Charles Babbage (UK) in 1854.

FIRST USE OF A CARDAN GRILLE

Mathematician Gerolamo Cardano (Italy) first employed a "Cardan grille" to disguise a secret message in 1550. The technique is used to hide a message in an ordinary-looking document. The writer of the message places a piece of card with irregular slots cut into it – a Cardan grille – over a sheet of paper and writes the message in the slots, then removes the grille and fills in the gaps to create a seemingly ordinary message. The message can be read later by someone with a copy of the grille.

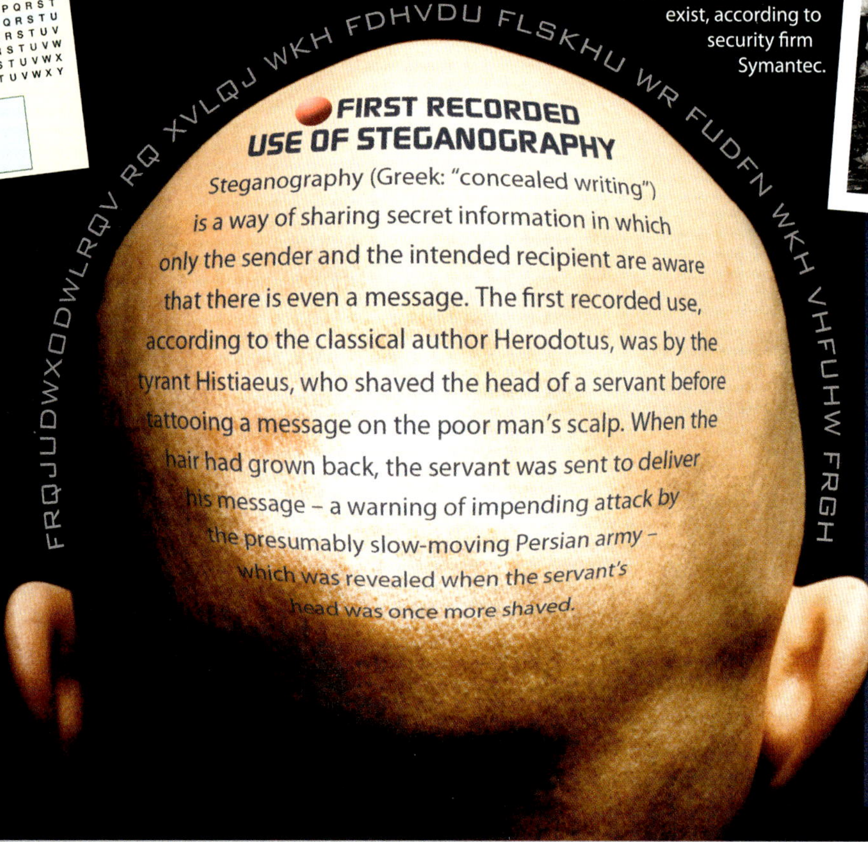

FIRST RECORDED USE OF STEGANOGRAPHY

Steganography (Greek: "concealed writing") is a way of sharing secret information in which only the sender and the intended recipient are aware that there is even a message. The first recorded use, according to the classical author Herodotus, was by the tyrant Histiaeus, who shaved the head of a servant before tattooing a message on the poor man's scalp. When the hair had grown back, the servant was sent to deliver his message – a warning of impending attack by the presumably slow-moving Persian army – which was revealed when the servant's head was once more shaved.

MOST DIFFICULT CODE TO CRACK

During World War II, the US Marine Corps developed a code utilizing the Navajo language in tandem with encryptions and word substitutions to produce an unbreakable code. The code substituted Navajo words for common military terms (so "tank" became the Navajo word for turtle), and it also spelled out letters using Navajo words based on the first letter of the English translation of the word, e.g., "Wo-la-chee" means "ant" so represents the letter "A."

Uri Gil (Israel, b. April 9, 1943), a brigadier general in the Israeli Air Force, flew from 1964 until his last flight in an F-16 on June 20, 2003 at the age of 60 years 72 days, making him the **oldest active fighter pilot**.

MOST ATTACKS IN A HACKING COMPETITION

A staggering 5.23 million attacks were made during eWeek's 17-day-long OpenHack III competition in January 2001, in which the latest security software, PitBull – by Argus Systems Group Inc. – was probed for weaknesses. Despite a $50,000 prize, no one could penetrate PitBull.

SMALLEST CODE-BREAKING SUPERCOMPUTER

Pico Computing (USA) has created a desktop-sized mini supercomputer by adapting difficult-to-program silicon chips to make them more powerful than those found in larger supercomputers.

At $400, it is also the **cheapest code-breaking supercomputer**.

LONGEST PRISON SENTENCE FOR COMPUTER HACKING

Brian Salcedo of Michigan, USA, was sentenced to nine years in federal prison in Charlotte, North Carolina, USA, on December 16, 2004 for computer hacking.

Salcedo was sentenced after pleading guilty to conspiracy and numerous hacking charges in August 2004 after he tried to steal credit card information from the computer systems of Lowe's hardware stores across the USA.

MOST POPULAR CHEAT CODE

The Konami Code debuted in the NES version of the video game *Gradius*, released in 1986, and has since been included in 151 games – either in the form of the same button presses, or subtle variations of them. The effect of the code differs from game to game, but in most cases entering the code while the game is paused grants the player most of the game's available power-ups. For those players who have not encountered it, or have forgotten about it, the sequence is: Up, Up, Down, Down, Left, Right, Left, Right, B, A.

FIRST HACK INTO A NETWORK PROTECTED BY QUANTUM CRYPTOGRAPHY

In April 2007, a team from the Massachusetts Institute of Technology (MIT) carried out the first reported hack of a quantum network. Quantum networks were thought to be uncrackable until the team managed to set up what they describe as a quantum-mechanical "wire-tap" and extract data that previously had been considered beyond the reach of even the most determined code-breaker.

FIRST PRESIDENT WITH A SECRET CODE NAME

Harry S Truman, who served as US President from 1945 to 1953, was given the Secret Service code name "General." Advances in telecommunications technology, and the newly present danger that potentially threatening forces might be listening in, required that all presidents, senior staff, and their families be issued with code names from this point onward in an effort to confuse anyone who might be listening to them illicitly.

FIRST SYNTHETIC GENOME TO CONTAIN SECRET MESSAGES

In 2008, the J Craig Venter Institute (USA) produced a manmade bacteria and placed five hidden "watermarks" within its genome (the complete list of its genetic material). This "secret" information was encoded in the form of single-letter amino acids (A, R, N, etc.), the names of which spelled out the Institute and people associated with the project: "CRAIGVENTER," "HAMSMITH," "CINDIANDCLYDE," "GLASSANDCLYDE," and "VENTERINSTITVTE" ("V" is used because there is no amino acid for the letter "U").

FIRST CONFIRMED USE OF SECRET CODES IN ONLINE PHOTOGRAPHY

On June 28, 2010, the US Justice Department announced charges against 11 people accused of working for the SVR – the Russian successor to the Soviet KGB. Among the charges was the accusation that they had slipped encoded messages into otherwise harmless-looking images on the internet (see right), the first confirmed use of this high-tech method of concealing data.

COLOR CODED

By altering the numeric values a computer assigns to the green, red, or blue in a pixel, the spies hid binary code in photos. Details about Baltimore Airport (main photo) were hidden in this photo of the Lincoln Memorial.

UPDATED RECORD
NEW RECORD

By contrast, the East Asian country of Laos has the **youngest official soldiers** – the minimum age for military service in the country is 15 years. And it's compulsory!

SCI-TECH & ENGINEERING

LARGEST MOTORIZED TRIKE

Swiss carnival band Guggä-Rugger Buus built a trike 26 ft 7 in (8.1 m) in length and weighing 13,300 lb (6,030 kg) as a mobile grandstand for all 30 members of the band. The machine has the 729-cu-in (12-liter) engine and chassis of a Saurer truck.

BAND MEMBER TOM BRODBECK RIDES THE TRIKE, WHICH WAS BUILT IN 2003 AND IS CALLED RÖSLI

Tektites are pieces of rock formed when large meteorites and asteroids hit Earth. The **largest recorded tektite** weighs 7.04 lb (3.2 kg). It was discovered in 1932 at Muong Nong, Laos.

The **largest known meteorite** is a block 9 ft (2.7 m) long by 8 ft (2.4 m) wide, estimated to weigh 65 tons (59 metric tons). It was found in 1920 at Hoba West, near Grootfontein in Namibia.

COMPUTING FIRSTS

THE STORY OF THE COMPUTER

The year 2012 has been designated "Alan Turing Year" in honor of the British code-breaker, mathematician, and computer pioneer, who was born on June 23, 1912. To mark the 100th anniversary of Turing's birth, and to acknowledge his contribution to computing, we look back over some key moments in the history of this now-ubiquitous invention.

ON YOUR MARKS...

Ten Colossus computers were built in total – a Mark 1, followed by nine Mark 2 models. So rapid was their development that the first Mark 2 was five times faster than the Mark 1.

COLOSSUS

Designed by a team of British engineers led by Tommy Flowers, the Colossus computers were used to decipher communications between German army commanders near the end of World War II and were the **first digital programmable electronic computing devices**. The first model began its work in February 1944.

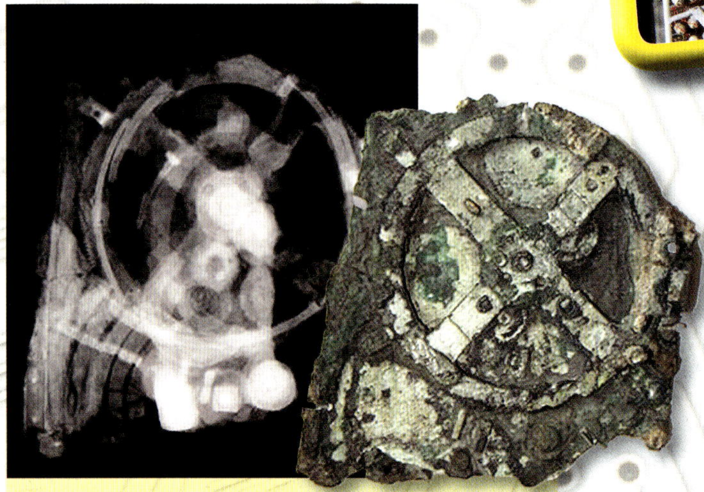

ANTIKYTHERA MECHANISM

The 2,000-year-old Antikythera Mechanism was discovered *c.* 1900 in a shipwreck close to the Greek island of Antikythera. It is a collection of bronze gears (X-ray, inset) built with a mechanical complexity not evident in any other object prior to the 14th century, though it is now encrusted with sea accretions. It is regarded as the **oldest analog computer**; experts believe that it was used to predict eclipses.

ALAN TURING
Born on June 23, 1912, one year after IBM was founded. During World War II, he worked as a code-breaker at Bletchley Park, UK. Died on June 7, 1954.

COMPUTER ACE

Turing designed the Automatic Computing Engine (ACE), an electronic computer with a stored program. (He likened it to "building a brain.") It first ran in 1950.

ENIAC

Developed for the US Army, the Electronic Numerical Integrator And Computer (ENIAC) was completed in 1946 and was the **first general-purpose electronic computer**.

1912

1912

1930 – Vannevar Bush (USA) creates the Differential Analyzer, a prototype analog computer.

1938 – Konrad Zuse (Germany) invents the Z1 Computer, a digital computer that uses punched tape.

1939 – John Atanasoff and Clifford Berry (both USA) create the **first electronic digital computer**; William Hewlett and David Packard form Hewlett Packard.

1950

1958 – Work by Jack Kilby and Robert Noyce (both USA), working independently, results in the **first integrated circuit**, or silicon chip. Noyce goes on to cofound Intel, in 1968.

1964 – The IBM 360 becomes the **first computer to use integrated circuits.**

1971 – IBM produces the **first floppy disk.**

1976 – Michael Shrayer (USA) develops the Electric Pencil, the **first word processor for microcomputers.**

The **fastest speed attained skiing on sand dunes** is 57.24 mi/h (92.12 km/h) by Henrik May (Namibia) in Swakopmund, Namibia, on May 31, 2010.

NY

ISLANDERS®

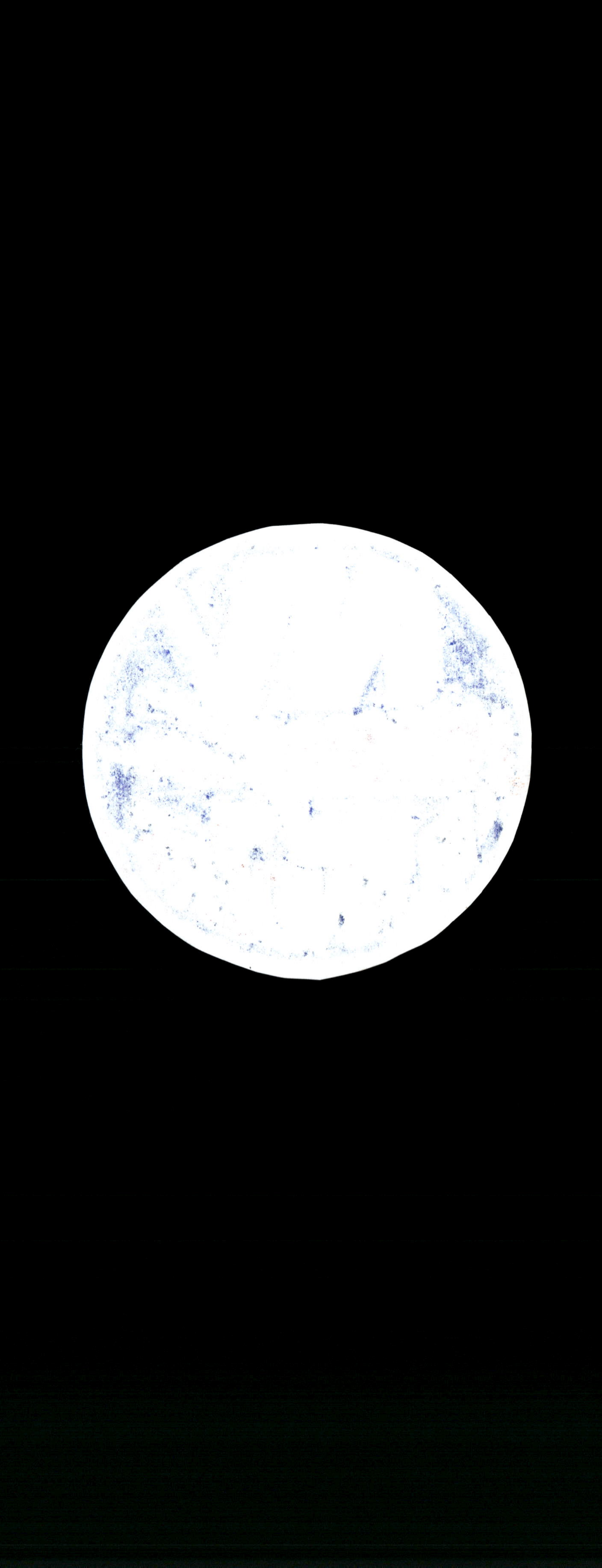

BABY

The Manchester Small-Scale Experimental Machine, known as "Baby," ran its first program at Manchester University, UK, in 1948 and was the ● **first computer to store its program internally**. Pictured is team leader Tom Kilburn (UK, 1921–2001) with a modern chip with the same capacity as Baby but a fraction of the size.

2012

1981 — IBM PC introduced.

1989 — Microsoft introduces Windows for IBM computers.

1990 — Tim Berners-Lee (UK) and Robert Cailliau (Belgium) kick-start the world wide web by proposing a hypertext system; the internet goes public in 1991. Microsoft and IBM stop collaborating on operating systems.

2001 — Approximately 1 billion PCs now sold. Apple sells its 5 millionth iMac.

2010 — Launch of Apple's iPad tablet. Nearly 15 million devices are sold in a year.

2012

THE MOUSE TALE

Douglas Engelbart (USA) created the **first computer mouse** in 1964. He was awarded a US patent for it in 1970. It was called a mouse because of the wire's resemblance to a tail.

● UPDATED RECORD
● NEW RECORD

POWER UP

The yellow timeline can also be viewed as a chart of computer processing power over time – this trend, known as Moore's Law, states that the number of transistors you can fit on to a circuit board doubles every two years.

SUPER COMPUTERS

In 1976, the first Cray-1 (right) was installed at Los Alamos National Laboratory, USA. It is the ● **first supercomputer**. The ● **fastest supercomputer**, China's Tianhe-1 (below right), is capable of 2.5 quadrillion flops. (A "flop" is the number of mathematical operations involving decimal fractions that a computer can make in a second.)

4004 CHIP

The **first microprocessor** was the 4004 chip, produced by Intel (USA) and dating from 1971. The size of a thumbnail, it was just as powerful as ENIAC (left), the room-sized first electronic computer.

PERSONAL COMPUTER

Today, PCs are everywhere – in our homes, schools, and workplaces – and we take laptops and tablet models with us wherever we go. Here's a brief guide to the history of the personal computer:

1950: Simon, the ● **first personal computer (PC)** (right), retails for $600. Memory is six 2-bit words – 12 bits in total.

1972: HP 9830, the ● **first all-in-one desktop computer**, is launched. Intel releases the SIM4, the **first microcomputer**, which uses the Intel 4004 microprocessor, capable of 92,000 instructions per second.

1979: Regarded as the **first true laptop**, the GRiD Compass (right) is designed by William Moggridge (UK) for GRiD Systems Corporation (USA). It is introduced in 1982 with a RAM of 512K.

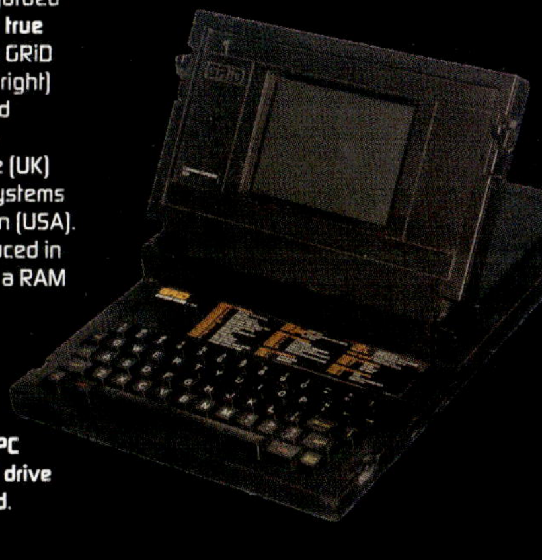

1983: The IBM PC/XT is the ● **first PC with a hard drive as standard.**

1984: The first Apple Macintosh (right) is launched, with an 8-MHz processor and 128 KB of memory. It becomes the ● **first commercially successful PC with a graphical user interface (GUI)** rather than command line (text-only interface).

1998: IBM demonstrates a prototype processor capable of operating at 1 GHz.

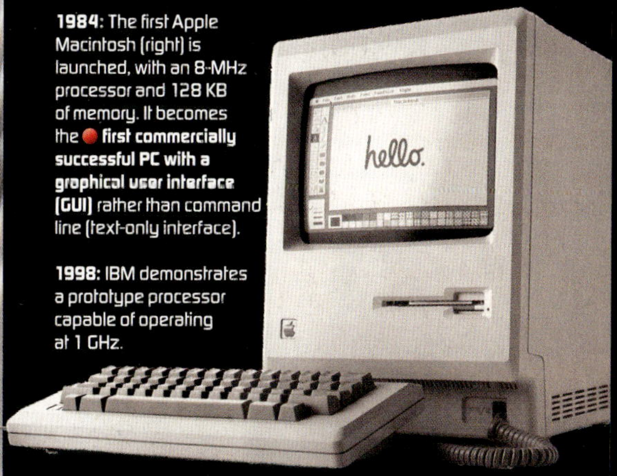

The ● **greatest distance traveled Nordic skiing in 24 hours** was 269.3 miles (433.4 km) and was achieved by Teemu Virtanen (Finland) at Kuortane, Finland, on November 16–17, 2010.

CUTTING-EDGE SCIENCE

LARGEST 3D EARTHQUAKE TABLE

E-Defense is a table used for research into the resilience of buildings and structures to earthquakes. Measuring 65 x 49 ft (20 x 15 m), it can support structures weighing 1,320 tons (1,200 metric tons) and shake payloads with an acceleration of 1 *g* in two dimensions horizontally and an acceleration of 1.5 *g* vertically. 1 *g* = acceleration of gravity at sea level. E-Defense is located in Miki City, Japan.

FIRST INDIVIDUAL TO WIN BOTH A NOBEL AND AN IG NOBEL PRIZE

Andre Geim (Russia) won an Ig Nobel Prize in 2000 for levitating a frog using magnets, and went on to win a Nobel Prize in Physics in 2010 for his research into graphene (see next entry), thereby becoming the first individual to win both prizes.

The Ig Nobels began in 1991 and are awarded for seemingly trivial advances in scientific research. They are organized by the *Annals of Improbable Research*, a US publication that takes a humorous approach to science. The Nobel Prize, considered a more illustrious award by some, has been handed out since 1901 in recognition of significant cultural and scientific advances.

LARGEST SHEET OF GRAPHENE

Graphene – discovered by Nobel Prize winners Andre Geim and Konstantin Novoselov (both Russia) – is a sheet of carbon atoms arranged in a pattern just one atom thick, and is the **thinnest man-made material**. Strong, flexible, and an effective conductor of electricity, graphene has great potential as an industrial material, but up to now it has proved impossible to produce in substantial amounts.

In June 2010, however, scientists at Sungkyunkwan University and Samsung (both South Korea) revealed they had devised a new method of increasing the amounts of graphene that can be made, and have produced continuous sheets with a width of 30 in (76 cm).

FASTEST MOVIE

Conventional movies run through a projector at a rate of 24 frames per second, creating the appearance of fluid motion. In January 2011, researchers using the FLASH X-ray laser in Hamburg, Germany, revealed their technique for molecular movie-making using ultrafast X-ray pulses to create a superfast movie. They made a two-frame movie of the Brandenburg Gate, reducing the rate from 24 frames per second to 0.00000000000005 seconds, or 50 femtoseconds, between frames. (A femtosecond is one millionth of one billionth of a second.)

LARGEST SEED VAULT

The Svalbard Global Seed Vault is an underground facility located on the Norwegian island of Spitsbergen. The facility is designed to store samples of the world's seeds as insurance against future threats to biodiversity. The heavily fortified vault opened on February 26, 2006 and has the capacity to store 4.5 million samples. On March 10, 2010, it received its 500,000th sample.

FIRST ANTILASER

In February 2011, scientists from Yale University, USA, unveiled their antilaser, the first device capable of absorbing and canceling out a laser beam. It uses an optical cavity made from silicon, which traps the laser energy and dissipates it as heat, and this prototype can absorb 99.4% of the laser light for a specific frequency. Researchers hope that the technology will have applications in the next generation of optical computing and in medical imaging.

TOXIC TASTES

The discovery that some bacteria can absorb arsenic is particularly surprising, as arsenic has long been used as a poison, notably in pesticides and insecticides.

FIRST ARSENIC-BASED LIFEFORM

Life on Earth uses six basic "building block" elements to make up its molecular structure: carbon, nitrogen, hydrogen, oxygen, sulfur, and phosphorus. In December 2010, a team of NASA scientists led by Felisa Wolfe-Simon (USA, pictured) announced its discovery of bacteria that shows the unique ability to incorporate arsenic into its DNA and proteins, as a substitute for phosphorus. It lives in the briny Mono Lake, California, USA.

The **fastest time to solve a Rubik's Cube using the feet** is 31.56 seconds and was achieved by Anssi Vanhala (Finland) at the Helsinki Open 2011, in Helsinki, Finland, on January 22–23, 2011.

HIGHEST MANMADE TEMPERATURE

In February 2010, scientists at Brookhaven National Laboratory's Relativistic Heavy Ion Collider on Long Island, New York, USA, announced that they had smashed together gold ions at nearly the speed of light, briefly forming a state of matter known as a quark-gluon plasma, which has properties more similar to those of a liquid than a gas. During the experiment the plasma reached temperatures of approximately 7.2 trillion °F (4 trillion °C), some 250,000 times hotter than the center of the Sun.

This substance is believed to have filled the universe just microseconds after the Big Bang – the **greatest explosion ever** – and is also thought to be the **earliest form of matter**.

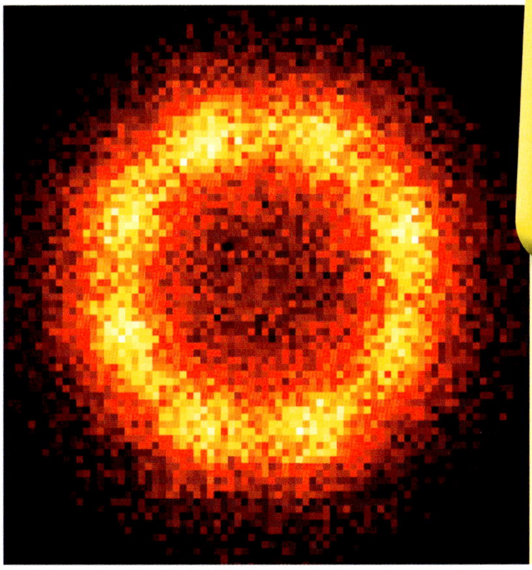

FIRST TRAPPING OF ANTIHYDROGEN

Antihydrogen – which consists of an antielectron (also known as a positron) and an antiproton – is the antimatter "opposite" of a hydrogen atom. In November 2010, researchers at CERN in Geneva, Switzerland, revealed that they had trapped and contained 38 atoms of this substance for around one-tenth of a second. Pictured is part of the "trap" where the positrons and antiprotons meet (above), and untrapped antihydrogen atoms annihilating on the inner surface of the trap (left).

SMALLEST SOLAR-POWERED SENSOR

In February 2010, scientists at the University of Michigan, USA, unveiled a solar-powered sensor measuring 0.09 x 0.1 x 0.03 in (2.5 x 3.5 x 1 mm). It consumes around one billionth of a watt of power and could operate indefinitely. This device could be used to monitor environmental conditions, or converted to run on body heat as a biomedical implant.

HIGHEST-RESOLUTION OPTICAL MICROSCOPE

On March 1, 2011, scientists at the University of Manchester, UK, announced that they had created an optical microscope that can see objects just 50 nanometers across, such as the insides of living cells. The instrument uses tiny spherical particles known as microspheres to amplify its optical power.

FIRST WEDDING CONDUCTED BY ROBOT

A humanoid robot named I-Fairy conducted the wedding ceremony of Tomohiro Shibata and Satoko Inoue in Tokyo, Japan, on May 16, 2010. The groom is a professor of robotics at the Nara Institute of Science and Technology, while his bride is an employee of Kokoro, the company that built I-Fairy.

FIRST HUMAN KILLED BY A ROBOT

On January 25, 1979, Robert Williams (USA) was killed by a production-line robot in a Ford Motor Company casting plant in Michigan, USA. The robot belonged to a parts-retrieval system that moved material around the factory. When the robot began running slowly, Williams climbed into the storage rack to retrieve parts manually and was struck on the head by the robotic arm.

LONGEST HI-FIDELITY SPACEFLIGHT SIMULATION

Mars500 is a collaboration between the European Space Agency, Russia, and China to simulate a 500-day manned mission to Mars. The crew of six entered their sealed facility (inset), located in Moscow, Russia, in June 2010, to begin their 520 days of isolated simulation.

UPDATED RECORD
NEW RECORD

The **fewest moves to complete a Rubik's Cube** in the usual way – with one's hands – is 22. Jimmy Coll (Belgium) set the record at the Barcelona Open 2009, in Terrassa, Spain, on April 24, 2009.

NANOTECH

Engineering the invisible

Join us on a journey down to the atomic level, where a single hair's width is considered colossal at 100 micrometers (µm) – millionths of a meter! Any smaller and we need to describe things in nanometers (nm) – billionths of a meter – or even picometers (pm), at a trillion to the meter! Here, scientists can manipulate individual atoms to create new objects and materials – pictured is a model of a toilet just 3 nm tall made by Takahashi Kaito (Japan). But there are also serious applications of this "nanotech," as our guide reveals...

SMALLEST...

ROBOTIC HAND

In October 2006, scientists at the University of California, USA, demonstrated a robotic hand only 0.039 in (1 mm) wide. Using silicon "fingers" and molecular balloons for joints, the hand could be made to flex and grasp objects by inflating or deflating the balloon joints. Inventors Yen-Wen Lu and C J Kim developed the robotic hand to perform complex manipulations at the sub-millimeter scale for applications that could include microsurgery.

SMALLEST TRANSISTOR

Researchers at Australia's University of New South Wales have made a transistor of crystalline silicon, with seven of the silicon atoms replaced by phosphorus atoms. It is 4 nm wide; conventional transistors are about 40 nm wide.

JET ENGINE

In September 2010, students at the Leibniz Institute for Solid State Physics and Materials Research in Dresden, Germany, produced a "nanorocket" measuring just 600 nm across and weighing 1 femtogram (10^{-15} g).

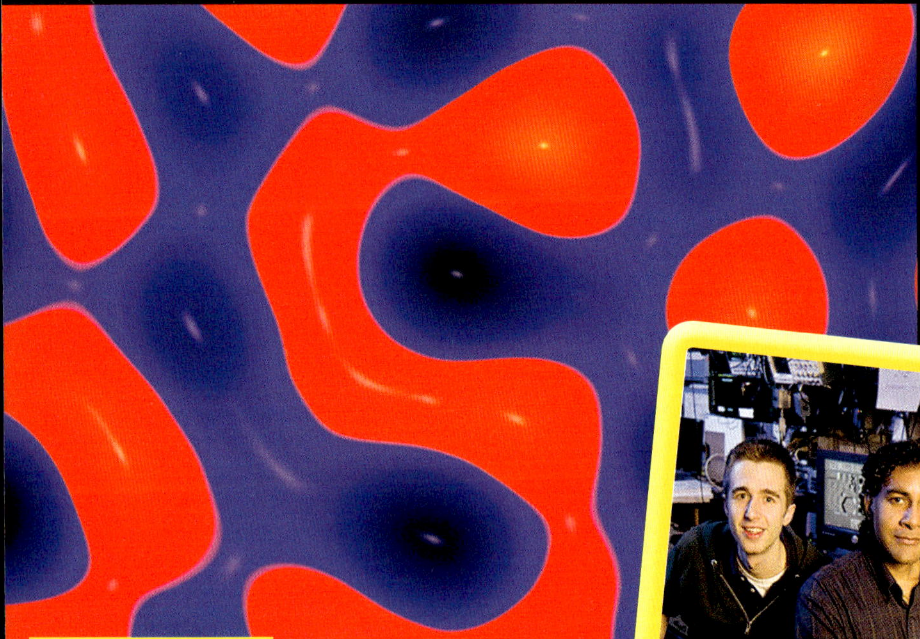

SMALLEST NANOCALLIGRAPHY

In March 2009, researchers at Stanford University (USA, left) were able to compose letters from subatomic pixels no bigger than 0.3 nm. The team arranged individual carbon monoxide molecules on a copper surface, then used a constant flow of electrons to form the letters "S" (pictured) and "U."

SMALLEST...

PERIODIC TABLE: 89 µm wide. Scientists at the University of Nottingham, UK, etched a table of element symbols into a strand of hair plucked from the head of Prof. Martyn Poliakoff (inset).

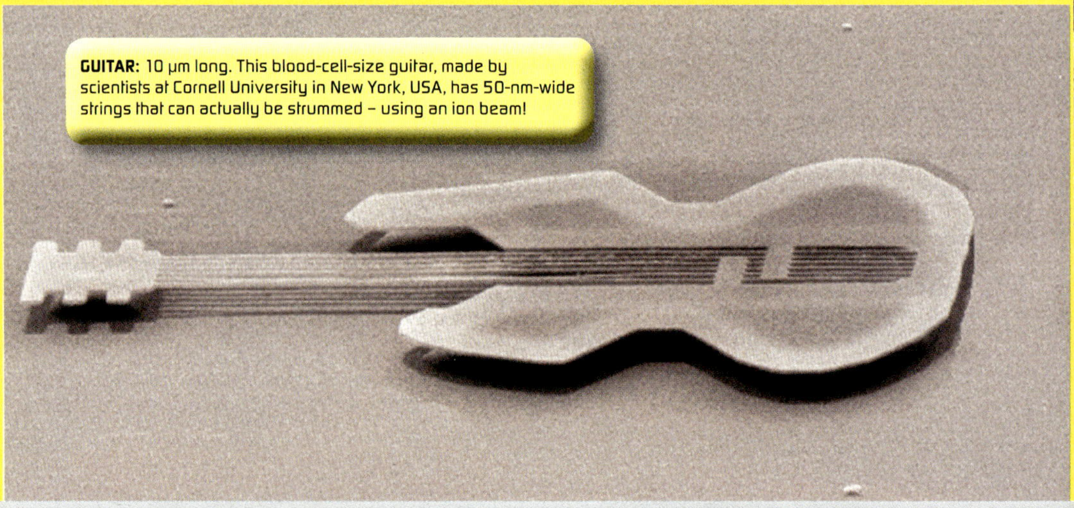

GUITAR: 10 µm long. This blood-cell-size guitar, made by scientists at Cornell University in New York, USA, has 50-nm-wide strings that can actually be strummed – using an ion beam!

Seven contestants from Belgium's *Big Brother* TV show built the **largest flaming image using matches**. The image depicted the show's logo and measured 107 ft² (10 m²) when the 329,700 matches were lit on November 19, 2000.

5.3 sextillion

Atoms of oxygen in every breath you take – the same atoms breathed out by the dinosaurs. In full, that's 5,356,800,000,000,000,000,000!

IT'S A SMALL WORLD The silicon cutting tip that created the 3D map is 100,000 times finer than a sharpened pencil tip, allowing scientists to recreate the Matterhorn (inset) at a scale of 1:50 million!

BOOK

Costing an enormous $15,000, the smallest book yet made comprises 30 micro-tablets carved on a pure crystalline silicon page, measuring just 70 x 100 µm. Etched using an ion beam at the Simon Fraser University, Canada, the book is called *Teeny Ted from Turnip Town*. It even has its own ISBN reference, ISBN-978-1-894897-17-4, though you will need a scanning electron microscope if you want to read a copy.

WORKING GEARS

Researchers at the Institute of Materials Research and Engineering in Singapore have developed working molecule-sized gears that can be fully controlled, rotating clockwise and counterclockwise. Based upon individual chains of molecules, they are arranged with arms issuing from each point on a hexagon.

BATTERY

Created in December 2010, the world's smallest battery was demonstrated at Sandia Laboratories, USA. Just 0.118 in (3 mm) long, the anode of the battery comprised a single nanowire of tin oxide only 100 nm in diameter by 10 µm long. Charged to 3.5 volts, the battery can sustain a current of only 1 picoampere (pA) – just a millionth of a microampere (mA). Work on miniaturization of batteries leads to better, smaller, and longer-lived rechargeable cells for cell phones and MP3 players.

SMALLEST ROBOTIC MEDICAL DEVICE

In April 2009, scientists at Zurich's Federal Institute of Technology (Switzerland) announced they had created a micro-robot capable of swimming in human arteries. The corkscrew-shaped robot has a maximum length of 60 µm. It will be used to repair damaged blood vessels and remove arterial deposits.

RADIO

Built using a single carbon nanotube, the world's smallest radio receiver measures only 10 µm in diameter by 100 µm in length. The carbon tube is electrically charged and can vibrate in harmony with incoming radio waves in the 40–400 Hz range. The precise tuning is achieved by changing the voltage applied to the tube to isolate individual radio frequencies.

CHRISTMAS CARD

Scientists at the University of Glasgow in Scotland, UK, saved on the cost of Christmas cards by making their own in 2010 – but recipients would need a high-power microscope to read them! At 200 x 290 µm in size, 8,276 cards would fit on a postage stamp. The card features a Christmas tree etched on to a tiny piece of glass. The technology used to produce the card could be used to make Christmas presents such as TVs and cameras of exceptional quality and performance.

SMALLEST 3D MAP OF EARTH

Scientists at IBM (USA) have created an accurate 3D map of Earth so small that 1,000 of them could fit on a single grain of salt. Patterns of the Earth's continents were created using an incredibly sharp silicon knife to carve features as small as 15 nm on a polymer substrate measuring only 22 x 11 µm.

AUTOMOBILE

In 2005, scientists at Rice University in Texas, USA, led by James Tour, revealed an "automobile" – made from a single molecule of mostly carbon atoms – measuring 3–4 nm wide. It includes four wheels made from "buckyballs" (carbon-60).

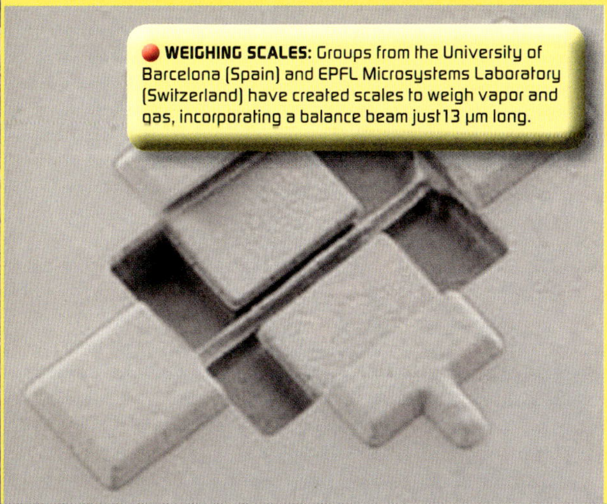

WEIGHING SCALES: Groups from the University of Barcelona (Spain) and EPFL Microsystems Laboratory (Switzerland) have created scales to weigh vapor and gas, incorporating a balance beam just 13 µm long.

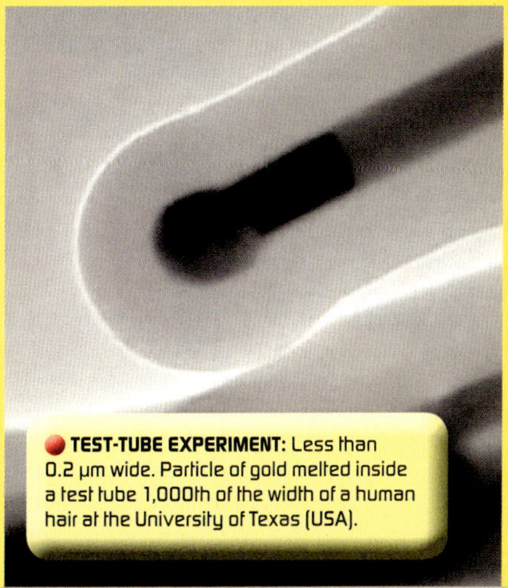

TEST-TUBE EXPERIMENT: Less than 0.2 µm wide. Particle of gold melted inside a test tube 1,000th of the width of a human hair at the University of Texas (USA).

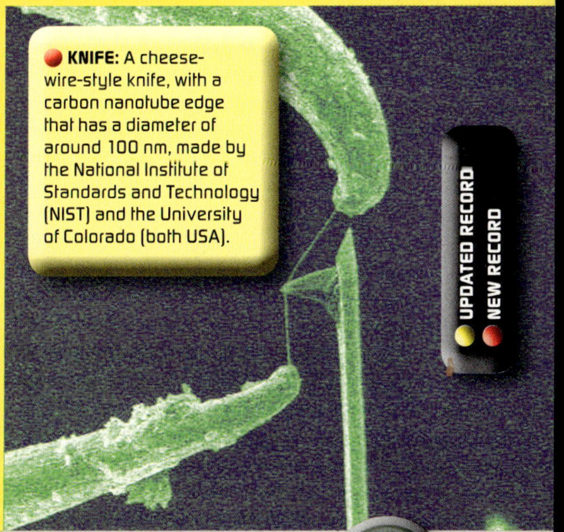

KNIFE: A cheese-wire-style knife, with a carbon nanotube edge that has a diameter of around 100 nm, made by the National Institute of Standards and Technology (NIST) and the University of Colorado (both USA).

UPDATED RECORD
NEW RECORD

On December 10, 2009, a total of 118 employees of the drug company Sandoz created the **largest flaming image using candles** at the Hotel Serena in Faisalabad, Pakistan. It had an area of 9,800 ft^2 (910.45 m^2) and included 35,478 candles.

CONSUMER TECH

LIGHTEST WI-FI PHONE
The modu W weighs 2.2 oz (62.7 g). Made by modu (Israel), it was measured at The Standards Institution of Israel (SII) in Tel Aviv, Israel, on September 21, 2010.

MOST EXPENSIVE CELL PHONE SERIES
Although more expensive limited-edition cell phones exist, the priciest handset that is commercially available is the Ulysse Nardin Chairman. Models range from $13,000 to $50,000 for precious-metal versions. It has a 3.2-in (81-mm) touch screen, 32 gigabytes of memory, and an 8-megapixel camera, and offers high-definition video playback. The phone includes a lacquered wooden docking station with built-in speakers.

This is also the **first cell phone with a self-winding rotor mechanism**, as in an automatic watch, which supplies backup kinetic energy to help keep the battery charged.

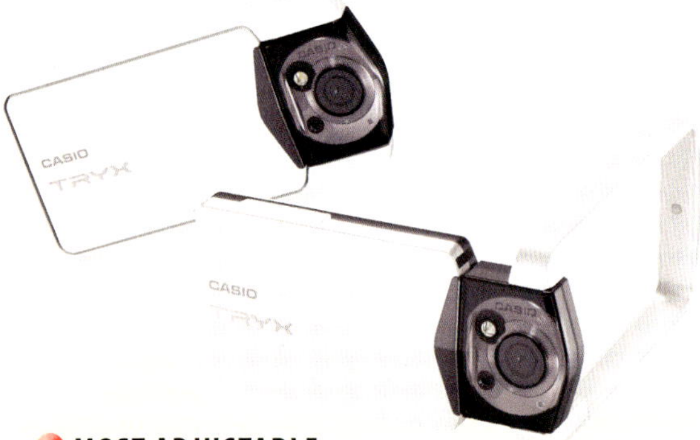

MOST ADJUSTABLE DIGITAL CAMERA
The 3-in (7.6-cm) touch-screen LCD on the Casio Tryx digital camera is swivel-mounted inside a frame, on which the lens and flash are affixed. The screen pops out of the frame and can be swiveled 270° around and through the frame in landscape mode, and swiveled simultaneously 360° on its frame-attached stem in portrait mode. The Casio Tryx launched in the USA and Japan in April 2011.

FIRST DUAL-SCREEN CELL PHONE
Instead of one large and unwieldy 4.7-in (11.9-cm) smartphone screen, the Kyocera Echo smartphone is equipped with twin 3.5-in (8.9-cm) displays with a hinge in the middle. When it is closed, the phone is no larger than a regular touch slab-style-screen smartphone. Each screen can run a different application or display a different web page; alternatively, a single app can be run or a single web page can be displayed across both screens. One screen can display a QWERTY keyboard as well. The Echo runs Android 2.2 and is powered by a 1-GHz processor.

LARGEST SCREEN ON A CELL PHONE
The Dell Streak 5 is a mobile 3G phone/tablet with a 5-in (12.7-cm) screen. It runs the Android 2.2 operating system, with a WVGA 800 x 480 thin-film transistor (TFT) LCD screen.

HIGHEST-RESOLUTION CELL PHONE CAMERA
In May 2009, Sony-Ericsson unveiled the Satio cell phone, equipped with a 12.1-megapixel camera. Shots can be framed in a 3.5-in (8.9-cm) 16:9 color LCD, lit with a Xenon flash, and brought closer with a 12x digital zoom, also the world's highest on a cell phone.

FASTEST-SELLING CONSUMER ELECTRONICS DEVICE
The concept of tablets – portable, lightweight, and thinner than conventional laptop computers – has existed for decades. The arrival of Apple's iPad, however – with its characteristic multitouch screen – proved a landmark release. Following its launch in April 2010, three million units were sold in the first 80 days, and thanks to the release of the iPad 2 on March 25, 2011, 4.69 million units were sold in the second quarter of the year – or 311,666 per day.

iBUY!
The sales figure of 4.69 million iPads includes both iPad and iPad 2 sales – and even if only half of the sales were iPad 2, this is 156,333 units per day, meaning that iPad 2 has sold faster than any other consumer gadget ever!

LARGEST PLASMA TV SCREEN
Launched on July 1, 2010, Panasonic's TH-152UX1 high-definition TV (HDTV) boasts a colossal 152-in (386-cm) plasma screen, which measures 5 ft 10.9 in (1.8 m) tall and 11 ft 2.4 in (3.41 m) wide to give a screen area equivalent to nine 50-in (127-cm) HDTVs arrayed in a three-by-three grid. It is also the **most expensive commercially available TV**, with a retail price of around $500,000.

In 1953, the Kutiah Glacier in Pakistan advanced more than 7.4 miles (12 km) in three months, averaging some 367 ft (112 m) per day – the **fastest glacial surge.**

$33,556 Your average lifetime spend on mp3 players, games consoles, computers, and related items of consumer technology.

FIRST HANDHELD 3D GAME PLAYER

On March 27, 2011, Nintendo unveiled the 3DS, a portable 3D game player that does not require the user to wear 3D glasses. The 3DS has two screens; an upper 800 x 240 pixel, 3.53-in (9-cm) widescreen 3D display and a lower 320 x 240 pixel, 3.02-in (7.7-cm) screen. Players can increase or decrease the 3D depth perception via a slider, or can simply turn off the 3D capability to play in 2D. The device also features a dual lens 3D camera on the rear.

LARGEST LCD TELEVISION SCREEN

Sharp's (Japan) LB-1085 is the world's largest LCD HDTV, with a screen measuring 108 in (274 cm) diagonally. Introduced at CES 2007, the HDTV without the stand measures 101.26 x 62.64 x 8.03 in (257.2 x 159.1 x 20.4 cm).

LARGEST LED SCREEN

The largest high-definition video screen is an LED display that measures 820 x 98 ft (250 x 30 m), giving a total surface area of 80,729 ft^2 (7,500 m^2). It is located at The Place, Beijing, China.

SMALLEST DIGITAL VOICE RECORDER

The Edic-mini Tiny A31, by Telesystems (Russia), measures just 1.14 x 0.47 x 0.59 in (29 x 12 x 15 mm) and weighs 0.21 oz (6 g). It was introduced in May 2009.

THINNEST LAPTOP

The Windows 7 Dell Adamo XPS ranges in size from 0.38 in (9.7 mm) at its slimmest point to 0.41 in (10.3 mm) at its thickest – an average of 0.39 in (9.99 mm). For comparison, an iPhone 4 is just 0.37 in (9.4 mm) thick. The Adamo stays skinny by repositioning key components and enclosing the keyboard fully inside the reinforced 13.4-in (34-cm) display area when the unit is closed. It measures 13.39 x 10.78 x 0.39 in (340 x 273.9 x 9.99 mm).

HIGHEST-CAPACITY DIGITAL MUSIC PLAYER

No other portable media player has ever had as much memory for music tracks, photos, or video as the Archos 5 Internet Tablet – a massive 500 GB, due to a built-in hard disk drive. The tablet runs the Android operating system, has a 4.8-in (12.2-cm) 800 x 480-pixel LCD screen and can connect to the internet via Wi-Fi. Up to 32 GB of extra memory can be added via the microSD card slot.

The Archos 5 is capable of storing up to 600 movies, 290,000 songs, or 5 million photos. It can record from any device with a standard video output (such as TVs, DVDs, and set-top cable boxes) via the optional digital video recording (DVR) station. It can receive FM radio, has built-in portable GPS navigation, an audio recording capability, and connects to an HDTV via a high-definition multimedia interface (HDMI) jack.

THINNEST BLU-RAY PLAYER

Samsung's BD-D7500 Blu-ray player is just 0.9 in (22.86 mm) thick. Wall-mountable, it plays 3D Blu-ray discs, runs 200 Samsung HDTV apps, and has built-in Wi-Fi to download these apps and to access their online content.

DEEPEST LIMIT FOR A DIVING WATCH

The 20,000-ft model CX Swiss Military Watch is a mechanical divers' watch made by Montres Charmex SA (Switzerland) that can function at depths of 20,000 ft (6,000 m). The wristwatch was tested at the Oceanographic Institute of the University of Southampton, UK, on January 5, 2009.

HANDS-FREE HEAVEN

Using a gadget similar to a web camera, Kinect enables players to interact with Xbox 360 using physical movements and verbal commands rather than a conventional games console.

FASTEST-SELLING GAMING PERIPHERAL

Kinect for Xbox 360 sold an average of 133,333 units per day in its first 60 days on sale in November–December 2010, and by March 2011, the "controller-free" peripheral had surpassed sales of 10 million units. Until iPad sales figures were released in April 2011 (see left), the Kinect also enjoyed the distinction of being the all-time fastest-selling piece of consumer tech.

UPDATED RECORD
NEW RECORD

A volcanic eruption under Europe's largest glacier, Vatnajokul in Iceland, in October 1996, topped Lake Grímsvötn with meltwater. This flowed from the lake at an estimated 1.6 million ft^3/s (45,000 m^3/s), the **fastest-melting glacier**.

INTERNET

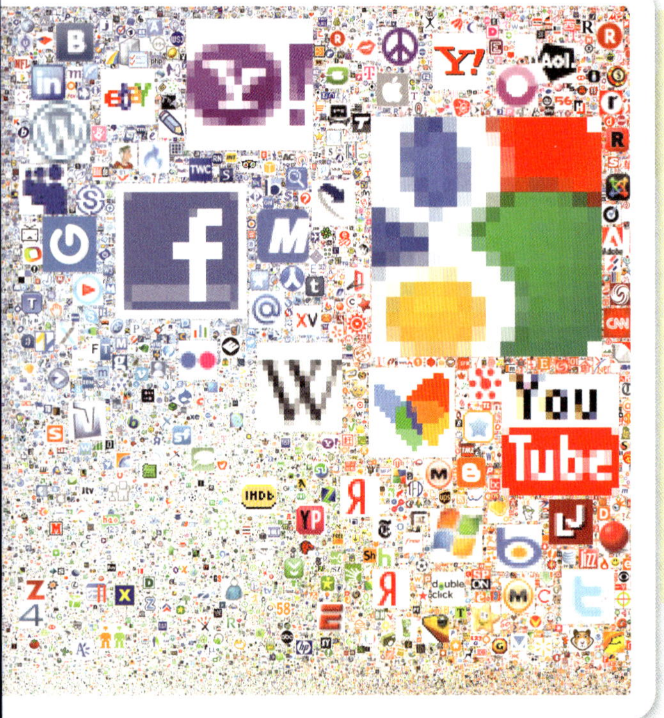

LARGEST INTERNET SEARCH ENGINE

Google no longer publishes its index size – owing, it says, to inaccurate data and duplicate sites. However, it remains the most popular search tool. In January 2011, Google enjoyed a 65.6% market share, with 11.1 billion searches that month in the USA alone.

Pictured is a pixelated "visualization" of the internet (left) created by nmap.org. It shows the logos of 328,427 websites, each scaled in proportion to the size of its web traffic. The largest icon, then, is Google's "g" (top right), with a total area of 11,936 pixels².

LARGEST ONLINE SOCIAL NETWORK

As of January 2011, Facebook boasted over 600 million active users, according to the global investment bank Goldman Sachs, and an estimated market value of $50 billion.

FIRST COMPUTERIZED SOCIAL NETWORK

The Community Memory project, established in Berkeley, California, USA, in 1973, used a teletype terminal in a record store, connected to an SDS 940 computer in San Francisco. It allowed visitors to the store to enter and view messages left by others and was the first public computerized bulletin board system (BBS).

MOST FREQUENT SOCIAL NETWORK USERS

According to market research company TNS, as of October 2010 social network users in Malaysia spend an average of nine hours a week on social network sites.

It therefore comes as no surprise to learn that Malaysia is the **country with the most digital friends** – in the same research study, TNS discovered that social network users in Malaysia have an average of 233 digital friends.

The **country with the fewest digital friends** is Japan, where social networkers have an average of just 29 friends.

MOST SEARCHED-FOR FEMALE ONLINE

Pop star Katy Perry (USA, b. Katheryn Hudson) was the highest-ranking female on the "fastest-rising people" list for 2010, according to Google's end-of-year report. Interest in the singer peaked at various times, notably around the announcements of the MTV and Grammy awards.

FIRST TWITTER TWEET

Twitter was invented by Jack Dorsey (USA) in 2006 as a microblogging and social networking tool. The very first tweet was posted by Dorsey at 9:50 p.m. (Pacific Standard Time) on March 21, 2006, and read: "just setting up my twittr."

BY 2009, FACEBOOK'S REVENUE WAS ESTIMATED AT $800 MILLION

FACEBOOK

The world's most popular online social network (see main record text) has spawned a few more records for its fans, followers, and founder:

Record	Achievement	Details
Youngest billionaire (present day)	Mark Zuckerberg (USA, b. May 14, 1984), CEO of Facebook	Estimated net worth of $1.5 billion when listed on Forbes.com on March 5, 2008
Most fans on Facebook	34,757,671	*Texas Hold'em Poker* (Zynga). Achieved on January 31, 2011
Most "likes" on a Facebook post in 24 hours	588,403, in response to a post made on February 15, 2011	Rapper Lil Wayne, aka Dwayne Carter, Jr (USA)

LARGEST MILITARY INTERNET LEAK

On October 22, 2010, the whistle-blowing website Wikileaks published online 319,882 field reports from the US Army, documenting its operations in Iraq from 2004 to 2009. Known as the "Iraqi War Logs," they outline events previously unpublicized concerning the activities of US and coalition troops in Iraq. UK-based Iraq Body Count, which attempts to monitor civilian casualties, claimed that the Iraqi War Logs reveal 15,000 extra civilian deaths that had not been included in public reports.

Wikileaks' editor-in-chief and spokesperson Julian Assange (Australia, pictured) was voted the 2010 Readers' Choice Person of the Year in *Time* magazine. At the time of going to press, he was living in the UK, appealing against extradition to Sweden, where he faces questioning about alleged assaults.

According to the Nobel Foundation, as of 2002 Iceland had 3.36 Nobel Laureates for every 1 million head of population – the **most Nobel Prize Laureates per capita**.

200 billion Neurons in your brain. Each neuron has 7,000 synapses, with each synapse making 1,000 connections. Your head contains more connections than all the computers, routers, and internet connections on Earth.

MOST "LIKES" ON YOUTUBE

Judson Laipply's (USA) "Evolution of Dance" viral video – in which Judson performs a dance routine featuring moves from the history of dance – was uploaded to YouTube in 2006 and was viewed 70 million times in less than eight months. As of May 4, 2011, the video has been viewed 171,571,560 times and has earned a record 739,956 "likes."

MOST COMMENTS ON A FACEBOOK POST

A post made on January 6, 2011 on the Facebook page for *CityVille* (Zynga, 2010) received 29,160 comments. The majority of the comments are requests for other players to link up, or "add," as friends on the game, which rewards community-based play. As such, the comment thread isn't so much a discussion of a topic but an open forum for players to attempt to attract people to add them as friends, thereby increasing their gameplay options.

LARGEST VIDEO SHARING WEBSITE

YouTube currently receives around 35 hours of content every minute, and in 2010, more than 13 million hours of video were uploaded to the site. Also in 2010, YouTube surpassed 700 billion playbacks.

MOST FRIENDS ON TWITTER

US President Barack Obama was following 703,744 friends as of February 14, 2011. But more important is the number of followers...

MOST FOLLOWERS ON TWITTER

Pop singer Lady Gaga (USA, b. Stefani Germanotta) had 7,942,058 Twitter followers as of February 1, 2011.

MOST RESPONSIVE BRAND ON TWITTER

The most responsive corporate account on Twitter is Microsoft's @XboxSupport, aka the "Elite Tweet Fleet." From March 12 to 18, 2010, the Fleet responded to more than 5,000 questions – taking an average of 2 min 42 sec per question – to illustrate their commitment to customer service.

MOST COMMON FORM OF MALWARE

Trojan-horse software performs unwanted tasks on a computer while masquerading as a useful application. It allows malicious software – aka malware or pestware – to be installed on a machine via a "back door." Data compiled by BitDefender in the first half of 2009 showed that Trojan horses accounted for some 83% of all malware on the internet.

MOST GOOGLE STREET VIEW APPEARANCES

The most verified appearances of an individual on Google Street View is 43, achieved by Wendy Southgate (UK), who was photographed repeatedly by the service's mobile camera while walking her dog in Elmswell, Suffolk, UK, in 2009.

"EVOLUTION OF DANCE" FEATURES 32 SONGS IN ALL

739,956 "LIKES"

DANCE, DANCE, DANCE! Judson's epic routine takes in landmark songs from the history of popular music, from Elvis Presley's 1956 hit "Hound Dog" to Jay-Z's "Dirt Off Your Shoulder" (2004).

UPDATED RECORD
NEW RECORD

In 1992, at the age of 33, Rigoberta Menchú Tum (Guatemala) became the **youngest-ever Nobel Peace Prize winner**; born in the Mayan village of Chimel, she was also the first indigenous person to receive the award.

NEED FOR SPEED

FASTEST LAND-SPEED RECORD

The official land-speed record, measured over 1 mile (1.6 km), is 763.035 mi/h (1,227.985 km/h, or Mach 1.020). Andy Green (UK) became the most recent holder of this famous record on October 15, 1997 in the Black Rock Desert, Nevada, USA, in *Thrust SSC*. When he set the land-speed record that day, Green also became the **first person on land to travel faster than the speed of sound** (usually around 768 mi/h, or 1,236 km/h, in dry air at 68°F, or 20°C). The resultant sonic boom shook a school in the nearby town of Gerlach. He set the record 50 years and a day after the sound barrier was broken in the air by Chuck Yeager (USA).

RACING TOWARD A NEW RECORD?

Bloodhound SSC has been built by the same team that created the record-breaking *Thrust SSC*. They hope to set a new land-speed record of around 1,000 mi/h (1,609 km/h) – significantly faster than the current record – in 2013. A site for the attempt has already been chosen at Hakskeen Pan, on the edge of South Africa's Kalahari Desert.

LAND-SPEED LANDMARKS

This table charts highlights from the history of the land-speed record, going back as far as the late 19th century. The speed is typically calculated over a two-way run measuring 1 km (0.6 miles).

Date	Vehicle	Driver	Location	Speed/Record
Dec 18, 1898	*Jeantaud Duc* (electric)	Gaston de Chasseloup-Laubat (France)	Achères, Yvelines, France	39.24 mi/h **First recognized land-speed record**
Aug 5, 1902	*Mors* (internal combustion [IC])	William Vanderbilt (USA)	Albis, near Chartres, France	76.080 mi/h **First internal combustion record**
Jul 21, 1904	*Gobron-Brillié* (IC)	Louis Emile Rigolly (France)	Ostend, Belgium	103.561 mi/h **First to exceed 100 mi/h**
Jun 24, 1914	*Benz #3* (IC)	L G "Cupid" Hornsted (UK)	Brooklands, Surrey, UK	124.095 mi/h **First two-way record attempt**
Mar 29, 1927	*Sunbeam 1000* (IC)	Henry Segrave (USA/UK)	Daytona, Florida, USA	203.792 mi/h **First to exceed 200 mi/h**
Sep 3, 1935	*Railton Rolls-Royce Bluebird* (IC)	Sir Malcolm Campbell (UK)	Bonneville, Utah, USA	301.129 mi/h **First to exceed 300 mi/h**
Sep 16, 1947	*Railton Mobil Special* (IC)	John Cobb (UK)	Bonneville, Utah, USA	394.194 mi/h **First to exceed 400 mi/h on one leg of two-leg run**
Aug 5, 1963	*Spirit of America* (jet)	Craig Breedlove (USA)	Bonneville, Utah, USA	407.518 mi/h **First to exceed 400 mi/h over both legs of two-leg run**
Nov 2, 1965	*Spirit of America Sonic I* (jet)	Craig Breedlove (USA)	Bonneville, Utah, USA	555.485 mi/h **First to exceed 500 mi/h**
Nov 15, 1965	*Spirit of America Sonic I* (jet)	Craig Breedlove (USA)	Bonneville, Utah, USA	600.601 mi/h **First to exceed 600 mi/h**
Oct 23, 1970	*Blue Flame* (jet)	Gary Gabelich (USA)	Bonneville, Utah, USA	631.367 mi/h **First record set by rocket-powered car**
Sep 25, 1997	*Thrust SSC* (jet)	Andy Green (UK)	Black Rock Desert, Nevada, USA	714.144 mi/h **First to exceed 700 mi/h**
Oct 15, 1997	*Thrust SSC* (jet)	Andy Green (UK)	Black Rock Desert, Nevada, USA	763.035 mi/h **First to break the speed of sound**

FASTEST LAND-SPEED RECORD (FEMALE)

The highest land-speed recorded by a woman is 512.710 mi/h (825.126 km/h), by Kitty Hambleton (USA) in the rocket-powered SM1 *Motivator* in the Alvord Desert, Oregon, USA, on December 6, 1976. In these record attempts, average speeds are calculated from a number of different runs. The highest speed measured during Hambleton's runs was 524.016 mi/h (843.323 km/h), although it is probable that she touched 600 mi/h (965 km/h) momentarily.

Guatemala boasts the record for the **oldest known Mayan writing**, with evidence that dates back to 300–200 BC at a site in the city of San Bartolo, Guatemala.

0.004 Number of seconds it takes images to travel from your eye to your brain. You live in the past. If you step on a pin, you won't find out about it until 0.2 seconds after it has happened.

FASTEST WHEEL-DRIVEN VEHICLE

The fastest speed ever reached by a vehicle powered through its wheels is 458.444 mi/h (737.794 km/h), by the turbine-powered *Turbinator* driven by Don Vesco (USA) at Bonneville Salt Flats, Utah, USA, on October 18, 2001. It is also the **fastest turbine-engine automobile**.

FASTEST AUTOMOBILE CRASH SURVIVED

In September 1960, during trials to set a new land-speed record at Bonneville Salt Flats, Utah, USA, Donald Campbell (UK) crashed his car *Bluebird* while traveling at 360 mi/h (579 km/h). The vehicle rolled over and Campbell fractured his skull, but against all the odds he survived.

In the 1950s and 1960s, he broke multiple world speed records. He was the son of Sir Malcolm Campbell (see table).

FASTEST SPEED BY A JET-POWERED MOTORCYCLE

On April 24, 2009, Kevin Martin (USA) achieved a speed of 202.55 mi/h (325.97 km/h) on his *Ballistic Eagle* jet-powered motorcycle at the Spring Nationals, Rockingham, North Carolina, USA.

FASTEST MOTORCYCLE WHEELIE

Sweden's Patrick Fürstenhoff hit 191.3 mi/h (307.86 km/h) on the rear wheel of a Honda Super Blackbird 1100 cc Turbo at Bruntingthorpe Proving Ground, Leicestershire, UK, on April 18, 1999.

FASTEST SPEED IN A DIESEL-ENGINE AUTOMOBILE

Driving the *JCB DIESELMAX*, Andy Green (UK) reached 350.092 mi/h (563.418 km/h) at Bonneville Salt Flats, Utah, USA, on August 23, 2006. In doing so, he broke his own record, which he had achieved the day before with a speed of 328.767 mi/h (526.027 km/h).

FASTEST MOTORCYCLE LAND-SPEED RECORD

On September 25, 2010, Rocky Robinson (USA) achieved an average speed of 376.363 mi/h (605.697 km/h) in his *Top Oil-Ack Attack* streamliner over a measured kilometer (0.6 miles) at Bonneville Salt Flats, Utah, USA.

HISTORY'S FASTEST SPEEDS

From speed on land to the all-time fastest methods of transport. Each entry on this bar chart was once the fastest way to travel, other than simply running. For more than 5,000 years, sledges were the fastest way to get around; and the air-speed record has not advanced since 1961. The Apollo 10 mission represents the fastest speed at which humans have ever traveled.

LIGHT FANTASTIC

We are still lagging far behind the speed of light, at 983,571,056 ft/s (299,792,458 m/s) in a vacuum. At that speed, you could travel around the world seven times in a second!

UPDATED RECORD
NEW RECORD

Going back even further, the Sumerians, who lived in what is now Iraq, created the **oldest surviving love poem** in the form of a clay tablet dating back to 3500 BC.

OIL

MOST WELLS SABOTAGED: In 1991, retreating Iraqi forces in Kuwait burned 700 oil wells, with a loss of up to 1.5 billion barrels of oil. Unburned oil formed a layer of "tarcrete" over 5% of the land.

HEAVIEST OFFSHORE OIL PLATFORM: With storage for 1.3 million barrels of oil, the 702,172-ton (637,000-metric-ton) Hibernia rig in the Atlantic can withstand iceberg impacts.

FIRST OIL WELLS

Humans first began drilling for oil in China as early as AD 347. Drilling was achieved to depths of 787 ft (240 m) using rudimentary drill bits attached to "pipes" made from bamboo.

OLDEST OIL

In August 2000, Australian scientists announced their discovery of minute oil droplets within fluid inclusions (microscopic liquid or gas bubbles) trapped inside mineral grains in rocks dating back some 3.2 billion years.

OLDEST OFFSHORE OIL PLATFORM

Neft Daslari is a town built in 1949 in the Caspian Sea 34.2 miles (55 km) off the coast of Azerbaijan. Oil production began there in 1951 and, at its peak, the town boasted hotels, a bakery, a power plant, and a total surface area of 17.3 acres (7 ha), consisting of separate "islands" connected by 124.3 miles (200 km) of bridges. Much of Neft Daslari has now been reclaimed by the sea, but its rigs still produce oil and its population remains around 5,000.

DEEPEST OIL WELL

While operating in the Tiber oil field in the Gulf of Mexico in 2010, the *Deepwater Horizon* semi-submersible drilling rig achieved a drilling vertical depth of 33,011.8 ft (10,062 m), working in water 4,130 ft (1,259 m) deep.

GREATEST DRILLING WATER DEPTH

In November 2003, the drillship *Discoverer Deep Seas*, owned by Transocean Inc. (USA), drilled for oil and gas in 10,011 ft (3,051 m) of water in the Gulf of Mexico.

LONGEST CRUDE OIL PIPELINE

The Interprovincial Pipe Line Inc. installation, which spans North America from Edmonton to Montreal (both Canada), covers a distance of 2,353 miles (3,787.2 km) and features 82 pumping stations, which maintain a flow of over 1.6 million barrels a day.

LARGEST OIL TANKER

The four T1 class ultra-large crude carriers – T1 Africa, T1 Asia, T1 Europe, and T1 Oceania – were constructed in 2002/03 by Daewoo Shipbuilding and Marine Engineering in South Korea. They are 1,243 ft (379 m) long and 223 ft (68 m) wide, and have a displacement of 570,621 tons (517,659 metric tons) fully loaded.

LARGEST TANKER SHIP HIJACKED

On November 15, 2008, off the coast of Somalia, pirates seized one of the world's largest tankers, the *Sirius Star* (UAE), along with its precious cargo of crude oil valued at $110 million. At 1,100 ft (330 m) long and with a gross tonnage of 162,252, the tanker is the largest ever hijacked, and a ransom of $3 million had to be paid for its release.

IN DEEP WATER

The flames from the *Deepwater Horizon* fire were up to 300 ft (91 m) high and could be seen 35 miles (56 km) away. The fire burned for 36 hours before the rig sank on April 22, 2010.

TO SEE THE FASTEST "GAS GUZZLERS" ON THE PLANET, TURN TO P.244.

UPDATED RECORD
NEW RECORD

The **first use of a graphite bomb** was during the Gulf War in 1991, when Allied forces used it to disable 85% of Iraq's power supplies. So-called G-bombs work by exploding thousands of ultrafine carbon-fiber wires over electrical installations, short-circuiting them.

LARGEST ACCIDENTAL MARINE OIL SPILL

On April 20, 2010, an explosion on the *Deepwater Horizon* oil drilling rig in the Gulf of Mexico killed 11 workers and caused an environmental and economic disaster that is still unfolding. The oil spill from a gusher on the seafloor continued to flow until July 15, when the well was capped. In the meantime, 4.9 million barrels, or 171 million gal (779 million liters), of crude had entered the ocean.

LARGEST OIL REFINERY COMPLEX

The Reliance Jamnagar complex in Gujarat, India, consists of two massive oil refineries adjacent to each other, completed in 1999 and 2008. Between them, the refineries have the capacity to process more than 1.2 million barrels (50 million gal) of crude oil each day.

BLACK GOLD

Fortunes are made and lost in the oil business. One of the industry's biggest winners was US tycoon John D Rockefeller (1839–1937), the **first dollar billionaire**, who made $1.4 billion from "black gold."

LARGEST OIL CONSUMPTION

A land full of road users, the USA is the world's most oil-thirsty nation, consuming an estimated 18.69 million barrels per day in 2009.

LOWEST FUEL PRICE

Despite the soaring oil price, motorists in Venezuela were paying just 2.3 cents per liter of gas in November 2010 – less than the market price of crude!

LARGEST OIL GUSHER

An oil gusher, or wildcat, is the uncontrolled release of oil from a well. On August 26, 1956, an enormous wildcat exploded to the surface near Qom, Iran, with some 120,000 barrels of crude oil per day spurting out in a fountain that reached 170.6 ft (52 m) high. The Qom wildcat was extinguished after 90 days.

LARGEST PROVEN OIL RESERVES

Residents of Saudi Arabia need not worry about the gas pumps running dry any day soon – the country has more proven oil reserves than any other, with 264.1 billion barrels, or almost 20% of the world's proven reserves, as of 2010.

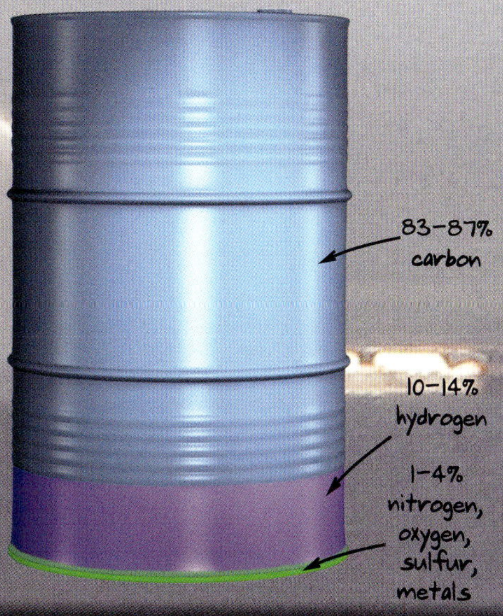

What is oil?

There are many types of oil, including those that we cook with, but the most useful – and sought after – is the dark, treacly "crude oil" that comes from deep within the Earth's crust. Crude is formed naturally from plants and animals that decayed under sand and mud millions of years ago, so it is known as a "fossil fuel." It is tricky to get to and has to be pumped to the surface by drilling rigs such as the Hibernia, then treated in an oil refinery to make it usable. The most common use for oil is as automobile fuel, but it is also found in plastics, clothes, fertilizers, foods, and almost everything else we use. Life without it would be very different.

ALTERNATIVE ENERGIES

GREENEST COUNTRY
Based on the Environmental Sustainability Index – which measures a country's water use, biodiversity, and adoption of clean energies, among other things – Iceland is the greenest country, with a score of 93.5/100.

In terms of the **greenest city**, Masdar City in Abu Dhabi, UAE, is the first city envisaged to have no carbon emissions and no waste. Designed by Foster and Partners (UK), all of its power will be generated from renewable resources, and all waste material recycled. Automobiles will be banned in favor of electric, driverless, underground vehicles, so the city's projected 50,000 citizens should leave no carbon footprint. Phase 1 is due to be completed in 2015.

LARGEST CNG FUEL STATION
The C-Nergy Compressed Natural Gas (CNG) station in Singapore has 46 filling hoses. It opened to the public on September 9, 2009.

HIGHEST-CAPACITY WIND FARM
Covering an area of almost 100,000 acres (400 km²), Roscoe Wind Farm in Texas, USA, has 627 wind turbines and can generate up to 781.5 megawatts (MW).

Located in Emden in northwest Germany, the **largest wind generator** is the Enercon E-126, with a hub height of 443 ft (135 m) and a rotor diameter of 416 ft (127 m). Its capacity is rated at 7 MW – enough to fuel 5,000 households of four people in Europe!

LARGEST SOLAR FURNACE
In Odeillo Font-Romeux, France, an array of heliostats direct the Sun's energy on to a 21,500-ft² (2,000-m²) parabolic reflector, which then reflects the rays of the Sun to a focal point. The concentrated rays can create temperatures of up to 6,872°F at the focal point, where they are used to conduct research into materials science and solar engineering. The furnace was built in 1969.

FIRST WAVE FARM
The Aguçadoura Wave Farm is located 3.1 miles (5 km) off the shore of Portugal. It uses three Pelamis wave energy conversion machines to generate up to 2.25 MW of electricity. These machines consist of connected sections that flex as waves pass and convert the flexing motion to electricity.

WOOD ALTERNATIVE
In Europe, *c.* AD 1500, the overuse of wood for burning led to shortages owing to deforestation. People began burning coal instead of wood, and coal became the **oldest alternative fuel**.

LARGEST SOLAR-POWERED BOAT
TÛRANOR PlanetSolar measures 101 ft (31 m) long – or 114 ft (35 m) with flaps extended. It has a beam, or width, of 49 ft (15 m) – 75 ft (23 m) with flaps – and a displacement of 93 tons (85 metric tons). The catamaran's upper surface is covered in 5,780 ft² (537 m²) of solar panels, allowing the vessel to be powered by solar energy alone.

WATER CRAFT
Hydro power – techniques of harnessing the energy created by moving water – remains the **largest contributor to renewable energy**, reaching a capacity of 980 GW by the end of 2009.

UPDATED RECORD
NEW RECORD

Although it had reached its full height of 1,082 ft (330 m), the Ryugyong Hotel in Pyongyang, North Korea, was not finished when construction was halted in 1992. Twenty years later, it remains the **tallest unoccupied building**.

VEHICLES

LONGEST JOURNEY BY COFFEE-POWERED AUTOMOBILE

In March 2010, a 1988 Volkswagen Scirocco was driven 209 miles (337 km) from London to Manchester, UK, powered by coffee. The coffee granules are heated in a charcoal fire, where they then break down into carbon monoxide and hydrogen. The gas is then cooled and filtered before the hydrogen is combusted to drive the engine. Nicknamed the "Car-puccino," it can reach a speed of 60 mi/h (96.5 km/h) and achieve a rate of 1 mile per 56 espressos (1 km per 35). The process works because coffee granules contain a small amount of carbon, which is why the trip required enough coffee to make 11,760 espressos!

LONGEST JOURNEY BY SOLAR ELECTRIC AUTOMOBILE

The *Midnight Sun* solar automobile team from the University of Waterloo in Ontario, Canada, traveled 9,364 miles (15,070 km) through Canada and the USA, leaving Waterloo on August 7, 2004 and finishing in Ottawa, Canada, on September 15, 2004.

On November 17, 2009, Tadashi Tateuchi (Japan) drove his electrically powered Mira EV for 345.23 miles (555.6 km), from Tokyo to Osaka, Japan, the **longest journey made by a non-solar-powered electric vehicle** without recharging the batteries.

FASTEST SOLAR-POWERED VEHICLE

Sunswift IV achieved a speed of 55.139 mi/h (88.738 km/h) at the naval base HMAS *Albatross* near Nowra, in NSW, Australia, on January 7, 2011. The car was built by the University of New South Wales Solar Racing Team and driven by Barton Mawer (Australia).

LONGEST JOURNEY BY WIND-POWERED AUTOMOBILE

Dirk Gion and Stefan Simmerer (both Germany) drove 3,106 miles (5,000 km) from Perth to Melbourne, Australia, in 18 days between January and February 2011. The *Wind Explorer* is powered by the wind; a wind turbine charges a lithium-ion battery pack to provide propulsion and, when the wind is strong enough, a kite resembling a parasail harnesses the power of the wind directly. Aside from about $10 worth of electricity when the wind was insufficient, the journey was entirely wind-powered.

FASTEST WATER-JET-POWERED AUTOMOBILE

The greatest speed attained in a water-jet-powered automobile is 16.65 mi/h (26.8 km/h) and was achieved by Jason Bradbury (UK) on the set of *The Gadget Show* at Wattisham Airfield, Ipswich, UK, on March 15, 2010.

FASTEST ELECTRIC AUTOMOBILE

The highest average speed achieved for an electric vehicle is 303.025 mi/h (487.672 km/h) by *Buckeye Bullet 2*. The vehicle was designed and built by engineering students at Ohio State University, USA, at the university's Center for Automotive Research (CAR), and driven by Roger Schroer (USA) at the Bonneville Salt Flats, Utah, USA, on September 25, 2009.

FASTEST ELECTRIC MOTORCYCLE

The *KillaCycle* can accelerate from 0–60 mi/h (0–96 km/h) in less than a second and is powered by the same battery as a cordless drill. On October 23, 2008, it reached 167.99 mi/h (270.35 km/h), driven in a race by Scotty Pollacheck (USA) at Bandimere Speedway in Morrison, Colorado, USA, and covered 0.25 miles (0.4 km) in 7.89 seconds.

BEST-SELLING HYBRID VEHICLES

Hybrid vehicles are powered by a combination of an internal combustion engine and an electric engine. They produce fewer harmful emissions than conventional cars and are highly energy-efficient. The best-selling hybrid vehicle is the Toyota Prius, launched in 1997. By September 2010, it had sold 2,011,800 units. The third-generation Prius was unveiled in 2009.

HYBRID HISTORY

Ferdinand Porsche (Germany) devised the Lohner-Porsche Mixte Hybrid – the first automobile powered by both gasoline and electricity – way back in 1899!

FASTEST SPEED ON A LAND YACHT

The highest speed officially recorded for a land yacht is 126.1 mi/h (202.9 km/h) by *Greenbird*, piloted by Richard Jenkins (UK), at Ivanpah Dry Lake, Prim, Nevada, USA, on March 26, 2009.

By contrast, the Nisiyama Onsen Keiunkan hot-spring hotel in Yamanashi, Japan, has been finished and entertaining guests for a very long time. The world's **oldest hotel**, it dates back to AD 705.

AUTOMOBILES

BEST-SELLING AUTOMOBILE

As of February 2011, the Toyota Corolla is the best-selling automobile, with more than 35 million sold since 1966.

The Volkswagen Beetle is the **best-selling automobile of a single design**; the core structure and shape remained largely unchanged from 1938 to 2003. It was also the **first automobile to achieve 20 million sales**. The Beetle's tally when production ended in 2003 was 21,529,464.

The Ford Model T is the second best-selling car of a single design, and the **first car to achieve sales of 10 million**; it has now exceeded 15 million sales. More than 16.5 million were built between 1908 and 1927.

Mazda has produced at least 900,000 Miata sports cars, making it the **best-selling sports car**. Production of the open-top two-seater began in April 1989 in Hiroshima, Japan. The Miata is expected to eclipse 1 million sales by 2015.

SPEEDY SERVICE

Automobiles are transported to the two steel-and-glass towers at the Autostadt straight from the Volkswagen factory. The robotic "shuttles" can process a vehicle every 45 seconds.

LARGEST VEHICLE MANUFACTURER

Japanese automobile manufacturer Toyota ended General Motors' 77-year reign as the best-selling vehicle manufacturer in 2008, selling 8.97 million vehicles compared with GM's tally of 8.35 million vehicles in that calendar year. Toyota continued to be the world's top-selling vehicle manufacturer for three years in a row (2008, 2009, and 2010), although its lead over General Motors narrowed in 2010.

FASTEST PRODUCTION AUTOMOBILE

The super-quick Bugatti Veyron 16.4 Super Sport achieved a two-way timed speed of 267.86 mi/h (431.072 km/h) at the Volkswagen proving grounds in Ehra-Lessien near Wolfsburg, Germany, on June 26, 2010.

LARGEST VEHICLE PRODUCER (COUNTRY)

The country that produces the most automobiles is China, which in 2010 manufactured 18.265 million vehicles out of a world total of 77.610 million, the biggest year on record according to provisional data supplied by the International Organization of Motor Vehicle Manufacturers (OICA). Japan was second with 9.626 million and North America third with 7.761 million.

LARGEST AUTOMATED PARKING FACILITY

The two 157-ft-tall (48-m) "automobile towers" at Volkswagen's Autostadt in Wolfsburg, Germany, can each store 400 automobiles. Buyers can watch as their new vehicle is retrieved from one of the 20-story towers by an automated system that travels at speeds of up to 3 ft 3 in/s (2 m/s).

OLDEST AUTOMOBILE IN PRODUCTION

The Morgan 4/4 has been produced since 1935. Apart from a break during World War II (and from March 1951 to September 1955), it has been in production ever since. The engine, transmission, and brakes have been redesigned many times, but the body has remained largely unchanged and is still hand-built by the Morgan Motor Car Company of Malvern, UK.

Japan is home to *PAC-Man*, the **most successful coin-operated arcade game**. A total of 293,822 *PAC-Man* arcade machines were built and installed in arcade venues around the world between 1981 and 1987.

15,250 Number of times you will honk your automobile horn during your lifetime. But the average driver will curse, or blaspheme, more than twice this amount – 32,035 times.

GUINNESS WORLD RECORDS 2012

FIRST AUTOMOBILE WITH A CRASH-AVOIDANCE SYSTEM

In 2008, Volvo (Sweden) released an automobile that constantly monitors the possibility of a nose-to-tail crash. A laser in the windscreen of the Volvo XC60 wagon monitors slow-moving traffic 19 ft 8 in–26 ft (6–8 m) ahead of the front bumper. At speeds less than 18 mi/h (30 km/h), the City Safety system will bring the vehicle to an abrupt halt if the driver does not brake in time.

LARGEST VEHICLE SALES (COUNTRY)

In 2009, for the first time since automotive mass production began, China overtook North America as the world's biggest automobile market, with 13.6 million sales compared to North America's tally of 10.4 million. In 2010, China's tally exceeded 18.3 million sales.

GREATEST FUEL RANGE

The farthest distance driven on a single standard tank of fuel is 1,526.63 miles (2,456.88 km), by a Volkswagen Passat 1.6 TDI BlueMotion in an event organized by *The Sunday Times* (UK). It was driven by Gavin Conway (UK) between Maidstone, UK, and the A26 in France between August 3 and 5, 2010.

GREATEST VEHICLE MILEAGE

A 1966 Volvo P-1800S owned by Irvin Gordon (USA) had covered more than 2,850,000 miles (4,586,630 km) by December 2010. It is still driven on a daily basis and covers more than 100,000 miles (160,000 km) per year, thanks in part to being driven to numerous automobile shows in Europe and the USA.

RECORD-BREAKING AUTOS

Some people will spend a fortune to secure their dream auto. But as the table below shows, you don't have to be a millionaire to buy a record-breaker!

Record	Price	Date
Most expensive automobile: Ferrari 250 GTO (above)	$17,275,000	Sold May 14, 2010
Most expensive veteran automobile: 1904 Rolls-Royce	£3,521,500 ($7,242,916)	Sold Dec 3, 2007
Most expensive production automobile: Mercedes-Benz CLK/LM	$1,547,620	Launched 1997
Least expensive present-day production automobile: Tata Nano (below)	100,000 rupees ($2,500)	Launched Jan 10, 2008
Least expensive production car ever: Red Bug	$122–$150 (approx. $1,600–$1,920 today)	Launched 1922

FIRST HYDROGEN-POWERED PRODUCTION AUTOMOBILE

Honda introduced its FCX experimental vehicle on public roads in North America and Japan in October 2002, but Mercedes-Benz was first to lease an automobile (the A-class F-Cell) under special arrangements to a paying customer, Tokyo Gas, in December 2003. Hydrogen powers a "fuel cell" that creates electricity.

NANO TECHNOLOGY
The groundbreaking Tata Nano was created to give poorer Indian families the chance to buy automobiles, rather than using motorcycles – often dangerously overladen – to get around.

FASTEST AUTOMOBILE ON ICE

On March 6, 2011, Janne Laitinen (Finland) drove an Audi RS6 at an average top speed of 206.05 mi/h (331.61 km/h) – less than 0.6 mi/h (1 km/h) faster than the previous record – on an 8.6-mile (14-km) section of highway in the Gulf of Bothnia, Oulu, Finland.

UPDATED RECORD
NEW RECORD

The Taiwanese gamer known only as "Little Gray" became the **first player to complete all the listed 986 quests and tasks in *World of Warcraft***, on November 27, 2009.

TRAINS & RAILROADS

FIRST PUBLIC ELECTRIC RAILROAD

Unveiled on May 12, 1881 at Lichtervelde near Berlin, Germany, the earliest public electric railroad was 1.5 miles (2.5 km) long, ran on a 100-volt current, and carried 26 passengers at a speed of 30 mi/h (48 km/h).

The Volk's Electric Railway, which runs along the seafront at Brighton, UK, is the world's **oldest electric railroad still in operation**. Designed by Magnus Volk (UK), the railroad first opened for business in August 1883.

LONGEST RAIL TUNNEL

On October 15, 2010, engineers working 6,560 ft (2,000 m) beneath the Swiss Alps drilled through the last remaining rock blocking the creation of the world's longest rail tunnel. The 35-mile (57-km) Gotthard rail tunnel will take up to 300 trains a day when it officially opens in 2016. Until then, the Seikan rail tunnel in Japan remains the world's longest, at 33.46 miles (53.85 km).

LARGEST TRAIN SET

The world's most extensive train set can be found in Hamburg, Germany. Its landscape is modeled on regions in Europe and the USA and it covers 12,378 ft^2 (1,150 m^2), but when completed in 2014, the 13 miles (20 km) of track will cover more than 24,756 ft^2 (2,300 m^2). The model comprises over 11,000 passenger cars and wagons, 900 signals, 3,500 buildings, and 200,000 figures.

LARGEST RAILROAD STATION

In terms of platform capacity, New York's Grand Central Terminal is the world's largest station. Currently covering 48 acres (19 ha), the station houses 44 platforms and 67 tracks over two below-ground levels. This is set to expand in 2016, when a new level will open beneath the existing ones, adding four new platforms and a further eight tracks. The station was constructed between 1903 and 1913.

SPEED

FASTEST RAIL LINK

The line between the cities of Guangzhou and Wuhan in China carries trains averaging 217 mi/h (350 km/h), which cover the 664-mile (1,069-km) distance in just three hours. In France, the average speed for high-speed trains is 172 mi/h (277 km/h), while in Japan high-speed trains travel at a relatively sedate 150 mi/h (243 km/h).

FIRST ALL-FEMALE PASSENGER CAR

For a number of years, female-only passenger cars have been a feature of Japanese rail travel, but in July 2002 the West Japan Railway Company (JR West), based in Osaka, Japan, introduced the first female-only cars at rush hour. Other companies soon followed, and all-female cars are now available all day long on trains supplied by Hankyu Railway.

FASTEST PASSENGER TRAIN

On December 3, 2010, a CRH380A-type unmodified passenger train reached 302 mi/h (486.1 km/h) on a stretch of track between Zaozhuang City in Shandong Province and Bengbu City in eastern Anhui Province, China. At the time of going to press, this is the fastest officially confirmed speed ever attained by an unmodified passenger train.

RUSH-RUSH HOUR!

China is planning an ambitious high-speed route to link the major economic centers of Beijing and Shanghai. It will reduce journey time between the two cities from 14 hours to just five hours.

Taiwan is home to the **first fully bioluminescent pigs**. Three glowing pigs were born in 2005, created by Taiwan University's Department of Animal Science and Technology, who added DNA from bioluminescent jellyfish to pig embryos.

LONGEST RAIL NETWORKS

Placed end to end, the 10 longest rail networks would extend for 417,157 miles (671,350 km) – enough to stretch from the Earth to the Moon and three-quarters of the way back again.

Country	Length of network
USA *(pictured is an Amtrak – government-owned stock)*	140,695 miles (226,427 km)
Russia	54,156 miles (87,157 km)
China	48,363 miles (77,834 km)
India	39,777 miles (64,015 km)
Canada	29,010 miles (46,688 km)
Germany	26,032 miles (41,486 km)
Australia	23,522 miles (37,855 km)
Argentina	19,516 miles (31,409 km)
France	18,152 miles (29,213 km)
Brazil	17,930 miles (28,857 km)

LONGEST HIGH-SPEED RAIL NETWORK

China had 4,679 miles (7,531 km) of high-speed track in service as of January 2011, according to the Chinese Ministry of Railroads. A further 10,560 miles (17,000 km) of track is being built, which by 2015 will extend China's high-speed network beyond 15,500 miles (25,000 km). (High-speed routes have an average speed of 124 mi/h [200 km/h] or higher.)

FASTEST MAGNETIC LEVITATION TRAIN IN REGULAR SERVICE

The Shanghai Transrapid "maglev" train links Pudong International Airport to the center of Shanghai (both China) and opened on January 1, 2004. It reaches a speed of 267 mi/h (431 km/h) in normal service. The **first maglev train in regular service** linked Birmingham International Airport and International rail station (both UK) between 1984 and 1995.

FASTEST SPEED BETWEEN TWO SCHEDULED RAIL STOPS

Between Lorraine and Champagne-Ardennes, France, trains reach an average speed of 173.6 mi/h (279.4 km/h), according to an official *Railway Gazette International* World Speed Survey study.

This figure is almost half the **highest speed ever recorded by a train on a national rail system** (rather than a dedicated test track). A French SNCF modified version of the TGV, called V150, reached 357.1 mi/h (574.8 km/h) on April 3, 2007.

HIGHEST SUSTAINED TRAIN SPEED FOR 1,000 KM

The highest average speed by a train over a distance of 1,000 km (621 miles) is 190.37 mi/h (306.37 km/h), by a French SNCF TGV train between Calais and Marseille on May 26, 2001. The train, which was unmodified and therefore identical to regular-service Eurostar trains, covered the 663 miles (1,067 km) between the cities in 3 hr 29 min, reaching a maximum speed of 227 mi/h (366 km/h). The feat was organized to mark the opening of a new stretch of high-speed line between Valence and Marseille.

BUSIEST RAILROAD STATION

An average of 3.64 million passengers per day pass through Shinjuku Station in Tokyo, Japan. The station has more than 200 exits and serves the city's western suburbs via a range of intercity, commuter-rail, and metro services.

LARGEST RAILROAD NETWORK UNDER A SINGLE MANAGEMENT

India may have only the fourth-largest rail network (see table above), but it has the distinction of being the largest in the world under a single management. It is also the world's largest commercial employer, with more than 1.6 million employees.

UPDATED RECORD
NEW RECORD

PETROL HEADS

FASTEST LAWNMOWER

Don Wales (UK), of Project Runningblade, rode a lawnmower at a world-beating speed of 87.83 mi/h (141.35 km/h) in Pendine, UK, on May 23, 2010.

SMALLEST ROAD-WORTHY AUTOMOBILE

Created by Perry Watkins (UK), the world's smallest roadworthy automobile is *Wind Up*, which measures 41 in (104.14 cm) high, 26 in (66.04 cm) wide, and 52 in (132.08 cm) long. It was measured in Wingrave, UK, on May 8, 2009.

FASTEST...

AMPHIBIOUS VEHICLE

With an engine based on the LS Corvette power train, the *WaterCar Python* is the fastest amphibious vehicle. It has a top speed of 60 mi/h (96 km/h; 52 knots) on water and can perform a 0–60 mi/h acceleration in 4.5 seconds on land. The *Python* is hand-built to order; prices start from $200,000.

BED

Created and driven by Edd China (UK), the fastest mobile bed reached a speed of 69 mi/h (111 km/h) along a private road in London, UK, on November 7, 2008 as part of Guinness World Records Day 2008.

CARAVAN TOW

A Mercedes Benz S600 driven by Eugene Herbert (South Africa) reached 139.113 mi/h (223.881 km/h) towing a caravan at Hoedspruit Air Force Base, South Africa, on 24 October 2003.

FURNITURE

Fast Food, a motorized mock-up of a fully laid dining table, reached 113.8 mi/h (183.14 km/h) at the Santa Pod Raceway, Bedfordshire, UK, on September 5, 2010. It was driven by its creator, Perry Watkins (UK).

HEARSE

Shane Hammond (Australia) covered 0.25 miles (0.4 km) in a hearse in 12.206 seconds on the TDRA Dragway in Tasmania, Australia, on February 20, 2010. (The time is an average from four runs.)

HOVERCRAFT

The highest recorded speed by a hovercraft is 85.38 mi/h (137.4 km/h), by Bob Windt (USA) at the 1995 World Hovercraft Championships on the Rio Douro River, Peso de Regua, Portugal. Windt was driving a streamlined 19-ft (5.8-m) Universal UH19P hovercraft named *Jenny II*, with a 110-hp (82-kW) V6 automobile engine driving its two fans.

Q. When was the first ever traffic-light system used?

A. Semaphore-type traffic signals were set up in Parliament Square, London, UK, in 1868, with red and green gas lamps for night use. However, it was perfectly legal to ignore them!

FASTEST MOBILITY SCOOTER

Colin Furze (UK) has supercharged a mobility scooter so that it can reach a top speed of 69 mi/h (111 km/h). It took Colin three months to convert the scooter, which features five gears, a 125cc motorbike engine, and twin exhausts.

69 MI/H

RACE TO P.172 FOR MORE HIGH-SPEED ANTICS.

The **largest dish radio telescope** is the partially steerable ionospheric assembly built over a natural bowl at Arecibo, Puerto Rico. The dish has a diameter of 1,000 ft (305 m).

LONGEST MONSTER TRUCK RAMP JUMP

On September 11, 1999, *Bigfoot 14*, driven by Dan Runte, jumped 202 ft (61.57 m) over a Boeing 727 passenger jet at Smyrna Airport, Tennessee, USA. During the runup, Dan also set the record for the **fastest speed for a monster truck**: 69.3 mi/h (111.5 km/h).

BIGFOOT TRUCKS WERE CREATED BY BOB CHANDLER (USA)

TOWED BIG WHEEL

On November 18, 2008, Jim DeChamp (USA) rode a towed Big Wheel to a maximum speed of 59 mi/h (94.9 km/h) at Miller Motorsports Park in Tooele, Utah, USA for the MTV show *Nitro Circus*.

TOWED TOILET

Garrett Olson (USA) rode a towed toilet at a speed of 49.6 mi/h (79.83 km/h) at the Dunn Tire Raceway in Lancaster, New York, USA, on September 2, 2009.

WASTE CONTAINER

The fastest waste container – built using a modified 0.43-gal (2-liter) turbo Subaru Impreza Type R rally car set within a 24-ft (7.3-m) debris box – achieved a land-speed record of 93.92 mi/h (151.15 km/h) on the 0.25-mile (0.4-km) dragster track at the Santa Pod Raceway, Northants., UK, on November 3, 2007. The vehicle was driven by its owner, James Norvill (UK).

FASTEST WEDDING CHAPEL

The *Best Man* achieved a speed of 62 mi/h (99 km/h) in Shelbyville, Illinois, USA, on September 30, 2010.

MOST CRASH TESTS ENDURED

By February 2003, traffic collision reconstructionist W R "Rusty" Haight (USA) had had 718 collisions in automobiles as a "human crash test dummy."

POWERED STREET LUGE

Joel King (UK) reached a speed of 112.7 mi/h (181.37 km/h) on his jet-engine-powered street luge at Bentwaters Airfield, UK, on August 28, 2007.

SNOWMOBILE

The speed record for the fastest snowmobile is 172.2 mi/h (277.13 km/h) and was set by Chris Hanson (USA) on Lake Nipissing in North Bay, Ontario, Canada, on March 13, 2004.

FASTEST...

OFFICE

Edd China (UK) built a roadworthy desk that can reach a speed of 87 mi/h (140 km/h). Edd drove it across Westminster Bridge into the City of London, UK, on November 9, 2006 as part of GWR Day.

FAST SERVICE

The mobile chapel includes stained-glass windows, pews, a pulpit, a pipe organ, a 1,000-watt stereo system, and a three-tiered back porch with wrought-iron hand railings.

AIRCRAFT

LARGEST FIRE-FIGHTING AIRCRAFT

The Evergreen International Aviation Company (USA) has modified a Boeing 747-300 aircraft for fire-fighting duties. The Evergreen 747 Supertanker has a capacity of 17,070 gal (77,600 liters) – more than eight times that of the commonly used P-3A Orion aircraft – and was first used in July 2009 to fight huge fires in Cuenca, Spain.

FASTEST PLANE (CIVIL)

In August 2010, a Gulfstream G650 jet flown by Tom Horne and Gary Freeman reached Mach 0.995 (757 mi/h; 1,219 km/h) in a 16–18-degree dive in Savannah, Georgia, USA. The US plane can carry four crew and eight passengers nonstop from London, UK, to Buenos Aires, Argentina – a distance of 6,916 miles (11,130 km).

FIRST COMMERCIALLY PRODUCED ELECTRIC AIRCRAFT

The two-seater Yuneec e430 is an eco-friendly plane that carries no fuel and emits no fumes and little noise. It is a single-engined monoplane that can fly for up to 3 hours at a cruising speed of 52 knots (60 mi/h; 96 km/h).

FIRST ELECTRIC HELICOPTER

Sikorsky unveiled the world's first all-electric helicopter on July 26, 2010. Called the *Firefly*, it is a modified Schweizer S-300C, weighing 2,125 lb (963.9 kg). Powered by two lithium-ion battery packs producing about 370 volts, it is capable of flying for up to 15 minutes at a speed of 80 knots (92 mi/h; 148 km/h).

MOST EXPENSIVE HELICOPTER

The cost for a proposed fleet of 28 Lockheed Martin (USA) VH71 Kestrel helicopters was estimated at a record $13.2 billion, making it the most expensive helicopter in the world at $471 million.

MOST EXPENSIVE AIRCRAFT SCRAPPED BEFORE BECOMING OPERATIONAL

In January 2011, nine new Nimrod MRA4 aircraft costing £450 million ($713 million) each were scrapped by the UK Ministry of Defence due to budget cuts.

FIRST FLAPLESS AIRCRAFT WITHOUT CONVENTIONAL CONTROL SURFACES

The UK aerospace company BAE Systems, in cooperation with 10 UK universities, has created an unmanned aerial vehicle (UAV) designed to fly without conventional control surfaces. The DEMON uses outputs from air jets to control airflow over the wing – based on a concept called "fluidic flight control" – manipulating lift and drag to control its flight path rather than using traditional mechanical elevators and ailerons. Its maiden flight took place in Cumbria, UK, on September 17, 2010.

FASTEST HELICOPTER (NON-FAI)

On September 15, 2010, the Sikorsky X2 set a new unofficial speed record for a helicopter, reaching 250 knots (288 mi/h; 463 km/h) at Sikorsky's Development Flight Center in Florida, USA. The X2, which took its first flight in 2008, has coaxial rotors – two sets of blades that rotate in opposite directions.

BLADES OF GLORY

The **fastest helicopter** according to the Fédération Aéronautique Internationale (FAI) is a Westland Lynx that hit a speed of 216 knots (249 mi/h; 400 km/h) in 1986.

UPDATED RECORD
NEW RECORD

Built in 2002 by Carlos Alberto Balbiani (Argentina), the world's **smallest pistol** is 2.1 in (5.5 cm) long, 1.3 in (3.5 cm) in height, and weighs just 0.91 oz (26 g). It fires 0.68 mm caliber bullets.

Q. Which aircraft manufacturer has produced the most aircraft to date?

A. Not Boeing or Airbus, but in fact the Cessna Aircraft Company of Wichita, Kansas, USA, which had built 192,967 aircraft up to 2010.

729 Balloons you will buy in a lifetime. If they were all filled with helium, they could together lift an average-sized newborn baby (7.5 lb). To fly an average adult (168 lb), you'd need more than 22 lifetimes' worth!

IN 2004, "ROCKET MAN" ROSSY BECAME THE FIRST HUMAN TO FLY HORIZONTALLY

BUSIEST AIRPORT (PASSENGERS, FLIGHTS)

According to the Airports Council International, 88,032,086 people flew in or out of Hartsfield-Jackson Atlanta International Airport in Georgia, USA, in 2009. Hartsfield-Jackson was also busiest by flight numbers, with 970,235 in and out.

BUSIEST AIRPORT (CARGO)

At Memphis International Airport in Tennessee, USA, 4,075,304 tons (3,697,054 metric tons) of cargo were loaded and unloaded in 2009.

FIRST AERIAL LOOP USING A JET PACK

On November 5, 2010, former fighter pilot Yves Rossy (Switzerland) became the first man to complete an aerial loop using a jet-propelled carbon-fiber wing. After launching from a hot-air balloon at 7,874 ft (2,400 m) over Lake Geneva, Switzerland, he performed two aerial loops before parachuting safely back to Earth.

FIRST HUMAN-POWERED AIRCRAFT WITH FLAPPING WINGS

The *Snowbird*, which has a wingspan of 105 ft (32 m) – comparable to a Boeing 737 – is the first aircraft to be able to fly like a bird (once launched by a tow vehicle). On August 2, 2010, Canadian student Todd Reichert flew the carbon-fiber-and-balsa-wood craft for 19.3 seconds, averaging 16 mi/h (25.6 km/h) over a distance of 476 ft (145 m) at the Great Lakes Gliding Club in Ontario, Canada.

LONGEST FLIGHT BY A SOLAR-POWERED UAV

At 6:41 a.m. on July 9, 2010, a Zephyr unmanned aerial vehicle (UAV) was launched from the US Army's Yuma Proving Ground in Arizona, USA, and flew for a record 336 hr 22 min – over two weeks – fueled only by solar power generated by paper-thin silicon arrays on the aircraft's wings. On the same flight, the battery-powered Zephyr also earned the record for the **highest altitude achieved by a solar-powered UAV**, soaring to an unprecedented height of 70,740 ft (21,561 m).

FIRST FLIGHT OF A MANNED SOLAR-POWERED AIRCRAFT

On April 7, 2010, German pilot Markus Scherdel flew the *Solar Impulse* on a 90-minute test flight at Payerne, Switzerland. The aircraft, the $93.8-million brainchild of Swiss adventurer Bertrand Piccard, is powered by 12,000 solar cells driving four electric motors and is destined for a future round-the-world record attempt.

FIRST ALGAE-POWERED AIRCRAFT

At the 2010 ILA Air Show in Berlin, Germany, the European defense company EADS showcased a twin-engine Diamond DA42 NG light aircraft powered by algae-derived biofuel.

LONGEST FLIGHT AT HYPERSONIC SPEED

Launched from a B-52 bomber on May 26, 2010, a Boeing (USA) X-51A Waverider was propelled to nearly Mach 6 – 4,567 mi/h (7,350 km/h), or six times the speed of sound – by its air-breathing scramjet motor, which burned for more than 200 seconds. Scramjets are powered by hydrogen fuel, which is ignited by oxygen rushing in through the engine at supersonic speeds.

LONGEST WINGSPAN OF AN AIRCRAFT IN PRODUCTION

The colossal Airbus A380 airliner has a wingspan of 261 ft 9.73 in (79.8 m), which is nearly as long as a full-sized soccer field.

FIRST PURPOSE-BUILT COMMERCIAL SPACEPORT

The construction of Spaceport America, by the Government of New Mexico, USA, is due for completion toward the end of 2011 at a cost of around $200 million. It will comprise a space-age terminal and hangar and a 10,000-ft (3,000-m) runway, and will be home to Virgin Galactic's (UK) space operations (see below).

FIRST COMMERCIAL PASSENGER SPACE AIRCRAFT

On March 23, 2010, the Virgin Space Ship *Enterprise* took its maiden test flight over California, USA. The craft, attached to the mothership, *WhiteKnightTwo*, flew for 2 hr 54 min and reached 45,000 ft (13,716 m). When passenger flights begin in 2012, the spaceship will rise to 50,000 ft (15,240 m) and then, powered by a single rocket motor, detach from the mothership and carry its six "space tourists" to the edge of the Earth's atmosphere.

Much larger by comparison is the **most powerful cell phone gun**, a 0.22 in caliber pistol disguised as a cell phone. Made in Croatia, the gun is triggered when the numbers 5, 6, 7, and 8 are pressed in quick succession.

WARSHIPS

LARGEST CLASS OF AIRCRAFT CARRIER

In terms of production numbers, the largest class of aircraft carrier is the Casablanca-class escort carrier. Between 1942 and 1945, a total of 50 were built for the US Navy. They were 512 ft (156.1 m) long with a displacement of 12,017 tons (10,902 metric tons) when fully loaded. Five Casablancas were lost during World War II and the rest have since been scrapped.

LARGEST AIRCRAFT TO LAND ON A CARRIER

In October 1963, a Lockheed KC-130F Hercules transport performed 21 unarrested landings and unassisted takeoffs on the USS *Forrestal* around 497 miles (800 km) off the US coast in the North Atlantic. Despite weighing up to 121,000 lb (54,844 kg), the aircraft managed to come to rest over a distance of just two wingspans without the aid of arresting gear to slow or stop it.

LARGEST SURFACE COMBAT SHIP IN ACTIVE SERVICE

Discounting carriers, amphibious assault ships, and subs, the largest combat ships are the Russian Kirov-class cruisers. At 827 ft (252 m) long with a beam of 93 ft 6 in (28.5 m), they displace 30,865 tons (28,000 metric tons) fully loaded and have a top speed of 32 knots (37 mi/h; 59 km/h). Pictured is the 24,300-ton (22,044-metric-ton) *Admiral Lazarev* (laid down 1978).

OLDEST AIRCRAFT CARRIER IN SERVICE

In 1959, the UK's Royal Navy commissioned the HMS *Hermes*, a Centaur-class carrier. Measuring 743 ft (226.5 m) long, it displaces 31,636 tons (28,700 metric tons) and can reach 28 knots (32 mi/h; 52 km/h). After serving as the UK's flagship in the Falklands War with Argentina in 1982, it was sold to India in 1986 and now serves as India's flagship under the name INS *Viraat*.

LARGEST AIRCRAFT CRUISER

Aircraft cruisers are capable of ship-to-ship combat as well as carrying aircraft. The largest of these is the Russian *Admiral Kuznetsov*, at 992 ft (302.3 m) long and displacing 64,595 tons (58,600 metric tons). Armed with 12 Granit antiship missiles, 192 Kinzhal surface-to-air missiles, an antisubmarine rocket launcher, and anti-air guns, it can also carry 12 Su-33 and 5 Su-25 jets, along with 24 helicopters.

LARGEST FLEET OF AIRCRAFT CARRIERS

Of the 22 aircraft carriers in service worldwide, the US Navy accounts for exactly half of them, boasting one Enterprise-class carrier (the USS *Enterprise*, the **first nuclear aircraft carrier**) and 10 Nimitz-class carriers (the **largest warships** ever built), including the USS *Truman*, pictured. The remaining 11 belong to the UK, Russia, France, Brazil, India, Italy, Spain, and Thailand.

The **largest truffle** was a white truffle (*Tuber magnatum pico*) found by Giancarlo Zigante (Croatia) near Buje, Croatia, on November 2, 1999. Weighing 2 lb 8 oz (1.31 kg), it was 7.6 in (19.5 cm) long and estimated to be worth $5,080.

LAST BATTLESHIPS TO SEE COMBAT

The growing dominance of airpower and guided missiles in naval combat has rendered battleships effectively obsolete. The US Navy's four Iowa-class battleships – *Missouri*, *Iowa*, *Wisconsin*, and *New Jersey* – were first commissioned in 1943 and, although they have spent much of their lives in mothballs, they have seen action in Korea (1950–53), Vietnam (1955–75), and the Persian Gulf (1990–91).

FASTEST SPEED BY A BATTLESHIP

The US Iowa-class ships were powered by eight fuel-oil boilers and four propellers, delivering 212,000 shaft horsepower. In 1968, the USS *New Jersey* achieved a record speed of 35.2 knots (40.5 mi/h; 65.2 km/h) for a duration of six hours. Following this feat, the *New Jersey*'s captain ordered an emergency stop, and the ship took 2 miles (3.2 km) to come to rest.

FIRST ALL-BIG-GUN BATTLESHIP

HMS *Dreadnought*, commissioned in 1906 by the UK's Royal Navy, revolutionized global battleship design. The vessel was the first to dispense with medium-calibre guns as main armaments, replacing them with more large-calibre main guns. In total, *Dreadnought* featured ten 12-inch guns mounted in five turrets.

LAST MONITOR TO SEE ACTIVE SERVICE

Monitor-class warships are named after the first of their class, USS *Monitor*, which was commissioned in 1862. They are slow, heavy, and characterized by a low profile and single main turret. The Brazilian Navy's riverine Monitor *Parnaíba* (U-17) was commissioned in 1937 and is still in active service.

LARGEST CRUISER FLEET

Just three nations have cruisers in active service: the USA, Russia, and Peru. The US Navy has by far the largest fleet with 22 ships to Russia's five and Peru's one. The US vessels are all Ticonderoga-class cruisers, built between 1980 and 1994. They are 568 ft (173 m) long with a displacement of 10,919 tons (9,906 metric tons) and are armed with a vertical launch system for surface-to-air, cruise, antisubmarine, and antiship missiles. They also have two 5-inch guns, antimissile defenses, and torpedo tubes.

LARGEST NAVAL EXERCISE

The Rim of the Pacific Exercise is an annual international maritime exercise that was first held in 1971. Its main participants are the USA, Canada, and Australia, with the UK, Chile, Peru, Japan, and South Korea also taking part regularly. Although the scale of the exercise varies annually, the US component can include up to 20,000 personnel and a full carrier battle group plus support ships.

MOST SHIPS SCUTTLED

During World War II, on November 27, 1942, the French fleet in Toulon, France, was sunk to avoid capture by the Germans. Of some 73 ships lost, 57 were major vessels, including two battleships, two battle cruisers, four heavy cruisers, two light cruisers, an aircraft transport, 30 destroyers, and 16 submarines.

CLASH OF THE TITANS

In the Battle of the Coral Sea on May 4–8, 1942, Japanese and US carriers fought the **first battle between aircraft carriers**. During the fray, neither ship caught sight of the other as the battle was fought by planes overhead.

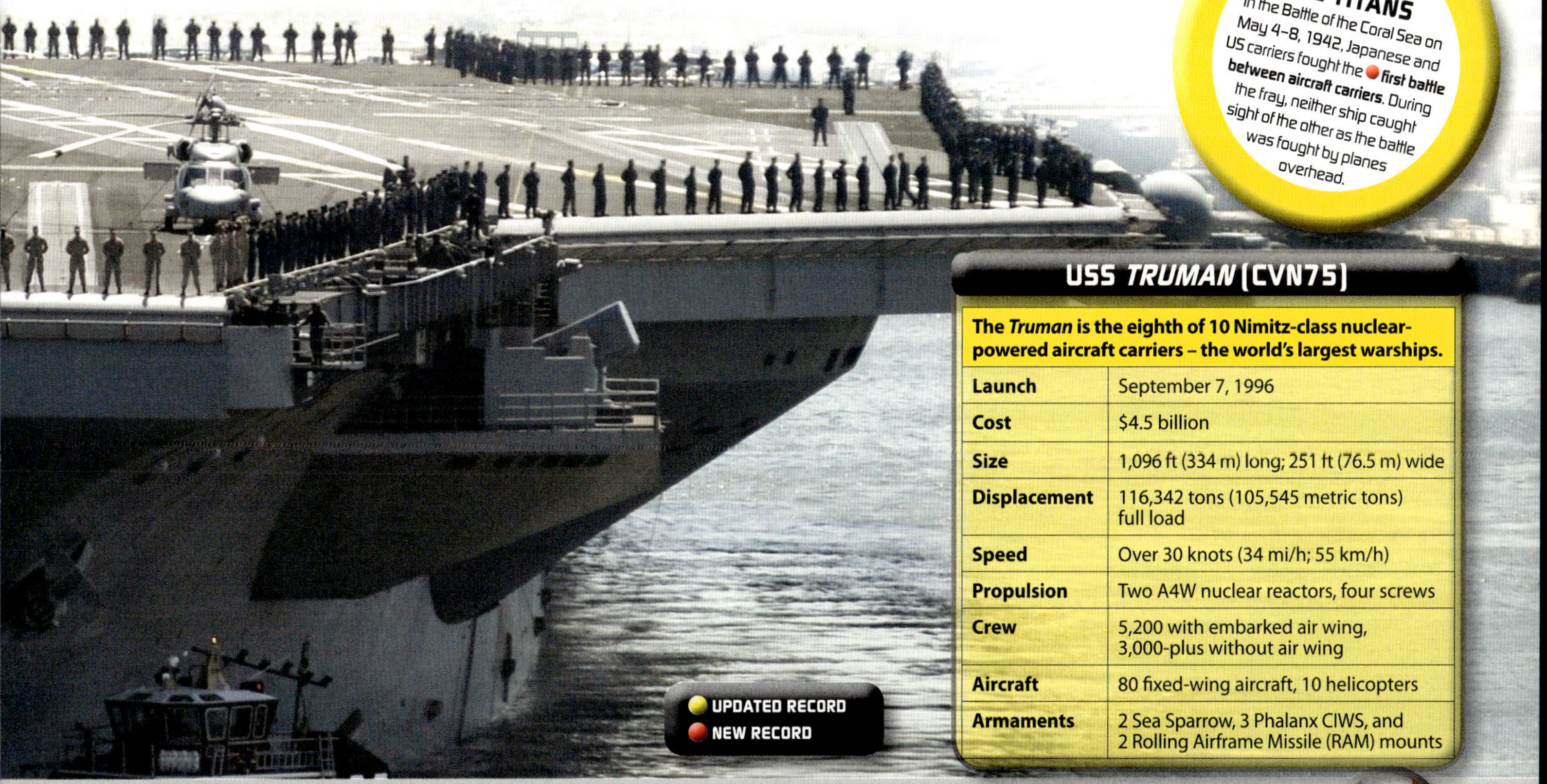

USS *TRUMAN* (CVN75)

The *Truman* is the eighth of 10 Nimitz-class nuclear-powered aircraft carriers – the world's largest warships.

Launch	September 7, 1996
Cost	$4.5 billion
Size	1,096 ft (334 m) long; 251 ft (76.5 m) wide
Displacement	116,342 tons (105,545 metric tons) full load
Speed	Over 30 knots (34 mi/h; 55 km/h)
Propulsion	Two A4W nuclear reactors, four screws
Crew	5,200 with embarked air wing, 3,000-plus without air wing
Aircraft	80 fixed-wing aircraft, 10 helicopters
Armaments	2 Sea Sparrow, 3 Phalanx CIWS, and 2 Rolling Airframe Missile (RAM) mounts

UPDATED RECORD
NEW RECORD

MILITARY HARDWARE

MOST EFFECTIVE BODY ARMOR

In July 2010, BAE Systems (UK) demonstrated the effectiveness of kevlar body armor integrating "shear-thickening fluid" (STF). This substance, dubbed "bulletproof custard," thickens when impacted and absorbs the energy more than three times more effectively than untreated armor. STF also offers a reduction in uniform thickness by 45%.

MOST ADVANCED ELECTRIC UNIFORMS

Intelligent Textiles Ltd (UK) have developed an "e-textile" with passive electronic circuits, allowing for electrical interconnectivity. In 2009, the e-textile was woven into an Osprey armor carrier vest, where it carried a current of 0.1–4 amperes. This technology helps lighten a soldier's load as it eradicates the need for heavy batteries and allows electrical equipment to be attached to powerpoints on their uniforms.

MOST ACCURATE ELECTRONIC SNIPER DETECTOR

The Boomerang Warrior-X system, made by Raytheon (USA), is just 4 in^2 (10.2 cm^2) and detects enemy shooters by triangulating the sound of their gunfire up to 3,000 ft (914 m) away. It displays the target's position on a screen and emits a warning signal.

MOST ECOFRIENDLY SPY PLANE

Powered by a highly efficient hydrogen propulsion system, the Phantom Eye is a prototype unmanned aircraft that was unveiled by Boeing (USA) on July 12, 2010. The reconnaissance plane can stay in the air for four days at 65,000 ft (19,800 m), while its only by-product is water.

CHINESE WHISPERS

In early 2010, China tested its new Chengdu J-20 Powerful Dragon stealth fighter, destined to enter service in around 2017 to challenge the world's only fully stealthy aircraft, the US F-22 Raptor.

LARGEST SPY SATELLITE

On November 21, 2010, a spy satellite, payload NROL-32, dubbed the world's largest by an official from the National Reconnaissance Office, was launched from Cape Canaveral, USA, on a Delta 4-Heavy rocket – the most powerful rocket in the US inventory. Although the satellite and its mission are top secret, the size of the rocket, which can launch payloads of up to 26.45 tons (24 metric tons), implies an extremely large satellite.

MOST EFFECTIVE ANIMAL MINE-CLEARER

In Tanzania, the giant African pouched rat is trained by APOPO, a Belgian nongovernmental organization, to sniff out landmines. The work is not overly dangerous for rats as they are very light and therefore highly unlikely to trigger a mine. Training the rats to recognize the smell of TNT explosive takes about nine months, but, once up to speed, two rats can clear an area of 2,150 ft^2 (200 m^2) in two hours, whereas human mine-clearers would take a day to cover the same area.

FIRST REMOTE-CONTROL SEARCH DOGS

Researchers at the Canine Detection Research Institute at Auburn University in Alabama, USA, have invented a harness that uses Global Positioning Systems (GPS) to remotely guide search dogs in dangerous situations. Carrying a GPS, a processor, spatial sensors, and a radio modem, the harness transmits vibrations to the dog on its left or right side so that it can be "steered" through extremely tight gaps in buildings such as airports or in other disaster scenarios.

MOST ECOFRIENDLY BOMB DETECTORS

The University of Colorado (USA) has developed a computer program that can "train" plants to respond to explosives in the same way that they react to other threatening stimuli, by releasing chemicals called terpenoids, which change the color of their leaves.

MOST ECOFRIENDLY AMMUNITION

Although lethal to humans, the US Army's new M855A1 Enhanced Performance Rounds are kinder to the environment as they are made of nonhazardous copper instead of lead. The bullets have been used by US troops in Afghanistan since June 2010.

On April 25, 2009, Italian Michele Pradelli performed the **longest standing jump on a motorcycle**, achieving a distance of 14 ft (4.26 m) on the set of *Lo Show dei Record* in Milan, Italy.

RC AIRCRAFT

The remote-control Black Hawk may be some way from service, but pilotless aircraft have been used in combat for years. The **first aerial battle involving a UAV** occurred when an Iraqi MiG downed a US Predator drone over Iraq in December 2002.

LARGEST OPERATIONAL UAV

In February 2010, Israel Aerospace Industries unveiled the latest development of the Heron TP unmanned aerial vehicle (UAV), named the *Eitan*. The size of a Boeing 737, it has a maximum takeoff weight of 10,250 lb (4,650 kg), a wingspan of 86 ft (26.2 m), and a length of 46 ft (14 m). Its 1,200-hp (895-kW) turbojet engine allows it to carry high-resolution cameras, electronic systems, and, possibly, weapons, while it can stay airborne for over 20 hours at 45,000 ft (13,716 m).

MOST POWERFUL ELECTROMAGNETIC RAILGUN

Electromagnetic (EM) railguns use electricity to fire projectiles at speeds greater than Mach 7 and are capable of destroying targets 230 miles (370 km) away. On December 10, 2010, an EM railgun at the Naval Surface Warfare Center in Dahlgren, USA, achieved a 33-megajoule shot – an amazing force, given that 1 megajoule can propel a 1.1-ton (1-metric-ton) vehicle at 100 mi/h (160 km/h).

FIRST PILOTLESS COMBAT HELICOPTER

The American, Connecticut-based helicopter manufacturer Sikorsky has embarked on a $1-billion program to produce the first pilotless combat helicopter, with a prototype set for 2011. Based on the same company's world-famous Black Hawk aircraft, the new helicopter is slated to enter service in 2015 at a cost of $17.25 million each.

SMALLEST GUIDED MISSILE

Weighing 5 lb 4 oz (2.4 kg), the US Navy's Spike missile is perfectly suited to small unmanned aerial vehicles (UAVs). With its precise laser-guided targeting system, it can lock on to a target as small as a motorcycle.

MOST ADVANCED AIRBORNE SURVEILLANCE SYSTEM

In December 2010, the US Air Force deployed its new Gorgon Stare surveillance system on an MQ-9 Reaper UAV in Afghanistan. The technology has nine cameras that can transmit 65 different live images at a time and can watch over an entire city.

FIRST SUCCESSFUL KILL OF A BALLISTIC MISSILE BY AN AIRBORNE LASER SYSTEM

In February 2010, a US prototype weapon system on board a modified Boeing 747-400F destroyed a ballistic missile in mid-flight off the coast of California, USA. Low-energy lasers were first used to detect and track the missile before it was then engaged by a megawatt-class high-energy laser fired through a telescope in the nose of the plane.

FASTEST LANDING VESSEL

In 2010, the UK agreed to test the Partial Air-Cushion Supported Catamaran, an aluminum landing craft capable of 30 knots (34.5 mi/h; 55.6 km/h).

UPDATED RECORD
NEW RECORD

BRIDGES

LONGEST BRIDGE

The Danyang-Kunshan Grand Bridge, on the Jinghu High-Speed Railway (aka Beijing–Shanghai High-Speed Railway), is 102 miles (164 km) long. This new line (open from June 2011) also crosses the 70.8-mile (114-km) Langfang–Qingxian viaduct, the second longest bridge in the world.

TALLEST BRIDGE

The Millau Viaduct, which crosses the Tarn Valley in France, is supported by seven concrete piers, the tallest of which measures 1,095 ft 4 in (333.88 m) from the ground to its highest point – more than twice the height of the Great Pyramid of Giza. *(See pp.194–195 for other Pyramid-related facts.)*

BRIDGE (DECK)

The deck of the suspension bridge over the Si Du River in Badong County, Hubei, China, is situated 1,549 ft (472 m) above the valley – more than high enough to accommodate the Empire State Building beneath it. When the bridge was being constructed, the first suspension cable to be secured was fired across the 1,600-ft-wide (500-m) valley, rather than flown across by helicopter, making it the **first suspension-bridge cable placed using a rocket**. The bridge was opened to traffic on November 15, 2009.

LONGEST BRIDGE FOUNTAIN

The Banpo Grand Bridge over the Han River in Seoul, South Korea, measures 3,740 ft (1,140 m) long. Running along its length are 380 nozzles that send 60 tons (54 metric tons)of water cascading 140 ft (43 m) horizontally and 65 ft (20 m) down into the river every minute. In the evening, LED lights illuminate the water spray, which "dances" in time to 100 different pieces of music.

MOST BRIDGES WALKED ACROSS

Donald H Betty of Lancaster, Pennsylvania, USA, has walked across 150 bridges (all suspension bridges), including 26 of the longest in the world. The longest bridge Betty has crossed is the Akashi-Kaikyo Road Bridge in Japan (see opposite).

OLDEST BRIDGE

Remnants of bridges dated *c.* 1600 BC exist over the River Havos in Mycenae, Greece. The oldest datable bridge still in use, though, is the slab-stone single-arch bridge over the River Meles in Izmir (formerly Smyrna), Turkey, which dates from 850 BC.

WIDEST BRIDGE

The 1,650-ft-long (503-m) Sydney Harbour Bridge in New South Wales, Australia, is 160 ft (48.8 m) wide. It carries two electrical overhead railroad tracks, eight lanes of roadway, a cycle track, and footway. It opened on March 19, 1932.

HIGHEST...

RAILROAD BRIDGE

The Beipanjiang River Railway Bridge, near Liupanshui in Guizhou province, China, is an arch with a maximum deck height of 902 ft (275 m).

LONGEST BRIDGE OVER WATER

The six-lane Qingdao-Haiwan road bridge, which spans Jiaozhou Bay in China's Shangdong province, is 26.4 miles (42.5 km) long. The earthquake- and typhoon-proof bridge opened in 2011 and is designed to withstand the impact of a 300,000-metric-ton vessel. It is 2.53 miles (4.07 km) longer than the former record holder, the Lake Pontchartrain Causeway in Louisiana, USA.

FOR MORE EPIC ENGINEERING, TURN TO P.192.

The record for the **largest collection of napkins** belongs to Antónia Kozáková (Slovakia), who had amassed 30,300 different ones as of April 27, 2007.

440 Length in miles of a lifetime's-worth of hair if placed end to end. Spin it into a single strand and it would measure four times longer than the world's longest bridge.

LONGEST...

ROAD BRIDGE

The six-lane elevated Bang Na Expressway (aka the Bang Na-Bang Phil-Bang Pakong Expressway or the Burapha Withi Expressway) runs for 33.5 miles (54 km) through Bangkok, Thailand, and was constructed using 63.5 million ft^3 (1.8 million m^3) of concrete. It was opened on February 7, 2000 at a cost of $1 billion.

TRANSOCEANIC BRIDGE

The bridge spanning the greatest expanse of open ocean is the 22-mile (36-km) Hangzhou Bay Bridge, which links the cities of Cixi and Zhapu in Zhejiang province, China.

SUSPENSION BRIDGE

The main span of the Akashi-Kaikyo Road Bridge linking Honshu and Shikoku, Japan, is 6,532 ft, or 1.24 miles (1,990.8 m) long. The overall suspended length with side spans totals 12,831 ft 8 in, or 2.43 miles (3,911.1 m).

FOOTBRIDGE

On October 3, 2009, the 6,767-ft, or 1.28-mile (2.06-km) Poughkeepsie Bridge (also known as the Walkway Over the Hudson State National Park) in New York, USA, was reopened to the public as the world's longest pedestrian bridge. (Hornibrook Bridge across Bramble Bay in Queensland, Australia, is longer but is now closed to the public.)

STEEL ARCH BRIDGE

The Chongqing-Chaotianmen Bridge over the Yangtze River in China is a two-deck, steel truss-arch bridge with a main span of 1,811 ft (552 m).

TIBETAN BRIDGE

A 1,227-ft (374-m) Tibetan bridge – a narrow walkway between two banks and supported loosely by cables or ropes – was strung across the Po River in Turin, Italy, in May 2004 by Experimenta (Italy).

MOST EXPENSIVE BRIDGE

The five-lane San Francisco–Oakland Bay toll bridge opened in 1963, but was left crippled by the Loma Prieta earthquake in 1989. In 2002, restoration and replacement work began on the bridge at an estimated cost of $6.3 billion.

BUILDING BRIDGES

The original Bay Bridge, built in 1936, cost $77 million – equivalent to $1.2 billion today. It needed more concrete than was used in the Empire State Building.

LONGEST ROAD-AND-RAIL BRIDGE

The Wuhu Yangtze River Bridge in Anhui province, China, is a road and railroad bridge with a total length of 6.2 miles (10.02 km) and a main span of 1,023 ft (312 m). The top deck carries four lanes of highway and a footpath, while the lower deck comprises a double-track grade-one railroad.

UPDATED RECORD
NEW RECORD

And those napkins would come in very handy at the Bawabet Dimashq (Damascus Gate) Restaurant in Damascus, Syria – with 6,014 seats, it is the **largest restaurant** in the world.

Sci-Tech & Engineering

EPIC ARCHITECTURE

TALLEST TOWER
The Canton Tower, also known as the Guangzhou TV & Sightseeing Tower, rises 1,968 ft 6 in (600 m) to the top of its mast – twice as tall as Paris' Eiffel Tower. It is located in the Haizhu District, Guangzhou, China, and was designed by Mark Hemel and Barbara Kuit (both Netherlands) of the Dutch firm Information Based Architecture.

TALLEST LIGHTHOUSE
The steel Marine Tower at Yamashita Park in Yokohama, Japan, is 348 ft (106 m) tall, has a visibility range of 20 miles (32 km), and contains an observatory 328 ft (100 m) above ground. It can project light with an intensity of 600,000 candelas.

HIGHEST BUILDING TO HOUSE A HOTEL
The Park Hyatt Shanghai in Pudong, China, occupies floors 79 to 93 of the Shanghai World Financial Centre.

The hotel also incorporates the **highest observation deck** in the world, a glass construction known as the Skywalk. It is located on the building's 100th floor at a height of 1,554 ft (473.9 m).

TALLEST BUILDING
On January 4, 2010, the Burj Khalifa, developed by Emaar Properties in Dubai, UAE, topped out at 2,716 ft 6 in (828 m). The architects were Skidmore, Owings, & Merrill LLP. Construction began on September 21, 2004, with the exterior being completed on October 1, 2009. The Burj Khalifa is also the **tallest manmade structure on land**.

TALLEST MANMADE LEANING TOWER
Completed in 1987, the Olympic Stadium Tower in Montreal, Canada, is 541 ft 4 in (165 m) high and curves at an angle of 45 degrees. The stadium was used as a venue at the 1976 Olympic Games, although the tower was unfinished at the time and the stadium did not have a retractable roof.

FARTHEST-LEANING MANMADE BUILDING
Capital Gate has an inclination of 18 degrees and is 524 ft 11 in (160 m) high. It was developed by the Abu Dhabi National Exhibitions Company and designed by RMJM. The external construction was completed in Abu Dhabi, UAE, in January 2010.

LEANS AT AN ANGLE FOUR TIMES GREATER

18 DEGREES

UPDATED RECORD
NEW RECORD

TALLEST RESIDENTIAL BUILDING

Q1 in Gold Coast, Queensland, Australia, has a structural height of 1,060 ft (323 m) and a roof height of 902 ft (275 m), making it the tallest building in the world used purely for residential purposes. The building's 80 levels accommodate 527 apartments. It opened in October 2005 and is the tallest building in Australia.

TALLEST TENSILE STRUCTURE

The Khan Shatyr Entertainment Centre, in Astana, Kazakhstan, soars 492 ft (150 m) from its elliptical base. The tent-like structure covers an area of more than 1,076,390 ft² (100,000 m²).

LARGEST HOTEL

The First World Hotel, in the Genting Highlands Resort in Pahang Darul Makmur, Malaysia, has 6,118 rooms. The hotel was completed in 2005.

HIGHEST RESIDENTIAL APARTMENTS

The Burj Khalifa in Dubai, United Arab Emirates, has the world's highest residential floor at 1,263 ft (385 m). Floors 77 to 108 of the 163-floor building are given over to its 900 apartments.

LARGEST RESIDENTIAL PALACE

The palace (Istana Nurul Iman) of HM the Sultan of Brunei in the capital Bandar Seri Begawan was completed in January 1984 at a reported cost of $422 million. It features 1,788 rooms, 257 toilets, and 2,152,780 ft² (200,000m²) of floor space – an area equivalent to 40 American football fields.

TALLEST STRUCTURE

The Ursa tension-leg platform is a floating oil-production facility operated by Shell in the Gulf of Mexico. The top of its drilling rig is 4,285 ft (1,306 m) above the seabed.

TALLEST HOTEL

The Rose Rayhaan by Rotana hotel in Dubai, UAE, stands 1,092 ft 6 in (333 m) from ground level to the top of its mast. The hotel consists of 482 rooms spread over 72 floors and it opened on December 14, 2009.

MOST LANDMARKS ILLUMINATED IN 24 HOURS

On October 1, 2010, as part of Breast Cancer Awareness Month, The Estée Lauder Companies organized the lighting of 38 landmarks in 24 hours. A host of iconic structures were turned pink, including the Zappeion (near right) in Athens, Greece; the Freedom Tower (far right) in Miami, USA; Tokyo Tower in Japan; and the Burj Al Arab in Dubai, UAE. The event culminated in New York City, USA, with the illumination of the Empire State Building.

PAINT THE TOWN PINK

The Estée Lauder Companies' record was in aid of breast cancer awareness, and on hand to flip the switch at the Empire State Building were Evelyn H Lauder and Liz Hurley.

THAN THAT OF THE LEANING TOWER OF PISA

Dating from AD 232, the **oldest surviving Christian church** is a house originally located in Qal'at es Salihiye (formerly Dura Europos) in eastern Syria.

The **largest monolithic church** is in Lalibela, Ethiopia: Bet Medhane Alem is 110 ft (33.5 m) long, 78 ft (23.5 m) wide, and 36 ft (11 m) high.

PYRAMIDS

WHAT IS A PYRAMID?

Technically, a pyramid is described as a polyhedron (a three-dimensional straight-edged shape) with a polygonal (many-sided) base and triangular faces that meet at the apex (top). The most famous examples are the giant stone buildings on the Giza Plateau in Cairo, Egypt (pictured), but pyramids come in all sorts of shapes and sizes, as this selection of records illustrates.

HUMAN PYRAMIDS

ON MOTORCYCLES

The Dare Devils Team of the Indian Army Signal Corps traveled a distance of 424 ft (129 m) while maintaining a pyramid formation of 201 men on 10 motorcycles at Gowri Shankar Parade Ground, Jabalpur, India, on July 5, 2001.

ON SKATES

A pyramid of 30 skaters from the NSA Roller Gymnastics Team (USA) traveled 155 ft (47.2 m) in eight seconds in Philadelphia, USA, in 1985.

LARGEST HUMAN WATERSKIING PYRAMID

Members of the Rock Aqua Jays Water Ski Team of Janesville, Wisconsin, USA, formed a 44-person, triple four-tier pyramid at the National Water Ski Show Tournament held in Rockford, Illinois, USA, in August 2003.

HIGHEST EIGHT-PERSON TIGHTROPE PYRAMID: The Flying Wallendas (USA) performed an eight-person pyramid suspended at a height of 25 ft (7.62 m) at Sarasota, USA, on February 20, 2001.

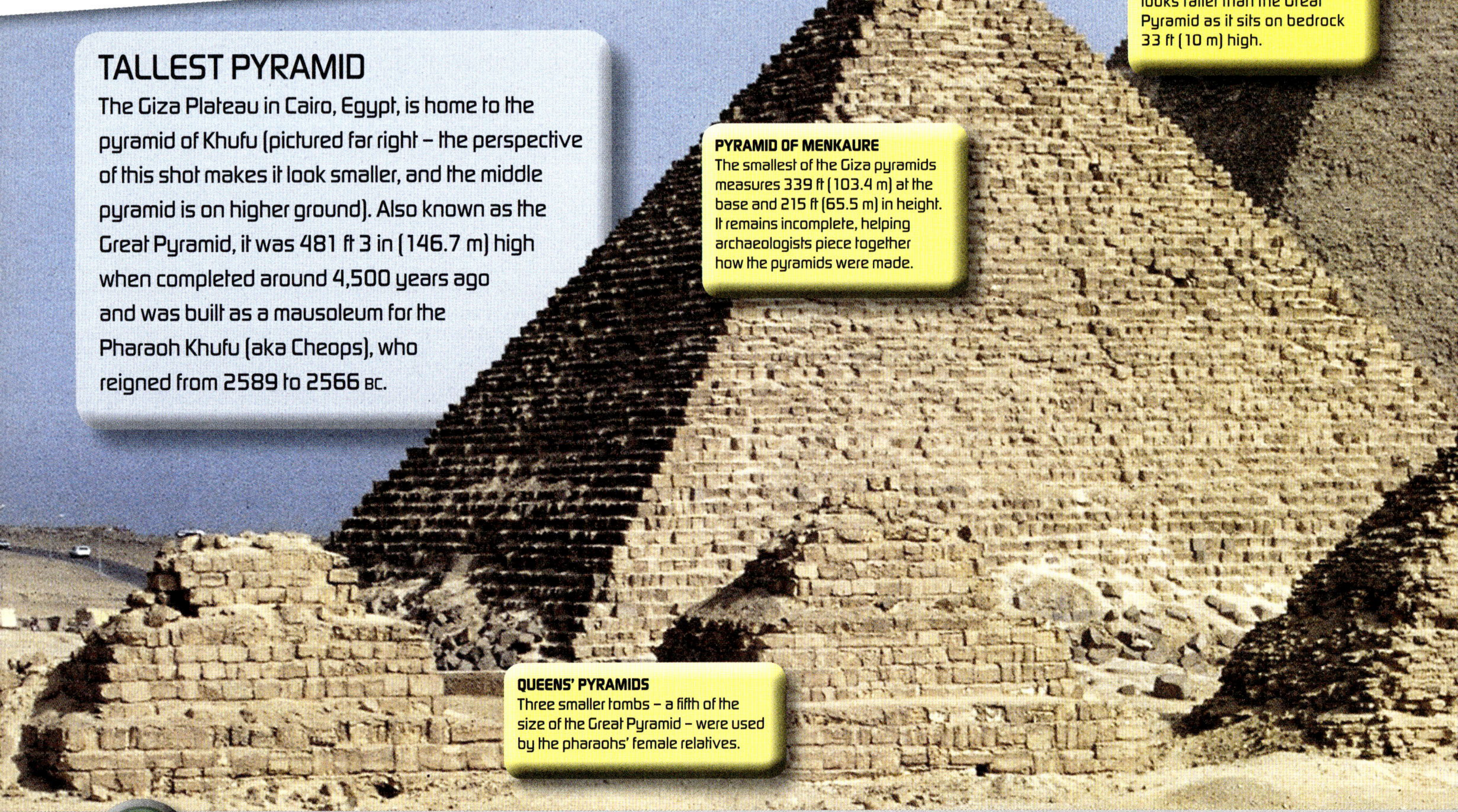

PYRAMID OF KHAFRE
Second-tallest pyramid at 706 ft (215.5 m) wide and rising to 448 ft (136.4 m); looks taller than the Great Pyramid as it sits on bedrock 33 ft (10 m) high.

TALLEST PYRAMID

The Giza Plateau in Cairo, Egypt, is home to the pyramid of Khufu (pictured far right – the perspective of this shot makes it look smaller, and the middle pyramid is on higher ground). Also known as the Great Pyramid, it was 481 ft 3 in (146.7 m) high when completed around 4,500 years ago and was built as a mausoleum for the Pharaoh Khufu (aka Cheops), who reigned from 2589 to 2566 BC.

PYRAMID OF MENKAURE
The smallest of the Giza pyramids measures 339 ft (103.4 m) at the base and 215 ft (65.5 m) in height. It remains incomplete, helping archaeologists piece together how the pyramids were made.

QUEENS' PYRAMIDS
Three smaller tombs – a fifth of the size of the Great Pyramid – were used by the pharaohs' female relatives.

Surprisingly, the **largest cowboy boot** was made not in the USA but in Ethiopia. The boot measured 8 ft 2 in (2.5 m) in height and 7 ft 9 in (2.38 m) in length and was made by Belachew Tola Buta (Ethiopia).

MANMADE PYRAMIDS

BOTTLE CAPS

On September 9, 2000, a group of 12 students from the Krasnystaw Cultural Centre in Krasnystaw, Poland, completed a pyramid of 308,945 bottle tops after nearly nine days of shift work.

TALLEST COFFEE-CUP PYRAMID

A pyramid of 22,140 coffee cups was built by Melanie Lütkefent, Vanessa Höft, Miriam Plümer, Arman Schlieker, and Damian Krey (all Germany) in association with Aral AG at the Du Mont Carre, Cologne, Germany, on October 8, 2010.

ALUMINUM CANS

It was thirsty work for the students of INTI College Subang Jaya (Malaysia) as they built a pyramid of 9,455 drinks cans in just 24 minutes in Kuala Lumpur on September 23, 2000.

BOTTLE CRATES

A team of 200 volunteers spent two days erecting a bottle-crate pyramid 63,365 crates strong at an event organized by Foundation Limmen Ludiek in Limmen, the Netherlands, on June 11–12, 2005.

PAPERBOARD BOXES

From caps, cans, and crates to paperboard boxes – the largest pyramid consisted of 43,147 Calgon boxes, which were stacked into 46 layers measuring 21 ft (6.44 m) tall. The towering structure was built by employees of the Reckitt Benckiser Cleaning Materials Industry and Trade Co. (Turkey) at CarrefourSA in Istanbul, Turkey, on October 30, 2010.

STRAW BALES

The largest straw-bale pyramid stood 94 ft 11 in (28.95 m) high with a base of 82 ft x 82 ft (25 m x 25 m) and was constructed using 1,500 bales. It was made by members of Le Cercle des Jeunes Agriculteurs du Pays de Sarrebourg, in Voyer, Sarrebourg, France, on August 22, 2004.

LARGEST CHAMPAGNE PYRAMID

Luuk Broos (Netherlands) and his team created a 63-story champagne fountain using 43,680 glasses at the Wijnegem shopping mall, Belgium, on January 25, 2008.

COOKIES

The record for the tallest pyramid of cookies is 4 ft 10 in (1.49 m) and was achieved by Jan Vinzenz Krause and members of the diocese Essen (Germany) at the Centro shopping mall in Oberhausen, Germany, on September 16, 2006. The pyramid may not sound that tall, but it was made using 12,180 Leibniz butter cookies!

PYRAMID OF KHUFU

The Great Pyramid, built *c.* 2560 BC, is eroded now to 451 ft (137.5 m) tall but is still the **tallest pyramid**. At its original height of 481 ft 3 in (146.7 m), it was the **tallest manmade construction** in the world until AD 1311 and the building of Lincoln Cathedral (UK).

TALLEST ICE-CREAM-SCOOP PYRAMID: Baskin-Robbins (USA) scooped the ice-cream pyramid title with 3,100 dollops of the company's own product in Hawaii, USA, on May 8, 2000.

SUPER-SIZED

The **largest pyramid** is the Quetzalcoatl pyramid near Mexico City, Mexico. Its base covers nearly 45 acres (18.2 ha) – about the size of 34 American football fields! – and its volume is estimated at 167 million ft³ (3.3 million m³).

ROCK LIKE AN EGYPTIAN

The Great Pyramid has a volume of 88.2 million ft³ (2.5 million m³) and is built from 2.3 million stone blocks (see inset photo), some of which weigh up to 88 tons (80 metric tons).

UPDATED RECORD
NEW RECORD

In terms of big boots, Latvian clown Coco (aka Nicolai Poliakoff) was clearly a step ahead. When he joined the Bertram Mills Circus (UK) in 1929, his 58½-US-size shoes went down as the **largest clown boots** in history!

BACKYARD BEHEMOTHS

LARGEST...

BEAD MOSAIC
A mosaic measuring 12 ft 3 in (3.74 m) wide by 8 ft 10 in (2.7 m) tall, with an area of 108.7 ft^2 (10.1 m^2) was made by the Fifth and Sixth grade of Scoil Naomh Iosaf Primary School (Ireland) in Baltinglass, Co. Wicklow, Ireland, on June 24, 2010.

CHANDELIER
Named "Reflective Flow," the largest chandelier weighs 39,680 lb (18,000 kg) and consists of 165,000 LED units. The chandelier was measured in the Ali Bin Khalifa Al Hitmi & Co. building in Doha, Qatar, where it is installed, on June 23, 2010.

SOCCER BALL
KIA Motors and Emperors Palace Resort and Casino (both South Africa) created a soccer ball with a diameter of 51 ft 4 in (15.66 m). It was displayed in Johannesburg, South Africa, on July 5, 2010.

INFLATABLE BEACH BALL
The world's largest inflatable beach ball is 48 ft 2 in (14.70 m) in diameter. Made by IDCL for MTN Nigeria (both Nigeria), it was presented and measured in Lagos, Nigeria, on August 10, 2010.

TABLE TENNIS BAT
Todd Thomas (USA) has constructed an outsize table tennis bat that is 8 ft 9.9 in (2.69 m) tall, with a diameter of 5 ft 9.9 in (1.77 m); its handle is 3 ft 5.5 in (1.05 m) tall. It was presented and measured at the DFW Table Tennis Club in Irving, Texas, USA, on May 3, 2010.

VOODOO DOLL
The largest voodoo doll was 21 ft 8 in (6.6 m) high, and was created by Catherina Williams (USA) at the Sugar Mill in New Orleans, Louisiana, USA, on November 17, 2010. The doll was blessed in the traditional manner of the voodoo religion, by a bona fide voodoo priestess.

LARGEST SKATEBOARD
Designed by Rob Dyrdek and Joe Ciaglia (both USA), the largest skateboard is 36 ft 7 in (11.14 m) long, 8 ft 8 in (2.63 m) wide, and 3 ft 7.5 in (1.1 m) high. It was unveiled on MTV, on February 25, 2009.

LARGEST RUBBER-BAND BALL
Weight: 9,032 lb (4,097 kg)
Height: 6 ft 7 in (1.99 m)
Made by: Joel Waul (USA)

LARGEST HAIR BALL
Weight: 167 lb (75.7 kg)
Height: 4 ft (1.2 m)
Collected by: Henry Coffer (USA)

LARGEST PAINT BALL
Approximately 17,994 paint layers around a baseball!
Circumference: 9 ft 1 in (2.77 m)
Made by: Michael and Glenda Carmichael (both USA)

LARGEST TAPE BALL
Weight: 1,862 lb (844.59 kg)
Circumference: 23 ft 9 in (7.23 m)
Made by: Tim and Ryan Funk (both Canada)

LARGEST PLASTIC-BAG BALL
Number of bags: 36,700
Made at: an event staged by the County of Los Angeles Department of Public Works (USA)

CHEERS!
The largest pom-pom was 4 ft (1.21 m) high and 10 ft 8 in (3.25 m) in diameter. It was made by the children of the Sixth grade of the Salesian Primary School (all Ireland) on March 16, 2010.

THINK BIG: CHECK OUT SOME GARDEN GIANTS ON P.140.

LARGEST BALL OF PLASTIC WRAP
Jake Lonsway of Bay City, Michigan, USA, created a ball of plastic wrap that had a circumference of 11.5 ft (3.51 m) and weighed 281 lb 8 oz (127.7 kg) as of June 14, 2007.

Eugene Gomberg (Latvia) bought the **most expensive picture postcard** in 2002. It cost $45,370.60 and dated from 1840.

6.5 Weight in tons of fruit you'll consume during your life – about the same weight as a bull elephant. Fruit is the only thing you eat that "wants" to be eaten – that's one of the ways it spreads its seeds.

YO-YO
Jerry Havill's Team Problem Solving course (USA) devised a yo-yo weighing 1,625 lb (738.64 kg) with an 11-ft 6-in (3.51-m) diameter at Bay de Noc Community College in Escanaba, Michigan, USA, on July 6, 2010. Launched by a crane, it yo-yoed 30 times.

LONGEST...

CROCHET CHAIN
Anne Vanier-Drüssel (France) created a chain of crochet 80.78 miles (130 km) long – the distance from New York to Philadelphia, as the crow flies. It was presented and measured in Aniane, France, on October 14, 2009.

PEARL NECKLACE
The world's longest single-strand pearl necklace was 728 ft 4 in (222 m) long. It was created by Shimashi Kanko Kyokai (Japan) at the 60th Pearl Festa in Kashikojima, Shima, Mie Prefecture, Japan, on October 22, 2010.

LARGEST BIRD-NEST BOX
The Heighley Gate Garden Centre in Morpeth, UK, created a bird-nest box 4 ft 1 in (1.25 m) long and 3 ft 11 in (1.20 m) wide, with a height of 5 ft 8 in (1.75 m) at the front and 6 ft 10 in (2.10 m) at the back. It went on display on January 16, 2008.

TABLECLOTH
Measuring 5,784 ft 1 in (1,763 m) long, the longest tablecloth was created by a group known as Gli Amici dell'Aia (Italy). On September 12, 2010, it was laid out along via Romana and via Della Noce between the towns of Albinea and Scandiano in Italy.

LONGEST PICNIC TABLE
On October 30, 2009, Deirdre Sargent (USA) created one continuous picnic table, measuring 248 ft 2 in (75.65 m) long and made from solid pine wood, at the New Orleans City Park, New Orleans, USA.

WHY "PICNIC"?
The word "picnic" comes from the French word *pique-nique*. First used in the late 17th century, it described the practice of diners each bringing a dish, or perhaps a bottle of wine, to a communal meal.

LARGEST ROCKING HORSE
On September 12, 2010, Ofer Mor (Israel) completed a rocking horse measuring an amazing 24 ft 11 in x 10 ft 6 in x 20 ft (7.6 x 3.22 x 6.10 m) in Kadima, Israel.

UPDATED RECORD
NEW RECORD

There are two contenders for the title of **rarest stamp**: the Swedish 3-skilling-banco yellow color error stamp of 1855 and the British Guiana (now Guyana) 1-cent black on magenta stamp from 1856. Both are unique.

BIG STUFF

LARGEST...

BACKPACK
Safta (Spain) has made a backpack 14 ft 1 in (4.31 m) tall, 10 ft 6 in (3.21 m) wide, and 4 ft 9 in (1.47 m) deep. It was measured at the Intergift IFEMA expo center in Madrid, Spain, on February 3, 2011.

BED
Mark Gerrick and Royal Sleep Products (both USA) created a bed 77 ft (23.47 m) long and 46 ft 6 in (14.17 m) wide in Fort Worth, Texas, USA, on September 11, 2008.

BELT BUCKLE
On February 3, 2011, the world's largest belt buckle was unveiled at "*ESPN The Magazine*'s NEXT BIG Weekend" in Fort Worth, Texas, USA. It is 6 ft 6 in (1.98 m) tall and 8 ft 6 in (2.59 m) wide and was created by ESPN with Kelly Graham (both USA).

FIREWORK ROCKET
Weighing 29 lb 8 oz (13.4 kg), the largest firework rocket was produced and launched by Associaçao Nacional de Empresas de Produtos Explosivos (Portugal) at the 12th International Symposium on Fireworks in Oporto and Vila Nova de Gaia, Portugal, on October 13, 2010.

FLASHLIGHT
Moon Way General Trading LLC (UAE) produced a flashlight 7 ft 5 in (227 cm) long and 1 ft 9 in (55 cm) in diameter. It was presented and measured in Sharjah, UAE, on August 25, 2010.

NATIVITY VILLAGE
El Pesebre Mas Grande del Mundo, the world's largest nativity village, was created by Fabian Rojas (Colombia) and opened on December 1, 2010 in Santiago de Cali, Colombia. It has an area of 185,440.6 ft^2 (17,228 m^2) – more than three times the size of an American football field – and features 339 figures.

ORIGAMI LEI
"Network of Fukuoka Universities" (Japan) created a 6,594-ft-long (2,010-m) origami lei (garland) at the Fukuoka City Hall, Fukuoka, Japan, on September 26, 2010.

POSTER
On December 8, 2010, a poster for Michael Jackson's *Michael* album was unveiled at Rectory Farm in Hounslow, UK. Measuring 171 x 170 ft (52.1 x 51.8 m), it was created by painter Kadir Nelson (USA) in 2009 as a commission from Sony Music UK.

SCRATCHCARD
The Golden Casket Lottery (Australia) created a scratchcard 32 ft 9 in (10 m) tall and 16 ft 4 in (5 m) wide. It was unveiled and scratched in Brisbane, Queensland, Australia, on February 5, 2011.

11 FT 5 IN TALL

LARGEST MOTORIZED SHOPPING CART
Edd China (UK) created a motorized shopping cart measuring 9 ft 10 in (3 m) long, 11 ft 5 in (3.5 m) tall, and 5 ft 10 in (1.8 m) wide. It was displayed at the Asda store, Watford, UK, on November 9, 2005.

LARGEST VUVUZELA
At 114 ft 9 in (35 m) long and 18 ft (5.5 m) in diameter at the front, the world's largest vuvuzela was created by Hyundai Automotive South Africa and was presented and measured in Cape Town, South Africa, on May 26, 2010.

UPDATED RECORD
NEW RECORD

BIG AND BEAUTIFUL, OR SMALL BUT PERFECTLY FORMED? YOU'LL FIND PEOPLE OF EVERY SIZE AND SHAPE ON P.84.

The **most successful attorney** is Sir Lionel Luckhoo (Guyana), senior partner of Luckhoo and Luckhoo of Georgetown, Guyana, who succeeded in securing 245 successive homicide acquittals between 1940 and 1985.

525 Height in yards of all the toilet rolls you'll use in your lifetime – approximately 4,000 – piled one on top of the other. That's about 328 ft taller than the Empire State Building.

LARGEST WATERING CAN

A giant watering can built from galvanized steel was constructed for Utica Zoo, New York, USA. The gigantic gardening tool arrived by truck on December 5, 2000. It weighs 2,000 lb (907.1 kg) and measures 15 ft 6 in (4.7 m) high, with a diameter of 12 ft (3.65 m).

WORRY BEADS

Also known as kombolói, worry beads are a set of beads threaded on to a string. They are designed as a tool to help people relax, by manipulating the beads.

A colossal set of worry beads measuring 47 ft 2 in (14.4 m) long was made by the Kuwait Oil Company (Kuwait) in Al-Ahmadi, Kuwait, and completed on January 15, 2011.

SNOWBALL

Wesley Fowlks and a team of nine other participants (all USA) rolled a snowball measuring 23 ft 2.5 in (7.07 m) in circumference at the University of Massachusetts' Dartmouth Campus, Massachusetts, USA, on February 1, 2011.

UMBRELLA

Measuring 56 ft (17.06 m) in diameter and 36 ft (10.97 m) tall, the largest umbrella was made by Max New York Life Insurance (India) and unveiled at Ishanya Mall in Pune, India, on August 14, 2010.

UNDERPANTS

The largest underpants in the world measured 65 ft 7 in (20 m) across the waist and 39 ft 4 in (12 m) from waistband to crotch. They were presented by Pants to Poverty (UK) in London, UK, on September 16, 2010.

WALLET

Produced by the Big Skinny Corporation (USA), the largest wallet measures 10 ft (3.14 m) long and 10 ft 5 in (3.06 m) high. It was presented and measured in Cambridge, Massachusetts, USA, on November 26, 2010.

LARGEST CHAINSAW

A working chainsaw measuring 22 ft 11 in (6.98 m) long and 6 ft (1.83 m) high was made by Moran Iron Works, Inc., of Onaway, Michigan, USA, in 1996. Named "Big Gus," it was shown at Da Yoopers Tourist Trap at Ishpening, Michigan, USA.

LARGEST BEACH TOWEL

Fateka SL manufactured a beach towel on behalf of the beverage group Compañía Cervecera de Canarias (both Spain) that measured 285 ft 10 in (87.14 m) long and 82 ft 8 in (25.20 m) wide. It was laid out at Playa de las Canteras in Las Palmas, Gran Canaria, Spain, on June 5, 2010.

ON THE BOARD

While you're on the beach, you could try out the **longest surfboard**. Made by Nev Hyman (Australia) in 2005, it was 39 ft 4 in (12 m) long, 9 ft 10 in (3 m) wide, and 11.8 in (30 cm) thick.

MAKING IT BIG

It took a month to plan how to create this huge beach towel, and eight days to actually make it. Hardly surprising when you consider that it's longer than a 747 jumbo jet.

By contrast, Pedro López (Colombia) was convicted of 57 counts of murder in Ecuador in 1980. Dubbed the "Monster of the Andes", he confessed to a total of 300 murders across Colombia, Peru, and Ecuador, making him the **most prolific serial killer** of all time.

HIGHEST BOX-OFFICE GROSS FOR AN ANIMATED MOVIE ON OPENING DAY

On its day of release in the USA on June 18, 2010, the hotly anticipated Disney/Pixar (both USA) movie *Toy Story 3* (USA, 2010) took $41 million at 4,028 locations across the country, beating the previous record of $38.4 million set by *Shrek the Third* (USA, 2007) on May 18, 2007.

Native to Ecuador (as well as Peru and Panama), the world's **largest winged cockroach** is *Megaloblatta longipennis*. A preserved female specimen in the collection of Akira Yokokura (Japan) measured 3.8 in (97 mm) in length and 1.75 in (45 mm) across.

The **largest aquatic insect** is the giant water bug (*Lethocerus maximus*), a carnivorous species that inhabits Venezuela (as well as Brazil). Although it can grow up to 4.53 in (11.5 cm) long, it is not as heavy as some of the continent's burly beetles and stick insects.

COMIC-CON

GUINNESS WORLD RECORDS VISITS THE WORLD'S LARGEST POPULAR CULTURE CONVENTION

More than 130,000 fans of comic books, movies, TV shows, and videogames descended on San Diego in California, USA, in July for Comic-Con 2010 – the globe's ● **largest pop-culture gathering**…and GWR was there to present some record certificates.

STAR WARS: THE CLONE WARS

The hit CGI TV series *Star Wars: The Clone Wars* pulled in an average viewership of 4 million at its launch on the Cartoon Network in 2008, making it the world's ● **most watched sci-fi animation series**. On hand to accept the GWR certificate were (left to right) producer Cary Silver, Turner Animation President and COO Stuart Snyder, and Supervising Director Dave Filoni.

FUTURAMA

With an average reviewer score of 80/100, the 6th season of the sci-fi comedy *Futurama* was the ● **most critically acclaimed animation on TV**. The show's creator – and multiple Guinness World Record-holder – Matt Groening (right) joined Executive Producer David X Cohen on stage to receive their official certificates.

ROCKY

Actor/director Sylvester Stallone made a guest appearance to promote his new movie, *The Expendables*, but it was for his *Rocky* movies that he received a record certificate. Having grossed $556 million at the domestic box-office alone, the *Rocky* series is the ● **most successful sports movie franchise**. Pictured is GWR's Craig Glenday (center) presenting to Stallone (right) and *Rocky IV* co-star Dolph Lundgren.

● UPDATED RECORD
● NEW RECORD

The **highest mudslide death toll** occurred in December 1999 after torrential rains fell in Vargas State, Venezuela. An estimated 10,000 to 30,000 people died in the disaster.

23,973 Hours you will spend reading newspapers, books, and comic books. At an average rate of 300 words per minute, that's more than 448 million words in a lifetime. Or 3,400 copies of this book!

GLEE

Stars of the musical TV show *Glee* were excited to learn that they'd made it into the *Guinness World Records* book for the **most simultaneous tracks debuting in the UK chart**, with five in January 2010. So, too, were the "Gleeks" who turned up to mob the overwhelmed cast!

TODD KLEIN

We were honored to meet record-breaking comic letterer Todd Klein, who won the **Most Eisner comic awards in one category** with 15. Here he is pictured with the 2011 GWR comic-books spread, for which Todd did the lettering.

SAW

With a total worldwide gross of $733 million over its first six installments, the *Saw* franchise is the world's ● **most successful horror movie series**. And who better to receive the award than the fearsome Jigsaw Killer himself – actor Tobin Bell.

STEAMPUNKS

Comic-Con attracts fans of all kinds of pop culture, including Steampunks – the subculture inspired by an alternative history of steam-age technology and Victoriana. The 2010 Con brought together 185 like-minded people to set the first ever record for the ● **largest gathering of Steampunks**. Congratulations everyone!

FOR MORE GARGANTUAN GATHERINGS, HEAD STRAIGHT TO P.102

The ● **most people receiving a mud treatment** was achieved by 50 participants in an event organized by Bad Saarow Kur GmbH in Brandenburg, Germany, on March 28, 2009.

VIDEO GAMING

FIRST GAME TO HAVE AN OFFICIALLY RECOGNIZED DAY OF CELEBRATION

On its release, *Sid Meier's Civilization V* (2K Games, 2010) was honored by the Governor of Maryland, USA, who stated that September 21, 2010 would henceforth be known as "Sid Meier's Civilization V Day."

MOST AUTOMOBILES IN A RACING VIDEO GAME

Sony's *Gran Turismo 5* (2010) features 1,000 licensed vehicles from the world's top marques – and all are included on the game disk. Downloadable content is expected to increase this number even further.

FASTEST LAP ON *CRASH NITRO KART*

On May 31, 2010, gamer Alex Herrera (USA) of Lilburn, Georgia, USA, achieved a lap time of just 37.77 seconds around the Jungle Boogie track on *Crash Nitro Kart* (Universal, 2003).

MOST DOWNLOADED CELL PHONE VIDEO GAME

The ever-popular puzzle game *Tetris* (Alexey Pajitnov, 1985) is still going strong after 25 years, notching up its 100 millionth cell phone download by October 2010.

RYOTA MADE 237 PERFECT STEPS!

LARGEST HANDHELD GAME CONSOLE PARTY

On January 23, 2011, 849 children, parents, and friends played the game *Tokutenryoku Gakushu DS* (Benesse, 2008) on Nintendo DS for 10 minutes. The event, hosted by TV star Takahiro Azuma and actress Wakana Aoi, was organized by Odawara Gakuryoku Koji Iinkai in collaboration with Benesse in Odawara, Japan.

FASTEST FINGERS

Ryota might want to try out the Venom Mini Dance Mat, which lets gamers play *DDR* with their fingers. Measuring just 4 in (10 cm) by 4.5 in (11.5 cm), it is the world's **first handheld dance mat.**

YOUNGEST GAMER TO ACHIEVE A PERFECT SCORE ON *DANCE DANCE REVOLUTION*

Aged just 9 years 288 days, Ryota Wada (Japan) achieved a perfect "AAA" rating on *Dance Dance Revolution* (Konami, 1998) when he mastered the song "Hyper Eurobeat" on the "Expert" difficulty setting at his home in Tokyo, Japan, on August 29, 2010.

UPDATED RECORD
NEW RECORD

Measuring 892 ft 3 in (271.97 m) in length, the world's **longest model train** was created by German model-maker Miniature Wunderland. Built in Hamburg, Germany, on July 25, 2008, the 1:87.1-scale train featured eight locomotives and 2,212 coaches!

34 Age of the average video game player. He (the average gamer is male) started playing 12 years ago and spends $126 a year on games. Curiously, the average video game buyer is 40 years old.

LONGEST MARATHON

In an epic session, Tony Desmet, Jesse Rebmann, and Jeffrey Gammon (all Belgium) played *Assassin's Creed Brotherhood* (Ubisoft, 2010) for 109 hours at the GUNKtv World Record Gaming Event in Antwerp, Belgium, on December 18–22, 2010.

LONGEST GAMING SESSION IN INDOOR FREEFALL

Suspended in a wind tunnel, the 6-ft 5-in (190-cm), 265-lb (120-kg) Jesse Moerkerk (Netherlands) enjoyed an aerial Nintendo Wii gaming session lasting 18 min 52 sec at Indoor Skydive Roosendaal, the Netherlands, on January 11, 2011.

LONGEST MARATHON (SOCCER GAME)

In the name of charity, soccer-mad Michael Puterflam (Australia) played *FIFA 11* (EA, 2010) for 30 hr 1 min at Westfield Bondi Junction, Sydney, Australia, on December 1–2, 2010. During the attempt, Michael faced more than 100 opponents, including celebrities, sports personalities, and the public.

LONGEST MARATHON (*GUITAR HERO*)

In a performance streamed live over the internet, Zach Wong (Canada) played *Guitar Hero* (Harmonix, 2005) for a record 50 hr 3 min in Vancouver, Canada, on August 25–27, 2010.

FIRST MAXIMUM SCORE ON *PAC-MAN*

Billy Mitchell (USA) completed the first "perfect" game of *PAC-Man* (Namco, 1980) on July 3, 1999, notching up the maximum 3,333,360 points in just over six hours. The feat is considered one of the most difficult in video gaming, requiring the player to eat every dot, energizer, flashing ghost, and fruit in all 256 levels without losing a single life.

FASTEST COMPLETION OF "SNIPER-FI" ON *CALL OF DUTY: MODERN WARFARE 2*

In 2010, a US gamer known as Janner, of online community weplayedcod.com, finished the special-ops mission "Sniper-Fi" on the PC version of *Call of Duty: Modern Warfare 2* (Infinity Ward, 2009) in a time of 1 min 39.5 sec – 16 seconds faster than the game's own developers!

FASTEST-SELLING PC GAME

Launched on December 7, 2010, *Cataclysm*, the third expansion for Blizzard Entertainment's *World of Warcraft*, sold 3.3 million copies in its first 24 hours, beating the previous record of 2.8 million set by its predecessor, *Wrath of the Lich King*, in 2008.

MOST EXPENSIVE VIRTUAL OBJECT

The greatest amount paid for a piece of virtual property is $6 million by SEE Virtual Worlds (USA) for Planet Calypso, a virtual planet within the online game *Entropia Universe* (MindArk, 2003). This "virtual real estate" was purchased on December 20, 2010.

ARCADE ACTION

Guitars first came to arcades in 1999 when Konami released *GuitarFreaks*, a rhythm game for up to two players. The franchise is still going strong a decade later, with *GuitarFreaks V8* released in 2011.

HIGHEST SCORE ON *GUITAR HERO III* (FEMALE)

On September 30, 2010, at her home in California, USA, Annie Leung (USA) proved she was a true guitar hero when she racked up a score of 789,349 playing the classic track "Through the Fire and Flames" on *Guitar Hero III: Legends of Rock* (Neversoft, 2007).

Speaking of models, the **largest collection of model automobiles** belongs to Nabil Karam (Lebanon), who had amassed 22,222 unique items by November 11, 2009.

COLLECTIBLE CARD GAMING

RAREST TRADING CARD

Created for Magic: The Gathering (Wizards of the Coast, Inc., USA), the most elusive cards on the planet are the 1996 World Champion (left) and the Shichifukujin Dragon (right) – only one of each exists. The former was awarded to the winner of the 1996 World Championships, Tom Chanpheng (Australia), while the latter was created to celebrate the opening of the DCI Tournament Centre in Tokyo, Japan, in 1996.

FIRST TRADING CARD GAME

The world's oldest trading card game (TCG) appeared way back in 1904. The Base Ball Card Game, published by the Allegheny Card Co. (USA), contained 104 player cards and eight team "ball counter" cards. As the game proved unpopular in its day, these hand-cut card sets are today extremely rare, with a mint condition deck likely to fetch around $500.

FIRST MODERN TRADING CARD GAME

Magic: The Gathering was unleashed on the world on August 5, 1993. Created by Richard Garfield (USA) and published by Wizards of the Coast, Inc., the game combines the excitement of competition with the thrill of trading and collecting. Players engage in combat to reduce their opponent's score from 20 to zero with a variety of attacks and defenses that unleash spells, artifacts, and mystical creatures. Still enormously popular, Magic is regarded as the origin of TCGs as we know them.

BEST-SELLING TRADING CARD GAME

The world's most popular trading card game is Yu-Gi-Oh!, created by Konami Digital Entertainment Co., Ltd (Japan) and based on the comic books and animated TV series by artist Kazuki Takahashi (Japan). Fronted by lead character Yusei Fudo (left), the game sold a phenomenal 25,175,567,833 cards around the globe between 1999 and April 1, 2011, and has spawned spin-offs including video games and movies.

MOST PLAYED TRADING CARD GAME

Since making its debut in 1993, the Magic: The Gathering trading card game has spread across the world while growing ever more popular. According to the publisher, Wizards of the Coast, Inc., the game, which has since been translated into nine languages, is now played in 52 countries by more than 6 million players.

FIRST ONLINE TRADING CARD GAME

When it went live on May 28, 1997, *Chron X*, developed by George Moromisato and published by Genetic Anomalies, became the first TCG to enter the virtual world. Free to play, *Chron X* is set on a dystopian Earth in the year 2096. The rights to the game were acquired by Darkened Sky Studios in 2007, who announced their plans for a sequel, *Chron X2*.

LONGEST-RUNNING DIGITAL TRADING CARD GAME

Magic: The Gathering has been available in computer format since the release of the PC game *Magic: The Gathering* (Microprose) on March 27, 1997.

COSTLY ERROR

In 2009, a misprinted Yu-Gi-Oh! card went up for sale on eBay with an asking price of $100,000! This rare "Clock Tower Prison" card – incorrectly titled as "Miraculous Descent" – failed to raise the outrageous sum.

Ashraf Makarem (Lebanon) and Khaled Othman (Kuwait) unveiled the world's **largest flag**, a huge 710,148-ft^2 (65,975-m^2) Lebanese flag, in Rayak, Lebanon, on October 10, 2010.

14,953 Sandwiches you will eat during your lifetime. Legend has it that the sandwich was invented as a convenient snack in 1760 by John Montague, the 4th Earl of Sandwich, so that he didn't have to leave the card table for meals.

LARGEST TRADING CARD

Produced by Panini America (USA), the world's largest trading card was revealed on February 13, 2010. Carrying the image of the basketball player Kobe Bryant of the Los Angeles Lakers NBA team (both USA), the card was embossed with a 15-in-by-15-in (38-cm-by-38-cm) swatch of an official game jersey and measured a vast 7 ft (2.13 m) tall by 4 ft 11 in (1.22 m) wide.

LONGEST TRADING CARD GAME MARATHON

From December 27, 2002 to January 1, 2003, William Stone, Bryan Erwin, and Christopher Groetzinger (all USA) played 154 games of The Lord of the Rings Trading Card Game over 128 hours at The Courtyard, Colorado Springs, Colorado, USA.

FIRST THREE-DIMENSIONAL TRADING CARD GAME

Canadian games company Spin Master took TCGs to the next level when they unveiled the world's first 3D trading card game, Redakai, at the American International Toy Fair in New York, USA, in February 2011. The game, which focuses on a group of teens searching for a mystical energy called Kairu, includes hologram cards that animate characters' attacks, as well as transparent cards that can be overlayed with others to create a variety of effects.

DISCOVER MORE COLLECTIBLES ON PP.150–53.

LARGEST CASH PRIZE FOR A TCG

The World of Warcraft TCG World Championship, held at the San Diego Convention Center (USA) between November 30 and December 2, 2007, saw Guillaume Matignon (France) beat over 400 of the world's best World of Warcraft warriors to claim a record payout of $100,000.

FIRST TRADING CARD GAME PATENT

On September 2, 1997, Magic: The Gathering's inventor, Richard Garfield (USA), was granted US patent 5,662,332 (A) for "the trading card game method of play" – the first-ever TCG patent.

HIGH STAKES

TCG tournaments are big business – just ask pro Magic: The Gathering player Kai Budde. To date, the German has racked up career winnings of $352,620 – the **highest earnings from TCG tournaments**.

LARGEST TRADING GAME TOURNAMENT

The Magic Grand Prix Madrid 2010, held over the weekend of February 27–28, 2010 in Madrid, Spain, saw 2,227 players battle it out over 19 rounds until just two remained: David Do Anh (Czech Republic) and Andreas Müller (Germany). In a close-fought final, Müller won through by a margin of 2–1, taking home $3,500.

UPDATED RECORD
NEW RECORD

A flag of that size would need quite a flagpole if it were to be flown, and a suitable candidate would be the **tallest unsupported flagpole**. It measures 531 ft 5 in (162 m) and was erected in Baku, Azerbaijan, on May 29, 2010.

PUBLISHING

LARGEST GOVERNMENT PUBLISHING COMPANY

In 1813, the US Congress decided that Americans should be kept informed about the workings of the government, leading to the creation of the US Government Printing Office (GPO) and the "Keep America Informed" program. In 2010, the GPO employed 2,300 staff (and up to 332,000 private sector contract staff) supplying 1,220 libraries; more than 250,000 titles were available online, and 25 million documents were downloaded per month.

FIRST CROSSWORD PUZZLE BOOK

The earliest collection of crossword puzzles was published in the USA in 1924. *The Cross Word Puzzle Book* was the first publication by a new partnership formed by Dick Simon and Lincoln Schuster. A compilation of crossword puzzles from US newspaper *New York World*, it was an instant success and helped to establish publishing giant Simon & Schuster, who still produce crossword books today.

MOST EXPENSIVE PUBLISHED BOOK SOLD AT AUCTION

On December 7, 2010, a rare, complete copy of John James Audubon's *Birds of America* sold for £7.3 million ($11.4 million) at Sotheby's in London, UK. It contains 1,000 life-size illustrations of 435 birds drawn and printed by Audubon between 1827 and 1838. The illustrations were originally sold a page at a time to collectors, and only 119 complete editions are known to exist.

HIGHEST WEEKLY NEWSPAPER CIRCULATION

Founded in 1978 in Moscow, Russia, *Argumenty i Fakty* ("Arguments and Facts") attained a circulation of 33,431,100 in May 1990, with an estimated readership of more than 100 million.

MOST BOOKS WRITTEN AND PUBLISHED IN A YEAR BY AN INDIVIDUAL

Ryuho Okawa (Japan) wrote and published 52 books between November 23, 2009 and November 10, 2010.

YOUNGEST PERSON TO HAVE A BOOK PUBLISHED

The youngest commercially published author is Dorothy Straight (b. May 25, 1958), of Washington, DC, USA, who wrote *How the World Began* in 1962, aged four. It was published in August 1964 by Pantheon Books.

LARGEST BOOK (TRIMMED PAGE SIZE)

On March 21, 2010, Béla Varga, Béláné Varga (both Hungary), and 25 volunteers completed *Fragile Nature* – a book about the Aggtelek National Park in Hungary – which measured 13 ft 8.5 in x 12 ft 4.3 in (4.18 x 3.77 m) and weighed 3,130 lb 9 oz (1,420 kg). It runs to a length of 346 pages.

THE BOOKS WE LEAVE BEHIND

A 2010 survey of the thousands of books that guests most often leave behind at rooms in 452 Travelodge hotels in the UK gave the following Top Ten.

Book title	Author(s)
1. *Simon Cowell: The Unauthorized Biography*	Chas Newkey-Burden
2. *Ooh! What a Lovely Pair: Our Story*	Ant & Dec
3. *The Storm: The World Economic Crisis and What it Means*	Vince Cable
4. *The Lost Symbol*	Dan Brown
5. *The Girl with the Dragon Tattoo*	Stieg Larsson
6. *Breaking Dawn*	Stephenie Meyer
7. *The Girl Who Played with Fire*	Stieg Larsson
8. *Eclipse*	Stephenie Meyer
9. *The Girl Who Kicked the Hornets' Nest*	Stieg Larsson
10. *Eat, Pray, Love*	Elizabeth Gilbert

LARGEST POP-UP BOOK

Measuring 13 ft 1 in x 9 ft 10 in (4 x 3 m) and featuring pop-ups 7 ft 9 in (2.35 m) tall, the largest pop-up book was made for a TV commercial advertising Pearle Opticiens (Belgium) in Ghent, Belgium, on September 6, 2010.

MY WORD! Entitled *My Word*, the book was a scaled-up version of a booklet available in the 160 Pearle Opticiens stores in Belgium. It took three months to complete the paper engineering and final build.

Azerbaijan and the area surrounding the Caspian Sea contain nearly 400 mud volcanoes. The **largest mud volcanoes** in Azerbaijan, and the world, are an average of 0.6 miles (1 km) across the base and hundreds of yards tall.

42 The meaning of life, the universe, and everything, according to writer Douglas Adams's memorable creation *The Hitchhiker's Guide to the Galaxy*. It's also how many years of your life are left over when you take off the time you'll spend sleeping and working.

FIRST AUTHOR TO SELL MORE THAN 1 MILLION E-BOOKS

On July 6, 2010, the Hachette Book Group announced that James Patterson (USA), creator of the Alex Cross and Women's Murder Club series of novels, was the first author to exceed 1 million sales in electronic books, moving 1.14 million units of his books for devices such as Kindle and the iPad.

HIGHEST-EARNING ADULT FICTION AUTHOR

In terms of book sales and earnings, James Patterson (USA) is currently the best-selling author of adult fiction. In the year to June 1, 2010, he earned $70 million from his writing, and has sold more than 200 million books since 1992.

HIGHEST INITIAL PRINT RUN (FICTION)

Harry Potter and the Deathly Hallows had an initial print run of 12 million copies, the biggest initial print run in history. It was released at midnight on July 21, 2007. It is also the **fastest-selling fiction book in 24 hours**, shifting 8.3 million copies (or 345,833 books per hour) on the day of its release in the USA, from 00:01 a.m. on July 21, 2007.

LONGEST-RUNNING CHILDREN'S MAGAZINE

Murzilka is a monthly literary and art publication for children aged six to 12, published by UAB "Editors Murzilka" (Russia). *Murzilka* launched on April 28, 1924 and has appeared monthly and without interruption for its 86 years of existence, except for 26 double issues in the years 1931 to 1933 and 1939 to 1946. Overall, 1,014 issues had been produced as of November 28, 2010.

FIRST DOLLAR-BILLIONAIRE AUTHOR

J K Rowling (UK) is one of only five self-made female billionaires, and the first billion-dollar author. Her seven Harry Potter books have sold 400 million copies worldwide. According to *Forbes*, Rowling has grossed more than $1 billion for her novels and from related earnings.

MAGIC AT THE MOVIES

Quite aside from her hugely popular books, J K Rowling also profits from the mega-successful Harry Potter movie series, which has earned $6.4 billion globally to date.

UPDATED RECORD
NEW RECORD

IF YOU LIKE LIFE ON A LARGE SCALE, TURN BACK TO P.198.

The **coldest erupting lava** is the natrocarbonatite lava of the volcano Oldoinyo Lengai, Tanzania, which erupts at temperatures of 930–1,110°F (500–600°C).

AT THE MOVIES

MOST PROFITABLE CINEMA INDUSTRY

The US cinema industry made more than $11 billion in domestic box-office takings during 2010. Japan is in second place with $2.5 billion while India is in third place, with $2.2 billion.

MOST EXPENSIVE MOVIE EVER PRODUCED

Pirates of the Caribbean: At World's End (USA, 2007) had an estimated budget of around $300 million. If the budgets of movies are adjusted for inflation to 2010 dollars, *Pirates of the Caribbean: At World's End* remains the most expensive production of all time, its $315-million budget narrowly beating *Cleopatra* (USA, 1963), starring Elizabeth Taylor and Richard Burton (both UK), which cost $44 million in 1963, the equivalent of $310 million in 2010.

HIGHEST-PAID ACTRESS

Star of the movies *The Proposal* and *The Blind Side* (both USA, 2009), Sandra Bullock (USA) earned $56 million in the 12 months to June 2010.

MOST SCREEN CREDITS FOR A LIVING ACTOR

Brahmanandam Kanneganti (India), usually known just as Brahmanandam, played an astonishing 857 credited movie roles from 1987 to June 24, 2010.

HIGHEST-PAID ACTOR

Pirates of the Caribbean star Johnny Depp (USA, seen above with costar Penélope Cruz) earned a treasure trove – $75 million – from June 2009 to June 2010.

HEAD TURNER

One of *Inception*'s most striking scenes depicts a zero-gravity fight in a corridor. No CGI here: the filmmakers used rotating sets, and 500 crew members, to produce the disorienting effect.

FASTEST $100-MILLION BOX-OFFICE GROSS FOR AN ANIMATION

Toy Story 3 (USA, 2010), the computer-animated movie from Walt Disney and Pixar Animation Studios, reached the $100-million mark at the US box office in three days from its release on June 18, 2010 at 4,028 movie theaters, making it the fifth fastest-grossing movie ever.

The movie also holds the record for the **highest box-office gross for an animation**, having taken more than $1.05 billion at the global box office from June to October 2010.

HIGHEST BOX-OFFICE GROSS FOR AN OPENING WEEKEND

Sci-fi action movie *Inception* (USA, 2010) racked up a record-breaking $62,785,337, across 3,792 theaters, on its opening weekend of July 16–18, 2010. Directed by Christopher Nolan and starring Leonardo DiCaprio, the movie was later nominated for eight Oscars, winning four.

The record for the **fastest group of Maasai warriors to complete a marathon** is 5 hr 24 min 47 sec and was achieved by six warriors from Tanzania at the Flora London Marathon, in London, UK, on April 13, 2008.

5,609 Number of movies you will watch in a lifetime, or one every five days. As the average Hollywood feature film costs $106 million to make, that's potentially $500 billion worth of entertainment.

THE OSCARS

MOST WINS (MOVIE)

Three movies share the record for the **most Oscars won**, with 11 wins each:

- *Ben-Hur* (USA, 1959) won from 12 nominations in 1960.
- *Titanic* (USA, 1997) won out of 14 nominations in 1998 (the **most nominations for a movie**, shared wth *All About Eve* (USA, 1950) in 1951).
- *The Lord of the Rings: The Return of the King* (NZ/USA, 2003) won all 11 of the categories in which it was nominated in 2004.

MOST WINS FOR BEST FOREIGN LANGUAGE FILM

Federico Fellini (Italy) won four Oscars for Best Foreign Language Film as a director, with *La Strada* (1954), *Nights of Cabiria* (1957), *8½* (1963), and *Amarcord* (1973).

If Special Oscars are also considered (awarded before the category of Best Foreign Language Film was opened), Fellini shares his record with Vittorio De Sica (Italy). De Sica won Special Oscars for *Shoeshine* (1946) and *Bicycle Thieves* (1938), and Oscars for *Yesterday, Today, Tomorrow* (1963) and *Il Giardino dei Finzi Contini* (1970).

MOST OSCAR NOMINATIONS WITHOUT WINNING BY AN ACTOR

Peter O'Toole (Ireland) has been nominated eight times for the Best Actor award, but has never won. O'Toole's nonwinning run has so far lasted 44 years, with *Lawrence of Arabia* (UK, 1962); *Beckett* (UK, 1964); *The Lion in Winter* (UK, 1968); *Goodbye Mr Chips* (UK, 1969); *The Ruling Class* (UK, 1972); *The Stunt Man* (USA, 1980); *My Favorite Year* (USA, 1982); and *Venus* (UK, 2006).

FIRST REMAKE TO WIN BEST PICTURE

The first – and only – remake to win Best Picture is *The Departed* (USA, 2006), a remake of *Infernal Affairs* (Hong Kong, 2002). Many films share the same source material, but *The Departed* is the sole Best Picture winner to have been based on another film.

BOX-OFFICE HALL OF FAME

GWR proudly presents the movies that have grossed the most. The first list is purely in terms of today's money; the second accounts for the number of tickets sold, contemporary seat prices, and inflation, giving a truer picture of success.

	Movie	Non-adjusted gross (million)	Movie	Adjusted gross (million)
1	*Avatar* (2009)	$2,782.3	*Gone with the Wind* (1939)	$3,301.4
2	*Titanic* (1997)	$1,843.2	*Avatar* (2009)	$2,782.3
3	*The Lord of the Rings: The Return of the King* (2003)	$1,119.1	*Star Wars* (1977)	$2,710.8
4	*Pirates of the Caribbean: Dead Man's Chest* (2006)	$1,066.2	*Titanic* (1997)	$2,413.8
5	*Toy Story 3* (2010)	$1,063.2	*The Sound of Music* (1965)	$2,269.8
6	*Alice in Wonderland* (2010)	$1,024.3	*E.T.: The Extra-Terrestrial* (1982)	$2,216.8
7	*The Dark Knight* (2008)	$1,001.9	*The Ten Commandments* (1956)	$2,098.6
8	*Harry Potter and the Sorcerer's Stone* (2001)	$974.7	*Doctor Zhivago* (1965)	$1,988.6
9	*Pirates of the Caribbean: At World's End* (2007)	$961	*Jaws* (1975)	$1,945.1
10	*Harry Potter and the Deathly Hallows Part 1* (2010)	$952.2	*Snow White and the Seven Dwarfs* (1937)	$1,746.1

MOVIE MAGIC

The seven Harry Potter movies have grossed $6.3 billion at the global box office to date, making them the **most successful movie franchise** of all time.

HIGHEST-GROSSING STUDIO

Warner Bros. (USA) claimed 18.2% of the movie market in 2010, its motion pictures grossing $1,923.9 million in all. The studio's impressive performance was helped by the fact that it distributes the highly profitable Harry Potter series, the penultimate installment of which appeared in November 2010 (see table above).

UPDATED RECORD
NEW RECORD

Jan Skorkovský (Czech Republic) juggled a soccer ball while running the 26.219-mile (42.195-km) Prague City Marathon in 7 hr 18 min 55 sec on July 8, 1990, the **fastest marathon juggling a soccer ball**.

WORLD CINEMA

THE GLOBAL BOX OFFICE

We've all heard about Hollywood and Bollywood. But what about the rest of the planet? GWR presents you with a guide to the biggest movie hits made (or, in some cases, co-produced) by some of the world's other film industries. All the figures listed are for the worldwide box-office gross of each film, unless otherwise stated.

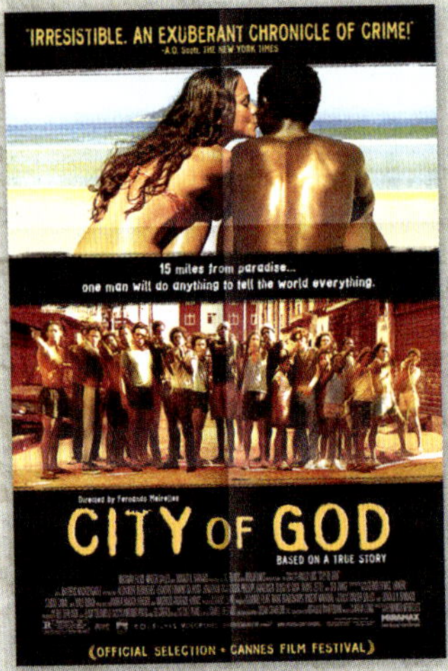

BRAZIL
City of God (2003)
Dir.: Fernando Meirelles and Kátia Lund (both Brazil).
Box office: $30.6 million.

CHINA
Hero (2004)
Dir.: Yimou Zhang (China).
Box office: $177.4 million.

FINLAND
The Man Without a Past (2003)
Dir.: Aki Kaurismäki (Finland).
Box office: $9.6 million.

ITALY
Life is Beautiful (1997)
Dir.: Roberto Benigni (Italy).
Box office: $229 million.

JAPAN
Spirited Away (2002)
Dir.: Hayao Miyazaki (Japan).
Box office: $274.9 million.

NEW ZEALAND
The Piano (1993)
Dir.: Jane Campion (NZ).
Box office (US): $40 million.

PORTUGAL
The House of the Spirits (1993)
Dir.: Bille August (Denmark).
Box office (US): $6.2 million.

BOLLYWOOD CINEMA

Although often applied to all Indian movies, the term "Bollywood" actually refers to the Hindi-language film industry based in Mumbai. Typical Bollywood films are colorful and romantic, with songs, action, and comedy. India has the **largest annual movie output**, with 800 to 1,000 features produced each year by Mumbai's Bollywood studios – roughly double the number of Hollywood movies made each year. In 2009, 1,288 movies were made in India, in 24 different languages. By contrast, Hollywood made 606 feature films in 2008.

HIGHEST-EARNING BOLLYWOOD STAR

As the salaries of Bollywood stars are never officially revealed, financial success is usually ranked by the tax they pay each quarter. Shah Rukh Khan, star of *Devdas* (2002) and *My Name is Khan* (2010), paid Rs 5 crore ($1.06 million) in tax for the second quarter of financial year 2011. (The term "crore" stands for 10 million.)

The Czech Republic is the **highest consumer of beer per capita**, with an estimated 35.3 gal (160.5 liters) quaffed annually by each citizen as of 2005.

UPDATED RECORD
NEW RECORD

300 Number of times a day you will be filmed on CCTV. At an average of three seconds at a time, you will rack up 7,186 hours on camera in a lifetime – or enough footage for 3,593 feature films starring you!

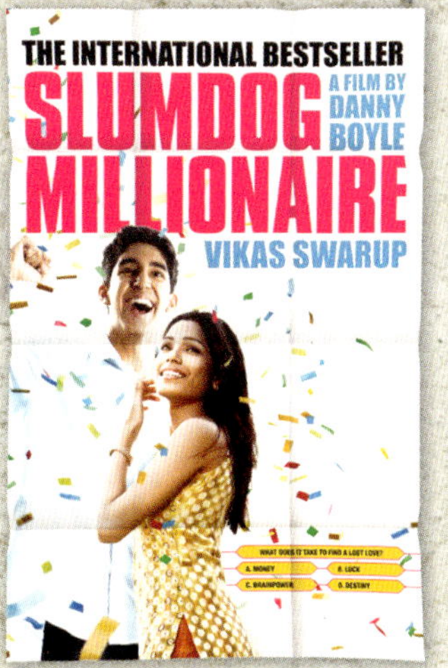

UK
Slumdog Millionaire (2008)
Dir.: Danny Boyle (UK) and Loveleen Tandan (India).
Box office: $378 million.

ESTONIA
The Singing Revolution (2006)
Dir.: James and Maureen Castle Tusty (both USA).
Box office (US): $335,700.

FRANCE
Amélie (2001)
Dir.: Jean-Pierre Jeunet (France).
Box office: $174 million.

GERMANY
Das Boot (1981)
Dir.: Wolfgang Petersen (Germany).
Box office: $84.915 million.

SWEDEN
The Girl with the Dragon Tattoo (2010)
Dir.: Niels Arden Oplev (Denmark).
Box office: $104 million.

AUSTRALIA
Crocodile Dundee (1986)
Dir.: Peter Faiman (Australia).
Box office: $328 million.

RUSSIA
Mongol (2008)
Dir.: Sergei Bodrov (USSR, now Russia).
Box office: $26.5 million.

MEXICO
Pan's Labyrinth (2006)
Dir.: Guillermo del Toro (Mexico).
Box office: $83.2 million.

HIGHEST-EARNING BOLLYWOOD ACTRESS
Bollywood budgets remain much lower than those of Hollywood blockbusters, but top Indian stars can command a high percentage of a movie's production budget – reportedly up to 40%. Katrina Kaif, star of *Singh is Kinng* (2008) and *De Dana Dan* (2010), paid Rs 1.3 crore ($289,000) in tax in the second quarter of 2011.

HIGHEST BOX-OFFICE GROSS FOR A BOLLYWOOD MOVIE
Starring R Madhavan, Sharman Joshi, and Aamir Khan (all India), *3 Idiots* (2009) has grossed Rs 202,57,00,000, or Rs 2.0257 billion ($44.9 million), at the box office to date, seeing off competition from the 2010 movies *Dabangg*, *Golmaal 3*, and *Raajneeti* by a considerable margin.

Muhamed Kahrimanovic (Bosnia and Herzegovina) holds the record for the **most cans crushed in one minute**, squeezing the life out of 65 full cans of beer with his bare hands in Vienna, Austria, on September 28, 2008.

MUSIC 1

RIHANNA IS THE "ONLY GIRL IN THE WORLD" TO HAVE ACHIEVED 10 NO.1 HITS ON THE US HOT DIGITAL SONGS CHART

MOST US NO.1 SINGLES IN A YEAR (FEMALE)

In 2010, Barbados-born singer Rihanna became the only female artist to have four US Hot 100 No.1 singles in a calendar year: "Rude Boy," "Love the Way You Lie" (featuring Eminem), "What's My Name?" (featuring Drake), and "Only Girl (In the World)." She is also the **first female artist to have UK No.1 singles in five consecutive years** (2007–11).

MOST CONSECUTIVE NO.1 SINGLES

KinKi Kids (Japan) – Tsuyoshi Domoto and Koichi Domoto (both Japan) – saw 30 singles in a row go straight to No.1 on the Japanese chart between July 28, 1997 and November 14, 2010. The duo's 30th hit was "Family – hitotsu ni narukoto."

BEST-SELLING SINGLE OF ALL TIME

Yuletide favorite "White Christmas," written by Irving Berlin (Israel) and first recorded by Bing Crosby (USA) on May 29, 1942, is estimated to have sold in the region of 100 million copies across all formats, including 78s, 45s, and albums. The popular single has been reissued every Christmas since 1942.

MOST R&B NO.1 SINGLES

Since accurate sales figures were introduced in the USA in 1991, no artist has amassed more R&B No.1 hits than the multitalented Usher (USA). The singer, songwriter, producer, actor, model, and designer has a total of 11 No.1s to his name, from 1997's "You Make Me Wanna..." to "There Goes My Baby," released on August 14, 2010.

LONGEST CHART RUN IN THE UK BY A GROUP (ONE SINGLE)

On March 26, 2011, Snow Patrol's (UK) "Chasing Cars" spent a world record 100th nonconsecutive week in the UK Top 75.

COUNTRY QUEEN

Although tied with Carrie for country No.1s, Reba McEntire is in a class of her own as the world's **best-selling female country artist**, with 23 gold, 19 platinum, and 9 multi-platinum albums as of February 2011.

MOST COUNTRY NO.1 HITS IN THE USA BY A FEMALE ARTIST

Since the introduction of accurate sales records in the USA in 1991, US stars Reba McEntire (above) and Carrie Underwood (top, winner of talent show *American Idol* in 2005) have each amassed a record 10 US Hot Country Songs chart-toppers.

MOST SIMULTANEOUS US HOT 100 HITS BY A FEMALE ARTIST

On November 13, 2010, Taylor Swift (USA) had 11 singles on the US Hot 100, with 10 of those tracks making their chart debuts – another record for a female artist.

LONGEST RUN ON THE US HOT COUNTRY SONGS CHART

By September 25, 2010, Lee Brice's (USA) "Love Like Crazy" had spent an incredible 56 weeks – more than a year – on the US Hot Country Songs chart.

MOST NO.1 SINGLES PRODUCED BY AN INDIVIDUAL

Johnny Kitagawa (Japan) has achieved the No.1 position more often than any other music producer, with a record 232 chart-toppers for over 40 of Japan's best-selling groups between 1974 and 2010. He also holds the record for the **most concerts produced by an individual**, having put on an amazing 8,419 shows between 2000 and 2010.

SOUNDS OF SILENCE

If you think today's music is just a lot of noise, you might enjoy "4'33"" (1952) by John Cage or the aptly titled "Two Minute Silence" (2010) by the Royal British Legion – not a note is played or sung on either.

On May 7, 2010, Bosnia and Herzegovina played host to the **largest waltz**, with 1,510 couples dancing up a storm at an event organized by Radio Kameleon in Tuzla's Freedom Square.

1,023 Hit singles that will make it to No.1 in your lifetime. The average hit is four minutes long, so it would take 4.25 days to listen to them all back to back, discounting the time you are asleep.

MOST US HOT 100 ENTRIES

By April 2, 2011, cast members of the TV show *Glee* (USA) had notched up 131 Hot 100 entries – beating Elvis Presley's (USA) 108, which remains the **most US Hot 100 entries (solo)** since the chart began in 1958. In 2010, Glee also claimed the **most hit singles in a year (UK)**, with 45 making the Top 75.

BEST-SELLING GROUP

The Beatles (UK) have sold more music than any other band in history. All-time global sales have been estimated at more than 1 billion disks and tapes, with around 177 million sales in the USA alone. Elvis Presley (USA) is the **best-selling solo artist**, with 1 billion sales worldwide (129.5 million in the USA).

HIGHEST-GROSSING MUSIC TOUR

By April 10, 2011, Irish rock band U2 had raked in over $558 million on their 360° world tour, making it the most lucrative on record. In total, over 7 million tickets have been sold for the tour's 110 shows between July 2009 and July 2011.

DOUBLE TOP

Adele (UK) is the **first female to reach the UK Top 5 with two singles and two albums simultaneously**, achieving the feat on February 26, 2011 with singles "Someone Like You" and "Rolling in the Deep" and albums *19* and *21*.

MOST US HOT 100 HITS BY A RAP ARTIST

Between December 4, 1999 and October 16, 2010, US rapper Lil Wayne (b. Wayne Carter) appeared in the Hot 100 chart on an incredible 64 different tracks, which roughly equates to a successful single release every two months for nearly a decade.

OLDEST GROUP TO ENTER THE UK ALBUM CHART

On November 20, 2010, The Chelsea Pensioners (UK) entered the UK album chart at No.14 with *Men in Scarlet*. The all-male group, British war veterans from the Royal Hospital Chelsea (UK), had an average age of 78.

BIGGEST HIT ACT (UK)

Rock Choir (UK), a gospel, pop, and Motown ensemble, entered the UK album Top 20 at No.5 on July 17, 2010 with *Rock Choir Vol.1*. The group has around 4,500 members, 1,000 of whom contributed vocals to the debut album.

WHERE THERE'S MUSIC, THERE'S DANCE – ON P.98.

BEST-SELLING CONTEMPORARY JAZZ MUSICIAN

American saxophone player Kenny G is the world's most popular jazz artist, with 15 gold, 11 platinum, and eight multiplatinum albums to his name, as well as total record sales of over 75 million.

HIGHEST-EARNING DECEASED ARTIST

According to *Forbes'* 2010 list of Top-Earning Dead Celebrities, the late Michael Jackson (USA) made more than the rest of the Top 10 combined, with $275 million for the year. In the 12 months following his death on June 25, 2009, his estate is reported to have earned $1.017 billion in revenue, with album sales of more than 33 million worldwide.

TOP TRACK

The movie soundtrack to *South Pacific* (USA, 1958) stayed at No.1 on the UK album chart for a record 70 consecutive weeks from November 8, 1958, eventually spending 115 weeks at the top – also a record!

MOST CONSECUTIVE WEEKS AT NO.1 ON THE UK ALBUMS CHART (FEMALE)

On April 9, 2011, Adele's (UK) second album, *21*, achieved its 10th consecutive week at No.1 on the UK albums chart, beating the 21-year-old record of nine weeks set by Madonna's (USA) *The Immaculate Collection* in 1990. Adele's album went on to spend 11 consecutive weeks at the top before dropping to No.2 on April 23, 2011. However, it returned to No.1 the following week, and at the time of going to press had spent a total of 16 weeks there – the **most non-consecutive weeks at No.1 on the UK albums chart (female)**.

The **longest single line of dancers** consisted of 2,354 participants performing the "Toe Dance" in an event organized by the Rääma Young People Union "Youth" in Audru, Estonia, on June 14, 2008.

Popular Culture

MUSIC 2

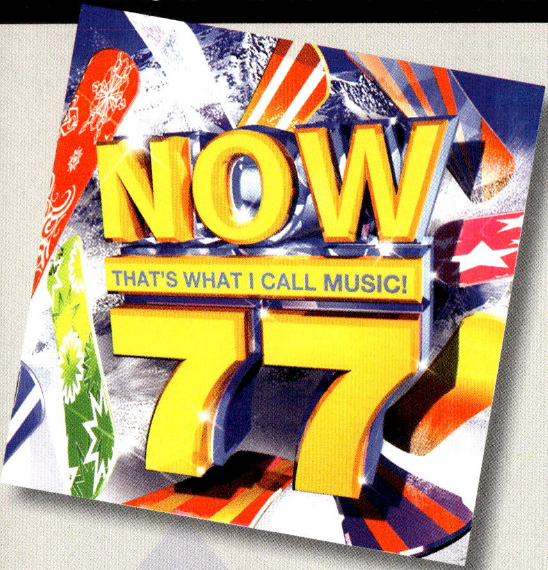

FASHION MIS-STEAK?
Trend-setter Lady Gaga pulled off another fashion first at the 2010 MTV Video Music Awards when she turned up to receive her eight awards wearing a dress and hat (below) made of raw meat!

MOST SUCCESSFUL COMPILATION SERIES

It was announced in May 2010 that the *Now That's What I Call Music!* series had passed the 200-million sales mark around the world. The series was launched by Virgin Records (UK) in the UK in 1983 and has since become a global phenomenon.

MOST SUCCESSFUL ALBUM SERIES BY A SOLO ARTIST

All five albums released by Rod Stewart (UK) in his Great American Songbook series (2002–10) have reached the US Top 5 and the UK Top 10, with *Stardust: The Great American Songbook, Volume III* topping the US chart in 2004.

FIRST SOLO ARTIST TO ACHIEVE FOUR UK NO.1 ALBUMS IN FOUR SUCCESSIVE DECADES

Australian vocalist Kylie Minogue first topped the UK chart with *Kylie! – The Album* in 1988, and she has revisited the No.1 slot four times, with *Enjoy Yourself* (1989), *Greatest Hits* (1992), *Fever* (2001), and *Aphrodite* (2010).

MOST ALBUM SALES IN THE 21ST CENTURY (UK)

As a solo artist, Robbie Williams (UK) has notched up an astonishing 13,339,555 album sales up to October 2010, achieving eight UK No.1 albums in the process.

MOST SUCCESSIVE US NO.1 ALBUMS BY A SOLO ARTIST

Eminem, aka Marshall Mathers III (USA), has hit the top spot in the US album chart six times in a row, with his latest success, *Recovery*, debuting at No.1 on July 10, 2010. He also holds the record for **most album sales in the 21st century (USA)**, with 32,241,000 sales by the end of 2009.

MOST WEEKS ON THE US HOT DIGITAL SONGS CHART

Lady Gaga's (USA) track "Poker Face" spent a record 83 weeks on the US Hot Digital Songs chart in the course of 2009 and 2010.

TAKE THAT SOLD A RECORD 1.3 MILLION TICKETS IN A DAY FOR THEIR 2011 TOUR

FASTEST-SELLING DOWNLOAD ALBUM (UK)

Take That's (UK) album *Progress*, which saw the return of ex-member Robbie Williams, sold a record 79,807 digital copies on November 15, 2010, its first day of release. Across all formats, the album's first-week sales hit 518,601 – more than any other album this century.

Intan Pragi (Estonia) spun a roulette wheel more than 1,650 times in a 48-hour period during the **longest croupier marathon** at the Olympic Casino in Tallinn, Estonia, on February 18–20, 2005.

$2,792 The amount you will spend on recorded music during your life. However, no recording can ever replace the experience of live music, so more of your cash will go on concert tickets: $3,163 in a lifetime.

GUINNESS WORLD RECORDS 2012

YOUNGEST TRANSATLANTIC TOP 20 ARTIST

Willow Smith (b. October 31, 2000), daughter of US actor and rap star Will Smith, is the youngest artist to have had a single in the US and UK Top 20s. At the age of 10 years 48 days, her single "Whip My Hair" entered the UK chart at No.2 on December 18, 2010, following a US debut at No.11 on November 13, 2010.

YOUNGEST US TOP 3 ALBUM ACT

On December 4, 2010, the album *O Holy Night* entered the US chart at No.2, making *America's Got Talent* runner-up Jackie Evancho (USA), at 10 years and 7 months, the youngest person ever to have a Top 3 album in the USA. Only *Britain's Got Talent* winner Susan Boyle prevented her reaching the No.1 spot.

YOUNG AT HEART

Before Willow was born, Jimmy Osmond (USA) took "Long-Haired Lover from Liverpool" to the top of the UK chart on December 23, 1972, making him the **youngest UK No.1 artist** at 9 years 250 days old.

FIRST BRITISH FEMALE ARTIST TO TOP THE US AND UK ALBUM CHARTS WITH TWO RELEASES

In 2010, Susan Boyle (UK) achieved her second transatlantic No.1 album with *The Gift*, matching the success of 2009's *I Dreamed a Dream*. On November 20, 2010, the 49-year-old Boyle also became the **oldest female to top the UK album chart with a newly recorded album**, while *The Gift* was also the **first Christmas album to top the UK chart**.

OLDEST CHART DUO

At the ripe old ages of 68 and 62, respectively, American singers Carole King (b. February 9, 1942) and James Taylor (b. March 12, 1948) hit No.4 in the US Billboard 200 chart with their album *Live at the Troubadour* on May 22, 2010.

OLDEST ARTIST TO ACHIEVE A US NO.1 DANCE HIT

Ono, aka Yoko Ono (Japan), widow of the late Beatle John Lennon, made chart history on March 12, 2011 when "Move On Fast" became the 78-year-old's eighth chart-topper and sixth successive No.1 on the US Hot Dance Club Songs chart.

MOST POPULAR MUSIC DOWNLOAD SITE

On February 25, 2010, "Guess Things Happen That Way" by Johnny Cash (USA) became the 10 billionth track to be downloaded from the iTunes music store since its launch in April 2003.

BEST-SELLING DIGITAL ALBUM (UK)

The Fame (2008), the debut album of American singer and fashionista Lady Gaga, passed the 300,000 mark in digital sales on March 1, 2011.

FASTEST-SELLING DIGITAL ALBUM BY A FEMALE ARTIST (USA)

Taylor Swift's (USA) album *Speak Now* shifted 278,000 digital copies in the week ending November 13, 2010.

HIGHEST CONCERT

Singer James Blunt (UK) played a concert at 42,080 ft (12,825 m) to a ticketed audience of over 100 people on June 29, 2010. The gig – which lasted 21 min 15 sec – took place on a Boeing 767-300 ER operated by Titan Airways that left Stansted Airport in London, UK, and flew in circles between Norwich and Cambridge until it reached maximum altitude.

FIRST SINGLE TO REACH 1 MILLION DOWNLOADS (UK)

A year after its release in June 2009, The Black Eyed Peas' (USA) "I Gotta Feeling" became the first song to be downloaded more than a million times in the UK, reaching the landmark in June 2010. Gwen Stefani's (USA) "Hollaback Girl" (2005) was the **first digital million-seller worldwide**.

MOST US NO.1 MUSIC VIDEOS

With the release of *Sticky & Sweet Tour* (2010), Madonna (USA) enjoyed her ninth No.1 on the US Music Video chart on April 24, 2010.

BIEBER WAS THE MOST SEARCHED FOR CELEBRITY ON THE INTERNET IN JULY 2010!

MOST VIEWED MUSIC VIDEO ONLINE

The video for the hit single "Baby", performed by Justin Bieber (Canada) and directed by Ray Kay (Norway), had been viewed 463,820,304 times by February 16, 2011, making it the most watched music video online and also the **most popular video of any kind online**. Alongside Bieber, the video also features R&B singer/actress Jasmine Villegas (USA) and US rapper Ludacris.

UPDATED RECORD
NEW RECORD

On the subject of gambling, the **longest time spent dealing blackjack** is 51 hr 33 min, achieved by Stephen De Raffaele (Malta) at the Oracle Casino, Qawra, Malta, from August 24 to 27, 2001.

MUSICAL MAYHEM

OLDEST DJ

Ruth Flowers (UK) played more than 38 sets at clubs and festivals worldwide in 2010, as Mamy Rock. GWR has established Ruth's date of birth, and precise age, but at her request we have decided to print only her "stage age": 69.

FASTEST FIDDLE PLAYER

Fiddler Frankie Gavin (Ireland) played "The Foxhunter's Reel" at 150 bpm. The live performance took place at the Aula Maxima at the National University of Ireland (Galway), in Co. Galway, Ireland, on September 20, 2010.

The **fastest violinist** is Guo Siyan (China), who sped through "Flight of the Bumblebee" in a mere 54.922 seconds in Beijing, China, on December 21, 2010.

MOST CONCERTS IN 12 HOURS

Weltrekorder (Germany) played 35 live concerts at venues across Cologne, Germany, between August 21 and 22, 2010.

The **most concerts performed in 24 hours** is 55, by Kesiraju Srinivas (India) at venues in and around Narasapur, Bhimavaram, and Palakol, India, from September 23 to 24, 2010.

MOST PEOPLE WHISTLING AT ONCE

On June 6, 2010, a group of 329 whistlers performed at Grandberry Mall, Tokyo, Japan, in an event staged by the TMD Corporation (Japan). They whistled the tune "Sapo," from the film *My Neighbour Totoro*, for over five minutes.

MOST PEOPLE SINGING LIVE ON A RADIO BROADCAST

In an event organized by the Children's Aid Society of Ottawa (Canada), 622 people sang "Lean on Me." The performance was broadcast by HOT 89.9 live from the Place D'Orleans Shopping Mall in Ottawa, Canada, on October 2, 2010.

LONGEST CONCERT BY A GROUP

From April 14 to 16, 2009, Bodhi Foundation & Maharashtra Youth Development Organization & Group (India) played a concert 64 hr 5 min 7 sec long at the Veterinary Hall, Seminary Hills, Nagpur, India.

Richard Deschamps (France) performed the **longest solo concert**, for 40 hr 40 min 40 sec, on guitar and piano in Caen, France, on December 4–5, 2010.

LONGEST DRUMROLL BY AN INDIVIDUAL

Mickey Grimm (USA) played a drumroll lasting 5 hr 20 min at the Coffee House, New Harmony, Indiana, USA, on October 24, 2009.

LONGEST SOLO SINGING MARATHON

On October 14–17, 2010, Swaradhika Dhari Pancham'Da (India) sang for 82 hr 15 min at Aarshiwad Complex in Vasna, Ahmedabad, India.

LARGEST ALPHORN ENSEMBLE

A group of 366 musicians played six songs on alphorns on the Gornegrat mountain near Zermatt, Switzerland, on August 20, 2009. The alphorn is a traditional Swiss instrument that was once used to enable people to communicate with each other over distance.

Q. What's the difference between a fiddle and a violin?

A. There is no real difference, but classical musicians are more likely to refer to their instruments as violins, while folk musicians tend to call theirs fiddles. This is why GWR recognizes records for both.

With 785 anglers, the **largest sea angling contest** took place at Malta's 2010 Blue Sea – Puttinu Fishing Festival.

LARGEST ENSEMBLES

Instrument	No.	Organized/Led by	Date
Barrel organ	82	On Leiden Barrel Organ Day (Netherlands)	May 3, 2008
Can drum	770	Pringles Xtreme and Jake Sasseville (USA)	October 10, 2010
Car horn	185	Funda Vanroy (Germany)	October 8, 2010
Dhol drum	632	King Gucharan Mall (UK)	May 2, 2009
Flute	2,320	Aomori Nebuta Festival and the Aomori Nebuta Executive Committee (both Japan)	August 1, 2010
Guitar	6,346	Thanks Jimi Festival (Poland)	May 1, 2009
Horn	264	Suffolk County Music Educators Association (USA)	January 15, 2010
Orchestra on recycled materials	617	Allegro gra Eko (Poland)	August 1, 2010
Saxophone	918	Taizhong City Government Cultural Department (Taiwan)	October 18, 2008
Spoons	888	Conducted by Tang-ChiChung (China)	July 6, 2009
Ukulele	851	DeQuincy Prescott (UK)	June 20, 2009

LONGEST SINGING MARATHON BY MULTIPLE SINGERS

A group of 389 artists sang 1,488 songs in 103 hr 9 min 26 sec at an event staged by nonprofit organization Titanus (Italy) at the Teatro Cinema Astra in Pesaro, Italy, between the dates of September 21 and 25, 2010.

LONGEST MARATHON PLAYING GUITAR

Guillermo Terraza (Argentina) played guitar for a finger-numbing 100 hours at La Fabrica in Comodoro Rivadavia, Chubut, Argentina, from May 12 to 17, 2010. Terraza has previously held this record four times, in 2000, 2003, 2005, and 2008.

LARGEST PIANO

Daniel Czapiewski (Poland) has built a piano 8 ft 2 in (2.49 m) wide, 19 ft 10 in (6.07 m) long, and 6 ft 3 in (1.92 m) high. It featured in a concert at Szymbark, Poland, on December 30, 2010.

LARGEST CONDUCTOR'S BATON

Harmonie Amicitia Roggel (Netherlands) made a 13-ft 11-in-long (4.25-m) baton. It was first used by Bas Clabbers (Netherlands) for a concert in Heythuysen, the Netherlands, on October 30, 2010.

UPDATED RECORD
NEW RECORD

LARGEST VIOLIN

The Vogtland masters of violin- and bow-making (Germany) created a violin 14 ft (4.27 m) long and 4 ft 6 in (1.4 m) at its widest. It was completed on June 14, 2010.

LONG BOW

This fantastic fiddle – plus its 17-ft-long (5.2-m) bow – is seven times larger than the real thing. It takes three people to play a tune on it – one to press the strings and two to move the bow.

WHAT'S ON TV

MOST HOURS OF TV WATCHED (NATION)

Americans watched more television than ever in 2010, according to media research company Nielsen. Viewing of broadcast networks and basic cable channels rose about 1% for the year, to an average of 34 hours per person per week.

HIGHEST-RATED NEW SHOW (US)

Crime drama *Hawaii Five-0* (CBS) drew an audience of 19.34 million for its highest-rated episode on January 23, 2011. The new series is a "reimagining" of the 1968 original.

FIRST SHOW BASED ON A TWITTER FEED

$h! My Dad Says* premiered on September 23, 2010 on CBS (USA) and is based on the hugely popular Twitter feed by Justin Halpern (USA).

The sitcom documents the life of a struggling author (played by Jonathan Sadowski) who finally finds work writing about his father's politically incorrect rants. Starring in the role of Dad is veteran TV actor William Shatner.

A new Japanese series, *Hard to Say I Love You,* aired in April 2010 and was inspired by Twitter but was not an actual feed.

MOST EXPENSIVE TV EPISODE

The opening episode of *Boardwalk Empire* (HBO), directed by Martin Scorsese (USA), is reputed to have cost $50 million. The Prohibition-Era drama, which aired on HBO on September 19, 2010, stars Steve Buscemi (USA, pictured left) as underworld kingpin Enoch "Nucky" Johnson.

MOST POPULAR TV SHOW (2010)

The first series of the ITV drama *Downton Abbey* scored 92 out of 100 on Metacritic, making it the highest-scoring reviewer-rated show of the year. The series, conceived and written by the actor Julian Fellowes (UK), follows the lives and loves of those living upstairs and downstairs in the estate of Robert, Earl of Grantham from 1912 to 1914.

UPDATED RECORD
NEW RECORD

BIGGEST-SELLING TV DVD

As of the end of 2010, the chart-topper on both sides of the Atlantic – and in some territories beyond – was the box-set of the 10-part mini-series *The Pacific* (HBO), a sister project to the hugely successful *Band of Brothers*. In 2010, US sales alone reached 1,488,763 units, generating a revenue of more than $65 million.

COST AN ARM-Y AND LEG

The Pacific cost an estimated $150 million to make, breaking the record for the **most expensive mini-series** held by its sister show, *Band of Brothers*.

The Okla natural fossil reactors, found underground in Gabon in 1972, are evidence of the **oldest nuclear chain reaction**. The fission happened 2 billion years ago, powered by natural uranium ore.

HIGHEST-PAID ACTOR IN A TV DRAMA

Hugh Laurie (UK) reportedly earns $400,000 per episode as the titular star of the US medical drama *House* (Fox). The success of the show (see below), now in its seventh series, currently makes Laurie **TV's most-watched leading man**.

HOUSEHOLD NAME

Medical drama *House* is currently the world's **most-watched TV show**, broadcast in 66 countries and watched by an amazing 81.8 million viewers.

LONGEST-RUNNING SITCOM (YEARS)

The UK's *Last of the Summer Wine* (BBC) finished in 2010 after a record-breaking 37 years and 31 series. Every single episode was written by Roy Clarke (UK), the world's **most prolific writer of sitcoms**.

LONGEST-RUNNING SITCOM (EPISODES)

It was announced in November 2010 that *The Simpsons* had been renewed for a 23rd season, which means that the series will rack up over 500 episodes. The show has featured the **most celebrity guests**, with at least 555 as of series 21.

LONGEST-RUNNING ANIMATION

The longest-running animated series by years is *Sazae-san* (Fuji Television), which first aired in October 1969 and continues to the present day.

LONGEST-RUNNING TV SOAP OPERA

With the ending of CBS's *As the World Turns* in 2010, the UK's *Coronation Street* (ITV) is now the all-time longest-running drama serial on TV. *"The Street"* first aired on December 9, 1960, and introduced us to the character of Ken Barlow – a role still played by William Roache (UK), the **longest-serving actor in a TV show**.

HIGHEST-PAID ACTOR ON TV

Charlie Sheen (USA, pictured below left), star of *Two and a Half Men* (CBS), remains at the top of the list of highest-paid TV stars, with his pay now up to $1.25 million per episode. At the time of going to press, however, Sheen had left the show amid much controversy and media attention.

HIGHEST-PAID TV CHILD STAR

Angus T Jones (USA, b. October 8, 1993), who stars as Jacob David "Jake" Harper (pictured above right) in the CBS hit comedy *Two and a Half Men*, is reported to earn $250,000 per episode. At the time of going to press, the 17-year-old's stellar pay cheques make Jones – aka the "Half" – the highest-paid under-18-year-old on TV, although other juvenile performers may earn more annually through endorsements, royalties, and appearance fees.

FIRST 3D DRAMA

Debuting in January 2011, Fuji TV's (Japan) *Tokyo Control* is a ten-part all-3D drama series about Tokyo's Air-Traffic Control Centre, airing on SKYPerfecTV's dedicated 3D channel. The technology behind the show was produced by Sony.

LONGEST GAP BETWEEN ORIGINAL TV SHOW AND SEQUEL

When costume drama *Upstairs Downstairs* (ITV) returned to UK screens in 2010, it was 35 years after the original series ended. Actress Jean Marsh returned as the same character (Rose Buck), verifying this as a direct sequel (i.e., one that features one or more members of the original cast).

LONGEST GAP BETWEEN TV APPEARANCES

When Philip Lowrie (UK) rejoined the cast of *Coronation Street* in 2011, he reprised the role of Dennis Tanner, a part he first essayed in 1960. The last time he played this role was 43 years ago in 1968.

HIGHEST-PAID ACTRESS ON TV

As of 2010, Mariska Hargitay (USA, below) – star of *Law & Order: Special Victims Unit* (NBC) – has regained her title as the world's highest-paid actress per episode, taking home a tidy $395,000 for every show.

The **highest-paid teen actress on TV** is Miranda Cosgrove (USA, b. May 14, 1993), who earns the sum of $180,000 per episode of Nickelodeon's sitcom *iCarly*.

TV ACTION HEROES

FIRST TV SPY SERIES
TV's first spy series was the USA's *Shadow of the Cloak* (DuMont, 1951–52), which featured Helmut Dantine as Peter House, an agent working for International Security Intelligence. Another spy series, *Dangerous Assignment* (USA, syndicated), starring Brian Donleavy as US Government Agent Steve Mitchell, was produced at the same time but didn't air until some months later.

LONGEST-RUNNING SPY SERIES
US series *The FBI* (ABC) was broadcast from 1965 to 1974, running to 240 episodes. The series featured adaptations of many real-life FBI cases and was partly inspired by the 1959 movie *The FBI Story*.

FIRST PRIVATE-EYE TV SERIES
Running from 1949 to 1954, the US series *Martin Kane, Private Eye* (NBC) was the first authentic private-eye show, though the character of a private investigator had featured in short dramatized segments as part of various guess-the-ending panel shows. In its five-year run, four different actors played Martin Kane: William Gargan, Lloyd Nolan, Lee Tracy, and Mark Stevens.

FIRST TV SUPERHERO
Superman – created by Jerry Siegel and Joe Shuster and sold to Detective Comics in 1938 – was the first comic-strip superhero to appear in his own TV series. *The Adventures of Superman* (syndicated, 1952) starred George Reeves as the Man of Steel and was sponsored by Kellogg's. Initially filmed in monochrome, the show was shot in color from 1955 onward.

MOST VALUABLE COSTUME FROM A TV SERIES
The Superman suit from the 1955 series of *The Adventures of Superman* (USA) – starring George Reeves (USA) – was sold for $129,800 at the Profiles in History auction in Los Angeles, USA, on July 31, 2003. Until 1955, the show was filmed in black and white, and a brown and white outfit was used to create extra definition.

FIRST FEMALE JUNGLE HERO
In the syndicated series *Sheena Queen of the Jungle* (USA, 1955–56), actress Irish McCalla played the lead. The character of Sheena had first appeared in comic strips in the 1930s, and was the **first female character to star in her own comic book**.

FIRST FEMALE TV SPY
British series *The Avengers* (ABC, 1961–69) pioneered the concept of the action spy heroine, but it was American agent April Dancer (played by US actress Stefanie Powers) who was TV's first female spy with her own show: *The Girl from UNCLE* (NBC, 1966–67).

JUNGLE GENTLEMAN
The character of Sheena borrowed heavily from Tarzan, a jungle-bred action hero created by Edgar Rice Burroughs (USA), whose adventures first appeared in print in 1912.

HIGHEST-RATED TV SPY SHOW
Season 1 of *Archer*, an animated series based on the exploits of spy Sterling Archer, scored a rating of 78 (out of 100) on Metacritic.com. The website assembles an average rating from reviews by a range of entertainment critics.

The Kiev dam across the Dnieper River, Ukraine, was completed in 1964. It has a crest length of 25.6 miles (41.2 km), making it the **longest dam wall** in the world.

UPDATED RECORD
NEW RECORD

9 Years of your life you'll spend watching TV. Five activities will take up 70% of your life: 27 years of sleep, 10 years of work, nine years of TV, 5.7 years lounging about at home, and 4.7 years of eating.

FIRST WESTERN ACTRESS TO PERFORM KUNG FU ON TV

In 1965, the combat choreographers Ray Austin (UK) and Chee So (UK/China) incorporated kung-fu moves into several action scenes performed by Diana Rigg (UK, later Dame Diana Rigg) in *The Avengers*.

MAN APPEAL

Diana Rigg (above) played the role of Emma Peel (a play on the words M-Appeal or Man Appeal) in *The Avengers* in the 1960s, a role for which the US *TV Guide* named her the "Sexiest TV Star of All-Time."

MOST PORTRAYED SUPERHERO ON TV

The character of Superman has featured in four live-action television series and been played by five different American actors:

- **George Reeves** (*The Adventures of Superman*, syndicated, 1951–57)
- **John Haymes Newton** and **Gerard Christopher** (*Superboy*, syndicated, 1988–91)
- **Dean Cain** (*Lois & Clark: The New Adventures of Superman*, ABC, 1993–97)
- **Tom Welling** (*Smallville*, Warner Bros., later CW, 2001–11).

A sixth actor, Johnny Rockwell (USA), played the character in *The Adventures of Superboy* (1961), an untransmitted pilot for an unrealized series.

FEMALE TV FIRSTS

ACTION HERO

Cowgirl Annie Oakley became the first female action-hero character to have a show built around her in the Western series *Annie Oakley* (USA, 1954–57), a syndicated show starring Gail Davis as the sharpshooter from the Buffalo Bill traveling show.

DETECTIVE

The earliest female detective (i.e. paid investigator, not amateur sleuth) character to front a television show was Stacey Smith (played by Hattie Jaques) in the UK series *Miss Adventure* (ABC, 1964).

The **first US female detective** to headline her own show was Honey West (played by Anne Francis, USA) in *Honey West* (ABC, 1965–66). The character of West had first appeared in books during the 1950s.

SLEUTH

The earliest female sleuth to front her own show was Mme Lui-Tsong in the US series *The Gallery of Mme Lui-Tsong* (DuMont, 1951). Lui-Tsong – played by Chinese-American actress Anna May Wong – was a globe-trotting art gallery owner who doubled as a sleuth and became involved in various international intrigues.

TV's **most prolific female amateur sleuth** was Jessica Fletcher (played by British actress Angela Lansbury), the hero of *Murder, She Wrote* (CBS, 1984–96), who investigated crimes over the course of 265 episodes and four feature-length movies. Agatha Christie's Miss Marple has had fewer small-screen cases, but in various incarnations has been on and off air since 1956. On that first occasion, she was played by Gracie Fields for the US one-off *A Murder is Announced* (NBC).

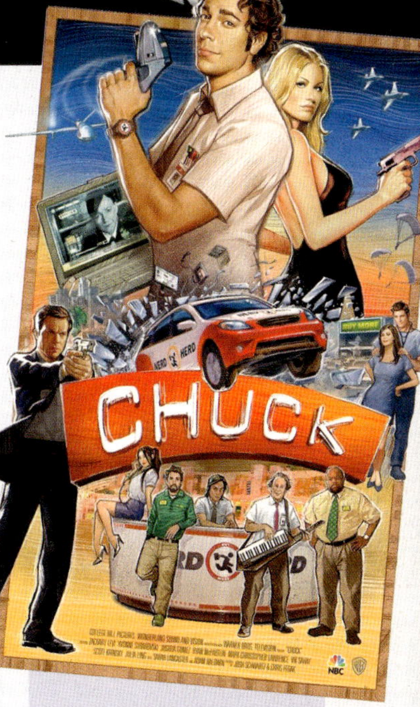

FIRST 3D SPY

On February 2, 2009, NBC presented *Chuck vs the Third Dimension*, an all-3D episode of the hit comedy spy series *Chuck*. Viewers accessed the 3D using glasses that had been made available from various retailers. Many viewers would have worn the glasses the day before, to enjoy an all-3D commercial break in the 2009 Super Bowl presentation.

SUPER SLEUTH

Created by Sir Arthur Conan Doyle (UK), Sherlock Holmes is also the **most portrayed literary character at the movies**, with at least 81 actors appearing in more than 220 movies.

DETECTIVE MOST OFTEN PORTRAYED ON TV

From early small-screen appearances on NBC experimental programming in 1937 to the present day, more than 30 actors have essayed the role of Sherlock Holmes. In the latest incarnation, *Sherlock* (BBC, 2010), Benedict Cumberbatch (above left) plays the cerebral hero alongside Martin Freeman as Dr Watson (right, both UK).

The world's **highest dam** is the Nurek dam on the Vakhsh River in Tajikistan. It is 984 ft (300 m) high and was completed in 1980.

TV DOCUMENTARIES

1. FIRST EMMY AWARD FOR SPECIAL EFFECTS

The 13-part series *Cosmos* (1980), produced and hosted by astrophysicist Carl Sagan (USA), won an Emmy for its impressive set, which was built to look like the inside of a space station.

2. LONGEST-RUNNING SCIENCE DOCUMENTARY SERIES

Canada's award-winning *Nature of Things* (CBC), hosted by geneticist David Suzuki since 1979, has been on TV screens since its debut on November 6, 1960.

3. LONGEST-SERVING TV HOST

Amateur astronomer Sir Patrick Moore (UK) is the most durable host in the history of television, having hosted his monthly astronomy show, *The Sky at Night*, since April 24, 1957.

4. LONGEST-RUNNING TV DOCUMENTARY SERIES

NBC's news interview series *Meet the Press* (USA) has been airing since November 6, 1947. The weekly show, which focuses on political interviews, has had 11 hosts in its history.

5. LONGEST CAREER AS A TV NATURALIST

Sir David Attenborough's (UK) career as a writer and host of TV nature programs dates back to 1954's *Zoo Quest* and continues today with *Frozen Planet*, scheduled for 2011.

The Pamir gardens near Khorog, Tajikistan, are the **highest botanical gardens** in the world, located at an elevation of 6,889–11,483 ft (2,100–3,500 m) above sea level. The 30-acre (12-ha) site features more than 2,000 species of flora.

$7,381 How much you will spend on buying six televisions in a lifetime. This means that your nine years of small-screen viewing will cost you about $820 per year or 9¢ per hour – so spend it wisely!

GUINNESS WORLD RECORDS 2012

● UPDATED RECORD
● NEW RECORD

The camera rolled on and on for these TV documentary record-holders...

● **Longest-running nonterrestrial TV documentary series:** *Explorer* (National Geographic) has been running on cable in the USA since its Nickelodeon debut on April 7, 1985.

Longest video documentary *The Definitive Elvis Collection* (Passport International Productions, USA) – released on July 16, 2002 – ran for 13 hr 52 min and featured over 200 interviews with Elvis Presley's friends, family, and fans.

● **Longest-running medical TV show** Hosted by Dr Jayalath Jayawardena (Sri Lanka), *Vaidaya Hamuwa* has been regularly broadcast for 14 years 7 months as of April 2011.

LONG HAUL

The 11-part series *Planet Earth* (BBC), screened in the UK in 2006, holds the record for the **most days filming on location for a natural world TV show**, with 40 crew shooting for 2,000 days in 200 locations on every continent.

6. ● HIGHEST-RATED TV DOCUMENTARY

According to review site Metacritic, *Beyond Scared Straight: Season 1* achieved an average rating of 84/100. The US show followed students visiting prisons to find out more about life behind bars.

7. ● LONGEST-RUNNING TV DOCUMENTARY SERIES – SINGLE SUBJECT

First aired in May 1964, *UP* is a UK series that has followed 14 people since they were seven years old; it returns every seven years to see how their lives have developed.

8. ● FIRST VIDEO GAME TO INSPIRE A HISTORICAL DOCUMENTARY

Telling the story of the US 101st Airborne Division in World War II, the History Channel's *Brothers in Arms* (2005) was inspired by a 2005 video game of the same name.

9. MOST EXPENSIVE TV DOCUMENTARY SERIES PER MINUTE

Depicting how dinosaurs lived, reproduced, and became extinct, the BBC's *Walking with Dinosaurs* (1999) cost over £37,654 ($61,112) per minute to produce.

10. LARGEST AUDIENCE FOR A TV DOCUMENTARY

CBS's *9/11*, broadcast in the USA on March 10, 2002, achieved the highest viewing figures for a documentary, with 39 million people tuning in to the documentary about the 2001 terrorist attacks.

One plant found at altitude that would suit the Pamir gardens is the giant bromeliad *Puya raimondii*, discovered at a height of 12,992 ft (3,960 m) in Bolivia. The flower cluster emerges after 80–150 years of the plant's life, making it the **slowest-flowering plant**.

ART & SCULPTURE

1

2

3

4

ART OR GRAFFITI?

In 1998, a vast "drawing" of an Aboriginal man appeared on the landscape at Finniss Springs, near Marree in South Australia. At 2.6 miles (4.2 km) long, it is the largest **human image ever**, but its artist remains a mystery.

1. HIGHEST INSURANCE VALUATION

The world's most famous painting, Leonardo da Vinci's (Italy) *Mona Lisa* was valued at $100 million ahead of its move from the Louvre in Paris, France, for a special US exhibition in 1962–63. In the end, the insurance was not taken up because the cost of security for the artwork was less expensive than the price of insuring it.

2. ● MOST HANDMADE ELEMENTS IN AN ARTWORK

Sunflower Seeds, by Chinese artist Ai Weiwei, comprises 100 million replica sunflower seeds, with each "seed" crafted in porcelain and hand-painted by a team of 1,600 skilled artisans. The work, laid out in a 10,764-ft² (1,000-m²) rectangle, was displayed in the Turbine Hall at Tate Modern, London, UK, between October 12, 2010 and May 2, 2011.

3. LARGEST GUM MOSAIC

A 209-ft² (19.4-m²) mosaic of Nelson Mandela made with 100,000 Cadbury Chappies was created by TBWA Digerati and ID Productions in Johannesburg, South Africa, on August 17, 2004.

4. ● LONGEST PAINTING

On May 28, 2010, a group of 3,000 school students created a painting on paper 19,690 ft (6,001.5 m) long in San Luis Potosí, Mexico.

5. ● HIGHEST ART GALLERY

Owned by artist-mountaineer Miguel Doura (Argentina), the Nautilus art gallery is located in a tent on Mount Aconcagua, Argentina, 14,108 ft (4,300 m) above sea level.

6. ● HIGHEST TOTAL AUCTION SALES

Long after his death in 1973, Pablo Picasso (Spain) continues to be a hit in the auction room, with sales of $2 billion to date. A significant contributor to this total was *Nude, Green Leaves, and Bust* (1932), which sold for $106.5 million in 2010 to become the world's ● **most expensive painting at auction.**

7. LEAST VALUABLE ART

The collection of the Museum of Bad Art (MOBA) in Boston, USA, has the lowest value of any public art collection. Its 573 works are worth a total of just $1,197.35!

● UPDATED RECORD
● NEW RECORD

The **highest restaurant** on the planet is found at the Chacaltaya ski resort, Bolivia, 17,520 ft (5,340 m) above sea level. Lake Titicaca, the world's **highest commercially navigable lake**, can be glimpsed through the restaurant's windows.

5.25 Area in square feet you could cover if you collected all the flakes of earwax you produce in a lifetime. That's enough for two 12.4-in-high hollow replicas of the Statue of Liberty – one for each ear!

5

6

7

TALLEST SCULPTURE MADE OF COAT HANGERS

Standing at an imposing height of 9 ft 11 in (3.02 m), *Silver Streak* is a male gorilla made out of 6,000 metal coat hangers and weighing 661 lb (300 kg). Created by British sculpture and installation artist David Mach, it was unveiled at the Royal Academy, London, UK, in June 2010.

WALKING TALL

Although smaller than *Silver Streak*, Alberto Giacometti's (Switzerland) *Walking Man I* (1961) is the world's **most expensive sculpture**, selling for £65 million ($104.3 million) at Sotheby's, UK, on February 3, 2010.

On December 14, 2009, food manufacturer Kraft Foods Philippines scooped the record for the **most different dishes on display**, serving up 5,845 plates of food – all containing Kraft Eden cheese – at Araneta Coliseum in Quezon City, the Philippines.

SPORTS

FIRST CLIFF-DIVING RUNNING TAKEOFF

On August 8, 2010, UK diver Gary Hunt executed the first running takeoff ever performed in cliff-diving competition, launching into four front-piked somersaults with 2.5 twists (captured here using time-lapse photography). Hunt's death-defying aerial feat, from a height of 88 ft (26.8 m) at Polignano a Mare (Italy), helped him clinch first place in the first Red Bull Cliff-Diving World Series.

"Today Gary tried a very difficult dive that isn't possible, maybe for anyone apart from him..."

World Series rival Artem Silchenko

On May 22, 1998, the Central Bank of Manila (Philippines) issued the world's **largest legal banknote**, a special 100,000-peso note measuring 8 x 11 in (22 x 33 cm).

The honor for the **largest denomination banknote** goes to Zimbabwe, which issued a $100-billion bill on July 22, 2008 – it was enough to buy two loaves of bread.

LONDON 2012

ALL EYES ON LONDON

Following in the footsteps of the phenomenally successful Beijing Olympics of 2008, London 2012 certainly has much to live up to – but so far it is shaping up to be one of the most spectacular Games ever. As the world's elite athletes, the global media, and millions of excited fans converge on the Olympic city in July and August, records are certain to be shattered – both in and out of the shiny new stadia.

OLYMPIC HERITAGE

London is no stranger to the Olympics – the city hosted only the fourth Games of the modern era in 1908, stepping in for Rome at the last minute when the Italian capital pulled out after the eruption of Mt Vesuvius. The Games returned to London in 1948, with a record 59 nations taking part as the world sought to put the trauma of World War II behind it. In winning the right to host the Games for a third time in 2012, London saw off the challenges of New York, Madrid, Paris, and Moscow to take the record for the **most Summer Olympics hosted**.

ONES TO WATCH

With the Olympics only coming around once every four years, the world's elite athletes will be going all out to make their mark in 2012. World and Olympic 100 m and 200 m record-holder Usain Bolt (Jamaica, below) has set his sights on smashing his own times of 9.58 sec and 19.19 sec, respectively, while fellow runner Haile Gebrselassie (Ethiopia, bottom right) is aiming to better the marathon record of 2:03.59 he set in Germany in 2008. In the water, former record-breaker Ian "Thorpedo" Thorpe (Australia, right) is set to return from retirement to renew his rivalry with the current king of the pool, Michael Phelps (USA).

NOTABLE FIRSTS

Women's boxing made its first and only Olympic appearance as a demonstration sport at the 1904 Paris Games. However, after a century on the sidelines, the sport will make its debut as an official Olympic sport at London 2012, with China's Dong Cheng (left) tipped for success in the 57–60 kg category.

SECURITY!

Despite the huge security operation at Beijing 2008 (left), London 2012 is set to go one step further, with the **largest security budget for an Olympics** – $1.3 billion (£838 million) as of December 2010.

The people with the **fewest toes** are members of the Wadomo tribe of the Zambezi Valley, Zimbabwe, who, along with the Kalanga tribe of the eastern Kalahari Desert, Botswana, have just two very large digits due to a hereditary genetic condition.

160 Days spent on sport and outdoor activities in a lifetime. This is 27 days less than the first London Olympics, which lasted for 187 days from April 27 to Halloween (October 31) 1908.

OLYMPIC ICONS

Launched in June 2007, the 2012 logo (left), designed by Wolff Olins (UK), is the **most expensive Olympic logo** ever, costing £400,000 ($645,645) to design. The Olympic mascots, Wenlock and Mandeville (below), are named after the British towns Much Wenlock, where modern Olympics founder Baron de Coubertin got his inspiration for the Games, and Stoke Mandeville, home of the hospital that was central to the birth of the Paralympics.

TAKE YOUR SEAT

With around 500,000 visitors expected to descend on London's Olympic venues every day during the 2012 Games, there will be plenty of competition for the 8.8 million tickets up for grabs. The organizing committee, led by former athlete Seb Coe (UK, above), hopes to raise £441 million ($710.5 million) from ticket sales, and a fair proportion of that will come from the opening ceremony on July 27. With a price tag of £2,012 ($3,250), the top seats are the **most expensive Olympic tickets** ever!

ECO-FRIENDLY GAMES

Located in the heart of East London, the brand new Olympic Stadium is the focal point of London 2012 and the place where, for the athletes, dreams will be made or dashed in the blink of an eye. However, the stadium is also central to London's aim to be the greenest Games on record, and as well as 80,000 seats for spectators, the stadium boasts 525 bird boxes, 150 bat boxes, and numerous otter holts. Elsewhere in the park, there will be 4,000 trees and 300,000 wetland plants planted, creating habitats for numerous bird and mammal species.

TOP VELO-CITY

London's 6,000-seat velodrome was the first 2012 venue to open, in January 2011, and the £100-million ($161-million) track has already been hailed as the world's fastest by cyclists who have tried it.

FOR MORE SPORTING FEATS, TURN TO P.258.

The Padaung and Kareni tribes of Burma engage in active body modification. The females are known to have the world's **longest necks**, measuring up to 15.75 in (40 cm), which they "grow" by adding successive copper rings over a number of years (see page 80).

OLYMPIC MILESTONES

THE OLYMPIC STORY BEGINS

The ancient Olympics, so called as they were held on the plains of Olympia in Greece, date back at least as far as 776 BC. They attracted famous names such as Socrates and Aristotle, who competed in events including running, discus, javelin, and wrestling. However, in AD 393, after 1,000 years of competition, the Games were terminated by order of Emperor Theodosius I, who considered them a "pagan cult."

First female Olympic athletes
Paris 1900 sees 22 women compete in tennis, golf, and croquet. Tennis player Charlotte Cooper (UK) becomes the **first female Olympic champion**.

Lowest attendance at an Olympic event
The women's croquet event is attended by just one paying spectator.

FIRST WINTER OLYMPIC GAMES

The Winter Olympics, originally established to support snow- and ice-based sports not suited to the summer, are held for the first time in Chamonix, France, between January 25 and February 5, 1924.

Last solid-gold medals
After Stockholm, gold medals are cast in silver and coated in 0.21 oz (6 g) of gold.

First Olympic torch relay
The torch is carried 1,980 miles (3,187 km) from Olympia to Berlin by 3,331 runners.

FIRST SOUTHERN HEMISPHERE GAMES

The Olympics travel south of the Equator for the first time when hosted by Melbourne, Australia, in 1956. It will be another 44 years before they will again visit such southerly climes, with Sydney putting on the event in 2000.

776 BC – AD 393 OLYMPIA | 1896 ATHENS | 1900 PARIS | 1904 ST LOUIS | 1908 LONDON | 1912 STOCKHOLM | 1920 ANTWERP | 1924 PARIS | 1928 AMSTERDAM | 1932 LOS ANGELES | 1936 BERLIN | 1948 LONDON | 1952 HELSINKI | 1956 MELBOURNE

FIRST MODERN OLYMPIC GAMES

Conceived by the French academic and sports enthusiast Pierre de Fredi, Baron de Coubertin (1863–1937), the modern Olympic Games are inaugurated in Athens, Greece, the birthplace of Olympic sport, on April 6, 1896. The first ever modern Games are a modest affair by today's standards, with just 241 participants representing 14 different countries and competing in 43 events.

First gold medals
Until St Louis 1904, just two medals were awarded to competitors: a silver for first place and a bronze for second.

First Olympic village
To keep all the athletes in one place and avoid the expense of hotels, a "village" of cabins is erected close to the Olympic Stadium.

First Olympic use of starting blocks
Previously, athletes had been forced to dig holes in the track to gain a foothold.

First Olympics to be broadcast live on radio
The 1924 Games are heard on the airwaves across the home nation of France.

First three-tiered victory podium
Los Angeles 1932 are the most lavish Games to date, with the first victory podium, the **first raising of the gold medalist's flag**, and the **first playing of national anthems**.

FIRST TELEVISED OLYMPIC GAMES

The 1936 Berlin Games are beamed out live in black and white to athletes in the Olympic village and to special viewing rooms in Berlin and Potsdam. Color pictures arrive on screens much later, in 1968, when Mexico City becomes the **first Olympics to be televised in color**.

ANCIENT RECORD
In 656 BC, the Spartan Chionis achieved the **first Olympic record**, a long jump of 21 ft (7.05 m). His leap would have won the 1896 event and placed in the top eight up to Helsinki 1952!

The **heaviest bell still in use** is the 101.4-ton (92-tonne) Mingun bell in Mandalay, Burma.

- UPDATED RECORD
- NEW RECORD

151,891 Kilowatt-hours of electricity you will use in a lifetime – that's enough to power the 532 floodlights of the London 2012 Olympic Stadium 24 hours a day for six days.

FIRST OLYMPIC TEAM SPORT FOR WOMEN

Volleyball is introduced at the 1964 Tokyo Games, becoming the first Olympic team sport for female athletes. The event is won easily by the hosts, who lose just a single set in the tournament.

MOST EVENTS AT A SUMMER OLYMPICS

The XXIX Olympiad held in 2008 in Beijing, China, featured a record 302 events, nine of which are new to the Games, including the discipline of BMX racing.

First "Fosbury Flop"
Dick Fosbury (USA) wins gold in the 1968 high jump with a revolutionary new technique, leaping over the bar back first (rather than head on) and changing the sport forever.

1960	1964	1968	1972	1976	1980	1984	1988	1992	1996	2000	2004	2008	*2012*	*2016*
ROME	TOKYO	MEXICO CITY	MUNICH	MONTREAL	MOSCOW	LOS ANGELES	SEOUL	BARCELONA	ATLANTA	SYDNEY	ATHENS	BEIJING	*LONDON*	*RIO DE JANEIRO*

First billion-dollar Games
One of the best ever Games, Tokyo comes with an eye-watering price tag of $1.9 billion!

First use of gender testing at summer Olympics
Testing introduced to stop male athletes competing as women.

LARGEST ATTENDANCE AT AN OLYMPICS

A total of 8.3 million tickets are sold for the 1996 Games held in Atlanta, Georgia, USA – often referred to as the "Centennial Olympics." This equates to more than half a million spectators watching on each day of the two-week event, which is dominated by Michael Johnson's (USA, pictured) gold-medal-winning runs in the 200 m and 400 m. By comparison, "only" 6.8 million tickets are sold for the 2008 Games in Beijing.

Most participants at an Olympics
Beijing attracts a record 10,942 athletes from 204 countries.

MOST EXPENSIVE OLYMPIC GAMES

The 2008 Games in Beijing, China, cost 295 billion yuan ($43 billion). Accounting for a small part of the cost are the 958 medals awarded to the athletes, comprising 302 golds, 303 silvers, and 353 bronzes – the **most medals awarded at an Olympics**.

AS SEEN ON TV
The Beijing Games also attracted the **largest TV audience for an Olympic Games**. Over the two-week period, 4.7 billion people tuned in – that's two out of every three people on the planet!

The world's **heaviest bell ever** was the Tsar Kolokol, cast on November 25, 1735 in Moscow, Russia. The 222.6-ton (202-tonne) bell was never rung – it was cracked in a fire in 1737 while still in the casting pit.

OLYMPIC LEGENDS

LONGEST TIME AS AN OLYMPIC ATHLETE
Four men have competed in the Olympics over a period of 40 years: Ivan Joseph Martin Osiier (Denmark) in fencing, in 1908–32 and 1948; Magnus Andreas Thulstrup Clasen Konow (Norway) in sailing, in 1908–20, 1928, and 1936–48; Paul Elvstrom (Denmark) in sailing, in 1948–60, 1968–72, and 1984–88; and Durward Randolph Knowles (UK, then Bahamas) in sailing, in 1948–72 and 1988.

MOST OLYMPIC DISCUS GOLD MEDALS
During a glittering Olympic career, Al Oerter (USA) won four discus gold medals in a row, in 1956 in Melbourne, Australia, 1960 in Rome, Italy, 1964 in Tokyo, Japan, and 1968 in Mexico City, Mexico. This feat also makes Oerter a joint holder of the record for the **most consecutive Olympic gold medals won in an individual event** (see also Carl Lewis on p.235).

OLDEST SUMMER OLYMPICS CHAMPION
Aged 64 years 258 days, Oscar Swahn helped the Swedish team win the Running Deer shooting event at the 1912 Games in Stockholm, Sweden. At the 1920 Antwerp Games in Belgium, he became the oldest silver medalist in the event at 72 years 280 days old.

YOUNGEST SUMMER OLYMPICS CHAMPION
At the 1936 Berlin Games in Germany, Marjorie Gestring (USA) became the youngest gold medalist when she won the springboard diving at the age of just 13 years 268 days.

MOST CONSECUTIVE OLYMPIC GOLD MEDALS
Fencer Aladár Gerevich (Hungary) won gold in saber events at every Games he competed in: a total of six, in 1932–36 and 1948–60.

MOST CONSECUTIVE OLYMPIC GOLD MEDALS IN AN ENDURANCE EVENT
Britain's most decorated Olympian, Steve Redgrave won five consecutive gold medals between 1984 and 2000, competing in the coxed four (1984), coxless pair (1988–96), and coxless four (2000). Redgrave also won a bronze in the coxed pair in 1988.

MOST OLYMPIC MEDALS
With 18 gymnastics medals (nine gold, five silver, and four bronze) won in 1956–64, Larisa Semyonovna Latynina (USSR) is the most successful Olympian ever. Her nine golds are also the **most Olympic gold medals by a female**, while her 14 medals in solo events rank as the **most individual Olympic medals**.

MOST MEDALS WON AT ONE OLYMPICS (FEMALE)
The record medal haul by a female competitor at one Olympics is gymnast Maria Gorokhovskaya's (USSR) two golds and five bronzes at Helsinki, Finland, in 1952.

MOST MEDALS WON AT ONE OLYMPICS (MALE)
Just two men in Olympic history have walked away from a single Games with eight medals: gymnast Aleksandr Nikolayevich Dityatin (USSR), who won three golds, four silvers, and one bronze at the 1980 Games in Moscow, Russia, and US swimmer Michael Phelps (USA), who has achieved the feat twice. Phelps won six golds and two bronzes at Athens 2004 in Greece, and a remarkable eight golds at Beijing 2008 in China. Phelps's overall tally of 16 medals is the **most Olympic medals by a male**.

NO.1 FAN
Since attending the 1932 Olympics in Los Angeles, USA, sports-mad Harry Nelson (USA) has gone on to attend every Games to date (except Berlin 1936), making the 89-year-old something of an Olympic legend in his own right.

MOST OLYMPIC GOLD MEDALS
US swimmer Michael Phelps has won a record 14 individual and team gold medals in the pool – six at the 2004 Games in Athens, Greece, and eight at the 2008 Games in Beijing, China. His 2008 tally was also the **most gold medals won at a single Olympic Games**, comprising titles in the 100 m butterfly; 200 m freestyle, butterfly, and medley; 400 m medley; 4 x 100 m freestyle and medley relays; and the 200 m freestyle relay.

UPDATED RECORD
NEW RECORD

Lake Baikal in eastern Siberia, Russia, is the **deepest lake** in the world. It is 385 miles (620 km) long and 20–46 miles (32–74 km) wide. In 1974, the lake's Olkhon Crevice was measured to be 5,371 ft (1,637 m) deep, of which 3,875 ft (1,181 m) is below sea level.

MOST OLYMPIC LONG JUMP GOLD MEDALS

Carl Lewis (USA) won the Olympic long jump four times in a row, in 1984 in Los Angeles, USA, 1988 in Seoul, South Korea, 1992 in Barcelona, Spain, and 1996 in Atlanta, USA. Alongside Paul Elvstrom (Denmark) and Al Oerter (USA) – see p.234 – Lewis holds the record for the **most consecutive Olympic gold medals won in an individual event**.

SEE MORE AERIAL ANTICS ON P.116.

MOST OLYMPIC TRACK AND FIELD GOLD MEDALS

Distance runner Paavo Nurmi (Finland), nicknamed "The Flying Finn," claimed a total of nine Olympic golds in track and field between 1920 and 1928. The only man to match this feat is Carl Lewis (USA), who took gold in the 100 m, 200 m, 4 x 100 m relay, and long jump from 1984 to 1996.

MOST OLYMPIC BOXING GOLD MEDALS

Boasting a trio of gold medals each, the most successful pugilists in Olympic history are Laszlo Papp (Hungary), Teofilo Stevenson (Cuba), and Felix Savon (Cuba), who all won titles in three consecutive Games, in 1948–56, 1972–80, and 1992–2000, respectively.

MOST OLYMPIC CANOE/KAYAK MEDALS

Birgit Fischer (Germany) paddled her way to 12 medals in canoeing and kayaking events between 1980 and 2004, securing an impressive eight golds and four silvers.

FIRST ATHLETE TO SET THREE SPRINTING WORLD RECORDS AT ONE OLYMPIC GAMES

At the 2008 Beijing Games in China, Usain Bolt (Jamaica) smashed the world records in three sprint events – the 100 m, 200 m, and 4 x 100 m relay – the first Olympian to do so in history. Bolt won the 100 m in 9.69 seconds, the 200 m in 19.30 seconds, and the relay in 37.10 seconds, alongside his Jamaican team-mates Asafa Powell, Nesta Carter, and Michael Frater.

MOST OLYMPIC ATHLETICS MEDALS (FEMALE)

Jamaican sprinter Merlene Ottey won nine Olympic 100 m and 200 m medals – three silver and six bronze – between the 1980 Games in Moscow, Russia, and the 2000 Games in Sydney, Australia. The bronze won in the individual 100 m in Sydney was awarded in 2009, after the gold medalist, Marion Jones (USA), was stripped of her title due to a drugs offense.

STAYING POWER

The **most durable Olympic torch bearer** is Pandelis Konstantinidis (Greece), who first ran in the 1936 relay for the Berlin Games (when Hitler ruled Germany), and ran again, 72 years later, in the Beijing 2008 relay.

FIRST PERFECT 10 IN OLYMPIC GYMNASTICS

Nadia Comaneci (Romania) was the first athlete to earn a perfect score of 10/10 at an Olympic gymnastics event, for her uneven bars routine in the team competition in Montreal, Canada, on July 18, 1976.

TOP-PERFORMING NATIONS

MOST MEDALS WON AT THE SUMMER OLYMPICS (1896–2008)		
1	USA	2,298 overall (931 gold, 729 silver, 638 bronze)
2	USSR*	1,010 overall (395 gold, 319 silver, 296 bronze)
3	Germany**	852 overall (247 gold, 284 silver, 321 bronze)
MOST MEDALS WON AT A SINGLE SUMMER OLYMPICS		
1	USA	239 overall (78 gold, 82 silver, 79 bronze) at St Louis 1904 (USA)
2	USSR*	195 overall (80 gold, 69 silver, 46 bronze) at Moscow 1980 (USSR)
3	Great Britain	145 overall (56 gold, 51 silver, 38 bronze) at London 1908 (UK)
MOST GOLD MEDALS WON AT A SINGLE SUMMER OLYMPICS		
1	USA	83 at Los Angeles 1984 (USA)
2	USSR*	80 at Moscow 1980 (USSR)
3	USA	78 at St Louis 1904 (USA)

* Includes USSR only (1952–80 and 1988); does not include Russia, Unified Team, or Russian Federation
** Includes Germany (1896–1912, 1928–36, 1952, 1992–2008), United Team (1956–64), and FRD (1968–1976, 1984–88)

The **deadliest lake** is Lake Nyos in Cameroon, where toxic gases have claimed nearly 2,000 lives in recent decades. One night in August 1986, up to 1,800 people and many animals were killed by a large release of carbon dioxide.

PARALYMPICS

UPDATED RECORD
NEW RECORD

MOST MEDALS WON AT THE SUMMER PARALYMPICS

Since the first Paralympics, in Rome, Italy, in 1960, the USA has been by far the most successful nation, with its athletes picking up a record 1,870 medals over the years.

MOST GOLD MEDALS WON AT A SINGLE SUMMER PARALYMPICS

The host nations dominated proceedings at the 1984 Games in New York (USA) and Stoke Mandeville (UK), with the USA winning 136 golds and Great Britain picking up 107. The USA has also won the **most Paralympic gold medals** overall – 665 to date.

FIRST TELEVISED SUMMER PARALYMPICS

The 1976 Games in Toronto, Canada, represented the first time that the Paralympics had been televised in its entirety. Events were broadcast daily to more than half a million viewers across Ontario, Canada.

FIRST AMPUTEE AND VISUALLY IMPAIRED ATHLETES AT THE PARALYMPICS

Blind, partially sighted, and amputee athletes competed in the Paralympics for the first time at the 1976 Games hosted by Toronto, Canada. Wheelchair racing over distances of 200 m, 400 m, 800 m, and 1,500 m was added to the lineup along with goalball, a sport aimed at visually impaired athletes (see button above left). The standout athlete was Arnie Boldt (Canada), an 18-year-old leg amputee, who won gold in the long jump and the high jump.

FIRST PARALYMPIC RACING WHEELCHAIRS

Wheelchair racing debuted at the 1964 Paralympic Games in Tokyo, Japan, but athletes had no option but to race in standard chairs, which were heavy and awkward to control. By Toronto 1976, however, things had changed, and the development of special racing chairs, which were lighter, faster, and far more maneuverable, led to a glut of new speed records.

GOALBALL
Invented as a rehab aid for blinded World War II veterans, goalball is similar to soccer. It is played indoors by teams of three players wearing blackout masks, who score by throwing the ball into the opposition net. Bells in the ball help players keep track of where it is.

PISTORIUS HOLDS THE 100 M (T44) WORLD RECORD WITH A TIME OF 10.91 SEC

PARALYMPIC COMPETITION

First held in 1960, the Paralympic Games is an international multisport event that runs every four years in parallel with the Olympics. Featuring many Olympic sports and several unique events (see buttons), the Paralympics sees athletes of all levels of disability compete for glory on the world stage.

CLASSIFICATION
Athletes are classified according to the nature and extent of their disabilities, to ensure that they compete on equal terms. The main categories listed below are further subdivided according to severity.

Amputee	Athletes with partial or complete loss of one or more limbs; must be missing a major joint
Cerebral palsy	Athletes with motor conditions that cause impaired movement, balance, or muscle control
Visual impairment	Athletes with any condition that impacts on vision; includes total blindness
Spinal cord injuries	Athletes who must compete in wheelchairs due to some loss of functioning in lower limbs
Intellectual disability	Athletes with impaired mental functioning, including communication or social disorders
Les autres	French for "the others"; applies to athletes with disabilities not covered above

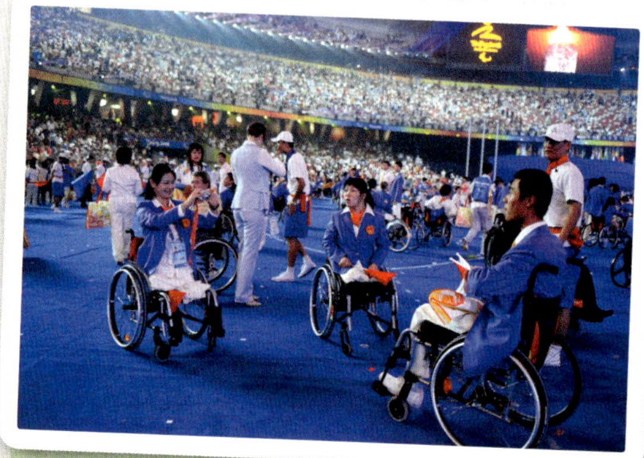

MOST COUNTRIES REPRESENTED AT A SUMMER PARALYMPICS

The best-represented Paralympics on record was the 2008 Games hosted by Beijing, China, which was attended by 146 nations from around the globe. Beijing also claimed the record for **most participants at a summer Paralympics**, with a total of 3,951 athletes turning up to compete for the 1,431 medals on offer.

FASTEST MEN'S 400 M (T44)

Dubbed the "Blade Runner," Oscar Pistorius (South Africa) set the track alight at the 2008 Paralympics in Beijing, China, winning the 100 m, 200 m, and 400 m titles and setting a 400 m record of 47.49 seconds on September 16, 2008. Born without his fibulae, Oscar had his legs amputated below the knees and today runs on carbon-fiber blades in the T44 class. He is bidding to become the first amputee sprinter to compete at the Olympics, in 2012.

FASTEST WHEELCHAIR MARATHON (T52)

At the 2008 Games in Beijing, China, Austrian wheelchair athlete Thomas Geierspichler won gold in the men's T52-class marathon (no lower limb function), setting a world-record time of 1 hr 40 min 7 sec on September 17, 2008.

The **first wheelchair marathon** took place at the 1984 Games cohosted by New York (USA) and Stoke Mandeville (UK).

The **most consecutive matches played in the Africa Cup of Nations soccer tournament** is 34, by defender Rigobert Song (Cameroon) between 1996 and 2010.

1.23 Gallons of blood your heart pumps during each one of the 41,393,520 minutes of your life. Plumbed into an Olympic-sized swimming pool, you would fill it to within 6.3 in of the regulation depth over the course of your life.

FIRST PARALYMPIAN TO COMPETE IN THE OLYMPIC GAMES

After representing her nation in the archery at the 1980 Paralympics in Arnhem, the Netherlands, Neroli Fairhall (New Zealand) became the first Paralympian to take on able-bodied athletes at the Olympic Games, competing with her bow at the 1984 Summer Olympics in Los Angeles, USA. Neroli, who won gold at the Paralympics, eventually finished 35th at the Olympics.

MOST MEDALS WON AT THE SUMMER PARALYMPICS BY A MALE ATHLETE

Sweden's Jonas Jacobsson has won more medals than any other male athlete at the Paralympics. Having competed at every Games since Arnhem 1980 in the Netherlands, Jonas has amassed a record 27 shooting medals, including 16 golds. At Beijing 2008, he won three titles, in the Air Rifle Standing, the Free Rifle 3x40, and the Mixed Free Rifle Prone.

MOST GOLD MEDALS WON AT THE SUMMER PARALYMPICS BY AN INDIVIDUAL

Trischa Zorn (USA) is the most successful Paralympian in history, racing to a record 32 individual golds and nine team golds in the pool between 1980 and 2004. The visually impaired athlete – who was born blind but later received two iris implants to boost her vision – has been almost unstoppable, winning 55 medals overall: 41 golds, nine silvers, and five bronzes.

FASTEST PARALYMPIC MEN'S 5,000 M (T13)

At Beijing 2008, Kenyan track star Henry Kiprono Kirwa claimed gold in the men's 5,000 m in a record time of 14 min 24.02 sec, competing in the T13 category – the minimum level of visual impairment.

FASTEST PARALYMPIC 50 M FREESTYLE SWIM (S12)

At the 2008 Games in Beijing, China, champion swimmer Maksym Veraska (Ukraine) set a new Paralympic record of 23.45 seconds in the S12 class of the 50 m freestyle. On the same day, September 14, 2008, Oxana Savchenko (Russia) won the women's category in a record 23.43 seconds. The S12 class is for those with an intermediate degree of sight loss.

MOST PARALYMPIC WHEELCHAIR BASKETBALL TITLES

The kings of the court in men's basketball are the Americans, with five titles won to date, in 1960, 1964, 1972, 1976, and 1988. More recently, the balance of power has shifted to Canada and Australia, with each country winning gold twice and silver once in the course of the last four Games. In the female category, Canada's women have replicated the success of its men by winning in 1992, 1996, and 2000.

FASTEST PARALYMPIC MEN'S 5,000 M (T46)

Abraham Cheruiyot Tarbei (Kenya) ran the quickest 5,000 m in the men's T46 class at the 2008 Games in Beijing, China, taking gold in 14 min 20.88 sec on September 13, 2008. The T46 class covers track athletes with impaired arm or trunk functioning or an amputation above or below the elbow.

BOCCIA

Similar to bowls, boccia is played in over 50 countries and made its Paralympic debut in 1984. Athletes with cerebral palsy and similar conditions throw balls as near as possible to a white target ball (the "jack") to win.

MOST FEMALE WHEELCHAIR BASKETBALL COMPETITORS

The 2008 Paralympic Games held in Beijing, China, saw the largest turnout of female wheelchair basketball players in the event's history, with 120 athletes from 10 nations competing for glory on the court. The tournament favorites, the USA (pictured in white), eventually won through, defeating Germany 50–38 in the final.

WHEELCHAIR RUGBY

Dubbed "murderball" due to its intense physicality, wheelchair rugby is played on a basketball court by teams of four, who must carry the ball across the opposing goal line to score. A cross between basketball and ice hockey, it is a hugely popular sport.

The record for the **fastest soccer goal by a substitute at the World Cup Finals** is 18 seconds, scored by Uruguay's Richard Morales against Senegal in Suwon, South Korea, on June 11, 2002.

HIGHEST EARNERS

THE INCREDIBLE INCOMES OF SPORT'S TOP TALENT

Meet the super-talented athletes whose hard work and natural ability have been rewarded with skyscraping salaries and lucrative sponsorship deals. This top ten, based on *Forbes* magazine's "Sports Money 50-50" list of the most powerful people in sports, is ranked according to total earnings between June 2009 and June 2010.

STRIKING IT RICH IN THE WORLD OF SPORT

- **$52M** Oscar de la Hoya's (USA) purse for his WBC Light Middleweight fight against Floyd Mayweather Jr on May 5, 2007
- **$30M** The spoils pocketed by the Spanish national soccer association when its team lifted the 2010 FIFA World Cup
- **$13M** The prize pot scooped by the Stanford Superstars on their victory in the 2008 Stanford Series of Twenty20 cricket
- **$12M** The record jackpot earned by Jamie Gold (USA) for winning the World Series of Poker Main Event in 2006
- **$10M** The huge haul for claiming the FedEx Cup, a points-based golf competition that spans several tournaments
- **$6M** The riches paid out by the most lucrative horse race in the world – the prestigious Dubai World Cup
- **$1.7M** The top purse in tennis, awarded to the men's and women's singles champions at the US Open
- **$1.5M** The glittering prize up for grabs in the biggest race of the NASCAR season – the Daytona 500
- **$1M** The windfall paid by the now-defunct IAAF Golden League to any athlete who won all of their events in a season
- **$400K** The cash on the table for the winner of the snooker World Championship, played at the Crucible, Sheffield, UK

$38.3M

TERRELL SUGGS USA, b. 10/11/82

A $63-million contract in 2009, and bonus of $33 million, made Suggs the best-paid National Football League (NFL) linebacker in history.

$39.9M

ELI MANNING USA, b. 1/3/81

Manning is now officially the highest-earning NFL player, following a $97.5-million, six-year contract signed with the New York Giants in August 2010.

$43.7M

DAVID BECKHAM UK, b. 5/2/75

The England soccer hero and celebrity is still a financial top draw. Of the $40 million he earned in 2009, almost $33 million came via sponsorship.

$46M

PHIL MICKELSON USA, b. 6/16/70

Mickelson is the world golfing number two, but his prize money is dwarfed by his lucrative endorsements from companies such as ExxonMobil, Rolex, and Barclays.

Emilio Arenas (Uruguay) has the **largest collection of pencils**. His collection, which he started in 1956, includes a total of 11,856 different pencils from 55 countries.

3 billion Number of people (almost half of the world's population) living on less than $2.50 a day. Of these, more than half live without electricity.

$42M

MANNY PACQUIAO Philippines, b. 12/17/78
Fights against Miguel Cotto and Joshua Clottey netted "Pac-Man" a cool $35 million alone. In 2010, he became a member of Congress in the Philippines.

$42.8M

LEBRON JAMES USA, b. 12/30/84
James enjoys lucrative deals with Nike and McDonald's, among others. In 2010, *Forbes* rated him the second most influential athlete, after US cyclist Lance Armstrong.

$43M

ROGER FEDERER Switzerland, b. 8/8/81
As of August 2010, Federer had won $56.9 million in prize money. His Nike deal is the most lucrative in tennis, worth over $10 million a year.

$48M

KOBE BRYANT USA, b. 8/23/78
With 25,970 points as of April 2010, Bryant is the Los Angeles Lakers' all-time top scorer. He is set to earn $30.5 million in the 2013–14 season just from playing.

$65M

FLOYD MAYWEATHER JR USA, b. 2/24/77
Undefeated in his professional career (his 41 wins include 25 knockouts), this boxing sensation can boast nine world titles in five different weight classes.

$105M

TIGER WOODS USA, b. 12/30/75
The golfing legend's income includes an annual $30-million payment from sponsors Nike. He has won the Masters four times, most recently in 2005.

The **largest collection of pencil sharpeners**, meanwhile, is held by Demetra Koutsouridou (Greece), who has amassed 8,514 different pencil sharpeners since 1997.

TOP MARKSMEN

HIGHEST FIELD GOAL PERCENTAGE IN AN NBA CAREER

As of April 12, 2011, Boston Celtics center Shaquille O'Neal (USA) boasted a career field goal percentage of .5823, making him the most accurate points-scorer in the history of the National Basketball Association (NBA).

MOST POINTS IN A TRI-NATIONS MATCH

Morne Steyn (South Africa) scored 31 points against New Zealand at ABSA Stadium, Durban, South Africa, on August 1, 2009.

MOST THREE-POINT FIELD GOALS IN AN NBA FINALS GAME

Ray Allen (USA) scored eight three-pointers for the Boston Celtics in game two of the 2010 NBA Finals in Los Angeles, USA, on June 6, 2010. He also scored the **most three-point field goals in an NBA playoff game**: nine.

MOST THREE-POINT FIELD GOALS (WBNA)

Between 1999 and the end of the 2010 season, Katie Smith (USA) scored 785 three-pointers for the Minnesota Lynx, Detroit Shock, and Washington Mystics (all USA).

MOST DROP GOALS IN THE FIVE/SIX NATIONS CHAMPIONSHIP

England rugby union fly-half Jonny Wilkinson scored 11 drop goals for his country between 1998 and 2011.

MOST POINTS IN AN NFL CAREER

Morten Andersen (Denmark) scored 2,544 points in his National Football League (NFL) career as a placekicker from 1982 to 2007. He played for the New Orleans Saints, Atlanta Falcons, New York Giants, Kansas City Chiefs, and Minnesota Vikings (all USA).

HIGHEST FIELD GOAL PERCENTAGE IN AN NFL CAREER

By the end of 2010–11, Nate Kaeding (USA) had converted 173 of 200 field goal attempts for the San Diego Chargers (USA), posting an 86.5% average. Mike Vanderjagt (Canada) lies in second place, averaging 86.47% (230/266) between 1998 and 2006.

SPORTING LANDMARKS

Record	Tally	Holder
Most goals in a single FIFA World Cup	13	Just Fontaine (France)
Most Test cricket centuries	51	Sachin Tendulkar (India)
Most UEFA Champions League goals	71	Raúl González Blanco (Spain)
Most NFL touchdowns	208	Jerry Rice (USA)
Most English Premier League goals	260	Alan Shearer (UK)
Most NFL field goals	565	Morten Andersen (Denmark)
Most MLB home runs	762	Barry Bonds (USA)
Most Rugby Union international points	1,195	Jonny Wilkinson (UK)
Most WNBA points	6,413	Tina Thompson (USA)
Most NBA field goals	15,837	Kareem Abdul-Jabbar (USA)

MOST GOALS IN A SOCCER CAREER

Edson Arantes do Nascimento (Brazil), known as Pelé, scored 1,279 goals in 1,363 games from September 7, 1956 to October 1, 1977. His best year was 1959, with 126 goals.

MOST CONSECUTIVE CHAMPIONS LEAGUE MATCHES SCORED IN

Marouane Chamakh (Morocco) scored in six UEFA Champions League games in a row for Bordeaux (France) and Arsenal (UK) between 2009 and 2010.

MOST DARTS WORLD CHAMPIONSHIPS

Phil Taylor (UK) has won 15 World Championship titles: the World Darts Organization (WDO) in 1990 and 1992, and the Professional Darts Corporation (PDC) in 1995–2002, 2004–06, and 2009–10.

MOST POINTS SCORED IN AN NHL CAREER

Wayne Gretzky (Canada) scored 2,857 points during his National Hockey League (NHL) career, playing for the Edmonton Oilers (Canada), Los Angeles Kings, St Louis Blues, and New York Rangers (all USA) from 1979 to 1999. This total comprises 894 goals and 1,963 assists, achieved in 1,487 games.

UPDATED RECORD
NEW RECORD

Sophia Vaharis of Athens, Greece, has gathered the **most labels from champagne and wine bottles**: 15,255 different items, representing 50 different countries.

1,735 Weight in pounds of a lifetime's supply of chocolate. You're going to eat 10 times your own body weight of chocolate. Alternatively, you could make it all into an edible, life-size model of a basketball team.

CHECK OUT THE CRAZIER SIDE OF SPORT ON P.264.

MOST COMPETITIVE 147 BREAKS IN SNOOKER

Ronnie O'Sullivan and Stephen Hendry (both UK) have both achieved a record 10 maximum 147 breaks in competitive snooker. The most recent was Hendry's (pictured) clearance in the opening frame against Stephen Maguire in their Welsh Open match on February 17, 2011.

MOST GRAND SLAM HOME RUNS IN A GAME

The Major League Baseball (MLB) record for the greatest number of grand slam home runs in one game is two and has been accomplished by 13 players. The most recent batter to achieve this feat was Josh Willingham (USA, right) for the Washington Nationals against the Milwaukee Brewers (both USA) on July 27, 2009.

MOST 180s SCORED IN A DARTS PDC CHAMPIONSHIP

The most maximum scores by an individual darter in a Professional Darts Corporation (PDC) World Championship is 60 by Adrian Lewis (UK) at Alexandra Palace, London, UK, in January 2011.

MOST ACES SERVED IN A PROFESSIONAL TENNIS MATCH

John Isner (USA) served 113 aces in his epic match – from June 22 to 24 – against Nicolas Mahut (France) at the 2010 Wimbledon Championships in London, UK. The feat also gives Isner the records for the **most aces in a Wimbledon match** and the **most aces in a Grand Slam tournament match**.

MOST GOALS IN AN NHL DEBUT

On October 9, 2010, Derek Stepan (USA) became only the fourth player in National Hockey League (NHL) history to score a hattrick on his debut, for the New York Rangers in a 6–3 victory over the Buffalo Sabres (both USA). He shares the record with Fabian Brunnstrom (Sweden) of the Dallas Stars (USA), Alex Smart of the Montreal Canadiens, and Real Cloutier of the Quebec Nordiques (all Canada).

MOST TEST CRICKET RUNS SCORED

Sachin Tendulkar (India) scored 14,692 runs in his Test match career between November 15, 1989 and January 6, 2011. He also holds the record for the **most runs scored in a one-day international career**: 18,111 runs, at an average of 45.16, between December 18, 1989 and the 2011 World Cup final on April 2, 2011.

MURALITHARAN'S 800TH WICKET CAME WITH THE FINAL BALL OF HIS LAST OVER IN TEST CRICKET

800 WICKETS

MOST WICKETS IN TEST MATCH CRICKET

Muttiah Muralitharan (Sri Lanka, left) took 800 wickets in 133 Tests from August 28, 1992 to July 22, 2010. He also has the **most international wickets**: 1,347, from 1992 to the World Cup final on April 2, 2011. Muttiah's compatriot, Chaminda Vaas, has the **most wickets in a one-day international match**, with 8–19 against Zimbabwe at Colombo, Sri Lanka, on December 8, 2001.

Commandaria, the sweet dessert wine from Cyprus, is the world's **oldest manufactured wine**. Its origins can be traced as far back as 2000 BC.

WORLD'S FASTEST...

FASTEST...

ENGLISH PREMIER LEAGUE GOAL BY A SUBSTITUTE
Playing for Arsenal, super-sub Nicklas Bendtner (Denmark) scored just six seconds after coming on against Tottenham Hotspur in a Premier League soccer match at the Emirates Stadium, London, UK, on December 22, 2007.

UEFA CHAMPIONS LEAGUE GOAL
Marginally slower than Bendtner, striker Roy Makaay (Netherlands) scored the opening goal for Bayern Munich against Real Madrid in just 10 seconds in Munich, Germany, on March 7, 2007.

FIFA WORLD CUP GOAL
Hakan Şükür's 11-second strike for Turkey against Korea Republic at Daegu, Korea, on June 29, 2002 is the fastest ever scored in a soccer World Cup finals match.

NFL TOUCHDOWN
Playing for the Dallas Cowboys against the Philadelphia Eagles on October 12, 2003, receiver Randal Williams (USA) ran in the NFL's fastest ever touchdown. On the opening play of the game, the Eagles tried an onside kick, but Williams caught the ball and returned it 37 yards for a TD. The play, which set up a 23–21 Cowboys win, took just three seconds off the clock.

NHL HAT-TRICK
Nobody has broken Bill Mosienko's (Canada) phenomenal record of smashing three goals in just 21 seconds playing for the Chicago Blackhawks against the New York Rangers (both USA) on March 23, 1952.

RUGBY UNION SUPER RUGBY TRY
The Super Rugby competition, contested by teams from Australia, New Zealand, and South Africa, saw its quickest ever try on May 12, 2001 when the Highlanders' (NZ) lock Vula Maimuri (Fiji) crossed the line just 12 seconds into a match against the Crusaders (NZ) at Christchurch, NZ.

CRICKET WORLD CUP CENTURY
During the 2011 World Cup, Irish all-rounder Kevin O'Brien hit 100 runs off just 50 balls – an average of 12 per over, or two per ball! O'Brien went on to score 113 in a three-wicket win over England at Bangalore's M Chinnaswamy Stadium, India, on March 2, 2011.

CRICKET WORLD CUP FINAL CENTURY
Australian wicket-keeper Adam Gilchrist chalked up the quickest ton in a cricket World Cup final, hitting 100 runs off 72 balls against Sri Lanka at Kensington Oval, Bridgetown, Barbados, on April 28, 2007.

CRAZY GOLF
On June 19, 2005, Ben Crosby, Andrew Crawford, John Lyon, and Russell Hayhoe (all UK) played the **fastest round of golf (fourball)** at Ponteland Golf Course, Northumberland, UK, finishing in 1 hr 4 min 25 sec.

SNOOKER MAXIMUM BREAK (147 POINTS)
True to his name, Ronnie "The Rocket" O'Sullivan holds the record for the fastest 147 break, recording a time of 5 min 20 sec in his first round match against Mick Price at the World Championships in Sheffield, UK, on April 21, 1997. Sinking 15 reds, each followed by a black, then all seven colors, he averaged a pot every 8.65 seconds!

FASTEST MEN AND WOMEN
Crossing land, air, ice, and water at breakneck speeds, these athletes are the fastest in their class. In the ultimate sporting showdown, we pitch rowers and runners against skiers, skaters, swimmers, and skydivers to discover the fastest sport on the planet!

Marathon (female) Over 26.2 miles, Paula Radcliffe (UK) is the queen of the road, with a record time of 2:15.25 achieved in the London Marathon (UK) on April 13, 2003.

50 m freestyle, long course (female) Britta Steffen (Germany) is the fastest woman in the pool over 50 m, finishing in 23.73 seconds at the World Championships in Rome, Italy, on August 2, 2009.

2,000 m row, single sculls At the 2009 World Championships in Poznan, Poland, Mahé Drysdale (NZ) won the 2 km sprint in style, beating his own world record in a time of 6 min 33.35 sec.

1 mile run Fastest over 1,500 m and 2,000 m, Moroccan running machine Hicham El Guerrouj also holds the mile record, setting a time of 3:43.13 in Rome, Italy, on July 7, 1999.

SPEEDS: AVERAGE/TOP	4.71 mi/h (7.59 km/h)	10.46 mi/h (16.83 km/h)	11.61 mi/h (18.68 km/h)	16.13 mi/h (25.96 km/h)

The **largest skewer of kebab meat** weighed 8,866 lb 15 oz (4,022 kg) and was prepared by Zith Catering Equipment Ltd and the Municipality of Pafos (both Cyprus) in Pafos, Cyprus, on December 31, 2008.

0.9 trillion Distance in miles you'll travel in space. Our galaxy spins through the universe at 360 mi/s, so don't ever let anyone accuse you of sitting still – right now you're going at 1,296,000 mi/h!

BIGGEST HITTERS

From pacey pitches to speedy shuttlecocks, check out some of the fastest throws, tosses, whacks, and smashes from around the world of sport!

Category	Speed	Holder	Date
Cricket bowl	100.2 mi/h (161.3 km/h)	Shoaib Akhtar (Pakistan)	Feb 22, 2003
Baseball pitch	100.9 mi/h (162.3 km/h)	Lynn Nolan Ryan (USA)	Aug 20, 1974
● Ice hockey shot	110.3 mi/h (177.5 km/h)	Denis Kulyash (Russia)	Feb 5, 2011
● Lacrosse shot	111.0 mi/h (178.6 km/h)	Paul Rabil (USA)	Jul 8, 2010
Soccer shot (UK)	114.0 mi/h (183.0 km/h)	David Hirst (UK)	Sep 16, 1996
● Tennis serve	156.0 mi/h (251.0 km/h)	Ivo Karlovic (Croatia)	Mar 5, 2011
Jai alai throw	188.0 mi/h (302.0 km/h)	José Ramón Areitio (Spain)	Aug 3, 1979
● Golf drive	204.0 mi/h (328.3 km/h)	Jason Zuback (Canada)	Dec 1, 2007
● Badminton smash	206.0 mi/h (332.0 km/h)	Fu Haifeng (China)	May 15, 2005

● Speed skydive
Thanks to gravity – and a 12,139-ft (3,700-m) plunge from a plane – speed skydiving is the world's fastest sport. On June 5, 2010, at the Speed World Series in Utti, Finland, Christian Labhart (Switzerland) hit a freefall speed of 327.41 mi/h (526.93 km/h) – fast enough to outpace a Bugatti Veyron supercar at full pelt (267.86 mi/h; 431.07 km/h).

327.41 MI/H

100 m sprint
Dubbed "the fastest man in the world," Usain Bolt (Jamaica) cruised to the 100 m record in 9.58 seconds in Berlin, Germany, on August 16, 2009.

1,000 m speed skate
In between winning two Olympic golds (2006, 2010), Shani Davis (USA) set a new record for the 1,000 m event, posting a time of 1:06.42 in Salt Lake City, Utah, USA, on March 7, 2009.

Speed skiing (female)
Sanna Tidstrand (Sweden), the world champion speed skier since 2006, reached a death-defying 150.73 mi/h (242.59 km/h) on the slopes of Les Arcs, France, on April 20, 2006.

110 m hurdles
Dayron Robles (Cuba) leaped into the record books with his 12.87-second finish over the sprint hurdles at the Golden Spike event in Ostrava, Czech Republic, on June 12, 2008.

● UPDATED RECORD
● NEW RECORD

19.12 mi/h (30.77 km/h) | 23.35 mi/h (37.58 km/h) | 33.69 mi/h (54.21 km/h) | 150.73 mi/h (242.59 km/h)

The **most meat consumed at an outdoor event** was 57,639 lb (26,145 kg), cooked up by La Pastoral Social Arquidiocesana de Asunción y amigos, at La Asociacion Rural de Paraguay, Mariano Roque Alonso, Paraguay, on October 26, 2008.

FASTEST ON WHEELS

FASTEST...

AVERAGE SPEED IN AN F1 GRAND PRIX

Michael Schumacher (Germany) averaged a record 153.842 mi/h (247.585 km/h) in his Ferrari on his way to winning the Italian Grand Prix at Monza on September 14, 2003. Despite advances in race technology, the German's speed remains unbeaten.

COMPLETION OF THE INDY 500

Dutchman Arie Luyendyk is the fastest driver ever to grace the 500-mile (804.5-km) race at the Indianapolis Motor Speedway in Indiana, USA. On May 27, 1990, his Lola-Chevrolet cruised home in 2 hr 41 min 18.404 sec, averaging 185.981 mi/h (299.307 km/h).

LAP IN THE LE MANS 24-HOUR RACE

On June 10, 1989, Alain Ferté (France) drove the fastest lap in the history of the 24 Hours of Le Mans, recording a time of 3 min 21.27 sec in his Jaguar XJR-9LM at the Circuit de la Sarthe, Le Mans, France, with his brother Michel also on board.

AVERAGE SPEED IN THE TOUR DE FRANCE

Lance Armstrong (USA) won the 2005 Tour de France in 86 hr 15 min 2 sec, averaging 25.882 mi/h (41.654 km/h) on the 2,241-mile (3,607-km) course. After his record-breaking 7th Tour victory in a row, Armstrong announced his retirement, only to return in 2010 to finish in 23rd place. One of the world's greatest athletes, he gave up pro sports for good in February 2011.

4 KM CYCLE, UNPACED STANDING START (MALE)

On February 2, 2011, Australia's Jack Bobridge broke Chris Boardman's (UK) 15-year-old 4 km record in the Cycling Australia Track National Championships in Sydney, Australia. Crossing the line in 4 min 10.534 sec, he was just half a second quicker than Boardman's 1996 record – a barrier once thought unbeatable.

3 KM CYCLE, STANDING START (FEMALE TEAM)

On May 12, 2010, Dotsie Bausch, Sarah Hammer and Lauren Tamayo (USA) won the 3 km team pursuit in Aguascalientes, Mexico, in 3 min 19.569 sec.

FASTEST 500 M CYCLE, UNPACED FLYING START (MALE)

On May 13, 2007, Chris Hoy (UK) raced round the Alto Orpavi velodrome in La Paz, Bolivia, to shatter the "flying 500 m" record in a time of 24.758 seconds – more than a second quicker than Arnaud Dublé's (France) 2001 record.

FASTEST INDY 500 OPENING LAP

The fastest start to an Indianapolis 500 was set by Brazilian driver Tony Kanaan, who fired his Honda round the opening lap of the 2007 race in a record 41.335 seconds, at an average speed of 217.728 mi/h (350.39 km/h). Pictured below left setting the pace for the Andretti Green team, Kanaan eventually fell back to finish eighth.

FASTEST OUTRIGHT SPEED IN AN F1 RACE

Driving a McLaren-Mercedes, Juan Pablo Montoya (Colombia) accelerated to 231.5 mi/h (372.6 km/h) at Monza in the Italian Grand Prix on September 4, 2005. Montoya started and finished the race in first place.

The **most recent tribal first contact** was with a subgroup of the Ayoreo-Totobiegosode peoples of Paraguay, who were forced from the forest in March 2004 when their land and waterholes were taken over by cattle ranchers.

FASTEST NEW YORK WHEELCHAIR MARATHON

On November 5, 2006, Australian Kurt Fearnley powered to victory in the wheelchair marathon in New York City, USA, in a blistering 1 hr 29 min 22 sec. A talented athlete, Fearnley also holds the record across the Atlantic, achieving the **fastest London Wheelchair Marathon** in 1 hr 28 min 57 sec in 2009. His most recent success was gold in the 1,500 m at the 2010 Commonwealth Games.

UPDATED RECORD
NEW RECORD

MARATHON MAN

Fearnley's big-race credentials were tested to the max at the 2004 Paralympics in Athens, Greece. With 3 miles (5 km) to go, Fearnley suffered a flat tire, but still pushed on to take gold.

COMPLETION OF THE LONDON WHEELCHAIR MARATHON (FEMALE)

Just months prior to winning a Paralympic bronze in the marathon at the 2008 Beijing Games, Swiss wheelchair athlete Sandra Graf saw off her rivals Amanda McGrory and Shelly Woods to win the London Wheelchair Marathon in a record time of 1 hr 48 min 4 sec on April 13, 2008.

FASTEST OUTRIGHT SPEED IN NHRA DRAG RACING, PRO STOCK MOTORBIKE

The highest speed for a gas-driven, piston-engined motorcycle (Pro Stock) is 197.65 mi/h (318.08 km/h), by Michael Phillips (USA) at Baton Rouge, Louisiana, USA, on July 18, 2010.

OUTRIGHT SPEED IN NHRA DRAG RACING, PRO STOCK CAR

On March 27, 2010, drag racer Greg Anderson (USA) tore up the tarmac to record a speed of 212.46 mi/h (341.92 km/h) in a gas-driven, piston-engined car (Pro Stock) at Concord, North Carolina, USA.

LAP AT THE ISLE OF MAN TT (FEMALE)

With a super-quick time of 19 min 22.6 sec and an average speed of 116.83 mi/h (188.02 km/h), Jenny Tinmouth (UK) is the fastest female rider ever to lap the daunting 37.73-mile (60.75-km) Isle of Man TT course. She claimed the record on June 12, 2009 and has since gone on to become the **first woman to race in the British Superbike Championship**, appearing for the Splitlath Motorsport team in the 2011 season.

FOR MORE THRILLS ON WHEELS, TURN TO P.178.

ISLE OF MAN TT

At the 2009 Isle of Man TT (UK), British Superbike rider John McGuinness won the Superbike category in a record time of 1 hr 46 min 7.16 sec on June 8, 2009.

McGuinness also achieved the double feat of **overall fastest lap** and **overall fastest average speed**, completing the arduous circuit in 17 min 12.3 sec and averaging 131.578 mi/h (211.754 km/h) on his Honda CBR1000RR.

SPEED BY A NEWCOMER AT THE ISLE OF MAN TT

The 2009 British Supersport Champion Steve Plater (UK) made his Isle of Man TT debut in 2007 and, despite his inexperience on the course, steered his 1,000-cc Yamaha into the record books with a top speed of 125.808 mi/h (202.468 km/h).

FASTEST FIRS INLINE SPEED SKATING ROAD 200 M (MALE)

On July 6, 2006, inline speed skater Gregory Duggento (Italy) set a new record of 16.209 seconds in the men's 200 m time trial at the 2006 World Road Championships held in Anyang, South Korea.

FIRS INLINE SPEED SKATING TRACK 10,000 M (MALE)

At the 2009 Fédération Internationale de Roller Sports (FIRS) World Roller Speed Skating Championships in Haining, China, Bart Swings (Belgium) won the track 10,000 m event in a record time of 14 min 41.425 sec. He achieved this incredible feat at the age of 18 on September 18, 2009.

FIRS INLINE SPEED SKATING TRACK 300 M (FEMALE)

On the same day of the same 2009 championships, South Korea's So Yeong Shin achieved a record of her own in the junior women's track 300 m. Finishing in a blistering 26.426 seconds, she even outpaced the winner of the senior race, and her time is the overall world record.

YOUNGEST & OLDEST

OLDEST NO.1-RANKED TENNIS PLAYER (MALE)

The oldest male tennis player to be ranked No.1 by the Association of Tennis Professionals (ATP) is Andre Agassi (USA, b. April 29, 1970), who became the highest seeded men's player on May 11, 2003 aged 33 years 13 days. During his career, Agassi was ranked No.1 for a total of 101 weeks.

OLDEST WIMBLEDON TENNIS CHAMPION

Martina Navratilova (USA, b. October 18, 1956) was 46 years 261 days old when she won the mixed doubles with Leander Paes (India) on July 6, 2003.

QUICK SILVER

When Dara Torres (USA, right) won silver at Beijing 2008 to become the **oldest Olympic swimming medalist**, she broke a record that had stood for a century, since 38-year-old William Robinson (UK) won silver at the 1908 Olympic Games.

REDDING WON ROOKIE OF THE YEAR FOR HIS LANDMARK WIN

OLDEST WINNER OF THE FRENCH OPEN TENNIS TOURNAMENT

Elizabeth Ryan (USA, b. February 8, 1892) won the 1934 women's doubles with Simone Mathieu (France) at 42 years 88 days old.

OLDEST DAVIS CUP TENNIS PLAYER

The oldest player ever to take to the court in the Davis Cup team tennis competition is Yaka-Garonfin Koptigan (Togo), who played for his country against Mauritius aged 59 years 147 days on May 27, 2001.

YOUNGEST PLAYER TO WIN A CAREER TENNIS GRAND SLAM (MALE)

Tennis ace Rafael Nadal (Spain) was 24 years 101 days old when he achieved a career Grand Slam – winning all four major tournaments: the French Open, the Australian Open, Wimbledon, and the US Open. He completed the feat by winning the US Open on September 14, 2010.

YOUNGEST RIDER TO WIN A GRAND PRIX

Scott Redding (UK, b. January 4, 1993) won his first Grand Prix motorcycle race aged 15 years 170 days when he took the checkered flag in the British 125 cc Grand Prix at Donington Park, UK, on June 22, 2008.

OLDEST PLAYER TO SCORE IN THE NFL SUPER BOWL

On February 7, 2010, Indianapolis Colts (USA) placekicker Matt Stover (USA) became the oldest American football player ever to score in the NFL's season finale, when, aged 42 years 11 days, he struck a 38-yard field goal against the New Orleans Saints (USA) in Super Bowl XLIV. In taking the field, he had also earned the record for the **oldest player to appear in the Super Bowl**.

YOUNGEST NBA SCORING CHAMPION

At 21 years 197 days old, basketball player Kevin Durant (USA, b. September 29, 1988) of the Oklahoma City Thunder (USA) became the youngest single-season scoring champion in NBA history, averaging 30.1 points per game in 2009–10.

YOUNGEST PLAYER TO HIT 600 HOME RUNS IN AN MLB CAREER

New York Yankees (USA) third baseman Alex Rodriguez (USA, b. July 27, 1975) hit his 600th home run aged 35 years 8 days against the Toronto Blue Jays (Canada) on August 4, 2010. In doing so, "A-Rod" broke the record set by baseball legend "Babe" Ruth (USA, 1895–1948) with a year to spare.

OLDEST ROWER TO WIN THE UNIVERSITY BOAT RACE

Mike Wherley (USA, b. March 15, 1972) was 36 years 14 days old when he helped Oxford beat Cambridge (both UK) in the 2008 river race in London, UK.

YOUNGEST ROWER TO WIN THE UNIVERSITY BOAT RACE

On March 25, 2000, Oxford's Matt Smith (UK, b. July 14, 1981) became the boat race's youngest victor, aged just 18 years 255 days.

YOUNGEST JUDO CHAMPION (MALE)

The youngest male Judoka to win a World Championship is Teddy Riner (France, b. April 7, 1989), who was 18 years 192 days old when he took gold in the Heavyweight category at the 2007 World Championships in Rio de Janeiro, Brazil.

OLDEST OLYMPIC SWIMMING MEDALIST

On August 9, 2008, 41-year-old Dara Torres (USA) defied the years to earn a silver medal for the Americans in the pool at the Beijing Olympics, swimming the anchor leg in the 4 x 100 m freestyle relay.

YOUNGEST FIGURE-SKATING CHAMPION

Tara Lipinski (USA, b. June 10, 1982) won the individual world title on March 22, 1997, aged 14 years 286 days.

The crater of the shield volcano Mount Nyiragongo in the Democratic Republic of the Congo holds the world's **largest lava lake**, measuring 820 ft (250 m) across.

$495 The amount you will spend on antiperspirant and deodorant in your lifetime. You'll spend most of it between the ages of 16 and 24, when you're at your most sporty – and your most self-conscious!

OLDEST PLAYER TO SCORE A GOAL IN THE UEFA CHAMPIONS LEAGUE

On April 26, 2011, Ryan Giggs (UK, b. November 29, 1973) made Champions League history by scoring the opener in Manchester United's (England) 2–0 semi-final win over German side Schalke 04 at the age of 37 years 148 days.

OLDEST PLAYER IN A FIFA WORLD CUP

Roger Milla (Cameroon, b. May 20, 1952) played against Russia at USA '94 on June 28, 1994 aged 42 years 39 days. During the game, he also scored, becoming the **oldest scorer in the FIFA World Cup finals**.

When it comes to sinking putts and pots, these youths are in a league of their own...

Youngest hole-in-one golfer (male):
Christian Carpenter (USA), 4 years 195 days on December 18, 1999.

Youngest hole-in-one golfer (female):
Soona Lee-Tolley (USA), 5 years 103 days on July 1, 2007.

Youngest century-break snooker player:
Michael White (UK), 9 years 268 days on March 24, 2001.

Youngest 147-break snooker player:
Ronnie O'Sullivan (UK), 15 years 98 days on March 13, 1991.

YOUNGEST F1 CHAMPION

Sebastian Vettel (Germany, b. July 3, 1987) clinched his first Formula One title aged 23 years 134 days when he won the Abu Dhabi Grand Prix, UAE, on November 14, 2010, the last day of the season. Before the race, he was trailing Championship leader Fernando Alonso (Spain) by 15 points, but his last-gasp victory saw him just edge past his rival in the standings.

OLDEST PLAYER TO MAKE A FIFA WORLD CUP FINALS DEBUT

David James (UK) made his first FIFA World Cup finals appearance at the ripe old age of 39 years 322 days, playing in goal for England against Algeria in Cape Town, South Africa, on June 18, 2010. The game ended 0–0, giving James a clean sheet on his debut.

YOUNGEST GOLFER TO WIN THE US MASTERS

One of the greatest golfers of all time, Tiger Woods (USA, b. December 30, 1975) was just 21 years 104 days old when he won the 1997 US Masters at Augusta National Golf Club, Georgia, USA, on April 13, 1997. Woods now has 14 major championships to his name, including three further US Masters: 2001, 2002, and 2005.

YOUNGEST GOALKEEPER TO APPEAR IN A UEFA CHAMPIONS LEAGUE FINAL

Iker Casillas (Spain) appeared for Real Madrid against Valencia (both Spain) at the age of 19 years 4 days at the Stade de France in Paris, France, on May 24, 2000. Casillas kept a clean sheet in Real's 3–0 victory.

YOUNGEST GOLFER TO MAKE THE CUT AT THE US MASTERS

Matteo Manassero (Italy, b. April 19, 1993) was just 16 years 355 days old when he made it through the first two rounds of the US Masters tournament held at Augusta National Golf Club, Georgia, USA, on April 9, 2010.

YOUNGEST DRIVER TO WIN AN F1 CHAMPIONSHIP POINT

Three years before he was crowned World Champion, Sebastian Vettel became the youngest driver to claim a point in the Championship, finishing eighth in the US Grand Prix on June 17, 2007, aged 19 years 349 days.

YOUNGEST DRIVER TO FINISH AN F1 WORLD CHAMPIONSHIP RACE

For the new drivers on the grid, the first aim is to get round the track without crashing out. On July 26, 2009, Jaime Alguersuari (Spain, b. March 23, 1990) became the youngest driver to pass this test, racing home in 15th place in the Hungarian Grand Prix, aged 19 years 125 days.

YOUNGEST WINNER OF THE LE MANS 24-HOUR RACE

Before switching to F1, Alexander Wurz (Austria, b. February 15, 1974) cut his teeth in the world's oldest and most prestigious endurance race: the Le Mans 24 Hours. On June 15–16, 1996, driving for Joest Racing (Germany), he became the French event's youngest-ever winner, aged just 22 years 123 days.

YOUNGEST DRIVER TO WIN A NASCAR RACE

On June 28, 2009, Joey Logano (USA, b. May 24, 1990) became the youngest driver to win a NASCAR event, speeding to victory in the Lenox Industrial Tools 301 at New Hampshire Motor Speedway, USA, aged 19 years 35 days.

OLDEST GOAL SCORER IN A UEFA CHAMPIONS LEAGUE FINAL

AC Milan (Italy) captain Paolo Maldini (Italy, b. June 26, 1968) was 36 years 333 days old when he scored the opener in the Champions League final against Liverpool (England) on May 25, 2005. This was the **fastest Champions League goal ever**, coming in the first minute; despite leading 3–0 at halftime, Milan went on to lose on penalties.

BURN RUBBER

Proving that age is no object in sport, Jeannie Reiman (Canada, b. April 19, 1913) became the world's **oldest female racing driver** when she competed in a 10-lap race at Sunset Speedway, Canada, on August 3, 2003, aged 90 years 106 days.

On December 18, 2009, US scientists revealed that they had filmed the **deepest volcanic eruption** on record, more than 3,900 ft (1,200 m) down in the Pacific Ocean, near Samoa. The footage, of the West Mata volcano, was captured by a robotic submersible.

DISTANCE & DURATION

LONGEST RUNNING RACE
The 1929 transcontinental foot race from New York City to Los Angeles, USA, covered a lung-busting 3,635 miles (5,850 km). Finnish-born Johnny Salo won in 79 days, with a time of 525 hr 57 min 20 sec, placing him just 2 min 47 sec ahead of Pietro "Peter" Gavuzzi (UK).

LONGEST INDIVIDUAL TEST CRICKET INNINGS
During a Test match against the West Indies played in Barbados on January 17–23, 1958, Pakistan opener Hanif Mohammad made up for a poor first-innings score of 17 by hitting 337 runs in a heroic knock that saw him remain at the crease for 16 hr 10 min.

LONGEST FEMALE GRAND SLAM TENNIS MATCH
At the 2011 Australian Open, Francesca Schiavone (Italy) beat Svetlana Kuznetsova (Russia) in an epic last-16 match on January 23, 2011. Level after two sets, the pair took 30 games to settle the third, with the Italian finally winning through 4–6, 6–1, 16–14 after 4 hr 44 min.

LONGEST NINE-INNINGS BASEBALL MATCH
On August 18, 2006, the second game of a double-header between fierce rivals the New York Yankees and the Boston Red Sox (both USA) lasted 4 hr 45 min at Fenway Park, Boston, USA, with the Yankees finally emerging victorious by a score of 14–11.

MOST CONSECUTIVE 30-WIN SEASONS TO START AN NHL GOALTENDER CAREER
Since joining the National Hockey League with the New York Rangers (USA), Henrik Lundqvist (Sweden) has become the only goaltender to record five straight seasons with 30-plus wins, achieving the run from 2005/06 to 2009/10.

LONGEST SOCCER TOURNAMENT
With the first ball kicked on January 2 and the trophy lifted on November 14, the 2010 Copa Telmex in Mexico was equivalent in duration to more than 11 back-to-back FIFA World Cups! The competition also qualified as the **largest football tournament**, with 201,287 players and 11,777 teams competing for glory.

LONGEST PRO TENNIS MATCH
On June 22–24, 2010, in the first round of the 2010 Wimbledon Championships (UK), John Isner (USA) and Nicolas Mahut (France) played out the longest match in tennis history, both in terms of time and number of games. After 11 hr 5 min on the court, and 183 games, Isner finally broke Mahut's spirited resistance, winning 6–4, 3–6, 6–7, 7–6, 70–68!

LONGEST GOLF PUTT IN A MAJOR TOURNAMENT
Two players have managed to hole out from 110 ft (33.5 m) in a major: Jack Nicklaus (USA) in the 1964 Tournament of Champions and Nick Price (Zimbabwe) in the 1992 US PGA.

LONGEST DROP GOAL IN RUGBY UNION
Gerald Hamilton Brand scored from 255 ft (77.7 m) for South Africa against England at Twickenham, UK, in 1932.

LONGEST NFL KICK RETURN BY AN OFFENSIVE LINEMAN
Although better known for his strength than his speed, 313-lb (142-kg) New England Patriots lineman Dan Connolly (USA) returned a kick 71 yards against the Green Bay Packers in Foxboro, Massachusetts, USA, on December 19, 2010. He made it to the 4-yard line, only just missing out on a touchdown.

ONLY SKI JUMPER TO WIN THE WORLD CUP THREE TIMES IN A ROW (2001–03)

MOST SKI JUMPS OVER 200 M
One of the greatest ski jumpers in the history of the sport, four-time World Champion Adam Małysz (Poland) passed the 200-m (656-ft) mark a record 106 times in competition between 1994 and 2011. His longest jump ever was 225 m (738 ft) in 2003, which places him joint 10th in the all-time list.

GOING THE DISTANCE
Before the Queensberry Rules brought in round limits in 1867, Jack Jones defeated Patsy Tunney (both UK) in a fight lasting 276 rounds in Cheshire, UK, in 1825 – the **most rounds in a boxing match**.

The **smallest spider** is the Patu marplesi (family *Symphytognathidae*) of Western Samoa. A male found at around 2,000 ft (600 m) in Madolelei on the island of Upolu in January 1965 had a leg-span of just 0.017 in (0.43 mm) – about the size of a period on this page.

449,061 Distance in miles you will travel in the 18,193 hours of your life spent in an automobile – enough to drive to the Moon and then travel around it 31 times at an average speed of 24.7 mi/h.

GUINNESS WORLD RECORDS 2012

FARTHEST HAMMER THROW

On July 6, 2010, Anita Wlodarczyk (Poland) gave the performance of her career to achieve a throw of 256 ft 10 in (78.3 m) at the Enea Cup in Bydgoszcz, Poland, thus breaking her own 2009 world record of 255 ft 9 in (77.96 m).

LONGEST FA CUP TIE

When Alvechurch met Oxford City (both UK) in the fourth qualifying round of the FA Cup in November 1971, the tie went to a record five replays, with Alvechurch breaking the deadlock after 11 hours of play by winning the sixth game 1–0.

LONGEST F1 CIRCUIT

The temporary road circuit at Pescara, Italy, was the longest ever to host a Formula One World Championship race, measuring 16 miles (25.8 km) for its only Grand Prix in 1957. Sections of the circuit ran along a cliff edge in the Abruzzi mountains, while there was also a 4-mile (6.4-km) straight beside the sea, leading many experts to contend that it was the most dangerous F1 track of all time.

LONGEST SOCCER PENALTY SHOOTOUT

In a nail-biting finish, the final of the 2005 Namibian Cup had to be settled by a record-breaking 48 penalty kicks, with KK Palace holding their nerve to defeat the Civics 17–16, following a 2–2 draw in regular time.

LONGEST UNBEATEN RUN AT HOME BY A SOCCER MANAGER

Wherever he has managed, José Mourinho's (Portugal) home ground has been a fortress. Incredibly, he did not taste defeat on home soil for over nine years, between February 22, 2002 and March 12, 2011, during which time he managed Porto (Portugal), Chelsea (England), Inter Milan (Italy), and Real Madrid (Spain). The record run finally came to an end on April 2, 2011, when Real Madrid lost 1–0 to Sporting Gijón (Spain).

LONGEST-SERVING PREMIER LEAGUE SOCCER MANAGER

Sir Alex Ferguson (UK) has managed Manchester United (England) for all 19 seasons since the birth of the Premier League in 1992.

SHORTEST F1 CIRCUIT

By lap distance, the prestigious Circuit de Monaco in Monte Carlo, Monaco, is the shortest on the Formula One race calendar. The course, which has staged races since 1929, has varied in length over the years, with its shortest incarnation between 1929 and 1979, when it measured just 1.9 miles (3.1 km) in length.

- UPDATED RECORD
- NEW RECORD

Far larger than a period, the **heaviest spider** was a captive female goliath bird-eating spider (*Theraphosa blondi*) named Rosi, who weighed 6.17 oz (175 g) on July 27, 2007 and belonged to Walter Baumgartner of Andorf, Austria.

SPORTING FIRSTS

IVANISEVIC HIT 213 ACES AT WIMBLEDON 2001, THE MOST EVER AT A GRAND SLAM

FIRST WILDCARD ENTRANT TO WIN A TENNIS GRAND SLAM

In 2001, Goran Ivanisevic (Croatia) won the men's singles at the Wimbledon Championships (UK). Ranked 125th in the world, Ivanisevic entered the competition as a wildcard and beat Pat Rafter (Australia) 6–3, 3–6, 6–3, 2–6, 9–7 in a nail-biting final.

WILD WOMAN

Ivanisevic's wildcard win has only been equaled once, by Kim Clijsters of Belgium, whose memorable singles victory at the 2009 US Open made her the **first female wildcard to win a grand slam.**

FIRST PERSON TO RUN A MILE IN LESS THAN FOUR MINUTES

On May 6, 1954, Roger Bannister (UK) became the first athlete to run a sub-four-minute mile. In front of a 3,000-strong crowd at Oxford University's Iffley Road track, the 25-year-old recorded a time of 3 min 59.4 sec, achieving what was then believed by many to be an impossible feat.

DECADE AT THE TOP

Joe Louis (USA) was the **first boxing champion to reign for a decade**, holding the heavyweight title for 11 years 252 days (1937–49). Supermiddleweight Joe Calzaghe (UK) achieved the feat in 1997–2007.

FIRST OFFICIAL 147 BREAK IN SNOOKER

On January 22, 1955, Joe Davis (UK) achieved an officially ratified maximum break against Willie Smith (UK) in London. The 147 break requires a player to pot all the balls in one turn and in a specified order – 15 reds (15 points), each followed by the black (105 points), and then all six colours (27 points). The **first televised 147** was achieved by Steve Davis (UK) at the Lada Classic on January 11, 1982.

FIRST BASKETBALL GAME ON TELEVISION

Basketball hit US TV screens on February 28, 1940, when Fordham's match against the University of Pittsburgh (both USA) was aired by broadcaster NBC. Pittsburgh won 57–37.

FIRST CHAMPION BOXER TO GO UNDEFEATED IN A CAREER

Rocky Marciano (USA, right), is the only champion of any division to have won every fight of his professional career, from March 17, 1947 to September 21, 1955. Of his 49 fights, 43 were by either knock-out or stoppage.

FIRST BROADCAST USE OF HAWK-EYE

Hawk-Eye, which tracks and predicts the path of a ball in flight using cameras placed around the playing field, has revolutionized sport. Developed in 1999, Hawk-Eye made its TV debut in 2001 in an England–Pakistan Test match at Lord's cricket ground in London, UK.

FIRST QUADRUPLE JUMP IN ICE-SKATING

On March 25, 1988, Canadian Kurt Browning landed a toe loop jump with four aerial rotations at the World Championships in Hungary.

FIRST PERSON TO RUN 100 M IN LESS THAN 10 SECONDS

At the 1968 Olympics, Jim Hines (USA) earned the title of "fastest man on the planet" when he broke through the 10-second barrier in the 100 m event. With a time of 9.95 seconds, Hines stormed to Olympic gold and set a new record that remained unbroken for 15 years.

The **largest hand-forged horseshoe** is 1 ft 10 in (56 cm) tall and 2 ft (61.5 cm) wide and was created by six clients and two employees of Caritas Tagesstätte Krumbach (all Austria) on June 21, 2008.

4 million

Tennis balls used at the Wimbledon Championships in your lifetime. An amazing 52,000 were supplied by Slazenger in 2010 alone – but what happened to them all afterwards? Each year, the All-England Tennis Club sells the used balls to raise money for charity.

GUINNESS WORLD RECORDS 2012

UPDATED RECORD
NEW RECORD

OLLIE WHO?
Tony Hawk may be the biggest name in skateboarding, but the first ever board trick came long before his time, when in 1976 Alan Gelfand (USA) pioneered the famous "Ollie," one of the most popular jumps in the sport.

FIRST ENGLISH PREMIER LEAGUE SOCCER TEAM TO GO UNBEATEN IN A SEASON

In the 2003/04 season, Arsenal FC emerged unbeaten from all 38 league games, winning 26 and drawing 12. In total, they netted 73 goals and conceded just 26, finishing the season with 90 points following a 2–1 win over Leicester City on May 15, 2004.

TONY HAWK WON 16 MEDALS IN HIS X GAMES CAREER

FIRST GOLDEN GOAL AT A FIFA WORLD CUP

On June 28, 1998, French defender Laurent Blanc scored the first golden goal in World Cup history in a match against Paraguay in Lens, France. Blanc scored in the 113th minute, in the second period of extra time, to give France a 1–0 win and send them into a quarter-final match against European rivals Italy. France went on to win the competition, defeating the favorites, Brazil, 3–0 in the final.

FIRST 900 ON A SKATEBOARD

On June 27, 1999, skateboard legend Tony Hawk (USA) became the first person to achieve a 900 in competition at the ESPN X Games in San Francisco, USA. The trick – two-and-a-half 360° aerial spins – is one of the most difficult in vert skateboarding.

FIRST NFL TEAM TO GO UNBEATEN IN A REGULAR SEASON

The New England Patriots (USA) achieved a 16–0 record in 2007, becoming the first team to finish the regular season undefeated since the NFL switched to a 16-game schedule in 1978. The Patriots eventually reached the Super Bowl, but lost 17–14 to the New York Giants.

FIRST OPENING KICKOFF RETURN FOR A TOUCHDOWN IN THE SUPER BOWL

In Super Bowl XLI, played on February 4, 2007, Chicago Bears receiver Devin Hester (USA) returned the opening kickoff the length of the field for a touchdown. Despite the best start in the history of the Super Bowl, the Bears went on to lose the game to the Indianapolis Colts 29–17.

FIRST ICE HOCKEY TEAM TO WIN WORLD AND OLYMPIC TITLES IN THE SAME YEAR

Having already taken gold at the 2006 Turin Olympics, Sweden's ice hockey team went on to win the world championship with a 4–0 shutout of the Czechs in Riga, Latvia, on May 21, 2006.

FIRST DRIVER TO WIN THE INDIANAPOLIS 500, DAYTONA 500, AND FORMULA 1 WORLD TITLE

Mario Andretti (USA) is the only driver to win the Indy 500 (1969), Daytona 500 (1967), and Formula One world championship (1978) – three of motorsport's most prestigious titles.

Q. Who made the **first double century in a one-day international?**

A. No, not Richards, Lara, or Botham. In fact, it was only in 2010 that a player finally hit a double ton, with India's Sachin Tendulkar making 200 off 147 balls vs South Africa.

Huaso ex-Faithful, the thoroughbred that made the **highest jump by a horse**, was wearing regular horseshoes. On February 5, 1949, the former Chilean racehorse leapt to a height of 8 ft 1.25 in (2.47 m)!

MARATHONS

FASTEST MARATHON

The official IAAF marathon world record is held by Haile Gebrselassie (Ethiopia), who raced home in 2 hr 3 min 59 sec in Berlin, Germany, on September 28, 2008. *(See also button below right and p.230.)*

FASTEST LONDON MARATHON

The fastest man over the London course is Samuel Wanjiru (Kenya, see right), who won the event in 2 hr 5 min 10 sec on April 26, 2009.

Set on April 13, 2003, Paula Radcliffe's (UK) time of 2 hr 15 min 25 sec remains not only the fastest London Marathon (UK) by a female runner but also the fastest marathon by a woman outright (see also p.242).

FASTEST TOKYO MARATHON

Viktor Rothlin (Switzerland) completed the Tokyo Marathon in Tokyo, Japan, in a record 2 hr 7 min 23 sec on February 17, 2008.

Japan's own Mizuho Nasukawa became the fastest female over the distance the following year, recording a time of 2 hr 25 min 38 sec on March 22, 2009.

FASTEST NEW YORK MARATHON

On November 4, 2001, Tesfaye Jifar (Ethiopia) won the New York Marathon in 2 hr 7 min 43 sec, setting a record time that remains unbeaten over a decade later.

Kenyan runner Margaret Okayo set the women's record on November 2, 2003, finishing in 2 hr 22 min 31 sec.

FASTEST CHICAGO MARATHON

Samuel Wanjiru (Kenya, see right) ran the Chicago Marathon in a time of 2 hr 5 min 41 sec on October 11, 2009, thus breaking Khalid Khannouchi's (USA) 10-year-old course record of 2 hr 5 min 42 sec by just one second.

Paula Radcliffe (UK, see left and p.242) holds the female record, winning in 2 hr 17 min 18 sec on October 13, 2002.

FAST FINISH

On April 18, 2011, Kenya's Geoffrey Mutai won the Boston Marathon (USA) in 2 hr 3 min 2 sec, beating Gebrselassie's world record time. However, his effort was not ratified, as the IAAF does not recognize times set in Boston due to the steep drops in elevation.

MOST WINS OF THE WORLD MARATHON MAJORS (MALE)

The World Marathon Majors comprises annual races in London (UK), Berlin (Germany), Boston, Chicago and New York (all USA), with athletes scoring points for top-five finishes over two calendar years. Kenya's Samuel Kamau Wanjiru (1986–2011) is the only man to have won the series twice, in 2008–09 and 2009–10.

MOST WINS OF THE WORLD MARATHON MAJORS (FEMALE)

Irina Mikitenko (Germany) is the most successful female runner in World Marathon Majors history, topping the leaderboard in both 2007–08 and 2008–09.

2011 VIRGIN LONDON MARATHON: NEW WORLD RECORDS

While marathon running is a serious business for elite athletes such as those featured above, for others it is a great excuse to have some fun on the run – and where better to have it than at the world's premier marathon event: the London Marathon?

Since the first London Marathon in 1981, athletes of all ages, shapes, and sizes have donned their running shoes (and many an outrageous costume) to raise some cash for charity. Here, we take a look at some of the key characters from the class of 2011...

- **Fastest in a bomb disposal suit** – John Bedford (UK), 9 hr 40 min 1 sec
- **Fastest on crutches** – John Sandford Hart (UK), 6 hr 24 min 48 sec
- **Fastest by a parent and child (mixed sex, aggregate)** – Libby and Richard Collinson (both UK), 6 hr 22 min 5 sec
- **Fastest by a married couple (aggregate)** – Jez and Lucy Mancer (both UK), 5 hr 46 min 53 sec
- **Fastest carrying a 60-lb pack** – Carl Andrew Creasey (UK), 4 hr 50 min 56 sec
- **Most Rubik's Cubes solved (100)** – Uli Kilian (Germany), 4 hr 45 min 43 sec
- **Fastest as Mr Potato Head** – Peter Barlow (UK), 4 hr 17 min 38 sec
- **Fastest in a wedding dress** – Eleanor Franks (UK), 4 hr 11 min 1 sec
- **Fastest as a vegetable** – Julie Tapley (UK), 4 hr 6 min 17 sec
- **Fastest as a Roman soldier** – Les Slinn (UK), 4 hr 5 min 34 sec
- **Fastest carrying a 40-lb pack** – Lee Riley (UK), 4 hr 1 min 17 sec
- **Fastest as a nun** – Ben Bradley (UK), 4 hr 0 min 28 sec
- **Fastest as an astronaut** – Darren Cox (UK), 3 hr 55 min 21 sec

The **largest bunch of grapes** on record weighed a hefty 20 lb 11.5 oz (9.4 kg) and was grown by Bozzolo Y Perut Ltda of Santiago, Chile, in 1984.

UPDATED RECORD
NEW RECORD

1,200 Pounds of pasta – the most common food eaten the night before a marathon – consumed by you in a lifetime. If your life quota of pasta was produced as a single strand of spaghetti, it would be 106 miles long.

MOST LINKED RUNNERS TO COMPLETE A MARATHON

Paris Centipede (UK) – a team of 53 runners tied together – completed the 2011 Paris Marathon in Paris, France, on April 10, 2011, raising $49,000 for charity.

OLDEST PERSON TO COMPLETE A MARATHON ON EACH CONTINENT

Margaret Hagerty (USA), who ran a marathon on all seven continents between 1995 and 2004, began her quest aged 72 years 225 days and finished aged 81 years 101 days. The **fastest marathon on each continent and at the North Pole (female)** was 324 days by Ginny Turner (USA), starting with the North Pole race on April 8, 2006 and finishing on King George Island, Antarctica, on February 26, 2007.

FASTEST COMPLETION OF 10 MARATHONS IN 10 DAYS (MALE)

Adam Holland (UK) ran 10 marathons in just 32 hr 47 min 3 sec to win the 2009 Brathay Challenge, held at Brathay Hall, Ambleside, UK, between May 8 and 17, 2009. Adam averaged 3 hr 16 min 42 sec per marathon, and beat the previous record holder, Steve Edwards (who came second in 2009), by over two-and-a-half hours.

FASTEST MARATHON BY A MARCHING BAND

The 20 musicians of the Huddersfield University Marching Band (UK) completed the 2011 Virgin London Marathon in 7 hr 55 min in London, UK, on April 17, 2011.

FASTEST MARATHON BAREFOOT

Running without shoes, Abebe Bikila of Ethiopia covered the marathon distance in a (blistering) 2 hr 15 min 16.2 sec at the 1960 Olympic Games in Rome, Italy, on September 10, 1960.

MOST MONEY RAISED BY A MARATHON RUNNER

Marathon man Steve Chalke (UK) raised over £2,000,000 ($3,264,480) in sponsorship money for the charity Oasis UK by completing the Virgin London Marathon in London, UK, on April 17, 2011. In raising the huge sum, Steve beat his own previous record of £1,841,138 ($3,669,325), which he set at the same event, for the same charity, four years earlier on April 22, 2007.

SLOWEST → FASTEST

- **Fastest in a gas mask** – Andy McMahon (UK) – 3 hr 54 min 55 sec
- **Fastest as a bottle (male)** – Gavin Rees (UK) – 3 hr 53 min 26 sec
- **Fastest as a gingerbread man** – David Smith (UK) – 3 hr 42 min 20 sec
- **Fastest as an animal (female, peacock)** – Barbara Stcherbatcheff (USA) – 3 hr 42 min 11 sec
- **Fastest as a sailor** – Subhashis Basu (UK) – 3 hr 24 min 12 sec
- **Fastest as a TV character (male, Captain James T Kirk)** – Simon Bryant (UK) – 3 hr 21 min 20 sec
- **Fastest as a fairy (female)** – Emily Foran (UK) – 3 hr 20 min 52 sec
- **Fastest as a Viking** – Ben Afforselles (UK) – 3 hr 12 min 11 sec
- **Fastest as a jester** – Alexander Scherz (Switzerland) – 3 hr 11 min 57 sec
- **Fastest as a fairy (male)** – David Hellard (UK) – 3 hr 10 min 56 sec
- **Fastest in a police uniform** – Paul Swan (UK) – 3 hr 9 min 52 sec
- **Fastest as an animal (male, ostrich)** – Martin Indge (UK) – 3 hr 4 min 0 sec
- **Fastest as Dennis the Menace** – David Ross (UK) – 3 hr 2 min 30 sec
- **Fastest as a nurse (male)** – Kevin Harvey (UK) – 2 hr 52 min 26 sec
- **Fastest as a superhero (male, Superman)** – David Stone (UK) – 2 hr 42 min 46 sec

Bozzolo's grapes would have provided ample ammunition for champion grape-spitter Anders Rasmussen (Norway), who achieved the world's **longest grape spit** – an astonishing 28 ft 7.25 in (8.72 m) – at Myra, Arendal, Norway, on September 4, 2004.

STRENGTH & ENDURANCE

MOST UFC MIDDLEWEIGHT CHAMPIONSHIPS

As of February 5, 2011, mixed martial artist Anderson Silva (Brazil, left) has won a record nine Middleweight title bouts in the Ultimate Fighting Championship. Known as "The Spider," he is a black belt in Judo, Tae Kwon Do, and Brazilian Jiu-Jitsu.

MOST BOXING TITLES IN DIFFERENT DIVISIONS

Manny Pacquiao (Philippines) has won world titles in eight weight divisions: WBC Super Welterweight, Flyweight, Super Featherweight and Lightweight; The Ring Featherweight; IBF Super Bantamweight; IBO and The Ring Light Welterweight; and WBO Welterweight.

MOST RUNNERS IN AN ULTRA-MARATHON

On May 30, 2010, a record 14,343 runners hit the road for the 85th Comrades Marathon, a grueling 56-mile (89.28-km) race from Pietermaritzburg to Durban, South Africa. The men's race was won by Stephen Muzhingi (Zimbabwe), while Elena Nurgalieva (Russia) was the leading female.

DISCOVER MORE TOUGH GUYS ON P.104.

MOST FLASH KNOCKOUTS

A flash knockout is when a boxer KOs his opponent less than a minute into a fight. Mike Tyson (USA) did this nine times in his pro career (1985–2006), against Trent Singleton (USA) in 52 sec, Ricardo Spain (USA) in 39 sec, Michael Johnson (USA) in 39 sec, Robert Colay (USA) in 37 sec, Sterling Benjamin (Trinidad & Tobago) in 54 sec, Mark Young (USA) in 50 sec, Marvis Frazier (USA) in 30 sec, Lou Savarese (USA) in 38 sec, and Clifford Etienne (USA, below) in 49 sec!

BOXING CLEVER

Another boxer with a killer punch is Tyrone Brunson (USA), who began his career with 19 first-round KOs in a row! His record run ended with a draw against Antonio Soriano (Mexico) on August 15, 2008.

UPDATED RECORD
NEW RECORD

The **longest knitted scarf** is 11,364 ft (3,463.73 m) in length and was completed after 23 years of knitting by Helge Johansen (Norway) in Oslo, Norway, on November 10, 2006.

FASTEST WIN OF THE TOUR DU LÉMAN

The annual Tour du Léman à l'Aviron is the **longest rowing race** in the world, covering 99 miles (160 km) around the circumference of Lake Léman in Switzerland – equivalent to crossing the sea between England and France five times without a break. The fastest race time on record is 11 hr 55 min 19 sec, achieved by Matthias Auer, Olaf Behrend, Jochen Domscheit, Christian Klandt, and Markus Neuman (all Germany), who won the men's coxed fours category in the 2007 race.

FARTHEST BREATH-HOLD SWIM UNDER ICE (FINS AND WETSUIT)

Nikolay Linder (Germany) swam 354 ft (108 m) under ice 1 ft (31 cm) thick at Lake Weissensee, Austria, on January 15, 2011, staying under the freezing water for 1 min 16 sec.

FARTHEST BREATH-HOLD SWIM UNDER WATER (FEMALE)

In Mexico on January 7, 2011, Ai Futaki (Japan) swam under water with and without fins for distances of 328 ft (100 m) and 295 ft (90 m), respectively.

MOST WINS OF THE YUKON QUEST

The Yukon Quest sled dog race, which runs 1,000 miles (1,600 km) between Fairbanks, Alaska, USA, and Whitehorse, Yukon, Canada, has been won four times each by Hans Gatt (Canada), in 2002–04 and 2010, and Lance Mackey (USA), in 2005–08.

MOST WINS OF THE SKYRUNNER WORLD SERIES (FEMALE)

Three athletes have won the women's Skyrunner World Series twice: Angela Mudge (UK) in 2006 and 2007; Corinne Favre (France) in 2005 and 2008; and Emanuela Brizio (Italy) in 2009 and 2010.

MOST WINS OF THE SKYRUNNER WORLD SERIES (MALE)

The annual Skyrunner series of high-altitude endurance races has been won three times each by the Catalan athletes Kilian Jornet Burgada (pictured), in 2007–09, and Agustí Roc Amador, in 2002–04.

ANETA WAS THE FIRST POLISH WOMAN TO LIFT 500 KG (1,102 LB)!

FASTEST CROSSING OF THE USA BY BICYCLE

In the 1992 Race Across America (RAAM), cyclist Rob Kish (USA) pedaled 2,911 miles (4,685 km) from Irvine, California, to Savannah, Georgia, in 8 days 3 hr 11 min – a record that still stands today. The race is one of the most arduous of all cycling ultra-marathons, requiring competitors to cover up to 22 hours per day with little rest or sleep.

MOST WEIGHT LIFTED BY ARM CURLS IN ONE HOUR

Multiple record holder Eamonn Keane (Ireland) curled a total of 51,314 lb 12 oz (23,276 kg) in an hour in Dublin, Ireland, on October 5, 2007. He performed 1,058 reps of a 48-lb 8-oz (22-kg) weight.

From powerful women to muscle-bound men, check out the world's strongest, youngest, oldest, and heaviest!

Most wins of the Strongman World Championships: Mariusz Pudzianowski (Poland) – five, in 2002, 2003, 2005, 2007, and 2008.

Youngest entrant in the Strongman World Championships: Kevin Nee (USA) – 20 years 37 days old at the 2005 competition held in China.

Oldest bodybuilder: Ray Moon (Australia) 81 years old at the 2010 NABBA championships held in Australia.

Heaviest living athlete: Sumo wrestler Emmanuel "Manny" Yarborough (USA) – 708 lb (321 kg).

MOST WINS OF THE STRONGWOMAN WORLD CHAMPIONSHIPS

Aneta Florczyk (Poland) began powerlifting in 1998 at just 16 years old, but by 2003 she had already earned her first Strongwoman world title. Since then, she has achieved three further wins in the competition, in 2005, 2006, and 2008, to become its most successful athlete.

MOST KING OF THE MOUNTAINS TITLES IN THE TOUR DE FRANCE

Richard Virenque (France) has been crowned King of the Mountains seven times, claiming the famous red-and-white polka-dot jersey in 1994–97, 1999, and 2003–04.

In 1995, Belarusian artist Alexander Kishchenko completed the **largest piece of needlework** – a hand-woven tapestry with a total area measuring 2,863 ft² (266 m²).

WINNING WAYS

MOST MATCH WINS IN THE RUGBY UNION SIX NATIONS CHAMPIONSHIP

Since the Five Nations became Six, with the addition of Italy in 2000, France has claimed 44 wins up to the end of the 2011 tournament. Despite England's victory that year, France still holds the **most Six Nations titles**, with five, in 2002, 2004, 2006–07, and 2010.

MOST RUGBY UNION TRI-NATIONS TITLES

New Zealand has won the annual three-way contest with Australia and South Africa a record 10 times, in 1996–97, 1999, 2002–03, 2005–08, and 2010.

MOST DAVIS CUP TENNIS TITLES

The US Davis Cup team has dominated the Davis Cup over the years, recording 32 wins between 1900 and 2007.

MOST CRICKET WORLD CUP TITLES

Since the cricket World Cup began in 1975, the standout team has been Australia, with a total of four wins from nine tournaments: the first in 1987 and the other three, in a row, in 1999, 2003, and 2007.

MOST INDIAN PREMIER LEAGUE TITLES

Cricket's glitziest tournament, the Indian Premier League, started in 2008 and has been won by three separate teams, the Rajasthan Royals (2008), the Deccan Chargers (2009), and the Chennai Super Kings (2010).

MOST SOLHEIM CUP GOLF WINS

The female version of golf's Ryder Cup is contested every two years between Europe and the USA's top players, with the USA coming out on top eight times, in 1990, 1994, 1996, 1998, 2002, 2005, 2007, and 2009.

MOST KITEBOARD FREESTYLE WORLD CHAMPIONSHIPS

The most Kiteboard Pro World Tour Freestyle World Championships won by a male rider is two, by Sebastien Garat (France), in 2006–07. The competition's most successful female is Gisela Pulido (Spain) with three wins, in 2004–06.

MOST CONSECUTIVE WINS OF THE FIS SPEED SKI WORLD CUP

North America's fastest speed skier, Tracie Sachs (USA) won Alpine skiing's greatest prize a record five times in a row, between 2003 and 2007.

MOST ESPN SUMMER X GAMES MEDALS

BMX biker and rally driver Dave Mirra (USA) has won more Summer X Games medals than any other athlete, with 24 as of March 2010.

MOST DAKAR RALLY WINS BY A MANUFACTURER

Between 1985 and 2007, a Mitsubishi Pajero (Japan) won the Dakar Rally on 12 occasions – an exceptional record in what is considered to be the world's most punishing off-road endurance race, covering 3,107 miles (5,000 km) through the deserts, canyons, and mountains of South America. (The rally was formerly held between Paris, France, and Dakar, Senegal, but was relocated in 2009 for security reasons.)

MOST WINS IN A WNBA SEASON

In 2010, the Seattle Storm (USA) won 28 of 34 games on their way to winning the women's National Basketball Association championship.

MOST CAREER WINS, NHRA DRAG RACING

John Force (USA) has finished first in 132 races as of the end of the 2010 season.

MOST HOCKEY ASIA CUP TITLES (MALE)

Two nations have won the Asia Cup a record three times: Pakistan and South Korea. Pakistan led the way in the early years, blitzing their way to three successive titles, in 1982, 1985, and 1989, each time defeating India in the final. South Korea enjoyed wins of their own in 1993 (again against India), 1999, and, more recently, in 2009. Incredibly, India have been in seven out of the tournament's eight finals, winning in 2003 and 2007.

3,368 WINS

McCOY HAS BEEN THE BRITISH JUMP RACING CHAMPION EVERY YEAR SINCE 1996

MOST CAREER STEEPLECHASE WINS

By the end of the 2011 racing season, the 15-times champion jump jockey Tony McCoy (UK, above and inset) had ridden a record 3,368 winners in the course of his career. McCoy brought up an unprecedented 3,000th win on the back of Restless D'Artaix at Plumpton (UK) on February 9, 2009.

UPDATED RECORD
NEW RECORD

On November 15, 1995, Aleksandr Bendikov (Belarus) built the world's **largest coin pyramid**, consisting of 880 coins stacked on the edge of a coin free-standing vertically on a table.

$863 The amount you will spend on soccer match tickets in a lifetime. With the average English Premier League player paid $1,117,480 per year, it would take the lifetime contributions of you and 1,294 of your closest friends to buy his services for a single season.

MOST MOTO GP WORLD TITLES

Valentino Rossi (Italy) has won motorcycle racing's most prestigious prize a record six times, in 2002–05, and 2008–09. He has also won the 125 cc, 250 cc, and 500 cc titles, giving him a total of nine different world championships in a glittering career that began in karting as a five-year-old.

LATEST GOAL TO WIN A FIFA WORLD CUP

In the FIFA World Cup final on July 11, 2010, Spain midfielder Andrés Iniesta (left) made history by netting the winner in the 116th minute to claim the Cup for Spain. The 1–0 victory, over the Netherlands in South Africa, was Spain's first ever World Cup title and the first by a European team on another continent.

MOST D1 GRAND PRIX TITLES

The only driver to win the Japanese Professional Drift Grand Series twice is Youichi Imamura (Japan), in 2003 and 2009.

MOST AFRICA CUP OF NATIONS TITLES

Egypt has proved itself to be the best soccer team in Africa seven times, winning the Africa Cup of Nations in 1957, 1959, 1986, 1998, 2006, 2008, and 2010.

MOST MATCH WINS IN THE UEFA CHAMPIONS LEAGUE

Between September 15, 1993 and May 4, 2011, Manchester United (England) notched up 93 European wins.

MOST UEFA CHAMPIONS LEAGUE TITLES (COUNTRY)

As of April 2011, the Champions League (formerly the European Cup) has been won 12 times each by teams from Spain and Italy. Spain's first triumph came through Real Madrid in 1956, while its most recent was in 2009, with Barcelona. Italy won for the first time with AC Milan in 1963, and is home to the 2010 champions, Inter Milan.

MOST CONSECUTIVE WINS OF A FINA DIVING WORLD CHAMPIONSHIP

Jingjing Guo (China) topped the podium in both the individual and the synchronized 3 m platform in 2001, 2003, 2005, 2007, and 2009. Between her last two victories, the talented diver also won gold in both categories at the 2008 Olympics in Beijing, China.

NEW START

Proving that everyone can be a winner, the Caltech Beavers (USA) college basketball team broke a 310-game losing streak on February 22, 2011 with a 46–45 win over Occidental College (USA). None of the players were alive when the team last won – in 1985.

MOST NBA CHAMPIONSHIPS

The Boston Celtics (USA) are the most successful team in basketball history, winning the NBA title 17 times, in 1956–57, 1958–66, 1967–69, 1973–74, 1975–76, 1980–81, 1983–84, 1985–86, and 2007–08. They have also finished runner-up on four occasions, in 1957–58, 1984–85, 1986–87, and 2009–10, when the Los Angeles Lakers (USA) beat them 4–3 in the NBA Finals, the seven-game season finale.

Tahar Douis (Morocco) supported 12 members of the Hassani Troupe on his shoulders to form the **largest-ever human pyramid**, weighing 1,700 lb (771 kg), at BBC TV studios in Birmingham, UK, on December 17, 1979.

GREAT ACHIEVEMENTS

MOST GAMES PLAYED IN A WNBA CAREER

Since she began her career in 1998, Tangela Smith (USA) has competed in 415 Women's National Basketball Association (WNBA) games, playing forward/center for the Sacramento Monarchs, Charlotte Sting, Phoenix Mercury, and, from February 2011, the Indiana Fever (all USA).

MOST APPEARANCES IN INTERNATIONAL HOCKEY MATCHES

Two-times Olympic hockey champion Teun de Nooijer (Netherlands) made 431 appearances for the Netherlands between 1994 and January 25, 2011.

MOST CONSECUTIVE TENNIS GRAND SLAM SEMIFINALS (MALE)

Between 2004 and 2010, Roger Federer (Switzerland) made a record 23 Grand Slam semifinal appearances in a row. His extraordinary run came to an end when he was beaten by Robin Soderling (Sweden) in the French Open quarterfinals on June 1, 2010.

MOST CONSECUTIVE BWF SUPER SERIES MASTERS FINALS TITLES (SINGLES)

Badminton world No.1 Lee Chong Wei (Malaysia) has won the Badminton World Federation Super Series Masters Finals in every year that it has been held, three times from 2008 to 2010.

MOST FIGURE-SKATING TRIPLE AXELS EXECUTED IN ONE COMPETITION (FEMALE)

During the 2010 Winter Olympic Games in Vancouver, Canada, champion figure skater Mao Asada (Japan) performed the notoriously difficult triple axel – three aerial spins, shown in time-lapse photography below – a record three times: once in her short program on February 23 and twice in her long program on February 25.

MOST CONSECUTIVE WINS IN TWENTY20 INTERNATIONALS

The England cricket team won eight 20-over matches in a row between May 6, 2010 and January 12, 2011, beating Pakistan three times, Australia twice, and South Africa, New Zealand, and Sri Lanka once.

MOST CANADIAN FOOTBALL PASS RECEPTIONS

The Canadian Football League (CFL) record for most career pass receptions is 1,017, by Ben Cahoon (USA) playing for the Montreal Alouettes (Canada) from 1998 to 2010.

MOST CONSECUTIVE MLB SEASONS WITH 200-PLUS HITS

Ichiro Suzuki (Japan) has recorded at least 200 hits in a Major League Baseball season for a record 10 consecutive years while playing for the Seattle Mariners (USA) from 2001 to 2010. Ichiro also holds the record for **most hits in an MLB season**, with an impressive 262 in 2004.

DANCING ON ICE

From the grace of figure skating to the power of NHL ice hockey, Alex Ovechkin (Russia) of the Washington Capitals (USA) is the **fastest player to reach 2,000 career shots on goal**, achieving the feat in 2011 after just 4.5 seasons.

TURN TO P.124 FOR MORE ICY ACHIEVEMENTS.

With 10 victories to his name (1997, 1999–2007), Lahcen Ahansai (Morocco) holds the record for **most wins of the Marathon des Sables**, a six-day ultradistance running race that covers 156 miles (254 km) across the Sahara Desert in Morocco.

78 billion

The incredible number of golf balls that will be produced in your lifetime, which is enough to circle the world 78 times. However, around half of these – 39 billion – will go missing, lost in trees, bushes, ponds, and other hazards.

MOST CONSECUTIVE WINS IN SPAIN'S TOP SOCCER DIVISION

Between October 16, 2010 and February 5, 2011, La Liga champions Barcelona achieved 16 league wins in a row. Spearheaded by Argentina striker Lionel Messi (pictured center), they outscored their opponents by a goal margin of 60–6.

GREATEST COMEBACK IN THE ENGLISH PREMIER LEAGUE

On February 5, 2011, Newcastle United earned a 4–4 draw with Arsenal at St James' Park in Newcastle, UK, after coming back from 4–0 down with four goals in the last 22 minutes.

MOST SCOTTISH PREMIER LEAGUE GOALS

Scottish striker Kris Boyd scored a record 164 goals for Kilmarnock and Rangers between 2001 and 2010.

MOST GOALS SCORED BY A GOALKEEPER

Better known for scoring goals than saving them, São Paulo FC's Rogério Ceni (both Brazil) netted his 100th career goal on March 27, 2011. His long-range free kick secured a 2–1 win over rivals Corinthians.

MOST RUGBY UNION HEINEKEN CUP POINTS

Ronan O'Gara (Ireland) is the most prolific points-scorer in Heineken Cup history, notching up 1,196 points for his province, Munster (Ireland), from 1997 to 2009.

MOST PASS COMPLETIONS IN AN NFL SEASON

In the 2010/11 season, Indianapolis Colts quarterback Peyton Manning (USA) set the National Football League record for most pass completions in a season, throwing 450 successful passes.

MOST KICK RETURNS FOR A TOUCHDOWN IN AN NFL CAREER

The most successful kick returner in American football history is the Chicago Bears' receiver/return specialist Devin Hester (both USA), who had run back a record 14 kicks for touchdowns by the end of the 2010 regular season. Hester's impressive haul came from 10 punts and four kickoffs.

MOST SUMO BOUTS WON IN A CALENDAR YEAR

Hakuhō Shō (Mongolia) grappled his way to a record 86 wins in his 90 regulation bouts in 2009. Promoted to yokozuna, sumo wrestling's top rank, in 2007, Hakuhō has won 18 championship tournaments in his career.

UPDATED RECORD
NEW RECORD

A less punishing but equally impressive feat, the **most wins of the IAAF Half Marathon World Championships (male)** is four, by Zersenay Tadese (Eritrea) in 2006–09.

CAPTAIN MARVELS

MOST SUCCESSFUL UEFA CHAMPIONS LEAGUE CAPTAIN

Carles Puyol (Spain) is one of just two soccer captains to have lifted the UEFA Champions League trophy twice, with Spanish giants FC Barcelona in 2006 and 2009. The only captain to have matched him is the now-retired Paolo Maldini (Italy), who led AC Milan to the title in 2003 and 2007. As of going to press, however, Puyol was in the running for an historic third title, with his side set to face Manchester United (England) in the 2011 final.

MOST CONSECUTIVE TEST WINS BY A CAPTAIN

Between December 26, 2005 and January 2, 2008, the Australia cricket captain Ricky Ponting (pictured holding the trophy) led his team on a record-equaling run of 16 consecutive Test match victories, matching the win streak achieved by his predecessor, Steve Waugh, between October 14, 1999 and February 27, 2001. Ponting skippered his side on the field in all 16 matches, whereas Waugh did so in only 15, having missed the 13th Test match because of a muscle injury.

MOST SUCCESSFUL TEST MATCH CAPTAIN

On December 19, 2010, Ricky Ponting won his 48th Test in charge of Australia in the third Test of the Ashes series against England in Perth, Australia. He is also the **most successful cricket World Cup captain** – with Clive Lloyd of the West Indies – having guided his team to glory in 2003 and 2007.

LONGEST-SERVING TEST MATCH CAPTAIN

Prolific batsman Allan Border led out the Australia Test cricket team 93 times in a row from 1978 to 1994.

OLDEST CAPTAIN TO WIN THE UEFA CHAMPIONS LEAGUE

When Paolo Maldini lifted the Champions League trophy for the second time, in 2007, he became the oldest captain ever to do so. Playing for AC Milan (Italy) at the age of 38 years 331 days, he presided over a 2–1 victory against Liverpool (UK) in Athens, Greece, on May 23. The next season, he broke his own record for the **oldest player to captain a UEFA Champions League team**, when, aged 39 years 239 days, his side drew 0–0 with Arsenal (UK) in London, UK, on February 20, 2008.

YOUNGEST TEST MATCH CRICKET CAPTAIN

On May 6, 2004, Tatenda Taibu (Zimbabwe) was promoted to captain of the Zimbabwe cricket team at the age of 21 years 2 days, taking the helm for a match against Sri Lanka in Harare, Zimbabwe.

MOST RUNS IN A TEST MATCH BY A CAPTAIN

In the first of three Tests against India in 1990, England skipper Graham Gooch smashed 456 runs – 333 in the first innings, 123 in the second – in a 247-run victory at Lord's, UK, on July 26–31.

FIRST MAN TO WIN THE FIFA WORLD CUP AS PLAYER AND MANAGER

Regarded as Germany's greatest ever soccer player, Franz Beckenbauer, aka *Der Kaiser* ("The Emperor"), is the only man to have won the game's premier event both as captain and manager, in 1974 and 1990, respectively. The 1974 triumph was particularly special as it was capped by a 2–1 win over the "Total Football" of the Dutch.

FOR MORE GREAT LEADERS, TURN TO P.156.

MOST MATCHES AS CAPTAIN IN THE FIFA WORLD CUP FINALS

The diminutive genius Diego Maradona led Argentina in 16 World Cup finals matches between 1982 and 1994. In this time, he experienced numerous highs and lows, including lifting the Cup in 1986, losing the final to Beckenbauer's West Germany in 1990, and being sent home for a failed drugs test in 1994.

JACK OF ALL TRADES

Alaa El-din Gabr (Egypt) has captained his country in no fewer than three different sports: swimming (1970–78), modern pentathlon (1980), and tenpin bowling (1997–98).

MOST ODI CRICKET MATCHES AS CAPTAIN

Australian Belinda Clark captained her country in 101 One-Day International matches between 1994 and 2005. Talented with a bat, she also holds the record for the **highest score at a World Cup**, racking up 229 against India in 1997.

According to the World Health Organization's first report on global road safety, Eritrea, in Africa, is the **deadliest place to travel by road** in terms of deaths per capita, with 48 deaths per 100,000 people in 2007.

140,000–1 The odds of you becoming a professional soccer player in your lifetime. Of the world's 7 billion people, only around 50,000 play the game professionally – so keep practising and perhaps one day you'll join them!

LONGEST-SERVING INTERNATIONAL RUGBY UNION CAPTAIN
Springboks legend John Smit skippered the South Africa rugby union team in a record 67 international matches between 2003 and 2009.

MOST SUCCESSFUL RUGBY UNION WORLD CUP CAPTAIN (FEMALE)
On beating England 25–17 in the 2006 IRB World Cup final, New Zealand's Farah Palmer took her title tally to three, having also guided the Black Ferns to victory in 1998 and 2002. Under her decade-long stewardship, from 1996 to 2006, New Zealand lost once – to England in 2001.

MOST RUGBY UNION TRI-NATIONS WON BY A CAPTAIN
Following on from Palmer's success in the women's game, Richie McCaw has demonstrated his own leadership qualities in the men's, steering the New Zealand All Blacks to four wins in the annual Tri-Nations tournament, against Australia and South Africa, in 2006–08 and 2010.

MOST BRITISH AND IRISH LIONS RUGBY UNION TOURS AS CAPTAIN
Only one player has led the Lions on two separate tours: Martin Johnson (UK) in 1997 and 2001. In 1997, the team triumphed in South Africa, while in 2001 they lost a tight series 2–1 in Australia.

- UPDATED RECORD
- NEW RECORD

FIRST CAPTAIN TO WIN THE NFL MVP AWARD UNANIMOUSLY
On February 6, 2011, the New England Patriots' captain and quarterback Tom Brady (USA) was voted Most Valuable Player of 2010, winning every one of the 50 available votes for the first time in the award's 53-year history.

MOST SUCCESSFUL STANLEY CUP ICE HOCKEY CAPTAIN
The only player to captain two teams to the Stanley Cup – the trophy awarded to the annual champion of the National Hockey League – is Mark Messier (Canada), playing center for the Edmonton Oilers (Canada) in 1990 and the New York Rangers (USA) in 1994.

YOUNGEST CAPTAIN TO WIN THE STANLEY CUP
At the age of 21 years 309 days, Sidney Crosby (Canada, b. August 7, 1987) became the youngest captain to win ice hockey's Stanley Cup, when the Pittsburgh Penguins (USA) defeated the Detroit Red Wings (USA) 4–3 in the final game of the 2009 playoffs on June 12. By this time, Crosby already held the record for the **youngest captain of an NHL team**, having been appointed to the position on May 31, 2007 at the age of 19 years 297 days.

MOST SUCCESSFUL RYDER CUP GOLF CAPTAIN
In his time as US captain, Walter Hagen (USA) orchestrated a record four wins in golf's prestigious Ryder Cup contest between the USA and Europe, outwitting his opponents in 1927, 1931, 1935, and 1937.

MOST SUCCESSFUL AFL PREMIERSHIP CAPTAIN
Three captains have won the Australian Football League Premiership title on four occasions: Syd Coventry (Australia) for Collingwood in 1927–30, Dick Reynolds (Australia) for Essendon in 1942, 1946, 1949, and 1950, and Michael Tuck (Australia) for Hawthorn in 1986, 1988–89, and 1991.

MOST CONSECUTIVE AFL MATCHES AS CAPTAIN
Stephen Kernahan (Australia) led the Australian Football League side Carlton 226 times between 1986 and 1997, becoming the club's all-time record goalscorer in the process, with 738 strikes.

LONGEST-SERVING ICE HOCKEY CAPTAIN
Steve Yzerman (Canada) served as captain of the Detroit Red Wings (USA) for 20 years, from 1986 to 2006, leading his team to three Stanley Cup championships (1997–98 and 2002). In recognition, his jersey number, 19, was retired in a ceremony at the team's Joe Louis Arena on January 2, 2007.

Avoiding the perils of the road, the world's **most expensive franked letter** traveled by sea from Mauritius in the Indian Ocean to Bordeaux, France, in 1847. It sold at auction in 1993 for CHF5.75 million ($3.9 million) due to its rare Mauritian stamps.

BIG AIR

FASTEST TIME TO COMPLETE A SKYDIVE ON SIX CONTINENTS

Martin Downs (UK) took 8 days 7 hr 30 min to perform a skydive on six continents: Africa, Europe, South America, North America, Oceania, and finally Asia. Martin completed his last skydive in Nha-Trang, Vietnam, on March 6, 2008.

LARGEST PARACHUTING CANOPY FORMATION (FEMALE)

An international team of 250 female parachutists took part in a canopy formation over Perris Valley, California, USA, on October 17, 1997.

The **largest women's free-flying head-down parachuting formation** consisted of 41 parachutists and was formed by an international team on November 26, 2010.

Eugene Andreev (Russia, then USSR) holds the official World Air Sports Federation (FAI) record for the **longest free-fall parachute jump**. On November 1, 1962, he fell 80,380 ft (24,500 m) – almost as far as the height of the highest mountain in the Solar System, Olympus Mons on the planet Mars – from an altitude of 83,523 ft (25,458 m) near the city of Saratov, Russia.

MOST PARAGLIDING WORLD CHAMPIONSHIPS (FEMALE)

Louise Crandal (Denmark) won three paragliding World Championships, in 1999, 2001, and 2005.

The **most paragliding World Championships won by a national team** is two, by two teams: Switzerland in 1991 and 1993, and the Czech Republic in 2007 and 2009.

MOST WORLD GLIDER AEROBATIC CHAMPIONSHIPS (TEAM)

The greatest number of wins at the World Glider Aerobatic Championships by a national team is eight, by Poland in 1985, 1987, 1989, 1991, 1993, 1999, 2001, and 2003.

MOST PILOTS IN A RED BULL AIR RACE WORLD CHAMPIONSHIP

Fifteen pilots took part in the six races of the 2009 installment of this competition – the seventh championship in the series to date. Paul Bonhomme (UK) won the title that year for the first time.

The **most wins of the World Glider Aerobatic Championships by an individual** is six, by Jerzy Makula (Poland) in 1985, 1987, 1989, 1991, 1993, and 1999.

MOST BASE RACE VICTORIES

The BASE Race is an annual BASE-jumping wingsuit flying contest that has been held three times. Launching themselves into midair from a high point, competitors race over a 2,460-ft (750-m) course; the fastest person to complete the course wins the race. Three Norwegian competitors share the record for most victories, with one win each: Ronny Risvik in 2008, Frode Johannessen in 2009, and Espen Fadnes in 2010.

HIGHEST FLAT SPIN ON INLINE SKATES

Sven Boekhorst (Netherlands) cleared a bar set at 15 ft (4.6 m) with a flat spin on inline skates on the set of *L'Été de Tous les Records* in Biscarrosse, France, on July 1, 2004.

The **highest 900-degree McTwist performed on inline skates off a halfpipe ramp** is 3 ft 9 in (1.15 m), by Kevin Marron (Belgium) on the set of *L'Été de Tous les Records* in La Tranche-sur-Mer, France, on July 28, 2005.

The **highest McTwist on inline skates** is 7 ft 8 in (2.35 m) and was set by Taïg Khris (France) on the set of *L'Été de Tous les Records* in Benodet, France, on August 2, 2004.

Taïg also registered an inline-skate jump of 10 ft 2 in (3.1 m) from a halfpipe on the set of *L'Émission des Records*, Paris, France, on December 6, 2000, the **highest indoor vertical air**.

LONGEST RAMP JUMP ON A SNOWMOBILE

On March 26, 2009, Paul Thacker (USA) carried out a huge 301-ft (91.7-m) jump on a snowmobile – greater than the length of a 747 jumbo jet – in Brainerd, Minnesota, USA.

UPDATED RECORD
NEW RECORD

The **first crossing of the Indian Ocean by a team of eight** was completed by team Pirate Row aboard the Mauritian vessel *Aud Eamus* between April 28 and June 25, 2009.

93 Speed in miles per hour at which the average sneeze leaves the average nose. Unless you catch it in a tissue, the fine mist of mucus and saliva from your nose and mouth can fly up to 16 ft through the air.

LONGEST BACKFLIP

Lukas Steiner (Germany) executed a 13-ft 6-in (4.11-m) backflip on the set of *Zheng Da Zong Yi – Guinness World Records Special* in Beijing, China, on May 25, 2010.

LONGEST JOURNEY KITE SURFING

Phillip McCoy Midler (USA) kite-surfed from South Padre Island to Matagorda (both Texas, USA) between May 10 and 11, 2010, covering 199.63 nautical miles (229.73 miles; 369.71 km).

The **fastest speed kite surfing** was 55.65 knots (64 mi/h; 103 km/h), achieved by Rob Douglas (USA) at the 2010 Luderitz Speed Challenge in Luderitz, Namibia, on October 28, 2010.

LONGEST JOURNEY BY POWERED PARAGLIDER

From May 15 to August 24, 2009, Benjamin Jordan (Canada, above and right) flew west to east across Canada from Tofino (British Columbia) to Bay St Lawrence (Nova Scotia) by powered paraglider, a distance of 4,976 miles (8,008 km).

FASTEST SPEED KITE SURFING (FEMALE)

Charlotte Consorti (France) registered a speed of 50.43 knots (58 mi/h; 93 km/h) while kite surfing at the 2010 Luderitz Speed Challenge in Luderitz, Namibia, on October 28, 2010.

HIGHEST-SCORED HIGH DIVE

In 2000, during the Cliff-Diving World Championships in Kaunolu, Hawaii, USA, Orlando Duque (Colombia) performed a double-back somersault with four twists from 80 ft (24.4 m). For this dive he earned a perfect 10 from all seven judges and scored 159.00 points.

HIGHEST HIGH DIVE FROM A BOARD

The world record high dive from a diving board is 176 ft 10 in (53.9 m) – higher than the Statue of Liberty – by Olivier Favre (Switzerland) at Villers-le-Lac, France, on August 30, 1987.

HIGHEST HIGH JUMP

Javier Sotomayor (Cuba) performed an 8-ft 0.45-in (2.45-m) high jump in Salamanca, Spain, on July 27, 1993.

The **highest indoor high jump** measured 7 ft 11.66 in (2.43 m) and was also achieved by Javier, in Budapest, Hungary, on March 4, 1989.

Stefka Kostadinova (Bulgaria) recorded the **highest high jump by a woman**, which measured 6 ft 10.28 in (2.09 m). She achieved the feat in Rome, Italy, on August 30, 1987.

The **highest indoor high jump by a woman** was 6 ft 9.8 in (2.08 m) and was performed by Kajsa Bergqvist (Sweden) in Arnstadt, Germany, on February 4, 2006.

HIGHEST POLE VAULT

On July 31, 1994, legendary Ukrainian athlete Sergei Bubka launched himself into history's highest pole vault: 20 ft 1.73 in (6.14 m). The feat took place in Sestriere, Italy. The previous year, on February 21, 1993, he had recorded the all-time **highest indoor pole vault**, in Donetsk, Ukraine, reaching 20 ft 2.12 in (6.15 m). The remarkable Bubka broke the world pole-vaulting record 35 times in a 20-year period.

The **highest pole vault by a woman** measured 16 ft 7 in (5.06 m) and was executed by Yelena Isinbayeva (Russia) in Zürich, Switzerland, on August 28, 2009. She also holds the world record for the **highest indoor pole vault by a woman**, clearing 16 ft 4 in (5 m) on February 15, 2009 in Donetsk, Ukraine.

VAULT TO SUCCESS

With two Olympic gold medals and five World Championships (three indoor, two outdoor) to her name, Yelena Isinbayeva has a claim to being the greatest female pole vaulter of all time.

Elsewhere in the Indian Ocean: Huvadhu Atoll in the Maldives covers an area of around 1,120 miles^2 (2,900 km^2) and contains some 255 islands within its boundary, the **most islands within an atoll**.

SPORTING MADNESS

FASTEST BOG SNORKELING TRIATHLON – MALE AND FEMALE

Daniel and Natalie Bent (both UK) are the world's top brother–sister bog snorkeling duo, with Daniel setting the men's triathlon record of 2 hr 21 min 5 sec in July 2009 and Natalie setting the women's record of 2 hr 45 min 40 sec in July 2010.

BOG STANDARD

The World Bog Snorkeling Triathlon, held in Llanwrtyd Wells, UK, consists of a 7.5-mile (12-km) run, a two-way snorkel through a 135-ft (41-m) peat bog, and finally a grueling 19-mile (31-km) cycle race!

Other fast finishes from the wacky world of sport:

Fastest 100 m on a space hopper: 30.2 sec
(Ashrita Furman, USA)

Fastest 100 m while throwing and catching a yo-yo: 13.9 sec
(Taro Yamashita, USA)

Fastest 50 m on can-and-string stilts: 9.7 sec
(Steven Bell, USA)

Fastest ferret over 10 m: 12.59 sec
("Warhol" the albino ferret, owned by Jacqui Adams, UK)

Fastest marathon with an egg and spoon: 3 hr 47 min
(Dale Lyons, UK)

MOST COMPETITORS AT THE WORLD BOG SNORKELING CHAMPIONSHIP

On August 31, 2009, a record 200 bog snorkelers took part in the World Championship at Waen Rhydd peat bog, Llanwrtyd Wells, Wales, UK.

FASTEST WORLD BOG SNORKELING CHAMPIONSHIP WINS

New men's and women's records were set at the 2010 World Championship, with Dan Morgan (UK) snorkeling to victory in 1 min 30.66 sec and Dineka Maguire (Ireland) finishing in 1 min 31.90 sec.

LONGEST-RUNNING MAN vs HORSE RACE

The Man vs Horse Marathon has been held annually since 1980 in Llanwrtyd Wells. The race, between runners and riders on horseback, covers 22 miles (35.4 km) of rugged Welsh terrain.

MOST WINS BY A RUNNER IN THE MAN vs HORSE MARATHON

Just two runners have ever beaten the riders in the Man vs Horse Marathon: Huw Lobb (UK) in 2004 and Florian Holzinger (Germany) in 2007. Lobb's victory earned him a prize of £25,000 ($45,777).

FOR MORE CONVENTIONAL SPORTING SUCCESSES, HAVE A LOOK AT THE GREAT ACHIEVEMENTS ON PAGE 258.

MOST COMPETITORS IN A HIGH-HEEL RACE

On September 11, 2010, 967 runners raced in high heels at Headwaters Park in Fort Wayne, Indiana, USA. The event, staged by Women's Bureau, Inc. (USA), smashed the previous record of 763.

MOST "RINGERS" IN A HORSESHOE-PITCHING WORLD CHAMPIONSHIP (FEMALE)

In the target sport of horseshoe pitching, the aim is to throw horseshoes over stakes in the ground. In 2008, Sylvianne Moisan (Canada) scored a record 126 "ringers" – the horseshoe-pitching equivalent of a bullseye.

LONGEST-RUNNING KUBB CHAMPIONSHIP

Held in Gotland, Sweden, the Kubb World Championship has been running annually since 1995. Kubb is a target sport in which competitors have to knock down wooden blocks by throwing sticks.

MOST MEN'S PEA SHOOTING WORLD CHAMPIONSHIPS

Deadeye Mike Fordham (UK) has blown his way to a record seven Men's Pea Shooting World Championships, in 1977–78, 1981, 1983–85, and 1992.

MOST PEOPLE EXTREME IRONING UNDERWATER

A group of 86 adventurous folk from the National Diving and Activity Centre near Chepstow, Gloucestershire, UK, donned their wetsuits and scuba gear for a 10-minute session of extreme ironing underwater on January 10, 2009.

The **longest milk tooth** is from Ahmed Afrah Ismail (Maldives): 0.91 in (2.3 cm) long, comprising a 0.39-in (1-cm) crown and a 0.51-in (1.3-cm) root.

0.3 Number of skateboards you'll buy in a lifetime – although the average person doesn't own or ride a skateboard. The average skater, however, will buy eight decks and 10 sets of wheels.

FARTHEST WINKLE SPIT

The farthest distance anyone has ever spat a periwinkle is 34 ft 1.4 in (10.4 m). The record is held by Alain Jourden (France), who retained his Winkle Spitting World Championship crown in Moguériec, France, on July 16, 2006 with a spit of 30 ft 9.2 in (9.38 m).

LONGEST-RUNNING FINGER WRESTLING CONTEST

Fingerhakeln (finger-wrestling contests) are known to have been staged in Bavaria, Germany, since the 14th century, when rivals competed for women's favors. The contests continue to this day, and the aim remains the same: to pull your rival (seated opposite) across a table using a finger lash wrapped around your fingers.

FARTHEST CELL PHONE THROW BY AN INDIVIDUAL

On August 12, 2007, Chris Hughff (UK) threw a cell phone a record 314 ft 5 in (95.83 m) at the UK Mobile Throwing Championships. The defending 2006 champ achieved his record throw on the first of three attempts.

HIGHEST BOBBAGE JUMP

In Association Bobbage, competitors wearing flippers must jump into a swimming pool without letting their heads go under the water. The highest ever successful jump is 7 ft 10 in (2.4 m), achieved by Laszlo Fazekas (Hungary) in 2002.

FIRST CHESS BOXING WORLD CHAMPION

The first Chess Boxing World Championship was held in Amsterdam, the Netherlands, in 2003 and was won by Lepe Rubingh (Netherlands). Chess boxing is a hybrid of chess and boxing, alternating between each discipline for a total of 11 brain- and body-bruising rounds. Only boxers who have at least a Class-A chess rating can take part.

MOST WINS OF THE MASHED POTATO WRESTLING CHAMPIONSHIPS

Steve O'Gratin, aka Steve Barone (USA), has won the Mashed Potato Wrestling title a record four times since 2006. The championship, which takes place in Barnesville, Minnesota, USA, is contested in a ring filled to the brim with lashings of mashed potato. Barone, a musician, filmmaker, and comedian, is also the founder of the Mashed Potato Wrestling Federation, which sanctions the event.

MOST GURNING WORLD CHAMPIONSHIP WINS (MALE)

The only male gurner to win the world title an amazing 12 times is Tommy Mattinson (UK), whose flexible face took the top prize at the annual Gurning World Championship at Egremont Crab Fair, Cumbria, UK, in 1986–87 and then 10 times between 1999 and 2010.

WHY THE LONG FACE?

Another face-pulling high-achiever is Anne Woods (UK), who has cringed and contorted her way to 27 Championship wins since 1977, the **most gurning world titles** ever won.

FASTEST 1,000 MARTIAL ARTS SWORD CUTS

Samurai Isao Machii (Japan) sliced through 1,000 rolled straw mats in 36 min 4 sec on the set of *The Best House 123* in Tokyo, Japan, on September 19, 2007.

UPDATED RECORD
NEW RECORD

The **most people brushing their teeth simultaneously in a single venue** is 13,380, at an event staged by Colgate Palmolive (Central America) Inc. at the Cuscatlaiun Stadium, City of San Salvador, El Salvador, on November 5, 2005.

SPORTING EXTREMES

HIGHEST BASE JUMP FROM A BUILDING
On January 5, 2010, Nasser Al Neyadi and Omar Alhegelan (both UAE) performed the highest BASE jump from a building, plummeting 2,205 ft (672 m) from the 160th floor of the Burj Khalifa tower in Dubai, UAE. The duo hit 137 mi/h (220 km/h) before their parachutes opened.

HIGHEST BASE JUMP
To perform the highest BASE jump on record, Australians Glenn Singleman and Heather Swan turned to the mountains of India. On May 23, 2006, they climbed Mount Meru and then, wearing wingsuits and parachutes, leapt from a cliff edge 21,666 ft (6,604 m) to the ground below.

HIGHEST BUNGEE JUMP (COMMERCIAL)
The world's highest bungee jump available to paying customers is the 764-ft (233-m) AJ Hackett Macau Tower Bungy Jump, located on the Macau Tower in Macau, China, and opened on December 17, 2006.

HIGHEST BUNGEE JUMP
Curtis Rivers (UK) performed a bungee jump from a hot-air balloon at 15,200 ft (4,632 m) over Puertollano, Spain, on May 5, 2002.

MOST ULTRA-TRAIL DU MONT BLANC WINS
The 166-mile (267-km) race through the Alps has been won twice by Marco Olmo (Italy), in 2006–07, and Kilian Jornet (Spain), in 2008–09.

HIGHEST SKI-JUMPING HILL
The most forbidding purpose-built ski-jumping slope to regularly host international competition is Vikersundbakken in Vikersund, Norway. Officially ratified at a height of 738 ft (225 m), it is the equivalent of nearly five Statues of Liberty stood one on top of another.

MOST CONSECUTIVE DAYS RUNNING AN ULTRAMARATHON
Extreme athlete Enzo Caporaso (Italy) ran seven ultramarathons in seven consecutive days between June 13 and 19, 2010. All the races covered 62.14 miles (100 km) in Ruffini Park, Turin, Italy, and were sanctioned by the Italian Athletics Federation. Caporaso ran the first in 11 hr 28 min 43 sec, but slowed to 19 hr 23 min 11 sec by his last.

HIGHEST MARATHON
The Everest Marathon in Nepal takes place every two years, setting out from Gorak Shep, at 17,100 ft (5,212 m), and finishing at Namche Bazar, at 11,300 ft (3,444 m). Hari Roka (Nepal) is the event's fastest man, with a time of 3 hr 50 min 23 sec in 2000, while Anna Frost (NZ) is the fastest woman, finishing in 4 hr 35 min 4 sec in 2009.

MOST NORTHERLY MARATHON
The North Pole Marathon has been held annually since 2002, and the course at the geographic North Pole has been certified by the Association of International Marathons and Road Races.

The fastest runner to date is Thomas Maguire (Ireland), who finished in 3 hr 36 min 10 sec in 2007, while the fastest woman is Cathrine Due (Denmark), who achieved a time of 5 hr 7 min 40 sec in 2008.

MOST SOUTHERLY MARATHON
The Antarctica Marathon and Half Marathon are the only sporting events that take place on the world's most southerly continent. Held every February on King George Island, the route runs from the Uruguayan Antarctic base through bases belonging to Russia, Chile, and China. Despite the extreme conditions, the intrepid runners must compete in ordinary running shoes.

LARGEST WAVE SURFED
On January 5, 2008, surfer Mike Parsons (USA) rode a huge wave estimated to be 77 ft (23.4 m) tall at Cortes Bank, an underwater mountain range 100 miles (160 km) off the coast of south California, USA. The fearsome wave was generated by a powerful storm in the area on January 4–6 that resulted in giant swells and buoy readings of 80–100 ft (25–30 m).

The **largest pupusa**, an El Salvadorian tortilla with cheese and meat, measured 10 ft 2 in (3.09 m) in circumference and was made by the Chamber of Commerce El Salvador-California and Liborio Markets, Inc. (both USA) in Los Angeles, USA, on June 3, 2007.

UPDATED RECORD
NEW RECORD

1.7 Weight in tons of cookies you'll eat in a lifetime. Cookies are not traditionally a key element of any athlete's training regime. In a lifetime, you will eat the weight of 10 sumo wrestlers in cookies.

DEEPEST FREEDIVE, NO LIMITS (FEMALE)

Tanya Streeter (UK) only took up freediving at the age of 25, but soon found she had a natural talent for it. On August 17, 2002, she plunged 525 ft (160 m) into waters off the Turks and Caicos Islands, briefly wresting from the men the overall no-limits record.

LARGEST ICE CANOEING RACE: Each year, the icy St Lawrence River in Quebec City, Canada, hosts the world's largest canoe race, with the 2011 event attracting 49 five-man teams.

DEEPEST MAN ON EARTH

Herbert Nitsch is truly the king of the deep, with 31 freediving world records. It is a phenomenal feat, given the risks – up to 40 people die each year diving without oxygen.

FASTEST ROAD RACE

The Silver State Classic, run on Route 318 in Nevada, USA, is the world's fastest road race, with drivers averaging speeds of over 190 mi/h (305 km/h) over the 90-mile (145-km) course. The 2010 winners in the unlimited speed category were Pal-Arvid Blytt and Vegard Robberstad (both Norway), who averaged 183.10 mi/h (294.67 km/h) in a 1986 Pontiac TransAM.

MOST DANGEROUS MOTORSPORTS CIRCUIT

Home to the Isle of Man TT and Manx Grand Prix motorcycle races, the Isle of Man's Snaefell Mountain Course is the most dangerous circuit in the world. Since racing began there in 1911, the treacherous, winding course has claimed 229 lives.

DEEPEST FREEDIVE, NO LIMITS (MALE)

Although Tanya Streeter briefly held the overall no-limits apnea record, it was soon regained by the men, first by Loïc Leferme (France) in 2002 and then by the "Deepest Man on Earth," Herbert Nitsch (Austria), who descended to 702 ft (214 m) near Spetses, Greece, on June 14, 2007.

LONGEST BREATH-HOLD SWIM UNDER WATER (OPEN WATER)

In a single breath, freediver Carlos Coste (Venezuela) managed to cover a record 492 ft 1 in (150 m) submerged in the Dos Ojos cave system in Quintana Roo, Mexico, on November 3, 2010. During the attempt, Coste stayed under for 2 min 32 sec.

HIGHEST-ALTITUDE SCUBA-DIVING

Scuba-dives have been made on several occasions at an altitude of 19,357 ft (5,900 m), in a lagoon in the crater of Licancabur, a volcano on the border between Chile and Bolivia.

HIGHEST-LATITUDE WINDSURFING

On July 14, 1985, Gerard-Jan Goekoop (Netherlands) windsurfed alongside the pack ice of the Arctic Ocean at a latitude of 80°40.3'N, 13°43'E, north of the Spitsbergen archipelago.

HIGHEST-ALTITUDE GOLF COURSE

Located at 13,025 ft (3,970 m) above sea level, the Yak golf course in Kupup, East Sikkim, India, opened to the public on October 10, 2006.

LONGEST SLED-DOG RACE

The Iditarod Trail sled-dog race covers 1,049 miles (1,688 km) across the icy wastes of Alaska, USA. Racers experience extreme weather conditions and temperatures as low as -100°F (-73°C). The **fastest time to complete the Iditarod Trail** is 8 days 18 hr 46 min 39 sec, by John Baker (USA) in 2011.

Another sizeable tortilla dish, the world's **largest flour taco** weighed 1,654 lb (750 kg) and was made by the city of Mexicali and Cocinex SA de CV, in Mexicali, Baja California, Mexico, on March 8, 2003.

SPORTS REFERENCE

MEN'S OUTDOOR 800 M

On August 29, 2010, David Lekuta Rudisha (Kenya) ran the men's 800 m in 1 min 41.01 sec at the IAAF World Challenge in Rieti, Italy, beating the record he had set in Germany a week earlier by eight seconds.

OFFICIAL WEBSITES

ULTRARUNNING
www.iau-ultramarathon.org

TRACK & FIELD
www.iaaf.org

ATHLETICS – OUTDOOR TRACK EVENTS

MEN	TIME	NAME & NATIONALITY	LOCATION	DATE
100 m	9.58	Usain Bolt (Jamaica)	Berlin, Germany	Aug 16, 2009
200 m	19.19	Usain Bolt (Jamaica)	Berlin, Germany	Aug 20, 2009
400 m	43.18	Michael Johnson (USA)	Seville, Spain	Aug 26, 1999
800 m	1:41.01	David Lekuta Rudisha (Kenya)	Rieti, Italy	Aug 29, 2010
1,000 m	2:11.96	Noah Ngeny (Kenya)	Rieti, Italy	Sep 5, 1999
1,500 m	3:26.00	Hicham El Guerrouj (Morocco)	Rome, Italy	Jul 14, 1998
1 mile	3:43.13	Hicham El Guerrouj (Morocco)	Rome, Italy	Jul 7, 1999
2,000 m	4:44.79	Hicham El Guerrouj (Morocco)	Berlin, Germany	Sep 7, 1999
3,000 m	7:20.67	Daniel Komen (Kenya)	Rieti, Italy	Sep 1, 1996
5,000 m	12:37.35	Kenenisa Bekele (Ethiopia)	Hengelo, the Netherlands	May 31, 2004
10,000 m	26:17.53	Kenenisa Bekele (Ethiopia)	Brussels, Belgium	Aug 26, 2005
20,000 m	56:26.00	Haile Gebrselassie (Ethiopia)	Ostrava, Czech Republic	Jun 26, 2007
1 hour	21,285 meters	Haile Gebrselassie (Ethiopia)	Ostrava, Czech Republic	Jun 27, 2007
25,000 m	1:13:55.80	Toshihiko Seko (Japan)	Christchurch, New Zealand	Mar 22, 1981
30,000 m	1:29:18.80	Toshihiko Seko (Japan)	Christchurch, New Zealand	Mar 22, 1981
3,000 m steeplechase	7:53.63	Saif Saaeed Shaheen (Qatar)	Brussels, Belgium	Sep 3, 2004
110 m hurdles	12.87	Dayron Robles (Cuba)	Ostrava, Czech Republic	Jun 12, 2008
400 m hurdles	46.78	Kevin Young (USA)	Barcelona, Spain	Aug 6, 1992
4 x 100 m relay	37.10	Jamaica (Asafa Powell, Nesta Carter, Michael Frater, Usain Bolt)	Beijing, China	Aug 22, 2008
4 x 200 m relay	1:18.68	Santa Monica Track Club, USA (Michael Marsh, Leroy Burrell, Floyd Heard, Carl Lewis)	Walnut, USA	Apr 17, 1994
4 x 400 m relay	2:54.29	USA (Andrew Valmon, Quincy Watts, Harry Reynolds, Michael Johnson)	Stuttgart, Germany	Aug 22, 1993
4 x 800 m relay	7:02.43	Kenya (Joseph Mutua, William Yiampoy, Ismael Kombich, Wilfred Bungei)	Brussels, Belgium	Aug 25, 2006
4 x 1,500 m relay	14:36.23	Kenya (Geoffrey Rono, Augustine Choge, William Tanui, Gideon Gathimba)	Brussels, Belgium	Sep 4, 2009

ATHLETICS – OUTDOOR TRACK EVENTS

WOMEN	TIME	NAME & NATIONALITY	LOCATION	DATE
100 m	10.49	Florence Griffith-Joyner (USA)	Indianapolis, USA	Jul 16, 1988
200 m	21.34	Florence Griffith-Joyner (USA)	Seoul, South Korea	Sep 29, 1988
400 m	47.60	Marita Koch (GDR)	Canberra, Australia	Oct 6, 1985
800 m	1:53.28	Jarmila Kratochvílová (Czechoslovakia)	Munich, Germany	Jul 26, 1983
1,000 m	2:28.98	Svetlana Masterkova (Russia)	Brussels, Belgium	Aug 23, 1996
1,500 m	3:50.46	Qu Yunxia (China)	Beijing, China	Sep 11, 1993
1 mile	4:12.56	Svetlana Masterkova (Russia)	Zurich, Switzerland	Aug 14, 1996
2,000 m	5:25.36	Sonia O'Sullivan (Ireland)	Edinburgh, UK	Jul 8, 1994
3,000 m	8:06.11	Wang Junxia (China)	Beijing, China	Sep 13, 1993
5,000 m	14:11.15	Tirunesh Dibaba (Ethiopia)	Oslo, Norway	Jun 6, 2008
10,000 m	29:31.78	Wang Junxia (China)	Beijing, China	Sep 8, 1993
20,000 m	1:05:26.60	Tegla Loroupe (Kenya)	Borgholzhausen, Germany	Sep 3, 2000
1 hour	18,517 meters	Dire Tune (Ethiopia)	Ostrava, Czech Republic	Jun 12, 2008
25,000 m	1:27:05.90	Tegla Loroupe (Kenya)	Mengerskirchen, Germany	Sep 21, 2002
30,000 m	1:45:50.00	Tegla Loroupe (Kenya)	Warstein, Germany	Jun 6, 2003
3,000 m steeplechase	8:58.81	Gulnara Samitova-Galkina (Russia)	Beijing, China	Aug 17, 2008
100 m hurdles	12.21	Yordanka Donkova (Bulgaria)	Stara Zagora, Bulgaria	Aug 20, 1988
400 m hurdles	52.34	Yuliya Pechonkina (Russia)	Tula, Russia	Aug 8, 2003
4 x 100 m relay	41.37	GDR (Silke Gladisch, Sabine Rieger, Ingrid Auerswald, Marlies Göhr)	Canberra, Australia	Oct 6, 1985
4 x 200 m relay	1:27.46	United States "Blue" (LaTasha Jenkins, LaTasha Colander-Richardson, Nanceen Perry, Marion Jones)	Philadelphia, USA	Apr 29, 2000
4 x 400 m relay	3:15.17	USSR (Tatyana Ledovskaya, Olga Nazarova, Maria Pinigina, Olga Bryzgina)	Seoul, South Korea	Oct 1, 1988
4 x 800 m relay	7:50.17	USSR (Nadezhda Olizarenko, Lyubov Gurina, Lyudmila Borisova, Irina Podyalovskaya)	Moscow, Russia	Aug 5, 1984

UPDATED RECORD
NEW RECORD

WOMEN'S INDOOR 4 x 800 M

The Russian team of Yekaterina Martynova, Aleksandra Bulanova, Anna Balakshina, and Elena Kofanova (pictured left to right) recorded a time of 8 min 6.24 sec in the 4 x 800 m at the Russian Indoor Championships in Moscow on February 18, 2011. In doing so, the quartet shaved more than six seconds off the previous record, set by another Russian team in 2010.

In 1997, Mexican Sergio Rodriguez Villarreal crafted the **largest ornamental Christmas candle**, measuring 12 ft 9 in (3.9 m) tall and 10 ft 2 in (3.1 m) wide. It featured 1,789 pieces of mirrored glass and 1,164 bottles.

TRACK AND FIELD – INDOOR TRACK EVENTS

MEN	TIME	NAME & NATIONALITY	LOCATION	DATE
50 m	5.56	Donovan Bailey (Canada)	Reno, USA	Feb 9, 1996
60 m	6.39 6.39	Maurice Greene (USA) Maurice Greene (USA)	Madrid, Spain Atlanta, USA	Feb 3, 1998 Mar 3, 2001
200 m	19.92	Frank Fredericks (Namibia)	Liévin, France	Feb 18, 1996
400 m	44.57	Kerron Clement (USA)	Fayetteville, USA	Mar 12, 2005
800 m	1:42.67	Wilson Kipketer (Denmark)	Paris, France	Mar 9, 1997
1,000 m	2:14.96	Wilson Kipketer (Denmark)	Birmingham, UK	Feb 20, 2000
1,500 m	3:31.18	Hicham El Guerrouj (Morocco)	Stuttgart, Germany	Feb 2, 1997
1 mile	3:48.45	Hicham El Guerrouj (Morocco)	Ghent, Belgium	Feb 12, 1997
3,000 m	7:24.90	Daniel Komen (Kenya)	Budapest, Hungary	Feb 6, 1998
5,000 m	12:49.60	Kenenisa Bekele (Ethiopia)	Birmingham, UK	Feb 20, 2004
50 m hurdles	6.25	Mark McKoy (Canada)	Kobe, Japan	Mar 5, 1986
60 m hurdles	7.30	Colin Jackson (GB)	Sindelfingen, Germany	Mar 6, 1994
4 x 200 m relay	1:22.11	Great Britain & Northern Ireland (Linford Christie, Darren Braithwaite, Ade Mafe, John Regis)	Glasgow, UK	Mar 3, 1991
4 x 400 m relay	3:02.83	USA (Andre Morris, Dameon Johnson, Deon Minor, Milton Campbell)	Maebashi, Japan	Mar 7, 1999
4 x 800 m relay	7:13.94	Global Athletics & Marketing, USA (Joey Woody, Karl Paranya, Rich Kenah, David Krummenacker)	Boston, USA	Feb 6, 2000
5,000 m walk	18:07.08	Mikhail Shchennikov (Russia)	Moscow, Russia	Feb 14, 1995
WOMEN	**TIME**	**NAME & NATIONALITY**	**LOCATION**	**DATE**
50 m	5.96	Irina Privalova (Russia)	Madrid, Spain	Feb 9, 1995
60 m	6.92 6.92	Irina Privalova (Russia) Irina Privalova (Russia)	Madrid, Spain Madrid, Spain	Feb 11, 1993 Feb 9, 1995
200 m	21.87	Merlene Ottey (Jamaica)	Liévin, France	Feb 13, 1993
400 m	49.59	Jarmila Kratochvílová (Czechoslovakia)	Milan, Italy	Mar 7, 1982
800 m	1:55.82	Jolanda Ceplak (Slovenia)	Vienna, Austria	Mar 3, 2002
1,000 m	2:30.94	Maria de Lurdes Mutola (Mozambique)	Stockholm, Sweden	Feb 25, 1999
1,500 m	3:58.28	Yelena Soboleva (Russia)	Moscow, Russia	Feb 18, 2006
1 mile	4:17.14	Doina Melinte (Romania)	East Rutherford, USA	Feb 9, 1990
3,000 m	8:23.72	Meseret Defar (Ethiopia)	Stuttgart, Germany	Feb 3, 2007
5,000 m	14:24.37	Meseret Defar (Ethiopia)	Stockholm, Sweden	Feb 18, 2009
50 m hurdles	6.58	Cornelia Oschkenat (GDR)	Berlin, Germany	Feb 20, 1988
60 m hurdles	7.68	Susanna Kallur (Sweden)	Karlsruhe, Germany	Feb 10, 2008
4 x 200 m relay	1:32.41	Russia (Yekaterina Kondratyeva, Irina Khabarova, Yuliya Pechonkina, Yulia Gushchina)	Glasgow, UK	Jan 29, 2005
4 x 400 m relay	3:23.37	Russia (Yulia Gushchina, Olga Kotlyarova, Olga Zaytseva, Olesya Krasnomovets)	Glasgow, UK	Jan 28, 2006
4 x 800 m relay	•8:06.24	Moscow (Aleksandra Bulanova, Yekaterina Martynova, Elena Kofanova, Anna Balakshina)	Moscow, Russia	Feb 18, 2011
3,000 m walk	11:40.33	Claudia Stef (Romania)	Bucharest, Romania	Jan 30, 1999

• Still awaiting ratification at the time of going to press

TRACK AND FIELD – ULTRA LONG DISTANCE (TRACK)

MEN	TIME/DISTANCE	NAME & NATIONALITY	LOCATION	DATE
50 km	2:48:06	Jeff Norman (GB)	Timperley, UK	Jun 7, 1980
100 km	6:10:20	Donald Ritchie (GB)	London, UK	Oct 28, 1978
100 miles	11:28:03	Oleg Kharitonov (Russia)	London, UK	Oct 20, 2002
1,000 km	5 days 16:17:00	Yiannis Kouros (Greece)	Colac, Australia	Nov 26–Dec 1, 1984
1,000 miles	11 days 13:54:58	Peter Silkinas (Lithuania)	Nanango, Australia	Mar 11–23, 1998
6 hours	60.4 miles (97.2 km)	Donald Ritchie (GB)	London, UK	Oct 28, 1978
12 hours	100.91 miles (162.4 km)	Yiannis Kouros (Greece)	Montauban, France	Mar 15–16, 1985
24 hours	188.59 miles (303.506 km)	Yiannis Kouros (Greece)	Adelaide, Australia	Oct 4–5, 1997
48 hours	294.21 miles (473.495 km)	Yiannis Kouros (Greece)	Surgères, France	May 3–5, 1996
6 days	645.51 miles (1,038.851 km)	Yiannis Kouros (Greece)	Colac, Australia	Nov 20–26, 2005
WOMEN	**TIME/DISTANCE**	**NAME & NATIONALITY**	**LOCATION**	**DATE**
50 km	3:18:52	Carolyn Hunter-Rowe (GB)	Barry, UK	Mar 3, 1996
100 km	7:14:06	Norimi Sakurai (Japan)	Verona, Italy	Sep 27, 2003
100 miles	14:25:45	Edit Bérces (Hungary)	Verona, Italy	Sep 21–22, 2002
1,000 km	7 days 1:28:29	Eleanor Robinson (GB)	Nanango, Australia	Mar 11–18, 1998
1,000 miles	13 days 1:54:02	Eleanor Robinson (GB)	Nanango, Australia	Mar 11–23, 1998
6 hours	57.7 miles (83.2 km)	Norimi Sakurai (Japan)	Verona, Italy	Sep 27, 2003
12 hours	91.71 miles (147.6 km)	Ann Trason (USA)	Hayward, USA	Aug 3–4, 1991
24 hours	158.09 miles (254.425 km)	Kudo Mami (Japan)	Taipei, Taiwan	Dec 12–13, 2009
48 hours	246.75 miles (397.103 km)	Inagiki Sumie (Japan)	Surgères, France	May 21–23, 2010
6 days	549.06 miles (883.631 km)	Sandra Barwick (New Zealand)	Campbelltown, Australia	Nov 18–24, 1990

WOMEN'S 48 HOURS (TRACK)

On May 21–23, 2010, Inagiki Sumie (Japan) broke the 48-hour track record at Surgères, France, with a distance of 246.75 miles (397.103 km). Above, she is seen completing a 24-hour race in Finland in January 2010.

Energisa Sergipe (Brazil) organized the creation of the **largest Christmas tree structure**, a 419-ft 10-in-tall (127.99-m) decorated tree that was exhibited in Aracaju, Sergipe, Brazil, in December 2009.

SPORTS REFERENCE

15 KM ROAD RACE

Leonard Patrick Komon (Kenya) won the 15 km road race in a record time of 41 min 13 sec in Nijmegen, the Netherlands, on November 21, 2010, adding to the 10 km record he achieved two months earlier.

TRACK AND FIELD – ROAD RACE

MEN	TIME	NAME & NATIONALITY	LOCATION	DATE
10 km	26:44	Leonard Patrick Komon (Kenya)	Utrecht, the Netherlands	Sep 26, 2010
15 km	41:13	Leonard Patrick Komon (Kenya)	Nijmegen, the Netherlands	Nov 21, 2010
20 km	55:21	Zersenay Tadese (Eritrea)	Lisbon, Portugal	Mar 21, 2010
Half marathon	58:23	Zersenay Tadese (Eritrea)	Lisbon, Portugal	Mar 21, 2010
25 km	1:11:50	Samuel Kiplimo Kosgei (Kenya)	Berlin, Germany	May 9, 2010
30 km	1:27:49	Haile Gebrselassie (Ethiopia)	Berlin, Germany	Sep 20, 2009
Marathon	2:03:59	Haile Gebrselassie (Ethiopia)	Berlin, Germany	Sep 28, 2008
100 km	6:13:33	Takahiro Sunada (Japan)	Tokoro, Japan	Jun 21, 1998
Road relay	1:57:06	Kenya (Josephat Ndambiri, Martin Mathathi, Daniel Mwangi, Mekubo Mogusu, Onesmus Nyerere, John Kariuki)	Chiba, Japan	Nov 23, 2005
WOMEN	**TIME**	**NAME & NATIONALITY**	**LOCATION**	**DATE**
10 km	30:21	Paula Radcliffe (GB)	San Juan, Puerto Rico	Feb 23, 2003
15 km	46:28	Tirunesh Dibaba (Ethiopia)	Nijmegen, the Netherlands	Nov 15, 2009
20 km	•1:02:36	Mary Jepkosgei Keitany (Kenya)	Ras Al Khaimah, UAE	Feb 18, 2011
Half marathon	•1:05:50	Mary Jepkosgei Keitany (Kenya)	Ras Al Khaimah, UAE	Feb 18, 2011
25 km	•1:19:53	Mary Jepkosgei Keitany (Kenya)	Berlin, Germany	May 9, 2010
30 km	1:38:49	Mizuki Noguchi (Japan)	Berlin, Germany	Sep 25, 2005
Marathon	2:15:25	Paula Radcliffe (GB)	London, UK	Apr 13, 2003
100 km	6:33:11	Tomoe Abe (Japan)	Tokoro, Japan	Jun 25, 2000
Road relay	2:11:41	China (Jiang Bo, Dong Yanmei, Zhao Fengting, Ma Zaijie, Lan Lixin, Li Na)	Beijing, China	Feb 28, 1998

• *Still awaiting ratification at the time of going to press*

TRACK AND FIELD – RACE WALKING

MEN	TIME	NAME & NATIONALITY	LOCATION	DATE
20,000 m	1:17:25.6	Bernardo Segura (Mexico)	Bergen, Norway	May 7, 1994
20 km (road)	1:17:16	Vladimir Kanaykin (Russia)	Saransk, Russia	Sep 29, 2007
30,000 m	2:01:44.1	Maurizio Damilano (Italy)	Cuneo, Italy	Oct 3, 1992
50,000 m	•3:35:27.2	Yohann Diniz (France)	Reims, France	Mar 12, 2011
50 km (road)	3:34:14	Denis Nizhegorodov (Russia)	Cheboksary, Russia	May 11, 2008
WOMEN	**TIME**	**NAME & NATIONALITY**	**LOCATION**	**DATE**
10,000 m	41:56.23	Nadezhda Ryashkina (USSR)	Seattle, USA	Jul 24, 1990
20,000 m	1:26:52.3	Olimpiada Ivanova (Russia)	Brisbane, Australia	Sep 6, 2001

• *Still awaiting ratification at the time of going to press*

50,000 M RACE WALK

Yohann Diniz (France) completed the 50,000 m race walk in a world record 3 hr 35 min 27.2 sec in Reims, France, on March 12, 2011.

TRACK AND FIELD – INDOOR FIELD EVENTS

MEN	RECORD	NAME & NATIONALITY	LOCATION	DATE
High jump	7 ft 11.66 in (2.43 m)	Javier Sotomayor (Cuba)	Budapest, Hungary	Mar 4, 1989
Pole vault	20 ft 2.12 in (6.15 m)	Sergei Bubka (Ukraine)	Donetsk, Ukraine	Feb 21, 1993
Long jump	28 ft 10.06 in (8.79 m)	Carl Lewis (USA)	New York City, USA	Jan 27, 1984
Triple jump	•58 ft 9.51 in (17.92 m)	Teddy Tamgho (France)	Paris, France	Mar 6, 2011
Shot	74 ft 4.12 in (22.66 m)	Randy Barnes (USA)	Los Angeles, USA	Jan 20, 1989
Heptathlon*	•6,568 points	Ashton Eaton (USA)	Tallinn, Estonia	Feb 6, 2011
WOMEN	**RECORD**	**NAME & NATIONALITY**	**LOCATION**	**DATE**
High jump	6 ft 9.8 in (2.08 m)	Kajsa Bergqvist (Sweden)	Arnstadt, Germany	Feb 4, 2006
Pole vault	16 ft 4 in (5.00 m)	Yelena Isinbayeva (Russia)	Donetsk, Ukraine	Feb 15, 2009
Long jump	24 ft 2.15 in (7.37 m)	Heike Drechsler (GDR)	Vienna, Austria	Feb 13, 1988
Triple jump	50 ft 4.72 in (15.36 m)	Tatyana Lebedeva (Russia)	Budapest, Hungary	Mar 6, 2004
Shot	73 ft 9.82 in (22.50 m)	Helena Fibingerová (Czechoslovakia)	Jablonec, Czechoslovakia	Feb 19, 1977
Pentathlon†	4,991 points	Irina Belova (EUN)	Berlin, Germany	Feb 15, 1992

* 60 m, 6.66 seconds; long jump, 7.77 m; shot, 14.45 m; high jump, 2.01 m; 60 m hurdles, 7.60 seconds; pole vault, 5.20 m; 1,000 m, 2 min 34.74 sec

† 60 m hurdles, 8.22 seconds; high jump, 1.93 m; shot, 13.25 m; long jump, 6.67 m; 800 m, 2 min 10.26 sec

• *Still awaiting ratification at the time of going to press*

The **largest published book** is a 128-page edition of Antoine de Saint-Exupéry's *The Little Prince* measuring 6 ft 7 in (2.01 m) high and 10 ft 1 in (3.08 m) wide when open. It was published by Ediouro Publicações SA (Brazil) in 2007.

● UPDATED RECORD
● NEW RECORD

29.5 Length, in feet, of your intestines. If you were to stretch them all out in a straight line, they would extend slightly farther than the current men's long jump world record of 8.95 m.

TRACK AND FIELD – OUTDOOR FIELD EVENTS

MEN	RECORD	NAME & NATIONALITY	LOCATION	DATE
High jump	2.45 m (8 ft 0.45 in)	Javier Sotomayor (Cuba)	Salamanca, Spain	Jul 27, 1993
Pole vault	6.14 m (20 ft 1.73 in)	Sergei Bubka (Ukraine)	Sestriere, Italy	Jul 31, 1994
Long jump	8.95 m (29 ft 4.36 in)	Mike Powell (USA)	Tokyo, Japan	Aug 30, 1991
Triple jump	18.29 m (60 ft 0.78 in)	Jonathan Edwards (GB)	Gothenburg, Sweden	Aug 7, 1995
Shot	23.12 m (75 ft 10.23 in)	Randy Barnes (USA)	Los Angeles, USA	May 20, 1990
Discus	74.08 m (243 ft 0.53 in)	Jürgen Schult (USSR)	Neubrandenburg, Germany	Jun 6, 1986
Hammer	86.74 m (284 ft 7 in)	Yuriy Sedykh (USSR)	Stuttgart, Germany	Aug 30, 1986
Javelin	98.48 m (323 ft 1.16 in)	Jan Železný (Czech Republic)	Jena, Germany	May 25, 1996
Decathlon*	9,026 points	Roman Šebrle (Czech Republic)	Götzis, Austria	May 27, 2001

* 100 m, 10.64 seconds; long jump, 8.11 m; shot, 15.33 m; high jump, 2.12 m; 400 m, 47.79 seconds; 110 m hurdles, 13.92 seconds; discus, 47.92 m; pole vault, 4.80 m; javelin, 70.16 m; 1,500 m, 4 min 21.98 sec

WOMEN	RECORD	NAME & NATIONALITY	LOCATION	DATE
High jump	2.09 m (6 ft 10.28 in)	Stefka Kostadinova (Bulgaria)	Rome, Italy	Aug 30, 1987
Pole vault	5.06 m (16 ft 7.21 in)	Yelena Isinbayeva (Russia)	Zurich, Switzerland	Aug 28, 2009
Long jump	7.52 m (24 ft 8.06 in)	Galina Chistyakova (USSR)	St Petersburg, Russia	Jun 11, 1988
Triple jump	15.50 m (50 ft 10.23 in)	Inessa Kravets (Ukraine)	Gothenburg, Sweden	Aug 10, 1995
Shot	22.63 m (74 ft 2.94 in)	Natalya Lisovskaya (USSR)	Moscow, Russia	Jun 7, 1987
Discus	76.80 m (252 ft)	Gabriele Reinsch (GDR)	Neubrandenburg, Germany	Jul 9, 1988
● Hammer	78.30 m (256 ft 10.67 in)	Anita Wlodarczyk (Poland)	Bydgoszcz, Poland	Jun 6, 2010
Javelin	72.28 m (253 ft 6 in)	Barbora Špotáková (Czech Republic)	Stuttgart, Germany	Sep 13, 2008
Heptathlon†	7,291 points	Jacqueline Joyner-Kersee (USA)	Seoul, South Korea	Sep 24, 1988
Decathlon**	8,358 points	Austra Skujyte (Lithuania)	Columbia, USA	Apr 15, 2005

† 100 m hurdles, 12.69 seconds; high jump, 1.86 m; shot, 15.80 m; 200 m, 22.56 seconds; long jump, 7.27 m; javelin, 45.66 m; 800 m, 2 min 8.51 sec

** 100 m, 12.49 seconds; long jump, 6.12 m; shot, 16.42 m; high jump, 1.78 m; 400 m, 57.19 seconds; 100 m hurdles, 14.22 seconds; discus, 46.19 m; pole vault, 3.10 m; javelin, 48.78 m; 1,500 m, 5 min 15.86 sec

WOMEN'S JAVELIN

Barbora Špotáková (Czech Republic) achieved a distance of 253 ft 6 in (72.28 m) in the first round of the 2008 IAAF World Athletics Final in Stuttgart, Germany, on September 13, 2008.

CYCLING – ABSOLUTE TRACK

MEN	TIME/DISTANCE	NAME & NATIONALITY	LOCATION	DATE
200 m (flying start)	9.572	Kevin Sireau (France)	Moscow, Russia	May 30, 2009
500 m (flying start)	24.758	Chris Hoy (GB)	La Paz, Bolivia	May 13, 2007
Team 750 m (standing start)	42.950	Great Britain (Chris Hoy, Jason Kenny, Jamie Staff)	Beijing, China	Aug 15, 2008
1 km (standing start)	58.875	Arnaud Tournant (France)	La Paz, Bolivia	Oct 10, 2001
● 4 km (standing start)	4:10.534	Jack Bobridge (Australia)	Sydney, Australia	Feb 2, 2011
Team 4 km (standing start)	3:53.314	Great Britain (Ed Clancy, Paul Manning, Geraint Thomas, Bradley Wiggins)	Beijing, China	Aug 18, 2008
1 hour	*49.7 km	Ondrej Sosenka (Czech Republic)	Moscow, Russia	Jul 19, 2005

WOMEN	TIME/DISTANCE	NAME & NATIONALITY	LOCATION	DATE
● 200 m (flying start)	10.793	Simona Krupeckaite (Lithuania)	Moscow, Russia	May 29, 2010
500 m (flying start)	29.655	Erika Salumäe (USSR)	Moscow, Russia	Aug 6, 1987
500 m (standing start)	33.296	Simona Krupeckaite (Lithuania)	Pruszków, Poland	Mar 25, 2009
● Team 500 m (standing start)	32.923	Australia (Kaarle McCulloch, Anna Meares)	Copenhagen, Denmark	Mar 25, 2010
● 3 km (standing start)	3:22.269	Sarah Hammer (USA)	Aguascalientes, Mexico	May 11, 2010
● Team 3 km (standing start)	3:19.569	USA (Sarah Hammer, Lauren Tamayo, Dotsie Bausch)	Aguascalientes, Mexico	May 12, 2010
1 hour	*46.065 km	Leontien Zijlaard-Van Moorsel (Netherlands)	Mexico City, Mexico	Oct 1, 2003

** Some athletes achieved better distances within an hour with bicycles that are no longer allowed by the Union Cycliste Internationale (UCI). The 1-hour records given here are in accordance with the new UCI rules.*

OFFICIAL WEBSITES

ATHLETICS & RACE WALKING
www.iaaf.org

CYCLING
www.uci.ch

● TEAM 500 M STANDING START

On March 25, 2010, Kaarle McCulloch (left) and Anna Meares (both Australia) achieved the fastest-ever team sprint by a female pair, winning the event in 32.923 seconds and breaking their own world record for a second time on the same day.

The **largest coloring book** is a super-sized version of a popular coloring book aimed at teaching young people to brush their teeth. It measures 5 ft 10 in (1.8 m) high and 4 ft 11 in (1.5 m) long and was created by Salma Al-Jeddi (Kuwait) in 2008.

SPORTS REFERENCE

WOMEN'S FREEDIVING, VARIABLE WEIGHT

On October 5, 2010, Annelie Pompe (Sweden) achieved a record depth of 413 ft 4 in (126 m) in the variable weight discipline in Sharm el Sheik, Egypt.

FREEDIVING

MEN'S DEPTH DISCIPLINES	DEPTH/TIME	NAME & NATIONALITY	LOCATION	DATE
Constant weight with fins	124 m (406 ft 9 in)	Herbert Nitsch (Austria)	The Bahamas	Apr 22, 2010
Constant weight without fins	101 m (331 ft 4 in)	William Trubridge (New Zealand)	The Bahamas	Dec 16, 2010
Variable weight	142 m (465 ft 10 in)	Herbert Nitsch (Austria)	The Bahamas	Dec 7, 2009
No limit	214 m (702 ft)	Herbert Nitsch (Austria)	Spetses, Greece	Jun 14, 2007
Free immersion	• 121 m (393 ft 8 in)	William Trubridge (New Zealand)	The Bahamas	Apr 10, 2011
MEN'S DYNAMIC APNEA	**DEPTH/TIME**	**NAME & NATIONALITY**	**LOCATION**	**DATE**
With fins	265 m (869 ft 5 in)	Dave Mullins (New Zealand)	Porirua, New Zealand	Sep 2, 2010
Without fins	218 m (715 ft 2 in)	Dave Mullins (New Zealand)	Porirua, New Zealand	Sep 27, 2010
MEN'S STATIC APNEA	**DEPTH/TIME**	**NAME & NATIONALITY**	**LOCATION**	**DATE**
Duration	11 min 35 sec	Stephane Mifsud (France)	Hyères, France	Jun 8, 2009
WOMEN'S DEPTH DISCIPLINES	**DEPTH/TIME**	**NAME & NATIONALITY**	**LOCATION**	**DATE**
Constant weight with fins	• 100 m (328 ft 1 in)	Natalia Molchanova (Russia)	The Bahamas	Apr 16, 2011
Constant weight without fins	62 m (203 ft 5 in)	Natalia Molchanova (Russia)	The Bahamas	Dec 3, 2009
Variable weight	126 m (413 ft 4 in)	Annelie Pompe (Sweden)	Sharm el Sheik, Egypt	Oct 5, 2010
No limit	160 m (524 ft 11 in)	Tanya Streeter (USA)	Turks and Caicos Islands	Aug 17, 2002
Free immersion	85 m (278 ft 10 in)	Natalia Molchanova (Russia)	Crete, Greece	Jul 27, 2008
WOMEN'S DYNAMIC APNEA	**DEPTH/TIME**	**NAME & NATIONALITY**	**LOCATION**	**DATE**
With fins	225 m (738 ft 2 in)	Natalia Molchanova (Russia)	Moscow, Russia	Apr 25, 2010
Without fins	60 m (524 ft 11 in)	Natalia Molchanova (Russia)	Aarhus, Denmark	Aug 20, 2009
WOMEN'S STATIC APNEA	**DEPTH/TIME**	**NAME & NATIONALITY**	**LOCATION**	**DATE**
Duration	8 min 23 sec	Natalia Molchanova (Russia)	Aarhus, Denmark	Aug 21, 2009

• Still awaiting ratification at the time of going to press

ROWING

MEN	TIME	NAME & NATIONALITY	LOCATION	DATE
Single sculls	6:33.35	Mahe Drysdale (New Zealand)	Poznan, Poland	Aug 29, 2009
Double sculls	6:03.25	Jean-Baptiste Macquet, Adrien Hardy (France)	Poznan, Poland	Jun 17, 2006
Quadruple sculls	5:36.20	Christopher Morgan, James McRae, Brendan Long, Daniel Noonan (Australia)	Beijing, China	Aug 10, 2008
Coxless pairs	6:14.27	Matthew Pinsent, James Cracknell (GB)	Seville, Spain	Sep 21, 2002
Coxless fours	5:41.35	Sebastian Thormann, Paul Dienstbach, Philipp Stüer, Bernd Heidicker (Germany)	Seville, Spain	Sep 21, 2002
Coxed pairs*	6:42.16	Igor Boraska, Tihomir Frankovic, Milan Razov (Croatia)	Indianapolis, USA	Sep 18, 1994
Coxed fours*	5:58.96	Matthias Ungemach, Armin Eichholz, Armin Weyrauch, Bahne Rabe, Jörg Dederding (Germany)	Vienna, Austria	Aug 24, 1991
Eights	5:19.85	Deakin, Beery, Hoopman, Volpenhein, Cipollone, Read, Allen, Ahrens, Hansen (USA)	Athens, Greece	Aug 15, 2004
LIGHTWEIGHT	**TIME**	**NAME & NATIONALITY**	**LOCATION**	**DATE**
Single sculls*	6:47.82	Zac Purchase (GB)	Eton, UK	Aug 26, 2006
Double sculls	6:10.02	Mads Rasmussen, Rasmus Quist (Denmark)	Amsterdam, the Netherlands	Jun 23, 2007
Quadruple sculls*	5:45.18	Francesco Esposito, Massimo Lana, Michelangelo Crispi, Massimo Guglielmi (Italy)	Montreal, Canada	Aug 1992
Coxless pairs*	6:26.61	Tony O'Connor, Neville Maxwell (Ireland)	Paris, France	1994
Coxless fours	5:45.60	Thomas Poulsen, Thomas Ebert, Eskild Ebbesen, Victor Feddersen (Denmark)	Lucerne, Switzerland	Jul 9, 1999
Eights*	5:30.24	Altena, Dahlke, Kobor, Stomporowski, Melges, März, Buchheit, Von Warburg, Kaska (Germany)	Montreal, Canada	Aug 1992
WOMEN	**TIME**	**NAME & NATIONALITY**	**LOCATION**	**DATE**
Single sculls	7:07.71	Rumyana Neykova (Bulgaria)	Seville, Spain	Sep 21, 2002
Double sculls	6:38.78	Georgina and Caroline Evers-Swindell (New Zealand)	Seville, Spain	Sep 21, 2002
Quadruple sculls	6:10.80	Kathrin Boron, Katrin Rutschow-Stomporowski, Jana Sorgers, Kerstin Köppen (Germany)	Duisburg, Germany	May 19, 1996
Coxless pairs	6:53.80	Georgeta Andrunache, Viorica Susanu (Romania)	Seville, Spain	Sep 21, 2002
Coxless fours*	6:25.35	Robyn Selby Smith, Jo Lutz, Amber Bradley, Kate Hornsey (Australia)	Eton, UK	Aug 26, 2006
Eights	5:55.50	Mickelson, Whipple, Lind, Goodale, Sickler, Cooke, Shoop, Francia, Davies (USA)	Eton, UK	Aug 27, 2006
LIGHTWEIGHT	**TIME**	**NAME & NATIONALITY**	**LOCATION**	**DATE**
Single sculls*	7:28.15	Constanta Pipota (Romania)	Paris, France	Jun 19, 1994
Double sculls	6:49.77	Dongxiang Xu, Shimin Yan (China)	Poznan, Poland	Jun 17, 2006
Quadruple sculls*	6:23.96	Hua Yu, Haixia Chen, Xuefei Fan, Jing Liu (China)	Eton, UK	Aug 27, 2006
Coxless pairs*	7:18.32	Eliza Blair, Justine Joyce (Australia)	Aiguebelette-le-Lac, France	Sep 7, 1997

** Denotes non-Olympic boat classes*

The **largest gathering of people dressed as nurses** was achieved by 116 participants at an event organized by the Kuwait Medical Students' Association at Dar Al Shifa Hospital in Kuwait on October 11, 2008.

1,491 Length, in miles, of the airways in your lungs – more than seven times as long as the New York City subway. Flattened out, your lungs would cover about 807 ft^2 – an area the size of half a tennis court inside your chest.

SPEED SKATING – LONG TRACK

MEN	TIME/POINTS	NAME & NATIONALITY	LOCATION	DATE
500 m	34.03	Jeremy Wotherspoon (Canada)	Salt Lake City, USA	Nov 9, 2007
2 x 500 m	68.31	Jeremy Wotherspoon (Canada)	Calgary, Canada	Mar 15, 2008
1,000 m	1:06.42	Shani Davis (USA)	Salt Lake City, USA	Mar 7, 2009
1,500 m	1:41.04	Shani Davis (USA)	Salt Lake City, USA	Dec 11, 2009
3,000 m	3:37.28	Eskil Ervik (Norway)	Calgary, Canada	Nov 5, 2005
5,000 m	6:03.32	Sven Kramer (Netherlands)	Calgary, Canada	Nov 17, 2007
10,000 m	12:41.69	Sven Kramer (Netherlands)	Salt Lake City, USA	Mar 10, 2007
500/1,000/500/1,000 m	137.230 points	Jeremy Wotherspoon (Canada)	Calgary, Canada	Jan 18–19, 2003
500/3,000/1,500/5,000 m	146.365 points	Erben Wennemars (Netherlands)	Calgary, Canada	Aug 12–13, 2005
500/5,000/1,500/10,000 m	145.742 points	Shani Davis (USA)	Calgary, Canada	Mar 18–19, 2006
Team pursuit (eight laps)	3:37.80	Netherlands (Sven Kramer, Carl Verheijen, Erben Wennemars)	Salt Lake City, USA	Mar 11, 2007
WOMEN	**TIME/POINTS**	**NAME & NATIONALITY**	**LOCATION**	**DATE**
500 m	37.00	Jenny Wolf (Germany)	Salt Lake City, USA	Dec 11, 2009
2 x 500 m	74.42	Jenny Wolf (Germany)	Salt Lake City, USA	Mar 10, 2007
1,000 m	1:13.11	Cindy Klassen (Canada)	Calgary, Canada	Mar 25, 2006
1,500 m	1:51.79	Cindy Klassen (Canada)	Salt Lake City, USA	Nov 20, 2005
3,000 m	3:53.34	Cindy Klassen (Canada)	Calgary, Canada	Mar 18, 2006
5,000 m	•6:42.66	Martina Sáblíková (Czech Republic)	Salt Lake City, USA	Feb 18, 2011
500/1,000/500/1,000 m	149.305 points 149.305 points	Monique Garbrecht-Enfeldt (Germany) Cindy Klassen (Canada)	Salt Lake City, USA Calgary, Canada	Jan 11–12, 2003 Mar 24–25, 2006
500/1,500/1,000/3,000 m	155.576 points	Cindy Klassen (Canada)	Calgary, Canada	Mar 15–17, 2001
500/3,000/1,500/5,000 m	154.580 points	Cindy Klassen (Canada)	Calgary, Canada	Mar 18–19, 2006
Team pursuit (six laps)	2:55.79	Canada (Kristina Groves, Christine Nesbitt, Brittany Schussler)	Calgary, Canada	Dec 6, 2009

• Still awaiting ratification at the time of going to press

WOMEN'S 500 M LONG TRACK

Jenny Wolf (Germany) sped to a new world record of 37 seconds in the 500 m event at the ISU World Cup Speed Skating Championships in Salt Lake City, USA, on December 11, 2009.

SPEED SKATING – SHORT TRACK

MEN	TIME/POINTS	NAME & NATIONALITY	LOCATION	DATE
500 m	40.651	Sung Si-Bak (South Korea)	Marquette, USA	Nov 14, 2009
1,000 m	1:23.454	Charles Hamelin (Canada)	Montreal, Canada	Jan 18, 2009
1,500 m	2:10.639	Ahn Hyun-Soo (South Korea)	Marquette, USA	Oct 24, 2003
3,000 m	4:32.646	Ahn Hyun-Soo (South Korea)	Beijing, China	Dec 7, 2003
5,000 m relay	6:38.486	South Korea (Kwak Yoon-Gy, Lee Ho-Suk, Lee Jung-Su, Sung Si-Bak)	Salt Lake City, USA	Oct 19, 2008
WOMEN	**TIME/POINTS**	**NAME & NATIONALITY**	**LOCATION**	**DATE**
500 m	42.609	Wang Meng (China)	Beijing, China	Nov 29, 2008
1,000 m	1:29.049	Zhou Yang (China)	Vancouver, Canada	Feb 26, 2010
1,500 m	2:16.729	Zhou Yang (China)	Salt Lake City, USA	Feb 9, 2008
3,000 m	4:46.983	Jung Eun-Ju (South Korea)	Harbin, China	Mar 15, 2008
3,000 m relay	4:06.610	China (Sun Linlin, Wang Meng, Zhang Hui, Zhou Yang)	Vancouver, Canada	Feb 24, 2010

OFFICIAL WEBSITES
FREEDIVING
www.aida-international.org
ROWING
www.worldrowing.com
SPEED SKATING
www.isu.org

WOMEN'S 1,000 M SHORT TRACK

On February 26, 2010, China's Zhou Yang broke the 1,000 m short track world speed skating record by almost half a second, achieving a time of 1 min 29.049 sec at the 2010 Vancouver Winter Olympics in Vancouver, Canada.

UPDATED RECORD
NEW RECORD

Laurence Wicks (UK) completed the **fastest marathon dressed as a doctor (male)** in 4 hr 16 min 9 sec at the Leicester Marathon in Leicester, UK, on August 10, 2010.

SPORTS REFERENCE

MEN'S 100 M FREESTYLE

On July 30, 2009, Cesar Cielo Filho (Brazil) broke the men's 100 m long-course freestyle world record by just 0.03 seconds, finishing in a time of 46.91 seconds in the event's final at the 13th FINA World Championships in Rome, Italy.

WOMEN'S 200 M BUTTERFLY

China's Liu Zige – pictured while competing in the 2009 FINA World Championships in Rome, Italy – claimed the world record in the 200 m long-course butterfly on October 21 of the same year, covering the distance in a time of just 2 min 1.81 sec in Jinan, China.

SWIMMING – LONG COURSE (50 M POOL)

MEN	TIME	NAME & NATIONALITY	LOCATION	DATE
50 m freestyle	20.91	Cesar Cielo Filho (Brazil)	Sao Paulo, Brazil	Dec 18, 2009
100 m freestyle	46.91	Cesar Cielo Filho (Brazil)	Rome, Italy	Jul 30, 2009
200 m freestyle	1:42.00	Paul Biedermann (Germany)	Rome, Italy	Jul 28, 2009
400 m freestyle	3:40.07	Paul Biedermann (Germany)	Rome, Italy	Jul 26, 2009
800 m freestyle	7:32.12	Zhang Lin (China)	Rome, Italy	Jul 29, 2009
1,500 m freestyle	14:34.56	Grant Hackett (Australia)	Fukuoka, Japan	Jul 29, 2001
4 x 100 m freestyle relay	3:08.24	USA (Michael Phelps, Garrett Weber-Gale, Cullen Jones, Jason Lezak)	Beijing, China	Aug 11, 2008
4 x 200 m freestyle relay	6:58.55	USA (Michael Phelps, Ricky Berens, David Walters, Ryan Lochte)	Rome, Italy	Jul 31, 2009
50 m butterfly	22.43	Rafael Muñoz (Spain)	Malaga, Spain	Apr 5, 2009
100 m butterfly	49.82	Michael Phelps (USA)	Rome, Italy	Aug 1, 2009
200 m butterfly	1:51.51	Michael Phelps (USA)	Rome, Italy	Jul 29, 2009
50 m backstroke	24.04	Liam Tancock (UK)	Rome, Italy	Aug 2, 2009
100 m backstroke	51.94	Aaron Peirsol (USA)	Indianapolis, USA	Jul 8, 2009
200 m backstroke	1:51.92	Aaron Peirsol (USA)	Rome, Italy	Jul 31, 2009
50 m breaststroke	26.67	Cameron van der Burgh (South Africa)	Rome, Italy	Jul 29, 2009
100 m breaststroke	58.58	Brenton Rickard (Australia)	Rome, Italy	Jul 27, 2009
200 m breaststroke	2:07.31	Christian Sprenger (Australia)	Rome, Italy	Jul 30, 2009
200 m medley	1:54.10	Ryan Lochte (USA)	Rome, Italy	Jul 30, 2009
400 m medley	4:03.84	Michael Phelps (USA)	Beijing, China	Aug 10, 2008
4 x 100 m medley relay	3:27.28	USA (Aaron Peirsol, Eric Shanteau, Michael Phelps, David Walters)	Rome, Italy	Aug 2, 2009
WOMEN	**TIME**	**NAME & NATIONALITY**	**LOCATION**	**DATE**
50 m freestyle	23.73	Britta Steffen (Germany)	Rome, Italy	Aug 2, 2009
100 m freestyle	52.07	Britta Steffen (Germany)	Rome, Italy	Jul 31, 2009
200 m freestyle	1:52.98	Federica Pellegrini (Italy)	Rome, Italy	Jul 29, 2009
400 m freestyle	3:59.15	Federica Pellegrini (Italy)	Rome, Italy	Jul 26, 2009
800 m freestyle	8:14.10	Rebecca Adlington (UK)	Beijing, China	Aug 16, 2008
1,500 m freestyle	15:42.54	Kate Ziegler (USA)	Mission Viejo, USA	Jun 17, 2007
4 x 100 m freestyle relay	3:31.72	Netherlands (Inge Dekker, Ranomi Kromowidjojo, Femke Heemskerk, Marleen Veldhuis)	Rome, Italy	Jul 26, 2009
4 x 200 m freestyle relay	7:42.08	China (Yang Yu, Zhu Qian Wei, Liu Jing, Pang Jiaying)	Rome, Italy	Jul 30, 2009
50 m butterfly	25.07	Therese Alshammar (Sweden)	Rome, Italy	Jul 31, 2009
100 m butterfly	56.06	Sarah Sjöström (Sweden)	Rome, Italy	Jul 27, 2009
200 m butterfly	2:01.81	Liu Zige (China)	Jinan, China	Oct 21, 2009
50 m backstroke	27.06	Zhao Jing (China)	Rome, Italy	Jul 30, 2009
100 m backstroke	58.12	Gemma Spofforth (UK)	Rome, Italy	Jul 28, 2009
200 m backstroke	2:04.81	Kirsty Coventry (Zimbabwe)	Rome, Italy	Aug 1, 2009
50 m breaststroke	29.80	Jessica Hardy (USA)	Federal Way, USA	Aug 7, 2009
100 m breaststroke	1:04.45	Jessica Hardy (USA)	Federal Way, USA	Aug 7, 2009
200 m breaststroke	2:20.12	Annamay Pierse (Canada)	Rome, Italy	Jul 30, 2009
200 m medley	2:06.15	Ariana Kukors (USA)	Rome, Italy	Jul 27, 2009
400 m medley	4:29.45	Stephanie Rice (Australia)	Beijing, China	Aug 10, 2008
4 x 100 m medley relay	3:52.19	China (Zhao Jing, Chen Huijia, Jiao Liuyang, Li Zhesi)	Rome, Italy	Aug 1, 2009

UK cricketer David Gower batted for 119 Test match innings in a row without being dismissed for a duck (zero runs) between 1982 and 1990, the **most consecutive Test match innings without a duck**.

SWIMMING – SHORT COURSE (25 M POOL)

MEN	TIME	NAME & NATIONALITY	LOCATION	DATE
50 m freestyle	20.30	Roland Schoeman (South Africa)	Pietermaritzburg, South Africa	Aug 8, 2009
100 m freestyle	44.94	Amaury Leveaux (France)	Rijeka, Croatia	Dec 13, 2008
200 m freestyle	1:39.37	Paul Biedermann (Germany)	Berlin, Germany	Nov 15, 2009
400 m freestyle	3:32.77	Paul Biedermann (Germany)	Berlin, Germany	Nov 14, 2009
800 m freestyle	7:23.42	Grant Hackett (Australia)	Melbourne, Australia	Jul 20, 2008
1,500 m freestyle	14:10.10	Grant Hackett (Australia)	Perth, Australia	Aug 7, 2001
4 x 100 m freestyle relay	3:03.30	USA (Nathan Adrian, Matt Grevers, Garrett Weber-Gale, Michael Phelps)	Manchester, UK	Dec 19, 2009
● 4 x 200 m freestyle relay	6:49.04	Russia (Nikita Lobintsev, Danila Izotov, Evgeny Lagunov, Alexander Sukhorukov)	Dubai, UAE	Dec 16, 2010
50 m butterfly	21.80	Steffen Deibler (Germany)	Berlin, Germany	Nov 14, 2009
100 m butterfly	48.48	Evgeny Korotyshkin (Russia)	Berlin, Germany	Nov 15, 2009
200 m butterfly	1:49.11	Kaio Almeida (Brazil)	Stockholm, Sweden	Nov 10, 2009
50 m backstroke	22.61	Peter Marshall (USA)	Singapore	Nov 22, 2009
100 m backstroke	48.94	Nick Thoman (USA)	Manchester, UK	Dec 18, 2009
200 m backstroke	1:46.11	Arkady Vyatchanin (Russia)	Berlin, Germany	Nov 15, 2009
50 m breaststroke	25.25	Cameron van der Burgh (South Africa)	Berlin, Germany	Nov 14, 2009
100 m breaststroke	55.61	Cameron van der Burgh (South Africa)	Berlin, Germany	Nov 15, 2009
200 m breaststroke	2:00.67	Daniel Gyurta (Hungary)	Istanbul, Turkey	Dec 13, 2009
100 m medley	50.76	Peter Mankoc (Slovenia)	Istanbul, Turkey	Dec 12, 2009
● 200 m medley	1:50.08	Ryan Lochte (USA)	Dubai, UAE	Dec 17, 2010
● 400 m medley	3:55.50	Ryan Lochte (USA)	Dubai, UAE	Dec 16, 2010
4 x 100 m medley relay	3:19.16	Russia (Stanislav Donets, Sergey Geybel, Evgeny Korotyshkin, Danila Izotov)	St Petersburg, Russia	Dec 20, 2009
WOMEN	**TIME**	**NAME & NATIONALITY**	**LOCATION**	**DATE**
50 m freestyle	23.25	Marleen Veldhuis (Netherlands)	Manchester, UK	Apr 13, 2008
100 m freestyle	51.01	Lisbeth Trickett (Australia)	Hobart, Australia	Aug 10, 2009
200 m freestyle	1:51.17	Federica Pellegrini (Italy)	Istanbul, Turkey	Dec 13, 2009
400 m freestyle	3:54.92	Joanne Jackson (UK)	Leeds, UK	Aug 8, 2009
800 m freestyle	8:04.53	Alessia Filippi (Italy)	Rijeka, Croatia	Dec 12, 2008
1,500 m freestyle	15:28.65	Lotte Friis (Denmark)	Birkerod, Denmark	Nov 28, 2009
4 x 100 m freestyle relay	3:28.22	Netherlands (Hinkelien Schreuder, Inge Dekker, Ranomi Kromowidjojo, Marleen Veldhuis)	Amsterdam, the Netherlands	Dec 19, 2008
● 4 x 200 m freestyle relay	7:35.94	China (Chen Qian, Tang Yi, Kiu Jing, Zhu Qianwei)	Dubai, UAE	Dec 15, 2010
50 m butterfly	24.38	Therese Alshammar (Sweden)	Singapore	Nov 22, 2009
100 m butterfly	55.05	Diane Bui-Duyet (France)	Istanbul, Turkey	Dec 12, 2009
200 m butterfly	2:00.78	Liu Zige (China)	Berlin, Germany	Nov 15, 2009
50 m backstroke	25.70	Sanja Jovanovic (Croatia)	Istanbul, Turkey	Dec 12, 2009
100 m backstroke	55.23	Sakai Shiho (Japan)	Berlin, Germany	Nov 15, 2009
200 m backstroke	2:00.18	Sakai Shiho (Japan)	Berlin, Germany	Nov 14, 2009
50 m breaststroke	28.80	Jessica Hardy (USA)	Berlin, Germany	Nov 15, 2009
100 m breaststroke	1:02.70	Rebecca Soni (USA)	Manchester, UK	Dec 19, 2009
200 m breaststroke	2:14.57	Rebecca Soni (USA)	Manchester, UK	Dec 18, 2009
100 m medley	57.74	Hinkelien Schreuder (Netherlands)	Berlin, Germany	Nov 15, 2009
200 m medley	2:04.60	Julia Smit (USA)	Manchester, UK	Dec 19, 2009
400 m medley	4:21.04	Julia Smit (USA)	Manchester, UK	Dec 18, 2009
4 x 100 m medley relay	3:47.97	USA (Margaret Hoelzer, Jessica Hardy, Dana Vollmer, Amanda Weir)	Manchester, UK	Dec 18, 2009

● MEN'S 4 x 200 M FREESTYLE RELAY

Nikita Lobintsev, Danila Izotov, Evgeny Lagunov, and Alexander Sukhorukov (all Russia) swam the men's 4 x 200 m freestyle relay in 6 min 49.04 sec at the 10th FINA World Swimming Championships (25 m) in Dubai, UAE, on December 16, 2010.

OFFICIAL WEBSITE

SWIMMING: Federation Internationale de Natation

www.fina.org

WOMEN'S 200 M BREASTSTROKE

On December 18, 2009, during the Duel in the Pool in Manchester, UK, Rebecca Soni (USA) swam the women's 200 m short-course breaststroke in a record time of 2 min 14.57 sec.

● UPDATED RECORD
● NEW RECORD

Sri Lankan Muttiah Muralitharan has recorded the **most man of the series awards in Test cricket by an individual player**, with 11 titles between 1992 and 2009.

SPORTS REFERENCE

● MEN'S 69 KG: CLEAN & JERK, TOTAL

Liao Hui (China) achieved records of 198 kg in the clean & jerk category and 358 kg in the total category at the World Championships in Antalya, Turkey, on September 21, 2010. These feats earned him a second 69 kg World Championships gold medal to add to the one he picked up a year earlier competing in Goyang, South Korea (pictured).

OFFICIAL WEBSITES
WEIGHTLIFTING
www.iwf.net
WATERSKIING
www.iwsf.com

● WOMEN'S 75 KG: SNATCH, CLEAN & JERK, TOTAL

On September 23, 2010, at the World Championships in Antalya, Turkey, Svetlana Podobedova (Kazakhstan) swept the board in the women's 75 kg competition, achieving new world records in snatch (134 kg), clean & jerk (161 kg), and total (295 kg).

WEIGHTLIFTING

MEN	CATEGORY	WEIGHT	NAME & NATIONALITY	LOCATION	DATE
56 kg	Snatch	138 kg	Halil Mutlu (Turkey)	Antalya, Turkey	Nov 4, 2001
	Clean & jerk	168 kg	Halil Mutlu (Turkey)	Trencín, Slovakia	Apr 24, 2001
	Total	305 kg	Halil Mutlu (Turkey)	Sydney, Australia	Sep 16, 2000
62 kg	Snatch	153 kg	Shi Zhiyong (China)	Izmir, Turkey	Jun 28, 2002
	Clean & jerk	182 kg	Le Maosheng (China)	Busan, South Korea	Oct 2, 2002
	Total	326 kg	Zhang Jie (China)	Kanazawa, Japan	Apr 28, 2008
69 kg	Snatch	165 kg	Georgi Markov (Bulgaria)	Sydney, Australia	Sep 20, 2000
	● Clean & jerk	198 kg	Liao Hui (China)	Antalya, Turkey	Sep 21, 2010
	● Total	358 kg	Liao Hui (China)	Antalya, Turkey	Sep 21, 2010
77 kg	Snatch	174 kg	Lu Xiaojun (China)	Goyang, South Korea	Nov 24, 2009
	Clean & jerk	210 kg	Oleg Perepetchenov (Russia)	Trencín, Slovakia	Apr 27, 2001
	Total	378 kg	Lu Xiaojun (China)	Goyang, South Korea	Nov 24, 2009
85 kg	Snatch	187 kg	Andrei Rybakou (Belarus)	Chiang Mai, Thailand	Sep 22, 2007
	Clean & jerk	218 kg	Zhang Yong (China)	Ramat Gan, Israel	Apr 25, 1998
	Total	394 kg	Andrei Rybakou (Belarus)	Beijing, China	Aug 15, 2008
94 kg	Snatch	188 kg	Akakios Kakhiasvilis (Greece)	Athens, Greece	Nov 27, 1999
	Clean & jerk	232 kg	Szymon Kolecki (Poland)	Sofia, Bulgaria	Apr 29, 2000
	Total	412 kg	Akakios Kakhiasvilis (Greece)	Athens, Greece	Nov 27, 1999
105 kg	Snatch	200 kg	Andrei Aramnau (Belarus)	Beijing, China	Aug 18, 2008
	Clean & jerk	237 kg	Alan Tsagaev (Bulgaria)	Kiev, Ukraine	Apr 25, 2004
	Total	436 kg	Andrei Aramnau (Belarus)	Beijing, China	Aug 18, 2008
105+ kg	Snatch	213 kg	Hossein Rezazadeh (Iran)	Qinhuangdao, China	Sep 14, 2003
	Clean & jerk	263 kg	Hossein Rezazadeh (Iran)	Athens, Greece	Aug 25, 2004
	Total	472 kg	Hossein Rezazadeh (Iran)	Sydney, Australia	Sep 26, 2000
WOMEN	**CATEGORY**	**WEIGHT**	**NAME & NATIONALITY**	**LOCATION**	**DATE**
48 kg	Snatch	98 kg	Yang Lian (China)	Santo Domingo, Dominican Republic	Oct 1, 2006
	● Clean & jerk	121 kg	Nurcan Taylan (Turkey)	Antalya, Turkey	Sep 17, 2010
	Total	217 kg	Yang Lian (China)	Santo Domingo, Dominican Republic	Oct 1, 2006
53 kg	● Snatch	103 kg	Li Ping (China)	Guangzhou, China	Nov 14, 2010
	Clean & jerk	129 kg	Li Ping (China)	Taian City, China	Apr 22, 2007
	● Total	230 kg	Li Ping (China)	Guangzhou, China	Nov 14, 2010
58 kg	Snatch	111 kg	Chen Yanqing (China)	Doha, Qatar	Dec 3, 2006
	Clean & jerk	141 kg	Qiu Hongmei (China)	Taian City, China	Apr 23, 2007
	Total	251 kg	Chen Yanqing (China)	Doha, Qatar	Dec 3, 2006
63 kg	Snatch	116 kg	Pawina Thongsuk (Thailand)	Doha, Qatar	Nov 12, 2005
	● Clean & jerk	143 kg	Maiya Maneza (Kazakhstan)	Antalya, Turkey	Sep 20, 2010
	Total	257 kg	Liu Haixia (China)	Chiang Mai, Thailand	Sep 23, 2007
69 kg	Snatch	128 kg	Liu Chunhong (China)	Beijing, China	Aug 13, 2008
	Clean & jerk	158 kg	Liu Chunhong (China)	Beijing, China	Aug 13, 2008
	Total	286 kg	Liu Chunhong (China)	Beijing, China	Aug 13, 2008
75 kg	● Snatch	134 kg	Svetlana Podobedova (Kazakhstan)	Antalya, Turkey	Sep 23, 2010
	● Clean & jerk	161 kg	Svetlana Podobedova (Kazakhstan)	Antalya, Turkey	Sep 23, 2010
	● Total	295 kg	Svetlana Podobedova (Kazakhstan)	Antalya, Turkey	Sep 23, 2010
75+ kg	● Snatch	145 kg	Tatiana Kashirina (Russia)	Antalya, Turkey	Sep 23, 2010
	Clean & jerk	187 kg	Jang Mi-Ran (South Korea)	Goyang, South Korea	Nov 28, 2009
	Total	326 kg	Jang Mi-Ran (South Korea)	Beijing, China	Aug 16, 2008

Measuring around 400 ft (120 m) tall, the Jetavanarama Dagoba in the ancient city of Anuradhapura, Sri Lanka, is the **largest Buddhist brick monument**.

● UPDATED RECORD
● NEW RECORD

16 The average age of the average body. Apart from your eyes, heart, and brain, your cells live less than 16 years before being replaced. At the age of 17, your first memory is already one of the oldest "parts" of you.

GUINNESS WORLD RECORDS 2012

LONGEST SPORTS MARATHONS

SPORT	TIME	NAME & NATIONALITY	LOCATION	DATE
● Aerobics	29 hr 5 min	Julian Hitch (UK)	London, UK	Apr 24–25, 2010
Baseball	48 hr 9 min 27 sec	Jonny G Foundation Cardinals and Edward Jones Browns (USA)	St Louis, Missouri, USA	Oct 9–11, 2009
● Basketball	107 hours	György Boronkay Technical and Grammar School (Hungary)	Vác, Hungary	Jul 1–5, 2010
Basketball (wheelchair)	26 hr 3 min	University of Omaha students and staff (USA)	Omaha, Nebraska, USA	Sep 24–25, 2004
● Bowling (tenpin)	134 hr 57 min	Stephen Shanabrook (USA)	Plano, Texas, USA	Jun 14–19, 2010
Bowls (indoor)	36 hours	Arnos Bowling Club (UK)	Southgate, London, UK	Apr 20–21, 2002
Bowls (outdoor)	170 hr 3 min	Goulburn Railway Bowling Club (Australia)	Goulburn, NSW, Australia	Jan 19–26, 2009
● Cricket	105 hours	Blunham Cricket Club (UK)	Blunham, Bedfordshire, UK	Aug 26–30, 2010
Curling	54 hr 1 min	The Burlington Golf and Country Club (Canada)	Burlington, Ontario, Canada	Mar 12–14, 2010
● Darts (doubles)	32 hr 4 min	Scott Maynard, Nathanael Hubbard, Chris Taylor, Shane Rose (Australia)	Chapel Hill, Queensland, Australia	May 22, 2010
● Darts (singles)	32 hr 25 min	Joanne and Danielle Tonks (UK)	Stafford, Staffordshire, UK	Apr 30–May 1, 2010
● Floorball	25 hr 13 min	London Sharks and friends (UK)	Haywards Head, West Sussex, UK	May 29–30, 2010
● Soccer	60 hours	Pink Panthers and Black Eagles (UK)	Loughborough, Leicestershire, UK	Oct 22–24, 2010
● Soccer (five-a-side)	33 hr 30 min	Youghal United AFC (Ireland)	Youghal, Ireland	Jun 5–7, 2010
Hockey (ice)	241 hr 21 min	Brent Saik and friends (Canada)	Strathcona, Alberta, Canada	Feb 8–18, 2008
Hockey (indoor)	50 hours	Bert & Macs and Mid-Town Certigard teams (Canada)	Lethbridge, Alberta, Canada	Mar 25–27, 2008
● Hockey (inline/roller)	25 hr 20 min	Roller Hockey Guernerin (France)	La Guérinière, France	Dec 3–4, 2010
Hockey (street)	105 hr 17 min	Molson Canadian and Canadian Tire teams (Canada)	Lethbridge, Alberta, Canada	Aug 20–24, 2008
Korfball	30 hr 2 min	Kingfisher Korfball Club (UK)	Larkfield, Kent, UK	Jun 14–15, 2008
Netball	58 hours	Sleaford Netball Club (UK)	Sleaford, Lincolnshire, UK	Jul 25–27, 2008
Pétanque (boules)	52 hours	Gilles de B'Heinsch (Belgium)	Arlon, Belgium	Sep 18–20, 2009
Pool (singles)	53 hr 25 min	Brian Lilley and Daniel Maloney (USA)	Spring Lake, North Carolina, USA	Oct 10–12, 2008
Skiing	202 hr 1 min	Nick Willey (Australia)	Thredbo, NSW, Australia	Sep 2–10, 2005
Snowboarding	180 hr 34 min	Bernhard Mair (Austria)	Bad Kleinkirchheim, Austria	Jan 9–16, 2004
Table soccer	51 hr 52 min	Alexander Gruber, Roman Schelling, Enrico Lechtaler, Christian Nägele (Austria)	Bregenz, Austria	Jun 27–29, 2008
Table tennis (doubles)	101 hr 1 min 11 sec	Lance, Phil, and Mark Warren, Bill Weir (USA)	Sacramento, California, USA	Apr 9–13, 1979
Table tennis (singles)	132 hr 31 min	Danny Price and Randy Nunes (USA)	Cherry Hill, New Jersey, USA	Aug 20–26, 1978
● Tennis (doubles)	56 hr 37 min 13 sec	Gavin White, Jeganathan Ramasamy, Simon Burk, David Sears (Australia)	Sydney, NSW, Australia	Sep 10–12, 2010
● Tennis (singles)	55 hr 55 min 55 sec	Christian Masurenko and Denis Heitmann (Germany)	Herford, Germany	Aug 6–8, 2010
● Volleyball (beach)	25 hr 39 min	Mateusz Baca, Sebastian Lüdke, Tomasz Olszak, Wojciech Kurczynski (Germany)	Görlitz, Germany	Jul 3–4, 2010
Volleyball (indoor)	76 hr 30 min	Zespól Szkól Ekonomicznych students (Poland)	Sosnowiec, Poland	Dec 4–7, 2009

WATERSKIING

MEN	RECORD	NAME & NATIONALITY	LOCATION	DATE
● Slalom	2 buoy | 9.75 m line | 58 km/h	Chris Parrish (USA)	Covington, USA	Jun 13, 2010
Barefoot slalom	20.6 crossings of wake in 30 seconds	Keith St Onge (USA)	Bronkhorstspruit, South Africa	Jan 6, 2006
Tricks	12,400 points	Nicolas Le Forestier (France)	Lac de Joux, Switzerland	Sep 4, 2005
● Barefoot tricks	12,150 points	David Small (GB)	Adna, USA	Jun 12, 2010
Jump	75.2 m (246 ft 8 in)	Freddy Krueger (USA)	Seffner, USA	Nov 2, 2008
● Barefoot jump	29.9 m (98 ft 1 in)	David Small (GB)	Brandenburg, Germany	Aug 11, 2010
Ski fly	91.1 m (298 ft 10 in)	Jaret Llewellyn (Canada)	Orlando, USA	May 14, 2000
Overall	2,818.01 points*	Jaret Llewellyn (Canada)	Seffner, USA	Sep 29, 2002
WOMEN	**RECORD**	**NAME & NATIONALITY**	**LOCATION**	**DATE**
● Slalom	1.5 buoy | 10.25 m line | 55 km/h	Regina Jaquess (USA)	Santa Rosa, USA	Oct 24, 2010
Barefoot slalom	17.0 crossings of wake in 30 seconds	Nadine de Villiers (South Africa)	Witbank, South Africa	Jan 5, 2001
● Tricks	9,690 points	Natallia Berdnikava (Belarus)	Winter Garden, USA	Oct 26, 2010
Barefoot tricks	4,400 points	Nadine de Villiers (South Africa)	Witbank, South Africa	Jan 5, 2001
● Jump	57.1 m (187 ft 4 in)	June Fladborg (Denmark)	Lincoln, UK	Aug 24, 2010
● Barefoot jump	21 m (69 ft)	Elaine Heller (USA)	Brandenburg, Germany	Aug 12, 2010
Ski fly	69.4 m (227 ft 8.2 in)	Elena Milakova (Russia)	Pine Mountain, USA	May 26, 2002
● Overall	2,945.85 points**	Regina Jaquess (USA)	Santa Rosa, USA	Jun 20, 2010

** 5@11.25 m, 10,730 tricks, 71.7 m jump **4@10.75 m, 7,920 tricks, 53.6 m jump; calculated with the 2006 scoring method*

● WOMEN'S BAREFOOT JUMP

Elaine Heller (USA), pictured at the 2009 Barefoot Ski Nationals at Mystic Lakes in Maize, Kansas, USA, jumped a record 69 ft (21 m) in the same event in Brandenburg, Germany, on August 12, 2010.

Our final connection brings us back to China, where we started – in Lushan County, Henan Province, you'll find the ● **tallest Buddha statue**, the Zhongyuan Buddha, which measures 418 ft 76 in (127.64 m).

SUBJECT INDEX

This year's index is organized into two parts: by subject and by superlative. **Bold entries** in the subject index indicate a main entry on a topic, and **BOLD CAPITALS** indicate an entire chapter. Neither index lists personal names.

SUPERLATIVE INDEX

SUPERLATIVE INDEX

the
POGO
DUDES

ACKNOWLEDGMENTS

Guinness World Records would like to thank the following individuals, organizations, groups, websites, schools, colleges and universities for their help and advice in compiling this year's edition:

3Run; Academy of Motion Picture Arts & Sciences; Shabir Ahluwalia; *Airboating Magazine* LLC (Matt Hartman); Carmen Alfonzo Portillo; Alfons Andresson Gidlöf; Vilgot Andresson Gidlöf; Ulla Anlander; Paulina Amaya; Arctic Kingdom; Ascent Media; Attenda (Charlotte, Phil, Mark and team); Bender Helper Impact (Eric Kanner, Alyson Hagert, Mark Karges, Brian Reinert); Back-to-back worldwide competition; BBC Radio 3; Bender Media (Susan and Sally); Maud Bissier; Baby Boatface; Joseph Boatfield; Luke Boatfield; Box Office Mojo; British Airways; British Film Institute; The Bronx Zoo (Linda Wied); Sarah Brown; Bureau of Indian Affairs, United States Department of the Interior (Dr Richard Meyers, Ms Teddi Penland); CAN Networks (Paul, Damaris and team); Angelo Carbone; Clara Chambers; Camille Chambers; Georgina Charles; Mark Chisnell; Christie's - London (Meg Ford); Simone Ciancotti; Vincenzo Di Cillo; Adam Cloke; Antonia Coffman; Collaboration (Mr Suzuki, Miho, Masumi, and all our friends); Comic Relief; Connection Cars (Tracey Dunkerley, Rob Dunkerley); Consumer Electronics Association (Carolyn Slater); *Coronation Street* (ITV); Council on Tall Buildings and Urban Habitat (Marshall Gerometta); CYCLO IMAGE Co. Ltd (Ken Arai); Deep Metal Piercing, Dortmund, Germany; Denmaur Independent Papers Limited; East Looe Town Trust, Cornwall, UK; The Eden Project, London; Louis Epstein; Kate Ereira; Europroduzione/Veralia (Marco, Stefano, Gabriel, Renato, Carlo, and all our friends); Amelia Ewen; Toby Ewen; Explorersweb (Tom and Tina Sjögren); Eyeworks Australia and New Zealand (Julie, Alison, and all); Eyeworks Germany (Kaethe, Andi, Michael, and all); Rebecca Fall; Benjamin Fall; Joanna Fells; Rebecca Fells; Simon Fells; *First Drop* magazine, European Coaster Club (Justin Garvanovic); F.J.T. Logistics Limited (Ray Harper, Gavin Hennessey); Alexis Forcada Zamora; Forbes; Formulation Inc (Marcus, Ayako, Kei, and all our friends); Fuji Television Network, Inc (Ryu Utsui); Gerontology Research Group; Thomasina Gibson; Gobierno Delegacional de Iztapalapa; Green Events, Llanwrtyd Wells, UK; Brandon Greenwood; Jordan Greenwood; Ryan Greenwood; Victoria Grimsell; Grover Cleveland Birthplace (Sharon Farrell); Hampshire Sports and Prestige Cars (Richard Johnston); High Noon Entertainment (Pam, Jim, Adam, Ian, Mark, Jeremy, and all); Hikone Castle, Shiga, Japan; Lorena Hinojosa; Tamsin Holman; Marsha Hoover; Hunter College of The City University of New York (Dr Richard Belsky); ICM (Michael and Greg); IGFA (Jack Vitek); IMDB.com; INP Media (Bryn Downing); Integrated Colour Editions Europe (Roger Hawkins, Susie Hawkins, Clare Merryfield); Intelligent Textiles; International Jugglers' Association; International Sport Juggling Federation; Anita Ives; Dominique Jando; Dr Lewis Jones; Juggling Information Service; Lambiek (Amsterdam); Orla Langton; Thea Langton; The Leigh Bureau (Jennifer Bird Bowen); London Cocktail Club, Goodge St, London; Sean Macaulay; Lourdes Mangas; Luke Meloy; Metropolis Collectibles, Inc. & ComicConnect, Corp. (Ben Smith); Miditech (Niret, Nivedith, Vidyuth, Tarun, Niraja, Komal, Nischint, Alphi, Mazin, Sunil, Denzil, Monil, Nikita, and all the production team); Harriet Molloy; Joshua Molloy; Sophie Molloy; Matilda Morales; Dora Morales; Moulin Rouge (Fanny Rabasse); Adrian Muscari; NASA; National Geographic Society (Michael Fry); National Oceanic and Atmospheric Administration; National TV Awards; New Jersey State History Fair (Beverly Weaver); New York Times (John Noble Wilford); Caroline Newby; Matilda Nieberg; Saúl Nuñez Sanchez; Shaun Opperman; Andrew Peacock; Charlotte Peacock; Stefano Perni; Clara Piccirillo; Robert Pullar; Queens College of The City University of New York (Dr Morris Rossabi); R&G Productions (Stephane, Jerome, David, Eric, and all our friends); Lauren Randolph; Elizabeth Rayner; Re:fine Group (Alex); David Rea; Restaurante Bismark; Martyn Richards; Ritz-Carlton Hotel, Bachelor Gulch, USA; Fabián Rojas y familia; Roller Coaster Database (Duane Marden); Rosa Romero Vélez; Royal Geographic Society (Dr Steven Toole, Lis Parham); Pablo Rubio; MTG Rummery Esq.; James Rushmere; Elley Rushmere; Scarborough Book Festival; Christopher W Schneider; *The Scottish Sun;* Abdulla Shareef; Mauro Di Sí; Richard Sisson; Society For American Baseball Research (Lyle Spatz); Sotheby's - London (Catherine Slowther, Peter Selley); Sotheby's - New York (Elizabeth R Muller, Selby Kiffer, Justin Caldwell); Ian Starr; Nick Steel; Stora Enso Veitsiluoto; The Sun Newspaper (Caroline Iggulden); Holly Taylor; Charlie Taylor; Kevin Thompson; Spencer Thrower; TomTom (Rosie Tickner); Top 8 Magic (Brian David-Marshall, Matthew Wang); TNR; truTV (Marissa, Robyn, Angel, Mark, Stephen, Michael, and all); UNESCO; University of Cambridge (Dr Lisa Maher, Dr Jay T Stock); Majorie Vallee; Andres Vallejo; Donna Vano; Lorenzo Veltri; Viacom18 (Vivek, Rmil, Ashvini, Smitha, Shivani, Sachin, Tanushree, and all); Visit Britain (Charlotte Tuffin); Screech Washington; The Water Rocket Achievement World Record Association; David White; Wildlife Conservation Society Library (Kerry Prendergast); Wildlife Conservation Society (Madeleine Thompson); Beverley Williams; Adam Wilson; Barry Woods; Dan Woods; Lydia Wood; World Juggling Federation; World Sailing Speed Record Council (John Reed); Xara Computers (Adnaan, Muzahir and team); X Games; Yale University (Dr Jonathan D Spence); YouTube; Preity Zinta; Zippy Production (Mitsue).

PICTURE CREDITS

1 Stewart Volland/National Geographic/AP; **2** Getty Images/Getty Images/Mykel Nicolaou/GWR; **3** Getty Images/Nick Obank/Getty Images/Paul Michael Hughes/GWR/Drew Gardner/GWR; **4** Ryan Schude/GWR; **8** (UK) Ranald Mackechnie/GWR/Jay Williams/GWR; **9** (UK) BBC; **10** (UK) Robbie Reynolds/CPR/Ken McKay/Rex Features/Brian Lawless/Sportsfile; **11** (UK) Luke Inman/Getty Images/Getty Images; **8** (USA) Brian Palmer/GWR; **9** (USA) Paul Drinkwater/NBC; **10** (USA) Scott Gries; **11** (USA) Brian Brantley/GWR/Kevork Djansezian/Getty Images/Tom Donoghue/David M Russell/Watershed Visual Media; **8** (CAN) Greg Henkenhaf; **9** (CAN) Doug Pensinger/Getty Images; **11** (CAN) Sam Yeh/Getty Images; **8** (INT) Paolo Valenti; **9** (INT) Phil Walter/Getty Images; **10** (INT) Mark Kolbe/Getty Images; **11** (INT) Christophe Simon/Getty Images; **12** Getty Images/Miguel Medina/GWR/Tim Anderson/GWR/Matt May/GWR/Luca Di Tommaso/GWR; **13** Jay Williams/GWR; **14** Paul Michael Hughes/GWR/Paul Michael Hughes/GWR/Edwin Koo/GWR; **15** Paul Michael Hughes/GWR; **16** Photolibrary/Awashima Marine Park/Getty Images; **17** Gerry Penny/Corbis/NASA/Martin Ruegner/Getty Images; **18** ESA/Herschel/**20** Mountain High/Getty Images/NASA/NASA; **21** NASA/NASA/NASA/Casey Reed/Penn State/NASA; **22** Getty Images/Science Photo Library/NASA; **23** NASA/NASA; **24** NASA; **25** NASA/NASA/NASA/NASA/NASA; **26** NASA/NASA/Ho New/Reuters; **27** NASA/NASA/NASA/John Foster/Science Photo Library; **28** NASA/Getty Images/Getty Images/Getty Images; **29** NASA/NASA/Getty Images/Getty Images; **30** NASA/NASA/Getty Images/NASA/Laurent Hamels/Getty Images; **31** Dr Scott Lieberman/AP/PA/Getty Images/Alamy/Ralph Morse/Getty Images/Getty Images; **32** Sean Heavey/Barcroft Media; **34** Mark A Garlick/space-art.co.uk; **35** Alamy/Alamy/smart-elements.com/Getty Images/Getty Images/Warut Roonguthai/Element Photo Gallery/Getty Images/smart-elements.com/David Wall/Alamy/Getty Images; **36** Thomas Kunz/Alamy/Getty Images/Gavin Hellier/Getty Images; **37** Charles O Cecil/Alamy/Getty Images/George Steinmetz/Corbis/Survival International/Reuters; **38** AFP/Alamy/Getty Images/Daniel Garcia/Getty Images/Russ Widstrand/Getty Images; **39** Alamy/NOAA/Alamy/Hannah Johnston/Getty Images/Getty Images/Alamy; **40** Getty Images/B O'Kane/Alamy/Philippe Bourseiller/Getty Images; **41** Gary Corbett/Alamy/Robert Frerck/Getty Images/Steve Bloom/Barcroft Media; **42** Getty Images/Getty Images/Getty Images; **43** Getty Images/Getty Images/Alamy; **44** Nati Harnik/AP/PA/Gerard Fritz/Getty Images/Arnar Thorisson/AP/PA; **45** Peter Caton/Artyom Korotayev/Getty Images/WENN; **48** Bruce Davidson/Nature PL/Gunther Michel/Still Pictures/Science Photo Library/Alamy; **49** Photolibrary/Stephen Dalton/NHPA/Pete Oxford/FLPA/Louise Murray/Science Photo Library; **50** Joseph Brown/University of Kansas/AFP/Durrell Wildlife Conservation Trust/Getty Images; **51** Robin Moore/iLCP/Robin Moore/iLCP/Russell A Mittermeier/Javier Garcí/Conservation International; **52** Robbin Thorp/AP/PA/Getty Images/Yeshey Dorji; **53** Adnan Moussalli and Devi Stuart-Fox/Bryson Voirin/Getty Images; **54** C & M Fallows/SeaPics/Photolibrary/Alamy; **55** Getty Images/Annie Katz/Getty Images; **56** Thomas Marent/Getty Images/Suzy Bennett/Alamy/FLPA/Alamy; **57** Photolibrary/Alamy/Photolibrary/Michael Giannechini/Science Photo Library; **58** Joel Sartore/National Geographic/Genevieve Vallee/Alamy/Martin Harvey/Corbis; **59** Alamy/FLPA/Tui De Roy/National Geographic; **60** Dr Jeremy Burgess/Science Photo Library/Science Photo Library/Photolibrary/Photolibrary; **61** Steve Gschmeissner/Science Photo Library/Photolibrary/Steve Gschmeissner/Science Photo Library/David Scharf/Science Photo Library; **62** Eric Vandeville/Getty Images/Photolibrary/Pink Tentacle; **63** Mark Bowler/Nature PL/Ezzal/Ifremer/A Fifis/Ken Catania/Visuals Unlimited; **64** Tom Gardner/Alamy/City & County of Honolulu/Walt Anderson/Getty Images/Howard Rice/Photolibrary; **65** Daniel J Cox/Alamy/Alamy/Getty Images/Getty Images; **66** Peter Horree/Alamy; **68** Getty Images/Getty Images/Alisdair Macdonald/Rex Features/Getty Images/Getty Images; **69** Getty Images/Getty Images/Getty Images/Getty Images/Getty Images/Getty Images; **70** Eric Vandeville/Getty Images/Getty Images; **71** Ray Tang/Rex Features/Getty Images/Stan Tess/Alamy/Timm Schamberger/Getty Images; **72** Davit Hakobyan/Getty Images/The Art Archive/Getty Images/Alamy/Erich Lessing/AKG/Erich Lessing/AKG; **73** Getty Images/AKG/Alamy/AKG/Davies and Starr/Getty Images/Alamy/John Cartwright/Alamy; **74** AKG/AKG/Art Archive/AKG/Getty Images; **75** Bridgeman Art Library/Art Archive/British Museum/Alamy; **76** Getty Images/Seth Joel/Corbis/Mary Evans Picture Library/Getty Images; **77** Danita Delimont/Getty Images/Alamy/NASA/Ted Soqui/Corbis/Ian Sanders/Alamy/Alamy; **78** Ranald Mackechnie/GWR; **80** Ranald Mackechnie/GWR/Thomas Mukoya/Reuters/Adrees Latif/Reuters; **81** Chris Lewington/Alamy/Ranald Mackechnie/GWR/John Wright/GWR/John Wright/GWR; **82** Ryan Schude/GWR/Paul Michael Hughes/GWR; **83** Ryan Schude/GWR/John Wright/GWR/Ranald Mackechnie/GWR; **84** Paul Michael Hughes/GWR/John Wright/GWR/Charlie Saceda/Getty Images/Gary Parker; **85** Ryan Schude/GWR/Barcroft Media; **86** Getty Images/Monica M Davey/Getty Images; **87** Rex Features; **88** Rex Features/John Wright/GWR/John Wright/GWR; **89** Richard Bradbury/GWR/Chris Granger/GWR; **90** Ranald Mackechnie/GWR/Ranald Mackechnie/GWR; **92** John Wright/GWR/Amy Sancetta/AP/PA; **93** Wong Maye-E/AP/PA/Ralph Crane/Getty Images/Alamy; **94** Nick Hannes/GWR/John Wright/GWR; **95** Ranald Mackechnie/GWR/John Wright/GWR; **96** Ranald Mackechnie/GWR/Mike Marsland/GWR; **98** K K Najeeb/Ranald Mackechnie/GWR; **99** David M Russell/Disney ABC/Ranald Mackechnie/GWR/Ranald Mackechnie/GWR; **100** AFP/Aman Sharma/AP/PA; **101** Franz Neumayr/MMV; **102** Toby Melville/Reuters/Ismael Mohamad/Eyevine; **103** Mark Ralston/Getty Images; **104** John Wright/GWR; **105** Paul Michael Hughes/GWR/John Wright/GWR/John Wright/GWR/John Wright/GWR; **106** Ranald Mackechnie/GWR/Paul Michael Hughes/GWR; **107** Ranald Mackechnie/GWR; **108** John Wright/GWR; **109** John Wright/GWR/John Wright/GWR; **110** Getty Images/Brian Thompson/Shinsuke Kamioka/

GWR; **112** Ranald Mackechnie/GWR/Tim Anderson/GWR/John Wright/GWR; **114** Paul Michael Hughes/GWR; **115** Craig Lenihan/AP/PA/Craig Lenihan/AP/PA; **116** Adam Moore/GWR; **118** Nicholas DeVore/Getty Images/PA/PA; **119** Bill Janscha/AP/PA/AFP/Getty Images/Getty Images/AP/PA/AP/PA/Getty Images; **120** Keith Ducatel/Keith Ducatel/Andy Sillaber; **121** Shinsuke Kamioka/GWR; **122** Galen Rowell/Corbis; **123** Namgyal Sherpa/Getty Images/Ryan Schude/GWR; **125** Richard Bradbury/GWR; **126** Rex Features; **127** Tony Cheng/AP/PA/Richard Bradbury/GWR; **128** Corbis/Vincent Yu/AP/PA; **129** Cate Gillon/Getty Images/Richard Bradbury/GWR; **130** USAF/Jay Williams/GWR/Reuters; **131** Carl De Souza/Getty Images/Thierry Boccon-Gibod-Pool/Getty Images/USAF/Ryan Schude/GWR; **132** Reuters; **134** Worldmapper.org/Getty Images; **135** Getty Images/Getty Images; **136** Reuters/Rodrigo Arangua/Getty Images/David Greedy/Getty Images/Jaime Saldarriaga/Reuters; **137** Larry W Smith/Getty Images/Maya Vidon/Getty Images/Getty Images/Veronique de Viguerie/Getty Images; **138** Mahmoud Ahmadinejad/Getty Images/Vitaly Armand/Getty Images; **139** Alexander Nemenov/Getty Images/Ben Stansall/Getty Images/Manpreet Romana/Getty Images/Chung Sung-Jun/Getty Images; **140** Paul Michael Hughes/GWR; **142** Ryan Schude/GWR; **143** Anwar Amro/Getty Images/Umit Bektaş/Reuters/Paul Michael Hughes/GWR; **144** Paul Michael Hughes/GWR; **145** Geoffrey Swaine/Rex Features/Rex Features/Rex Features; **146** Paul Michael Hughes/GWR/Ryan Schude/GWR; **147** Lu Liang/Paul Michael Hughes/GWR/Jacob Chinn/GWR; **148** Ryan Schude/GWR/Ryan Schude/GWR; **149** Rex Features; **150** Ranald Mackechnie/GWR; **151** Ryan Schude/GWR; **152** Shinsuke Kamioka/GWR/Ranald Mackechnie/GWR; **153** Ranald Mackechnie/GWR/Stuart Hendry/GWR; **154** Geoff Pugh/Rex Features/Amit Dave/Reuters/Divya Bhaskar/Barcroft Media; **156** Paula Bronstein/Getty Images/Rex Features/Sukree Sukplang/Reuters/Getty Images; **157** Alastair Muir/Rex Features/Miramax/Kobal/Nils Jorgensen/Rex Features/Fox TV/Getty Images/Fred Duval/Getty Images/Paul Grover/Getty Images; **158** Alamy/Alamy/Getty Images/Betsie Van der Meer/Getty Images; **159** AP/PA/Scott J Ferrel/Getty Images; **160** Stuart Hendry/GWR; **162** AFP/Getty Images/Alamy/Alamy/Los Alamos National Laboratory/SPL; **163** PA/Getty Images/Getty Images/Los Alamos National Laboratory/PA/Kevin Murrell/Getty Images; **164** Colorado State University/Steve Allen/AFP/Ho New/Reuters; **165** CERN/CERN/ESA/Alexander Nemenov/Getty Images; **166** SII Nanotechnology Inc/M Fuchsle/AFP/Hari Manoharan/Stanford University/Periodic Videos/Periodic Videos/D Carr and H Craighead/Cornell University; **167** Advanced Materials/Science/AAAS/NIST/CU; **170** Alexa Reach/Getty Images/Getty Images/Ian Dagnall/Alamy; **171** zynga/youtube.com/Judson Laipply; **172** Vanderbilt Cup Races/Getty Images/E Bacon/Getty Images/Corbis/Getty Images/Corbis/Corbis/Troxx/AP/PA; **173** Nathan Allred; **174** John Gaps/AP/PA/Ho New/Reuters/NASA; **175** Rajan Chaughule/Getty Images/AP/PA/Alamy; **176** Alamy/Joao Abreu Miranda/Getty Images; **177** PA; **178** Charlie Magee/Sean Gallup/Getty Images/Tim Wallace/Newspress; **179** Getty Images; **180** Miniatur Wunderland/Yoshikazu Tsuno/Getty Images/Getty Images; **181** Getty Images/Photolibrary/K K Arora/Reuters; **182** WENN/Patrik Stollarz/Getty Images/Geoffrey Robinson/Rex Features; **183** Richard Bradbury/GWR/David Torrence/GWR; **184** Jack Guez/Getty Images; **185** Todd Reichert/Todd Reichert/Laurent Gillieron/Getty Images; **186** US Navy/US Navy; **187** Getty Images/Getty Images; **188** Patrick H Corkery/Unitel Launch Alliance; **189** Jo Yong/Reuters/David Silverman/Getty Images; **190** Photolibrary/WENN; **191** Mitchell Funk/Getty Images; **192** Chris Cheadle/Alamy/Getty Images/Mosab Omar/Reuters/Ho New/Reuters; **193** Michael James Brown/Alamy/Phil Roche/MDC; **194** Getty Images; **195** Getty Images; **196** WENN/Ranald Mackechnie/GWR; **198** Tim Anderson/GWR; **199** Ranald Mackechnie/GWR; **200** Disney/Pixar; **202** George Doyle/Getty Images/Lucasfilm Ltd/Ronald Grant Archive/20th Century Fox/Rex Features/Chelsea Lauren/Getty Images; **203** Daniel Sakow/PA; **204** Shinsuke Kamioka/GWR; **205** Ryan Schude/GWR; **206** Wizards of the Coast/Sonny Meddle/Rex Features; **207** Wizards of the Coast/Wizards of the Coast; **208** Getty Images; **209** Timothy A Clary/AFP/Alamy; **210** Warner Bros./Warner Bros./Warner Bros./Disney; **211** 20th Century Fox/Warner Bros.; **212** Getty Images/Globo Films/Kobal Collection/Melampo/Kobal Collection/Touhoku Shinsha/Kobal Collection/Kobal Collection/Getty Images; **213** Kobal Collection/Rex Features/Paramount/Rex Features/Kobal Collection/Kobal Collection/Yogen Shah/Getty Images; **214** Michael Tran/Getty Images/Kevin Winter/Getty Images/Rex Features; **215** Tom Watkins/Rex Features; **216** Carlos R Alvarez/Getty Images/Kevin Winter/Getty Images; **217** Ian West/PA/Kevin Winter/Getty Images/Charlie Gray; **218** Marjorie Curty; **219** Ranald Mackechnie/GWR; **220** CBS/HBO/ITV/HBO; **221** NBC/Rex Features/Rex Features/Rex Features; **222** Kobal Collection/Rex Features; **223** Popperfoto/Getty Images/BBC; **224** Alamy/Rex Features/Roger Bamber/Rex Features/Getty Images/Rex Features; **225** ITV/Rex Features/BBC/CBS; **226** Getty Images/Peter Macdiarmid/Getty Images; **227** Gjon Mili/Getty Images/Peter Macdiarmid/Getty Images/Julian Andrews/Getty Images/Getty Images/Getty Images/Getty Images/Getty Images/Getty Images; **228** Red Bull; **230** Getty Images/Getty Images/Andy Lyons/Getty Images/Reuters/Mike Blake/Reuters/Philippe Huguen/Getty Images/Getty Images; **231** Rex Features/Christopher Lee/Getty Images; **232** Alamy/British Museum Images/Getty Images/Getty Images/Getty Images/Getty Images; **233** Getty Images/Getty Images/Phil Walter/Getty Images/Getty Images/Jason Lee/Reuters; **234** Getty Images/Stuart Franklin/Action Images/Adam Pretty/Getty Images; **235** Ron Kuntz/Getty Images/Daniel Garcia/Getty Images/Jerry Cooke/Getty Images; **236** Mark Ralston/Getty Images/Frederic J Brown/Getty Images; **237** Bob Thomas/Getty Images/Scott Barbour/Getty Images/Ng Han Guan/AP/PA; **238** Dennis Flaherty/Getty Images/Joe Robbins/Getty Images/Nick Laham/Getty Images/Victor Decolongon/Getty Images/Donald Miralle/Getty Images; **239** Al Bello/Getty Images/Jamie Squire/Getty Images/Jonathan Nackstrand/Getty Images/Ethan Miller/Getty Images/Jed Jacobsohn/Getty Images/Robyn Beck/Getty Images; **240** Allen Einstein/Getty Images/Lee Warren/Getty Images/Reuters/Rex Features; **241** Getty Images/Morry GashAP/PA/Hamish Blair/Getty Images/Tim Wimborne/Reuters; **242** Phil Walter/Getty Images/Shaun Botterill/Getty Images/Clive Mason/Getty Images/Jewel Samad/Getty Images; **243** John MacDougall/Getty Images/Doug Pensinger/Getty Images/Getty Images/Gerard Julien/Getty Images; **244** Aizar Raldes/Getty Images/Matthew Stockman/Getty/Damien Meyer/Getty Images; **245** Don Emmert/Getty Images/Patin Carrera/Brian Bahr/Getty Images; **246** Timothy A Clary/Getty Images/Jose Jordan/Getty Images/Guillaume Baptiste/Getty Images; **247** Patrik Stollarz/Getty Images/Fred Dufour/Getty Images/David Cannon/Getty Images; **248** Torsten Blackwood/Getty Images/PA/Nancy Lane/AP/PA/Stanko Gruden/Getty Images; **249** Adam Nurkiewicz/Getty Images/Matthew Peters/Getty Images/Getty Images/Robert Riger/Getty Images; **250** Gerry Penny/Getty Images/Getty Images/Getty Images/Walter Iooss Jr./Getty Images; **251** Clive Mason/Getty Images/Brendan McDermid/Reuters/Getty Images/Getty Images; **252** Julian Finney/Getty Images/Shaun Curry/Getty Images; **254** Rogan Ward/Reuters/Josh Hedges/Getty Images/Peter Jones/Reuters/Richard Bouhet/Getty Images; **255** Stefano Rellandini/Reuters; **256** Albert Gea/Reuters/Julian Herbert/Getty Images/Alan Crowhurst/Getty Images; **257** Vincent Jannink/Getty Images/Paul Gilham/Getty Images/Al Bello/Getty Images/Jesse D Garrabrant/Getty Images; **258** Christian Petersen/Getty Images/Mark Dadswell/Getty Images/Shuji Kajiyama/AP/PA/AP/PA; **259** David Ramos/Getty Images/Graham Stewart/Getty Images/Sankei/Getty Images; **260** Shaun Botterill/Getty Images/Emmanuel Dunand/Getty Images/Paul Kane/Getty Images; **261** Alexander Joe/Getty Images/Getty Images/David E Klutho/Getty Images; **262** Tom Lovelock/AP/PA; **264** Richard Bradbury/GWR/Images Of Life; **265** Miguel Villagran/Getty Images/Emma Wood/Shinsuke Kamioka/GWR/Paul Michael Hughes/GWR; **266** Terje Bendiksby/Getty Images/PA/Robert Brown/Billabong XXL.com; **267** Heinz Kluetmeier/Getty Images/Alamy/Andy Hooper/Rex Features; **268** Tiziana Fabi/Getty Images; **269** Esko Anttila; **270** Wim Van Hemert/Francois Nascimbeni/Getty Images; **271** John MacDougall/Getty Images/Vincent Jannink/Getty Images; **273** Jonathan Ferrey/Getty Images/Ivan Sekretarev/AP/PA; **274** Clive Rose/Getty Images/Clive Rose/Getty Images/Shaun Botterill/Getty Images; **275** Jamie McDonald/Getty Images; **276** Lee Jin-man/AP/PA/Mustafa Özer/Getty Images; **277** Paul Adams; **286** Marwan Naamani/Getty Images/Emmanuel Aguirre/Getty Images; **287** Sean Bell/Mark Allan/BBC.

IN MEMORIAM

A Alexander (**longest magic show**), Walter Breuning (**oldest man**), Herbert Fischer (**one half of the oldest living married couple**), Fluffy (**longest snake in captivity**), James Fuchs (**most shot-put competitions won**), Oscar (**oldest ever pig**), Eunice Sanborn (**oldest woman**), Valerio De Simoni (**longest journey by ATV**), Jack Stepham (**highest combined age for four siblings**), Grete Waitz (**most wins of the New York Marathon, female**), Samuel Wanjiru (**fastest London** and **Chicago Marathons**).

END PAPERS

FRONT (left to right):

Largest serving of salsa
Farthest distance walking on stilts in 24 hours
Most models in a fashion show
Largest hayride
Most people patting heads and rubbing stomachs
Most people solving Rubik's Cubes
Most eggs cracked in one minute with one hand
Most people shaking hands
Fastest time to lay 12 m² of carpet
Greatest distance 24 hours Nordic skiing (men)
Most artists contributing to the same painting simultaneously
Largest nativity village
Most wet sponges thrown in one minute (two people)
Longest book series – travel guides
Largest beach towel
Longest tongue on a dog ever
Fastest waterskiing (women)
Most high-fives in 24 hours (individual)
Most two-finger push-ups (one arm) in one minute
Largest collection of toy soldiers
Longest marathon playing accordion
Most head spins in one minute
Fastest string/can stilt walking – 50 m
Largest collection of pencils
Most hugs given in one hour by an individual
Largest parade of electric cars
Most people twirling flags
Largest collection of dictionaries
Most knots undone by a dog in three minutes
Largest boat tie-up
Largest dirndl dress
Largest serving of rice pudding

BACK (left to right):

Largest robot dance
Most people hula hooping (multiple venue)
Longest moving line of wheelchairs
Longest rubber band chain – individual
Most eggs cracked in one hour with one hand
Most people in a custard pie fight
Most rice eaten in three minutes
Shortest time to travel the New York City Subway (underground)
Most people treading grapes
Largest barefoot walk
Largest gathering of Elvis impersonators
Most bicycle wheelies in one minute
Largest origami lei
Longest barbecue
Fastest time to make one litre of ice-cream
Longest marble track
Largest seashell ensemble
Farthest distance covered on a waterslide in 24 hours (team, female)
Longest nose wheelie (manual) on a motocross bike
Largest sculpture made of soap
Most people modeling on a catwalk
Longest solo drum roll
Largest steel pan
Largest melodica ensemble
Largest silver ring
Most ballet dancers *en pointe*
Largest cannolo
Longest bicycle wheelie in one hour
Largest gathering of people dressed as cartoon characters
Largest art lesson (multiple venues)
Most nails hammered into a block of wood in one minute

STOP PRESS

LONGEST TIME WITHOUT A GOVERNMENT IN PEACETIME
As of May 16, 2011, Belgium had gone 337 days without a government, following elections in June 2010. The record (which may have been beaten by the time you read this) is 354 days – on July 27, 2003, the National Assembly elections in Cambodia failed to give any one party the two-thirds majority of seats required to form a government, a stalemate that was not resolved until July 15, 2004.

LONGEST JOURNEY ON AN ATV
At the time of going to press, the Expedition Squad – Valerio De Simoni, Kristopher Davant, and James Kenyon (all Australia) – had exceeded the previous record distance of 16,864 miles (27,141 km) to register the longest journey on an ATV. The group continued their tour, hoping to complete an estimated 31,070 miles (50,000 km).

MOST DOWNLOADED PODCAST
The Adam Carolla Show (USA) received 59,574,843 unique downloads from March 2009 to March 16, 2011.

FARTHEST DISTANCE LIMBO SKATING UNDER AUTOMOBILES
Rohan Ajit Kokane (India) limbo-skated for a distance of 126 ft 11 in (38.68 m) under automobiles for *Guinness World Records – Ab India Todega* at the Juhu Aerodrome in Mumbai, India, on February 17, 2011.

MOST COMMENTS ON A FACEBOOK POST
A post on the Facebook page for Roberto Esposito (Italy) on January 10, 2011 drew 389,141 comments.

MOST PEOPLE DYEING EGGS
A group of 317 people dyed eggs together at Carowinds (USA) in Charlotte, North Carolina, USA, on April 23, 2011. The Easter-themed record attempt launched a summer 2011 partnership between Guinness World Records and Cedar Fair Entertainment Company.

LONGEST RIDE THROUGH A TUNNEL OF FIRE
Shabir Ahluwalia (India) took his motorcycle on a death-defying ride through a 224-ft 8-in (68.49-m) tunnel of fire on the set of *Guinness World Records – Ab India Todega* in Mumbai, India, on March 13, 2011. Even more impressively, he went through the tunnel twice.

MOST ESPRESSOS MADE IN ONE HOUR (TEAM)
The Coffee Club Aspley (Australia) brewed up 5,061 espressos in Brisbane, Australia, on October 7, 2010. Five espresso machines were used, with four team members to each machine.

HEAVIEST WEIGHT LIFTED WITH BOTH EYE SOCKETS
On April 28, 2011, Yang Guang He (China) lifted an eye-watering 51 lb 12.96 oz (23.5 kg) – in the form of two buckets of water – using only his orbits on the set of *Lo Show dei Record*, in Milan, Italy.

GWR IPAD CHALLENGES
Following the launch of the *Guinness World Records at Your Fingertips* app, three individuals set new iPad world records: **fastest time to type the alphabet backward**: "Neurojc", 2.03 seconds (January 31, 2011); **fastest 100 metres**: "Kenny!", 6.28 seconds (April 23, 2011); **most color sequences memorized**: "ilyas.isk", 67 (March 29, 2011).

LARGEST 3D-MOVIE SCREEN
LG Electronics (South Korea) unveiled a supersized 3,196.87-ft² (297-m²) 3D-movie screen at the Grand Palais in Paris, France, on April 21, 2011. The screen was created to showcase their latest 3D technology and was 88 ft 6 in (27 m) long and 36 ft 1 in (11 m) wide.

At the same event, the company also assembled the **largest attendance at a 3D-film screening**. An audience of 1,148 watched the animated film *Rio* (USA, 2011) in stereoscopic 3D.

FASTEST TIME TO CLIMB THE BURJ KHALIFA TOWER SOLO
Alain Robert (France) took 6 hr 13 min 55 sec to top the Burj Khalifa tower, the world's **tallest building**, in Dubai, UAE, completing his task at 12:17 a.m. on March 29, 2011.

Alain had not climbed the building before and sought permission from real-estate developer Emaar Properties, who convinced him to wear safety equipment during the attempt. Alain did so, but chose his own method of climbing, using only his bare hands and rubber shoes.